D1234337

exciting book. Dr. Goode describes how people and organizations gain, lose, invest, and exchange respect and how our efforts to win prestige at every social rank shape our behavior powerfully and continually.

In the final chapters the author turns to the practical and philosophical problems of justice and equity raised by his analysis of prestige. In direct and compelling language he goes well beyond the usual boundaries of exchange theory, which is commonly restricted to analysis of distributive justice, to discuss need, sacrifice, and proportionality.

Professor Goode draws upon the empirical and theoretical work of anthropologists, economists, and psychologists, as well as that of sociologists to create a comprehensive and highly original statement on a subject of vast importance. Students and researchers in many areas of human behavior will be challenged for years to come.

William J. Goode is Professor of Sociology at Stanford University.

The Celebration of Heroes

The
Celebration of Heroes

Prestige as a Social Control System

William J. Goode

University of California Press

Berkeley • Los Angeles • London

For my beloved children

University of California Press
Berkeley and Los Angeles, California
University of California Press, Ltd.
London, England
Copyright © 1978 by
The Regents of the University of California
ISBN 0-520-03602-6
Library of Congress Catalog Card Number: 77-20322
Printed in the United States of America

1 2 3 4 5 6 7 8 9

Contents

Preface

Prestige is a system of social control that shapes much of social life. All people share the universal need to gain the respect or esteem of others, since without it they can not as easily elicit the help of others, and all individuals and groups give and withhold prestige and approval as a way of rewarding or punishing others. The foundations of social life rest in part on the universal need for respect, esteem, approval and honor.

This book is the first extensive treatise on prestige as a social control system. It explores the prestige processes that shape much of social life, and it develops many empirically linked propositions and hypotheses about prestige. It demonstrates the pervasive influence of prestige processes by drawing on a wide array of observations from historical and field research and from the experimental laboratory. One of my aims is to alert the reader to this pervasive influence, even in the interaction among large-scale organizations and agencies. Social analysts have long recognized, either implicitly or explicitly, the importance of prestige or esteem in social behavior. Together with wealth and power, honor or prestige has always been viewed as one of the three major axes of class systems and an important base for the social control all people and all groups have over one another.

Since prestige processes can be observed in any concrete situation, there is no end to the number of topics that could be analyzed by considering how people's behavior is shaped by the wish to obtain the respect of others. Thus, we are forced to choose which patterns or relationships are more important than others. We must also move beyond the concrete or particular situation, to social regularities or generalizations that can help to explain or illuminate specific social behavior, not only in the twentieth-century United States, but also in other epochs and places.

Among the more general questions that command our attention are the following: First, how is prestige or respect distributed? How highly is it correlated with some other variable such as family nobility or individual achievement? If, as seems apparent, at some points the increase of prestige is greater than the increase in achievement, what are the consequences for gossip and reputation, the giving of awards or prizes, or the allocation of personnel in an organization?

Next, how are prizes and honors used to shape social behavior? A very large minority—perhaps even a majority—of the population in this country win some kind of small or large prize or honor at some time in their lives, but most of the important awards, ribbons, and prizes are given to a few people, who are in fact more productive than others. Because prizes have many personal and social consequences, groups and organizations can use them to shape the behavior of their members. However, the formal giving of awards and honors is itself highly structured by social rules that implicitly state not only who may be given such rewards, but also which kinds of organizations may give them, and in which fields of human activity.

Since everyone at times suspects that the successful have not fully merited the esteem they receive, we also ask, how is prestige "subverted" by both individuals and groups? Obtaining respect from others is immediately rewarding, and it is likely to be useful as well. However, some people perceive that the social standards for winning approval are too difficult to meet. As a consequence, everyone is tempted at times to improve the apparent facts about himself or herself, to avoid merited punishment, or to gain unmerited rewards. This "subversion" of prestige processes has many consequences for individual lives, but it is of great political importance as well. To the extent that people come to believe the social system is simply rigged against them, they are more likely to withdraw their loyalty and support for it. How much subversion is tolerated varies from one field of activity to another, and from one historical era to another. These differences suggest the importance of exploring not only the interpersonal dynamics of prestige subversion, but also the subversion that is created by the social structure itself. Indeed, as we weigh the extent to which subversion on a wide scale is successful in any society, we come to the conclusion that the most successful subversion occurs as a result of active efforts by groups and organizations in power to prevent others from obtaining adequate opportunities for advancement.

How do prestige and the processes of attaining and losing prestige change over time? Here, the analysis of long-term changes in prestige processes considers two types of cases, both of which occur throughout history. In one of these, meeting the standards for obtaining the respect of others becomes easier (or harder) because of technical changes of various kinds, as when new training techniques make it easier to achieve new sports records, or widespread education makes it easier for almost everyone to master schoolroom English. In the other more general category new standards for obtaining the respect of others are proclaimed, as during the revolution, or when a new religious sect announces new rules for achieving a satisfactory degree of piety. When most people improve their behavior, and move the average level of, say, piety to a higher level, often the standard for a merely adequate performance rises too, so that behavior once considered adequate is now dispraised. Sometimes, by contrast, when the average level of performance rises or falls over time, the rule or standard simply loses its social importance.

How can praise and dispraise be used to deliberately shape behavior? What are the different effects of praise and dispraise? In some experimental learning situations, the behavior of the subjects (whether animals or human beings) is deliberately shaped by rewards or their absence. However, considerable evidence suggests that punishment has consequences that are different from the mere absence of reward. Since experimental data now suggest that rewards (or praise) are much more effective at shaping behavior than punishments are, I have tried to formulate some hypotheses to explain why dispraise is more widely used in some settings (training for the performing arts, athletics) than in others (science).

How are groups and individuals linked throughout society by the flow of esteem or prestige, and by the movement of people as they gain or lose prestige? Social life is shot through with dilemmas, tensions, and contrary effects, not the least of which is that giving respect or admiration is fundamentally an individual response, but that response comes from and flows back to various social groups and organizations. For that reason, we attempt to uncover and present some of the regularities that are observable in the myriad interlinkages among people and organizations in the society; that is, how prestige flows from one part of the society to another, and how people do so as well. Both these processes, and their corresponding social structures, help to shape individual movement from one group to another, the rise or decline of families in the class system, and the success or failure of organizations.

Under what conditions do people believe that prestige and honors and rewards are "just"? Whatever debate this inquiry stimulates about the meaning of prestige or respect, its processes must rest on beliefs about *worth*, or the justice of giving rewards to this or that organization or person, the rightness of privileges that are enjoyed by different classes in the stratification system. We are thus required to consider the ancient problem of justice. Although we suggest how sociological knowledge can contribute to its solution, no science can solve it; for what is defined as justice is at bottom determined by people's preferences, values, and attitudes. We consider whether talk of justice is no more than a rhetorical mode, or instead rests on some kinds of principles. If people and groups do believe in some principles of justice, we need to ascertain what they are, and more specifically what are the social forces that determine whether one principle of justice rather than another is applied under given circumstances—for example, in a survival situation, at a monarch's banquet, in decisions about who should be given a loan. These factors are of much consequence, of course, for the contemporary thrust toward greater equality.

In this, as in other substantive work I have done over the past two decades, I have continued to develop what seems to me a complex but realistic version of exchange theory.[1] For readers who are unfamiliar with this term, a comment is in order. All versions of exchange theory begin with the observation that an individual who wants another to do something must do something for that other person in turn. This may be as formal as giving money for goods, or as informal as an exchange of friendly greetings. Both parties value some things more than others, and thus are willing to pay more or less for them, just as they are more or less willing to give up some things to get what they want. Presumably, they will not continue to exchange if one or both parties learn that better bargains can be obtained elsewhere. Other things being equal, people will seek better terms for their social exchanges, as presumably they do for their economic exchanges. Just how the terms of exchange are agreed upon, why some people obtain good bargains more easily than others, where the evaluations come from, and how individual is the bargaining are the subjects of some controversy in this area.[2]

Since the theoretical orientation that I have been developing seems less open than others to the objections that some sociologists make against this approach, a brief description of it may be useful.

Although much social interaction occurs between two persons, they do not typically act as free-floating individuals; instead they act as members of a larger social structure or group. Thus, what one person does for another is often not "paid for" by that other person, but by an organization or other members of the group. Or, one person does something for another, who carries out some further service for still another individual, all of them being rewarded in some way by an organization, a family, a group, or a community.

Besides the payments themselves, the very terms of the exchange are not usually created or determined within the dyad, even when the exchange seems to occur between two people. The terms are mainly set before the transaction occurs, often before the two have even met. They are also shaped further by what I have called "third parties"—people (or groups) who are not immediately part of that transaction but who are socially linked with one or both of these persons.

Nor are the terms simply the outcome of a free market, of an unrestrained interaction of supply and demand. They are partly or mainly determined by norms or standards that answer the question, What is it

---

1. In company with a number of other social scientists, my rediscovery or recognition of exchange theory began in the late 1950's. Some of my grander aspirations of that time have since been chastened. My first two articles on these topics appeared in 1960: "A Theory of Role Strain," *American Sociological Review*, 25 (August, 1960): 438–496; and "Norm Commitment and Conformity to Role-Status Obligations," *American Journal of Sociology*, 66 (November, 1960): 246–258.

2. Two thoughtful critiques of exchange theory may be mentioned here: Anthony Heath, *Rational Choice and Social Exchange* (Cambridge: Cambridge University Press, 1976), and Peter Ekeh, *Social Exchange Theory: The Two Traditions* (London: Heineman, 1974). The most influential exposition remains that of George C. Homans, *Social Behavior: Its Elementary Forms* (London: Routledge & Kegan Paul, 1961). See also the experimental test in Philip Brickman, "Preference for Inequality," *Sociometry*, 40 (December, 1977): 303–310; and Toby Lee Parcel and Karen S. Cook, "Status Characteristics, Reward Allocation and Equity," *ibid.*: 311–324.

worth?—and those in turn reflect pre-existing distributions of resources and opportunities, including power. As a consequence, exchanges may continue even though one or both parties feel that the terms are not very fair. How voluntary or free the exchanges are is always a question to be answered by specific inquiry.[3]

All these comments call into question the use of a classical market model for social exchange. Moreover, although economic man has been assumed to pursue his own interests rationally (a view widely criticized) in most social exchanges, people are not likely to calculate closely how much they can gain. To be sure, they do know or learn whether they have done well over a period of time, and under some circumstances they may become very rational in their calculations. The notion of exchange also suggests a contractual relation, but social exchanges and especially friend-ship and prestige transactions are not mostly contractual. For example, we cannot truly promise a certain amount of respect or esteem to someone, because we cannot force ourselves to feel it or to avoid feeling it. We cannot will admiration any more than we can will the feeling of love.

Thus, social exchanges are not simply contracts or rational economic transactions. Social exchange is the more general form of social relation-ship, and market exchange only a subtype. On the other hand, as I shall later point out, certain types of economic exchanges in real life are closer to the general forms of social exchange than to the pure market of econometrics.

Of course, people and organizations also use both market and contract to control each other, and both are widely thought of as the most impor-tant modes of social control in modern urban industrial societies. So-ciologists sometimes use the term *Gesellschaft* for such a society as dis-tinguished from the rural, tribal, or traditional community labeled *Ge-meinschaft*. For centuries, social scientists have pointed out that these two types of social structures use different forms of social control.

But though contract and market do play a large role in the urban or *Gesellschaft* type of society, all the modes of social control are also found within it that are thought of as typical of the traditional community or *Gemeinschaft*: primary or personalistic relations, kinship, friendship, es-teem payments within the small group. These ways of controlling people's behavior are not simply residues of an older form of interaction; nor are they wiped out by contract, market, or industrialism generally. They spring up spontaneously in many settings. Since the larger focus of this study is on social control, I try to specify the social conditions under which people may press toward the use of either of these two patterns of shaping others' social action.

This inquiry also contributes to the continuing debate about the place of norms or values in social life, as well as the place of self-interest and

3. By contrast, Peter Blau specifically excludes from his version of exchange both the exchanges determined by threat and those determined by the individual's wish to conform to a norm he or she affirms. See his *Exchange and Power in Social Life* (New York: Wiley, 1964), pp. 91–92.

rationality. It thus throws some light on contemporary criticisms made against mainstream sociology, which some critics have charged with making the unrealistic assumptions that all members of a society feel committed to the same set of values and norms and that social behavior can be generally predicted from those consensual evaluations.[4] Certainly no ranking sociologist ever asserted such views. Nevertheless, it is fair to say that in the period between the two world wars, mainstream or consensual sociology did neglect somewhat the importance of self-interest and rationality, in part because it was exploring fruitfully the ways that norms, values, or beliefs of different groups help to shape social behavior. Modern sociologists are now redressing that neglect, primarily through a more elaborate analysis of exchange theory.

If we bring rationality and self-interest back into sociological theory (without forgetting that both are directed by norms and values), we are not asking whether social behavior is rational, nonrational, or irrational. Obviously it is all of these. Our next step is rather to ascertain the social conditions under which people are more or less rational, that is, when do they calculate closely the most effective means toward a given end.[5]

Much social science is now evaluated by whether or not it is Marxist in orientation. If an analysis is Marxist that lays bare the social forces of power and dissidence, this analysis does that, for it repeatedly calls attention to the situations in which people's power or class position manages to command more prestige than their performances might justify. However, if it is Marxist to assert that social action is "fundamentally" or "ultimately" economic, then this treatise is anti-Marxist. It suggests that we return rather to the common facts of observation when we ask what are the fundamental roots of human behavior. It is a curious perversion of reality to suppose that it is tough-minded or hard-nosed to believe that economic factors are so fundamental as to determine all others, including prestige processes. We can easily concede that starving people are somewhat less attentive to honor or pride than other people, but it is also obvious that when people seek profits, they do so *for* the things that profits can bring them—deference, ostentation, vulgar comforts, the love and friendship of people they esteem, political influence—which suggests again the weight of these "noneconomic" factors. This is so for organizations, groups, communities, and nations.

The tragedies of nationalist wars would have been greatly lessened if nations and the elites who directed them had merely sought profits or even

---

4. Although I have never made such extreme charges, and instead have pointed out that they are incorrect, I am of course to be numbered among the critics of mainstream sociology, as witness the two articles of mine in note 1. For some of the attacks, see my two articles "The Place of Values in Social Analysis" and "Functionalism: The Empty Castle," in William J. Goode, *Explorations in Social Theory* (New York: Oxford University Press, 1973), chaps. 2, 3.

5. For a cogent argument that economic theory need not be based on the strong assumption of maximizing rationality, because several *different* assumptions lead to similar economic conclusions, see Gary S. Becker, "Irrational Behavior and Economic Theory," in his *The Economic Approach to Human Behavior* (Chicago: University of Chicago Press, 1976), chap. 8.

plunder, and had not cared about glory or bowing and scraping from others. Religious wars and persecution would have been far less savage, if the people who set them into motion had only concerned themselves with maximizing their wealth. Of course, people desire money in part for the material benefits it will bring, but also because they need and want the admiration of others. They will engage in chicanery, violence, self-sacrifice, and even hard work in order to get that admiration.

In this inquiry I have stated systematically a large number of general relationships which are based, as far as that is possible, on observable facts, both contemporary and historical. However, the precise data needed to test many of these hypotheses do not yet exist. It is especially evident that we need far more *quantitative* data: we need to work out various operational indexes that will yield quantitative measurements of how *much* esteem is given for *which* kinds of behavior or qualities, and how much respect is acquired, lost, or traded for various kinds of help or services.[6]

Such quantitative developments would be useful not only as a basis for more precise tests of these related propositions in themselves, but also for the analysis of *power*. As I have noted here and elsewhere, the analysis of power has been handicapped by a loose conceptualization, which defines power simply as getting one's way against opposition, no matter what the sources of that influence might be. Clearly, power in that sense includes the resources of prestige. However, if we wish to make a distinct analysis of power itself, especially in the sense of force and force threat, we need to be able to separate out the influence of prestige (or love and friendship) from the great array of legal and quasi-legal factors that permit people to call upon others for support in the form of force threat. If we can develop quantitative statements about prestige processes, then we can analyze power more fruitfully.

Since the 1950's, several lines of theoretical work have been converging toward a more realistic analysis of social behavior. One such line is to be found in the extension of economic analysis to many types of nonmonetary behavior such as fertility, time, marriage and divorce, crime, and discrimination. Although I have written some criticisms of that development,[7] I have also welcomed it. The greater elegance and power of economic analysis both generates new hypotheses and offers a different foundation for many sociological research findings.

In addition, developments in social psychology have moved toward one or another form of exchange theory and equity theory and a wide variety of

6. Perhaps the closest approximation to such an analysis is Gary S. Becker's theorizing about how much people are willing to pay in order to indulge their wish to discriminate against others—i.e., how much they will pay to avoid contact with disesteemed others. See his *The Economics of Discrimination*, rev. ed. (Chicago: University of Chicago Press, 1971).

7. See my "Comment: The Economics of Nonmonetary Variables," in Theodore W. Schultz, ed., *Economics of the Family: Marriage, Children, and Human Capital* (Chicago: University of Chicago Press, 1973), pp. 345–351. For a severe criticism of econometric analysis of fertility, see Judith Blake, "Are Babies Consumer Durables? A Critique of the Economic Theory of Reproductive Motivation," in *Population Studies*, 22 (March, 1968): 5–25.

hypotheses about social control. We have often drawn on this largely experimental research, which is of course open to all the usual criticisms against the artificiality of social processes within a laboratory.[8] Nevertheless, that research contains numerous fruitful hypotheses, and many of them fit our day-to-day observation.

In sociology itself, of course, still other developments have been pursued. The work of J. Berger, Blau, B. Cohen, Coleman, Emerson, Goode, Homans, Zelditch, Zetterberg, and many others has increasingly moved to integrate various elements of role and exchange theory into a broader theoretical orientation that encompasses large-scale social structures as well.

In the past, the optimism of sociologists about the developments of the future has all too often been dashed by the less than momentous research findings that eventually appeared. Now, by contrast, we have some modest grounds for a realistic optimism about what can be built on the work of these decades.

Because this investigation has been under way for some two decades, and has been applied to much of my work on the professions, illegitimacy, force and force threat, divorce, family change, and role theory, many colleagues and strangers have helped me develop it, although it is safe to say many did not know that was happening. One unfortunate consequence of this complexity and errant time is that now I am simply not able to list the many who have clarified my thinking or stimulated me to improve the analysis through discussions or their publications. They number far more than the few I have mentioned in footnotes.

Of more direct importance are the many students who have criticized parts of this manuscript over the years. Important contributions have come from the many professorial and student colleagues who took part in our continuing "free-floating" uncatalogued seminar in theory at Columbia University, where I and others presented our research for commentary. I hesitate to mention any individuals for fear of overlooking others equally deserving of my gratefulness, but shall nevertheless venture to note a few: Angela Aidala, Andrew Beveridge, Ray Bradley, Mary E. Curran, Cynthia Fuchs Epstein, Carol Ann Finkelstein, Walter Goldfrank, Mark Johnson, Eugene Litwak, Stanley Raffel, Nicholas Tavuchis, Jerald G. Schutte, Joel Telles, Lenore J. Weitzman, James Wendt, Benjamin Zablocki.

In oral or epistolary discussions, others have been helpful, though again not all were aware that thereby they became responsible for some part of this work. Some of them are: Mark Baldassare, Peter Blau, Erich Goode, Alvin W. Gouldner, George C. Homans, Alex Inkeles, Paul F. Lazarsfeld, Robert K. Merton, James Coleman, Robert Hamblin, and Erving Goffman.

---

8. For a defense of such work see Morris Zelditch, "Can You Really Study an Army in the Laboratory?" in A. Etzioni, ed., *Complex Organizations,* 2d ed. (Holt, Rinehart, Winston, 1969), pp. 528–539.

I wish to thank Charlotte A. Fisher once more for her jolly efficiency in unscrambling the literally thousands of pages of this manuscript she has typed over the years.

At various phases in the development of this inquiry, I have received material support from the National Institute of Mental Health, the National Science Foundation, the Russell Sage Foundation, and the Hoover Institution. I am especially grateful for the generous gift of time that came from NIMH in the form of a Senior Scientist Career Award (1969–1974). Over the past two decades, I have again and again received help on this work from Columbia University. Even after numerous drafts, this manuscript was substantially revised after I came to Stanford University, which has willingly assumed the burden of yet another complete retyping and still more checking of data or footnotes by my conscientious research assistant Stephen Stedman and my secretary Linda Collins. For all this help I express my great thanks.

I apologize to others whom I have inadvertently omitted, and also thank them. I had not anticipated that this book would be so long in the making, but it was often exciting to watch it develop. I now give it to the reader, with the hope that the hard work of much rewriting has made the reading easier; and that much rethinking has increased the richness and validity of the analysis.

W. J. G.

Chapter 1
Social Control Through Prestige Processes

PRESTIGE AS A BASIS
OF SOCIAL CONTROL

One of the earliest bits of wisdom that infants acquire is an awareness that whatever they want must be obtained through other people. Adults believe they are more independent than infants, but there is little they do, from making love to murder, without enlisting the aid of others. Saint Simeon Stylites may indeed have lived alone on top of a pillar in a desert, but he had to persuade others he deserved the gift of whatever was necessary for survival. Some hermit saints have instead retired to caves, but they do not live long unless believers come and give them food. The reclusive "mountain men" of the American west had to come down to a trading post from time to time to obtain the salt, bullets, and flour that only other people could provide. People have aimed at the stars, aspired to the hearts of queens, and commanded empires while using a range of techniques from love magic to atomic bombs, but always they have needed the help of others.

Indeed, in considering the wide variety of human activities, it seems clear that a large and critical part of all human action is *social action*, that is, behavior that affects or shapes others' actions. That behavior can be examined in many ways, but a most fruitful way is to view it as *social control*. We lay bare its most important meaning when we focus on how social behavior moves (or fails to move) people to act in ways other people want them to act.[1] Social control is the general topic to be explored in this study, and it has been a central concern of sociology from its beginnings as social philosophy over two millennia ago.

1. Most sociologists who have written on this traditional topic have emphasized only one of its aspects: how groups or societies try to make individual members conform. However, even they are forced to consider individuals' resistance, i.e., how individuals also try to affect group behavior or the behavior of other people. Thus, although I am deliberately broadening this traditional topic in order to include the ways all social actors (collective or individual) affect one another's actions, the essential meaning of the topic is not being violated. One of the earlier American sociologists to give major attention to it is Edward A. Ross in his *Social Control* (Cleveland: Case Western Reserve University Press, 1969 [orig. ed. 1901]).

To assert that the analysis of social control is a principal sociological task is not to take a singular or odd theoretical position. The central problem of any science is the discovery of whatever order or regularity exists in the phenomena it studies, and of the processes or factors that govern that order. In sociology, the observable social order is created by social control processes, that is, the efforts people make to shape one another's behavior. To achieve their goals, people and groups, organizations and nations constantly try to control what others do, using any techniques or resources they can muster: an infant's cry, a raise in salary, a teacher's smile of approval, a dictator's threat of exile.

In this inquiry, the focus will be on one special set of control techniques and processes: the allocation of prestige, respect, or esteem.[2] Specifically, how people's behavior is shaped or affected by the esteem that others give to them or withdraw from them will be analyzed. Observed in any continuing social interaction, at high and low social ranks, in formal and informal settings, among egalitarians and elitists, the social processes by which esteem or respect is generated, accumulated, expended, or lost have a great effect on most social behavior. These processes have not yet been analyzed systematically. To do so is the aim of this book.

THE SOCIAL CONTROL PROCESSES

For centuries, social analysts have intuitively perceived that the multiplicity of concrete goods and services exchanged, the threats and rewards people give one another, the persuasions and payoffs, could be categorized as examples of four general control resources or sets of factors. They can even be viewed as analytically distinct social realms. From Plato onward, social scientists and philosophers have given different names to these sets of factors; but their disagreement has been more in the naming alone than in the notion of what the control resources or factors actually are.

If a general resource or set of related factors is to be widely effective in eliciting desired behavior from others, it must have several social attributes. The main ones are these:

1. It must be wanted or needed by almost everyone because of its utility in gaining one's ends.

2. It must be obtainable, usable, and observable in a wide range of social interactions, from informal play among boys and girls to religious ceremonies, from war to the stock exchange.

3. People must be able to generate, accumulate, lose, or expend it in some fashion.

4. It must be exchangeable, under some conditions, for the others; or at least, the possession of any one type should increase the likelihood of obtaining any of the others.

Social analysts have also agreed that three control factors in particular

---

2. Throughout this analysis, I use these terms in their usual English sense and do not impose on them any esoteric or technical meanings. In subsequent pages, I shall define my central concept, but that definition does not depart from ordinary usage.

are important because they are the fundamental bases of social stratification, that is, they determine which social strata or classes actually exist in any society. Besides *force and force threat*, they are *wealth* and *prestige*. A fourth has appeared less often (but, as usual in sociology, beginning with Plato), which could be loosely labeled *friendship-love-affection*.

Because I believe the processes of control are somewhat different in each realm, separate sets of propositions should be developed for each,[3] though here I shall try to demonstrate the fruitfulness of a separate development of only one: prestige. In fact, the distinction among these four realms is often made in daily observation; and of course, all have repeatedly figured in classical social theory. For example, the range of weapons from the clenched fist to the hydrogen bomb can be viewed as one type of resource, under the rubric of force or the threat of force. In some terminologies, this category is often confused by using the term "power" to designate it.[4] The confusion occurs because power is typically defined in a Weberian sense, meaning getting one's way against some resistance. But since an individual can impose his or her will through love, force, money, or prestige, the term then means no more than "getting compliance."[5] Despite all the confusion engendered by so loose a definition—which could refer to almost any kind of control over others from whatever source—"power" suggests coercion and domination, and the realm of resources sometimes covered by the term has long been recognized as basically comprising all the processes of force and force threat.

In Plato's *Republic*, the people who achieved the highest levels were to be given great honor, but they were not to indulge in mere physical comforts. Those who were to use force—who were younger and had not yet passed through all the trials and examinations that yielded the highest positions—would not be given as much honor. But only the lowest class of the four-class system were to enjoy the vulgar pleasures of material wealth.

In his *Muqadima*, Ibn-Khaldun described the cyclical process by which tribal groups, scorning the wealthy decadence of urban people and united by a care for honor and for close personal and kin ties, conquered great cities but were in turn corrupted by the wealth and power they obtained.

3. I have in fact been engaged in that task for many years. See, for example, "The Place of Force in Human Society," *American Sociological Review*, 37 (October, 1972): 507–519; "The Economics of Nonmonetary Variables," in T. W. Schultz, ed., *Economics of the Family* (Chicago: University of Chicago Press, 1974), pp. 345–351; "Violence between Intimates," in *Explorations in Social Theory* (New York: Oxford University Press, 1973), pp. 145–197; "The Theoretical Importance of Love," *American Sociological Review*, 24 (February, 1959): 38–47.

4. For an analysis based on the notion of power as force or its threat, see my article "The Place of Force in Human Society."

5. For an example, see Peter M. Blau, *Exchange and Power in Social Life* (New York: John Wiley, 1964), pp. 21ff., 118ff., where Blau—following Emerson—defines the generating condition for power as one in which an individual wants something, he cannot obtain it from another source, and he cannot do without it. This condition merely defines a difficult bargaining situation, and in fact few occasions so dire are encountered in real life. However, the more important point is that it simply refers to *any* kind of influence over another; and it is confusing to use the term "power," which in

In *The Prince*, Machiavelli wrote in concrete, not abstract terms; but he often distinguished carefully among good reputation or honor, force and force threat, and wealth. He warned the Prince to leave unsullied the virtue of his subjects' women, else he would risk losing control over them: Subjects will rebel if their honor is attacked. He noted the usefulness of esteem, of being perceived as truthful, generous, kindly, pious, and basically deserving of respect.

In his usually clearheaded fashion, Hobbes asserted in *The Leviathan* that when there are no bases for dependence or cooperation among human beings, that is, for social order, they will rely upon force to control one another. But this could not be a foundation for an orderly society: the hand of every man would be turned against every other man, and any man has the ability to kill any other. His solution was the creation of a monarch with a monopoly of force, but one whose authority could also command great deference from his subjects, one whose prestige would overawe his people.

Modern sociologists have followed Max Weber and other classical writers in distinguishing among the first three of these realms of control, namely, "party" (force, power, political authority), class (economic factors), and status (honor, prestige). They have done so because daily observation discloses that an individual may rank high on one of these but less high on another, and each realm exhibits somewhat different patterns of behavior.[6]

For example, Weber and many others have pointed out that an individual may achieve great wealth, but elite circles may nevertheless reject him if he has not yet earned much personal prestige, or if his life style is not admirable. In discussing the processes through which "homogamy" occurs, that is, husband and wife are likely to have similar social backgrounds, analysts also point out that a man who enjoys high prestige for his achievements but possesses little money may be acceptable as a bridegroom for a woman whose family is wealthy but commands less esteem.[7]

English possesses many connotations of force, coercion, and domination. See Richard M. Emerson, "Power-Dependence Relations," *American Sociological Review*, 27 (1962): 31–41.

6. For example, almost all extensive analyses of stratification systems point out that these three are correlated, but independent, and they sometimes devote separate chapters to the importance of wealth or political influence. To illustrate that independence, they sometimes note the examples of the rich, politically powerful, but disesteemed racketeer, or the esteemed, politically unimportant, but modestly well-to-do professor. The most important collection of essays in this area remains that of Reinhard Bendix and Seymour M. Lipset, *Class, Status, and Power*, 2d ed. (New York: Free Press, 1966). See also T. H. Marshall, *Citizenship and Social Class* (Cambridge: Cambridge University Press, 1950); T. B. Bottomore, *Classes in Modern Society* (New York: Vintage, 1966); Leonard Reissman, "Social Stratification," in Neil J. Smelser, ed., *Sociology*, 2d ed. (New York: Wiley, 1973), pp. 127–190; and Edward O. Laumann, Paul M. Siegel, and Robert W. Hodge, eds., *The Logic of Social Hierarchies* (Chicago: Markham, 1970).

Max Weber's formulation is in "The Distribution of Power within the Political Community: Class, Status and Power," in *Economy and Society: An Outline of Interpretive Sociology*, trans. Guenther Roth and Claus Wittich (New York: Bedminister, 1968 [1922]), II, 926–940.

7. Sociologists have sometimes defined prestige by reference to a class of positions, such as the

Systematic empirical data, daily ordinary observation, or our own intuitions and introspections make the distinction among these three factors, elements, or social realms relatively clear.[8] As to the fourth: The social control aspects of friendship, affection, and love have not been totally ignored in sociology, but as far as I know there is no systematic treatise on it[9] and none on prestige.

The one realm that separated long ago from the other three is of course that of economic processes, and it contains the theoretically most sophisticated body of propositions. By contrast, the realm of force and force threat has only rarely, except for empirical studies of war and mathematical formulations in game theory, been analytically distinguished as a formal area for the development of linked empirical propositions.[10] Instead, analysts (usually political scientists or political sociologists) have focused on the concrete phenomena of government and political parties, and on political influence generally. Here, as in economics, the main lines of inquiry have been developed by a separate academic discipline.

Clearly, both people and corporate agencies use all four types of resources to elicit cooperation from others, even though the four can be analytically distinguished. Citizens accuse prison wardens at times of "coddling the prisoners," but wise prison wardens know that a system based on force alone is explosive. Corporations emphasize economic pay-

---

prestige of occupations, and have reserved the term esteem for the approval or respect that an individual enjoys by virtue of his performance within that position or occupation; but in this inquiry I shall not use separate terms. For a definition of that distinction, see Kingsley-Davis, *Human Society* (New York: Macmillan, 1949), p. 94.

8. Sociologists will also recognize that these four classical realms of action overlap in part with Parsons' AGIL schema: Talcott Parsons, R. F. Bales, and E. A. Shils, *Working Papers in the Theory of Action* (Glencoe, Ill.: Free Press, 1953), pp. 180–185; although the precise definitions of each of his four phases seem too obscure to permit exact delineation. The four are still closer to the variables laid out by Amitai Etzioni in *Complex Organizations* (New York: Free Press, 1961), pt. 1, although we seem to differ in minor ways in our usage of the concept "coercion vs. force and force threat," and "allocation and manipulation of acceptance and positive response" vs. friendship-affection love. In his empirical analysis, the fourth realm drops out altogether.

9. My colleague Allan Silver has for some years been analyzing this phenomenon and has amassed a considerable bibliography on the topic. Sociologists have contributed to it, but their work is a tiny part of the whole. Social psychologists have been investigating these relations recently. However, up to now there is no systematic analysis that presents a series of propositions which separate the independent effect of friendship on control processes, or the conditions under which friendship or love arises—though approximations of this latter goal do exist. See, e.g., Edward E. Jones, *Ingratiation* (New York: Appleton-Century-Crofts, 1964); Ellen Berscheid and Elaine H. Walster, *Interpersonal Attraction* (Reading, Mass.: Addison-Wesley, 1969); and Kenneth J. Gergen, *The Psychology of Behavior Exchange* (Reading, Mass.: Addison-Wesley, 1969).

10. See in this connection Ted R. Gurr, *Why Men Rebel* (Princeton, N.J.: Princeton University Press, 1970). For a mathematical treatment of international force and threat, see Thomas C. Schelling, *The Strategy of Conflict* (New York: Oxford University Press, 1963). Of course, threat has been experimentally studied. See, e.g., Morton Deutsch and R. Krauss "The Effect of Threat upon Interpersonal Bargaining," *Journal of Abnormal and Social Psychology*, 61 (1960): 181–189; and C. S. Fischer, "The Effect of Threats in an Incomplete Information Game," *Sociometry*, 32 (September, 1969): 301–314. See also H. Andrew Michener *et al.*, "Factors Affecting Concession Rate and Threat Usage in Bilateral Conflict," *Sociometry*, 38 (March, 1975): 62–81; and James Tedeschi *et al.*, "Compliance to Threats as a Function of Source Attractiveness and Esteem," *ibid.*: 81–99.

ments, but wise managers attempt to foster both interpersonal friendships and prestige-giving in order to create more effective organizations.

Close friends express their affection and respect for one another, but it is observable that they also exchange gifts and services, which will be roughly balanced over time.[11] People try to consolidate growing affection through material gifts. In the more purely economic of relations, wise businessmen will present gifts and favors to one another as tokens or perhaps real expressions of friendship. A political leader who engages in tough bargaining about who can deliver the votes in exchange for money or for a counter-offer of power takes care to pay some respect and deference to those with whom he bargains.

Though this analysis focuses primarily upon one of these sets of processes—the giving, withholding, and utilization of prestige—it does not suggest that it is more important than the others.

WHY PEOPLE SEEK ESTEEM

We need only introspect to recognize how important others' approval and respect are to us. We have been socialized to need this deference or esteem, and those responses from others become *ends* in themselves, or psychological needs. At the earliest period of childhood socialization, approval is accompanied by love and affection and disapproval by anger, rejection, and sometimes physical hurt.[12] In simple terms, we are un-happy if people do not give us approval, and we feel pleased if they do, whether or not that respect can be used for other purposes. If others do not recognize our worth, we are dismayed, annoyed, or bitter, even if we do not need another person's esteem as a means toward some end.

In addition, prestige is obviously a *means* to the goals of individuals, groups, and corporate agencies. If we command higher prestige than others, we enjoy entree into socially more desirable circles. People are more pleased to receive our telephone calls, letters, or visits. More re-munerative jobs are offered us. We are more likely to be consulted about changes in policies within our organization, group, or community.[13] Organizations that have low prestige are less able to command political or financial resources when they need them. Potential employees are less willing to join their staffs. Employees are less proud of working for such associations.

11. Indeed, in his classic essay *The Gift* (1925), Marcel Mauss speaks of the "obligation" of repaying, which in any event is a matter of common observation: trans. J. Cunnison (New York: Norton, 1967), pp. 10, 37ff.

12. "Social approval" also appears in behavioral psychology, where it is viewed as one of several "secondary reinforcers"—i.e., because of earlier association with primary reinforcers such as goods, it comes to have an influence of its own. See B. F. Skinner, *Science and Human Behavior* (New York: Free Press, 1953), pp. 77–78; and F. S. Keller, *Learning-Reinforcement Theory* (New York: Random House, 1954), pp. 55–62.

13. Studies of public opinion and of fashion changes have noted for decades that people of higher social rank have a greater influence than do others on public opinion and acceptance of innovations. Experiments by social psychologists have yielded similar data; see, e.g., E. E. Jones and Harold P. Gerard, *Foundations of Social Psychology* (New York: Wiley, 1967), pp. 436–439.

Consequently, one individual or group can control another to a degree by responding with esteem or disapproval to the other's acts, policies, philosophies, and so forth. When people fail to comply with the wishes or values of others, they know that they run the risk of some kind of disapproval and that eventually they will encounter resistance or lack of cooperation.[14] Knowing this, they are less likely to run that risk. Since having others' esteem is both desirable and useful, people will act to increase it, if that is not too difficult.

DEFINING PRESTIGE

A fully satisfactory formal definition of prestige is not easily stated. But for the purposes of this analysis *prestige is the esteem, respect, or approval that is granted by an individual or a collectivity for performances or qualities they consider above the average.*[15] An individual may, for example, make a *contribution* to a group by sacrificing his or her life, or by paying for religious rituals. An individual may generate deference or respect for achieving an above-normal level of performance in an area that is valued highly by the group: splitting the atom, singing a Bach cantata brilliantly, or winning a stickball game. Prestige (negative or positive) may also be granted for *qualities* with which the individual is endowed by birth, such as nobility, membership in an ethnic group, or perhaps musical genius. Some qualities that are approved or disapproved can be acquired without achievement—qualities such as age or various physical or mental disabilities. Sociologists often lump these together as "ascribed" traits.

Later, we shall analyze how exhibiting approved qualities or performances above the average is frequently viewed as contributing to the group; and how groups share somewhat in the prestige their members receive for their achievements. But here it is to be noted only that an exceptional performance or quality approved by the group will yield some esteem.

As is often the problem in definitions, this one is also open to the charge of circularity: a group pays prestige, that is, approval, for the things it approves. At a deeper level, the term is also partly indefinable and primitive, like many other terms that ultimately refer to feeling tones (love, hate, awe).[16]

But that circularity can be broken by taking note of a wide variety of behaviors that can be considered indexes of prestige: formal awards, hon-

14. Every reader has had this experience, which has also been tested in social psychology experiments on social conformity. See Leon Festinger, Stanley S. Schachter, and Kurt Back, *Social Pressures in Informal Groups* (New York: Harper, 1950).

15. Of course we must not forget that the definition ignores the obvious, theoretically trivial exception: e.g., being born with six green legs is certainly "above the norm" of two pink ones, but it is empirically ascertainable that this is not a desired or approved trait.

16. Most such definitions fail to satisfy critics because operational or nominal definitions so clearly fail to capture the critics' actual experience. Critics are less severe on definitions of "negative" emotions, such as hate, hostility, or envy. With reference to this problem, see my article "The Theoretical Importance of Love," pp. 251ff.

ors, gestures of deference or respect paid to those who achieve well. It can also be ascertained empirically that some organizations enjoy more prestige than others. We can find out whether group members do hold certain values, and whether individuals or groups who live by such values to a high degree are paid more respect than the others. (Technically, this last test would of course no longer be a definition but a postulated, empirical regularity.) We can also ask individuals whether they do in fact feel esteem or approval toward them, and whether they pay that overt esteem to others because those others have certain qualities or have achieved beyond the average.[17]

It is important to keep in mind that approval or praise is also given *for the right kinds of approval*. That is to say, not only do we give approval to socially approved kinds of performances, activities, and qualities; but also, the people around us give us approval for our evaluations. We learn from their response that we have reacted "correctly." If we praise what is considered vulgar, meretricious, ugly, or immoral, then parents, friends, and teachers inform us that we have responded "incorrectly," that is, we do not have the "right values."

From the earliest age, children not only learn to which action standards they are required to adjust, but they also acquire the appropriate *responses* to others' behavior, traits, and activities.[18] In the first stages of acquaintanceship as adults, people typically sound out one another by various comments, expressions of attitudes, or gestures, through which they communicate how they evaluate different tastes in music, fashion, or sports. Thereby they learn one another's class position, particular cliques or circles, political and esthetic allegiances, and so on. As a consequence, they may decide early in the interaction to retreat to the banalities and platitudes of cocktail talk. Or, they may instead agree on each other's excellence, and move on to deepen and widen the relationship. In short, we are constantly evaluating others' evaluations.

DISTINCTIONS IN
PRESTIGE INTERACTION

At the simple experimental level a prestige response seems to be individual; obviously, when we speak of a "group" response we simply mean that most individuals within that group experience a feeling of esteem when someone has performed well.[19] A community may esteem Mr. X, for

17. And of course we can ask them about their feelings of self-esteem or self-worth when they believe they have done very well.

18. For an analysis of these processes from a "social exchange" perspective, see Robert L. Hamblin, ed., *The Humanization Processes* (New York: Wiley, 1971).

19. In such responses, in social exchanges, and in social interaction generally, it cannot be assumed that one dominant person, or "the group," controls fully the response or the action. People can and do leave; dominant people "need" subordinates; subordinates need not agree or yield; and concessions from both sides may be required to keep the relationship stable. In any of its various meanings, power is never completely in the hands of one party.

example, because he has bequeathed his excellent art collection to the local museum; or a work team may respect Mr. Y because he has carried out an elegant statistical computation. But sociological analysis reveals that these apparently individual responses are not only maintained by the groups within which the individual acts and lives, but that they are initially generated and acquired through a socialization process that teaches the individual to value or respect such arts or achievements.

In most analyses, of course, we need not go back to the sources of those values, either in the history of the group or in that of the individual; we need only ascertain what they are and how much people will sacrifice to live by such values. That has been the traditional position of economists, for example, who need only to ask how much something is valued on the market, not how the evaluation arose which makes that market value high or low.

In daily observation we make a further distinction between a prestige *response*, and the *act* of paying prestige. An individual may feel admiration for another's work or performance but for various reasons hide that admiration. A person may enjoy a high rank as a creative scientist, but his colleagues may decide on political or personal grounds not to give him a medal for his achievements. A football coach may feel his quarterback's performance deserves no praise but decide to evoke a still higher level of performance by complimenting him warmly.

In addition, at times we can and do pay more deference to some people than we actually feel. At a political rally one leader may introduce another whose policies he deplores and whose character he detests; nevertheless he publicly expresses great respect for the man. Posts, honors, degrees, and other expressions or payments of prestige are sometimes given to those who have earned only modest admiration. We need only observe the overt deference any boss enjoys in his office to recognize that the amount of prestige payment is not always equivalent to the amount of esteem (or disapproval) that people actually feel.[20]

Obviously, this distinction introduces the possibility of manipulation or subversion, which is complex enough to require more systematic attention in later chapters (on the subversion of prestige processes and on public awards). At this point it should merely be noted, however, that for the most part people are not manipulative in their gestures and acts of respect toward one another. Not only are they not insincere; I believe that in general most people are not even conscious of the ways in which they express esteem for others, whether peers or superiors. But at various points

---

20. For some of the dynamics or processes by which such payments can be made when modest performance has been achieved, see my "Protection of the Inept," in *Explorations in Social Theory*, pp. 121–144. Even a group that respects a man's work may not like him, or they may feel that he is not a true member. A later section analyzes participation or membership as a factor in granting *public* prestige payments.

we shall find that the distinction between manipulative and spontaneous prestige payment, and between overt esteem and inner respect, is of considerable empirical importance.

Not only may an individual pay prestige he does not feel, or withhold the expression of esteem he does feel. In addition, the performance of a person deserving esteem according to the criteria of the people who observe it may not become well known, whereas the achievement of another individual may be given great prominence by design or accident.[21] In these two instances, the amount of deference overtly expressed may actually be as much as the inner individual prestige response, but it may not correspond with the actual achievement. We must then be alert both to the possibility of *manipulation* and to the problem of *contingency*, the chance that performances actually become well enough known to be admired.

CONSCIOUS VERSUS SPONTANEOUS EXPRESSIONS OF RESPECT

Because we are concerned with the overt *payment* of prestige as a control process, we must at least take brief note of how the insincere gesture or act of esteem may affect others' actions. Blau and Homans take somewhat different positions on this point. Homans bases his theorizing on the notion of psychological reinforcement and asserts:

> Those who read this book are taken by that fact to be men of the world, who know that when Person thanks Other he may not really feel grateful. As social scientists we may also believe that skilled questioning of Person might bring out how sincere he was. But sincerity is not a problem for us. The real question is this: Whether or not Person is sincere, does his expressed sentiment reinforce Other's behavior? What Other doesn't know won't hurt him, and so far as he takes the thanks at face value and acts as if it were a sign of approval, we care not if it be sincere.[22]

By contrast, Blau seems to assert that the influence of insincerity is substantial:

> The social approval of those whose opinions we value is of great significance to us, but its significance depends on its being genuine. We cannot force others to give us their approval, regardless of how much power we have over them, because coercing them to express their admiration or praise would make these expressions worthless . . . . Simulation robs approval of its significance, but its very importance makes associates reluctant to withhold approval from one another and, in particular, to express disap-

21. In science, these accidents and manipulations often appear in the raging controversies about who should get credit for a discovery. For some dramatic cases, see Robert K. Merton, *The Sociology of Science*, ed. Norman W. Storer (Chicago: University of Chicago Press, 1973), pt. 4, "The Reward System of Science."

22. George C. Homans, *Social Behavior: Its Elementary Forms* (New York: Harcourt, Brace & World, 1961), p. 34.

proval, thus introducing an element of simulation and dissimulation into their communications.[23]

Without analyzing these two positions in detail, I should like to summarize my general position on how conscious people are about their prestige-giving when they try to control others, and what effect that consciousness has. Most expressions of respect are not only genuine but uncalculating. To be sure, some individuals are frequently conscious or even Machiavellian about giving praise to others as a way of obtaining an end, whether it is the general goodwill of other people or some future specific benefit.[24] Indeed, there are few true "innocents" (or insensitives) who almost invariably respond spontaneously with praise or blame without being at least aware that those expressions might have adverse or favorable effects on their own plans. All people are at times conscious of these effects upon others; thus all try at times to affect others' behavior by giving or withholding praise or blame. In some situations, this consciousness is salient, especially in anger or disappointment. Then, individuals do calculate whether they have been given enough respect, or whether they have given more praise than deserved. If people are receiving about what they think they deserve they are less likely to be conscious of how much that is, while the person who praises them is not forced to be very conscious about the control results of his praise. This may also be phrased thus: there is a definite floor but a much less firm ceiling, to the level of praise individuals feel they should get, below which they are likely to become very conscious of how much they "deserve" or how much they are giving. Stated differently, if individuals get a good bit more than they feel they deserve, they are less prone to be guilty about not deserving the praise than they are to be indignant when they get too little.[25]

Dissimulation, expressing approval without feeling it, is likely to have some effect on others, as does failure to express approval even when it is genuinely felt. Both types of dissimulation will have some effect, though it will be less when the target person is sure that the praise, dispraise, or nonpraise is not what the other person really feels.

Similarly, people may correctly penetrate the dissimulation, and they have a strong motivation to do so. It is possible, nevertheless, that false praise, correctly perceived as false, may achieve some control over the target person. How much control is a question to be determined by empirical investigation.

23. Blau, *Exchange and Power in Social Life*, p. 17.

24. For analyses of Machiavellianism, see Richard Christie and Florence Geis, eds., *Studies in Machiavellianism* (New York: Academic Press, 1970), and Stanley S. Guterman, *The Machiavellians* (Lincoln: University of Nebraska Press, 1970).

25. What one believes one deserves may be Thibaut and Kelley's Comparison Level, the standard by which one values what one gets. Their CLalt, or Comparison Level Alternative, is the lowest level of acceptable outcome, below which one will simply leave the relationship. My emphasis here is simply that as the rewards drop, one becomes much more conscious of how much one "deserves," and

Some social transactions will be unsuccessful unless people *can* pene-trate others' conscious attempts at dissimulation to some extent. For example, one individual may follow good form by openly stating his or her admiration, but intend that the other should know that it is not meant. A common pattern of flirtation is double dissimulation, when each intends that the other should know the opposite is meant—as when a man and woman engage in ironic verbal (or other symbolic) attacks on each other.

But what is most important is that the amount of consciousness, or even calculation, in the use of approval as a control action does not usually determine whether the control attempt succeeds. Individuals vary from one moment to the next in the amount of their alertness to the possible effects of giving approval to others, although it is probably usually given spontaneously and without much thought.[26] Whether calculated or not, prestige-giving is likely to have some effect. How much (and in which direction) can be empirically investigated. If sincerity of the sentiment is important, sincerity can also be studied as an independent factor. Indeed, as will be reported later, data on some of these points do exist.

IDEAL IDEALS AND WORKING IDEALS

It can usually be said that performing at the level of a *working ideal* means that the individual earns an average amount of prestige and con-tinues to be acceptable in a certain group; if the individual performs far above that level, he or she gains an increasing amount of prestige and might be viewed as performing at the level of an *ideal ideal*. Still, it must be kept in mind that, with reference to some activities, people will view a performance beyond some working ideal as not admirable, heroic, or saintly, but as neurotic, obtrusive, or annoying. For example, in any given group there is an acceptable level of cleanliness. Below that level, one is disapproved of as "dirty." Above it, one is not admired but viewed as silly. Similarly, all subgroups or relationships have some norm of how much truth is permitted or encouraged. To pay out less truth than that will likely earn a person the reputation of being a fibber or even a liar. However, above that working ideal, one is not so much viewed as noble but as blunt, tactless, or even cruel.

In some contexts it is necessary to specify *whose* working ideal one is to follow. To perform beyond the norm in many work groups is to earn the

---

that is more likely to occur than if one gets *more* than is deserved. See John W. Thibaut and Harold H. Kelley, *The Social Psychology of Groups* (New York: Wiley, 1959), pp. 21–23.

26. Mark Baldassare points out that this is because we have been taught to give approval on the appropriate occasions, thus we do so automatically, without thinking. Under different conditions, people's ability to make correct judgments about others' feelings or dispositions will also vary. See E. E. Jones and K. E. Davis, "From Acts to Dispositions: The Attribution Process in Person Percep-tion," in L. Berkowitz, ed., *Advances in Experimental Social Psychology*, II (New York: Academic Press, 1965), pp. 220–266; and Kelley Shaves, *An Introduction to Attribution Processes* (Cambridge, Mass.: Winthrop, 1975).

enmity or deprecation of one's fellow workers but the praise or approval of superiors. This is not so much a conceptual distinction as an empirical one, however. It merely requires that we sometimes specify which group ideals are being used as the criteria to measure prestige.

PRESTIGE VERSUS ECONOMIC EXCHANGES

The most general basis of prestige generation is the overfulfillment of a social norm, or some approximation to an ideal ideal as distinguished from the working ideal.[27] Since all societies rank both ascriptive qualities and achieved performances, they also grant prestige for both.

This group emphasis underlines the fact that although prestige processes can be viewed as exchanges, they are not fundamentally *dyadic*, meaning that one person does something for another for which the other pays him back. Individuals do not typically try to achieve *for* another specific person. The most central relationship is most fruitfully seen as *triadic*: a relation among Person, Other, and Group or Community. A person may feel hurt if specific other persons do not give appropriate praise for an excellent performance, but that standard is set by the group or social set of which they are both members.[28] Overpraise by an especially significant other person is welcome, as underpraise is unwelcome, but both are perceived and evaluated by reference to the real or hypothetical responses of others.

Individuals engage in prestige processes if they interact with others at all. Everyone is constantly under judgment, being evaluated for his or her qualities and performances, if only as a normal by-product of everyone's concern as to whether others are fulfilling their obligations. But though this pervasiveness appears to be similar to that of economic phenomena[29]—for the economist asserts that a wide range of social acts can be called economic—in several ways the prestige processes are different.[30]

First, we are all consumers in both systems (we must obtain goods, and we cannot avoid evaluating other people), but in the economic sphere some can avoid being producers. If they are wealthy, or are supported by others, they do not have to sell goods or services. By contrast, to live is to act; and some of one's acts will inevitably be evaluated by others. Second,

27. For further comments on the distinction between these types of ideals, see my "Norm Commitment and Conformity to Role-Status Obligations," *American Journal of Sociology*, 66 (November, 1960): 246–258. See also Marion J. Levy, Jr., *The Structure of Society* (Princeton, N.J.: Princeton University Press, 1952), pp. 157–166.

28. See also the discussion of the collective aspects of exchange in Peter Ekeh, *Social Exchange Theory: The Two Traditions* (Cambridge, Mass.: Harvard University Press, 1974), pt. II.

29. For the theoretical importance of such comparisons—i.e., how one is rated by reference to others—see Leon Festinger, "A Theory of Social Comparison Processes," *Human Relations*, 7 (May, 1954): 117–140.

30. A brief analysis of these differences is also to be found in my article "A Theory of Role Strain," in *Explorations in Social Theory*, pp. 97–120.

an individual can be a specialist producer in the economic realm; but in the area of prestige a person produces not only whatever his or her job calls for, but a wide range of other acts—friendly greetings, paternal behavior, neighborly cooperation, for example—and all will be approved to some extent or not. Third, one can leave the economic market, except for consumption, but one cannot leave the realm of prestige, for even in old age one's behavior will be weighed and found acceptable or wanting.

These contrasts are presented as an illustration of basic distinctions between the economic and prestige processes, but in chapter 3 those differences will be examined in more detail and other important differences will be presented.

CONCLUSION

All social structures, institutions, organizations, or processes that endure—the preparation and execution of military campaigns, the production and allocation of goods, the socialization of the succeeding generation, the worship of the gods—do so mainly because people want to carry out the specific, concrete acts or tasks that make up those larger social patterns. People want to do so because their childhood socialization makes those actions preferable to other acts, and because they are rewarded by other people for carrying them out or punished for not doing so.

Specifically, people are willing to comply with others' wishes or needs in return for compliance with theirs, or for rewards from still other people for their actions. That is, the specific link between individual actions and the larger needs of the society is created by all the ways by which individuals are persuaded or forced to do what others want, in return for which they get cooperation and help from those others. Since the 1950's, these processes have been called "social exchanges." As emphasized in the Preface and spelled out in more detail in chapter 3, they do not follow a simple economic pattern and cannot be easily deduced from microeconomies. Prestige exchanges and distributions do not follow a contractual model, either. People do not ordinarily think of their social behavior with others as "social exchanges," just as they do not think of them as ways of controlling others; but both exchange and control processes are observable within social interaction just the same.

If people can achieve their goals only to the degree that those whose help *they* need reciprocally need *their* help, they must spend some of their energy and skill in obtaining or giving resources that others want: flattery, expertise, tenderness, land. Or, they must force others to cooperate. As in all exchanges, each of us would perhaps like to pay out or concede things that are not of great value to us. Perhaps in most our secret hearts we would like to be given deference, love, wealth, and influence simply for being our own true selves, rather than working hard for any of these things.

Unfortunately, our lot is different, and harder. Coleman takes note of this important condition for exchanges aimed at social control by postulating (for political control) that the individual "will lack power [in his sense, influence] over actions which interest him, together with a surplus of power over actions which interest him little or not at all."[31] Thereby, the individual is moved to yield in the latter areas, in exchange for which other persons may yield in the former areas.

Since the case of "little or no interest" may be too rare, Coleman's postulation can be emended toward greater realism by stating that: the individual can obtain some control over people if he has some control over matters less important to him, which he can exchange for others' actions that are more important to him. This emendation is also closer to the conception of the economist, who needs to assume only that: people are willing to exchange when what they possess is less valuable to them than it is to others—who in turn control goods or services that are less valuable to *them* than what the first set of people offers.

Of course many individuals may be in the still less advantageous position that they value greatly what they must pay out in services and influence, and what they can get in return seems a poor bargain indeed though the best bargain they can get. Nevertheless, whether our exchanges yield us favors or goods that are less or more valuable than those we now have, we must all exchange with one another, since we cannot survive alone. Just how we control one another through these exchanges is the general focus of this analysis; the specific focus is the acquisition, accumulation, expenditure, and loss of esteem or respect, and how *granting or withdrawing prestige or esteem controls the actions of both individuals and groups*.

Because these exchanges are not simply contracts between two actors, they can be better understood by analyzing the differences between social control exerted through contractual relations and control exercised through other kinds of exchanges. That is the theme of the next chapter.

31. James S. Coleman, "Collective Decisions," in Herman Turk and Richard L. Simpson, eds., *Institutions and Social Exchange* (Indianapolis: Bobbs-Merrill, 1971), p. 276; see also Coleman, *The Mathematics of Collective Action* (Chicago: Aldine, 1973).

Chapter 2
Contractual and Noncontractual Bases of Control in Social Systems

It was asserted in chapter 1 that prestige processes can be viewed as some kind of social exchange; but they neither form a *contract* system nor do they follow the pattern of *market* economics. Let us, then, consider how the realm of prestige is different from both, focusing here on the first of these themes and in the next chapter on the second. Prestige processes should be considered here in a broad view, as one among several modes of social control used by all societies. Thereby not only will prestige processes be illuminated, but also some lesser known theoretical patterns in social systems generally will be uncovered.

THE SOCIAL DEFINITION OF CONTRACT

Although a contract system appears relatively simple, to examine it adequately requires entrance upon some broad problems of classical social theory. Our concern here is not with the complex legal definition of contract, to which whole libraries of dicta, monographs, and published cases are devoted. Rather, our focus is upon how contract exchanges are socially viewed as different from other social exchanges (especially prestige), and of course upon how those differences affect the ways in which people try to control one another.

The changing legal conceptions of contract shape some sectors of social life (for example, it is no longer possible to indenture oneself; a woman can now make an independent contract), just as changing norms and attitudes shape the terms of contracts (for example, what is a minimum wage or maximum workday). Nevertheless, the broad social definition of what a contract is does not alter quickly from one generation to the next, and its social impact does not depend on the lawyer's technical knowledge of contract.

People can and do make a distinction between social exchanges that are contractual and those that are not, even if they never use the term at all. The relationship between a customer and the seller of a newspaper is perceived as contractual, but that between a host and a guest is not; exchanging a cord of wood for medical services is contractual, but a campaign contribution to a political candidate often is not, although that line can be thin indeed.[1]

The essential elements in the *social* definition of a contract are probably these (subject to some emendation whenever data from an adequate opinion survey is collected): 1. a specific offer and acceptance (I shall do this if you will do that); 2. a clear specification or at least understanding of the penalties if one side fails to perform as agreed (if some pages of the newspaper I buy are missing, I have the right to demand another); 3. a specification or at least an understanding of the conditions under which the agreement can be terminated; and 4. freedom after termination of this contract to enter a new one with another person, or the right to renegotiate this one if the original terms were not satisfactory.

Since real life is somewhat more fluid than concepts, the distinction between contractual and noncontractual exchanges cannot be viewed as a clear-cut dichotomy.[2] Contractual expectations often intrude in noncontractual situations and vice versa. Continuing contractual relations, as when someone works for the same company for many years, almost always come to include many understandings that are technically or legally noncontractual but that are socially perceived as contractual (for example, the "right" to park in a certain place, the right to job continuity, permission to brew coffee on the job). Over time, buyers and sellers come to view their relations as somewhat personalistic and their contract as broader than specifications of price and quantity; either may feel betrayed if the other rationally seeks a new partner who will make a better bid. That is, their interaction and thus control over one another is also based on esteem, trust, and friendship.[3]

Similarly, in the noncontractual realm of prestige processes the rhetoric of contract is often used, both on formal occasions such as testimonial dinners, and when a person feels he has been paid less than he deserves. When public prestige payments such as medals or offices are awarded, the laudatory speeches in these ceremonies describe the honors as "rewards" that were "earned," suggesting some kind of exchange or contract. They emphasize what the awardee has done to deserve the payment. Similarly, the language of love and friendship often implies some kind of contract: you must love me because I love you. This rhetoric is especially used, of course, when a friend, spouse, or sweetheart is angry and reviews all that

1. To give financial support to a candidate whose principles one approves is viewed as proper; to buy a change in his principles (thus, a contract) is not, and he is thereby judged to be corrupt. In politics, sometimes those who contribute believe they have made a purchase but the politician does not. Whether a politician will deliver, having been bought, is worthy of some research.

2. For comments on the noncontractual bases of contract, see Emile Durkheim, *The Division of Labor in Society,* trans. George Simpson (Glencoe, Ill.: Free Press, 1949 [1892]), pp. 200–229. See also Marcel Mauss, *The Gift* [1925] trans. J. Cunnison (New York: Norton, 1967).

3. For evidence of the extent to which many business transactions, even between corporations, are precisely stipulated in formal contracts, see Stewart Macaulay, "Non-Contractual Relations in Business: A Preliminary Study," in Lawrence M. Friedman and Stewart Macaulay, eds., *Law and the Behavioral Sciences* (New York: Bobbs-Merrill, 1969), pp. 145–165.

he or she has done for the other person, along with all the failures of the other to make appropriate counterpayments.

Nevertheless, the use of that rhetoric does not convince others that a real contract existed, and it is well understood that "deserving" something in a social exchange does not mean that a contract exists. The differences between these two types of exchange should be examined more closely, in order to understand better their consequences for social control.

ACCOMPLISHING "FOR" PRESTIGE IS NOT CONTRACT

Getting prestige is structurally different from contracts or even many social exchanges because the essential relationship is not dyadic, but triadic. Prestige is thus the outcome of interaction between one person, another, and significant third parties. If a plumber is very efficient, or a professor makes learning an exciting activity for students, each is doing something "for" specific others. Those others pay admiration or respect for competence or dedication although they have not made a contract to do so. Prestige evaluations are not only personal and individual; they are shared by and ultimately come from the several groups who learn of those performances and validate any esteem given. Similarly, specific partners may like or admire what they are doing for one another but the relevant third parties or community disesteem them for it, as when a man and woman engage in adultery, or two politicians figure out a clever scheme for stealing votes.

People may express gratitude for a performance that also elicits admiration (a pilot's skillful crash landing), but the complex rules for thanking as a way of redressing an imbalance in social exchanges are not the same as the rules for giving respect. A wide range of personal favors is socially defined as calling for some recompense—such as the return of a similar favor (invitations to parties, borrowing cups of sugar), or an expression of thanks or an even deeper gratefulness that can be shown in elaborate ways. Some of the many ways of paying back are not onerous (a simple "thank you"), and the rules are complex enough to permit many types of response that will not be judged as boorish or unfeeling. The rules are also flexible, permitting many individual decisions as to what is "owed."

The rules do not—contrary to the opinion of many social analysts—state that an individual owes obedience to another if a favor cannot be paid back.[4] More important, favors, gifts, or services do not necessarily generate either "power" or respect. One respects another person because he or she has done something very well or possesses outstanding qualities.

Favors and obligations are part of social exchanges between two or more persons, or even groups and organizations. But whether or not the same

---

4. Peter Blau is especially prone to this error. See, e.g., his statement, "Unreciprocated exchange leads to the differentiation of power," *Exchange and Power in Social Life* (New York: Wiley, 1964), p. 7; see also pp. 21–22 and esp. p. 28.

acts also generate prestige is a separate question. One may be thankful for a present, and also admire the style with which it was given—or admire a performance, and not feel that it was a gift calling for a return gift. If someone risks his or her life to rescue another, the rescued person will likely feel thankful, while outsiders or the community will feel respect for that selfless bravery. In short, the performances that generate esteem or prestige may or may not also make a person feel obliged to return the favor; and the performances that are defined as creating an obligation to pay back may or may not also be viewed as outstanding enough to merit respect, when weighed by the standards of the community or group.

Besides the distinction between dyadic and triadic patterns, a second major difference between contractual relations and social exchanges in which prestige is earned is that, in contracts, individuals stipulate what they will do if the others do something, whereas in the social processes of prestige, that promise would be illusory. It is clear that, in the latter, *no contract is possible because it is simply not in our power to control a response* and thus make a promised "delivery" of respect, though we can always display it insincerely. It is not possible to will admiration, any more than one can will an esthetic thrill, or friendliness or love.[5] Rulers have always been able to command the external trappings of deference and medals and even laurel wreaths for their poems; but no one can command even one's own, much less others', esteem responses. The granting or withholding of feelings of esteem is to this extent not one side of a contract.

A third difference is that, if an individual or group cannot promise a specific amount of prestige response, *neither can an individual make a real contractual offer of a future performance of high quality*—the offer being the other side of a hypothetical contract. Few of us can with any assurances contract to produce a brilliant essay, or virtue under great temptation, or a wise solution to a governmental crisis, in exchange for a given amount of esteem from our relevant group; at best we can promise to try hard. Of course we *can* contract to produce an essay or a bookshelf if the contract calls for only a competent performance, closer to the working ideal of our group.

In the professions the ideal, for which high prestige is paid, *is* to produce "brilliant solutions"; but the professional does not make contracts to do so. Since the outcome contingencies are high in several of the professions—in almost half of all military battles one side loses, in most

---

5. One can promise or contract to pay overt deference or respect. Certainly in the past, as de Tocqueville asserted was true in America, a servant made that implicit contract. He or she was not required to feel respect, however: *Democracy in America* (New York: Doubleday, Anchor, 1969), p. 579. Some analysts have argued that in the traditional Chinese marriage the emphasis was on overt acts, carrying out respect obligations such as bringing a mother-in-law her slippers or hot tea in the morning, rather than on the much more difficult task of feeling love for one's family members. Arlie Hochschild is investigating, nevertheless, the circumstances in which people do accept the *obligation* to "feel," as at funerals or in marriages, and the extent to which some actually succeed at this.

law cases one side loses, and all patients eventually die—the professional does not guarantee a solution at all, as the carpenter can. The physician will not contract to cure his patient, nor will the lawyer contract to win the case.[6] Of course, here as everywhere, exceptions are sometimes encountered, since some creative people are so confident in their powers that they will make such contracts. Certainly Mozart felt at times that he *could* promise his next quartet or piano concerto would astound his listeners.

A fourth difference between contracts and prestige relationships is that by social rule *people are not supposed to specify in advance a prestige "price"* for performing well, because part of the esteem others pay is for selfless dedication to the activity and the norm itself, not alone for the level of achievement. That is, the performance is supposed to express some commitment to the group evaluation of the activity as an end in itself. Even the professional athlete, who plays for money, will lose some of his prestige if he proclaims that he is interested only in the material rewards he can get out of the sport.[7] In T. S. Eliot's *Murder in the Cathedral*, this notion is stated clearly in the exchange between Thomas à Becket and one of the Tempters, who suggests that Thomas might welcome martyrdom in order to obtain eternal bliss and become a saint. However, to accept that exchange is to fail of entrance into heaven. Similarly, although the scientist does work for pay, he or she ought not, under penalty of criticism, to announce the intention of solving a problem merely to win public acclaim or triumph over others (or even worse, money). Many reviews of Watson's *The Double Helix* expressed dismay at his disclosure that he was trying to beat out the American team, or win in the race against Pauling.[8] Although Americans view politicians with some cynicism, a mayor who admits that he is administering well simply because soon he wants to make a race for the governorship or presidency will be paid less esteem by ordinary citizens.[9]

Social attitudes, then, oppose the introduction of an overt contractual element into the prestige payoff, since a main thrust of both socialization and social control is that we should do good things because they are

6. It is possible that the steady rise in malpractice suits for the past two decades is partly caused by the growing belief that physicians view medicine as a purely economic and contractual relationship and therefore should be held responsible when they fail to cure the patient. Nevertheless, the medical Code of Ethics considers a "contract to cure" a violation. Patients may now feel, however, that since good medical care is a right, they have made a contract with their physicians for a cure.

7. See Joe Namath, *I Can't Wait until Tomorrow Cause I Get Better Looking Every Day* (New York: Random House, 1969); Jim Bouton, *Ball Four: My Life and Hard Times Throwing the Knuckleball in the Big Leagues* (New York: World, 1970); Dave Meggyesy, *Out of Their League: Why I Quit Pro Football* (New York: Simon & Schuster, 1971); Bernie Parrish, *They Call It a Game* (New York: Dial, 1971); Johnny Sample *et al., Confessions of a Dirty Ball Player* (New York: Dial Press, 1970).

8. James D. Watson, *The Double Helix: A Personal Account of the Discovery of the Structure of DNA* (New York: Atheneum, 1968). Compare the reviews by Peter Caws in *Commentary*, 45 (June, 1968): 88ff.; R. C. Cowen in *Christian Science Monitor*, May 7, 1968, p. 12; John Lear in *The Saturday Review*, 51 (March 16, 1968): 86ff.; Erwin Chargaff in *Science*, 159 (March 29, 1968): 144ff.

9. In a personal communication, Mark Baldassare suggests an interesting exception: when an individual is thought to have a "destiny" (e.g., the Roosevelts or Kennedys), so that to view each step as only a way upward is actually to help fate along.

intrinsically good. That emphasis also supports the existing value system, since one consequence is that at least a good part of the group will want to do well even when being good or doing well does not yield much payoff (we should not kill our enemy even if no one is watching). In turn, if people indeed come to love virtue for itself, we do not have to reward them so much for acting virtuously.

PRESTIGE CLAIMS IN HONOR-SENSITIVE SOCIETIES

It follows from the foregoing analysis that to claim the "just reward" of prestige as though a contract had been made violates a set of social understandings. It arouses some resentment and reduces the admiration already given, at least in Western society and possibly in most others as well. But because, without question, the norms for making public claims to prestige do vary from one society to another and across time, these differences should be briefly considered.

Concretely, some societies of the past have exhibited a strong sense of personal honor. In Homeric Greece, for example, heroes felt no hesitation in claiming their rights to trophies as well as esteem.[10] In societies where class divisions were sharper than in our own, it was more permissible to assert one's rights to minor privileges. In the courts of great monarchies, people expressed openly their concern for glory, for the niceties of prece- dence, for the justice of esteem allocations. Among the Plains Indians, the Homeric Greeks, and the Vikings, where personal courage and skill in battle yielded high esteem,[11] such matters were closer to the center of social and individual attention than in modern industrial or industrializ- ing societies. In the latter, by contrast, the norm within peer groups is to mask cut-throat competition by surface modesty.[12] In "honor-sensitive" societies or classes, people were (and are, where they still exist) constantly alert to their own reputations and those of others. They drew sharp distinctions as to who was most courageous or skillful in battle or danced the quadrille most gracefully. Where everyone made such judgments constantly, the sheer number of overt disagreements would probably be greater than in a modern industrial society.

10. M. I. Finley, *The World of Odysseus*, rev. ed. (New York: Viking, 1965), pp. 114ff., 129ff.
11. The modern reader may find it worthwhile to remember that army officers once did speak openly of their chances of achieving "glory" on the battlefield. See also Finley, *ibid.* It is not at all cynical to keep in mind, too, that battlefield glory (if not posthumous) frequently led to civil posts, titles, and wealth. The rise of the Duke of Marlborough (excellently narrated by his descendant and biographer, Winston Churchill) was only one dramatic instance among many. And Shakespeare puts this not unlikely exhortation into the mouth of "Harry the King":

> If we are mark'd to die, we are enow
> To do our country loss; and if to live,
> The fewer men, the greater share of honor.
>> The Life of King Henry V
>> Act IV, Scene III

12. In the villages described in F. G. Bailey, ed., *Gifts and Poison* (Oxford: Blackwell, 1971), members of the community are constantly sensitive to matters of reputation but expend much effort in preventing anyone from successfully claiming to be superior.

But though each aspirant might be permitted to assert his claims, and the rhetoric of "what is owed to whom" might be used, the previously stated differences from contract would still apply. Even in such societies, to have asked less in deference than others believed one had earned doubtless aroused kindliness and approval; to claim more than others believed one had earned surely aroused annoyance and deprecation.

Among honor-sensitive groups, as well as in industrial societies, there is a special humiliation in asking for an overt expression of respect ("please tell me how wonderful you consider my painting") and then being refused, because the rejection explicitly states lower esteem than the individual believes he or she should enjoy.[13] We usually suppose that others esteem our work and worth; to be refused that recognition destroys the illusion, for then our lower prestige is made public. Moreover, to demand and then be rejected forces the person to confront his or her dependence on others' judgments.

FOCUS OF CONTRACT

Contract differs from prestige processes because in the latter the essential relationship is not dyadic but triadic; because neither the prestige response nor the level of performance eliciting it can truly be promised; and because social attitudes disapprove of one's demanding a particular prestige price for doing something. A further difference between contractual and prestige exchanges is that the focus of the contract is on what is done, not on the social traits of the individual who does it. In the technical jargon of sociology, the contract relationship is "functionally specific": all the characteristics of the performer are supposed to be irrelevant except those relating to the function or the task. This is the social ideal—though reality deviates from it. Primarily, we pay for the value of a project or commodity, not for the social standing of the seller, or his or her particular relation to us. By contrast, in prestige processes, more or less esteem for the same achievement will be paid because of other traits of the performer, such as general prestige ranking, sex, ethnic standing, or personal character.

For example, doing good is virtuous, and Christian doctrine expresses greater joy over one strayed sinner who returns to the fold than over those who remained virtuous all along. But real communities have not behaved that generously.[14] They have instead examined suspiciously the motives of

13. See also George C. Homans' remarks on the indignation people feel when they believe that their payoff is less than that of others whose investment was no more: *Social Behavior: Its Elementary Forms*, 2d ed. (New York: Harcourt, Brace, 1974), chap. 11.

14. At least partly contradictory to this widespread observation is the experiment of Stanley Schachter reported in "Deviation, Rejection, and Communication," *Journal of Abnormal and Social Psychology*, 46 (1951): 190–207, where the "slider" (the person with a deviant opinion who later comes to agree with the others in the artificial group) is not rejected. That kind of experiment probably does not recreate the real life situation of the genuine deviant, sinner, or criminal. However, in real life, too, "returned sinners" are typically not rejected, and some of them have made a comfortable living from lecturing or preaching about their conversion. The question is whether their rank is as high as that of the steadily virtuous person, and the answer seems clearly negative.

the scoundrel who later sought honor as a philanthropist or engaged in prestige-generating acts. More than one reformed criminal has learned to his sorrow that his good deeds generate less respect than those of men who already bask in the deference of their fellow citizens and whose practice of virtue is less onerous. Outsiders earn less prestige for their achievements than insiders. Every endeavor in the United States, except perhaps those of lowest prestige, is studded with the names of black performers of high achievement (cowboys, scientists) who were not given as much honor as their white counterparts or who were later ignored in historical accounts.

In general terms, any given prestige-generating act commands a varying "market price," depending on whose act it is.[15] At the extreme, a charismatic leader will be given deference for a performance that would be viewed as trivial if a less magnetic man or woman executed it. (Indeed, this pattern can be viewed as a fair index or definition of charisma.) Since *who* does the act determines in part the approval given, a group cannot specify in advance exactly how much prestige it will pay for a given *act*, unlike the price of a given economic commodity or service on the market.

In line with that general view, some have argued that people of high rank need not conform as much to group rules as do members of low or middle rank.[16] That assertion is not completely confirmed by observation. With reference to class differences, some behavior (for example, speaking schoolbook English) yields no esteem for middle-class members, while failure to behave thus will lower others' respect for them. That is, different activities will yield more or less prestige, depending on who the doer is; but the behavior must be specified first to make a correct prediction of prestige.

Of course, the crude observation that people of higher rank can get away with more deviation is correct, for several reasons. First, it is more difficult to attack them openly; they have more resources with which to protect themselves when they are accused of not conforming. But, even though it may be unwise for lower-ranking people to pay them less overt

15. For example, various experiments have proved that the same essay is more likely to be rated excellent if it is identified as having been written by a male rather than a female, or by someone with a "WASP" rather than a "foreign" name. A person will also be more respectful in a telephone interaction—even with the same words spoken—if he or she is told the other person has a higher rank. Some of these experiments are summarized in Sandra L. Bem and Daryl J. Bem, "We're All Unconscious Sexists," *Psychology Today*, 4 (November, 1970): 22–26, 115–116.

16. For a review and discussion of this point, see Richard L. Simpson, *Theories of Group Exchange* (Morristown, N.J.: General Learning Corporation, 1972), pp. 6–9; Simpson gives special attention to Thibaut and Kelley's and Homans' views—John W. Thibaut and Harold H. Kelley, *The Social Psychology of Groups* (New York: Wiley, 1959), and George C. Homans, *Social Behavior* (New York: Harcourt, Brace & World, 1961).

Nor is this a new observation: "The first thing that strikes me is that in the feudal world actions were not always praised or blamed with reference to their intrinsic worth, but were sometimes appreciated exclusively with reference to the person who was the actor or the object of them, which is repugnant to the general conscience of mankind. Thus some of the actions which were indifferent on the part of a man in humble life dishonored a noble; others changed their whole character according as the person aggrieved by them belonged or did not belong to the aristocracy" (Alexis de Tocqueville, *Democracy in America*, trans. H. Reeve, F. Bowen and P. Bradley [New York: Vintage, 1945], II, 243.

deference, the inner feelings of respect of these underlings will nevertheless be less. Second, people of higher rank enjoy a longer period of time in
which their main performances are not closely evaluated—for example, it
may be supposed by others that what seems to be deviation is done for
good reasons—so that within that period the deviations are not given
much weight.[17] Third, having already accumulated a substantial amount
of prestige, these people do not usually lose all of it quickly, or for a few
small deviations; but they can and do lose it. It does not, in any event,
seem likely that people of high rank are held to a less high standard than
others.[18]

SIMILARITIES BETWEEN CONTRACTUAL
AND NONCONTRACTUAL RELATIONS

Despite the important differences discussed above, prestige and contractual exchanges are similar in two major ways: 1. the terms change over
time, and 2. the terms are more or less forced on any given individual or
group, and little can be done to alter them.

In general, group or individual judgments about what deserves more or
less prestige do not change rapidly and do not all change at the same speed
in all groups or all activities, but they all do change. In this generation,
athletic performances that once would have excited national admiration—a hundred-yard dash in 9.8 seconds, a pole vault of 16 feet—
will now generate high prestige only in local school track meets. The
professor who spoke out on controversial political issues fifty years ago
gained more peer esteem for his courage than now. Of course he was also
more likely to be fired for that action.

With reference to the terms encountered by the individual or group
when performances or qualities are evaluated, it seems clear that little can
be done to alter them in the immediate situation by haggling or demanding more, although people do make that attempt. Haggling is partly
ineffective because those who admire cannot respond more than they in
fact do. In addition, their refusal is supported by third parties, who have
some stake in preventing others from paying higher esteem.

This resistance to individual haggling does not mean, of course, that
the individual is pleased with the terms; and one response is to try to get
better terms from others. In fact, some of the dissidence in any society is
created by the belief or sense that the terms themselves are unfair. The
individual feels that he or she *should* get more for his kinds of performances
or qualities.[19] Subsegments of the society, such as lower-class men,

17. Eliot Jacques, *The Measurement of Responsibility* (Cambridge: Harvard University Press, 1956).

18. Perhaps, again, it is necessary to specify in advance *which* kind of job or achievement is in
question. Certainly most people do "forgive" people in political office for some kinds of deviations—
though here, once more, it is usually because people believe the deviant act was carried out because of
some "higher" value or aim. Most American citizens will, e.g., forgive a governor who violates the
constitutional rights of a known criminal, if that was done in order to convict him.

19. This problem comes up again in later chapters, esp. in Chapter 12 on justice. See also
Homans, *Social Behavior*, 2d ed. 1974, chap. 11.

women, blacks, and artists, not only want more than they actually get, but a high percentage of those who suffer from social disadvantages feel that they do not receive even their just rewards for particular traits or behavior. Correspondingly, a major revolution, when dissidents come to rule, typically proclaims that the rules for earning rewards have been changed, that new terms have been set.

The extent to which any contract is "free" and open to haggling between two independent parties is a matter of empirical fact to be ascertained by investigation. For theoretical purposes, the economist postulates that customers set prices in a free market; but he knows this is only partially so, since both customers and prices are manipulated by corporations. Yet at a deeper level customers do set prices, in that if they stop buying, or evaluate commodities or services as worth less, prices will indeed fall. Similarly, members of groups collectively set prestige rewards as well as economic prices by their own continuing evaluations. This is true even if one keeps in mind that those in high positions have far more influence on prestige-granting than those in low positions; for people mostly yield to that influence without coercion, often without even being aware of the influence.

The *structure of opportunity*, or position and influence, that permits some to gain easier access to the kinds of competition in which high prestige can be earned, will be reserved for later discussion.[20] But over longer periods of time, as in the price-setting mechanisms of the marketplace, it is the demand for certain qualities and behaviors that, in interaction with supply, determines whether much or little prestige will be granted.

GENERAL BASES OF SOCIAL ORDER

My aim in this chapter is to distinguish prestige processes from those of contract with reference only to the problem of control, as it is in the next chapter to compare prestige processes with simple supply and demand mechanisms in the marketplace. But several issues of general theory demand attention at this point. Their resolution will help us to understand better the place of prestige processes in all social systems, especially in two "types" of societies, *Gemeinschaft* and *Gesellschaft*, described by social analysts many times over the past centuries.

That social analysts have focused on the phenomenon of social order and thus on the social control processes that create it is a tribute to their insight, for order is statistically most improbable and therefore needs to be explained. This is so for any system, not alone social ones. A social system is a creation of relative order, forged from disparate, contrary, and cen-

---

20. Because those in high ranks enjoy privileges in any social interaction, their opinions as well as their contributions may count for more than they are actually worth. Aside from the finding that their vote counts for more on juries, see the data in Harold H. Kelley and John W. Thibaut, "Group Problem Solving," in G. Lindzey and E. Aronson, eds., *The Handbook of Social Psychology*, 2d ed. (Reading, Mass.: Addison-Wesley, 1968), IV, 41–42, on how positive responses to rank may impede effective solutions when the suggestions of people in high rank are not excellent.

tripetal forces that, if not checked by one another, would tear it apart. It is held together by its contrary tensions, as well as by some forces that are in harmony. Thus the orderly work of the society (production, distribution, child-rearing, worship) could not be accomplished if its members could not control or check in part each other's aims, plans, activities, and desires.

For certainly over half a century, and in a less and less systematic way throughout history, social analysts have perceived that social order had two somewhat different bases: *socialization*, by which children (and thus adults) come to internalize the norms of the society, that is, actually to value highly, to desire, to get satisfaction from, the social patterns followed by fellow group members ("as the twig is bent, so the tree will grow"); and *social exchanges* of various kinds, by which virtue is rewarded and evil punished (an eye for an eye). Social mechanisms are created for distinguishing between who does evil and who does good. Granted, socialization does not stop at the end of childhood, and control mechanisms based on social exchanges are also applied to children; but the distinction is nonetheless real and observable, while its full importance has not yet been noted in prior analyses.[21]

Parallel to this distinction is the commonsensical observation, surely as old as cities, that people act differently toward one another in town and country. The description and explanation of those differences has been the main topic of social analyses. Indeed, one critic has sneered that the history of sociology is only an extended commentary on those different social patterns. Various labels have focused on one or another aspect of the distinction: rural/urban, port cities/inland cities (Plato), obligations based on status/contract (Sir Henry Maine), *Gemeinschaft/Gesellschaft* (Ferdinand Tönnies), mechanical/organic solidarity (Emile Durkheim), substantive/formal rationality (Max Weber).[22] For decades, American sociologists cross-tabulated their data by rural/urban, negro/white, and immigrant/native-born categories.

These crude but useful variables corresponded to traditional or folk patterns on the one hand, and urban or contractual patterns on the other.

---

21. The most effective learning and therapeutic technique for children whose socialization has failed in some way has been explicit social exchanges. See Robert L. Hamblin *et al.*, *The Humanization Processes* (New York: Wiley, 1971). For a critique of sociological theories about how norms are internalized, see John F. Scott, *The Internalization of Norms* (Englewood Cliffs, N.J.: Prentice-Hall, 1971).

22. Compare Henry J. S. Maine, *Ancient Law: Its Connection with the Early History of Society and Its Relation to Modern Ideas* (Boston: Beacon, 1963 [1861]); Ferdinand Tönnies, *Gemeinschaft und Gesellschaft: Grundbegriffe der Reinen Soziologie* (Darmstadt: Wissenschaftliche Buchgesellschaft, 1887), trans. as *Community and Society* by Evans Charles Loomis (New York: Harper and Row, 1963); Charles H. Cooley, *Social Process* (Carbondale, Ill.: Southern Illinois University Press, 1966 [1918]); Emile Durkheim, *The Division of Labor in Society*, trans. George Simpson (Glencoe, Ill.: Free Press, 1949 [1893]); Max Weber, *Economy and Society*, ed. Guenther Roth and Claus Wittich (New York: Bedminster Press, 1968 [1922]), I, 85–86; Robert Redfield, "The Folk Society" (1947), in R. Sennett, ed., *Classic Essays on the Culture of Cities* (New York: Appleton-Century-Crofts, 1969), pp. 180–205; and Robert E. Park, "The City" (1925), *ibid.*, pp. 91–130.

Dissecting the components of these two patterns, Parsons elaborated this ancient dichotomy into his five pattern-variables. In each of them, the first is more commonly found in a folk or traditional society: affectivity-emotional neutrality, diffuseness-functional specificity, ascription-achievement (or quality-performance), particularism-universalism, and collectivity orientation-self interest.[23] Although not all these terms refer in detail to the same phenomena, all refer to the same two basic patterns of social control. In the tribal, folk, rural, or *Gemeinschaft* pattern, sociologists have asserted that the primary basis of control is the individual's firm commitment to traditional group norms or behavior, inculcated by socialization and shared by the adult members of the group. Because social order is said to be based on consensus, there is no need to pay much attention to the problems of social control, except for controlling the rare "deviant."[24]

In contrast to such societies, urban society or *Gesellschaft* is made up of diverse people whose values differ and who take part in an extensive division of labor. As a consequence, according to sociological doctrine during much of the past century, social order and integration in such societies are based on explicit contracts, economic exchanges, formal legal systems, and specially designated regulatory bureaucracies (policemen, unions or guilds, railroad commissions).

We need not explore in detail the inadequacies seen by a modern sociologist in such a traditional formulation of folk and urban societies. For example: The harmony, the commitment to the group or to one another, and the consensus among modern villagers seems low, and it is not clear that the past was really very different; urban neighborhoods sometimes show some traits of a village; and so on.[25] Nevertheless, various of these differences have been observed ever since there were cities; and they cannot be blamed on the inadequacies of sociology, for they arise from the experiences of ordinary people. Even if the classical dichotomy seems to be less distinct in modern life, becoming a continuum or a gradation, we can still perceive broad behavioral differences at the two extremes. But arguments over whether there are really two types of societies have not been of great intellectual importance during the past half-century. Far more important changes in theory have occurred during that period, which implicitly erased much of the meaning of the theory.

23. Compare Talcott Parsons, *The Social System* (Glencoe, Ill.: Free Press, 1951) and T. Parsons and E. Shils, eds., *Toward a General Theory of Action* (Cambridge, Mass.: Harvard University Press, 1951); see in this connection also R. Dubin, "Parsons' Actor: Continuities in Social Theory," *American Sociological Review*, 25 (August, 1960): 457–466.

24. And this is why the topic of social control still has a bad name: over many decades, it referred primarily to the efforts by groups or societies to press the nonconformist (whether criminal or idiosyncratic) back into the standard social mold. Now we are more sympathetic to the deviant, while the term must be used to refer to *all* aspects of control, by anyone, in relation to anyone or any organization.

25. See, e.g., Bailey, *Gifts and Poison;* Edward C. Banfield, *The Moral Basis of a Backward Society* (Glencoe, Ill.: Free Press, 1958); Oscar Lewis, *Life in a Mexican Village: Tepoztlan Restudied* (Urbana: University of Illinois, 1951); Ronald Blythe, *Akenfield* (New York: Dell, 1970); John K. Campbell, *Honor, Family and Prestige* (Oxford: Clarendon, 1964).

Sociologists began to espouse the belief (to be encountered here and there in both Durkheim and Weber) that even modern societies are essentially "communities."

That is, the view emerged by the 1920's and became standard sociological doctrine by the end of the 1930's[26]—certainly in part as a way of differentiating sociology from other fields—that social order in *all* societies is based on shared values or the integration of values. That doctrine, denying the validity of self-seeking, individualist "economic man," underlay most sociological analyses until the late 1950's. The attacks on it did not swell into a flood until the late 1960's, often under the guise of assaults on "functionalism."[27]

But the "new" orientation, which has come to be called social exchange theory, did not simply reassert the validity of the rational economic man, whose behavior is ruled by contract and market and by the principle of getting the most from every transaction. The roots of exchange theory are older than economics. As Homans pointed out: "In its vulgar form, it must be the oldest of all theories of social behavior."[28]

The new orientation recognizes that formal control systems (contract, law, and the market) play a larger role in industrial societies than in folk societies, and it denies that consensus or shared values within these societies are adequate as a basis for social order. But it also asserts that we must explore a wide variety of social exchanges that do not seem to be contractual or to follow the market patterns assumed in economics.

Thus, in analyzing the processes of prestige allocation, we can view them as belonging to a very general category of social exchanges, without at all supposing that they can be distorted into pure contractual or market behavior.[29] Nevertheless, the succeeding section raises the issue of *how* the social processes that focus on prestige do control people's behavior. That is, what are the processes of feedback and control? More generally:
1. How do either contractual or noncontractual relations achieve social

26. At which time Ralph Linton's *The Study of Man* (New York: Appleton-Century-Crofts, 1936) and Talcott Parsons' *The Structure of Social Action* (New York: McGraw-Hill, 1937) offered magisterial formulations of it.

27. For other elements in this attack, see my detailed comments in "Functionalism: The Empty Castle," in *Explorations in Social Theory* (New York: Oxford University Press, 1973) pp. 64–94. Those who were questioning traditional doctrine on this topic in the late 1950's, as they moved toward exchange theory, include Homans, Zetterberg, Thibaut and Kelley, Goode, Coleman, Blau, D. Cartwright, and J. R. P. French. At the same time, some economists (notably Gary Becker) were reaching out to analyze nonmarket variables econometrically.

Summary statements of the objections to consensus as the main basis for social control or order can be found in William J. Goode, "Norm Commitment and Conformity to Role-Status Obligations," *American Journal of Sociology*, 66 (November, 1960): 246–258; and "A Theory of Role Strain," *American Sociological Review*, 25 (August, 1960): 483–496 (repr. in my *Explorations in Social Theory*, pp. 97–120).

28. George C. Homans, *Social Behavior*, 2d ed., 1974.

29. For further comments on these processes, see Peter Ekeh, *Social Exchange Theory: The Two Traditions* (Cambridge, Mass.: Harvard University Press, 1974, esp. pt. 2, and Mauss, *The Gift*, chap. 2.

control, in this or any other society? And: 2. Under which conditions will a contractual or noncontractual pattern emerge or become more widespread in part of a social system?

FEEDBACK AND SOCIAL CONTROL

Although the second question above will be discussed here, the focus will be more on the first: How does social control differ, when the process rests on economic, formal, legal, bureaucratic, or contractual relations, from when it rests on personal affection, respect, or traditional exchanges? This question assumes the point of view, already stated, that even in a nonindustrial, nonurban, or tribal society we might expect to observe some contractual relationships (such as silent trading),[30] just as in an industrial society, and even in a highly bureaucratic corporate life, we find many noncontractual exchanges. The question also suggests that the two forms of social control can achieve somewhat different ends, and that only under particular conditions can part of a social system—never an entire society—maintain itself on the basis of only contract and market. Finally, the question implies that in *any* social system or subsystem some individuals or groups may press in the direction of either a contractual or noncontractual system of exchange if they perceive that thereby they can obtain better overall terms. We can therefore ask under what conditions people press toward one or the other type of control. The differences in the control processes of the two systems should be considered before commenting on the deeper question of the social conditions under which each might arise.

The biases of an industrial society suggest that contractual, formal, or bureaucratic patterns would create better or more efficient controls than a more tribal, *Gemeinschaft*, or rural system, because these patterns yield more immediate and specific feedback. The other person is quickly told where and how much he or she has failed to meet the terms of the agreement. Since the person thereby faces penalties, he is motivated to correct matters. Punishment and reward seem to be more certain and more exact. Quick and clear feedback is thought to be necessary for an effective control system, and thus a contractual pattern offers important advantages if the members of a society want effective control. Are there other advantages?

Under contract, both parties, whether groups, bureaucracies, or individuals, presumably know in advance what the terms are; thus, a clearer line is drawn between the acceptable and the unacceptable. A contract specifies minimum performance levels, so that neither will feel betrayed, but only pleased, if the other performs at that level. By contrast, in much of noncontractual social exchange, although both may come to expect that

---

30. Karl Polanyi, *The Great Transformation* (Boston: Beacon, 1957). For various types of trading, see Karl Polanyi *et al.*, eds., *Trade and Market in the Early Empires* (Glencoe, Ill.: Free Press, 1957).

only a minimum is forthcoming, standards are set higher so that both parties may feel dissatisfied with each other's minimum.[31]

In a contract system, and especially in the economic or bureaucratic relations that form most of it, it is easier to ascertain that we are being unwise or not doing well, for example, by drawing up a balance of profits and losses, or inputs and outcomes, than to learn we are being socially foolish and therefore losing prestige.[32] Again, the control mechanics seem to be more effective in a contractual system.[33]

Moreover, if the contract terms turn out badly we can haggle for better terms next time, alter our performances, or locate and enter new relations or a new bureaucracy. Thereby, further control messages are distributed among third parties who observe; and people learn what the appropriate market terms are.

Nevertheless, the facts that even in contemporary life most human relations have not become contractual, that essayists and philosophers deplore the unsatisfying quality of contractual life, and that most people resist its intrusion in many areas of their lives should at least suggest that contract relations are not so clearly advantageous or desirable as the above sketch asserts, possibly not even as a control device. Let us then compare how individuals or groups control one another in a noncontractual system.

PSYCHOLOGICAL BASES OF CONTROL

An old but fruitful intuition asserts that socialization and nonmarket social exchanges use somewhat similar social controls. They do so because both aim at shaping not only the acts or performances of others (which economic, contractual, or formal-legal controls also do), but their emotions, commitments, and attitudes as well.

The basic differences in these social patterns, which in turn rest on somewhat different bases of control, should be considered. In contract (including the formal economic market and bureaucracy) one is more likely than in either socialization or ordinary social exchanges to assume a task or duty voluntarily, with the belief that one can carry it out adequately. By contrast, in many of our informal social exchanges, as husband, kinsman, friend, neighbor, or community member, we often

31. For the reader whose memory does not furnish immediate illustrations: the potlatch among the Northwest Pacific Indians (Wayne Suttles, "Affinal Ties, Subsistence, and Prestige among the Coast Salish," *American Anthropology*, 62 [April, 1960]: 296–305); offering and expecting gifts in Homer's *Odyssey*; the earning of esteem by giving more yams than required to one's married sister among Malinowski's Trobrianders; or gifts to groom and bride in contemporary weddings. See also Mauss, *The Gift*, chaps. 1, 2.

32. For example, "saving another's face" is so much a social norm that finding out how well one performed at a social gathering may be difficult. People both try to smooth over our blunders and later deny that anything was really amiss. See Erving Goffman, "On Face Work: An Analysis of Ritual Elements in Social Interaction," *Psychiatry*, 18 (August, 1955): 213–231; repr. in Warren G. Bennis *et al.*, *Interpersonal Dynamics* (Homewood, Ill.: Dorsey, 1968), pp. 226–249.

33. See James B. Rule, *Private Lives and Public Surveillance* (London: Allen Lane, 1973), esp. pp. 343ff.

feel that others impose duties on us. Second, in the latter type of social interaction, informal or nonmarket exchanges, what is to be done is not fully specified in advance, but is continually being renegotiated while the relationship continues. What is to be done, and when, and what are the limits at which one is told one has failed—all are likely to be imprecise and changing.

In contract, to do the minimum is adequate. If one does more, the contract typically does not call for any extra reward. In social exchanges and socialization, it is more likely that the other person will be disappointed with a minimum performance, while an above-average fulfillment calls for extra respect or show of gratefulness. On the other hand, in such interactions it is also more likely than in contract that doing adequately, or even very well, may not elicit approval at all: all of us at times feel we have been unrewarded after performing beyond the norm.

Even if contracts call for a penalty for failure, that penalty does not provide for denunciation or a show of disesteem. In socialization and much of social exchange, any punishment or penalty is likely not to have been precisely specified in advance; it is invented when failure has occurred ("we shall not invite you again") and is usually accompanied by scolding or a show of disapproval. Indeed, if a child or adult is punished coldly, without some expression of anger or disesteem, either one is likely to be puzzled.

Such control patterns in social exchange (including prestige transactions) seem far removed from the accuracy, efficiency, and speed of control mechanisms that are said to be typical of a bureaucratic, urban, industrial society; and so they are. Nevertheless, it is through such control patterns that much of the daily action of any society gets done. They fit the necessary conditions for the psychological learning processes of cognitive dissonance, random reinforcement, and punishment. All of these have considerable effect on people's attitudes and norm commitments (as distinguished from cognitive learning). Without attempting a deep inquiry into the psychological details, it should here be noted how each of these is important.

In both socialization and social exchange processes people are more likely than in contract to take on a task or duty that they had no great wish to assume, or did not even believe they could do well. The theory of cognitive dissonance asserts that people's behaviors, and especially their attitudes, are more likely to be shaped or altered if they are faced with contrary alternatives between which choice is difficult, and are somewhat gently but successfully pressed to follow one of them.[34] These alternatives

---

34. Although I am not as yet convinced that "cognitive dissonance" is what causes these effects, the experimental data uncovered by Leon Festinger and his associates are persuasive with respect to the empirical regularities, and thus I am drawing upon the main hypothesis here. The correctness of these descriptions will not be vitiated even if it is some other variable than cognitive dissonance that creates these effects.

may be bending to a mild threat versus grabbing a forbidden but desirable toy, or one activity or object versus one or more others. After the choice, if it was not precipitated by a definite, substantial loss or threat, or by a barrier too difficult to surmount, people are likely to find that the choice they discarded (under mild pressure) is now less attractive and the one they followed is more attractive.

The "dissonance" that is postulated arises from the discrepancy between the course they followed or the choice they made and their previous norms or attitudes (that is, *formerly* they did *not* unequivocally prefer that particular choice). Little or no dissonance is created when the threat is great or the anticipated loss is definite and substantial. If people see in advance that one of the courses of action is clearly less advantageous, of course they will rationally pursue the other; but then they need not change their self-conceptions or attitudes. If strong external threats, costs, or substantial rewards are used to press people toward one course of action that seems somewhat less than desirable in itself, but if these are later removed (that is, when other people are not around to observe and correct their behavior), they will then act just as they would have without such rewards or threats. Strong negative or positive rational inducements, as are common in contractual relations (or the market, or criminal law), do not change beliefs and attitudes, or even behavior, except while those inducements are present. They do not create any commitment to the social patterns so induced.

In childhood socialization, at least one of the necessary components of dissonance is present. The child is constantly pressed to do what he or she would prefer not to do. Childhood contains many delights, but socialization is not one of them. From eating and speaking "properly" to general obedience, the child is moved in directions that are not necessarily unpleasant, but that are not typically preferred. Thus a dissonance is created between what he or she in fact did and alternatives that seemed more attractive (eating with the fingers, not going to sleep just now, not going to school).

It is commonly assumed, correctly no doubt, that socialization plays a lesser role in adulthood than in childhood, but adults do change many of their attitudes as they enter new jobs, organizations and clubs, groups, neighborhoods, or phases of life. For daily social exchanges to proceed without each person calculating how to best the other, but instead with each one *wanting* to do what the other needs, some attitudinal changes are necessary. Adults will generally attest to a common experience that is central to cognitive dissonance: they are constantly being pressed, without

For an early statement of these relationships, see Leon Festinger, *A Theory of Cognitive Dissonance* (New York: Harper and Row, 1957).

See also Leon Festinger, Henry W. Riechen, Jr. and Stanley Schachter, *When Prophecy Fails* (Minneapolis, University of Minnesota Press, 1956); and Leon Festinger and J. Carlsmith, "Cognitive Consequences of Forced Compliance," *Journal of Abnormal and Social Psychology*, 58 (1959): 203–211.

strong coercion or inducements, to engage in tasks or role performances that they do not seek or want—both on the job and in much social interaction. Indeed, the gradual acceptance of these activities as desirable is often called "adjustment" or "maturity."

How the child, or the adult, is pressed to conform is therefore crucial here. The conditions for the inculcation of attitudes or moral commitment, judging by many socialization studies over the past few decades, seem close to what is required by cognitive dissonance: taking for granted a person will assume the burden (rather than threatening him or her); praise inducements rather than physical punishment; social rejection or the threat of withdrawing love or respect rather than deprivation of material things; close physical and emotional contact that permits mild pressures, rather than severe threats at a distance; persuasion rather than physical barriers; permitting temptation and giving trust, with an injunction to conform, rather than removing entirely what is forbidden.[35]

It seems only common sense to suppose that precise patterns of reward and punishment would induce at least behavioral conformity and perhaps attitudinal change as well. By contrast, in especially prestige processes but more generally in socialization and social exchange, we observe much imprecision with regard to: a) the limits of what is forbidden or praised; b) whether penalty or reward will be forthcoming; and c) how much punishment or reward will be handed out. Contingency is encountered in all social relations, contractual and noncontractual, but it plays a different role in the acquisition of *attitudes*, as contrasted with *cognitive knowledge* or rational calculations. In solving physical problems, which can be considered the epitome of the purely cognitive or rational learning situation, one tries to ascertain the chances of success, making one's bets accordingly: for example, this beam will tolerate a stress of a certain magnitude and an overload of a still higher quantity, and so forth. If we are wise, we also make such calculations in the economic market. However, we do so to a much lesser extent in noncontractual relations.

Our knowledge is most certain when the schedule of payoff is most clear and definite. Then, for a given amount and likelihood of either low or high payoff, we are most likely to act in a certain way if the schedule of rewards seems a good risk. It would be irrational to do otherwise.

By contrast, we now know from learning experiments that a pattern of behavior or attitude is hardest to extinguish if its schedule of rewards or reinforcement is random—not definite, as in cognitive learning, contract, or the market. The experience of children or adults in receiving praise or

35. For further data on these points, esp. on a possible "boomerang" when strong pressures are used, see J. W. Brehm, *A Theory of Psychological Reactance* (New York: Academic, 1966); E. Aronson, "The Theory of Cognitive Dissonance: A Current Perspective," in L. Berkowitz, ed., *Advances in Experimental Social Psychology*, vol. IV (New York: Academic, 1969), pp. 1–34; P. Steiner, "Perceived Freedom," *ibid.*, V (1970), pp. 187–248; and D. Bem, "Self-Perception Theory," *ibid.*, VI (1972), pp. 1–62.

blame for a specific action is often closer to randomness than to definiteness. Although on average we are esteemed for goodness and disesteemed for failure to conform, whether we experience either one for any given act is highly contingent. That is precisely the learning situation in which attitudes and behavior are most likely to become firmly grounded, internalized, and least likely to be wiped out by later experiences.

This fact may seem paradoxical to laymen, and even to sociologists who are not familiar with the theory of random reinforcement, which now enjoys much empirical support.[36] It can be at least made intelligible, if not explained adequately, by an illustration. If every time we press the button our car's motor starts (that is, there is low contingency), we are likely to keep on doing that if we want it to start. But if even once we experience a negative result, we are then likely to suppose that the system has broken down in some way: It does not work at all. Consequently we soon give it up as a waste of time. By contrast, the sports fisherman often catches no fish, or only a few, and for any ten casts of his line he is almost certain not to catch any. However, sometimes he does get a strike, and because he never knows whether it will be *this* time, he compulsively continues to cast. When a fisherman goes fishing, it is not only the fish that is hooked.

As a more extreme illustration, the Nazi technique of arresting possible dissidents here and there, with little visible order or sense to the choices made (minor violations might lead to arrest, major ones might not), appeared to be somewhat random, but therefore powerful in its consequences. The randomness seems to have had a greater fear and control effect on the German population than a clearly defined, rigorous, and certain system of humiliation and destruction might have had.[37]

Modern learning theory has emphasized the greater effectiveness of reward as against punishment. Surely this is in part because what rewards accomplish best—for example, accuracy and swiftness of learning, creativity and exploration, pleasure in personal growth—seem praiseworthy; and because the finding that punishment is a poor teacher fits the modern bias against treating others harshly. But let us consider some of the effects of punishment on attitudes, as distinguished from cognitive learning.[38] In

36. See B. F. Skinner, *Science and Human Behavior* (New York: Free Press, 1953), and F. S. Keller, *Learning-Reinforcement Theory* (New York: Random House, 1954), pp. 19–22. For a classic statement of the work in random reinforcement, see B. F. Skinner's *Schedules of Reinforcement* (New York: Appleton-Century-Crofts, 1957), *Science and Human Behavior* (New York: Macmillan, 1953), and *Walden Two* (New York: Macmillan, 1962); as well as F. S. Keller, *Learning and Reinforcement Theory* (New York: Random House, 1960).

37. Eugene V. Walter, *Terror and Resistance: A Study of Political Violence* (New York: Oxford University Press, 1969). Random stress (e.g., sudden noise) has a negative effect on task performance: D. Glass and J. Singer, eds., *Urban Stress: Experiments on Noise as Social Stressors* (New York: Academic, 1972).

38. See Byron A. Campbell and Russell M. Church, eds., *Punishment and Aversive Behavior* (New York: Appleton-Century-Crofts, 1969); Erling E. Boe and Russell M. Church, eds., *Punishment: Issues and Experiments* (New York: Appleton-Century-Crofts, 1968); and A. Bandura, *Principles of Behavior Modification* (New York: Holt, Rinehart, and Winston, 1969), esp. with respect to aversive conditioning as a technique for "curing" deviants. In the present study, see my later chapter on dispraise.

crude terms, the notion of reward or operant conditioning asserts that in order to control others, it is most effective to seize or create an occasion when a person (or an experimental animal) does what is desired, then to reward him or her for it. He or she will therefore be more inclined to do it again in similar circumstances. In effect, such rewards give a control message: you are doing right; do it some more. By contrast, punishment merely says: Stop!—but the person cannot be sure what it is that he is doing wrong, and he may not ever find out what is right.

Nevertheless, no social system has been founded on the wisdom of modern operant conditioning. Although it cannot be supposed from this that human beings are wiser than psychologists, what punishment accomplishes in ordinary social relations and in socialization should at least be considered.

Unlike the perfect teaching machine—which would so structure the progression of learning that the student never makes a mistake, is always rewarded for doing well, and is never scolded—the processes of social control over adults or children operate in situations in which: mistakes are nearly certain (in part because others choose one's tasks); neither rewards nor punishments are certain; and punishment and disapproval go together. Only in special circumstances—such as at the early stages of learning new ways—does the person who corrects another simply explain the "error." Certainly, continued correction is typically accompanied by scolding, anger, deprecation (that is, loss of esteem), and loss of love.

Punishment—typically, hurt and disapproval—is usually imprecise, but it is massively effective in inducing both animals and people to avoid the behavior that is punished. For much of social control, quick, deep avoidance-learning is indeed the social goal. Punishment is of course less effective in stimulating people to exploration, creation, leadership, or positive action, but few social groups or dyads welcome much of that type of behavior.

Social punishments are effective *because* they are imprecise. They do not teach people that they can safely come close to the limit of disapproved behavior (as contract does), but rather that they should avoid even an approach to it.[39] Social prohibitions are more successful when the individual feels threatened, anxious, or uneasy at even coming near forbidden taboo areas, acts, temptations, and so on. If by contrast individuals could be sure of the exact amount of punishment they would suffer if they violated a rule within a narrow, specific margin (as they can in contract), they would then be more inclined to calculate the costs rationally and to approach the forbidden as closely as seems profitable. Punishment learning is cognitively crude but emotionally powerful. Prestige punishment (humiliation, rejection, dispraise) may confuse individuals, but it does

---

39. Punishment causes persons and animals to avoid a whole series of behaviors as well as the environment around those possible acts. See F. S. Keller, *Learning and Reinforcement Theory* (New York: Random House, 1960), p. 71.

inculcate deeply the importance of trying to please others, as well as a general aversion to various taboo areas of behavior. Indeed, so deep is this inculcation that many people spend years on an analyst's couch trying to unlearn some of it.

Finally, the effect of a random system of rewards and the crude impact of punishment have been emphasized, but one further extreme type of emotional learning situation should be noted: continuous and steady dispraise, hurt, humiliation, or contempt. There are some individuals, and in perhaps all major societies some subsegments, castes, or classes, much of whose behavior patterns elicit deprecation, punishment, and sparse material rewards from others. Such uniformly negative inducements are perhaps the least effective stimuli to learning. This is not randomness. In a technical sense, the social environment does not differentiate among the individual's behavior responses—whatever the person does, punishment follows. Under those conditions, neither animals nor human beings learn accurately. Human beings become alienated from the system, and are more likely to obey the norms only when that seems profitable. Then the result is that social learning or social control creates confusion and ambiguity, low motivation, apathy, and rejection of the system. Many ethnic and racial groups have had this type of experience, and so have many children who have been the victims of child abuse.[40]

In drawing upon psychological findings, I have tried to show that some of the common prestige processes in social control and socialization may be better grounded in psychological principles than is apparent. The general aim in this section has been to explain how noncontractual processes, especially those in the realm of prestige, can achieve powerful control effects even though they do not have the clarity and definiteness of feedback that are observable in contractual relations. Since groups do not mainly aim at a specific, narrow, "technically correct" behavioral conformity with the rules, but rather some emotional commitment to them, this broad-band pattern can be fairly effective for much of social control.

THE CHOICE: CONTRACTUAL OR NONCONTRACTUAL CONTROL PROCESSES

Before concluding this chapter I wish tentatively to answer the question raised earlier, why do some subgroups or classes move toward a contractual or instead toward a noncontractual system of social control? Although the trend in Western society over several centuries has been toward a greater emphasis on contractual relations, even within contemporary society with its many contractual settings, large scale bureaucracies, and buyer-seller relationships, many human beings try to alter their relations

40. See my article "Force and Violence in the Family," in *Journal of Marriage and the Family*, 33, no. 4 (November, 1971): 624–636.

in the direction of noncontractual processes, especially those of esteem or personal liking.

The question really asks, which groups profit if the society begins to move in one or the other direction?[41] Some light can be shed by considering one special instance of this movement, the trend of Western society toward contractualism over the past several centuries.[42] The social conflicts that created an industrial working class out of the serfs and peasants of the later middle ages will illustrate this. If, as appears to be true, no class or group has ever entered slavery, serfdom, or even the rank of outcaste except under force and force threat, we can at least know whose advantage was served by those earlier versions of noncontractual arrangements. Obviously, anyone who possesses superiority in force, as did feudal lords, can pay less for what he receives, that is, make better economic or social bargains than he could in a free market. Indeed, if his superiority is great, as in the early stages of a conquest, he need not pay money, goods, or services at all. The force embodied in a slave system, too, gives advantageous economic terms to the slaveowner.[43]

Some similarities to the parent-child relation are evident here. These patterns of potential and real economic and legal exploitation bring other social benefits of deference, attention, and loyalty; thus, when those in power try to move away from such noncontractual arrangements toward explicit contract, they are giving up substantial advantages. Consequently, we can look for the kinds of alternative, larger advantages they hope to find in the new system, which in recent centuries has become more explicitly contractual.

Those noncontractual relations in preindustrial society yielded many advantages to the superordinate but also imposed certain burdens on them, although with our contemporary democratic biases we tend to ignore these when analyzing absolutist monarchies or feudal systems. These burdens were not, to be sure, as great as the advantages they brought (however much the lords may have commiserated with one another about those burdens). However, political and economic conditions did arise in which these burdens pressed superordinates to move toward a more contractual pattern, that is, to give away some of their

41. Although businesses often do not make formal contracts, some factors increase the likelihood of their doing so. See Steward Macaulay, "Non-Contractual Relations in Business," *American Sociological Review* 28 (February, 1963): 55–67.

42. Within the lifetime of individuals, the parent-child relationship moves somewhat in this direction; within the spousal relationship there may be some similar movement, but that analysis is omitted here.

43. A single datum—the continued rise in slave prices in the U.S.—would have shown even long ago that the American slave system was profitable to slaveholders. Additional and more complex data, still in dispute, are to be found in R. W. Fogel and Stanley L. Engerman, *Time on the Cross: The Economics of American Negro Slavery* (Boston: Little, Brown, 1974). For critiques of this work, see *New York Review of Books*, 21, no. 7 (May 2, 1974), and subsequent issues.

obvious advantages, to cast off the corresponding duties, and to seize still greater opportunities.

The burdens of which the lords wished to divest themselves were closely linked to the disadvantages suffered by their tenants or serfs. For though the holder of power, the feudal lord, had some freedom to change the terms of exchange arbitrarily, and the subordinate could not end the exchange as he would later under a free contract system, neither could the superordinate simply abandon his responsibilities. The peasant and serf lived under poor terms, but they did have claims that were recognized as custom or law (gleaning, commons grazing, food) and were sometimes expressed in rebellions, revolts, riots, and other violence when those claims were violated.[44]

An index of that responsibility can be seen in phenomena that are usually interpreted as evidence of the power of the English landowners, the enclosure movement and rack rents. By the former, communities as well as individuals were dispossessed of customary land rights, permitting lords and gentry to use the land more economically for their own purposes (especially for growing sheep). Through rack rents, tenants holding land in fief and under other terms were transformed into tenants for limited periods, that is, given a land contract. In a generally expanding economy over several centuries, this permitted landowners to raise rents steadily or to rent land to the highest bidder after the term had expired. Both processes were well under way by Elizabeth's reign. Indeed, Lawrence Stone asserts that the consequent destruction of lord-tenant loyalty and of esteem for the upper classes, as their relations became contractual rather than traditional, created one of the elements generating the Protestant Revolution.[45] In contractual relations, after all, each owes to the other only a set of specific performances and money for a limited time, but not the fringe acts or commitments such as responsibility, deference, protection, or loyalty. If lords were to treat the lower orders as mere customers, the prestige and deference of the old system would no longer be paid.

But though all this did happen, it should not be forgotten that the process took place over hundreds of years, culminating in the eighteenth but continuing into the early nineteenth century, against substantial resistance. That is, though the earlier system gave advantages to the landowner, obviously it gave fewer advantages than the new one that gradually emerged, and correspondingly his tenants believed they were *losing* much by the change, however we may now deplore the older order. They fought

44. Charles Tilly, "Collective Violence in European Perspective," in *Violence in America: Historical and Comparative Perspectives*, eds. Hugh Davis Graham and Ted R. Gurr (New York: New American Library, 1969), pp. 4–42. Both Wayne Suttles, "Affinal Ties, Subsistence, and Prestige among the Coast Salish," and F. G. Bailey, *Gifts and Poison*, offer cases where especially the giving of presents or help yields political advantages or influence in tribal society or peasant villages.

45. Lawrence Stone, *The Crisis of the Aristocracy: 1558–1641* (Oxford: Clarendon, 1965), p. 259. Far more land was enclosed during the eighteenth century, but conflict about the process was centuries old by then.

against the contractual freedom being thrust upon them, although they eventually gained in civic rights and prestige thereby.[46] The gentry could not and did not divest themselves quickly or easily of an array of responsibilities and duties that were essentially noncontractual.

Marx expressed scorn of the "freedom" of the worker when the early factory system began to appear, noting that he was indeed free, but in the cruel sense that he could either make a contract to work at low wages or starve. But his implicit contrast was with an earlier system in which the rural lower class was not free, but neither was the great landowner. The new industrial system "freed" both, the one to starve or work at low wages, the other to exploit successfully in a contractual system or to go bankrupt. This was also the result of freeing the slaves in the Civil War of the United States.

We are asserting, then, that people choose or move away from noncontractual controls under different social and economic conditions, and the advantages they seek in such changes are not alone economic in the market sense. More specifically, they are more likely to move toward noncontractual social interaction and controls when they are concerned with another's emotions, attitudes, and motivations as much as his or her overt acts; with loyalty, emotional security, deference or respect, love or affection, centrality, and continuity; with a wide range of indulgences and tolerances for one's idiosyncracies and changes of mood and attitude, not easily specifiable in a contract; with performances ideally above some minimum; with less calculation of the most advantageous terms the other can extort:[47] with the relation as an end in itself rather than with its output; and with a series of transactions that do not require much managerial or planning skill.

THE LIMITED REALM OF CONTRACT

If this theoretical sketch is correct, it is not surprising that societies characteristically restrict contractual controls to a small part of all social interaction. Such controls are more satisfactory to their participants when a minimum performance is adequate; when those who participate in supervision acquire managerial and planning skills (note that they were not so necessary in a feudal system); when one or both sides prefer to be free to renegotiate terms whenever more advantageous ones are offered; when the aim is the actual performance or activity that is paid for, not the

---

46. De Tocqueville makes a similar observation about English landowners, saying: "I have often heard the great landed proprietors of England congratulate themselves on getting much more money from their lands than did their fathers . . . . Perhaps they are right to be pleased, but for certain they do not understand in what it is that they take pleasure. They think they are clearing a net profit, when they are only making an exchange. They are selling their influences for cash down, and what they gain in money they will soon lose in power," *Democracy in America* (New York: Doubleday, Anchor, 1969), pp. 581–582.

47. Compare the discussion of "minimax" in John Rawls, *A Theory of Justice* (Cambridge: Harvard University Press, 1971), pp. 152–157.

attitude or motivation of those who sell a commodity or service; or when (as in modern industry) the system can tolerate people's freedom to leave.

Such a contractual system offers certain types of guarantees with respect to needed commodities or services but conspicuously fails to offer many fringe benefits. It thus relieves individuals of some side burdens that cannot be specified in a contract. Since the contractual system of controls creates a degree of competition in which no one has much responsibility for those who fail, even in modern economic transactions the buyer or seller tries to bind the other to a more continuous, morally obligated relationship in which this competitiveness is reduced somewhat. The most "modern" corporations are precisely the ones that succeed in controlling their markets and their top managers through political and personal ties.

These preliminary considerations have carried us into complex areas of social order, although our primary focus has remained the same: description of the fundamental prestige processes in a society. Here these are viewed as processes of social control, by which individuals move each other toward living up to ideals set by themselves, their groups, or the larger society. They are always reciprocal; no single one is without some influence. They are essentially noncontractual, frequently entail giving or getting esteem from others, and may be viewed as exchanges, even though they are not often dyadic, for "third parties" or the community as a whole is also part of the relation. They form part of the larger structure of social controls aimed at creating some orderliness in human relations, made up of both contractual and noncontractual social patterns.

Chapter 3
Market and Nonmarket
Bases of Social Control

In this chapter, we shall examine to what extent the processes of getting or allocating prestige may be like those of the economic market. Our general problem is how the amount of prestige given affects the willingness of people to do what others want, or how doing what others want affects the amount of respect paid. Since contemporary social exchange theory, in its many varieties in many fields (political science, social psychology, sociology, economics, anthropology, and even history), is so often expressed in economic terms, it is imperative to this discussion that we consider how fruitful the economic model is to an understanding of prestige processes and (by implication) other social exchanges as well.

Indeed, thinking about prestige processes in economic terms helps to understand those processes better, because economic terms alert us to some general social patterns (supply, demand, elasticity) that are observable and call for explanation.[1] But the larger thesis here is more important and indeed has implications for all of social exchange theory. It is that when we consider prestige processes in economic terms, it is clear that standard formulations of microeconomic processes are deficient precisely because they omit some significant social control regularities. Thus, the analysis of *real* economic behavior (as against its idealized version in textbook formulations) would be improved by utilizing observations or data on general social exchange processes. In short, each can profit from the other. Social exchange theory has profited from economic formulations in the recent past, because economic behavior is one subbranch of social exchange behavior, and at many points they are likely to be similar in form.

Let us first note some crude ways in which prestige processes are similar to economic ones, to show that there is some justification for the explora-

1. In *Exchange and Power in Social Life* (New York: John Wiley, 1964), chaps. 4–7, Blau has applied many technical notions of elementary economics to social exchanges. But not all of his conclusions seem to be borne out by empirical data, and some economists have asserted that not all of the economic formulations are correctly applied. On this point, see Anthony Heath, *Rational Choice and Social Exchange* (Cambridge, Mass.: Harvard University Press, 1976).

tion we are making. Then we can consider one important foundation of social or economic exchanges, that is, values, norms, and evaluations, as a step toward examining prestige processes in terms of supply and demand.

On a crude observational level, some likenesses are apparent between the processes of the prestige "market" and those of the economic market. That is, people at some level perceive the daily social process as in part a type of exchange, if a risky one, in which they are giving various kinds of performances in order to receive praise or approval. Individuals and groups, knowing full well that no definite, clear contract has been made, do feel at times they are working hard "in order to get" honors, praise, offices, and so forth. Not only do they use that vocabulary of rhetoric internally, but they use it in conversation and speeches. People exhort one another to work hard not only for money but also "for" the respect of others. Good performance on the job, though it is mainly viewed as yielding economic benefits, is also viewed as "deserving" esteem. Moreover, as noted earlier, people feel morally indignant or angry if they are not praised when they feel they deserve it, just as they feel angry if they are not paid money that is owed them.

It is also observable over time that people can accumulate prestige and rise in prestige ranking, just as in the market realm they can acquire wealth over time.[2] If they have acquired more prestige, they can use it as a "commodity" or even as risk capital.[3] For example, a highly respected scientist can sometimes obtain a research grant even when he or she cannot specify in advance precisely the research techniques to be used or where the research inquiry will eventually go. The granting board may well feel that his or her prestige justifies that kind of risk. Here, both are making an investment and taking a risk. Similarly, if a person has more prestige than others, he or she can fail at some task or enterprise for a longer period of time without incurring censure. Others may also hope that in the long run what seems at the moment to be a failure will later be revealed as a clever set of moves for the advantage of the group.

Just as it can be accumulated, prestige can be variously expended (as wealth can) to obtain such pleasures as a society may offer, from the company of attractive men and women to generous salaries and lavish expense accounts. When people have greater prestige, they are more likely

2. And, of course, we can sometimes ascertain whether a given transaction has yielded prestige. We can also note the consequences for the group if the leader is given much esteem. See, e.g., the "great men" (those with high task and socioemotional leadership qualities) in the Bales experiments: E. F. Borgatta, A. S. Couch, and R. F. Bales, "Some Findings Relevant to the Great Man Theory of Leadership," in A. P. Hare, E. F. Borgatta, and R. F. Bales, eds., *Small Groups: Studies in Social Interaction* (New York: Knopf, 1955), pp. 568–574.

3. Bringing high-ranking people into an organization convinces others that the other aspects of the organization (which cannot easily be seen) will be run well. Thus, in the days before the war research organization RAND began to frighten people with its inquiries and suggestions, it had to obtain an outstanding board of directors so as to convince the government that it would be directed competently and that the scientific and industrial communities would back it: Bruce L. R. Smith, *The Rand Corporation* (Cambridge: Harvard University Press, 1966), p. 72.

to be entrusted with important jobs and offices.[4] They are welcome in higher ranking social networks.[5]

Like money, prestige is in short supply. People usually feel that they do not have enough prestige. They generally strive for it when they perceive some chance of obtaining it.

Moreover, as in the economic market, people can decide *not* to continue to maximize in that realm, but to gain more in another. Some people decide that they will not strive ever upward in the corporation, but will spend more time in civic or family activities. Similarly, people may decide that they will not aim at higher prestige levels, but turn instead to money-making, friendship, or politics.[6] As with money, however, even people who feel they have enough respect already will nevertheless feel that they cannot do without the respect or approval of others.[7]

Thus we can observe at least some rough similarities between economic and prestige markets: in both, a resource is gained or distributed that is widely useful but limited in supply, and people will do things for others in order to get it.[8] Let us now consider an important basis of all such transactions.

FOUNDATIONS OF SOCIAL ACTION

An important basis of all social action, and thus of both economic and prestige systems, is a *set of group or individual evaluations* that prescribe what anything is worth, that is, how desirable it is: wheat, time, self-sacrifice, ethnic membership. In Western society, with rare exceptions in particular social circles or regions, the ability to fall into a trance or to make black magic is worth little; and so is (among adults) a talent for moving one's ears. Although social commentators often exclaim cynically or indignantly over the deference given the rich, wealth alone confers only a modest amount of prestige (but considerable overt deference). As can be inferred from the statues, biographies, and histories in any civilization,

---

4. Compare Max Weber: "Social honor, or prestige, may even be the basis of political or economic power, and very frequently has been," in "Class, Status, and Party," in Reinhard Bendix and Seymour M. Lipset, eds., *Class, Status, and Power,* 2d ed. (New York: Free Press, 1966), p. 21.

5. W. Lloyd Warner and Paul S. Lunt, *The Status System of a Modern Community*, Yankee City Series vol. II (New Haven: Yale University Press, 1942), esp. pp 3–24.

6. Casanova opted for a whole-hearted investment in the realm of love, reasoning that since men seek prestige, power, or wealth mainly to attract lovely women, it would surely be more sensible to go directly toward the goal.

7. Samuel Butler does express a dissenting view, asserting that the loss of money is not only the worst pain, but the parent of all others. Of the three most serious losses, money is the most severe, then health, then reputation. ". . . A man may grow a new reputation as easily as a lobster grows a new claw, or, if he have health and money, may thrive in great peace of mind without any reputation at all," *The Way of All Flesh* (New York: Hartsdale House, 1935), p. 298.

8. Since prestige is in these (and some other) respects something like money or wealth, it is tempting to call it a *medium of exchange*. However, so many analysts have called so many things "media"—even *values*, which makes no sense at all—that I will not succumb. Moreover, prestige is not so separable from the person as money or wealth, and it is experienced far more as a direct pleasure.

politics and the arts yield far more. It may be useful here to make some elementary comments about values and norms as a way of illuminating their role in prestige processes.

Since sociologists have so often used values and norms to explain social action, much of their survey research has attempted to find out which values and norms people hold, in different groups, organizations, or social strata.[9] Sociologists have also carried out many experiments designed to change those normative commitments, especially in race relations. However, they have not often inquired systematically into the social conditions that alter values and norms over a longer period of time, that is, why ideologies, evaluations, values, or norms have changed over several generations.

Sociologists claim, on the basis of both self-examination and reliable data, that: social action is mostly set into motion by values and norms, attitudes and evaluations, since they express or describe what people feel is worth doing; and, wherever those evaluations may come from ultimately, each individual acquires them in a continuing process of socialization and social control, that is, in social interaction with many other individuals and groups; further, however evaluations may change, we can at any given time use fairly reliable research tools to find out how people believe or feel or evaluate at that time.

For economics, this evaluative foundation creates no theoretical problems, except for a few perceptive economists whose work is viewed as somewhat deviant. Economics does not even have to ask what these evaluations are, much less what creates them, since it is believed that any evaluation relevant to economic behavior can be stated as market demand: if people value it, they will pay for it.[10]

By contrast, sociology views the problematics of values, that is, their influence on social action, as a central focus of inquiry.[11] Sociologists cannot infer others' evaluations from observing people's overt behavior, or predict future behavior from people's assertions about their own values.[12]

9. Jack Gibbs analyzes why the more usual definition of "norm" as only a *group* standard cannot be applied to real behavior, in *Social Control*, Warner Modular Publications (Module 1, 1972), p. 3.

10. Alfred Marshall was wise enough to recognize that society determines much of what people want and thus will pay for. Nevertheless, he did not attempt to build those elements into a formal theory of demand. In more recent years, George Katona's research has focused on actual economic behavior and attitudes, but it, too, has not been assimilated into formal economic theory. See Alfred Marshall, *Principles of Economics*, 9th ed. (New York: Macmillan, 1961 [1890]), I, esp. 102–116; and George Katona, *The Powerful Consumer: Psychological Studies of the American Economy* (New York: McGraw-Hill, 1960). For more extended comments on the introduction of sociological theory or data into economic analysis, see Neil J. Smelser, *The Sociology of Economic Life* (Englewood Cliffs, N.J.: Prentice-Hall, 1963), esp. chap. 4.

11. For the importance of that focus in the history of sociology, see Talcott Parsons, *The Structure of Social Action* (New York: McGraw-Hill, 1937).

12. For a strong attack on the assumption that people's statements about their norms or values can be used to predict behavior, see Irwin Deutscher, *What We Say/What We Do* (Glenview, Ill.: Scott, Foresman, 1973). Ethnomethodological research has especially challenged any assumption of sociologists that they already know the group norms without making tests. They have of course also informed us of many norms that traditional sociology had not previously taken into account. On the question of how we know that a norm exists, see D. H. Zimmerman and Melvin Pollner, "The

They must ascertain both internal and external behavior, and, as Weber pointed out, their problems become more complex and their data richer.[13] As a consequence, the sociologist cannot assume, for example, that we can know the amount of real respect a person enjoys by simply observing how much deference others pay him or her; or even how much demand there is for a given type of performance or behavior by noting the apparent price or amount of prestige paid. In both cases the amount actually paid may be partly a function of the force or force threat, or the political influence (or other resources) that person can command.[14]

Economics seems to be in a safer position, while sociology has taken a more difficult road by asserting that its data include people's inner evaluations and norms. In both prestige and economic markets one would like to know how much underlying demand there is for a given level of behavior or type of commodity (lyric poetry, good plumbing, virtue). In economics, that problem seems to be solved by the claim that demand is simply measured by a set of demand schedules, that is, how much people will actually buy at different price levels. In short, what is their behavior?

Thus, the economist will present a curve that shows people will purchase 100,000 bushels of wheat at $10 a bushel, 120,000 bushels at $8, or only 90,000 at $11.[15] Presumably, these hypothetical purchases define demand at that time. In fact we have no such data, however, if "the" price of a given quality of wheat is $10: no one would be so foolish as to sell his wheat for $8 (and thus test whether 120,000 bushels *would* be bought) or to try to sell it at $11 (at which price probably no one would buy at all).[16]

But if the economist does not possess so crucial a factual base, neither does the sociologist. That is, even if sociology is correct in asserting that data on inner evaluations and norms might yield such a measure of demand, it is still not possible to ascertain exactly, that is, quantitatively, how much respect really would be paid for different levels or types of performances or traits. Nevertheless, we can assume from crude, ordinary intuition and introspection that people do change their behavior in response to guesses and data about their prospective payoffs from working

Everyday World as a Phenomenon," in Jack Douglas, ed., *Understanding Everyday Life* (Chicago: Aldine, 1970), pp. 80–103.

13. However, since both psychologists and sociologists are sensitive to the problem of finding out what other people are experiencing inside themselves, some do assert their intention of using behavior alone. See, e.g., the essays (and some criticism) in Don Bushell and Robert L. Burgess, *Behavioral Sociology* (New York: Columbia University Press, 1969), and J. F. L. Scott, *The Internalization of Norms* (Englewood Cliffs, N.J.: Prentice-Hall, 1971).

14. For some empirical analyses of these control processes, see Herbert J. Gans, *The Urban Villagers* (New York: Free Press, 1962), esp. re the "external caretakers," pp. 142–159; or Gerald B. Suttles, *The Social Order of the Slum* (Chicago: University of Chicago Press, 1968), re territory, respect of the gang's "turf," and the goal of social order, pp. 9, 10, 31–38.

15. For an elementary but elegant presentation, see Paul A. Samuelson, *Economics*, 9th ed. (New York: McGraw-Hill, 1973), chap. 4.

16. But in the economic view of this matter, since thousands of people are constantly deciding to sell or not, as the price fluctuates, they are at least testing whether that really is "the" price. Nevertheless, that still does not yield real data for such a hypothetical curve of demand at very different prices.

hard or not, conforming to group ideals or not, and seeking a better market or not.

SUPPLY AND DEMAND IN
THE PRESTIGE MARKET

In the prestige market we (like the economist) can observe that *if the evaluation of a given trait or performance is high, demand by definition is also high; but if the supply of a given behavior is high, even if it is given a moderate evaluation, then the payoff will be low.* For example, we strongly disapprove of murder, and place a high value on our control over our own and (especially) others' murderous impulses; but since most of us do control ourselves (that is, the supply of this behavior is high) we gain no prestige from not murdering our fellow human beings—while we incur much disesteem if we give in to that temptation. By contrast, the evaluation of scientific discoveries is high, but few can supply them, so that the prestige paid for this form of creativity is high.

In the economic view, the ever-shifting elements of supply and demand as exhibited in prices asked and paid carry control messages to those in the market. As textbooks sometimes explain it, when a buyer learns that the entire wheat market can be bought at $10 a bushel, he or she knows the abundant supply conveys the message that the price of $10 is far too high. Demand, on the other hand, gives an important message to the seller; if no one will buy any wheat at, say, $12 a bushel, the seller has learned that the price set is too high. The seller tries to learn what is the maximum price he or she can get while selling all he or she wants to sell. The prices offered give both buyer and seller the needed information about the market.

Similarly, the amount of respect paid for a Ph.D. informs us what it is "worth" on the prestige market, that is, how much demand there is for it in different social circles or organizations. In some circles, the individual learns that others view him or her as an oddity for even having a Ph.D. In a prestigious university, the degree may be necessary if the individual wants a regular professorial job. During a time of shortage, however, universities, as "buyers" of Ph.D.'s, may be willing to hire a person who has not completed the doctorate. The demand is higher for the doctorate from a high-ranking university. In short, those who are in the market learn from others' behavior just what the current prestige value of the doctorate is. Those who have the Ph.D. (the sellers) as well as the universities, agencies, or companies who hire them (the buyers) learn from one another whether they are setting their prices too low or too high. The recent Ph.D. who demands too high a price may not be hired; the college that will give only a lecturer's rank to a Ph.D. from a highly respected university may find few or no takers.

With these examples in mind, we can succinctly restate in economic terms of supply and demand some elementary parallels between prestige and economic processes:

1. Other things being equal, people prefer to obtain more prestige from others, and they will alter their behavior to gain it if they can without undue cost. In economic terms, this means that they will supply more of one kind of behavior if the demand for it makes others willing to pay a satisfactory "prestige price" for it.[17]

2. Other things being equal, people will feel or pay esteem, respect, or deference to an individual or group that exhibits qualities or performances that people perceive as excellent according to their own values and norms. In economic terms, this means that if people's demand for some kind of performance is high, they are willing to pay more for it.

3. Since earning prestige requires effort (aside from those admired ascriptive qualities, such as being born of "a good family," which almost no amount of effort can procure), people must choose whether the amount of prestige they see as possible is really worth the effort. In economic terms, they will anticipate whether a given allocation of energy, skill, or investment will yield a prestige price that is higher than a different allocation or investment.

In these traditional formulations, then, people engage in transactions when the amount one person is willing to buy at the market price will be supplied by another at that price. Or, each is willing to give up something he or she wants *less* (money, hard work) in order to get something he or she wants *more* (frisbees, esteem from others). The amount offered will then "equal" the amount demanded. Demand, translated into willingness to buy at the market price, will be equivalent to supply, translated into willingness to sell at that price.

Although social exchange theory has not utilized this economic tautology of supply (at market price) = Demand (at market price), it has used the tautology on which the economic one is based; moreover, much of psychology is based on a similar tautology. In general, in all these theoretical orientations, it is asserted that the individual (or group, or white rat) will engage in certain kinds of behavior if they are rewarding, or pay more, or perhaps are given a higher evaluation, and will avoid courses of action that yield a lesser or a negative outcome. It would not be sensible to do otherwise. If an animal or human being seems to do otherwise, we do not reject this general assumption, but search for other reasons for that behavior. That is, no matter what the animal does, we suppose it *preferred* that action to the available alternatives.

Learning that social analysts sometimes engage in circular reasoning is useful, for then we are less likely to confuse a restatement with a discovery. Most important, however, for much analysis we do have some independent measures outside that circularity: for example, people can (if white rats cannot) tell us whether they wanted or valued something or later found it rewarding and would like to do it again sometime. Or, we can observe an increase in demand for, say, nuclear physics, and then a rise

---

17. We shall consider at length the conditions under which they will conform more to others' norms or evaluations to gain prestige. We shall also analyze the conditions under which they will attempt, by various forms of "subversion," to avoid that conformity when it is too costly, but *appear* to conform just the same.

in the prestige of nuclear physicists. Moreover, if we remain fully aware that often our predictions will be confounded by other variables, we can nevertheless state many regularities of prestige behavior, and check them by observation. The best test of any theoretical orientation is whether it generates many powerful relationships that can be tested by real data; I believe that in this case subsequent analyses will do just that.

THE NONECONOMIC STRUCTURE
OF PRIMITIVE ECONOMIES

While exploring prestige processes from the perspective of social exchange, and seeing parallels between prestige and economic processes, we have argued that the textbook formulations of microeconomic patterns are properly to be regarded as a special subset of all social exchanges. We have also suggested that realistic descriptions of some economic patterns in even modern societies are closer to ordinary social exchanges than to the assumption of a free market.

For these reasons, it is valuable at this point to consider a set of market patterns that do not appear to fit the textbook descriptions of a free market. For many decades anthropologists have denied that the formulations of economics are general explanations of economic behavior, for they fail when applied to the economies of primitive societies. Few economists have altered their theories because of those data.[18]

Aside from a few exchanges that seem to be genuine market transactions, the economic patterns in primitive societies appear to be similar to the ordinary social transactions between kin, friends, or neighbors in a modern society. Exchanges in a primitive economy have been described in the following ways.

First, exchanges in societies without fully developed market systems occurred mainly between persons who were designated by explicit status or position as the appropriate partners, for example, chiefs, mother's brothers or other kin, age-group members, or religious leaders.

Second, both the amount and timing of exchanges were set by tradition more than by the fluctuations of supply and demand. This applies as well to much gift-giving in modern societies among friends and kin (Christmas, birthdays, Hannukah, marriages). It seems likely that some part of price determination at the retail level of the small store in the United

18. For a good summary of the differences between a market economy and a tribal one, see the extended notes to chap. 4 in Karl Polanyi, *The Great Transformation* (Boston: Beacon, 1957 [1944]), pp. 269ff. Bronislaw Malinowski viewed his *Argonauts of the Western Pacific* (New York: E.P. Dutton and Co., 1922) as an attack on formal economics. See also Raymond Firth, *Primitive Polynesian Economy* (London: Routledge & Kegan Paul, 1939), and Karl Polanyi *et al.*, *Trade and Market in the Early Empires* (Glencoe, Ill.: Free Press, 1957), as well as Marcel Mauss, *The Gift* [1925], trans. J. Cunnison (New York: Norton, 1967), and Peter Ekeh, *Social Exchange Theory: The Two Traditions* (Cambridge, Mass.: Harvard University Press, 1974). Wilbert G. Moore, "Economic and Professional Institutions," in Neil Smelser, ed., *Sociology*, 2d ed. (New York: Wiley, 1973), pp. 375ff., notes some of these differences as well.

States and other countries is affected by traditional notions of what is a "fair" or a "traditional" price. Economists do not, however, view this as an appreciable element in market exchange. In primitive societies, religious rituals specified that accumulations of food be made at certain times of the year for later redistribution, and those customs specified how much food was to be accumulated and of what quality it should be, as well as who was to receive which portions of it later.[19]

Third, since so many of the transactions were determined by custom, the people engaged in them were clearly not aiming at maximizing their monetary gain—although the social exchange theorist might comment that they may well have been trying to increase their total *social* gain, in respect as well as friendship.

Fourth, minimum performances within those economies were well understood, but to pay more than custom specified yielded esteem. The man of rank returned more than he got. This social pattern has been reported by many analysts of nonmarket societies.[20]

Fifth, the consequences of making foolish or wrong transactions were not typically market penalties (for example, going bankrupt), but were more likely to be supernatural punishments or the loss of social esteem.

Finally, in such primitive economies the person who did not like the terms of such exchanges typically did not have the freedom to renegotiate them as in a free market. To try to choose other partners would have caused a loss of respect. To try to change the terms (since they were presumably fixed customs) would be socially costly and over the long run economically disastrous.

Anthropologists who have criticized formal economics have claimed nevertheless that primitive peoples were rational. These peoples calculated how much time and energy to allocate to producing food, and they made clever adaptations to their environment. They often produced and sold in local markets. Objects of great value were likely to embody considerable work and skill. They were, in short, capable of precise, sensible calculations. But their *evaluations* of what was more or less worthwhile were different from those of a market economy: Specifically, the maximization of money (or its equivalent) received at best a modest ranking. We would now assert that they evaluated social esteem, political influence, and friendly social relations as higher in importance than increases in material wealth.

Even rational economic exchanges, then, need not aim at maximizing wealth but can maximize other kinds of resources such as political influ-

---

19. For some details of this process viewed as the effect of religion on economic behavior, see William J. Goode, *Religion among the Primitives* (Glencoe, Ill.: Free Press, 1951), chaps. 5, 6.

20. For example, a Trobriand brother tried to give more yams to his married sister than custom called for; among the Northwest Pacific Coast Indians the potlatch furnished an extreme version of "overgiving"; Finley, in *The World of Odysseus*, rev. ed. (New York: Viking, 1965) notes that generosity beyond the customary earned people's respect; and Mauss discusses this point as well (*The Gift*, chaps. 1–3).

ence or prestige. In noting this, we become alert to similar patterns in the modern economies with which we are more familiar.

DIFFERENCES AND SIMILARITIES
IN ECONOMICS AND PRESTIGE

If we observe prestige processes in a modern society (socialist or capitalist), some important structural differences from the free economic market can be seen. These can be stated briefly, before noting similarities:

1. In the economic market, the individual can be highly specialized as a producer or seller, offering only one commodity or service. By contrast, almost anything the person is likely to do will be esteemed or disapproved by others who observe him or her.

2. It is possible to accumulate enough wealth to drop out of the supply side of the market (though of course one remains a consumer). However, no matter how respected one becomes, one is constantly being evaluated as long as one lives. One cannot even temporarily drop out of the prestige market, as some younger people claim to do in order to avoid the rat race of competition; even avoiding competition is also approved or disapproved.

3. In the economic market, no transaction takes place at all if the parties do not agree on the price, thus one can refuse a job or an offer. By contrast, one cannot refuse to be evaluated in the prestige realm.

4. The economic market rests on contract, but there are various ways in which prestige processes differ from contractual patterns (they are not dyadic, people cannot control their "delivery" of esteem to others, payoffs depend on who performs well, and so on).

These are important differences, and they generate other differences in social behavior that we shall note as we pursue this analysis.

But economic transactions are one subset of the general category of social exchanges; thus prestige processes and economic behavior are not likely to be radically different in many ways. Those ways are important, but so are the similarities. Specifically, social exchanges, including prestige processes, are likely to be somewhat closer to social behavior in the *real* economic market than to the ideal, rational economic behavior of formal economic analysis.

In real economic behavior, the seller cannot bear the costs of waiting very long for better prices and thus cannot leave the economic market or drop out of it in order to get a better price. In this respect, the real seller is close to the real person in the prestige realm. Workers can and do refuse jobs that do not pay well enough, but few can stop working for long. In a parallel way, the individual cannot easily put off his or her achievements until the "prestige price" goes up, because that price will not change much over a short period of time.[21] Avant-garde artists hope for an

---

21. Of course, individuals in some social experiments may rise in esteem over even the short period of such interactions, but not by "holding off their excellence" from the market. More typically, the

improvement in public taste, which will then raise their esteem. But they cannot retire from the market while waiting; their paintings and sculptures are part of the educational process. They must continue stubbornly to create, while preaching the merits of their new vision. They must act as does the prophet, who offers a message that brings no prestige at first, but who cannot withdraw from the prestige market as a strategy. Although in these cases the hypothetical "pure" market permits people or groups to wait for better economic conditions or a better price, in real life the prestige and the market realms are closer to one another: it is difficult to stay out of either, even for short periods.

That the distinction is real, however, can be illustrated by noting that some artists *can* stay out of the economic market for a while, once a genuine market for their specific art work has emerged. Then they are in the position of a monopoly supplier and can manipulate the sale of their goods. On the other hand, artists can hardly stay out of the prestige market by withholding their creations, for they would be in the sad position of scientists who failed to announce their discoveries in order to save some for a later and better prestige market. Both would run the risk that others would be honored instead: other tastes in art would appear, or other scientists would make similar discoveries. Thus, whereas Picasso withheld some of his paintings from the economic market to maintain his high prices, he made sure that admiring people saw his latest creations even if they could not buy them.

Part of the definition of a free market in economics is that no individual seller can influence price much by offering all of his product at one time, or withholding it. This hypothetical free market is like the real market in both small-scale economic and prestige transactions. Any buyer or seller who enters will face a set of "going prices" and by his or her individual efforts can do little to change them. The farmer who dumps all his wheat on the market will not lower the price; that supply is too little to affect prices. Similarly, small-scale sellers or buyers in the real economic or prestige markets must accept the prices they receive or pay as realities they cannot easily alter.

On the other hand, in either type of market the individual can decide which submarkets might yield a better payoff. People can, for example, select the areas where their special skills or talents might be more highly rewarded (for example, athletics rather than mathematics, local politics rather than a corporation). People can and do choose to try harder or not,

---

prestige given may not change much. For example, leaders who emerge almost at the beginning of the group formation have a high participation rate from beginning to end, and they remain leaders. In groups that are initially undifferentiated, and where participation is more or less equal, some individuals may gradually become dominant over the course of the session, but then there is less agreement among participants about who are the leaders. See E. E. Jones and H. Gerard, *Foundations of Social Psychology* (New York: Wiley, 1969), p. 671, and Richard Ofshe and M. Fisek, "The Process of Status Evolution," *Sociometry*, 33 (September, 1970): 327–346.

to aim high or not, to overconform or to deviate, depending on how much they want that payoff. One might decide, for example, that to become a dedicated physician is too long and costly a road to pursue for the esteem it could bring.

As a similar choice in allocating energies, people can seek out other groups that might pay more in esteem. For example, a man with a flair for interior decoration might leave a small southern town for New York City; or a professor who does not engage in research might move from a university to a small liberal arts college that emphasizes teaching. In these respects, too, both types of market offer similar possibilities of allocating one's abilities or resources in a different way in order to achieve some gain, whether in monetary or prestige payoffs.

Although prestige processes differ from free market behavior in that the price in esteem varies according to who is being evaluated (for example, a child of six who shows good manners in meeting family friends is praised, whereas an adult, unless he has a reputation as a boor, is not), these processes do resemble market behavior in primitive economies. As noted earlier, in economic transactions in primitive societies it was more common for specific people in particular social positions to trade with certain others rather than seeking the best possible bargain from just anyone. This is one reason why anthropologists have asserted that formal economics does not apply to primitive economies.

Real economic behavior in modern societies, however, offers both trivial and important parallels with those "primitive" patterns, and such parallels suggest that prestige processes are closer to market behavior than textbook formulations would indicate. For example, in local neighborhood markets, who the seller or buyer is does make a difference with respect to price and quality, and this can be often observed in specialty markets as well. Resort property is sometimes not sold to people who "would not fit," and such restrictions may exclude many social groups other than ethnics.[22] In addition, sellers often try to convince buyers that they will sell only to special people (for example, members of the "jet set"); it is common for fancy butchers to try to persuade their customers that they are being especially favored. All these efforts suggest that many people believe the principles of the free market can be bypassed in favor of special relations between buyer and seller—and in most such cases it is evident that factors of prestige play a role in defining who should sell to whom.

Thus in at least some segments of all modern economies, who is permitted to sell to whom, or more crudely whose money is good enough to buy, does make a difference, just as it does in prestige processes. And the relation between these processes and modern economic behavior may be closer than these small cases suggest. Although they may not weigh

---

22. For example, owners of island property on the east coast of the U.S. may want some assurance that the possible buyer will uphold good ecological principles, is not buying in order to sell quickly at a higher price, or enjoys sailing.

heavily in the aggregate, their importance has probably not been systematically calculated.

Nor is the pattern confined to small markets. It is also encountered in governmental contracting, which is a large segment of the corporate market. Especially in defense purchases, not everyone may compete. Government officials work in close collaboration with corporate management and often draw up specifications and contracts that only one or a few suppliers could possibly fit (the "favored contractor"). Former government officials establish personal relations with corporate officials and later move into the corporation, where their earlier links with the government make them more useful, precisely in restricting who may sell to whom. Much corporate activity aims at manipulating officials by bribes, gifts, and campaign contributions, so that they will arrange for government purchases from a particular seller. This is also a prime aim of racketeers in their quasi-commercial transactions: to use force and force threat in order to "persuade" someone to buy only from them.

Thus it is clear that, at least in some major respects, prestige processes are akin to real economic behavior at both large- and small-scale levels and to economic processes in primitive societies. A second departure from formal economics that brings the modern real economy closer to prestige processes is to be found in complex manipulations of supply and demand. In the hypothetical free market, the individual seller or buyer cannot affect price. By contrast, in the advanced sectors of modern industry (for example, steel, aluminum, oil, electronics), corporations do shape both supply and demand. They do so typically as small groups, since a small number of corporations are large enough to dominate those particular submarkets, and their leaders can work together informally because of the trust, esteem, and friendly relations they share. As John Kenneth Galbraith has remarked in *American Capitalism* (p. 105), European visitors who come here to learn the latest techniques of management or production are likely to visit precisely the corporations that the Justice Department is examining for evidence of monopolistic collusion, that is, personal ties among leaders in an industry, with the aim of reducing competition. Corporations attempt to manage the market in various ways, for example, through advertising campaigns, private arrangements with other producers, keeping new inventions off the market, avoiding or preventing competition, or close and personal relations with a favored seller or buyer.

Few individuals can manipulate others very effectively in prestige transactions, although most people do try from time to time. However, as in the economic behavior noted above, groups and organizations do try to organize and execute plans that aim at increasing the respect they will get. People as a group in many occupations have made such attempts, and a few have succeeded.[23] Every professional group has tried, through public

---

23. Relevant here is the analysis in William J. Goode, "The Theoretical Limits of Professionalization," in *Explorations in Social Theory*, pp. 341–382.

speeches, brochures, lobbying, and so on, to upgrade the respect it enjoys from society.[24] Since these efforts aim at improvement in both prestige and economic ranking, their particular success in the prestige market is not clear. Moreover, many such efforts include substantial investments of energy, time, and money in raising the real performances of the members of that professional group.

For example, in the decade after the 1910 Flexner Report, the medical profession made substantial efforts toward improving the education of physicians, eliminating charlatans and the untrained, upgrading reputable medical schools, and attempting to introduce legislation that would raise medical standards.[25] Over the succeeding decades, the prestige (and income) of the medical profession grew. But physicians *did not succeed* in simply manipulating the amount of prestige paid to them; in fact, they also improved their performances. The public paid them more prestige because by the standards of the society they earned more. Limiting the number of charlatans also increased average incomes.

Organizations from clubs to nations constantly try to change their own internal prestige payments (as they try to alter external economic or prestige market prices in their favor) so as to reward and thus support one type of activity rather than another, or one job rather than another. Prizes and awards are offered to raise the usual prestige responses of members, as well as the public. Some of these are little more than empty symbols, such as honors paid to Father of the Year, Neighborhood Clean-Up Champion, or Heroine Mother. Uniforms are issued or redesigned. Titles of jobs are changed to make the incumbents feel their jobs are paid more respect and to make others feel that the job deserves more respect.

These efforts are a form of advertising. As a mode of manipulation, they usually have little impact, because it is difficult to change underlying evaluations or demand processes. Without doubt, changing the real qualities of a job has more effect than manufacturing new symbols. Nevertheless, such manipulative efforts form part of the daily prestige processes we observe, and they merit some attention.

All these efforts are based on people's guesses or hypotheses about what will create higher evaluations or (in the economic market) greater profit. Presumably, people believe they have a fair chance of succeeding, else they would not try. But it seems evident that large corporations in the advanced sectors of the economy have more control than other groups over their economic outcomes. Occupations and voluntary organizations sim-

24. Thibaut and Kelley, *The Social Psychology of Groups* (New York: Wiley, 1959), p. 121, call this "building up the value of one's product"; but the phrase is ambiguous, since obviously they are referring to advertising and manipulation. Most successful efforts at upgrading the prestige of occupations have focused on building up the *real* value of the product—actually offering a better product. This has been true for medicine, dentistry, and social work, as I note in my analysis of professionalization, noted above.

25. William J. Goode, "Encroachment, Charlatanism, and the Emerging Profession: Psychology, Sociology, and Medicine," *American Sociological Review*, 25 (December, 1960): 902–914.

ply do not possess as high a percentage of the total resources within their sectors of activity. I suggest, finally, that the reason why much real behavior in the modern economy parallels that in primitive economies, and thus behavior in prestige processes, is that in both types of economies the dominant figures (corporation leaders in the one and chiefs or medicine men in the other) do control those transactions, and their aim is often not maximum material gains. Both seek political influence, personal and group prestige, the staving off of interference from outsiders, stability, and continuity—and these are often best obtained through social transactions much like prestige processes, rather than through pure market transactions.[26]

ELASTICITY IN ECONOMIC AND PRESTIGE BEHAVIOR

Any attempt to compare prestige processes with economic processes— and thus to look at both as modes of social control—requires that we consider this elementary problem of daily life in almost any society:[27] will the demand rise much or little if the price is changed a given amount? Exploring the question as it applies to prestige processes yields some fruitful observations, and in economics the question generates many complexities.

The term *elasticity* refers to the quantitative aspect of change in demand: specifically, if the price for automobiles drops by ten percent, or rises by that amount, will the demand increase by that amount or more, or drop by that amount or more? If demand increases or drops more than the price does, it is said to be elastic, and the amount of change can be stated quantitatively. If demand rises more than the price is decreased, the total amount of revenue does not drop.[28]

Obviously, both corporate and national planners need this information in order to develop adequate programs of production and allocation. In the United States, if the price of oil is increased will the drop in consumption be proportionately as great as that increase, or are Americans so wedded to their automobiles that they will pay any price (and guarantee shortages in the near future)? In a socialist economy, will a modest decrease in the price for automobiles increase greatly the market demand for them (and thus create other problems)? A corporation planning group must decide whether a rise in the price of their product will send all their customers to other companies, or instead bring in more total revenue. Or, they may

---

26. On these points, see the persuasive arguments in J. K. Galbraith, *Economics and the Public Purpose* (New York: Signet, 1973), esp. pt. 3, "The Planning System."

27. Including primitive economies, where traditionally set prices may suggest high inelasticity; but the general social exchange problem exists as stated here.

28. Strictly speaking, one speaks of the amount of elasticity at one particular point or another along a demand-price curve; it may be high at one point but low at another. Generally, the reference is to a prevailing price, thus the definition stated above is adequate.

find that a decrease in price does not increase the number of purchases by much and actually decreases the total revenue.

The problem is also encountered in the economics of personal services, but its structure is altered; and it is altered even more in prestige processes. People who sell their services, such as social workers, physicians, or hairdressers, can fix their prices high or low and await the results, but their time is limited. They cannot, like the manufacturer, simply turn out more production. If they are serving all the customers they have time for, lowering their price could not increase the number of customers or the total revenue. A salaried person could lower his or her "price," and get more job offers, but what could be done with them? Such people could, as a group, also make such predictions about the total demand for the services of their occupation as a whole if they were to raise or lower prices, although in that case those who were already fully employed would benefit only from a rise in prices.

But in prestige processes the structural differences are still greater. For the most part, we do not ourselves set or fix the respect or esteem others are willing to pay us. In addition, those others are not customers, who could decide to feel more or less esteem depending on how much we ask. How much prestige we want for our achievements has, in general, little effect on how much respect others feel. If we desire only a modest amount of esteem for our substantial achievements (or noble birth), others will not (as they would in the economic market) simply feel that lower amount of respect.

But if we focus on the amount of deference, or *overt* respect, that people exhibit, we can see that the concept of elasticity does apply. Everyone constantly gives small or large cues to others about how much civility or respect he or she demands. Individuals or groups can ask for a lower or higher amount of overt respect, and one can at least estimate (even if unrealistically) whether a given increase in the prestige price would decrease commensurately the number of people who would pay that much. Examples are not hard to find. In the past, movie stars asked for (and sometimes received) many deferential services on their personal appearances, and in some cases all this was specified in contracts. For a rising star, and even more for his or her agent, it was important to know whether increasing that price by ten percent would simply decrease the number of invitations by an equal or greater amount. Refugees of high rank have often had to decide that since people in the United States would not pay them all the deference they had been accustomed to in their own countries, they would have to lower their demands in order to be accepted socially. They have had to predict by how much they should lower the overt respect asked for in order to obtain a needed social circle of adequate rank. In the opposite direction, aspiring artists or writers sometimes decide that they should be treated with the respect accorded to great talents or authentic geniuses. Some people may pay it; but the number who pay respect at all may then be so reduced that the total amount of esteem received will actually be less than before.

Although these illustrations show that the notion of demand throws some light on the processes of exchange, the elasticity of *supply* is of more consequence for prestige processes. That is, microeconomics gives more weight to the elasticity of demand because in modern economies supply is not very problematic (except, recently, for raw materials), whereas demand is; the opposite is true in prestige processes. Supply is less problematic in a highly productive technology because economies of scale can frequently be achieved. That is, if planners believe that reducing the price will be rewarded by a more than commensurate increase in the amount purchased, at a higher level of production it may be possible to make the product more cheaply: unit costs may be lower. Factories often operate at less than full capacity, and can increase the level of supply quickly if the demand is available.[29]

On the other hand, the problematic nature of supply in prestige processes can be illustrated by reflecting that we are often doubtful whether, by paying a higher amount of respect or approval to another person or group, he or they will respond by offering a still higher level of performance or achievement. The parent may consider whether giving more praise to a child before the child has actually earned it will elicit a still greater amount of conformity, obedience, or achievement—or whether perhaps it will instead simply confirm the child's sense that his or her previous level of achievement was satisfactory. If an organization offers new prizes and honors to its salespersons, will they respond by achieving a level of sales well beyond that increase in honor?

Whether or not individuals or organizations face this problem consciously, their acts and decisions deal with it just the same. If a modest increase in prestige paid will increase the supply of approved behaviors a great deal, supply is elastic. If, for example, the prestige given to nuclear physics is increased during a wartime crash program for developing the atomic bomb, and the supply of significant discoveries in that field increases by a still greater amount, supply could be called elastic.[30] Apparently, that did happen during World War II.

The "servant problem" of recent generations illustrates the processes further. In Western societies generally, the overt deference given to people of higher rank has steadily dropped for many decades, and it continues to drop.[31] Employers of servants have lowered their deference

---

29. Of course, as noted above, many types of professional and personal services offer few economies of scale; unit costs do not drop under conditions of high production.

30. Increased rewards might also increase the supply of people who call themselves "nuclear physicists," or who enrol in retraining courses.

31. See Edward A. Shils' comment: "It is one of the features of modern Western societies that they are moving in the direction of deference-indifference, deference-equality, and deference-attenuation," "Reflections on Deference," in Arnold A. Rogow, ed., *Politics, Personality and Social Science in the*

price, that is, they no longer require as much overt respect from their household employees. The number of potential domestic servants willing to pay even that lesser amount has not increased, however: The supply is *inelastic*. In prestige processes, inelasticity of supply means simply that if the amount of prestige offered or given is increased by a certain amount, people may not respond by a still higher increase in performance. Often they do not because that level in performance is too difficult. Eighteenth-century European dukes and princes tried to hire resident geniuses as composer-musicians to adorn their courts, and it must be conceded that the list of talented musicians in that period is remarkable. But the apparently higher price in respect offered very likely did not elicit a commensurate increase in the number of great artists. Yearning for a football championship, a college may be quite willing to offer a large increase in acclaim and respect to its players or new recruits, but they may not be able to make so large an increase in their own achievement.

Cases of supply inelasticity following a decision to pay less overt prestige than before seem to be uncommon in the corporation, for modern managers try instead to offer extra prestige in order to increase production. On the other hand, they seem to be frequent in socialist countries, where at times a decision is made to pay less respect to an occupational group (professors, managers) or a political group ("right-wing revisionists"). It is typical of any revolution that certain segments of the population will be officially given less respect than before. In all these instances the question arises whether the expected drop in performance will be commensurate with the drop in prestige. If performance does not drop that much, supply would be said to be inelastic.

In at least some of the examples just noted, very likely performance did not drop much, and in most the decision-makers believed that if any such drop occurred it ought to be punished. But I believe that a much more common occurrence is a more than commensurate drop in performance when deference or overt respect is reduced by a given amount. Generally, people are very sensitive to drops in prestige but very little troubled when the amount of respect given seems to rise suddenly and without apparent cause. Workers, members of an organization, or friends in a social network are likely to experience such a drop as insulting, hurtful, or punishing. They do not simply view the change as a mere alteration of the market price, to which one makes a calculating market response. Instead, they are more likely to withdraw more of their loyalty or contribution.

People do not often calculate that the possible supply of approved behaviors is inelastic and thus decide there is no point in paying more prestige; or that performances will not drop much if less prestige is paid.

Twentieth Century (Chicago: University of Chicago Press, 1969), p. 312; as well as Paul Blumberg, "The Decline and Fall of the Status Symbol: Some Thoughts on Status in a Post-Industrial Society," *Social Problems*, 21 (April, 1974): 480–498.

We shall explore later how thoughtful individuals in some cases *will* rationally calculate that giving more praise to a child or a friend may move that person to conform, to try harder, or to shape his or her course of action more nearly by the ideals or norms of the group.

Formal organizations do sometimes respond to people's setting a higher deference price by enacting programs through which some jobs are upgraded in prestige or uniforms, robes, or other symbols are introduced. That is, individuals are given greater respect in order to elicit better performances from them. And such external accoutrements may yield more respect for those people, either from outsiders or members of the organization. Pascal affirmed this point indirectly by his wry comment that judges and other high officials need their robes and accoutrements of office, since people would not otherwise pay them that much deference, for as human beings they do not actually deserve it.

Without regard to the problem of elasticity, people do decide in a calculating way not to work too hard, or perform too well, for a given level of prestige. Thus, they will refuse to compete or try, or they will try less hard than they could. On the other hand, some may decide rather to accept the risk of trying harder. In either of these types of unconscious or intuitive decision, however, changes in either supply or demand are likely to be relatively slower than in the economic sphere, largely because evaluations or preferences do not alter quickly.

As a consequence of these relations in handing out esteem or dispraise, people do not typically calculate (if they are conscious of the question at all) what would be the most effective technique for eliciting a higher supply of approved behavior. To select a common example: If members of the lower classes (or children, prisoners, members of a minority group) fail to meet even the working norms of the larger society and of the higher-ranking people who hand out esteem or disesteem to them, the latter do not ordinarily decide that the price they are willing to pay, that is, the amount of respect they are willing to give, is too little and that they should therefore raise the price.

It is especially unlikely that they will calculate that raising the prestige they pay by a given amount will elicit a still greater supply of approved behavior. Instead, they are more likely to express strong disapproval and threaten still more. They do not usually test whether the supply of approved behavior is inelastic at that social level.

COST OF PRODUCTION: AN INDEPENDENT VARIABLE

In this chapter, the extent to which some elementary formulations of economics may be useful in understanding social exchange processes has been considered. As a last step, let us examine two further questions, which some social analysts believe are not settled although formal economics gives a definitive answer. They are: whether the cost of production affects price directly, and whether the price of a service or commodity may have an independent effect on its perceived desirability. In this section, the first of these questions is discussed.

What is the role of the cost of production in the prestige system and in the economic market? At the most fundamental level, economic theory asserts simply that the cost of production does not affect the price level directly. Price is instead determined by the interaction of supply and demand. In the hypothetical economic market the question is, simply, how much demand is there for the product; that is, how much will people buy at given price levels? Or, how much will people pay at a given level of supply? The economist assumes that the buyer does not care how much the product costs the manufacturer to make. If the buyer wants it, he will buy it. If the supply is high relative to demand the price will be low, and if the supply is low the price will be high.

That fundamental relationship presumably does not change when the product is costly to produce. If it is expensive to make or to obtain, the seller must charge more for it or there will be no profit. If the price is high, the demand will be lower. However, if the seller has miscalculated that demand, so that not enough can be sold at a profitable price, he will have to sell unprofitably, and again the customer will not care that the manufacturing or production costs were high.

Usually, matters are somewhat less stark and cruel than that formulation suggests. For if the cost of production is high, then manufacturers will be sensible enough to turn out a smaller amount, knowing already what the likely price will be. That is to say, a lower or higher set of production costs will raise or lower the supply and thus alter the price. At higher cost levels, less will be supplied (because sellers know that fewer people will pay the higher price), which hypothetically adjusts supply to demand: the lower supply will increase the price and thus lower the demand. Or, the reverse may occur: higher costs increase the price and thus reduce the number who will buy at the new price, so that supply must be kept low to fit that lower demand.

Because of this disinterest on the part of the buyer as to how much a product costs the manufacturer to make, the manufacturer is under some competitive pressure to cut costs and increase his sales by advertising, persuasive packaging, or various kinds of controls over the market. In the developing technology that is characteristic of industrial societies, manufacturers can take advantage of a wide range of improvements that may decrease the costs of production. They may attempt to integrate all the phases of production, from raw materials to finished products, in order to take advantage of each possible profit margin at each new phase of production. They may invest in a research and development unit, to speed the process of technical improvement and decrease manufacturing costs. Since they are all competing with other manufacturers, who themselves would like to command the allegiance of sellers, who in turn prefer lower prices, manufacturers in both ideology and fact typically believe that one way to solvency or success is to cut their costs of production or at least keep them down.

Although it is possible that the underlying dynamics are similar in prestige processes, they do appear to be observably different in two important ways: As contrasted with the production process and the economic market, there seem to be almost no general methods by which the difficulties of achieving greatly in saintliness, athletics, science, or the arts can be reduced substantially—although intensive promotion and advertising seem to produce temporary stars at times; and, there seem to be no economies of scale or organization comparable to the manufacturing economies that occur when large-scale production is engineered.

Some heroes of the past did seem to produce their honored work with great facility. Mozart could dash off a sonata in a few hours, with no apparent loss to the beauty of the music. But no one can study Mozart's productive techniques and thereby learn how to reduce his or her own agonies and difficulties in artistic creation. In some athletic events, such as the pole vault, new techniques do make a difference; but since everyone soon acquires these techniques, the difficulty of the highest level of achievement remains beyond the reach of ordinary people. Moreover, since talent seems to play so large a role at the higher level of performances, no amount of hard work or effort on the part of less able people will make those achievements any less difficult or impossible.

In the realm of prestige transactions we cannot easily locate techniques for reducing the "cost of production," but we can nevertheless ask whether apparent difficulty or the personal costs of higher achievement will yield a greater amount of respect or admiration from others. The question is complex, and I can do no more here than offer several comments on it.

Certainly, whether a given achievement is really difficult is not of great significance for the amount of admiration paid, and most people will not know what that investment was anyway. For example, if one plays the piano with great difficulty, but poorly, few will admire that performance. Parents sometimes do, and close friends, sweethearts, and spouses—but then we suspect that their apparent admiration is generated by other emotions. As a painter said to Gertrude Stein at an exhibition: People exclaim over the agonies of creation the greatest painters suffer; we suffer as much, but our paintings are mediocre just the same. Indeed, with reference to real difficulty, in some areas, especially the arts and athletics (Joe DiMaggio, Picasso) some admiration is given to those who seem to achieve with great ease; they appear to enjoy a special grace precisely because of this facility.

Mere difficulty, like mere rarity, arouses little admiration unless it is a kind of achievement that is respected or admired. Reciting from memory whole pages of the telephone directory is difficult but little admired; so is playing Beethoven's sonatas backwards. Such skills are difficult to master, and the supply is therefore low; but the demand is also low among one's friends and in the larger society; thus the respect paid for them is low.

By definition, "difficulty" in any usual sense does not increase or decrease the admiration of ascriptive traits such as sex, age, or membership in an ethnic group. Some of these, like being born into an aristocratic family, can be viewed as difficult, since they are the result of effort made by persons and family members in the past, but for the most part the notion of felt difficulty seems irrelevant to this category of admired or disesteemed traits.

By contrast, the individual's cost for some kinds of achievement, as perceived or guessed by others, seems to raise directly the amount of respect paid. Thus, even when chastity was more generally respected than now, women (or men) who were never exposed to temptation reaped less admiration than those whose attractiveness generated many opportunities for sin. A rich man whose philanthropies are no more generous than those of ordinary middle-class people will be admired less, and some people will disesteem him for his stinginess, though the amount of money given may be as much as is given by others in more modest circumstances.[32] Saints have mostly come from the upper classes, and justifications of sainthood emphasize that since they could have continued to enjoy the alternative life of riches, indulgence, and power, they achieved more virtue by choosing a pious, self-denying road.[33] After all, only the formerly rich can convince others that they *chose* to be poor.

It may well be that "felt or imagined difficulty" is no more than a guess or a perception about how far above the normal potential or real skill a given performance or achievement is, whereupon this perception becomes almost equivalent to rarity of supply. For at that point, the person who admires is essentially placing an admired performance along some total distribution of achievement, perceiving it as being far out on the curve of a normal distribution. That is, at the extreme end of such a distribution, where the number of people who can perform well is rare, a folk or lay view about difficulty can be translated into distributional terms and may well be perceived at some level as a matter of rarity—though once again, rarity of something that is desired or applauded. Whether, then, difficulty per se raises the prestige paid still seems empirically unclear.

32. Here, the psychological "theory of attribution" is relevant, for it suggests that people are more likely to make judgments (and correct ones) about others when these others' behavior is unusual in intensity. From observing a rich person making a donation of $100, we can infer little or nothing; but we are likely to suppose that a poor person who makes an equal donation is "generous," for his behavior is unusual compared with that of his peers. See E. E. Jones and K. E. Davis, "From Acts to Dispositions: The Attribution Process in Person Perception," in L. Berkowitz, ed., *Advances in Experimental Social Psychology*, vol. II (New York: Academic, 1965), pp. 220–266.

33. Katherine George and Charles H. George, "Roman Catholic Sainthood and Social Status," in Reinhard Bendix and Seymour M. Lipset, *Class, Status, and Power*, 2d ed. (New York: Free Press, 1966), pp. 394–401.

PRICE: AN INDEPENDENT VARIABLE

In traditional economics, price is set by the interaction of supply and demand; in technical terms the price is the intersection of the two curves of supply and demand. In most of the commonsensical explanations used in economics textbooks, price changes will have some independent effect. For example, it is asserted that lowering the price demanded will increase the sales; and the economic and managerial question may be asked whether the total amount of revenue will then be greater or smaller (depending on elasticity of demand). Economics texts do not, however, typically ask or answer the question that Thorstein Veblen asked half a century ago: Does the price itself alter desirability? Similarly, I wish to ask that question with respect to prestige transactions: if individuals or social groups or organizations demand more prestige, does this higher price also increase their value, rank or admiration?

Veblen asserted that an independent effect of costliness or price (whether from higher costs of production or from overpricing is not clear) *is* to be observed in the economic market. Since, he asserted, the aim of buying and exhibiting costly goods is precisely to yield prestige, to prove one's prowess in the pecuniary field, their very costliness makes them desirable. Common observation seems to affirm this emendation of economic doctrine, since people do strive to let others know that a given trip, coat, or gift was expensive, hard to get, difficult to make, and so on. In more refined circles, this information may be allowed to emerge gradually, obliquely, or with subtlety; but one can make this type of observation in most circles, whether or not they deprecate any explicit discussions of expensiveness. Are those observations correct as applied to prestige dynamics?

Veblen was focusing on the interaction of the prestige system with economic processes. He asserted that the expensiveness itself generates prestige or the lack of it. For example:

> The marks of superfluous costliness in the goods are therefore marks of worth—of high efficiency for the indirect, invidious end to be served by their consumption; and conversely, goods are humilific, and therefore unattractive, if they show too thrifty an adaptation to the mechanical end and do not include a margin of expensiveness.[34]

Veblen recognized that people do become skilled in distinguishing the expensive real from the inexpensive (or, anyway, less expensive) imitation: for example, diamonds from paste, a Balenciaga original from a Seventh Avenue copy. He did not, however, pay much attention to the likelihood that those observable differences might create demand or high evaluation

34. Thorstein Veblen, *The Theory of the Leisure Class* (New York: Modern Library, 1934), p. 155; see also pp. 111, 115, 116, 126–128 and passim; also, chap. entitled "Pecuniary Canons of Taste," pp. 116–166.

in other ways than through costliness. For example, mink may well be warmer and is more durable than rabbit. He did not treat sensuous pleasure as an economic variable, either; but many expensive commodities rank high on that scale. A Ferrari will perform, by almost any engineering criteria, better than the standard American or European car. To musically trained ears, a Steinway produces a tone superior to that of most pianos.

In contrast to Veblen's notion that expensiveness in commodities may independently generate high evaluation, the types of products Veblen scoffed at because they did not seem to "do the job" any better than cheaper ones *also* typically require more skill and energy to produce. Specifically, the sometimes small improvements observable at the higher levels of quality products are increasingly harder to achieve at each successive level of increase in quality. They cost much more to produce because the cost curve rises sharply at higher levels of quality. If that is the process operating in the apparent desirability of a high price, then the greater costliness actually exhibits the normal processes of a free market and no intrusion at all of a false hankering after expensiveness per se. Few people can or will produce this higher level of quality in a commodity, as in any other kind of performance; and potential buyers or admirers know that at such levels each unit of improvement will eliminate still more producers. The supply will be low and thus the price will be high.

Of course the more fundamental test is whether we can find any two commodities or performances known to be of equally high quality, but offered at different prices. Could sellers ask a higher price, knowing that some purchasers would choose the more expensive, believing that it would bring them prestige; and would the purchasers receive that greater esteem? Or, with reference to the prestige transactions focused on here, if two men achieve scientific breakthroughs of equivalent value, will people honor more the man who demands more deference? If we compare two bosses of equivalent position, salary, and achievement in an organization, will the boss who demands more esteem from others receive more real esteem (not just more overt deference)?

We are using the term "demand," or "require," in a testable sense, that is, not merely that the individual *asks* for more admiration, compliments, or praise, but that if others do not pay it, he or she will not engage in social transaction with those people, or will move away from them.

The economist would predict that the higher-priced commodity would be driven from the market. Applying that to prestige transactions, we would have to predict that individuals who simply require more admiration from others than their performance seems to justify will not get that much; and indeed, people may focus their admiration on other people of equivalent capacities or achievements who did not make such demands. A sociologist would similarly predict that those who expected to be admired by their friends for spending more for a luxury commodity when they could obtain the equivalent for less money would hear derisive laughter instead.

On the other hand, whether an adequate test case could be found is open to question. As is typical in prestige-generating acts, two persons who are very similar in many ways may nevertheless be viewed as different in other important ways. Even the same product from a more expensive store may be rated by some people as worth the added cost because they believe, erroneously or not, that the store might be more likely to back its merchandise.

Nevertheless, it is observable that acquaintances will admire the more expensive label more. If we examine gifts made to kings, jewel-studded gold church relics, knightly armor, or the decorations in great houses of the past, the suspicion does remain that costliness has often triumphed, not only over efficiency, but also over artistic taste; the expensiveness of the object demonstrated its prestige value, rather than the reverse.

However, we have posed the economic question—can a higher price actually increase the desirability of at least some presumably high-quality products—in order to consider the correlative question in prestige transactions: can individuals or organizations get more prestige, seem more worthy, or be paid more respect, by demanding more esteem than others receive for the same qualities and performances? Perhaps the correct answer to both is no, *if* everyone has perfect knowledge. Then no one could presume to claim more prestige than he or she merits, because the individual would know others' inner judgments, they would know one another's judgments, and they would know the individual's own judgments. If two performances or commodities were truly equivalent, everyone would know this and thus would not impute more worth to the one with the higher "price."

But since perfect knowledge is not to be found in the real world, some people do convince others by their greater demands for esteem that they are worth it, while some people instead do the opposite: by their unpresuming ways they elicit less deference or respect than their performances or qualities would seem to justify. As the cynical philosopher has remarked, the meek will *have* to inherit the earth, for that is the only way they will get it.

In both these categories, the presuming and the unpresumptuous, some people fail in such false presentations of self. The farther removed from reality false presentations are, the greater the likelihood that other people will not accept them at face value. Both generate other by-products: for example, demanding too much will annoy some people, and demanding too little will arouse friendly feelings in some people. Nevertheless, these minor processes are important in enumerating the complexities of supply and demand in prestige transactions, while also raising some questions that require empirical inquiry, to be discussed later.

Chapter 4
Prestige Allocation

Although people evaluate each other constantly, and for everything from general demeanor[1] to achievement in some specialty such as chess or baseball, in modern societies the most easily observable and finely graded judgments focus on some major specialty, usually an occupational one. In this chapter we examine the processes of allocating prestige to people who rank high or low on some single and salient type of performance or quality. Our basic question continues to be how that allocation or distribution affects one person's control over another's behavior.

To begin with the problem of who gets how much: Will people who exhibit some admired single trait or performance in a high degree be given admiration exactly correlative with their amount of real or supposed superiority over others? Or, to use hypothetical (if ludicrous) quantities, if an individual possesses, say, twenty percent more knowledge than others, or has leaped twenty percent further into the unknown, or has a twenty percent higher rate of success in repairing radios, will his or her respect in those areas be as much as twenty percent higher? Or, more broadly, of the total amount of prestige given by a group for certain specific types of activities, how is it allocated among those who are considered eligible for any of it? Do a few get almost all?

A preliminary answer based on day-to-day observation would seem to be clear enough: Those few who are viewed as leaders in any given field seem to receive a large part of whatever public prestige payments are made, and the winners in various kinds of competition, even when they are marked off from the losers by minute differences in performance, or (as in science) by narrow differences in the time of discovery or achievement, seem to be given far greater amounts of prestige than those differences would appear to justify.

For example, we give recognition to Darwin's, not Wallace's, theory of evolution. By far the largest amounts of prize money and newspaper coverage go to the winner of a sports competition. In concert music, there are few stars. Most people find it difficult to remember the names of presidential candidates who lost in past elections or who were the winning

---

1. For excellent analyses of this aspect of behavior, see Erving Goffman, *Interaction Ritual* (New York: Anchor, 1967 [1956]); and *Behavior in Public Places* (New York: Free Press, 1963). See also Joel Telles, "Deference Processes in Intensive Care Units" (Ph.D. diss., Columbia University, 1976).

vice-presidents, and still fewer can remember who were the vice-presidential candidates who lost. All this suggests that *prestige payments rise more sharply than increments of quality at higher levels of performance*.

This commonsensical observation deserves rather extensive treatment, since the apparent distribution of prestige is the outcome of several distinct processes, each of which merits some attention. I wish therefore to proceed by focusing first on this general distribution and its causes. Then we shall consider in a more complex manner the impact of this distribution of prestige on how well people try to perform in a specific activity.[2] Because people must calculate their possible payoffs by reference to chances of getting them, and not merely their magnitude, we shall consider as well the effects of contingency on their attempts to earn prestige.

Thereafter, we shall consider how people adjust to the rank to which their efforts seem to have carried them. Finally, it will be asked whether a different allocation of prestige might be possible, and with what result. This latter question will be pursued more extensively in the chapter on justice.

GENERAL DISTRIBUTION OF PRESTIGE

Two major patterns are widely observed in human and nonhuman action. First, performances above the average become increasingly difficult to improve with each upward step even if the reward is great; consequently, the number who can or will achieve such higher levels drops off sharply.[3] Second, if a substantial number of people are engaged in the activity (because the rewards in influence, money, or prestige are high), there are, nevertheless, likely to be some performers at the top level, separated by small differences, but not typically one person who is unequivocally superior to all the rest.

To perform and be ranked at the highest levels, whether in saintliness or shooting marbles, demands both talent and dedication which only a few can muster. Such "heroes" are given more prestige or admiration because both the level and type of performance are rare and evaluated highly within the relevant group. Most admirers recognize that such performances are possible for only a few people. The supply is and remains low.

2. In this chapter, we shall not consider primarily those norms, easy to meet, that require almost everyone to act in a certain way—such as obeying certain traffic signals, or eating with the propriety acceptable in a given family or network. These may be viewed as minimal performances, and the minimum is considered adequate. Obedience to such norms yields little or no esteem, except the average amount of respect needed to maintain one's acceptability as a group member. Generally, overconformity to this range of norms is usually viewed with some disapproval (as noted in Chapter 1): e.g., to be clean is required, but to be excessively clean is viewed as persnickety, odd, or even neurotic.

We shall also ignore here those cases in which individuals are willing to give deference temporarily to authority figures, expecting to be approved for it, but in which outsiders would view that obedience or deference as meriting disapproval. For experiments of this kind, see Stanley Milgram, "Some Conditions of Obedience and Disobedience to Authority," *Human Relations*, 18 (February, 1965): 57–75, and his *Obedience to Authority: An Experimental View* (New York: Harper and Row, 1974).

3. This is one more illustration of what Kenneth Boulding calls the Law of Diminishing Everything: nothing increases indefinitely; all real curves fall off as they rise.

Millions of people can ice skate or play tennis, but a champion in either sport has usually spent years of his or her childhood at a gruelling, almost daily, work schedule. Hundreds of thousands "take lessons," but few can tolerate the increasingly rigorous demands of higher performance levels.

This is a general phenomenon, as noted above, not confined to processes dealt with in economics or social science generally. One of its forms appears in economics as the law of diminishing returns. A concrete illustration is the increasing cost per bushel of wheat produced at higher levels of production with increasing amounts of labor, fertilizer, and machinery. At lower levels, of course, the increase in production is worth more than the cost of such increments, but finally the cost rises more rapidly than production.

Trees cannot grow indefinitely higher, even in the most propitious environments. Practice will improve the playing of an ordinary violinist, and assiduous training of great talent will lead to still finer playing; but the ultimate limitations of the human animal make the progress asymptotic. Thus, the few individuals at the highest levels of achievement, where effort is very great, find that they as well as their closest competitors have approached their physical, mental, or moral limits.

But though there are only a few who are outstanding at the upper levels of performance, in activities where competition is keen the highest achievements are usually close in rank. In sports, where quantitative measurement is taken for granted, the winning racer can be separated from the next man by a few tenths or even hundredths of a second. Only a handful of people can distinguish the minute differences in excellence that separate the ten, or more likely eighty, finest concert pianists in the world. Indeed, in perhaps most fields, including ditch digging, the most astute critics might argue instead that there is no "top" man or woman but rather a handful of first-rate people, each distinguished from the other by complex differences of quality rather than simple degrees of excellence. Although the differences in excellence among the top performers are small, the disparity in acclaim is large between a few leaders and those very close to them in accomplishment; or between the "winner" and those who fall short by microscopic differences. The most creative of scientists knows that at any given time the new idea that he or she is entertaining may well be approaching fruition in another person, perhaps as yet unknown.[4]

This phenomenon can also be observed more generally in a technical trait of the curve of normal distribution (the "bell-shaped" curve), which appears to encompass most human abilities. The mass of men and women will cluster (with reference to any ranked characteristic) near the average,

4. Robert K. Merton, "The Role of Genius in Scientific Advance," *New Scientist*, 12 (November, 1961) 306–308, suggests that all discoveries are potentially "doubletons or multiples." In modern races of all kinds, technical inventions (electronic and photographic systems of measurement and recording) are used to determine who really won, because so often the difference is so small.

but toward the higher or lower levels the number drops off sharply, so that only about five percent will be found above or below a point two sigmas from the mean. However, the curve does *not* drop rapidly after that. In concrete terms, in a large population there will be not one, but some, individuals at the upper (or lower) reaches of any such curve of quality or achievement. That is, as we move toward the point where the fundamental limitations of the human being (psychological, physical, and so on) are approached, in a large sample there will be few people, but it is likely that there will be at least a few, who are distinguished from one another by small differences.

PAYOFF INCREMENTS

Granted that those who rank higher in an admired trait or performance are more esteemed, how large is that increment of prestige toward the upper levels of achievement? We can sometimes give almost a numerical description of the extent to which a relatively small apparent difference in achievement yields a large increment in prestige. Sports furnishes many illustrations. The move from a .250 batting average to, say, .300 is a numerical increase of 20 percent, but that step eliminates almost all the batters in the major leagues in any given year; then the smaller upward step of another 10 percent to .330 will eliminate all contemporary batters in most years (1977 being an unusual year) except those on a batting streak, or those who simply fail to complete a full year of play, plus a few of the all-time great baseball players. With reference to acclaim, it would be relatively easy to show that if a batter moves his average up by 20 percent from .250 to .300, he will receive a large increase in attention and respect paid to him by fans, baseball analysts, managers, other players, and of course newspaper writers. The latter group affords a possible numerical comparison, the number of column inches devoted to the player over a period of time if he becomes, say, a steady .300 or .330 hitter. The sharp rise in attendance or in the size of the television audience when such a batter or a correspondingly effective pitcher appears also provides a numerical illustration of the substantially higher rewards at the top levels of performance. Baseball stars are also interviewed by reporters about "how it feels" to be given such recognition.

If the distribution of prestige reward parallels that of monetary income in business, the top men receive far more than those below. We do not know how they rank in achievement—that is an imponderable.[5] Indeed, their salaries may well be determined more by their esteem than by quantitative proof of their productivity. The president of a corporation is likely to receive 50 to 100 percent more than the second or third in command. One compilation of such data appears in chart 1.

5. For some data supporting the thesis that corporate leadership is not the main determinant of profit levels, see Stanley Lieberson and James F. O'Connor, "Leadership and Organizational Performance: A Study of Large Corporations," *American Sociological Review*, 37 (April, 1972): 117–130.

CHART 1
Average Before-Tax Salaries and Bonuses Profile, 1940-1963

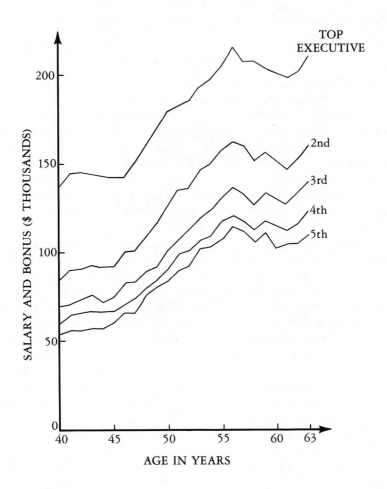

Wilbur G. Lewellen, *Executive Compensation in Large Industrial Corporations* (New York: Columbia University Press), 1968.

It cannot be unquestioningly assumed that the prestige pattern is the same as the economic pattern, but I must assert my conviction here that the rise in prestige payment is at least as steep as that of the economic, and possibly steeper, at the upper end of the achievement curve.

Do these statements also apply to ascriptive traits? Perhaps these are differentially rewarded, but some, such as traits of sex and race, are only minimally scaled because the socially recognized categories are few. It would be then difficult to claim there is any "upward" end of the "curve" where there are sharp increments in prestige. Other differentially evaluated traits, such as age, nationality, ethnic membership, or family honor, are scaled somewhat more. The differential rewards paid for age are usually smaller in Western societies than in traditional Eastern societies such as China or Japan in the past. Within a given country, some nationalities or ethnic memberships are given more or less prestige than others,[6] but in Western societies they are less rewarded or punished than in the past.[7] Inherited family honor is scaled, although because Western societies are no longer monarchies and aristocracies, differences in family honor seem to be less than in the past.

To the modern mind the most striking scaled ascriptive trait is nobility. In an epoch in which those who reach the top may not all be the "best" or ablest, but have nevertheless usually fought or struggled to get there, the notion that some people were once believed to be born not only rich (as they can be today) but also endowed with innate refinement, courage, the ability to rule, and so on, seems nothing short of startling. Within that system, placement was scaled, a matter of degree, and the curve of prestige rose greatly with each formal step upward—for example, from gentleman to baron to earl to marquis to duke to king. The separate quality of prestige is difficult to analyze out, since the increases in ascribed wealth, income, and political influence were also great. For wealth, the upward steps were especially steep.[8] For example, the minimum wealth required for the senatorial level of the Roman elite was over twice that of the second level.

That is to say, where the ascriptive traits are not merely dichotomous (male/female, black/white) but are also scaled and admired, the same

6. For an early study of the relative prestige or social acceptability of different nationality groups in the U.S., see Emory S. Bogardus, *Immigration and Race* (New York: Heath, 1928). See also an application to other countries: Harry Triandis and Leigh Triandis, "A Cross-Culture Study of Social Distance," *Psychological Monographs*, 76, no. 21 (1962).

7. However, the overt conflict among them may be even higher, since so many ethnic groups will no longer tolerate passively the disesteem they had to bear in the past. On this change, see Daniel P. Moynihan and Nathan Glazer, *Beyond the Melting Pot* (Cambridge, Mass.: M.I.T. Press, 1963), and D. P. Moynihan, ed., *On Understanding Poverty: Perspectives from the Social Sciences* (New York: Basic Books, 1968).

8. Lawrence Stone, *The Crisis of the Aristocracy: 1558–1640* (Oxford: Oxford University Press, 1965), apps. VII, X, XII. Keith Hopkins also asserts that the amount of wealth (and of course the prestige) of the Roman nobility was strikingly higher than even that of the apparently rich nonaristocrats: "Elite Mobility in the Roman Empire," *Past and Present,* 32 (December, 1965): 12–26.

phenomenon is observed, a rather sharp upward step in the amount of prestige paid for each step in the respected trait at higher levels.

LIMITED SPACE, COST-FREE CHOICE, AND THE "FAILURE" OF THE LESS POPULAR

These patterns of prestige allocation exhibit a process that can be thought of as typical of the economic market in a mass society but that appears to have a broader application: "the failure of the somewhat less popular." Perhaps the best illustration is the disappearance of good products from grocery store shelves, fairly popular programs from radio or television, excellent automobiles from the market, and so on.[9] Grocery stores have only so much shelf space and thus only so much for each type of soap, cornflakes, or maple syrup. If the aim is to maximize profit on each item, obviously the most popular of any class of products or programs will shoulder the less popular off, although in quality these may be close to the most successful in popularity.

In the world of solo concert artists, such as pianists, violinists, cellists, and so on, reputation as a "great" performer (that is, respect given for achievement) is highly correlated with popularity and rapidly transformed into financial success. On the other hand, if a concert artist fails to become very popular, and this may occur even if fellow artists concede his or her high musical ability, he or she may not be able to make an adequate income in that specialty. The artist does not, of course, disappear entirely, since he or she does have to earn a living. Many do, however, "disappear from the shelves" in the specific sense that they give up concert work almost entirely. The market does not support many of them. In the world of scientific research, again the aspirants to the highest rewards do not disappear either, since those who stay in the field are usually teachers as well, but they do not rise into prominence to be rated among the top men and women in the discipline.[10]

Different as some of these failures may be, they share at least one major process, the disappearance of a commodity from a single unified market because of marginal differences in consumer evaluations. Aiming at a single market, which will support only so much production of a given type of commodity—whether concert playing, scientific research, or becoming governor of a state—and in competition with somewhat similar products or people, it is not enough to be somewhat popular.

This gap between the most highly ranked and the somewhat less esteemed is partly created by the commonsensical unwillingness of most people to buy any worse commodity, to admire any less competent person,

9. For mathematical treatments of this phenomenon, see William N. McPhee, "Survival Theory in Culture," in his *Formal Theories of Mass Behavior* (New York: Free Press, 1963).

10. For data on this process, see Stephen Cole and Jonathan Cole, "Scientific Output and Recognition: A Study in the Operation of the Reward System in Science," *American Sociological Review*, 32 (June, 1967): 377–390, and their *Social Stratification in Science* (Chicago: University of Chicago Press, 1973); see also Robert K. Merton, *The Sociology of Science*, ed. Norman W. Storer (Chicago: University of Chicago Press, 1973), pt. 4.

than the one they rate highest, *if the choice is without cost.* If there are perceptible, evaluated differences, those marginal differences can be sufficient to drive the product with even slightly less desirable qualities from a given market, or at best to yield a much lower economic or prestige return. The matter of choice without cost should be considered for a moment, for it is very important and it is one major process by which a favored few in a given field are ranked far above the rest.

If microeconomic explanations are correct, a choice can sometimes be without cost because the constant effort of producers to gain or control a market forces them to adopt the most efficient techniques, so that almost every producer is forced to sell at the same low price in order to survive at all. Alternatively, some analysts would hold, producers try rationally to avoid price competition among themselves and constantly seek new markets by the proliferation of minute differences in the product, supported by heavy advertising expenditures. Consequently, competitors do not sell their products at a slightly lower price in order to dominate the market.[11]

Under either explanation the result is the same: with reference to a wide variety of mass products in the modern economic system, consumers are not faced with the choice of paying somewhat less for a product of lesser quality. Rather, they are faced with an array of products at roughly the same price, but with somewhat different types of characteristics—and these often are not even real differences, but imputed or claimed by advertising, and certainly not in any way known as facts to the consumer. Products in this category include a range of commodities such as cigarettes, gasoline, detergents, aluminum, breakfast cereals. Similarly, the less attractive, pleasing, or funny performer on television costs no less to watch than one who is viewed as a top performer. It costs no more to admire what we consider the best than to admire the worst.

Of course, there are apparent exceptions to this fact, if we focus on *actions.* In all groups, people are partly evaluated by the evaluations they express, and thus to state outlandish or deviant evaluations usually elicits disapproval from other group members. To be sure, most group members continue to associate with one another because they do share most values, thus few people feel they have to pay any costs for their prestige responses. In an organization, to admire openly the "wrong" person or achievement can be costly if one's boss is likely to feel less respect for anyone who holds such an opinion; subordinates will usually choose discretion as less costly than valor.[12]

An authoritarian or totalitarian political system, where the expression of some opinions may be viewed as politically dangerous and thus deserving of punishment, is more threatening. There, individuals can make

---

11. See John K. Galbraith, *The New Industrial State* (Boston: Houghton Mifflin, 1967), pp. 120–125.

12. In social networks made up of individuals very interested in a special activity, the arguments often seem vigorous but they rarely lead to rejection or real hostility. An admirer of Hank Aaron may sneer at a friend who esteems Jackie Robinson more, but after all they need each other as audiences too much to let that disagreement become enmity. The argument is part of the fun of being a fan.

prestige judgments without cost, but they may decide it is wise to keep them private. Next, to express one's admiration or respect for a social circle by intruding into it without being invited will elicit disapproval, but the admiration or respect itself does not cost anything. In most situations, one's cost-free inner prestige responses, or evaluations, can be expressed without much cost.

Economics wisely focuses not on evaluations, but on actions, that is, as foregone alternatives. Thus, to give up one alternative in favor of another is to incur a cost. On the other hand, what creates the market demand that constitutes those actions is a set of cost-free evaluations. They do not cost anything because we need not buy even what we view as desirable. When we do command enough resources to buy what we like, those evaluations can be expressed as market demand; before that time, they are simply inner responses. Indeed, most market demand is based on the continuing process of cost-free inner evaluations, before the problem is faced of translating that preference into action.

All the above minor exceptions do not alter the general fact that simply esteeming another person or achievement does not cost much, if anything, whether it is only an inner feeling or an open expression of esteem. Thus people are likely to give most of their admiration to those who seem to be at the top in their special activities.[13] The few top achievers or "the champion" will dominate the attention and interest of those who care at all and will push the less esteemed to the sidelines of concern—again the "principle of limited space."[14] Consequently, the most esteemed receive a high percentage of the total amount of the respect people give to that activity, and the amount of respect given to those just lower in performance is much less. That is, the curve of respect rises sharply at the upper levels of achievement.[15]

13. In scientific work, where in modern research the problem of *visibility* often arises in large-scale experiments in physics, that is, which one ought we to admire most? Zuckerman points out that in multiple authorship of a paper, the social system of rewards in science is frustrated to some extent, since it is difficult to ascertain who made which contribution. One possible solution has been variations in the ordering of names among authors; see Harriet A. Zuckerman, "Patterns of Name-Ordering among Authors of Scientific Papers: A Study of Social Symbolism and Its Ambiguity," *American Journal of Sociology*, 74 (December, 1968): 276–291. Note that if outsiders misinterpret the meaning of name-ordering, then some people will get more credit than the members of the collectivity believe they should get.

14. Illustrating neatly the connection between "real" and symbolic room for other people is what is called in France the forty-first chair (of the French Academy), i.e., a suggestion that in addition to those in the Academy there is someone who is at least that talented. The phenomenon, as Merton reminds us, is well known ("The Matthew Effect in Science," in Merton, *The Sociology of Science*, p. 441).

15. Arthur L. Stinchcombe suggests, without separating money from prestige, that a highly skewed *reward* pattern is more likely to be found when an individual's contribution is complementary or synergistic with others, so that his excellence makes a big difference in the organizational outcome; in other situations, his or her contribution is only "additive." Movie stars and research scientists would be in the first of these categories, teachers and manual workers in the second. See "Some Empirical Consequences of the Davis-Moore Theory of Stratification," in Reinhard Bendix and Seymour M. Lipset, eds., *Class, Status, and Power.* 2d ed. (New York: Free Press, 1966), pp. 70–72. Note also that the Matthew Effect (to them that hath, shall be given) implies the pattern we are describing; Merton, "The Matthew Effect in Science," pp. 439–459.

Each person's investment or concern in a given field (even his or her own) is limited. Most people are satisfied to know the names of a few baseball players, scientists, bartenders, sculptors, or political figures. Ordinary group conversations do not continue for long on any one of these topics, and all parties are satisfied in making a small number of evaluative remarks about them. If everyone admired completely different "heroes" in each activity, they could not all hold an adequate or satisfying conversation. Consensus about a few leaders is itself a source of pleasure in informal talk among friends.

Indeed, if we examine the conversations of any subgroup, whether a neighborhood gathering, a family dinner, or a group of women, it is clear that only a few names come into prominence, and only those of high evaluation or notoriety are discussed at length. That is, in both a psychological and temporal sense, people do not possess sufficient time and energy—enough "shelf space"—to focus on any but the top competitors.

PRESTIGE-GIVING AT LOWER LEVELS

Discussion and esteem are thus largely centered on a few top men and women in any given activity. That outcome is based on complex processes and should be examined in more detail. Although we can easily observe the extreme peakedness in the distribution of prestige that has been the focus of this discussion, we can also observe an apparently contrary phenomenon or at least one that qualifies that general regularity. If we observe our own daily behavior or that of others, it is evident that at almost any level of competence, and at high or low occupational levels, people are paying some esteem to one another. We cannot know without empirical study how sincere this is, but it is at least observable—and introspection suggests it is mostly spontaneous and sincere. Whether we are dealing with the butcher or the automobile mechanic, the manager of a local bank or an aspiring artist, we are likely to show some respect for the occupation itself and for the level of competence that the person seems to exhibit.

At most levels of skill, and at most occupational levels, people are not only responding with more or less inner feeling, esteem, or respect but they are also making visible gestures of esteem or respect, whether it is saying "good job" to the automobile mechanic for quickly repairing a sticky carburetor valve, praising the flower garden a neighbor has produced, or complimenting a village leader for the political position he or she has taken. Even if the general skew of prestige allocation we assert is correctly described, it is clear that at most points along the curve people do receive some daily esteem for their level of achievement.[16]

16. Although Erving Goffman's analysis of these patterns focuses on informal social interaction rather than work or buyer-seller behavior, it applies to these situations, too. See (among others) his essays in *The Presentation of Self in Everyday Life* (New York: Doubleday, Anchor, 1959); and his "On Face Work: An Analysis of Ritual Elements in Social Interaction," *Psychiatry*, 18 (August, 1955): 213–231. As E. A. Shils remarks: "The deference system of a society extends throughout the length

Let us summarize here the several patterns of this aspect of prestige allocation. Since everyone who engages in an activity of any kind, especially the activities that are occupationally important, is observed by someone, everyone is rated by someone. On the other hand, not everyone is rated by everyone. That is not possible because of time, space, energy, and so on. At some point, everyone is rated by someone or some group, but those persons or groups are not in direct communication with everyone else who is also interested in the same field but who lives in a different place or is concerned with a somewhat different level in the total range of skill. Thus, the people in a small Texas town may evaluate all the youngsters there who play the piano, but their judgments are not noted, nor are those performances, by New York critics. They are not that "important."[17] On the other hand, many activities do constitute a "national system" or even an international system—examples are the higher levels of the performing arts, show business, sports, politics, art, and scientific research—while many other types of skills are not structured as a national system (radio repairing, school teaching, plumbing, hairdressing). In the latter set of skills and qualities, people are not ranked on a single national scale, but only locally.[18]

Although most people make some evaluations in the international, national, and local systems, some of their most refined evaluations are of people who are important to them in daily interaction. These are persons who form part of their immediate social network, but these refined evaluations are not extended indefinitely beyond that point. For example, people in a given division of a corporation or a science department within a university make rather close evaluations of those about them; know or affirm a few evaluations of people still further out in their social network; but beyond that will be able to list only the top people in their relevant activity or skill.

With reference to these closer judgments, it is obvious that the performances of these people are important to all of us on a day-to-day basis—whether they are television repairmen, physicians, fellow workers, or neighbors who play in our string quartet. Thus we give some overt esteem on a regular basis to those important to us, whether or not they rank high in that activity as a whole.[19]

---

and breadth of that society. Everybody falls within it . . . " *Center and Periphery: Essays in Macrosociology* (Chicago: University of Chicago Press, 1975), chap. 16, "Deference" (p. 296).

17. Perhaps the only apparent exception is sports, where performances can be measured to some extent, and a small industry has arisen to keep records of performances in national track meets, baseball, prize fighting, and so on. However, although the published records take account of thousands of performances, even people who are well versed in a given sport have not heard most of the performers' names.

18. For the differing patterns of influence of cosmopolitans and locals, see Robert K. Merton, "Patterns of Influence: Local and Cosmopolitan Influentials," in his *Social Theory and Social Structure* (New York: Free Press, 1968), pp. 441–474.

19. Mark Baldassare, in a personal communication, reports that in small group experiments the subjects often would prefer not to state "who is best," and he suggests that social pressures from others cause us to state openly more such evaluations than we really want to make.

Indeed, if people paid prestige only to the best, most of us who take part in a given occupation would be starved for esteem. Those who think of going into a given activity would not be convinced of future rewards if they could not observe any present ones for modest performances. In any event, the pleasures of the future are never enough. And the great prestige paid to leading figures cannot be a real and driving motivation for most people; that is beyond their horizon. Thus, some smaller amounts of esteem must be given at earlier or lower levels of achievement.

On a day-to-day level, the people at modest levels of achievement contribute without question far more to our own immediate pleasure and comfort (or dismay) than the heroes of the field, who nevertheless serve important functions. People at every level of accomplishment must receive some daily esteem payoffs, else they would not feel inclined to contribute much in their own activities, or even to perform adequately.[20]

CONTINGENCY OF REWARDS

Up to this point, allocation has been examined with reference primarily to peakedness, the extent to which a few get a lot. We have been analyzing both the structure of this allocation and the processes that create it: That is, why is a large part of all prestige paid to a few people? We have done so because we take for granted the commonsensical notion that people will strive harder if the payoff is greater.

But people decide whether the rewards are worth striving for, by measuring not only desirability of the rewards but also chances of success, that is, the *contingency* of any given payoff.[21] This aspect of aspiration is noted in ordinary conversation, as when someone weaves a fantasy about success and friends remind him how unlikely that outcome is. Thus, before considering in detail how the distribution of prestige affects human beings, we must also explore the effects of contingency, or how people perceive the chances of success.

When people know that the chances of obtaining some type of reward are low, they are less willing to strive harder—and may be sensible to be so.[22] They are likely to discount in advance the value and reality of that

20. In simple behaviorist psychological terms, behavior that is not rewarded is eventually extinguished.

21. For an analysis of the psychological complexities in this variable, see B. F. Skinner, *Contingencies of Reinforcement: A Theoretical Analysis* (New York: Appleton-Century-Crofts, 1963). However, people can base their decisions on some experience with contingencies, i.e., knowing about them, whether or not those contingencies affect them as they do white rats' learning processes.

22. With reference to the "rationality of dropping out," see Stephen Thernstrom, "Poverty in Historical Perspective," in Daniel P. Moynihan, ed., *On Understanding Poverty* (New York: Basic Books, 1969), pp. 160–168, n. 31. Thernstrom cites the work of Samuel Bowles, based on 1960 census data, and the investigation of G. Hanoch, "Personal Earnings and Investment in Schooling" (Ph. D. diss., University of Chicago, 1967), as showing that "many legal school dropouts are in fact behaving in an economically rational manner in that for Negroes but not for whites the income lost by remaining in school will not necessarily be made up later. Of course, well-educated Negroes earn more than less-educated ones, but at some educational levels short of graduate school the gap has not always been large enough to make up for the additional years the educated remain outside the labor market." (Bowles' argument is to be found in his "Toward Equality of Educational Opportunity?" *Harvard*

reward and will invest less of their energy, work, and skill in any high endeavor. The amount of contingency an individual perceives is a function of both his class and individual position and of the height of his aspiration: for example, a talented boy whose father is a physician will perceive much less contingency in his aspiration of becoming a physician.[23] However, that security is not usual in modern industrial societies. For most people, at most class levels, the distribution of prestige at especially the upper levels seems both peaked and highly contingent. No one, for example, is "born" to be a fine scientist or baseball player. Some are indeed heirs to great fortunes, but not even they are born to be skilled corporation executives. Even with much financial backing, a symphony orchestra or ballet company may never become great; the chances of that happening are low.

We can imagine by contrast a society that does not exhibit either much peakedness *or* much contingency in its distribution of prestige, and indeed many primitive societies have been viewed as "classless," or egalitarian. A closer examination will disclose that people in them are ranked by age, achievement, lineage, honor, sex, possessions; but the peakedness is less than in modern industrial societies. That is, the curve of prestige allocation is flatter. By and large the amount of the difference among individuals is also relatively noncontingent, that is, people can count on receiving a certain amount of deference for their sex, age, or even skills without excessive striving, and without great concern that they can fail by much.

It is hard even to imagine a prestige system in which the curve of allocation would be both flat *and* contingent for much of the population. However, caste and estate societies have been described as peaked and noncontingent, that is, few people are at the top, most people are more or less born to a given rank and they are trained throughout childhood to fit the demands of that level of performance. The chance that any given person will get a high payoff is low, but one can predict with accuracy about where most people will eventually arrive: about where they started. Just how accurate this description is we do not know, but the ideology of such societies has asserted that people should remain where they were born.[24] In such a society, even the less talented can become fair cobblers, farmers, merchants, or barons if they are taught those skills from birth.

Nevertheless, contingency is high at the highest levels of every position in a highly stratified society. Not all children of beautiful parents are

Education Review, 38 [Winter, 1968]: 88–99.) This historical situation is changing, but in the early 1970's it had changed little—though more for black women than for black men.

23. Such a boy may also perceive less contingency in a second sense, as Joel Telles suggests in a personal communication, since he will also be aware of a *range* of high level posts to which he may reasonably aspire.

24. For reports on social mobility in the caste society of India, see Bernard Barber, "Social Mobility in Hindu India," in James Silverberg, ed., *Social Mobility in the Caste System of India: Comparative Studies in Society and History* supp. III, pp. 18–35; Man S. Das and Gene F. Acuff, "The Caste Controversy in Comparative Perspective: India and the United States," *International Journal of Comparative Sociology*, 11 (March, 1970): 48–54; and M. N. Srinivas, *Social Change in Modern India* (Berkeley: University of California Press, 1966).

handsome, and saints do not typically pass on their rare qualities to their children. A family name can carry much prestige, as in politics and generally in class, but this is not a specific ability, and even the son of a prestigious man has to create his own prestige to a considerable extent. For example, in a monarchy, the king has typically inherited his prestige, political power, and wealth. Here, again, however, the king's chance of enjoying high prestige among all known kings past and present, that is, his chance of achieving the kind of excellence that the "great kings" have achieved, will be relatively low. The highest levels of performance even within such an ascriptive system remain contingent: no one can be certain that he will become a first-rate duke, a great silversmith or troubadour, or a victorious admiral.

Western social systems may well create greater contingency than others, higher of course for the higher levels of almost any kind of activity (not only do most of us never learn to sing brilliantly, but most of us never learn to polish shoes nearly as well as the best can). But for those who are born with considerable disadvantages, such as being poor, living in a ghetto, or belonging to a denigrated ethnic or racial group, the contingencies are great even in aspiring to middle positions in activities that enjoy either high or middle amounts of prestige. Correspondingly, the actual impact of prestige allocation is affected not only by how much respect an activity or occupation generally earns, but also by people's calculations about the chanciness of that payoff.

Thus, peakedness and contingency vary according to the type of society. They also vary according to the type of occupation and they vary at different points on the total curve of distribution within a single occupation. For example, in academic life until recently the upper levels of prestige were (as they remain) highly peaked and highly contingent, but the middle and lower levels were relatively noncontingent, in that with a modest amount of effort and talent most determined aspirants could become full professors at some college or another. By contrast, as noted earlier, below the upper level of the concert artist, the failed competitor must in effect change his occupation. He does not remain a solo concert artist, except sporadically.[25]

Not only may contingency vary in an occupation at different points on the curve, but it may also vary according to the perception of each individual, who may discount the risk at a different rate from others. In a family network that contains many professionals, a young man is likely to consider as minimal the risk of not entering and attaining a professional career.[26] He has learned what he should do, which school he should attend, the kind of career line he should follow, and which kinds of

25. Charles Kadushin, "The Professional Self-Concept of Music Students," *American Journal of Sociology*, 75 (November, 1969): 389–404.

26. Even at present, that person is likely to be a "he"—another contingency to be considered by anyone choosing an occupation.

sponsors he ought to gravitate toward as he advances in his training. By contrast, a slum boy of equal talent may view the contingencies as nearly hopeless. Not only does he not have the relevant knowledge, and has seen almost no one attain such an eminence, but the chances against him seem far too great to be worthy of much investment. The first of these two persons views the rewards as peaked but relatively noncontingent; the second sees them as peaked and contingent.[27]

It can be supposed that personality factors also operate to change the perception of contingencies. From research on the need for achievement, it appears that persons who rank high in that personality trait do not typically choose competitions in which the risk is high. They are much more likely to choose situations of moderate risk in which their extra efforts will pay off.[28] On the other hand, there are gamblers in every social stratum, people who are willing to take a considerable risk, as their peers see it, in order to aim high. Thus they discount the high contingency more than others do, because they have either some stubborn faith in themselves, a more optimistic view of their chances, or a lesser fear of failure.[29]

Analysts generally suppose that the ideology of any society affects how people judge their chances of success. Modern industrial societies (both socialist and capitalist) in sermons, editorials, rhetoric, and propaganda, present the contingencies of high achievement as not only worth the effort and morally obligatory, but as capable of being overcome by anyone with talent and willingness to work hard. By contrast, the rhetoric of caste and estate societies urges that each person not aim at a higher rank, but instead adjust to the situation in which fate has placed him or her. Accepting that ideology, the individual reduces the perceived contingency by lowering his or her aspirations, and thereby also reduces the competition that more favorably placed people have to face. In most tribal societies, with a less peaked distribution of rewards, such ideological defenses play a much smaller role.

Similarly, in most large societies the common rhetoric among those at lower social ranks, where there are many social pressures against striving very hard toward perhaps unscalable heights of achievement, emphasizes the importance of the small virtues and pieties—for example, friendship, loyalty to kin, neighborliness, or parental virtues.[30] These attainments

---

27. Although here we consider the individual's view of the situation, doubtless most outside observers would also describe the contingencies in this way.

28. David C. McClelland, *The Achieving Society* (Princeton, N.J.: D. Van Nostrand, 1961), pp. 211–225.

29. Differences in socialization and thus in personality may also affect peoples' needs for affection or personal response from others. See Stanley S. Schachter, *The Psychology of Affiliation* (Stanford: Stanford University Press, 1959).

30. See the relevant data in Herbert Hyman, "The Value Systems of Different Classes: A Social Psychological Contribution to the Analysis of Stratification," in Bendix and Lipset, *Class, Status and Power*, pp. 488–489.

appear much less contingent.[31] With little effort, most people can meet the standards imposed, for they are not high. Accepting that perception, many individuals do not aspire as high as they otherwise might; thus they avoid the risk of failure. On the other hand, because some in the lower ranks who accept that view are talented, people at higher positions are less likely to be threatened by stiff competition.

In making their decisions about how much to strive to earn prestige by meeting the norms of their group or society, individuals weigh the available payoffs. Their decisions are also shaped, however, by their perceptions of the chanciness of success. In turn, those perceptions will vary by their social position, for the chances are greater or smaller at different positions in the society. People of different temperaments will also give greater or lesser weight to that low or high chance of success. Consequently, when we think of how low or high rewards may affect striving for prestige, we must take into account people's varied judgments about contingency, or the likelihood that they may be able to meet the standards of excellence imposed by the society.

HIGH PRESTIGE PAYMENTS
AND TOP PERFORMERS

People do not typically react with esteem or deference because they seek control through making a bargain with others, that is, offering so much respect in order to get that high a performance. Instead, as emphasized previously, they pay so much esteem because they spontaneously feel the performance is worth that much. By contrast, those whose performances are being weighed can consciously decide whether to work or perform at their highest level, in order to gain that added spontaneous acclaim which they cannot obtain by any amount of haggling. Thus, the pressure or control through prestige allocation exists and is fundamental in understanding why people will try harder or not.

At least at the higher levels of competition, what happens is clear: people do expend greater effort to do their best, as hundreds of personal accounts, interviews, and novels testify. People expect a "real champ" to rise to still greater heights under pressure. Being Number One yields a big enough reward differential to arouse still more effort when close competitors threaten to win. Both the close competitors and those who get the highest honor recognize to some degree that their accomplishments are similar in level, even though the last few increments may be

31. Just as those virtues are praised where ambition seems barred, so does the display of ambition elicit some disapproval, for it informs others that the individual is willing to abandon neighborhood, kin, and friends for "higher" goals. Reports on peer or kin pressures against ambition may be found in: Elizabeth Bott, *Family and Social Network* (London: Tavistock, 1957); Michael Young and Peter Wilmott, *Family and Kinship in East London* (Baltimore: Penguin, 1957); Herbert J. Gans, *The Urban Villagers* (New York: Free Press, 1962).

difficult. All are aware that any one of them may be able to supplant the leader at some time, and perhaps soon. All must look to their laurels.[32]

This pattern is most obvious in professional sports, where rules and rituals of camaraderie gloss over the savagery of interpersonal competition, and even top performers are soon dethroned. A goodly handful of novels have described a similar pattern at the highest levels of corporate life.[33]

The phenomenon can also be observed in revolutionary processes.[34] Members of the stratum just under the top are likely to feel they are as able as the rulers and thus deserve as much respect, while they are also more likely than any other stratum to be able to muster adequate resources, political influence, and prestige for mounting a rebellion. Examples include colonial upper strata (who were the leaders in the New World revolutions), as well as local chieftains of tribal colonies. Here, then, political instability grows from the peakedness we have analyzed, that is, the great rewards paid to the top leaders, which tempt those just below to attempt a dethronement.

The able person who is close to seizing the great rewards for yet another step upward is stimulated to sacrifice his time, energy, and even social relations to make that last successful effort. Although one need not accept fully the time budgets reported by people in various kinds of activities, all such studies show that from the higher levels of corporate life to those of academic or artistic life, the leaders work long and hard.[35]

Obviously, of course, *some* at the top do not do their best, and some are protected from displacement by their money, class position, political influence, or friendship. Some worked hard once to get to the top or near it but now find that extra effort does not gain much. Sportswriters sometimes say to a faltering champion boxer that he is not as "hungry" as he once was. Or, a lesser effort is more comfortable, and one can avoid great loss by manipulating the system. Nevertheless, on the whole, to get to the top or to remain there in almost any competitive activity requires great effort, and this effort is at least in part generated by the marginally greater payoffs: a relatively small amount of additional achievement elicits a large additional amount of esteem.

---

32. An example of the awareness of high-level competitors that new aspirants may be breathing on their heels is the prototypical and perhaps not entirely apocryphal story told about any of several musicians, which can be stated in this version: When the precocious Menuhin made his New York debut in Carnegie Hall, the somewhat older Heifetz turned to Rubinstein and commented: "It's very hot in here, isn't it?" Rubinstein, secure in his métier, answered, "Not for pianists."

33. For novelistic accounts of the struggle for the top posts, see Cameron Hawley, *Executive Suite* (Boston: Houghton Mifflin, 1952); and John Brooks, *The Big Wheel* (New York: Harper, 1949). For data on the traits thought to be useful in this struggle, see Paul E. Hoden, Carleton A. Pederson, and Gayton E. Germain, *Top Management* (New York: McGraw-Hill, 1968), esp. pp. 16ff.

34. William J. Goode, "Social Mobility, Family, and Revolutionary Potential," in *Explorations in Social Theory* (New York: Oxford University Press, 1973) pp. 287ff.

35. For an example of time-budget data for executives, see Osborn Eliot, *Men at the Top* (New York: Harper, 1959), pp. 112–130.

PRESTIGE PAYMENTS AND
LOWER OCCUPATIONAL RANKS

What of the people in less esteemed activities, or those whose performance or qualities are ranked very low? They are not offered much increase in potential prestige for any likely improvements in their performances. By the time such people are adult, many have learned that additional payoff will be hardly worth the effort. Lower-class children, for example, have relatively high fantasy aspirations but relatively moderate real expectations. As they grow older, they learn the harsh social reality that improving their various skills and competencies will yield little increase in wages, stability of income, or prestige.[36] If they become ditch-diggers, migratory farm workers, or domestics, for example, even their best performances will not elicit much applause from anyone. Their friends reinforce them in the belief that only the foolish aim high. Their peer groups aim at creating social and emotional defenses against outside social pressures to produce any more than economic necessity dictates, and they argue against viewing the dangling baubles as prizes to be won by real people. Moreover, because these people face so many barriers, at least some of them will turn to deviant careers that seem more easily available and that may pay more in money and even in locally-based prestige—as dealers in drugs, pimps, hustlers, gamblers, or organizers of the numbers game.[37]

Similarly, blacks and women[38] find that even when they have entered relatively prestigious occupations, they are likely to be fixed in subordinate positions, given less than full opportunity to utilize their highest skills, and paid lesser rewards than whites or males for what they actually do. They learn or come to believe that an increase in output or a higher level of performance will not yield the higher level of prestige that males or whites in the same types of jobs would get.[39] People in occupations that are generally paid lower esteem are motivated still less because they know how little prestige they will get from any improvement in output;

36. Roberta G. Simmons and Morris Rosenberg, "Functions of Children's Perceptions of the Stratification System," *American Sociological Review*, 36 (April, 1971): 235–249. See also Elliot Liebow, *Tally's Corner: A Study of Negro Streetcorner Men* (Boston: Little, Brown, 1967).

37. For discussions of differential opportunities, social networks, and deviance patterns, see Richard A. Cloward and Lloyd E. Ohlin, *Delinquency and Opportunity* (New York: Free Press, 1960); and Mark Lefton, J. K. Skipper, and C. H. McCaghy, eds., *Approaches to Deviance* (New York: Appleton-Century-Crofts, 1968).

38. Of course, these are not mutually exclusive categories. For a provocative hypothesis about those who are both, see Cynthia F. Epstein, "Positive Effects of the Multiple Negative: Explaining the Success of Black Professional Women," *American Journal of Sociology*, 78 (January, 1973): 912–935.

39. The income discrepancy between whites and blacks in the late 1960's and early 1970's was greatest among those with college educations. And, if a black comes from a higher *class* position, this gives him much less of an advantage in competing later on than it would give a white. See Otis Dudley Duncan, "Inheritance of Poverty or Inheritance of Race," in Daniel P. Moynihan, ed., *On Understanding Poverty: Perspectives from the Social Sciences* (New York: Basic Books, 1968), pp. 85–110.

at best, they avoid some disesteem by performing at a minimally adequate level.

EFFECTS OF PRESTIGE

Up to this point, we have mainly compared the top performers in the most esteemed jobs with those at the other end of the scale. Now we can look more intensively at the full range of esteem allocation in order to examine its impact upon people's willingness to contribute and to perform at a higher level. We are leaving aside, in this discussion, the special activities in which the audience is very small and largely irrelevant to the main demand structure of the society—activities such as skillfully shooting marbles, doing card tricks, or playing a kazoo.

Our concern here is, then, with the further categories of activities, jobs, and performances in which the best achievement does arouse some esteem but the activity itself is viewed as of only middling importance to the society—and this includes most of the activities for which people receive wages, such as cooking in a roadside diner, operating a cash register in a supermarket, serving as a filling station attendant, repairing radios. An activity that is ranked may be viewed as generally deserving high, middle, or low prestige; in addition, the actual achievement reached by individuals within any one of those categories may also be viewed as high, middle, or low.

Thus, an individual may achieve a high performance in a high-ranking occupation such as medicine, but most do not. They have only a moderate or low ranking in that occupation, though the occupation itself has a high ranking in all nations. Correspondingly, there are middle-level occupations and activities in which one may make a high personal achievement, but even an excellent individual achievement cannot change the basic ranking of the occupation itself. In addition, of course, there are many relatively low-ranking activities, from shining shoes to mopping floors, in which again some individuals may perform outstandingly while the fundamental ranking of the occupation remains low. These categories are presented in Chart 2.

CHART 2
How Much Esteem is Paid to People in
These Cells, with What Results?

Society-wide ranking of the skill or occupation	Achievement of the individual in the activity		
	High	Middle	Low
High			
Middle			
Low			

What is the effect of the highly peaked allocation of prestige upon people in each of these cells? It has already been pointed out that this allocation pattern does not motivate people equally in all the cells. For example, it does not motivate people much in the lower right cell, that is, people whose personal achievement is low in a low-ranking activity, to perform much better; but it doubtless stimulates those whose personal achievement is high in a high-ranking type of performance. What can be said about the other cells?

Since some of these activities are not ranked high by society as a whole—in our society they are mostly encompassed in jobs, thus we focus on those cases—the people in them do not, as a collectivity, receive much prestige which can be distributed. Thus, even the best performers are not likely to earn much by working harder, while of course they do earn much more than the performers viewed as less able.

Those who occupy a middle or low position in a high-ranking activity do get at least some prestige from being there at all. A village physician may get no national prestige or rewards, but he or she is at the top level of the local occupational ranking. Even in a town with several physicians, the lowest ranking among them is likely to have a loyal clientele and to receive local deference for being "the doctor." One can make similar assertions about other professionals, academics, and heads of small corporations, who are not known beyond their local networks.[40]

It seems likely that most such people feel little or no social pressure to aspire high, or even to live up to the highest standards of their professions. In part making up for this lack of pressure is a prior socialization during occupational training, which emphasizes dedication, and the aim of which is to persuade practitioners to feel less self-respect if they fall low in devotion to the job. Moreover, as editorials and speeches about such occupations constantly emphasize, if a high percentage of such people perform poorly over a long period, the prestige ranking of the occupation itself will begin to drop. It is likely that that process has already happened to some extent in the field of medicine.[41] Nevertheless, they are threatened with no loss of local respect unless they flagrantly violate the occupational norms that the local society recognizes as legitimate. This will be true both in the local network of a county or village and in a neighborhood of a large city. If they are inept, exposure is difficult and unlikely. Their colleagues protect them, while outsiders or clients are not often in a position to press home their accusations.[42]

40. For example, research shows that people who occupy positions of prestige even in local settings have considerable influence on social change. See Elihu Katz and Paul F. Lazarsfeld, *Personal Influence* (New York: Free Press, 1964), pp. 219–334, and James S. Coleman, Elihu Katz, and Herbert Menzel, *Medical Innovation: A Diffusion Study* (Indianapolis: Bobbs-Merrill, 1966), pp. 69–138.

41. For the dynamics of this process, see my article "The Theoretical Limits of Professionalization," in *Explorations in Social Theory*, pp. 341–382.

42. For a thoughtful account suggesting that colleague control in medicine is not adequate, see Eliot Freidson, *Profession of Medicine: A Study of the Science of Applied Knowledge* (New York: Harper and

Of course if our analysis of the prestige allocation patterns is correct, those in the middle-ranking types of activities (bookkeepers, truck drivers, railroad conductors) do receive more for a modicum of extra effort than those in lower-ranking activities, although once again the highest performers in mid-ranking activities cannot hope to be paid the same amount of esteem for each additional level of achievement that is to be given to those in higher-ranking activities: The curve of increments is higher at those higher levels, but these middle-ranking activities as a whole do not receive that much esteem from the society that can be distributed.

Those at high or middle levels of *achievement* in middle-ranking or lower-ranking types of *activities* can expect to receive, as a result of the prestige they earn, standard or somewhat better than average pay, stability in their jobs, and some respect from their superiors and some from their peers, together with a slight amount of disesteem and annoyance from peers who feel they are rate-busting. In addition, for those who perform well in the middle-ranking activities, there is at least some chance of moving to still higher occupational levels, where the payoff for added effort will be still greater. There, because the position of the activity itself yields more prestige, the successful person may then get still more for added effort; on the other hand, as the Peter Principle affirms, some people simply do poorly at that higher level because the job itself is different.[43]

Of course, in all of these subcells, members of a working group make reasonable efforts to protect the lesser performers, since thereby they are themselves protected in their own jobs.[44] By keeping the working ideal relatively modest, both superior and average performers are less threatened by a strong competition.

Indeed, only if there is a local shortage in economic demand, or an oversupply of people available for such activities (so that a hard-driving competitor can garner most of the available business or the one slightly better job in an office), are persons in such positions likely to feel much pressure to improve their performance substantially; and then only if they recognize that their performance is not respected much, and that as a consequence their economic security is in some danger. If demand is adequate, and if the normal social processes of protection for the less able operate well, moderate differences in performance do not change greatly the prestige rating of any individual. His or her payoff in money or prestige is not likely to suffer much.

Row, 1970), as well as his *Professional Dominance: The Social Structure of Medical Care* (Chicago: Aldine, 1970).

43. Although the analysis is meant to be humorous, like other social science humor (cf. the brilliant analyses of C. Northcote Parkinson) it contains a core of valid observation. See J. Laurence Peter and R. Hall, *The Peter Principle: Why Things Always Go Wrong* (New York: Morrow, 1969). Some people do indeed get promoted to a level where they are incompetent.

44. For this process, see my analysis "The Protection of the Inept," in *Explorations in Social Theory*, pp. 121–144.

As a consequence, the normal pattern of prestige allocation does not motivate a substantial part of the people in these occupations to try as hard as possible. Note that at middle- and lower-level activities especially, when individuals may recognize that they might gain some esteem (from superiors) by trying harder, that amount may not seem more rewarding than the continuing approval of their peers for supporting *their* lower work demands. The reward payoff from superiors is somewhat uncertain, but quite certain is the disapproval or annoyance from peers who feel threatened by the striver.[45]

The highly skewed allocation of prestige, and the chances of failure or success, confront people with choices about which career step to take next. It is clear that at every step of life people are making small or large decisions about how much effort they wish to invest in gaining or holding on to prestige, by reference to the likely outcome of that striving. They are engaging in various forms of social adjustment to their options, and what they choose determines which positions in the society they will enter. The other side of these processes of choice, evaluation, and social sifting is the allocation of people to various positions.

REALITY VERSUS AIMS

In a highly skewed system of chancy prestige allocations, with fine differentiations of rank in a given admired activity, even those toward the top must adjust at some point to the fact that they will not reach the top, or stay there long if they do, whatever their judgments may be about their own competence and worth. And, whether the ranking is by some ascriptive quality or performance, few of even those who rank fairly high with respect to any specific prestige-generating trait or skill will be judged by others to be at or near the top. Thus, even the relatively successful see their expectations or hopes frustrated by reality.[46]

More generally, because in modern societies most people aim higher than they can achieve, all but a few will have to adjust to a somewhat lower level of success. Few in our society have managed to follow the wise rule for spiritual serenity that tells us to keep our aspirations as low as our achievements.[47] Doubtless, some throw off the virus of ambition by the

45. For an example of the literature on rate-busting and norms of output, see: William A. Faunce, ed., *Readings in Industrial Sociology* (New York: Appleton-Century-Crofts, 1967), esp. sect. 4, "The Industrial Work Group and Informal Organization" (pp. 281–377). Norms for modest output are not, of course, found only among blue collar work groups.

46. For an ingenious confrontation of apparent "prestige success" (in this case, election as president of a learned society), and the reality of being unknown to many members of that society just the same, see Frank R. Westie, "Academic Expectations for Professional Immortality: A Study of Legitimation," *American Sociologist*, 8 (February, 1973): 19–32.

47. The question of whether people "aim" higher, in different kinds of class systems, is not fully answered as yet. People "desire" or want more in modern societies than they have, and I suppose that even in supposedly feudal systems most people did, too. However, "aim" suggests a definite purpose. They may "try" to move higher, without truly *aiming*; they might "aspire" without doing much of either. One might aspire, try, and aim, without really believing the higher goal is possible. In

time that they have tried one or two adult jobs, but few escape entirely the necessity of coming to terms eventually with the fact that their goals are higher than they are likely to reach.[48]

Doubtless, most could accomplish more than they do in a given activity, but they are insufficiently attracted by the rewards offered for additional effort. Some see that the social barriers they face will prevent their getting the rewards that others in more favorable social positions will garner. Others are tantalized for most of their lives by the glittering prestige rewards that lie just beyond their reach. Still others attain great acclaim, but only for a brief time. Common to all these varied types, however, is the necessity of accepting with more or less grace some degree of failure, whether it is toward the top or middle ranges of prestige-bearing accomplishments or in the least prestigious ones.

Both philosophical and empirical problems can make the definition of "failure" very troublesome. (For example, is a person a "failure" who serves humanity well at a lowly task, but who could have been a poet?) Here we use the term in an operationally simple sense: does the person feel that he or she has not achieved as high a performance as he or she had genuinely hoped to achieve; and therefore must make some adjustment to a lower level? This does not depend on whether the individual's ratio of rewards to investments or costs turned out to be high or low.

In our own type of society, as the individual decides (earlier or later) that the payoffs in prestige are not likely to be as great in a chosen activity, he or she may move over to less demanding activities, or to activities better suited to his or her skills. These calculations may or may not be based on adequate data or reasoning, but most people do actually calculate explicitly: about long-term versus short-term payoffs, security versus risk, monetary versus prestige rewards, job challenge versus one's potential skills, or which style of life to follow.

Doubtless, most people decide at some point that they will not rise further in the occupational world. They must accept whatever it offers. They must, to be wise, invest their time and attention in job and pension security, and enjoy the material and prestige rewards they can secure. They also try to maintain their local neighborhood respect and friendship network. It should be emphasized, however, that just as they cannot "drop out" of the economic market, so are they unable to avoid the continuing evaluations of others, about their worth as workers, neighbors, citizens, or family members. On the other hand, they can and do decide not to invest any more in trying to move upward in either occupational level or general esteem.

---

modern societies, people are encouraged to try for higher achievements, and to discover from experience whether they are possible rather than lower their aspirations before defeat.

48. See, for example, the data on how the auto worker adjusts to his failure to move upward in the plant hierarchy, or to establish a successful business on his own, in Eli Chinoy, *Automobile Workers and the American Dream* (Garden City, N.Y.: Doubleday, 1955), esp. chap. 10.

Nevertheless, it is characteristic of people in the United States that they do change jobs many times in the course of their lives.[49] Indeed, so much is this the case that up to the present time most workers have never received anything from corporate pension funds because they have not worked long enough on any one job to qualify under the pension rules.[50] In view of this high turnover, then, a fairly high percentage of the working population will at times consider many alternative opportunities that organizations and the society as a whole offer.

Thus, in making such changes, and as a mode of adjustment, people may decide:

1. to remain in the same activity but accept the lower rank and prestige they can earn; that is, they begin to view their present task as better than any alternative they can actually achieve;[51]

2. to move into somewhat different types of activities where the prestige payoff is somewhat or much lower; or

3. to use different talents, that may yield as high or higher rewards in prestige, in different activities.[52]

Those who experience a lesser discrepancy between expectation and reality face a lesser adjustment, but the patterns observable among those whose aims are greatly frustrated are doubtless to be found to a lesser degree among almost all those who strive.

ACCEPTANCE OF LOWER RANK

The decision to remain in the same activity but at a lower rank and prestige than one had hoped for can be illustrated by the dramatic instance of those who study to be concert artists. Because most were singled out in their early years as persons of extraordinary talent, they typically dedicated most of their childhood and youth to the acquisition of a rare set of skills.

49. Data from two decades ago show this trend clearly even at that time: Seymour M. Lipset and Reinhard Bendix, *Social Mobility in an Industrial Society* (Berkeley: University of California Press, 1959); see also Harold L. Wilensky, "Work as a Social Problem," in Howard S. Becker, ed., *Social Problems: A Modern Approach* (New York: Wiley, 1966), pp. 117–166.

50. Leaving aside, of course, the numerous cases in which companies have manipulated layoffs so as to avoid such payments.

51. This group comes closest to Merton's "ritualists" (*Social Theory and Social Structure*, in the chaps. titled "Social Structure and Anomie" and "Bureaucratic Structure and Personality"). Note that even they are trying to make the best of their situation.

52. As various analysts have noted, from de Tocqueville to the present, this alternative may include revolution—which is more likely to occur when a whole class has been led to expect upward movement but does not experience it, or experiences instead a lesser set of opportunities. The upward prestige strivings of the bourgeoisie are thus analyzed in Elinor Barber, *The French Bourgeoisie in Eighteenth Century France* (Princeton, N.J.: Princeton University Press, 1955). The more general relations of family and prestige with revolution are discussed in William J. Goode, "Social Mobility, Family, and Revolutionary Potential," in my *Explorations in Social Theory*, chap. 12. See also James C. Davies, "The J-Curve of Rising and Declining Satisfaction as a Cause of Some Great Revolutions and a Contained Rebellion," in H. D. Graham and T. R. Gurr, *Violence in America* (New York: Signet, 1969), pp. 671–709.

At every phase of their training they received considerable applause and were told that eventually they would make it to the top. There is great attrition over the years, but some actually make a formal debut. A high proportion of such people still receive considerable acclaim at that point. Critics make allowances for their youth and often write encouraging reviews. Strangers and friends applaud them.

Nevertheless, most of those who have survived the attrition to this point will not enjoy a successful solo concert career. They are not in great demand. Each concert seems a fair success, especially to the artist's friends. But there is no clear movement forward and upward. Only a handful succeed in realizing their career dreams. As a consequence, their adjustment problems are greater than those of persons who have much lesser career investments. Not only do they see that their investments are not likely to pay off as they had been led to expect. They must also change their self-images as "great artists," as well as their presentation of self to others. Each concert artist has spent much of his or her life preparing for that career, and is likely to move to another type of position in the music industry. He or she is not like, say, the first year graduate student in chemistry who learns that his or her talents are run-of-the-mill and easily switches to another field; or someone who in a first job in an advertising agency learns that he or she simply does not like the trade and wants to try another.

Thus, would-be concert artists may become private music teachers, members of symphony orchestras or quartets, or professors of music. Would-be scientists can also become teachers, or obtain jobs as laboratory technicians, while some shift to what they view as the less demanding social sciences. People who entertain literary ambitions can move into a wide variety of positions in which their craft in words will pay them adequately, from advertising to editing. They may use much or only some of the skill they have developed in that type of activity.[53]

DIFFERENT CHOICES AT A LOWER RANK

We have just been noting the case of people adjusting to a lower level of prestige than they had aimed at in their chosen field of activity. On the other hand, others may accept lower levels of prestige in activities quite different from the ones they sought to excel in. Perhaps most people do not end up in the same type of work, or at as high a level, as they aimed for when young. Many owners of small businesses, or door-to-door salespersons, once thought of themselves as aspiring lawyers or novelists, professors or political figures. Those who cannot become excellent actors may decide that they can nonetheless obtain much pleasure plus a modicum of prestige in activities behind the stage, from advertising and ticketing to handling costumes. (Actors may adjust with less personal disappointment to these shifts, as well as to entirely different types of

---

53. Stephen and Jonathan Cole show that in the physical sciences the reward system diverts "the energies of the less creative scientists into other channels," *Social Stratification in Science*, p.111.

activities, because they are more convinced than people in most other occupations that luck plays a large role in gaining stardom, and because few have made large investments of time and energy in training.) An athletic club, whose admiration is mainly focused on the success of its athletic "heroes," needs managers, publicity agents, secretaries, and the like. Voluntary organizations of all kinds need the skills of people at all levels, not alone those who are at the top; and all pay some amount of esteem for those contributions, just as outsiders do.

Moreover, far more of such alternative but lesser jobs are available than jobs at the top. It is not only in the United States Army that the men on the fighting lines are outnumbered by the support staff. Typically, in competitions that yield much prestige the staff outnumbers the competitors by a large margin. The ratio is especially large in the America Cup races, where a host of people engage in developing and testing new equipment or materials, designing hulls, raising money, and organizing elimination races, so as to select a small crew to sail one boat (which will probably never appear again in a Cup race) once in three years. However, all these people gain some prestige from participation in the match.

ALTERNATIVE HIGH-LEVEL ACTIVITIES

By offering alternative positions, and alternative if lower amounts of prestige, groups move their members to accept positions that are within their capabilities and thereby to contribute to the group goals. In addition, to the extent that some group members change to alternative but high-ranking activities, the group itself may gain prestige on a broader front, and all its members can share somewhat in that increment of earned prestige. The larger the group or organization, the wider the range of activities it encompasses, and as a consequence the more opportunities it will offer for alternative activities at a higher *or* lower level of prestige.

Some of these other activities may yield considerable prestige to the group or organization. A college, for example, may pay greater prestige to its handful of football stars, but the school receives far more prestige as a whole if its students strive for academic honors, or try newspaper writing, basketball, or political action, for example, as well. The top few in each such activity may not receive as much prestige, publicity, or deference as the few football heroes, but they get a considerable amount just the same; and the group or system receives a greater total amount of prestige because of the achievements of these people along a broad front of prestige-generating competitions.

Some people move to lower-level or ancillary tasks in the same activity when they are not satisfied with the prestige payments they receive after aiming (but failing) at the highest levels. Very different kinds of activities will also attract allocations or influxes of talent. Of course, each additional activity is an investment and uses both funds and available personnel. Thus the larger and richer associations can more easily follow such a strategy, but no organization can indefinitely expand such activities.

Many of those who do receive prestige at nearly the top level may nevertheless feel that they should receive more prestige than they in fact get. They feel so because they believe, correctly or incorrectly, that those who enjoy the highest accolades are not really much superior to them. Indeed, some would deny that the top persons *are* their superiors. Further, they may have committed enough investment to an activity to be unwilling to leave it totally, so do not feel that they must step down to ancillary or lesser activities. Since they are already esteemed, they are thought to possess skills and information that may be useful, and they are not likely to feel any pressure to leave the activity or organization.

As a consequence, such people may feel attracted to alternative activities at a broader or higher level of action, where somewhat different skills are necessary and the prestige rewards are great.[54] The professor who believes the prestige from his or her own research is not enough may attempt to become more active in the larger American Association for the Advancement of Science. Alternatively, some may decide to move into the higher levels of university administration, or into advisory or planning committees for the government.

There is, as noted, a high demand for such persons in these alternative posts. That demand, in turn, affects the different cost/reward ratios people see at these later career phases. Some persons may actually calculate these factors, while others simply feel less zest in continuing to try hard, without giving much thought to the fact that the ratios have changed. They change because, in a wide range of tasks, people who have been relatively successful will not receive large increments of prestige for the new work they are doing. Over time, they become better known and respected and thus receive some honors that appear to be given for a body of work over a whole career: membership in the National Academy of Sciences or the American Academy of Arts and Sciences, presidencies of their guild associations, or testimonial dinners. However, specific accomplishments or awards that would have raised their prestige substantially if done at an early age will not add much to their esteem once they have achieved fairly high standing. The increments are small, compared with the difficulty of trying to accomplish at an even higher level.

This special subprocess is intensified by a set of beliefs about the decline of creative powers with increasing age. The belief is especially strong among physical scientists, but people in acting as well as business are generally convinced of the truism ("this is a young man's game").[55]

In almost any field, achievement does decline with age, but for many

54. Specifically, they see that they possess valuable resources for which they will be paid well: In H. Kelley and J. Thibaut's terms ("Experimental Studies of Group Problem Solving and Process," in G. Lindzey and E. Aronson, eds., *The Handbook of Social Psychology*, 2d ed. [Reading, Mass.: Addison Wesley, 1968], pp. 735–785), others will be "information-dependent" on them.

55. Business executives may move into government service or philanthropy, or their corporations may move them into posts where the challenges seem less harsh (Frederick C. Haas, *Executive Obsolescence* (New York: American Management Association, 1968); and Frank L. Bird, "The Displaced Executive or the Man on the Shelf," *Business Topics* (Summer, 1966), p. 34.

other causes than the physiological. One creative person remarked that if anyone does a first-rate piece of work, the world instantly springs into action to prevent him or her from ever doing so again.[56] The black scientist is urged to become a political leader, the promising writer is tempted to become an editor, the excellent artisan to become a foreman. The higher the initial achievement, the greater the number of alternative opportunities offered that will undermine to some extent the person's time schedule as well as his or her dedication to a specialty.[57]

In a complex set of relations, two facts seem clear about the purported decline of accomplishment with age: For those who continue to work at their specialties throughout a normal span of years, the decline does not occur very early, even in mathematics; but the belief in that decline is strong enough to convince some people that since their chances of accomplishment are diminishing, it would be wise to turn to other activities.

It should be emphasized, however, that though the kind of process we are describing (that is, moving to alternative high-level activities) may generate more prestige for the individual as well as for the organization, it is a respect given for a different kind of activity. The actor who becomes a director may, if successful, gain in prestige, but not prestige in acting. The master teacher who becomes an assistant principal has been promoted, and will be esteemed more, but that person will not continue to earn still more prestige for excellent teaching. Moreover, the individual's peers typically believe that the new, higher, and more prestigious job is actually less demanding, is less "heroic" than continued dedication to the special activity.

SOCIAL ALLOCATION

As people continue to aspire within the same specialty, adjust at the level they have already achieved, or seek prestige in an alternative type of activity, the differential allocation of prestige generates processes that affect how people come together in sociable activities.

Those at the top are in high social demand, because in general people wish to have social interaction with the more esteemed. At the same time, these more esteemed people feel the same attraction toward their peers of high prestige, and are usually able to gain admittance to their company.

56. Frederick Mosteller, in a private communication.
57. The earlier work by H. C. Lehman, *Age and Achievement* (Princeton, N.J.: Princeton University Press, 1953), assured most readers that their prejudgments were correct, without raising the question of whether many creative people slow down after age thirty-five for the same reason that Mozart did. Wayne Dennis showed that if we begin instead with creative people who live, say, eighty years, and then ask about *their* curves of creativity, a very different pattern appears: "The Age Decrement in Outstanding Scientific Contributions," *American Psychologist*, 13 (August, 1958): 457–460. See also Matilda W. Riley and Anne Foner, *Aging and Society* (New York: Russell Sage Foundation, 1972), I, chap. 18; and Robert K. Merton and Harriet Zuckerman, "Age, Aging, and Age Structures in Science," in Merton, *The Sociology of Science*, esp. p. 512. But though creative scientists continue to be creative in their mature years, they do not receive large increments of prestige for their new work.

On a more obvious level, of course, this takes place naturally, since these are likely to be the kinds of people who already inhabit the same social and geographical space; so that even without a conscious pattern of choosing, homophily would be observable, that is, people of roughly the same social ranking would be found together.[58]

On the other hand, because individuals with less prestige are also attracted to those with more, some of the former are willing to pay the various kinds of additional costs to be admitted to the company of the latter: a considerable amount of overt deference, gifts, hospitality, services, and so on. Not everyone is willing to pay such costs, but many are. Conversely, some prestigious people want to have such deferential people around them, in part because those with equal prestige would make far greater demands upon them and would compete with them for available deference. Although deferential persons of lesser prestige do not contribute much prestige by their personal presence, they do remind the person of high rank that indeed he possesses that rank.

Note that this is an ordinary cost/reward action (very likely not usually a conscious calculation). That is, it is less costly and risky to obtain deference from others lower in social rank, but their deference is worth less, too. Deference from people closer to oneself in rank is worth more, but one may get less of it from them, or have to exert oneself to get it. It is more pleasing to control others (absolute power is absolutely delightful), and that is easier if they are of lower rank; it is still more pleasing to control people closer to one's own rank, though unfortunately they are less controllable.[59]

All the above processes of sifting and allocation occur, to a less obvious extent, at all levels of prestige; for example, the neighborhood leader may be accompanied by local stooges or retainers. On the other hand, such differences in evaluation between top- and lower-level people may create an alternative social relations pattern: some will pay admiration to a second or even a "third-best" person, since the cost of being close to that person is less than that of being close to the most admired person. Consequently, those who are at a somewhat lower level (that is, a second or third level) will still be able to attract a coterie of relatively deferential people.

Hence, more than one kind of sifting process in social relations is

58. Robert K. Merton and Paul F. Lazarsfeld, "Friendship as a Social Process: A Substantive and Methodological Analysis," in M. Berger, T. Abel and C. Page, eds., *Freedom and Control in Modern Society* (New York: Van Nostrand, 1954), pp. 18–66. Laumann has shown, on both subjective and objective measures of social distance, that while same-rank and higher-rank choices for friendship are both operative, the latter effect is somewhat stronger. Edward O. Laumann, *Prestige and Association in an Urban Community* (Indianapolis: Bobbs-Merrill, 1966), chaps. 3, 5.

59. For some evidence and argument that people of higher rank do seek and enjoy the deference of less esteemed others, see: Richard L. Simpson, *Theories of Social Exchange* (Morristown, N.J.: General Learning Press, 1972), pp. 1–19; Fritz Heider, *The Psychology of Interpersonal Relations* (New York: Wiley, 1958), pp. 258–263; Elihu Katz and Paul F. Lazarsfeld, *Personal Influence* (New York: Free Press, 1964), pp. 221–223, 272–275, 294–295; and Peter M. Blau, *Exchange and Power in Social Life* (New York: Wiley, 1964), pp. 62–69.

generated. The more usual pattern, as noted, is homophily. The individual who would like to be in contact with the most admired person recognizes that he simply does not have enough to offer. He may feel that he cannot rank in attractiveness (based on any kind of resource) with the most admired person, and may not wish to pay the deference that might seem to be appropriate in such a one-sided relationship. As a consequence, social circles are likely to be made up of prestige-equals.

Indeed, so much is this a common understanding among people that individuals of considerable prestige, therefore in high demand, may have the experience of being in a city temporarily where they are relatively well-known but having few people call on them, since these people all suppose that the respected person is already surrounded by others with high prestige or other resources.

FEUDAL SOCIETIES

It is not possible to ascertain whether the adjusting and allocative processes described here have been as pervasive or as fraught with personal hurt in caste or estate systems of the past.[60] According to classical descriptions, the social ideology of such systems impressed upon everyone his or her duty to stay at the social rank where he or she was born. The skewedness in prestige rewards was as great as in a modern industrial society, but the contingencies presumably were lower. Each individual was fairly certain about not only what kinds of skills he would acquire, but how high a level of skill he needed to acquire to maintain the level of prestige he was expected to earn. In neither caste nor estate society was occupation fully ascribed, although officially rank was. In both, the individual was typically trained from childhood to assume the traditional occupation in which he was placed. Thus one's entire youth could be devoted to the acquisition of the skills necessary for his job; so few would fail entirely. Presumably, in such a system the amount of later personal adjustment or social sifting among networks would be less extreme than in our own society.

On the other hand, we cannot suppose that these descriptions correspond entirely to reality, especially with respect to the day-to-day processes of adjustment. This skepticism cannot be tested because our data are unfortunately confined mostly to descriptive materials that focus on the life of people higher in the social scale than peasants and the urban poor.[61] From such descriptions of higher social levels it is quite clear, however, that life was a struggle and highly contingent. Strife, the honor of victory and the shame of defeat, intrigue, and aspiration are to be found in all the classical literature of the past that describes the daily lives of

60. For a complex analysis of the hurt in a modern class society, see Richard Sennett and Jonathan Cobb, *The Hidden Injuries of Class* (New York: Vintage, 1973).

61. However, as noted earlier, many studies of modern peasant villages have been carried out and it is clear that their inhabitants are studiously jealous of each small success of others, and spend much of their energy and gossip in preventing anyone from claiming to have risen above the others. (See esp. F. G. Bailey, *Gifts and Poison* (Oxford: Blackwell, 1971).

mythical heroes. All these abound in the stories found in the *Ramayana* or the *Mahabharata*, the two great Hindu epics. The Germanic sagas depict a high concern with honor, primarily in battle and personal intrigue. Lady Murasaki's *The Tale of Genji* is full of contingency, striving, and a concern for seeking victory or adjusting to defeat as one could find in any account of court life in the West at even a much later period than her tenth-century Japan.

A similar comment could be made of the *Chin P'ing Mei*, which indeed depicts aspiration and failure, among not merely Chinese court officials, but people in all walks of life. The Tokugawa period in Japan is usually described as feudal and certainly was an estate society according to classic definitions, but again a man's position in life was likely to be contingent at best.[62]

True enough, these accounts are typically of people in higher positions. Every study of any specific epoch in the past for which mobility can be measured shows that there was considerable turnover of people at the top.[63] Of course, since nine-tenths or more of the population would have been poor farmers or worse, most people could not rise far. On the other hand, it is at least possible to speculate that in, say, Sung China, Heian Japan, or eleventh-century France those who were peasants, poor independent farmers, or the urban poor might have aspired to at least a somewhat better or more secure position, have risen a bit or fallen somewhat, and have invested in those slight rises and falls as much emotion, torment, or hurt, as people of the same class level might in our own society with reference to far greater ascents or catastrophes.[64] Would such smaller increments or losses loom as large to those people as do the much larger changes in modern lives? Did small failures require as much or more social and personal adjustment? We cannot know, but it is at least possible to imagine that those differences may have seemed as great, and required as much adjustment in individuals' personal ambitions, social networks, and evaluations, as they do in modern life.[65]

ACCEPTING ONE'S POSITION

Societies do have, of course, some mechanisms by which people are persuaded that adjustment is a wise choice. For example, all societies give

62. See, e.g., Charles D. Sheldon, *The Rise of the Merchant Class in Tokugawa Japan: 1600–1868* (Locust Valley, N.Y.: J. J. Augustine, 1958), for his descriptions of not only the merchant strivers, but also the samurai and princes whose ascents and falls are noted here and there.

63. For data on historical China, see Robert M. Marsh, *The Mandarins: The Circulation of Elites in China, 1600–1900* (New York: Free Press, 1961).

64. For a savage account of the struggle over tiny losses and increments, see Emile Zola's account of nineteenth-century French farm life in *The Earth*.

65. The question of how much people's reference groups determine their feelings of success or failure, or their resentment against those who hold higher positions in wealth or prestige, has not been answered. W. G. Runciman's data (*Relative Deprivation and Social Justice* [Berkeley: University of California Press, 1966], chaps. 10, 11) suggest that the English social classes judge their own economic, political, and prestige situation mainly by reference to the standards of their own network.

subsidiary rewards to those who reach positions near the top, though doubtless without explicitly aiming at reducing their resentment at not receiving the top rewards, and without explicitly recognizing that it does. Those rewards may be minor honors, estates, jobs in a corporation with less authority but some prestige, counseling posts in a college, or high-sounding job titles.

In addition, all societies emphasize, as a kind of secondary adjustment to the failure that is inherent in high-contingency situations, the duty of serving the *collectivity*. That is to say, the rhetoric of caste, estate, and class systems emphasizes everyone's duty to serve the group in whatever capacity, and all these societies pay at least some amount of deference for this service. To what extent groups manage to mollify the hurt from small or large failures by telling people that they have contributed to the group by serving in a modest capacity is not known. Since Emile Durkheim's study, *Suicide* (1895), however, investigations of labor turnover, anomie, absenteeism, morale, and social cohesion have consistently shown that organizations and social groups gain more allegiance and dedication from their members if they convince them that their modest efforts do contribute to the collectivity. Propaganda to that end is especially widespread during a period of revolutionary change, that is, when people's efforts and loyalty are especially needed.

In addition, of course, all societies manage to contain some of the frustration that arises from these contingent and peaked allocations by making it clear that there is nowhere else to go. Short of a revolution that might change the system entirely, each person must find his or her "own place" and accept what he or she has managed or failed to achieve, since no other alternatives are better.

Finally, although in these paragraphs we have spoken of what "society" does, it should not be forgotten that this is largely the decision of the higher social strata. It is in their interest to maintain at least some commitment from those at lower levels: They need their services and contributions. Leaders are powerless without their followers. As in other kinds of social relations, these mechanisms for inducing commitment or adjustment among people who receive lesser rewards may not be enough and in any event will fall far short of equity. But unless some of the mechanisms discussed here work to some extent, the discontent of even the lowly can become dangerous.

Chapter 5
Interlinkages

The term "social structure" suggests a whole made up of parts that are interdependent in a coherent and organized fashion. The concept raises a complex question: How do the parts link together to form a whole? In this book that question becomes: How do these interconnections affect prestige processes?

We have, of course, already offered many propositions, comments, and data that bear on this general problem, for example, the different evaluations of people or achievements in different social circles or groups; the flow of people from one stratum or organization to another as they seek or get more (or less) prestige. Indeed, it is difficult to analyze social interaction without making mention of how some part of the society is related to another.

In our earlier discussions, however, these connections themselves and their effects on prestige processes were not the central focus, as they are in this chapter. Such a focus helps us to understand better the flow of respect or esteem in the society. However, our 'analysis will bypass—because of limitations in time and space—a set of important problems that have not been adequately addressed by contemporary sociology. Among these are the following: 1. the lack of *descriptive* data about the interaction among different parts of the society (for example, among organizations, classes, or groups); 2. the lack of *concepts* for describing or analyzing social structures or systems of interconnections; and 3. the lack of a body of *general* hypotheses or propositions about the interrelations of social institutions, organizations, networks, or groups. The complex reasons for this underdevelopment need not be pursued here, but the lack does make our task somewhat more difficult and the result more primitive.[1]

Much of sociological research describes how membership in some social category (sex, race, the Democratic party), or a commitment to a norm or value (belief in free speech, property rights, or chastity) is related to some

---

1. "Structuralism," the much-vaunted term invented by Claude Lévi-Strauss, though doubtless of considerable literary interest, does not advance our understanding of structural interconnections, or links among parts of the society. For more useful comments and attempts at analysis, see the various essays in Peter Blau, ed., *Approaches to the Study of Social Structure* (New York: Free Press, 1975). For critical analyses of Lévi-Strauss, see also Raymond Boudon, *The Uses of Structuralism* (London: Heineman, 1971), and E. Leach, *Lévi-Strauss* (London: Fontana [Collins], 1970).

individual behavior or attitude (participation in riots, occupational mobility, support of the right to have an abortion). Far less research is devoted, on the other hand, to how people in different social positions interact with one another directly, or affect one another's behavior indirectly—for example, to the interrelations of people in different classes, races, or occupations.[2] Still less research is devoted to how organizations, groups, occupations, or classes interact with one another. For some of these relations, indeed, it is not clear in what sense, or how, such segments of the society truly do interact.

How do we find out how any one thing is connected with any other? In mechanical devices (an automobile motor) we ascertain which parts actually touch one another, and through which linkages their motion or force is transmitted from one part to another. In electrical systems, we trace the flow of electrical energy as well as its transmutation into light, heat, or motion. Tracing out even one of such chains has often required the work of generations. In both organisms and ecological systems, researchers often begin without even knowing that a set of processes or parts *is* connected to other sets in any important way or ways.[3]

To ascertain how such social interlinkages might affect prestige processes is very likely as difficult as discovering the electrochemical chain of events that forces most mammals (not the cetaceans) to breathe, whether conscious or unconscious. But we may suppose that there are simpler links as well, some of which are open to elementary observation; and we can begin with such interconnections. Common sense, for example, takes note of such stepwise links as these:

Talent and skill in most of the performing and creative arts "flow" toward New York City.

As a consequence, New York is a major prestige center of the United States; esteem bestowed by New York City critics is "worth more" than respect granted elsewhere.

Individuals who move to different social circles, schools, corporations, research institutes, or cities are evaluated at each step in this movement, but so are the groups, places, or organizations that sent them, as well as the social units that received them.

Information and evaluations about people or groups flow from one social setting, group, class, or organization to another, and as they flow they are altered.

Groups and organizations may develop their own evaluations by which they confer esteem, but their ability to elicit what they want from other social units

---

2. One of the few pieces of research available on this problem is the Yankee City Series; see vol. I, *The Social Life of a Modern Community*, by W. Lloyd Warner and Paul S. Lunt (New Haven: Yale University Press, 1941).

3. Recent statistical analysis and elaboration of citation patterns in scientific literature have been used to map specialty areas in science and examine the flow of information in the sciences. See H. G. Small and B. C. Griffith, "The Structure of Scientific Literature, I: Identifying and Graphing Specialties," *Science Studies*, 4 (January, 1974): 17–40, and B. C. Griffith, H. G. Small, J. A. Stonehill and S. Dey, "The Structure of Scientific Literatures, II: Toward a Macro- and Micro-Structure for Science," *Science Studies*, 4 (October, 1974): 339–365.

depends on how well they meet the standards of those other groups or organizations. Thus, even when individuals, groups, or organizations exchange very little with specific others, those they do exchange with are linked directly or eventually with almost every other social unit. Thus, the various resulting social pressures are not confined to only *direct* interaction or exchanges.

Prizes, medals, and awards are mostly given by organizations to their members; but organizations also inform the public of these events, which suggests that they are trying to link their prestige-giving to a larger audience.

Such commonsense observations are not at all weakened by the possible charge that this view is "functionalist." The issues raised by that charge need not be debated here, for they are adequately analyzed elsewhere.[4] The observations above, and most of those to be found in the subsequent discussion, can be tested in their own right, just as the interconnectedness of social processes or structures can be tested, whether or not functionalism as a general theoretical orientation is viewed as fruitful. In any event, it is obvious that even the most implacable of antifunctionalists *act* in their daily behavior as though the various social units in a society are interconnected.

LINKS, NETWORKS, AND OTHER STRUCTURES

Structures appear in many forms. The biochemical structures alluded to previously are essentially chains of events or processes. More than a century ago, organic chemical analysis began to reveal the fact that the different ways in which various atoms bond together make very different compounds, even when the proportion of elements (carbon, hydrogen, oxygen, and so on) in them is the same. That is, different geometric structures of compounds create great differences in their chemical behavior. Sociometric analyses of who interacts with or likes whom show that the persons in some groups are extensively interconnected, while in others they form clusters or cliques only weakly linked one with another. Studies of communication flow report that groups structured as wheels (one central source connected with each and every person) function differently from those that are tightly connected networks or that are no more than a chain of persons. In modern geography, spatial studies of markets suggest the existence of hexagonal territories.[5]

Two large types of questions can be asked of social structures. Very likely, the first can be answered only after many decades of complex

4. See especially William J. Goode, "Functionalism: The Empty Castle," in *Explorations in Social Theory* (New York: Oxford University Press, 1974), pp. 64–94.

5. See Ronald Abler, John S. Adams, and Peter Gould, *Spatial Organization* (Englewood Cliffs, N.J.: Prentice-Hall, 1971), pp. 364–374. A methodological tool, sociometric blockmodels, recently elaborated by Harrison C. White, Scott A. Boorman, and Ronald L. Breiger in a set of articles in the *American Journal of Sociology*, holds promise of greater insights into social structures gathered from analyses of networks of links, but work with such tools has thus far been merely illustrative: White, Boorman, and Breiger, "Social Structure from Multiple Networks, I" *American Journal of Sociology*, 81 (January, 1976): 730–780, and Boorman and White, "II," *American Journal of Sociology*, 81 (May, 1976): 1384–1446.

inquiry: What are the social behavioral consequences that can be deduced from the mathematical or geometrical characteristics of the structures themselves? To answer that kind of question requires that we be able to make a real map of a whole social structure. It is unlikely that we can follow this line of inquiry very far at present, although I believe that some such consequences can be derived by mathematical sociology, from hypothetical social structures.[6]

Our earlier list of linkages points to a second, more basic set of questions. At this more elementary level—implied by the weak term "interlinkages"—we examine part of a social structure by asking how reputations change as they are passed on from one social group to another, or what calculations people make as they decide to move from a less to a more esteemed organization, or to recruit a new member. The analysis of how prestige processes are affected by linkages or structures must, I believe, begin at this level with ordinary observations of the *flow of prestige through reputation and membership*.

This view begins with the simple fact that even when the interaction observed seems to occur between two people, it may really be occurring between: one person or more in interaction with someone who represents an organization; two sets of such representatives; one or more persons and others who are viewed as members of a social group or category (country club set, upper class, Americans of Chinese background). Much interaction is made up of exchanges and evaluations among social categories, groups and groupings, occupations, classes and castes, clubs and corporations, cliques, neighborhoods and cities.

This fact has many consequences. One is that because people first perceive one another as "members" of such social units, their initial behavior and attitudes are determined most by the respect or dispraise they usually give to such social categories or groups. It is only when people know the other's individual achievements or traits better that they modify their behavior from this stereotyping or categorizing to pay more or less esteem than the stereotyped membership usually receives in the society.

We wish to consider, then, the processes by which people make reputations outside or inside their groups or networks, and are then accepted or rejected by others; and how groups, classes, or organizations maintain, lower, or enhance their prestige standing by recruiting new members of higher or lower rank. The focus is on the flow of prestige and of people from one social grouping to another, and on how the links among groups affect that flow.

Using this imagery is not distorting social or economic reality, for these processes are observable daily. For example, the New England country

6. Note that this possibility is suggested by André Weil, "Sur l'Étude algébrique de certains types de lois de mariage (système Murngin)" app. to pt. 1, in Claude Lévi-Strauss, *Les Structures élementaires de la parenté* (Paris: Presses Universitaires de France, 1949), pp. 278–285.

craftsman learns eventually that somewhere else an alternative, nonlocal, esthetically sophisticated market awaits his artisan products. Similarly, a husband may learn that he is being paid far less respect for his social and emotional contributions to his family than is common in his neighborhood, ethnic group, or class—and seek another "market" that will pay more.

Every day, people move from and to different sectors of the society, interacting with different persons and being evaluated by them. People make judgments about members of their families in the morning, about other people on the way to work, and about clients, customers, or fellow employees on the job. By telephone, people interact with others in different social positions about people in still other social groupings. They interact with employees of faceless corporations and owners of small businesses. They engage in sports or recreation, visiting, and movie-going. In all these activities, people gain knowledge of other people who are similar or different in various ways. They develop their own map of the social structure.[7] Thereby they learn what are the myriad prestige rankings that others make concerning ascribed traits, achievements, qualities, or memberships. Similarly, people make at least rudimentary calculations about how much esteem they are given for their own qualities and performances, compared to people like themselves or different from themselves.

Over an entire career or lifetime, people interact with a still wider set of other individuals, corporations, and people in different social positions; they make evaluations and are the objects of others' evaluations.

In those different settings, sharp differences of prestige ranking exist alongside substantial agreement. A man may be widely admired in a slum area as a hustler who makes a good living by chicanery, fraud, and threat, but in other circles he may encounter abhorrence or contempt. In some art circles the work of Rauschenberg, Oldenburgh, and Warhol may be given respect, but in others it may be evaluated as vulgar and fraudulent. That is, the prestige given in one group may not be transferable over group boundaries. On the other hand, scientific discoveries and medical skills are admired in the ghetto as well as in the academy. There are few groups in which physical bravery is not esteemed. Moreover, data on the prestige rankings of occupations show that all social classes generally agree; that is, the differences in standing of most jobs are not great from one class to another.

Whether the differences are large or small, people are concerned about their reputations outside their intimate networks. So are corporations. Top people in the corporation hierarchy are interested in studies of their

7. And, of course, people make their personal or group maps of geographical areas or whole countries. For geographic techniques used in constructing such maps, see Abler, Adams, and Gould, *Spatial Organization*, pp. 519ff. As Erving Goffman has noted, people also maintain a highly complex map of the microstructure they both inhabit and construct, in their interactions with other persons. See his *Frame Analysis* (New York: Harper, 1974).

rankings,[8] just as university presidents read with dismay or pleasure the latest national inquiries into the academic rankings of their departments. Corporations with high prestige can more easily recruit the abler graduates of prestigious schools, or people who have already been successful in other companies. Thereby they are more likely to maintain their high ranking, because abler employees are likely to achieve more. Companies have engaged in elaborate educational or public relations programs in efforts to enhance their public image—to maintain or increase their prestige ranking within their subsystem of related corporations as well as within the larger social structure.

We can observe in many contexts the concern of groups or social categories about the evaluations that people in other social positions make about them. For example, members of ethnic groups in the United States have created organizations to mount propaganda campaigns that are designed to lessen the disesteem they suffer. One of the results has been an evaluative change: ethnic jokes have come to be viewed as "bad taste," at least in public. In the past, when middle-class families had servants, elders frequently admonished others and one another to watch their behavior when servants were about, so that the lower orders would not see them behave badly.

The evaluations of individuals, organizations, groups, and members of social categories affect people's decisions to enter or leave a group or organization if they have that opportunity. Those judgments determine the national rankings of groups, persons, or organizations. They also determine some part of the success or failure that people or groups experience in their goal-seeking. Whatever agreement is observable in the amount of respect given to different occupations, classes, organizations, or groups is the resultant of many social transactions within a multiplicity of submarkets of prestige, and of the transactions between and among such social units. All of these are interlinked by virtue of the fact that all social actors (whether persons or organizations) engage in a wide variety of interactions with others, directly or indirectly, over shorter or longer periods of time, and thus there is a flow of evaluations and people from one part of the social structure to other parts.

Any given face-to-face interaction is shaped to some extent by people who are not there physically at the moment, as the structural concepts of "reference groups" and "third parties" remind us.[9] Tracing the flow of

8. For a commentary on such "industry-wide corporate image profiles," see David Finn, *The Corporate Oligarch* (New York: Simon and Schuster, 1969), chap. 8, esp. pp. 199ff. Sunday eds. of the *New York Times* contain several pages of listings of high-level jobs. Many of these advertisements include assertions, implied or explicit, that the corporation advertising the job is esteemed. For a market analysis of ethnic discrimination, see Gary Becker, *The Economics of Discrimination*, 2d ed. (Chicago: University of Chicago Press, 1971 [1957]).

9. See Herbert H. Hyman and Eleanor Singer, eds., *Readings in Reference Group Theory and Research* (New York: Free Press, 1968). With reference to third parties, see the two articles by William J. Goode, "Norm Commitment and Conformity to Role-Status Obligations," *American*

information or evaluation outward from a face-to-face interaction, we move to other circles and networks, other agencies and organizations, where the same individuals interact with a wider range of people and report to them what they have been doing. People talk about their bowling or bridge partners with people who never meet these partners. People evaluate their coworkers in family conversations. Neighbors talk about one another in conversations with other people in another city. Thereby a flow of reputation is generated.

Reputation, then, may begin with a direct interaction—the first link in its outward flow. But some of it is passed on to another set of people (neighbors, fellow workers, formal organizations) who constitute a second linkage. Gossip, anecdotes, racist or sexist comments, reports of observations, and work experiences are passed on to others as part of our informal social life. Talk is a large part of society's business. Through it we learn of others' evaluations and judgments, but often we do not expect to become acquainted with those others. Moreover, we do not usually have much opportunity to test what we have heard about them, and we are likely to have a low stake in the validity of those evaluations.

In a third type of linkage we do encounter a person about whom we have heard, and hence we may have an opportunity to reexamine whatever opinion we hold about that person. In most cases that opinion concerns character, personality, or likeableness (and thus we can decide whether our prior opinion is correct). In others, we may encounter a person of whose abilities we have heard—a Pulitzer Prize winner, a concert pianist, the winner of a sailing race—but in such instances we have no easy method for testing the opinion previously acquired. Very likely, most people nevertheless do try to relate these new social experiences to information heard earlier.

In a fourth type of flow and feedback, especially common in the world of work, people pass on their evaluations to others (often at higher levels in an organization) who can and do actually test the validity of those rankings in direct observation. In that case, those who pass on the information and those who receive it have a substantial stake in its validity. People who recommend want others to consider their judgments to be good. After all, they are being evaluated as evaluators while the person they recommend is being tested.

This situation is most obvious for "gatekeepers" of all kinds, such as

Journal of Sociology, 66 (November, 1960): 246–258, and "A Theory of Role Strain," *Explorations in Social Theory*, pp. 97–120.

The term "third parties" was used in my *After Divorce* (Glencoe, Ill.: Free Press, 1956), p. 206, but was not given special attention there. Robert K. Merton affirms that he had been using the term even earlier, and of course it is widely used now. I assume it was generally understood before my use of it. Simmel also makes reference to the various consequences of a third person entering or playing a role in what was formerly a dyad. See, e.g., "The Expansion of the Dyad," in Kurt Wolff, *The Sociology of Georg Simmel* (New York: Free Press, 1950), pp. 135–136.

baseball scouts, whose jobs are dependent on making reasonably accurate assessments. But such linkages are common in other kinds of activities: professors at a small college who recommend a colleague to a prestigious university department; an individual or group who reports to a talent agency his or their delight in an as yet little-known nightclub performer; a parole officer who tries to convince a businessman that his parolee has business talent and should be given a chance.

Further: this fourth type of link is not confined to the world of work. People who move from one city to another may go with letters from friends or former work associates to people in their destination city. The letters may call on members of the new groups to invite the migrant to dinners, parties, worship services and so on, in which the criteria for membership and acceptance are not based on technical competence at a specific job, but manners, charm, credit rating, character, or even piety.

CHANGES IN REPUTATION
THROUGH LINKS

Because each person, network, or group may have different aims in ranking people or telling others about them, or in utilizing rankings when they hear them, at every phase of these linking processes the information will be changed or filtered in various ways. We pass on only part of the information we know about a friend or acquaintance, and a different part to a different person. In turn, individuals hear it and respond to it selectively. Then they pass on only part of it again, somewhat differently, to still other networks or groups.

A person may be viewed among his poker-playing friends as a jolly, witty companion, one who holds his drinks well: but such a report might be received with little approval by members of a fundamentalist Protestant church or a loan officer at a bank. Or, standards applied by another network may be simply more rigorous: for example, a nonskiing person may express admiration for another because that person skis at all, but if that admiration is expressed to a member of a ski club, the ski-slope ranking of "expert" will be barely acceptable.

On the other hand, when both reporter and listener know one another's standard and aims, the evaluations given by one are tailored more carefully to the other's needs. For example, if a faculty member in a small liberal arts college talks to a professor at a major university, he or she is not likely to mention local faculty members who excel at committee work, cooperate with the administration, and are popular among townspeople. He or she is much more likely to pass on information about a talented young faculty member who shows promise of doing fine research work.[10] That praise

10. For a discussion of the different orientations of "professors" and "teachers," see the classic comments by Willard Waller, *The Sociology of Teaching* (New York: Wiley, 1932), pp. 58–66; and William J. Goode, Larry Mitchell, and Frank Furstenberg, *Willard Waller on the Family, Education and War* (Chicago: University of Chicago Press, 1970), pp. 233–245.

may be tempered somewhat, because the reporter knows the standards for good research may be higher at a major university. The praise would be greater, or have a different content, if the reporter were to discuss the same faculty member with other local colleagues.[11]

In all such exchanges, at least three kinds of information are being passed on: Information about a person; information about *what is valued or approved*; and information about the evaluator. It is through the constant exchange of information about how others evaluate different activities, achievements, and qualities that some general agreement is created, even over an entire nation, about the rankings in and around occupations, sports, styles of cookery, or forms of dress. One of the results is that "American" cultural or social patterns remain different from, say, Canadian or Spanish, and people in different social strata or groups can at least recognize the cues that distinguish other classes or neighborhood patterns from their own.

These tertiary or quaternary processes of evaluation may come to outweigh the primary processes over time, as a person's reputation moves into somewhat different or wider social groupings. Those who make the primary evaluations cannot control them once they enter other networks. A scholar's reputation may fall among experts while it remains high or even increases among outsiders whose information and evaluations are acquired much later. A person who becomes known outside his own field as an expert may also attempt to capitalize on such an "external" reputation, by appealing to that wider network on a different basis, and interacting directly with the people in it in an entirely new role. Thus both businessmen and professors may be able to obtain fairly high positions in government circles because their reputations have preceded them there. Thereupon, they succeed or fail in establishing a new basis for esteem. But in either case, the group who first validated those persons' achievements loses influence over their later reputation; it now has a new base.

HOW FAR EVALUATIONS FLOW

How far the reputation of a specific person or organization will be passed on is partly a function of prestige ranking. That is, the higher the prestige of a person (or organization) within his or her own network or group, the farther the evaluation will travel, as measured by the numbers of links or boundaries the information will pass through and very likely the physical distance as well. The more esteemed the person, the more likely it is that he will be known to a large number of others who have had no direct experience with his performances or qualities.

11. For a discussion of these relations with related theoretical import, see Peter M. Blau, "Structural Constraints of Status Complements," in Lewis A. Coser, ed., *The Idea of Social Structure* (New York: Harcourt, Brace, Jovanovich, 1975), pp. 117–138.

To add another proposition to this: Within any given type of activity, the higher the prestige of the person or organization that transmits the evaluations, the farther those rankings will travel. These hypotheses can be combined and expressed in formal mathematical terms.[12]

That such evaluations will travel farther if the individual enjoys greater esteem does not arise only from the well-known finding that people at higher prestige rankings know more people because they are more likely to be members of voluntary organizations, to participate in a larger network of acquaintances, and even to interact with more kin.[13] Rather, I am pointing to the related but different fact that more people know about an individual who enjoys higher prestige than about one in the same network or type of activity who enjoys less esteem. The people who are ranked toward the top of any group, organization, or social circle (whether or not that social unit is itself ranked high) are more likely to be known to people in other groups or organizations.

These relationships are partly caused by a simple social fact: Although almost no persons escape some rankings made by others who only hear about them (made through persons in a better position to observe), the greater the number of links distant from any given network or circle, the lower the percentage of people about whom gossip or evaluation is socially defined as worth the telling. With each more distant link, moving away from any given person, the higher the percentage of people who have little or no interest in any evaluations or information about that person.[14]

But though this regularity is generally observable, it must be qualified by another structural regularity, that reputations do not flow in all directions equally. In more figurative language, the boundaries of some social groupings are more permeable than others; that is, people are more willing to listen to information about a given person, depending primarily on how much their groupings care about the activity in which the reputa-

---

12. Various mathematical formulations of such relationships are possible. One may also state in formal terms the likelihood that a given person will have heard of another person, as a function of the prestige of the person being evaluated, the prestige of the person transmitting the evaluation, and the number of people of different prestige rankings who form the intervening links. For similar equations, see the work of Ronald Abler, John S. Adams, and Peter Gould, *Spatial Organization*, pp. 217ff. Earlier work on this relationship was done by George K. Zipf. For a more comprehensive listing of work, see Gunnar Olsson, *Distance and Human Interaction: Review and Bibliography*, Regional Science Research Institute Bibliographical, ser. no. 2 (Philadelphia, 1965). Our formula applies to networks or classes of people and organizations that share an interest in a given activity.

13. Although this relationship appears to be generally correct, recent data suggest that at *lower* class levels, *blacks* belong to more voluntary organizations than do whites. See J. A. Williams, N. Babchuk, and D. R. Johnson, "Voluntary Associations and Minority Status: A Comparative Analysis of Anglo, Black and Mexican Americans," *American Sociological Review*, 38, no. 5 (October, 1973): 637–646; but see also F. Clemente and W. J. Sauer, "Voluntary Associations and Minority Status—Comment and Extension," *American Sociological Review*, 40, no. 1 (February, 1975): 115–117.

14. This pattern is of course parallel with the general regularity, noted earlier, that the top few persons in any type of achievement get much of the prestige available and are talked about more frequently.

tion is created. If they care little about it, they resist information or evaluation about a specific reputation.

ESTEEM, FAME, AND INTEREST IN AN ACTIVITY

But how are we to account for the relatively greater ease with which some reputations cross barriers defined by separate activities and interests? This question leads us unwillingly into at least some analysis of fame, a phenomenon with many elusive facets on which philosophers have mused for ages. I do not propose to explain it adequately, and my modest aim is only to distinguish it from esteem.

The distinction is both simple and operationally clear, however much they overlap concretely. People (or organizations) are more or less famous if they are known to many or few; they enjoy more or less esteem if people respect them more or less. Ordinary people can easily make this distinction between being well known and being well thought of, and often they do. They have, after all, heard of famous scoundrels, and they take for granted that some highly specialized, obscure activities (for example, mathematics, astronomy) exist in which esteem, but little public renown, can be gained for achievement. But ordinary usage is much less precise, not because ordinary individuals are muddled but because these and related factors overlap. To exclaim, "He's famous!" usually means, for example, that the person is both well known *and* esteemed. The remark also assumes that the person is probably successful in the prosaic sense of having a good job or income. The term can carry that much meaning because in fact fame, prestige, and success are correlated in most social settings.

Our formula for the flow of prestige applies to networks or chains of people and organizations that are linked by a shared interest in a given activity, whether it is solid state physics or baseball. It does not apply to the flow of reputation from one activity to a very different one. This limitation can be clearly seen by considering a few concrete examples.

That people within a given type of activity (as participants or as part of the audience) are more likely to know its more esteemed performers is a normal by-product of their interest in that activity. They interact more with others who care about it and who want to talk about it than with those who do not. This selective attention can be widely observed: People read newspapers with a greater interest in some things than others—people who sail will "find" far more news items about sailing than will outsiders who consider that activity a bore.[15] Piccolo virtuosos at the highest levels are known to but few, while many baseball fans will read

15. And, in a parallel regularity, as Paul F. Lazarsfeld *et al.* reported long ago in *The People's Choice*, 3d ed. (New York: Columbia University Press, 1968 [1944]), political partisans read and remember far more information about their favorite candidates or party than about their opponents.

with interest about the performances of modest pitchers in bush league teams.

Correspondingly, since far more people are more interested in some activities than in others, far more are likely to know who the great ones are in those fields. Most will not know, for example, even one star lacrosse player, unless they happen to live in one of the states where Indians once played that game. By contrast, almost everyone knows that Babe Ruth was once a great hitter, John Barrymore a fine actor, and Al Capone a racketeer much respected within his own specailized métier. In some activities, persons of even modest attainments are known to many people simply because what they do exposes them to many people—in politics, sports, the performing arts both popular and highbrow, wartime battles, and popular writing. They are so exposed because their kind of activity is of great interest to many, who demand news about the people in it. To explore the psychological dimensions of that interest is beyond the scope of this book, although it seems clear enough that some of these activities (the performing arts, sports, popular writing) simply give pleasure to at least the audiences; and others (war, politics) are seen both as dramatic and as having immediate consequences for almost everyone. By contrast, in spite of the fact that a high percentage of the American population has been engaged in some kind of business (and should thus be "interested" in it), public relations experts must work hard to make any businessmen well known.[16]

It hardly needs emphasis as well that what people view as fameworthy will vary across cultures. Russians follow chess tournaments with more excitement than Americans do. Countries with no more concern about animal suffering than Spain's have nevertheless not given much attention to bull fighting. Sumo wrestling outside Japan has not generated a great following. In such cases, the reputation of even the best will not easily cross national boundaries because beyond them the audience is not very interested in the activity itself.

All these contrasting examples underline the effect of the kind of activity on fame, and they once more suggest why a given reputation will cross some group boundaries more easily than others. Our interest in people makes them newsworthy, and we may be interested in hearing about a person or an organization because of his prestige in a given activity—but only if we are interested in that activity. It is not, of course, the prestige of that activity that primarily determines our interest—an

16. Bennett M. Berger, "Ecstatic Youth," in *Looking for America* (Englewood Cliffs, N.J.: Prentice-Hall, 1971), pp. 118–140, argues that a society "apparently unable convincingly to glorify those men who manifest its most representative virtues may be said to be a society which doesn't like itself very much" (p. 133). John K. Galbraith, in *The Affluent Society* (London: Penguin, 1965), pp. 80–84, 162–164, states that businessmen do not enjoy much acclaim, as evidenced by the rise of the public relations industry.

interest that may be highly personal or instead shaped much by national culture (for example, baseball).[17]

We have noted how prestige within an activity and people's interest in the activity itself increase the fame of an individual or an organization. But, by referring to especially famous individuals, it has been intimated that still more subtle factors may also affect how far reputations can travel.

The journalistic aphorism "people make news" refers implicitly to one of these factors: Some people are newsworthy because they are viewed as glamorous, exciting, or charismatic. In almost any kind of activity, some persons arouse more attention than others, even at the same apparent level of competence. Many essays and comments have been written about this personal trait, and it is safe to say that no explanations of it are satisfactory. A star in show business, for example, is defined by the responses of audiences, not by qualities seen in the star. Specifically, stardom is not measured by competence in acting, but by whether audiences are excited when a given person steps on the stage.[18] In politics as in the university, in baseball as in the ministry, gossip and stories are more frequent, and travel farther, about some people than about others—but it should be understood that to say such persons are more glamorous or charismatic is merely to label that response without explaining it. Whatever the cause, such a response certainly increases the fame of an individual and probably his or her esteem as well.

DIFFERENT GROUPS AS INDEPENDENT
SUBMARKETS OF PRESTIGE

Just as individuals compete with one another for admiration, so do organizations and groupings of all kinds. They compete in various ways. One important way is by attempting to become the main dispenser of prestige or other rewards. That is, if group members can convince each other that one another's respect is the only esteem worth working for, they can control each other more easily, and more fully harness each other's energies toward group goals. To the extent that a given organization or group becomes a more or less closed prestige market, its members will find each other's esteem worth far more than that of any other group. Some communes and religious sects have tried to do this, often by isolating themselves from the larger society. Of course, nations accomplish it by restricting who may enter or leave their boundaries.[19]

17. Although the hypothesis that there is a rough correlation between prestige of activity and its being known might seem likely, closer examination suggests that it contains difficult conceptual problems. It cannot be easily formulated in any way that permits real testing.

18. So, similarly, one is recognized as a star, not by the critics' concession that one is a fine performer, but by having one's name put in lights *above* the title of the play. Potential ticket buyers are thought to be more likely to come to the theater upon learning that a certain person is in the play than on learning the title of the play.

19. However, some theorists have argued that some colonial societies were really "dual societies," since the colonial rulers and the natives interacted, but both segments of the whole maintained

Few ordinary groups can achieve so happy a state. Members and their group as a unit can most easily avoid competition with others if their own norms and evaluations are quite different from those of the larger society; then, by that standard, outsiders must rank low. But unless the group is willing to isolate itself it must engage in social and material exchanges with other groups, thus face the evaluations of others, with the attendant risk that the group and its members will *not* be granted much esteem. To the extent, in turn, that the group's allocation of esteem cannot fully control the flow of benefits to members—because outsiders also determine that flow—it cannot command the allegiance of members as much. That is, as it accepts the standards and responses of the larger society and its other subgroups, the group becomes less distinctive and less able to persuade its members that they should continue to give time, energy, and money to their group.[20]

These tensions are exhibited in many groups. That is, the group may be able to achieve a "monopoly," but only by becoming isolated and losing the benefits of exchanging with other subgroups. Or it can maximize the benefits of interaction and exchange with other groups, meeting their standards and evaluations, whereupon it is less able to maintain control over the acts and commitments of its members.

As soon as social transactions occur across the social boundaries of other subgroups, those others are not bound to accept one another's self-evaluations, and instead they impose their own evaluations. Since they, too, want to be esteemed for their qualities and performances (which are likely to vary from one group to another), the subgroups of a society are not likely to be fully in accord with each other. More succinctly, they must be in some degree of accord to interact at all; but each will have its own somewhat different set of evaluations. That flow and change in evaluation is accentuated by the fact that human beings may be members of several groups, and thus carry their esteem judgments from one to another; they may also leave one group or organization to join another.[21]

The differences among such subgroups or subsystems support the assertions of contemporary sociologists that there is no "value consensus" to be observed in industrial societies. Such a consensus, Shils asserts, is one of

---

divergent value systems and social structures. On this point, see Julius Herman Boeke, *Economics and Economic Policy of Dual Societies, as Exemplified by Indonesia* (New York: International Secretariat, Institute of Pacific Relations, 1953); and Peter P. Ekeh, "Colonialism and the Two Publics in Africa," *Comparative Studies in Society and History*, 17 (January, 1975): 91–112.

20. For a discussion of the dynamics outlined here as they pertain to the position of scientists working in industry, see Herbert A. Shepard, "Nine Dilemmas in Industrial Research," in Bernard Barber and Walter Hirsch, eds., *The Sociology of Science* (Glencoe, Ill.: Free Press, 1962).

21. Similar processes are observable in family interaction. George P. Murdock pointed out long ago, for example, that the rules of incest and exogamy require young adults to obtain spouses outside their own families. Consequently, any special information that a given family possesses may be spread through the society; deviant attitudes or practices are subjected to others' scrutiny; and the family unit itself is prevented from being wholly independent. See his *Social Structure* (New York: Macmillan, 1949), chap. 10, esp. pp. 296ff.

the necessary conditions for being able to rank social positions along a unitary distribution of deference or prestige.[22] On the other hand, the necessity for exchanges and transactions across the social boundaries of groups explains why, in fact, there is considerable consensus just the same.

The differences also suggest that to the extent that a subgroup really does form a social subsystem, it is partly a monopoly. One of the noneconomic benefits of remaining within one's neighborhood ethnic group or organization is precisely the avoidance of a free social market, that is, the avoidance of unremitting and full-scale competition in court-ship and marriage, friendship groups, social clubs, and general esteem.[23] Occupations, organizations, and social groups generally give themselves a somewhat higher rank than others do, even when they accept their general ranking in the larger society.[24] Most of them are not international markets.[25]

There are technical reasons for not insisting that each group, social category, or organization can be viewed as a market in the strict economic sense.[26] On the other hand, the *disagreements* among different groups, social strata, or organizations do not in themselves negate the existence of "economic" market-like behavior, especially with reference to: the move-ment of people from one market to another in order to increase their prestige; the effort of organizations or groups to recruit people with more esteem; or the effect of various submarkets on the esteem that each may give for various traits or behaviors.

In fact, the commodity market works very well with a similar pattern of widespread disagreement. For example, even if Cadillacs or Kawasaki 750

22. Edward A. Shils, "Deference," in Edward Laumann, Paul Siegel, and Robert W. Hodge, eds., *The Logic of Social Hierarchies* (Chicago: Markham, 1970), pp. 436–437. For Shils' other essays on values and consensus as they relate to deference, see *Center and Periphery: Essays in Macrosociology* (Chicago: University of Chicago Press, 1975). See also Randall Collins and Joan Annett, "A Short History of Deference and Demeanor," in Collins' *Conflict Sociology: Toward an Explanatory Science* (New York: Academic, 1975), pp. 161–224.

23. See Gerald B. Suttles, *The Social Construction of Communities* (Chicago: University of Chicago Press, 1972).

24. This pattern was observable in the 1947 North-Hatt NORC study of occupational prestige. Robert K. Merton also notes it in his article "Insiders and Outsiders," *American Journal of Sociology*, 77 (July, 1972): 9–47, where he takes note as well of Theodore Caplow's examination of thirty-three different kinds of organizations, ranging from dance studios and Skid Row missions to big banks, and finds that members overestimated the (actual) prestige of their organization some eight times as often as they underestimated it, as compared with outsiders' judgments. See Caplow, *Principles of Organization* (New York: Harcourt, Brace & World, 1964), pp. 213ff.

25. A NORC study of blue collar workers and managers found that workers define the importance of any increase in pay or prestige of their jobs by reference to their immediate social context, while managers define it by reference to the overall system of income and prestige in the United States as a whole, the managers emphasizing job prestige much more than do blue collar workers: Curt Tausky, "Occupational Mobility Interests," *Canadian Review of Sociology and Anthropology*, 4 (November, 1967): 242–249. Arthur Stinchcombe uses as an index of the separateness of sociology departments whether they exchange graduate students with one another. Departments in different countries do not typically exchange students, and low-prestige and high-prestige departments in this study do not. See Stinchcombe, "A Structural Analysis of Sociology," *American Sociologist*, 10 (May, 1975): 57–64.

26. For example, there is no monetary unit; the market is not free; and people cannot easily find out what "the" price is.

motorcycles were given away, not everyone would wish to own one; and so for black olives, dishes of raw fish, and simple black dresses. The flow of personnel, money, and products within a market *depends* in part upon such widespread disagreements as to their relative worth. Total agreement that only certain products are desirable would wreak temporary havoc on the market and ultimately change it fundamentally. There would then be no elasticity of demand, and no one would be willing to substitute one product for another, so that the demand for that narrow set of commodities would surge, with corresponding steep rises in prices. The products not chosen would plummet in value. The number of products sold would drop greatly, and much of the marketing structure would disappear.

Instead, while one person, subgroup, or class is avidly shopping for Product X, another seeks Product Y. So, similarly, some people admire those who can play baroque recorder music, while others give their esteem to the stars of the Little League team. People who disagree may become less friendly toward one another than they were, or admire each other less. Or, they may come to share one another's opinions.[27] Since everyone acts in very different role relations over the course of a day or a year, everyone also admires very different people or activities at different points in time.

Such a view assumes as unproblematic the fact that some commodities may not be desired at all here and there. In some neighborhoods, philosophical treatises and artichokes will not be sold at all. Most people, correspondingly, give little attention to the possible prestige rankings of most people, as well as to many activities.

On the other hand, they *are* concerned with the evaluations of other groups and organizations about *themselves*, either as individuals or as a group. People are only rarely content to be totally self-enclosed within the system of evaluations in their own social groups. They bring their concerns, opinions, and pressures to bear on others. They are aware of the prestige rankings that other people, groups, and organizations make and see the effects of those evaluations upon their own fate.

One of these sets of consequences is the movement of individuals from one social group or organization to another—the flow of people to different positions in the social structure over time. This process is in part determined by the decisions people make about whether they might gain or lose in prestige by moving to different social positions.

MOVING TO A DIFFERENT SUBSYSTEM

Most changes in social networks or groups occur as a by-product of geographical or occupational mobility or take place gradually as a result of other people's decisions over time. Few people spend much time deliberately altering their social circles in order to increase their prestige

27. Paul F. Lazarsfeld and Robert K. Merton, "Friendship as Social Process: A Substantive and Methodological Analysis," in Monroe Berger, Theodore Abel, and Charles Page, eds., *Freedom and Control in Modern Society* (New York: Van Nostrand, 1954), pp. 18–66.

ranking.[28] Of course, almost everyone engages in fantasies about how one's life would be changed if one moved in different circles. Everyone makes real calculations as well, about the advantages of particular moves such as changing jobs. In any event, whether people plot a campaign for their own advancement or are the pawns of others' decisions, they are aware of the losses and gains that occur thereby. They cannot easily avoid learning about them, precisely because in their new social positions they interact with many others in different positions and thus observe how much respect or deference others pay them when they change. Moreover, they are likely to know in advance of those evaluations.

Even if, in general, people *would* move to different groups or organizations in order to obtain more respect, in an imperfect world one must as usual consider whether one *could* make such a move, and for how much investment and at what real costs. In general, the more esteemed a person is within his or her own group or organization (except for highly disesteemed groups) the easier it is for him or her to enter a more prestigious organization or grouping, even a supposedly ascriptive one such as the stratum of dukes. The advantage of doing so may seem obvious, since others evaluate persons at first mainly by their memberships. Joining a more highly respected grouping or organization will (with some qualifications to be noted later) increase the esteem received from others.

But the investments and costs are also likely to be high, and these may become the focus of conscious calculation. As Paul A. Samuelson has remarked, there *is* room at the top, simply because it is so hard for anyone to get there. One may have to perform better, and at very different activities, if one enters a more highly esteemed organization or group. A different social circle may, for example, be made up of people from varied ethnic or class backgrounds, tastes, and patterns of recreation, and one's formerly applauded social routines may be received by them in awkward silence. A new job setting or promotion—and especially later promotions, after that—may be hedged about with many restrictions that do not rest on excellent performance alone. Formal education may be used as a criterion for later promotions even after one has been given an initial job, and it is often used as a basis for social acceptance. Medical schools have practiced various forms of sex, age, and ethnic discrimination in their admissions policies, but entrance into medical school is only the first step in medical training. At many later stages of study, sponsorship and establishment of practice, these and other criteria will still play a role. A person from Arkansas who is made editor of a magazine will find it harder to be taken seriously by the New York intelligentsia than will a person reared in New York City.

That is, even an invitation to join a more esteemed organization or

28. That so many novels give such prominence to people who coolly calculate how best to climb socially is not an index of their prevalence in real life, but it is evidence that people are fascinated by that effort even while deploring it.

social group does not erase all the barriers the individual may experience at further stages. The initial increase in esteem that one may get by entering a somewhat more respected group or organization may be only a prelude to a later failure. Consequently, even the person who believes in his or her own capacities may well do some calculating before setting forth on that road.

Part of the risk calculation is of course the problem of getting information in advance. In social perhaps even more than in economic calculations the information is likely to be costly, or impossible to get. Whether one has enough talent, whether the social barriers are too high, how one will feel about the decision later on, and so on, only future experience will disclose. In a close approximation to a free economic market, by contrast, people need not invest much in the cost of information to make a rational decision; there is a known price, for known qualities of the product. Individual ignorance costs much less in such a market, and one can buy or sell at the public price with little risk that someone else is getting a much better deal. In decisions about how to choose one's social or occupational memberships, by contrast, people cannot predict in advance what the total costs over time will be, or the chances of an acceptable payoff. The cost of being ignorant is high, but it may be impossible to obtain adequate information; or the cost of getting it may be prohibitive.

Another common type of calculation is classical, indeed Aesopian: Is it better to be a good-sized frog in a small pond, or a small one in a more esteemed, big pond? Both Aesop and more recent social research suggest that the former alternative may well be wiser.[29] For example, to enter a highly esteemed college yields some prestige to the individual. Unless that person is outstanding in some way, however, it is likely that he or she will, confronted by so many other able people, begin to settle for much lower aspirations. Since others are very able, and some are much abler than oneself, one sees that it is sensible not to compete with the best of them. But this may actually be an error; for other people of similar abilities, but in a less challenging and prestigious college, may set higher aspirations for themselves and go on to achieve them.

Even if we omit the problem of later aspirations and achievements, a similar result may occur. People who are just able enough to enter a more esteemed group or organization may accept that opportunity, but then find that they are ranked in the new setting at a considerably lower level than in their former group or organization. The esteem they get from outsiders may be somewhat higher than before. However, the esteem they get from their peers and fellow members is usually much more important, since this is their reference group, and within that setting they now

---

29. See James A. Davis, "The Campus as a Frog Pond: An Application of the Theory of Relative Deprivation to Career Decisions of College Men," *American Journal of Sociology*, 72 (July, 1966): 17–31. See also Michael S. Bassis, "The Campus as a Frog Pond: A Theoretical and Empirical Reassessment," *American Journal of Sociology*, 82 (May, 1977): 1318–1326.

receive less respect than they formerly did. For many people, the net result is eventually experienced as a loss.

A decision to enter a large college or university (or other organization) may lead to a similar result. If students go to small colleges, they are more likely to be satisfied with their success in them than if they go to large colleges. In the smaller setting, the ratio of positions to people is much higher than in the larger college. For example, there has to be a certain number of students on the first team in basketball, tennis, or football; there are so many posts on the daily newspaper; there is a limited number of positions in the student government—and all of these must be distributed among a small population in the one instance but a large population in the other. Or, more generally, in a large organization there are far more able competitors for any given set of higher-level posts. The larger number of people available for any given position may well have a depressing effect upon individual self-esteem.[30]

In addition to the problem of deciding whether one may gain esteem by entering a more respected subsystem and being successful in it, or gain esteem among outsiders by entering it even though one is not very respected by its members, an additional set of calculations may focus on which kinds of gains or losses the new position will bring. Some subsystems offer more political influence than esteem, or more money than respect, or more friendly interaction but less of other gains. A research chemist may consider whether the added prestige of being a university professor is worth more than the added income of working in an industrial laboratory. Many socially mobile people have had to consider whether they should drop their congenial set of friends in favor of a new network of higher social rank; or, if they are downwardly mobile, whether they should hang onto their old acquaintances of higher rank even though to move in that social network is now too expensive, and they suffer from feeling disesteemed. But in these decisions the individual is no longer weighing only the possibility of gains or losses in prestige, but the gains and losses in other resources as compared with a rise or fall in prestige.

THE FREE RIDER

The foregoing discussion assumes as correct the general finding that when individuals enter a more esteemed group or organization their own prestige rises, since in the eyes of others they share in the group esteem once they become members. Data on prestigious university departments show that for any given quantity of productivity, scientists at a more esteemed university receive more recognition than those at a less esteemed one.[31] At present, we do not know whether most people accept the

30. See the research of R. Barker and P. Gump, *Big School, Small School* (Stanford: Stanford University Press, 1964). This finding may also be related to crowding processes, where the competition is at least partly for space, but also for position.

31. Whether that would also be true for quality has not, as far as I know, been tested. Jonathan

opportunity of joining a more esteemed group when it is offered, although it is my impression that most do. The data suggest, and people seem to believe, that by joining a more respected group or organization they will gain in prestige, whatever their present level of esteem. Some people also suppose that the accepting organization validates the higher evaluation of recruits no matter what their quality may be. This analysis will question that belief, and will also move on to the still more general theoretical problem of whether, on average, to enter an organization is to lose (or gain) in esteem. Exploration of these relationships should further clarify the processes by which people and reputations flow from one part of the social structure to another.

Although research now suggests what common sense assumes, that a person does gain prestige simply by moving into a more respected social unit than his or her present one—and, leaving aside the problem of possible failure after entering—can we be sure this holds for everyone? Does anyone ever *add* prestige to the more esteemed group upon entering it?[32] Is everyone who enters a free rider? If an esteemed organization or group can confer prestige on everyone who enters it, that regularity seems akin to the Matthew Effect (challenged in the chapter on subversion). According to both patterns, presumably, persons are given additional honor because they have already been honored.

But the two patterns are not the same; they are complementary. If both are correctly described, they form an especially subversive evasion of rules about how people should obtain prestige. That is, according to the Matthew Effect, having received some honor or prestige leads to getting more. One way to get more is to join an esteemed organization. Then, having got that additional esteem, the individual will get still more. These two supporting processes would thus permit some people to over-step their equals in talent or achievement, if they received some honor at an early phase of their career. Indeed, many critics believe that it is precisely by such jumps that the most esteemed people arrived at eminence.

My later reformulation of the Matthew Effect is that those who receive higher honors are more likely than those who did not to have already received honors. Or: those who receive honors at Time 1 are more likely at Time 2 to receive still another honor than are those who receive no honors

---

and Stephen Cole have shown that at a given level of quality, the amount of productivity explains very little additional variance. See their *Social Stratification in Science* (Chicago: University of Chicago Press, 1973), pp. 104, 197, for data showing that visibility of the scientist is influenced by rank of the department. Whether or not a new Ph.D.'s first job is in a high-ranking department is greatly affected by the rank of the department from which he or she received the degree.

32. Of course this question is meant to be rhetorical, for one can think of extreme cases in which the new person obviously brings prestige, though he or she moves from a less esteemed department— e.g., the instance of Nobel Prize winners. On the claims of various organizations to distant or close connections with such honored scientists, see Harriet Zuckerman, "The Sociology of the Nobel Prizes," *Scientific American*, 27 (November, 1967): 25–33.

at Time 1. However, the examination of careers in any field will show that most people who receive honors at one stage of their careers do not continue indefinitely to receive more. Indeed, if that were so, a high percentage of the entire population would eventually end at the top. In fact almost everyone, including those who are honored early, falls far short of that rank.

The implicit assertion that everyone is a free rider who joins a more esteemed organization can also be questioned. That claim seems unlikely even at first glance, because then no organization could ever drop in esteem even if it continued to recruit incompetents; it could continue indefinitely to confer esteem on its new recruits without regard to their achievements. (And, again, some critics make that accusation against elite organizations.) It is also evident that members of respected organizations do not act as though they believe this assertion, since they typically show concern about who is to be recruited and feel that bringing in less esteemed recruits will reduce their collective rank.[33]

Note that the correlative question about the lower end of prestige rankings can be asked: Does everyone lose who joins a low-ranking collectivity, no matter what his or her prior esteem was? It seems evident that if a collectivity makes wise judgments, it will gain somewhat in prestige from new members whose contributions are greater than its average. If the ranking of any organization is not to fall, those who contribute more will have to furnish the increment that new members of lesser eminence and achievement cannot bring. It may also be observed that organizations do not typically suppose that all recruits have somehow been raised in esteem by entrance; for when newcomers fail to live up to the standards expected, they may be asked to leave—again suggesting that the prestige of the collectivity can exist only if it is actively maintained. That is, it cannot be maintained if recruits do not contribute on average as much as present members, or even more.

To consider the various possibilities:

1. The collectivity loses because it has accepted a person who is viewed as less able; but the person gains. In that case, he or she is a free rider.

2. The person who joins is viewed as more distinguished or potentially more distinguished than others.[34] At a minimum, the organization either gains in prestige or maintains its standing.

---

33. That groups or organizations do attempt to protect their less able members, as they also try to protect themselves against those members, is easily observable. However, precisely because they do make that effort, they show that they do not really believe that everyone who enters can be automatically raised in rank without regard to his or her qualities. On the protective processes, see William J. Goode, "The Protection of the Inept," in *Explorations in Social Theory*, pp. 121–144.

34. John K. Galbraith [Mark Epernay] has noted in *The McLandress Dimension* (Boston: Houghton Mifflin, 1963) that in Washington (and this may be generalized to almost all other career situations) an individual enjoys greater esteem if he or she is judged to be rising in influence and prestige.

3. The recruit is no higher in prestige than the average in the collectivity but goes on to achieve more; he or she is a free rider for a while, then helps to keep up the standing of the organization. But for the career as a whole, that individual has contributed to the esteem of the collectivity, and it would be difficult to prove that he or she had gained an unearned increment merely by joining it.[35]

RECRUITMENT DECISIONS

Dr. Samuel Johnson, asserting his own city's rank, once commented that the fairest prospect a Scotsman ever sees is the highroad leading to London. However enticing that prospect, the aspirant must still face the decisions of others as to whether his or her qualities and performances will yield more respect in the new groups and organizations he or she desires to enter.

In the recruitment process, as in most continuing linkages, most alterations in personnel do not substantially alter the prestige rankings of either the individuals or their groups and organizations. Even if a group tries to make the best decisions in order to maximize the prestige of new recruits, and individuals try to do the same when making the choice of which groups or organizations to join, the outcome will not be greatly different from the rankings beforehand. The group can only command so many resources, including prestige, in order to attract new members; and these potential members can obtain entrance mainly to groups or organizations at about their own level. Here then, as in mate choice, where the process yields homogamy (like marries like), the result follows not mainly from wanting to associate with others of like rank, but from the inability to obtain higher-ranking members or to join higher-ranking groups.

Since organizations and groups are evaluated both by what activities they excel in and which people they recruit (except for ethnic and racial groups, who do not recruit), and these in turn determine in part what other resources they obtain and how much control or influence they enjoy over events of importance to them, they seek to obtain as excellent a flow of newcomers as they can. As in all such choice and information processes, they run the risk of overlooking excellent potential members, or of allowing people to enter who will perform poorly. Even when they are aware that their own rank or other resources do not permit limitless excellent recruits, they can nevertheless calculate the best tactics to pursue.

The prestige ranking of organizations or groups changes even more slowly than that of individuals. As a consequence, a collective can attempt to persuade an individual to join by offering him or her a somewhat higher

35. Talcott Parsons seems to suppose that in the typical case the younger professor is "lent" some prestige capital and later "pays it back." From the perspective of senior Harvard professors, that may be a common instance. More dispassionate observers might deny that even at Harvard this cell is so well populated. See Talcott Parsons and Gerald M. Platt, "The American Academic Profession: A Pilot Study," mimeograph (National Science Foundation, Grant GS 513: March, 1968), p. I 30.

rank or post than he or she holds already, but it is not possible to change quickly the basic esteem or disesteem of belonging to the group itself. A group may attempt some kind of mix of prestige and money, by offering a somewhat higher rank and less money or vice versa, but since the basic esteem of belonging to the group at all does not change quickly, corporate bodies or informal networks do not have much freedom in contriving such mixes.

They are especially limited in such tradeoffs because, if the prestige of a group is relatively low, typically the group is also short of money—which might otherwise make joining it more desirable than the prestige alone would. Sometimes, of course, new organizations that are heavily capitalized can make tradeoffs. A few universities (for example, the University of Chicago in the 1890's) have succeeded in following this tactic, that is, offering much larger salaries than usual even though the basic prestige of belonging to a university at its inception has typically not been high.

In general, organizations or groups can offer or pay out to both their members and newcomers only what they possess in prestige, money, or influence, or what they can earn by current accomplishments. If they attempt to offer more to an incomer than current members feel is justified by reference to their own positions, the result may be considerable disaffection inside the unit. It the amounts paid out to newcomers are too high, the organization may lose too much of its basic capital or its resources. For these reasons new organizations try to begin with as large a capital of prestige as they can. They may attempt to recruit highly esteemed boards of directors or advisors, or seek the auspices of already existing, esteemed organizations, groups, and leaders.[36]

An alternative mode of prestige capitalization can be used by a political or religious sect, which attempts to create a subsociety whose standards will supersede those of the surrounding society, so that the group or organization becomes the major source of esteem for its members. In effect, they create their own "coinage" in a closed market. They reject the standards by which people give respect in the surrounding society, paying respect to one another on the basis of their own norms and values. A conspicuous recent example of this religiopolitical process is the formation of the Black Muslims, and its sudden rise to prominence during the 1960's, after many similar organizations had enjoyed less success in prior decades.

Large organizations with a high prospective turnover can efficiently recruit newcomers, expecting to reject most of them eventually. Some instead invest much energy and time in the search for adequate information about potential recruits. Perhaps the simplest type of information

36. Even the research organization RAND, backed by the U.S. government, did this in its early period of organization in order to obtain better contracts. See Bruce L. R. Smith, *The RAND Corporation* (Cambridge: Harvard University Press, 1966), p. 72.

obtainable is how the individual is respected by others, but this can lead to many incorrect judgments. One study ascertained that many assistant professors were hired by major universities that paid little attention to their actual work, the hiring decision being made primarily on the basis of senior professors' reports, that is, the candidates' prestige ranking among the outgoing crop of Ph.D.'s.[37] Indeed, that report led to increased investments in information-seeking on the part of many departments.

With reference to some types of groups and activities, even fairly good information may be only partially relevant, since the newcomer will be engaged in tasks that he or she had not done before. Some people, that is, move upward (in accordance with the Peter Principle) to a level where they are incompetent, although no data suggest this as the most common pattern.

As noted earlier, ethnic and racial groups cannot decide whom they will accept—though of course where an ethnic group is dominant within a society (for example, "WASPS" in the United States until fairly recently) it may decide to "overlook" an alien background if the person in question has earned enough esteem. On the other hand, ethnic groups can embark upon a strategy of investment, in which they attempt to build a wide variety of group-related activities that will encompass even members who might ordinarily leave the group for other social circles. They can also embark upon antidefamation programs, aimed at raising their esteem in the society as a whole. These programs typically take the form of both political protest against discrimination and prejudice, and propaganda that extols the contributions of members of the group—thus emphasizing that as a collective they deserve more respect than they now get. On a more trivial level, of course, esteem-raising is the prime aim of public relations and political propaganda campaigns that corporations pay for. These campaigns are also structurally similar to the efforts of former members of a private school, college, or philanthropic organization toward obtaining funds in order to develop new programs and gain sponsors and recruits to enhance the prestige enjoyed by the organization.

If the newcomers and the older members fail in their efforts to accomplish any widely respected goals, both they and the group or organization will lose in prestige. Generally, the group will also lose if its more esteemed members leave.[38] This can be pursued a step further (following our earlier suggestion that top-level personnel receive a large amount of the esteem allocated within an organization) by asking how much prestige an organization loses if a leader dies or leaves the organization voluntarily. It is rare that the death or retirement of a corporation president has any

37. Reece McGee and Theodore Caplow, *The Academic Marketplace* (Garden City, N.Y.: Doubleday, 1965).

38. Jane Jacobs asserts that a prime "cause" of slums is that a neighborhood fails to hold some of its more able and respected members. See *The Death and Life of Great American Cities* (New York: Vintage, 1961), chap. 15, "Unslumming and Slumming."

effect on either its prestige or its stock value. This suggests that the amount of esteem embodied or inherent in the collectivity (like its capital) is massively greater than that of the leadership.

By contrast, smaller organizations may expend much of their available resources in order to recruit one or more "stars" who will, it is hoped, enhance greatly the prestige of the collective unit. A university department may drop quickly in prestige with the loss of two or three of its respected professors, or may react to such losses by intensive recruiting efforts. In professional sports, it is widely thought that two or three key players can turn a team's losses into victories, which are the coin of prestige in that realm. Consequently, purchases and trades of players are thought to be crucial events in the changing ratings of teams. The fate of collectivities and their members is especially clear when an organization or group enjoys a great success, either temporarily or over a longer period. If a baseball team wins the World Series, everyone associated with it rises in prestige, while those who performed especially well are temporary stars whatever their usual ranking. It is much less clear that any but the top leadership gain much esteem when a corporation has an especially outstanding year. Few people outside a small segment of the business community will grant much respect for that. Within that subgroup, of course, the top corporate leadership is not only identified with the success; it is also thought of as responsible for it.

A correlative question can be raised at this point: If an organization or social group fails, or drops greatly in prestige, do all its individual members lose? If an organization fails, or a corporation goes bankrupt, it loses greatly in esteem (to the extent that people know about the event at all), but not all its members suffer a corresponding loss in prestige. Lower-level employees typically believe that their chances of raises or promotions are determined by their superiors, not by success of the organization, and they are basically correct. A typist may lose his or her job if the company fails, but that failure does not affect by much his or her rating as a typist. Indeed, this generally applies to all employees whose competence can be measured, and so it holds as well even for some high-level technical staff (accountants, chemists, lawyers).

Of course, top-level leaders will suffer loss of prestige if their performances have caused the company to fail, and if this is known to others. As in the case of a very successful year, the "public" that knows the facts is likely to be made up only of a small network of peers in the business world; and their esteem for those leaders will drop considerably. On the other hand, in the larger society outside that network, such leaders lose far less esteem than the organization that failed, for their performance is not typically well known, and they can still be identified as "the former president of X Company," or "former chancellor of Y University." That is, they are still identified as members of a highly-ranked occupation, even though their competence within it is not known. Outsiders assume their performance is average.

Quite parallel with the hypothesis that top leaders will lose some prestige among the people who identify them as having contributed to the downfall of an organization or collectivity is Schumpeter's assertion that it is especially the upper classes who lose their positions when a country suffers a massive catastrophe such as a conquest or an unsuccessful war.[39] Since members of those classes hold the key political positions in a society, and they are likely to be held responsible for the national humiliation, they may well lose their positions. Indeed, a large number of revolutions have been preceded by unsuccessful wars.

JOINING A CORPORATE BODY

The question of who gains or loses when anyone joins an organization can be phrased in a broader form by asking two distinct questions: whether joining a collectivity generally yields a gain in prestige; and, since one aim in seeking prestige is the ability to control social events, whether that gain (if any) yields more or less control than the individual would enjoy outside the collective over events the individual cares about. The first question asks whether joining will generally cause a loss or gain in a reward or resource, such as money, political influence, or respect. The second asks whether the individual will gain or lose in his or her ability to control decisions about important events.

The second question is a specification of Coleman's query about the loss of power an individual suffers when he or she joins a corporate body (a family, the state, a labor union, a corporation).[40] He uses "power" in the traditional sense of being able to get one's way, without respect to the resources used (friendship, money, prestige, force or the threat of force).[41] Since prestige is a major component of power in that broad sense, my formulation here does not represent a distortion, and Coleman's answer should (as it is stated, without distinction between these resources) apply to prestige or any other component of power, or control over social events.

In raising the second question, Coleman both points to many links among individuals and corporate bodies, and phrases with mathematical precision a lament that humanists have been expressing for generations. They proclaim that we have been selling our birthright for a mess of pottage: We have been giving up our freedom, our ability to control events, by yielding our resources when we join corporate bodies, which in turn pay us many benefits (health insurance, money for material goods and travel) for those resources.

The corporate body, having now so many resources to deploy as a collective, can execute vast enterprises of which an individual is not

39. Joseph Schumpeter, *Imperialism and Social Classes* (New York: Augustus M. Kelley, 1951), p. 177.

40. James S. Coleman, "Loss of Power," *American Sociological Review*, 38 (February, 1973): 1–17.

41. And for these reasons, I have suggested that the use of the term in this sense reduces the clarity of sociopolitical analysis. See "The Place of Force in Human Society," *American Sociological Review*, 37 (October, 1972): esp. pp. 510ff.

capable, and it has gained in its ability to control events *it* cares about. Unfortunately, as both Coleman and many social philosophers have pointed out, these are likely to be the same events as those which concern individuals. As a consequence, given certain assumptions about the voting rules of such a corporate body, people as individual actors feel they have much less influence over events than individuals once had, and indeed their feeling represents an objective reality: In fact they do enjoy less control over events they care about. The free-lance writer who becomes a regular employee of a magazine, the farmer who joins a giant cooperative, the plumber who becomes part of the maintenance staff of a school system usually feel this way: They have lost some prestige, and have less control over what they do. The effect arises from the cause stipulated, but many people are troubled by that experience—Tawny commented about such trade-offs by remarking that ". . . since even quite common men have souls, no increase in material wealth will compensate them for arrangements which insult their self-respect and impair their freedom."[42] Coleman sees the impairing process as somewhat more complex: People do accept the compensation, but they vaguely or consciously feel a loss of freedom just the same.

However, Coleman's answer to our second question requires some emendation and expansion, which have bearing on our first question of whether joining a corporate body or organization yields a gain in prestige. To consider these questions, we must distinguish among several relationships: Over time, have individuals lost influence or prestige, relative to various corporate bodies? Second, do they have a feeling of loss? And third, do they actually lose now, when they enter an organization?

Let us first note that over historical time people have lost control generally, because the ratio between the ability of individuals to control events they care about and the magnitude of those events has grown much smaller. This has happened because the second term in that ratio has become larger: In the modern world, we have come to care about more events and larger events. War, highway and railroad construction, presidential campaigns, and even starting a small business all seem to require far more resources than they once did, and thus they continue to move farther out of reach of the individual's control. The events that corporate bodies wish to control have also increased in size faster than the resources of these groups, although that ratio is smaller for corporations than for individuals. Whether or not they have actually lost, people feel such a loss. At least part of that feeling arises because far more persons in the modern world feel they *should* be able to control more events and larger events than felt that way in the past. The lower and middle classes in most industrial societies have an enlarged sense of their rights, as compared with the past. They enjoy more respect from others. They do not give as

---

42. R. H. Tawney, *Religion and the Rise of Capitalism* (New York: Harcourt, Brace, 1926), p. 284.

much overt deference to those higher in rank. Far fewer accept the notion that "others" or "the rulers" should have complete authority to make decisions on all matters; instead, they feel they too should be consulted and should have some control.

That is, some part of the modern sense of losing control is not from actually having lost it (since the mass of the people never had it), but from a growing gap between the control people feel they have and what they feel they should have. Far more citizens hold a stronger belief than in the past that they should be consulted, should have a voice. In short, the *standard* for an acceptable level of control over events has risen substantially with the spread of citizenship and general participation in national affairs.

A historical dimension accentuates this feeling of loss, especially among people at higher ranks. They believe that people like themselves should have more power, since people like themselves once did have a considerable amount of control, while they see that they do not have much now. Their sense of deprivation comes not so much from their actually having lost anything in their own lifetime (or perhaps not much) as from comparisons they make with people of the same ranks in the past. This sense of loss does not, however, come even primarily from corporate gains in power.

Over the past century, people at any social rank have probably lost prestige relative to corporate bodies (including state agencies). Although this time comparison is to some extent falsely based, because measurement of the two amounts of esteem may not be possible, one can at least suggest some indices of increased respect for corporations: legal standing in court cases, freedom to engage in a wide range of activities, and deference given to those who speak for a corporate body. Collective agencies have grown in resources and have made great achievements, so that they enjoy more prestige now than in the past.

However, those patterns are distinct from losing or gaining prestige by simply joining such a corporate body, either at the time of joining or over a period of some years. The acquisition of prestige, like the development of other resources, is not a zero sum process, with only so much over time being divided among a limited number of actors whether corporate or human. An organized system, a group, or a corporation may, like a society, actually create more prestige than its aggregate members could command individually, and so many members may gain from taking part in its activities.

On the other hand, very likely a successful corporate body increases its prestige (as it certainly does its political influence) at a faster rate than do its members. Thus, even though each individual member also increases in prestige somewhat during this same period—that is, joining may bring a gain, not a loss—the members lose *relative* to the prestige gains of the corporation. This relative difference is probably greater in some realms than in others: For example, government bodies and business corporations probably gain more, relative to their individual members, than do hospitals or universities. [43]

Whether, by joining a corporate body, the individual loses any prestige or any ability to control events outside the collective—as was asked at the beginning of this discussion—will depend on how much the corporation can control the flow of prestige, or punish the individual who attempts to act contrarily to corporate decisions. As to the first, many writers, creative artists, and researchers in the sciences are members of corporate bodies that do not determine their prestige as much as do their peers or the larger society. They are therefore freer than people in other fields to act independently of those corporations. By contrast, government agencies or business corporations are better able to control the esteem their employees receive. They are also more likely to frown on or punish individual actions against their policies and decisions.

Most important in both these questions is, what are the real alternatives? If joining a corporate body causes some loss, but not joining one causes a greater loss, the choice is one of greater or lesser evils. In fact, the modern structure of opportunity for either gaining or expanding any resources, including prestige, makes any purely "individual" course of action largely illusory. [44] Most ways of earning or using esteem are closed, except within corporate bodies of some kind (businesses, schools, the government, sports teams). The real choice is not "independent, free action to control events" versus "less autonomy but more material rewards." It is instead almost no control *or* rewards for the actor as an individual person, versus some as a corporate member. A useful inquiry would be how different kinds of activities vary in the amount of individual autonomy permitted within them. [45]

In this section we have been exploring interlinkages between individuals and various collectivities, with a primary focus on whether persons gain or lose in prestige and thus influence when they enter an organization. It has been useful to ask whether individuals have lost prestige and

---

43. Of course, since both prestige and influence are unequally distributed, a few members are likely to gain, relative to others, within almost any organization that commands resources. Here, however, we are considering the general question, with reference to the average member.

44. Coleman points out the difficulties of withdrawing from various memberships, such as the state or a labor union. It is worth noting that only under very particular circumstances can this be a real option. In some nineteenth-century African kingdoms, among them the Zulu, especially despotic kings sometimes faced the problem that some part of their subjects did not rebel, but simply voted with their feet by disappearing into the bush, to settle elsewhere. Many historians have believed that the American frontier functioned similarly to some extent during most of American history; people who felt they were being controlled too much simply drifted westward. For centuries, Russian governments have restricted that choice severely, and despotic governments typically try to prevent individuals from rejecting their membership in the state. In modern Russia many people choose to work in frontier towns, where they enjoy more freedom.

45. See Peter M. Blau, *Exchange and Power in Social Life* (New York: John Wiley, 1964), p. 29: "The greater the external power of an organization, the greater are its chances of accumulating resources that put rewards at the disposal of the leadership for possible distribution among the members."

influence over time, relative to various corporate bodies; whether they experience a feeling of loss; and whether at present they actually lose or gain when they do join, if the real alternatives they face are properly weighed. The reality is somewhat more complex than our original questions revealed and suggests the usefulness of further inquiry into these social patterns.

THE CONSPIRACY HYPOTHESIS

It is often alleged that various groups and organizations are interlinked so as to deny esteem to the worthy and keep it for the privilege of the few dominant persons in those structures. People who intensely believe in any extreme political ideology, whether left or right, are also likely to believe that some small groups conspire to achieve their evil ends by manipulating the social structure. Many analysts believe that the upper class consciously plots, more or less as a unit, to consolidate or maintain their prestige and their political and economic influence over the other classes and the nation as a whole. Many graduate students believe that the more prestigious colleges and universities maintain a set of gentlemen's agreements by which they give special advantages to the products of those schools and overlook their lack of merit. Testing the conspiracy hypothesis in two activities widely regarded as conspiracies—organized and white collar crime—enables us to understand better the linkages among various groups and organizations that enable them to work together as though they were engaged in a plot.

Beliefs in conspiracies are not all self-evidently false. They are, in one form or another, widely believed by reasonable analysts. Moreover, they fit the facts. That is, a goodly number of social patterns can be observed (for example, the failure of income taxation to reduce the relative advantages of the well-to-do, and their active efforts in support of those advantages; the preference of prestigious universities for hiring one another's Ph.D.'s) that could be so interpreted. Specifically, we can see 1. how the outcome is often to the advantage of the conspirators; 2. how they could get together and control events; and 3. how the outcome does fit their wishes for the most part. Some part of the necessary facts is missing: In fact, *do* they get together and conspire? At present, most social scientists believe the answer is "mostly no," but the facts are not in.

The conspiracy hypothesis often plagues any kind of structural analysis, both in actual observation and in the language one uses to describe the behavior. Indeed, it caused problems for biologists prior to the twentieth century, since the neat connections between parts and processes of the body seemed to fit some kind of plan.[46] In biology, scientific caution eventually rejected the notion that "nature" or the body plan these intricate arrangements, because kidneys and pituitary glands are very likely not capable of conspiring.

46. Embodied, as many readers will recall, in the twentieth-century title by an eminent physiologist: *The Wisdom of the Body*, by Walter B. Cannon (New York: Norton, 1939).

However, that caution does not apply to the many linkages we believe we see in daily life. They are made up of real people, whose interests seem to be served by those connections, and people *can* plot. Moreover, it is difficult to describe any such structure, whether a system of communications flow or a set of market interconnections between wheat farmers and international monetary exchanges, without using the language of planning or intention. As a consequence, economics textbooks must frequently repeat that "no one planned it that way." Nevertheless, they also show that in fact each person who participates anywhere in an entire set of connections does concoct plans for his or her individual activity, and does carry them out with the aid of other people who are part of the whole structure. That is: Analysts in both economics and sociology are asserting that, though a social structure seems to be created and maintained by the people it serves, and the people in it do cooperate with one another to maintain their part in it, *no one group actually plans the structure as a whole*. There is no real conspiracy.

That may be generally true (and the problem will be considered again in a later chapter, on class), but I believe the linkages among groups can be better understood by considering cases where the charge of conspiracy seems much more likely and in fact is sometimes successfully prosecuted in court: "organized" crime, and high-level white collar crime.[47]

Wherever a police system is created, some of the police and some of the civilian population promptly begin to establish exchanges that will benefit them personally at the expense of civic rectitude. Moreover, some of these interconnections are almost certain to become known to some outsiders.[48]

When Lincoln Steffens investigated political corruption at the turn of the century in the United States, he described what analysts of deviance have emphasized ever since, that political corruption always links up a wide range of networks or circles, both criminal and noncriminal, which for this discussion can be considered as a set of prestige interlinkages.

The many networks and groups which make up the complex structure of political corruption enjoy varying degrees of esteem or disesteem: fences, pawnshop owners, police, judges. In an efficiently run corruption system all these occupational positions are necessarily linked, but their individual relationships to the flow of prestige are different. Most people prefer to be esteemed; but because not all who are involved in corrupt activities are engaged in transactions with one another, who esteems them and for what varies greatly. The main source of respect for known criminals is their own network. There they are ranked by their competence in illicit activities as well as their character or trustworthiness. If they earn enough in money or political power, they will receive overt deference in

47. I use the quotation marks not because there is no organized crime but because I believe with Cressey that the analyst must observe carefully how *much* organization, of what *kinds*, there is in any given instance of criminal behavior. See Donald R. Cressey, *Organized Crime and Criminal Organization* (Cambridge, Mass.: Heffner, 1971).

48. For brief comments on the historic problem of corruption, see Jonathan Rubinstein, *City Police* (New York: Ballantine, 1973), chap. 1.

their local neighborhoods and in many commercial places that cater to their needs (they will avoid the others). They are, true enough, disesteemed by the larger public as well as by most of the police, but that disesteem does not cost them much in their careers.[49] Judges and police, by contrast, depend on public esteem and may not even be able to play an effective role in a set of illegal transactions if they lose the respect of others.

People in illicit or shady transactions must exchange with bondsmen, lawyers, police officers, prosecutors, politicians, or judges—and, on occasion, with all of them; for each is in a different position in the social structure, with a command over different kinds and amounts of resources, and variously open to exposure. (It is probably harder, for example, to win a court case against a judge than a known criminal, but it is easier to hurt his or her public standing).

Both parties to any interaction across these various boundaries have a high stake in minimizing the flow of derogatory information, especially to outsiders. Judges can be most useful if no one knows they have any such contacts, so that their public esteem remains high. The greater the number of such cross-boundary interactions, the greater the likelihood that more respectable citizens will know of them. To avoid the disesteem that would inevitably result, interactions between those labeled as criminals and corrupt but publicly respectable citizens (judges, business people) are likely to be kept as secret as possible, or to be conducted through intermediaries who can see either party without losing prestige.

Each such transaction is likely to be a "conspiracy," and the same people may engage in many of them over time. However, typically no one person or group created the *system* of exchange and protection that is observable. That grows from an opportunity structure that is made up of illicit supply and demand on the one hand, and its use of the existing legal and policing system on the other. Since these are similar in all large cities in the United States, similar patterns of corruption are likely to be reported, in which key people spend resources to prevent anyone from taking formal steps toward disesteeming processes aimed against them.

The protection of corporate crime is legally more complex but structurally simpler, in part because it does not usually require illicit transactions with criminals, judges, or politicians. The violations themselves are the result of managerial decisions to violate the law, usually at the expense of the public. To that extent, they are the outcome of a conspiracy. But the processes by which the prestige of the corporation or its managerial personnel is maintained are guided by the ordinary procedures of legal defenses. They are available, as is typical in the law, to anyone who is very rich. A battery of lawyers attempts to prevent such violations from being

---

49. I believe, however, that Francis A. J. Ianni is correct in asserting that Mafia families want public respect, too, and over time try to shift more of their personnel to legitimate businesses. See Ianni (with E. R. Ianni), *A Family Business: Kinship and Social Control in Organized Crime* (New York: Russell Sage, 1972), and *Black Mafia* (New York: Simon and Schuster, 1974).

viewed as crimes, and to concede at most that the corporation will cease doing what it denies was wrong anyway. Such legal teams are aided by the inability of most citizens to understand the laws and by the reluctance of both citizenry and government legal staffs to treat these violations as "real" crimes.[50] This restrained stance is observable even when (as in the asbestos industry and mining) the corporation has violated health laws that have actually caused the deaths of many people.

These processes are not likely to be challenged because few people feel they have a large, direct, personal stake in insisting on prosecution. The social actors who have both the resources and a strong interest in the matter are more likely to be other corporations, and they are more likely to seek redress merely through civil suits. These extreme categories of crime committed by organized groups form a limited test of the conspiracy hypothesis, that is, that the allocation of respect or prestige is fixed by a system created by a small group, usually the upper class. Both cases are striking because real conspiracies do occur in both, that is, people actually plot to evade the law as well as its penalties. The exchange of money for political influence is common in both, and those who commit the crimes try through illicit as well as licit means to keep or enhance their esteem by hiding their derelictions from the public.

However, in even such extreme cases the structure of opportunity is typically not set in motion by the participants. As in an ordinary market, the flow of services, goods, and payoffs is determined by the preexisting chances for profit as well as for potential costs such as public disesteem and loss of influence. No one needs to create that structure of possibilities, for it exists already: the likelihood of profits from supplying a demand for illicit services and goods or manipulating a market, resources for both executing a crime and for protecting against its penalties, and the existing set of laws. Clearly, conspiracy is widespread in both types of crimes, and it occurs in many other settings. However, those who profit do not create that structure of opportunity; they simply exploit it successfully.

DOMINANT AND SUBORDINATE MARKETS

The continuing success of many prestigious groups or organizations is based on the equilibrating and interlinking processes already noted. Having more resources of all kinds to begin with, they can recruit people with more and more esteemed qualities and performances, who will in turn contribute to future achievements. They can offer higher rewards, including more prestige, and greater opportunities for making the achievements that will yield further prestige to the organization and its members.

As noted earlier, however, like people they can and do fail. This points to a broader dynamic of the linkages that we have alluded to from time to

---

50. On the evaluation or ranking of criminal behavior in many of its forms, see Peter H. Ross *et al.,* "The Seriousness of Crimes: Normative Structure and Individual Differences," *American Sociological Review,* 39 (April, 1974): 224–237.

time. Although it is true that high-level people, groups, or organizations can confer prestige, since they possess it and are permitted to make the important judgments about who has earned it by his or her achievements, they can never control that flow of prestige fully. Of course, the higher levels in the markets of prestige in any area of activity are dominant: for example, staff generals in the military system, the most creative professors in scholarship and science, art and literary critics of all kinds in the major cities, the numerous award-giving organizations.

Nevertheless, the small ones have their innings as well. The social history of organizations and groups is strewn with the debris of reputations. Art and music critics, kings, patrons, public relations departments of wealthy corporations—indeed, a wide range of supposedly influential "validators" both corporate and individual—have announced the rise of new stars, only to learn that people at "lower levels" or in subordinate prestige markets did not concede that greatness. A high rank is not self-created; it rests on some concession from people in lower positions that those in higher positions do possess greater qualities or have achieved more than they. (To what extent that is so for social classes will be considered in the next chapter.) It should be emphasized that though the high-ranking groups or individuals in the society do confer prestige, and thus create or maintain a kind of dominant market, that dominance is in turn maintained by the little markets that are linked with it.

This should not be surprising, for a similar pattern can be observed in the commodity market, as well as in politics. There too, for example, the financial or political decisions made by corporate giants in the United States have much effect on political action and economic markets all over the nation or world.[51] Nevertheless, a corporate president forgets at his peril the truth that at some ultimate remove individual consumers will decide not to buy an Edsel or a Nash, will ignore a well-recommended stock, or will reject "the dramatic, new, lower hemline." So similarly, in spite of the proclamations by music critics, most "modern" music has not been given much acclaim even by serious concertgoers. And, in spite of their apparent dominance over most of the resources of prestige, wealth, and force threat, the aristocrats in almost every society in the world have not succeeded in eliciting continued respect from the lower orders and have been cast out or killed. If little people will not pay that deference, grand people cease to be aristocrats.

51. See Richard J. Barnet and Ronald E. Muller, *Global Reach* (New York: Simon and Schuster, 1975), for some of the chilling consequences of the influence of transnational corporations.

Chapter 6
Class

Because prestige is a major component of class position, the analyses in this book have constantly made reference to class dynamics. Here class appears in a special context, for we must view it as a kind of structure and then ask how that set of interlinkages affects prestige processes. My intent here is not to give a general theory of stratification systems, or even of the general place of prestige in them (for that is a major theme of the entire book). Rather, we shall note some of the structural differences among stratification systems, and suggest how they might affect prestige processes. The narrow view requires that we further specify some of the relationships we take for granted as background or foundation, but that we shall not be dealing with in any detail.

ASSUMPTIONS ABOUT CLASS SYSTEMS

First, we take for granted that all large-scale societies are stratified, that is, that the rewards of the society are unequally distributed and people can roughly be ranked into higher or lower layers or strata according to how much they receive. No large-scale society has ever allocated its rewards equally to its members, and none will ever do so.

However ubiquitous a social pattern this is, it cannot be viewed as a social institution in any classical sense, like religion, education, or the family. It is not a set of beliefs and activities organized about certain goals that most people believe should be carried out. No one is "in charge" of it. Nor is it "created" by anyone, though of course many small-scale class systems have been engineered by founders of colonies[1] and communes; and revolutionary leaders have made significant changes in the class systems of their societies.

Next, prestige is a major component of all stratification systems, as it is of all individual positions in them. We know how occupations (in most large societies the most important basis for class position) are ranked, and thus the extent to which people esteem them. We do not know, on the

1. See the astute analyses of what happened to several such created colonies in Sigmund Diamond, "Old Patterns, New Societies: Virginia and French Canada in the Seventeenth Century," in W. Cahnman and A. Boskoff, eds., *Sociology and History* (New York: Free Press, 1964).

other hand, how much the members of different classes respect one another.[2] We do know from ordinary observation that ambivalent attitudes are encountered at all class levels, that some grudging respect is paid upward and some restrained deprecation or denigation downward. We cannot assume that most people below the top in any society, either in the feudally integrated manors of Europe or the religiously supported caste societies of India, have felt as much respect or deference as they have had to exhibit toward their superiors.

With reference to the class patterns of esteem, the following regularities can be noted. 1. Each stratum, occupation, clique, or group has its own norms, and these determine how much prestige is given for different qualities and behaviors. A clear bias is visible in these evaluations, in that each group evaluates more highly than do other groups the traits its own members possess. 2. Nevertheless, this self-protectiveness is not sufficient to shield social strata, occupations, groups, or even individuals from the harsh knowledge that others do not fully share such self-evaluations.[3] Moreover, 3. members of a stratum do know how others rank them; in fact, their own rankings do not vary much from those of any other group. For example, carpenters give their own occupation a slightly higher rating than others do, but they rank medicine, law, and other professions much higher, in conformity with the evaluations of people in other occupations or at any class level.[4]

In broader terms, not only do the members of any higher social class agree that they rank higher than others, but those lower in the scale also make that concession to them and show it in their behavior. That is not an assertion that the members of the upper class "deserve" their advantages, but merely that toward the upper strata people have in fact more of whatever is valued by the society, whether it is blue blood, the ability to fight in armor on horseback, or highly ranked positions in government, the professions, or philanthropic institutions.

The next regularity to be noted is that the greater esteem obtained by the higher social strata also has more control effect. That is, esteem has more control effect over fellow upper-class members than does lower-class prestige over fellow members of the lower class.

To a member of the upper classes, the esteem and respect of fellow members is worth more because, first, they control far more resources. The potential loss from their disapproval is greater and the potential reward from their approval is greater. Second, they are more likely than lower class members to be linked into a network, so that the disapproval

---

2. Peter Rossi has, however, been engaged in precisely this inquiry.

3. See Richard Sennett and Jonathan Cobb, *The Hidden Injuries of Class* (New York: Vintage, 1973).

4. See Theodore Caplow, *Principles of Organization* (New York: Harcourt, Brace & World, 1964), pp. 213ff.

of one person may well persuade others to concur. True enough, to be at such levels at all means that each individual has more resources with which to counter disapproval; but the enterprises to be mounted are also typically greater and beyond the capacities of any single person. Many require the trust and cooperation, and thus the respect, of fellow members of the upper class.

In addition, controls are likely to be weaker when there is not much distinction made among most performers, that is, when they are all ranked about the same. It seems likely that members of lower classes rank one another far more on less finely graded performances, that is, what I have called the "small virtues." Few people obtain very high or very low rankings in these areas, and most people get little payoff in prestige or material goods from them. By contrast, members of the upper classes spend more of their time and attention on getting prestige in areas that are more finely graded, such as business or the professions. Since the payoffs are potentially greater, they are more likely to adjust their behavior to one another's norms or standards.

As a final relationship that is taken for granted: Although whole classes do rise in prestige or political influence over time, as when British and American workers fought for and achieved civic, political, and economic rights in the second half of the nineteenth century, or the middle classes in many European countries gradually assumed posts in the expanding governmental bureaucracy, it is only in radical revolutions that any class rises "above" another. Even then, it is only because the top stratum is eliminated. All but a few revolutions leave intact most of the class structure, although the individual membership of those classes may change during the turmoil. As noted before, however, radical revolutions do proclaim a new set of norms or bases for earning prestige, as when socialist or communist governments attempt to promote higher respect for workers.

The class structure can be viewed as a set of linkages that affects the flow of prestige and of persons who acquire that prestige. It is a structure, even if a loose one, and is not simply the resultant of individual competition within the existing inegalitarian social system. Let us now consider how that structure can affect the allocation of prestige.

HOW SHARP ARE CLASS BOUNDARIES?

One characteristic of class structure that might affect the allocation of respect is how definite or sharp are the boundaries between classes. Feudal Europe and Tokugawa Japan are examples of societies with relatively distinct boundaries. Sociologists sometimes refer to such strata as "estates." Where they have occurred—most have disappeared now—whatever the actual rate of social mobility, official ideology proclaims that people should be content with the rank in which they were born. Sumptuary laws forbid people of lower ranks to consume certain foods or to wear clothing inappropriate to their station. Laws or customs do not give "equal rights" to all citizens, but they specify different rights and obligations (for example, the Magna Carta asserts the right of nobles to be tried only by their peers). A more extreme example of sharp boundaries is, of course, the Indian caste system. Let us consider some of the possible implications of this variable.

Almost by definition, of course, nearly anyone in such a society would know fairly accurately the social rank of anyone he or she encountered. Costumes were more likely to be distinctive, as were language and life styles. Any cross-class interactions were more likely than in our own society to be governed by well-accepted rules of deference. Ideally, everyone was placed in a hierarchy so that he or she owed allegiance and service to specific persons upward, and protection downward. The boundaries were sharper because each individual was in a reciprocal relationship with *specific* other persons (a lord and his peasant), not merely in a general rank or position. There was, then, less doubt as to where an individual stood with reference to a class boundary.

In India's large-scale caste system, the boundaries have been sharp among all castes, but there too it was once (and to a lesser extent now is) typical for large numbers of people to be locked into enduring obligations and rights with specific others. Again as a consequence, there was little doubt as to who owed respect, and to whom, and thus where each stood in the caste hierarchy. Though much changed, this system persists today in part.

Although in such systems anyone could perceive the broad structure of caste or class relations, the more salient day-to-day interaction was guided by the prestige and authority of specific occupations and posts. In this sense, one might even claim that one's job had more impact on daily life than in modern society, since so much else was integrated with it. People were blacksmiths and fletchers on a barony, peasants holding land rights from a secular lord or bishop, warriors bound to aid their chief in battle, or bloodletters and bonesetters attached to a castle. Again the class boundaries were distinct because the social rank and attributes of those occupations were likely to be socially defined within narrow limits.

In such a system, achieving prestige by living up to the standards of the class, caste, or guild rules was socially defined as more important than gaining wealth, but we should be wary of accepting that view as the total reality. Poor fiscal management ruined many nobles, while rich merchants in Japan, medieval Europe, and India often enjoyed much more deference than official ideology prescribed.

In any event, the more important fact is that subgroups or classes in such a system were more likely than in modern society to have definite norms and customs of their own; not everyone was supposed to be measured by similar standards. Merchants earned respect from fellow merchants by living up to the rules of such groups. They were under less pressure than in modern society or, say, eighteenth-century France and Europe to acquire the culture and life style of higher classes. That is, the estates formed subcommunities (as castes in India did) in which individuals and families competed for prestige within the group more than across the entire range of the class structure. To be sure, people of a somewhat lower rank could not earn as much prestige as those in a higher estate, but their likelihood of feeling defeated—as many people do in our own society—because they could not meet the standards of a higher class or estate would be much lower.

When individuals and families did rise, their formal rights and obligations also changed, because these were much more closely defined by their new positions. Another difference may be noted. With few exceptions (for example, the success of a merchant), upward movement usually occurred when a specific person of higher rank gave land to or conferred a post or other rank upon another. Even when rights to land and title passed to a son in the feudal system, a higher-ranking person (usually a nobleman) formally gave him these rights (and in Europe was in turn given an oath of fealty plus gifts or promises of future payments in services or kind).

CONTROL OF UPPER STRATA OVER LOWER CLASSES

A second major interclass link that affects prestige allocation is how much control the higher social ranks have over upward social mobility. Although sociologists commonly assume that modern industrial societies exhibit a much higher class mobility than those of the past, this assumption is not based on solid empirical data. Where we have such studies—as in China—we know there was once substantial mobility at the higher ranks.[5] That is, a substantial percentage of the upper stratum was made up of "new families." As to mobility among lower ranks we cannot say, except for the obvious fact that if most of the population were poor farmers, it was arithmetically impossible for a large percentage to move a *large* step upward. We cannot infer from that fact, however, how much control the upper ranks had over the chances of a modest step upward.

That control has, in any event, taken many forms. Where military glory was the path to rank, the privileged classes were able to obtain most of the command posts. When sainthood was a possible career, the higher ranks furnished most of the saints. In Republican Rome, as in feudal Europe and Japan, the aristocracy had a near monopoly over the military,

5. For data on mobility in the historical dynasties of China, see Robert Marsh, *The Mandarins* (New York: Free Press, 1961). See also Jonathan Kelley and Melvin L. Perliman, "Social Mobility in Toro: Some Preliminary Results from Western Uganda," in *Economic Development and Cultural Change*, 19, no. 2 (January, 1971): 204–221. In his *Social Stratification* (New York: Harcourt, Brace, 1957), Bernard Barber assembles such data for the post-Reformation period in several European countries. Keith Hopkins also notes that the Roman Empire "promoted mobility in the fourth century to an unprecedented degree" in "Elite Mobility in the Roman Empire," *Past and Present*, 32 (December, 1965): 13.

civil, religious, and governmental posts that yielded high prestige (as well as licit or illicit wealth). In most great societies of the past, rank was based on land, whose control was determined mainly by the family laws of inheritance. In modern societies social mobility requires education, which cannot be as easily controlled as land used to be; but even so the educational advantages of the well-to-do are adequately documented.

There is no way to prevent the appearance of *talent* at any class level, and few ways of preventing respect from being given to high *skills* once they appear, but it is possible to prevent a talent from being trained into a high skill. All that is needed is to control access to opportunity. It is rare that a society has ever rejected its victorious generals because they were of lowly birth, but it is easy to keep people of lowly birth from ever being victorious (or defeated) generals by closing the road upward before that talent can be shown. Almost certainly, millions of British citizens could have become better rulers than their kings and ministers were, but they were never permitted to discover that fact or to obtain any training for it.

An examination of this lowered effectiveness which comes from high control over upward mobility discloses several important relationships. To elicit the best performances, a stratification system has to reward skills wherever they are shown; and indeed, it is to everyone's interest (except that of direct competitors) to reward the best. Few would prefer poor service from a waiter or a physician, if there were a good alternative. Few would prefer to listen to a poor violinist, even if he were a certified member of the Violin Caste. That bias is doubtless a universal human weakness, always slightly undermining the attempts of rulers to maintain a system in which the lower orders will be content to remain in their place. However, at every class level but the lowest, all stratification systems seem to find at least a partial solution: to praise those below for their excellent performances at *lower* tasks, but not to interpret any excellence as proving the right to move upward. A system of high control over upward movement need not deny merit where it appears. It is only necessary to be blind to *potential* merit. Since potential merit is often, perhaps even typically, ambiguous, that blindness can apparently be achieved quite easily.

That is more easily done than the rational mind might suppose, and several techniques seem to be used in all large-scale societies. People want to praise the excellent performances of those below them but restrict their perception of their ability to move upward. One way is to view any skill, any concrete evidence of talent, as proving different things, depending on the class (or caste) rank of the individual. The plantation slave who was efficient could be esteemed, but that excellence was not viewed as evidence that he should eventually own a plantation of his own. The black or white lower-class boy who understands motors might be praised for his skill at repairing them but not be encouraged to think about being an engineer. For some generations, middle-class and upper-middle-class parents in American society have eagerly looked for some evidence of talent, of potential merit in their children, so that they could press them to rise high in one or another profession or occupation; they have not, for example, viewed their children's skill at growing house plants as evidence that they might become efficient farm laborers, but more likely botanists or biochemists. Since real opportunities, recommendations, job offers, and economic support have been linked with these judgments, in most societies the people in disadvantaged positions do not usually prove those perceptions and judgments are wrong.

This general pattern can be stated in a more formal manner: 1. In any large-scale stratification system, at successively lower class levels an individual's talents must be more obvious for them to be viewed as evidence that he or she ought to be helped to obtain high occupational or class rank. 2. In stratification systems where the upper strata have a high control over the mobility chances of other ranks (as in feudal societies) this relationship is still more pronounced: that is, at successively lower social levels the individual's talents had to be even more conspicuous than in modern societies for them to be recognized and encouraged.

Control over the paths to prestige is generally easier where, as in most large societies of the past, few of the more prestigious positions require high technical expertise—skills that can be easily measured (accountancy, commanding a ship). Consequently, people from lower-class levels could not as easily prove that they had the talent or skill for most positions, while people at higher social ranks did not have to prove they had any special aptitude for court posts, diplomacy, dispensing justice, or directing their own estates. Whatever the judgments about individual skills, it was taken for granted that few people from lower ranks could achieve them.

Several additional regularities can be observed in the kind of society where higher social strata have more control than in other societies over the mobility chances of the lower strata. One is that *families* have more control over the individual's mobility, with reference to how decisions are reached and the resources invested in the individual. That is, elder kin are more likely to decide who will enter which kinds of adult activity, such as war or diplomacy. High-control societies are also more likely to be ascriptive societies, but it is worthwhile to emphasize this regularity: When a stratification system is based on ascription, it is highly likely that legal controls will also be used over who may obtain certain kinds of property (farmland, for example), enter certain occupations or positions, engage in certain kinds of trades (silver, wool, shipping), or even consume or display certain kinds of goods.

Such laws are also violated, of course. Indeed, the upper strata would not consider them desirable if the social rules against class mobility were operating to their satisfaction. Legal rules implicitly deny, of course, the strong upper-class belief that the lower orders are simply not competent; penalties are required, in order to reduce the number of those who will not keep their place.

Where the upper strata have high control over the upward flow of people below them, an ideological regularity is encountered: The philosophic view is widely asserted that those at lower levels owe service and care to those higher up (the peasants should feed the lord); while those higher up owe protection (and, sometimes, justice) to the lower classes. This is part of the ancient theory that the classes are part of an organic whole and are engaged in a kind of social exchange.

Some control is achieved over people at lower levels by virtue of the fact that upward movement is likely to occur through sponsorship, for example, the lord's support of a bright peasant lad's wish to enter the clergy. Even where that pattern of individual sponsorship is common, however, classes as units or collectivities do not—and even aristocracies do not—"decide" to recruit or reject a member, though specific groups such as country clubs, a guild of silversmiths, or a social network may do so. It was not the aristocracy but kings who decided who was to become a noble. A nobleman might create a knight, but knights as a social unit did not decide to reject or receive him.

In modern societies, this pattern is even more pronounced. First, the sponsorship by a specific person is of lesser weight where one can independently prove one's ability (computer programming, typing). Second, even when a trade union, corporation, or occupational gatekeeper has control over an individual's entrance into a particular job, he or they cannot usually reject or accept that person as a member of a class, or even as a practitioner of a given occupation.[6]

As a final, speculative point, it is possible that the steady loss of deference by the upper stratum in most Western countries over the past several centuries is partly caused by the loss of control over the access to opportunities for mobility. In order to show one's capacities, it is much less necessary now to obtain the help of specific persons who are higher in the class system. Effective sponsors can and do help, of course, especially in getting a chance at posts that either require no special skills (many beginning factory jobs) or high skills that are not easily measurable (directing a philanthropic agency). Nevertheless, the opportunity to gain prestige in the modern era is far less dependent on having a higher-stratum sponsor than in the past.

BASES FOR PRESTIGE

In asking how the links among classes affect the prestige processes of a society we raise again the question of the bases of prestige. In warlike tribes and societies, courage and competence in war have determined the respect men paid to one another. For centuries, the French nobility held to their (erroneous) self-definition as the shield and sword of the kingdom. In classical China, achievements in philosophy, calligraphy, and literature

6. For a discussion of this process in science see: L. Hargens and W. O. Hagstrom, "Sponsored and Contest Mobility of American Academic Scientists," *Sociology of Education*, 40, no. 1 (Winter, 1967): 24–38.

were viewed as essential to a mandarin's rank. Landed wealth, and thus family lineage, was required in order to be a senator in republican Rome, but a senator's sons were also expected to serve as military commanders and magistrates.

As yet, no systematic analysis has been made of how such differences affect prestige processes.[7] It is possible that the differences have had little effect, since whatever the bases of prestige, the upper strata will contrive to obtain most of the highest posts and a goodly share of other rewards as well. If military glory is important, it will also be a major road to wealth and political influence. If mandarin learning is the way to high prestige, it will also lead to great office and high income.

Whatever the official bases of prestige allocation at the upper levels, other bases will also be of some importance, and the upper strata must control them as well if they wish to keep their privileged position. They must do so for another reason: The sons of high-ranking families may do poorly in the special area of high prestige (war, for example), thus other kinds of opportunities (administration, law) must also be controlled to their advantage. Essentially, then, no single foundation of prestige is possible in any large society, simply because many areas of achievement are important for its control and maintenance. Hence there will be many arenas of possible prestige opportunities.

Most people do not, in any event, find their prestige opportunities in the arena of highest prestige. After all, only a tiny percentage of the Chinese population ever attempted to acquire mandarin learning, just as most Roman citizens were not engaged in conquest. Most people in any large society aim at earning the respect of others by simply doing reasonably well in the various lower-level occupations (farming, artisanship) that produce the goods and services the population needs. It does not seem likely, then, that the variation from society to society with reference to the main basis of prestige (religion, war, learning) has more than a modest effect on the processes or dynamics of prestige allocation by class.

CLASS DIFFERENCES IN PRESTIGE ALLOCATION

The main regularities of process seem to be the following. First, within each class some behaviors are valued but are so common as to yield little prestige. Lacking them may reduce one's esteem, but possessing them does not raise it. Performance below that working norm may bring disesteem from people at other class levels as well. In the middle class it is taken for granted that members will wear clean clothing, speak standard English, and work at a steady job; and correspondingly those advantages

7. It will be noted that I omit a variable traditionally used for comparing different class systems, the distance from the top to the bottom of the stratification system. I do this in part because in all large-scale societies that gulf has been enormous, and different effects from a similar enormity do not seem obvious. As to the "shape" of the system, i.e., its curve of distribution, I view that as primarily a resultant, and its few effects are already noted in this section.

will elicit little esteem from peers. On the other hand, such advantages will reap a modest amount of respect or envy from lower-class individuals who do not possess them.

Second, some traits will elicit admiration from lower-class peers but will generate little from middle- or upper-class members, not because those qualities are oversupplied at higher levels, but because they are simply less valued there. These might include the willingness to forego a job opportunity that requires leaving one's friends or family behind; exhibiting great physical strength or endurance in a manual job; or success in making one's children obedient. Note that in a modern society with no sharp divisions between classes, not very many characteristics can be put into this category. That is, it is difficult to locate many distinctively lower-class patterns in which the members of the lower class actually take pride. The most important one is that some will assert, as against their knowledge that they do not rank high in social esteem, that they do "most of the work of the society."

Third, losses in prestige are greater at upper social levels for some traits or behaviors that would elicit less depreciation at lower levels. This of course is no more than a specific phrasing of the more general regularity that many types of acts will generate prestige at most class levels; but a different *level* of performance in some behaviors is considered adequate in one class and not another, and a much lower level is required for disparagement in one class than another; and, correspondingly, some types of behavior that might be judged as "honorable" or prestige-generating in higher social circles might be seen as verging on the quixotic in lower social strata.

A few examples will make these patterns clear, for they correspond to much daily experience: A lower-class male who will not read books and makes little use of his high school classes will lose little or no respect among his peers, while the rarer one who reads difficult books and philosophy will be considered a bit odd, though a few friends may pay that behavior some grudging respect. A patrolman who rejects a small bribe or gift in a slum area may be given some admiration for being honest (and a cynical smile of disparagement from some people for being foolish), but a Wall Street lawyer who does not bribe a judge will receive none, nor will the judge if he turns one down. The Wall Street lawyer is held to somewhat higher standards of legal ethics and is disesteemed more for a level of behavior that would hardly be viewed as improper among the type of lawyers who once were labeled "ambulance-chasers."[8] In general, a highly esteemed occupational subgroup can ask a somewhat higher standard of ethical behavior (a greater "supply") because the costs are so low. Members of such groups have no excuse for their poor behavior since they are not in real need; they can prosper without it. The depreciation is greater because toward such higher levels one's peers will also suffer some

8. See Jerome E. Carlin, *Lawyers' Ethics* (New York: Russell Sage Foundation, 1966), pp. 66ff.

prestige loss when a fellow member cannot live up to even the standards that have been made easy to meet.

On the other hand, as noted earlier, there is little evidence that this statement applies at all to the range of corporate crime at upper levels. Loss of prestige is very substantial when such a person is actually sent to jail, but this rarely happens. Most malefactors are never brought to the bar of justice, or they escape if they are. This escape from denigration occurs in part because a wide variety of white collar crime is not viewed by businessmen as genuinely criminal.

Fourth, as a corollary to our earlier analyses of how prestige payments rise steeply with higher levels of achievement in particular skills, I suggest that generally the already highly rewarded posts and positions held by the upper classes offer the opportunity for still higher rewards in prestige. That is, such posts are highly esteemed, but in addition they are more likely than tasks at more modest levels to be somewhat open-ended in their challenge. They give more scope to the unusual talent, hence a higher range in prestige rewards. The higher-level tasks in government, business, or the university can be done at a modest level of competence, and often are; but they permit the use of very high ability, which is rare. Brilliant judgments may save our lives or fortunes, and poor performances may hurt us badly. There is never an oversupply of people who can adequately meet the challenge of the more highly ranked positions in the society.

A fifth class pattern in prestige processes is that persons toward higher class levels receive more esteem for their valued performances and qualities that are viewed as *marginal* to their occupations than do persons toward lower class levels. People in such positions are more likely to have many other positions which are not part of an occupation, such as serving on the board of trustees of a private school, taking part in community fund-raising, or serving on a committee of inquiry for the government on a temporary basis. Thus they are engaged in additional tasks, for which they receive a still greater amount of prestige. The amount is correspondingly greater because it is viewed as beyond the norm.

Whether people actually view such marginal contributions as deserving special recognition because they are extra, we do not know. I do not suppose, for example, that people actually calculate that large increments of prestige are necessary to elicit this increase in contribution. They may, however, consider quite consciously that people in high positions already enjoy much political influence, money, and prestige and thus merit larger amounts of deference or prestige for such extra activities, which must be given if their help is to be secured.

COMPETITION WITHIN AND AMONG CLASSES

A most important part of class dynamics is two independent processes that operate in some tension with one another and at all class levels. The first is the normal competition among people at roughly the same rank, often engaged in similar activities. However exploited the lesser folk may have been in the past, and however intensely they hated their lords, far more nobles have fallen at the hands of their peers than at the hands of rebellious peasants. Similarly, corporation presidents compete with one another far more than with the clerks in their offices. Failure in this competition, at any level, is sometimes serious enough to cause an individual family to lose its class position. How commonly this occurs will of course vary in different positions within the social structure—for example, it is very common in small businesses in the modern world, as it was once in farming, but it is uncommon in the professions.

The second process is political and economic competition *among* classes and occupations viewed as aggregates or collectivities. The former competition, that *within* a class, can be reduced somewhat if the class or subclass can obtain or protect its group rights to various franchises, opportunities, training facilities, monopolies, and privileges rooted in law and custom. Then, each member has greater assurance that "outsiders" will not compete successfully. In modern industrial society, no class can be neatly delineated from another, and no class as a whole (even very likely the upper class) acts as a unit to serve its own interests. Nor has it a legal right to such a monopoly. Nevertheless, those in any class position are more likely than others to share similar attitudes, political convictions, and perceptions of what should be done. As a consequence, they are likely, if they act at all with reference to this matter (even when members suppose they are acting as individuals), to support those social patterns that give them advantages while denying them to others. This applies as much to the craft unions' denial of opportunities to blacks as it does to the reluctance of prestigious law firms to hire young lawyers from state university law schools, or that of exclusive country clubs to admit Jews.

In one of these processes, the competition occurs *within* the class or occupation; in the other, it occurs among sectors, classes, or occupations of the whole society. The second aims at protecting the interests of the class, but it puts pressure on other individuals, classes, or occupations as well. If an advantaged class makes it more difficult for members of another to compete on equal terms, as when it controls the means of production or education, those within the disadvantaged group must compete more intensely with one another, and they will find it more difficult to achieve the more esteemed positions.

CONTROL EFFECTS OF PRESTIGE ALLOCATION

Since members of different classes pay esteem or disesteem as a way of affecting the behavior of other classes, we need to know what the control effects are, if any. It is first necessary to ask whether people *can* alter their behavior or qualities so as to increase their prestige rewards; and, if so, how they perceive the cost of doing better, as compared with the potential rewards. Both factors are of course class-linked. We must also consider the costs of paying prestige to a person from a different class. Even if a member of the upper class might be able to elicit improved behavior from one of the lower class by praising him or her, would the upper-class person make the payment, or would he or she view it rather as costing too much to pay that deference? Reciprocally, members of lower classes might affect upper-class behavior through dispraise, but it would be a costly tactic.

Of course, many class-linked qualities cannot easily be changed. In most societies to be darker than average or an immigrant is negatively valued. The ability to solve engineering or political problems is highly valued, but it cannot be acquired by simply trying hard. Education, skill, or bravery in battle can perhaps be improved, but at considerable cost.

As noted earlier, part of the cost-reward calculation centers on whether the individual believes that he can succeed at the challenge, and whether he will reap the rewards of success if the performance is excellent. Here the perception of high contingency or low chances for success is clearly class-linked and affects the dedication and motivation with which people begin a long period of training for upward mobility. Slum children typically do not believe that they can get into college and are not convinced that the payoffs others get at higher-class levels for their college education would eventually accrue to them. They are of course largely correct.[9] They discount in advance part of the prestige reward that the society might be willing to pay for a particular achievement or for acquiring many of the social traits of higher social strata. Thus, in most large-scale societies, the prestige differentials by class do not motivate many at lower-class levels to plan for positions in the upper social strata, although they may desire them. They are likely to calculate that the costs of self-improvement are higher than the probable rewards, and observe that though some of their number do "make it" these are probably uniquely fortunate cases or persons endowed with powerful friends.[10]

By contrast, the increasingly higher reward-cost ratio toward the upper social strata may well heighten the motivation to perform well at the top. However, many upper-level tasks can be performed only modestly well and still yield a substantial payoff. As Tumin has argued, perhaps at such levels, and for such tasks, people would perform them relatively well even

9. Joel Telles suggests that this interpretation can be applied to a number of studies of the educational and occupational aspirations of school children, those, e.g., of: Donald Q. Brodie and Edward A. Suchman, "Socioeconomic Status, Students' Evaluations and Educational Desires," *Social Science Quarterly*, 49, no. 2 (September, 1968): 253–261; Aaron Antonovsky, "Aspirations, Class and Racial-Ethnic Membership," *Journal of Negro Education*, 36, no. 4 (Fall, 1967) 385–393; William H. Sewell, Archie O. Haller, Murray Straus, "Social Status and Educational and Occupational Aspiration," in B. C. Rosen *et al.*, *Achievement in American Society* (Cambridge, Mass.: Schenckman, 1969), pp. 581–595; Roberta G. Simmons and Morris Rosenberg, "Functions of Children's Perceptions of the Stratification System," *American Sociological Review*, 36, no. 2 (April, 1971): 235–249. After personal communications with Simmons and Rosenberg, Telles suggests further that children in higher classes learn quite early that the cards are stacked in their favor, before those in the lower class learn they are stacked *against* them.

10. For data on this point, see Herbert Hyman, "The Value Systems of Different Classes," in Reinhard Bendix and Seymour M. Lipset, *Class, Status and Power*, 2d ed. (New York: Free Press, 1966), esp. p. 496.

with far lesser rewards.[11] Moreover, I believe that the threat of deprecation or prestige *loss* (for not performing well) would be more effective in controlling behavior at that level than the offer of greater marginal rewards.

What is striking about existing class differentials in prestige payoffs is that neither alternative suggested above is systematically tried—higher prestige to the lower classes for greater conformity with society-wide ideals, or greater dispraise threats to members of the higher social strata for failing to live up to social ideals or to the somewhat higher demands of those positions.[12]

With reference to the second of these, the more common pattern is considerable protection of the inept.[13] In the other direction, not many people are willing to try the experiment of scolding their boss in order to find out whether his or her behavior might improve a bit as a result.[14] To scold subordinates or members of the lower social strata has not been very costly in most societies. The lower castes, serfs and villeins, colonial subjects, and natives have all had fewer resources with which to defend themselves against deprecation. For them, flattery upward is safer, in order to avoid counterattacks.

Of more fundamental importance is that in general rulers or members of the upper social strata *do not really aim at "improving" the behavior of the lower classes*, as judged by the standards of excellence or propriety that are widely held within that social system. There is no general commitment on the part of most social strata to move the members of any lower strata very far toward higher achievements or virtue. On the contrary, most members of successively higher social classes have a stake in keeping those at any lower social levels in a disadvantaged position, competing ineffectively.[15]

11. Melvin M. Tumin, "Some Principles of Stratification," *ibid.*, pp. 56ff.

12. However, this ideological position has at least been promulgated in Maoist China. For some reports on the reward system in contemporary China, see Martin King Whyte, "Bureaucracy and Modernization in China: The Maoist Technique," *American Sociological Review*, 38 (April, 1973): 156–157; A. Doak Barnett and Ezra F. Vogel, *Cadres, Bureaucracy and Political Power in Community China* (New York: Columbia University Press, 1966); and G. William Skinner and Edwin A. Winckler, "Compliance Succession in Rural Community China: A Cyclical Theory," in Amitai Etzioni, ed., *A Sociological Reader on Complex Organizations*, 2d ed. (New York: Holt, Rinehart, and Winston, 1969), pp. 410–438. The modern Chinese experience suggests that these techniques may lose somewhat in efficiency, but they may well yield greater loyalty to the society as a whole, and perhaps a much higher motivation from the lower social strata.

13. William J. Goode, "The Protection of the Inept," in *Explorations in Social Theory* (New York: Oxford University Press, 1973) pp. 121–144.

14. Frantz Fanon has pointed out that to denounce one's superiors may be psychologically useful for colonial peoples, as a way of freeing them from their fears of people in high places. In the late 1960's, students in most advanced countries engaged in many such denunciations, and did succeed for a while in inducing a large number of organizations to change their surface behavior. See Fanon, *L'An V de la révolution algérienne* (1959), trans. as *A Dying Colonialism* by Haakon Chevalier (London: Penguin, 1970).

15. For extensive comments made by the English ruling class about workers, and especially about the need for keeping them in their place, see E. P. Thompson, *The Making of the English Working Class* (New York: Vintage, 1963). For a subtle analysis of the *problem* of keeping them in their place and "improving" their habits, while simultaneously divesting responsibility for the poor from the shoul-

Even if they knew that a different program of control would raise performances, it is unlikely that they would carry it out. In perhaps all epochs but our own, the advantaged classes have openly admitted that they had no stake in raising the general achievements of the lower classes. In the nineteenth century, for example, it was widely believed that to teach lower-class children to read would make them discontented workers and possibly lead to sedition or revolution. Members of the upper classes are now criticized if they admit in public that they do not want members of the lower classes to move upward. But in the present and past, dominant classes have been slow to make any large investment in improving the achievements of the lower classes—though they have often expressed a desire to improve the *virtue* of those classes, most commonly with respect to drinking and sex.

Upper-class social opinion in every stratification system and almost every colonial conquest has asserted that the lower classes, lower castes, natives, and the conquered are not *able* to improve, so that no payoff schedule would really change their behavior.[16] They are thought to be lazy, stupid, immoral, and irrational. This remarkable uniformity suggests how significant are the lower social strata for the upper: the whites have needed the blacks, the French settlers the Algerians, and the upper and middle classes the people who live on the wrong side of the tracks. Those who are deprecated confirm the higher rank of others by their failure to achieve or even strive for the highest possible levels of self-development.[17]

Since they so typically do fail, the upper strata (who believe that they themselves do not fail as often) conclude that those at lower levels simply do not have the capacity to improve: either their character is poor or their abilities are low. Since they are unable to rise (as proved by their poor responses to punishment or potential reward), those who are higher in the social scale can feel even more justified morally in their own possession of higher social rewards.[18] I assert, then, that members of the upper social strata are not willing to pay any more than they do in prestige to elicit a higher level of performance from those in lower social strata; and they do

---

ders of the upper classes, see Reinhard Bendix, "The Self Legitimation of an Entrepreneurial Class: The Case of England," *Zeitschrift für die Gesamte Staatswissenschaft*, 110, no. 1 (1954): 48–71.

16. With one kind of exception, for it should not be forgotten that not all conquests were carried out by the "advanced" nations against the "primitive" ones. Certainly the Mongols and the Manchus as conquerors of China used a very different rhetoric: The Chinese were soft, effete, decadent, corrupt, and so on. Doubtless the successive conquerors of Rome in the last days of the empire would have held similar opinions.

17. A tangential argument is sometimes made that there is a true "culture of poverty," and that members of the lower social strata have a distinct set of norms and evaluations, reject those of the middle and upper strata, and punish and reward each other by reference to those cultural ideals. So far, that assertion seems to be more of a political plank than an empirical observation. It is certainly an exaggeration with respect to family behavior.

18. For some of these justifications— even as applied to people who receive welfare payments, by members of the "respectable" working class or lower-middle class—see Peter Binzen, *White Town U.S.A.* (New York: Random House, 1970); and Sennett and Cobb, *The Hidden Injuries of Class*.

not in any event want a much higher level of performance, for that might then challenge their own domination.

DOES "EXCHANGE" BETWEEN CLASSES EXIST?

The notion that social classes owe both esteem and services to one another, in exchange for their contributions to the larger society as well as to each other, is in fact the oldest extant theory of stratification. It is encountered in the writings of Confucius or Plato, or in the Law of Manu in India. According to this view, each class should get higher or lower honors and perquisites, depending upon its contributions. For example, mandarins in Chinese society were not supposed to work in the fields, but peasants were. In feudal European societies, the lords were to guard their peasants, care for them in need, and dispense justice; villeins, serfs, and peasants were to till the fields and pay deference and loyalty to their rulers. Each class, then, has different tasks assigned to it, for which others give appropriate honor and remuneration, graded by the importance of those duties for the society as well as for each class.

This has always been the most prevalent official ideology, promulgated constantly by the leaders of most major societies. It is an organicist view, according to which the whole society is a kind of organism in which each part plays its role. It is conservative and defends the rank and privileges of the higher orders. Perhaps at times it persuaded some members of the lower social strata that they should respect and work for people in the upper social strata; in any event, it very likely persuaded many of them that what they were told they properly owed was somehow an outgrowth of the cosmic order. Such a view removes any guilt the privileged might feel about exploitation. It proclaims justice as the foundation of the stratification system and thus the society. It is compatible with an open class as well as a caste system; a republic or a monarchical polity; a village trading economy or the early stages of a capitalist one.

Moreover, many textbooks and analyses have stated that any system must rest upon that kind of mutual respect and exchange, and especially on the belief by the lower social strata that people at the upper levels deserve their rank; otherwise force or threat would have to be utilized continuously.[19]

Generally, in modern nations, that rhetoric is considered archaic or anachronistic in private and offensive in public. Few of the upper class would now agree that they should have any personal responsibility for the lower social strata, and most would assert that they have little ability to help them anyway. People in the lower classes would reject even more emphatically any obligation of loyalty or deference to people at upper social levels. Of course, in many contemporary authoritarian regimes such

19. During the nineteenth century, mainly as an outgrowth of Social Darwinism or Malthusianism, some asserted that the classes (meaning especially the upper social strata) do not really owe anything to one another as parts of a social organism. For one exposition of this view, see William Graham Sumner, *What Social Classes Owe to Each Other* (Caldwell, Idaho: Caxton, 1952 [1883]).

phrases may be used, for often the dictator-ruler asserts his personal benevolence and demands loyalty from his subjects. In democratic countries it is the state or government that proclaims concern and responsibility for the disadvantaged, but it is simultaneously asserted that getting that care is a civic right of each citizen, not simply a class right; and the obligation to give that care does not belong to any particular class. Correspondingly, if loyalty is owed, it is owed to the state, not to members of any one class and not even to specific political leaders.

These changes both illuminate the present relations among classes and remind us of other historical changes. The most important change is that people at any class level below the top would not now agree that they are obligated to show any special deference, or to feel any special respect, to members of any higher class—although they do in fact show some deference and probably feel some respect. They might agree that they owe respect to members of high-ranking occupations (doctors, lawyers, professors), however.

In this, as in so many other ways, World War I is a historic watershed. In most European countries until that time, it was taken for granted that men in the upper social strata could use force on men in the lower social strata, lower castes, colonials, or natives, without being questioned much about it.[20] The gentry did not have that right in England, for they had lost it long before. In the United States they did not have that right either (except in encounters with blacks, Indians, and Chicanos). Richard Hofstadter states that upper-class whites paid a kind of deference to lower-class whites even in eighteenth-century Virginia, in part as a way of "cementing the social bonds of white men."[21] Now, women no longer curtsey before a person of higher rank or age, men do not doff their caps to superiors, and people no longer get off the sidewalk to make way for those of higher rank.[22]

That overt deference concealed both real respect and much hostility. Casanova remarks, for example (of eighteenth-century England), that people who went abroad in daylight in court dress often ran the risk of being pelted with mud by lower-class Londoners. It can be argued that the generally "harmonious exterior of rural society often hid a guerrilla class warfare"[23] in England, as evidenced by poaching, nighttime burnings of hayricks, hostile or ironic ballads, and sabotage.

20. On this point, see Leonard Woolf, *Beginning Again* (New York: Harcourt, Brace, Jovanovich, 1963).

21. See *America at 1750* (New York: Vintage, 1973), p. 162.

22. In the rural southern U.S., probably until World War II, white men continued to assert their right to dispense rough justice to blacks on the street without being questioned about it. Of course individual instances of that violence did not cease at once. A rough index of the change can perhaps be seen in the decline of lynching, which began in the interwar period.

23. For part of a debate on the issue of deference in British farming areas, see Howard Newby, "Deference and the Agricultural Worker," *The Sociological Review*, 23 (February, 1975): 51–60. E. P. Thompson's *The Making of the English Working Class* (New York: Vintage, 1966) is a detailed analysis of much covert hostility along with some daring overt disrespect. In the Restoration period, Nell

It would be a rash analyst indeed who would assert that modern people feel any less hostility about their class positions, but it does seem likely that not as much of it is directed at a particular class; it is more likely to be directed at harassing social institutions (schools, the police) or at the society generally. Even Sennett and Cobb, who lay bare much of the sense of injustice among the "respectable" working class, report that very little of it is directed at the upper classes, or even at leaders of the society.[24]

Both disrespect and respect have to be justified. Those who have less riches or privileges do not much respect those who have more merely because they have more. If they did, those at the top would not spend any energy in proclaiming how well they deserve those benefits; the benefits would be self-validating. If they were self-validating, those who have less would not feel injured by the injustice of that arrangement, or denounce the privileged for not meriting those rewards. Prestige does not come from mere profits; it comes much more from having deserved the profits.

It is partly for this reason that when people were much more conscious of their class positions, and the differences in classes were much more visible, they sometimes told fellow class members to conform to class ideals in various ways, so as to maintain not only their own class standing, but the standing of the class itself. It was common in colonial systems, for example, for whites to remind one another of their duty to comport themselves so as to maintain their position of high influence and esteem.[25] Individuals were not only chided at times as traitors to their class (Franklin Delano Roosevelt, for example), meaning that they had violated their own economic class interests, but also as bringing shame on their class by bad behavior. When servants were more common, upper-class people were reminded that they could be observed in intimate settings by members of the lower class and thus should comport themselves well. Sometimes the rhetoric takes the form of "people like us don't do such things," or "in our family we don't do such things," but the meaning is apparent just the same.

Individual failure to live up to class standards does not affect the prestige paid to the class itself, for such people typically drop to a lower rank. Just as classes as units or wholes do not "accept" or "reject" new members, so they do not hold on to old ones who are failing. Individual families, usually kin, may attempt to bolster their sagging position, but the class as a unit has little concern over such failures. If families cannot live up to the norms that determine rank (landed wealth, government or corporate position, education) it is not the class that loses esteem. Of

Gwynn once disarmed a hostile crowd surrounding her carriage by sticking her head out the window and informing them that she was not a lady, but "only the King's whore."

24. Sennett and Cobb, *Hidden Injuries of Class*, pp. 130ff. and chap. V.

25. L. S. B. Leakey incurred such a rebuke when on one of his field expeditions he did his share of heavy work, such as water carrying, along with his native helpers, even though his critic knew that Leakey was accepted as a "white Kikuyu." See *White African* (New York: Ballantine, 1966 [1937], p. 162.

course, sometimes a revolution or conquest may undermine the prestige of an upper class, but the incompetence of an individual family has no such effect.[26] A ruling class will lose prestige, however, if its protective system is so entrenched that even the incompetent members do not fail (although whether it will then lose its dominance is not dependent on prestige alone).

I believe that in no system, now or in the past, have those toward the lower social strata fully acquiesced in their less esteemed position (believed that their class was given as much in exchange as it gave).[27] They have doubtless felt some respect for those in higher ranks because they seemed more refined, better able to rule others or cope with larger problems, more competent in war, better educated, or well-versed in the high arts—but it has been a resentful or grudging esteem. It is not a full acquiescence because it is never possible to convince all who have not achieved much that they could not have done better if the social system had been arranged differently. If that assertion seems unlikely, a radical challenge to the common belief that once classes or castes lived in harmony together, there are at least some data that bear on it, most notably the outbreak of denigration against the formerly privileged, and a general joy, when the system itself seems to totter or fall.[28]

Thus it is that though the more privileged strata proclaim the justice of a system that rewards them well by asserting that their contributions to the society have merited respect and other privileges, we face the unfortunate historical fact that it is difficult to locate any historical periods in which an upper class lived up to its supposed obligations to contribute adequately to the society for the rewards received. There are few if any periods when subjects have not groaned under the political and economic burdens of the ruling class. At each successively higher social stratum, people in it did perceive that those above them were somewhat superior—but not *that* superior; many have expressed the view, in the quiet security among trusted friends, that the system itself was not a fair exchange.

26. Consequently, the class may maintain itself staunchly while individual families come and go. It is the maintenance of stability that most people perceive. Thus Joseph A. Schumpeter's classic comment is especially apt: " . . . each class resembles a hotel or an omnibus, always full, but always of different people" (*Imperialism and Social Classes*, trans. Heinz Norden (New York: Kelly, 1951), p. 165. For historical data on these changes, see B. Barber, *Social Stratification* (New York: Harcourt, Brace & World, 1957); and B. Barber and Elinor G. Barber, eds., *European Social Class* (New York: Macmillan, 1965).

27. For further analysis of this statement, see William J. Goode, "Social Mobility, Family, and Revolutionary Potential," in *Explorations in Social Theory*, pp. 287–315.

28. For a striking analysis of the underlayer of resentment against the higher orders even in the fourteenth century, see Rodney Hilton, *Bond Men Made Free: Medieval Peasant Movements and the English Rising of 1381* (New York: Viking, 1973). For notes on denigration or joy, see any account of the French or Russian revolutions, as well as Leon Litwak, "Free at Last," in Tamara A. Hareven, ed., *Anonymous Americans* (Englewood Cliffs, N.J.: Prentice-Hall, 1971), pp. 131–171.

Chapter 7
Prizes, Awards, Ribbons, and Honorific Offices

FORMAL REWARDS: PART OF THE PRESTIGE PROCESS

In all great civilizations, philosophers and religious teachers have warned against chasing after the glittering gewgaws the world offers, its medals, decorations, prizes, and ribbons, even though they are supposed to be given in recognition of merit, not fame.[1] After all, a crown of laurel did not make Nero's poetry greater, while the lack of blue ribbons did not reduce for long the esthetic impact of the early Impressionist paintings. To seek a decoration is to forsake the substance for the shadow; to be proud of a medal, rather than the achievement, to be tricked by worldly success. We should be pleased by what we learn, not the grades we get.

At one time or another, many people experience some confirmation of that wisdom. We are amused on reading historical accounts (in Pepys' diary, for example) of people's machinations toward getting a decoration or prize. We feel cynical at perusing a list of the honors a head of state has received, knowing that such exalted figures can, upon giving a medal to a visiting Excellency, expect in turn to receive an equivalent decoration at a suitable time. Professors can be forgiven some skepticism about honorary degrees, when they read the list of such degrees after the names of their university presidents; those degrees, too, have been given and received in a pro forma way. Many people have mused over the meaning of formal awards and prizes upon finding a drawer with old medals (their own or someone else's) in it. When we now look at old photographs or paintings of beribboned men, still famous or (more often) now unknown, we are likely to view those trinkets as pretentious and faintly ludicrous.

Nevertheless, the warnings of philosophers have restrained others from aspiring to formal honors about as much as their arguments for the possible spiritual benefits of poverty have restrained others from seeking

---

1. Although all such baubles are socially defined as *rewards*, the various kinds of prizes, loving cups, plaques, ribbons, medals, and awards are set apart from the ordinary payoffs for excellence, most notably by their *contest* pattern. Within this general class of prizes and awards many further distinctions can be made, e.g., between honorific titles or offices and prizes, but I do not as yet see any typology of awards that would be theoretically fruitful.

wealth. The hollowness of past prizes does not reduce by much the glitter of future ones. Specific awards and decorations lose their prestige-giving qualities over time, since the social system that once endowed them with respect diminishes in credence—for example, doubtless a modern British peer does not view the Garter as so desirable a gaud as did a sixteenth-century Elizabethan—but other prizes take their place as symbols of worthiness.[2] The man who now disdains his Boy Scout medals may nevertheless be working hard to earn a plaque for selling the most insurance in one month. Military medals have recently lost some of their luster in the United States, not merely because of the political opposition to the Vietnam War (people are not given as much honor when they do a bad thing well, and even less when they do a bad thing poorly), but also because many medals were falsely given. Nevertheless this situation does not lower by much the motivation to win awards for most achievements. It is not possible now to ascertain who first created this social invention, but it is safe to predict that as long as societies offer such formal prizes, people will work hard to garner them. Moreover, societies will always feel the need to offer them.

Formal awards, prizes, and other honors are mostly given to individuals, but they are simultaneously *public announcements*, typically made by an organization, and meant to convey information to as many people as possible in as many different social networks as possible. They assert the importance of the *activity*. They proclaim the esteem due to the recipients. They remind people (however subtly) that the organization is a judge of achievement, possesses prestige to confer on others, and also deserves some prestige for its support of that activity.

Prestige in one group (philanthropists, intellectuals, the upper class) can be obtained by giving a formal prize to people in another (artists, scientists). If one group or organization selects people as award recipients whom other networks also accept as worthy, the group will itself be esteemed, just as it (and the award) will lose some esteem if it frequently gives awards to people whom others judge as less worthy than other possible contenders. An examination of formal awards discloses some further regularities in the dynamics of prestige processes. Most important, it sheds further light on how the different parts of the social structure are connected, or on what we have been calling interlinkages.

FORMAL AWARDS VERSUS EVERYDAY PRESTIGE EVALUATIONS

Before analyzing the social conditions that generate such awards, let us note how they differ from the ordinary judgments that people constantly

---

2. Melbourne's quip, ascribed to others as well, about the Order of the Garter, was that he liked the Garter: There was no damned merit about it. But of course he was wrong. It was not given at random, and gossip often took the form of guessing that Minister X would receive the Garter for something he had done.

make about each other's performances and qualities. Most of these differences are centered in the formal quality of an award as an event, set apart from day-to-day evaluations. This event can be seen as the crystallization of opinion about who most deserves prestige at one point in time. It is to be distinguished from both the general prestige rankings that could be ascertained at one time point; and from a promotion, which is also an event.

At any given time, of course, the prestige rankings among a specific population or group can be ascertained, and the results announced. Indeed, this is sometimes done in the form of citation studies in a scientific field.[3] Sociometric inquiry can yield such a ranking within a fraternity house, a class, or any group whose members will (privately) express their choices about one another.[4] Recently, such an investigation was made of the intellectuals in the United States. Some decades ago "popularity contests" were held in many schools, and the vote represented a mixture of prestige ranking and "liking." Popular magazines sometimes devote several pages to "Young Business Leaders" or "Woman of the Year."

However, the top-ranking persons in such descriptive inquiries only rarely get prizes or awards.[5] The data merely show the state of opinion about certain individuals at one time, and even those who are pleased about who is the "winner" (mostly they do not find out) do not view the occasion as calling for any medal. It is of course imaginable that such a "vote" might be taken each year, and the winner given a ribbon or medal, but in fact that is not common.

Several additional elements are needed to transform such an event into one for which a formal award is viewed as socially appropriate. Most of these can be classed under two rubrics: contest reality and formality. Awards or prizes are given for the outcome of a confrontation of prestige opinions or claims, with reality as defined by a set of judges. The fact that some people may protest the judges' decision does not alter this social definition. The definition is most obvious in the cases where the opinions of judges are given the least freedom, for example, in person-to-person downhill ski racing when speeds are measured by electronic devices. Observers, friends, kin, and the racers themselves all have prior opinions

---

3. There are over 3,000 articles on the use of citation studies in science today: one which is particularly apt here is Daryl Chubin's "On the Use of the 'Science Citation Index' in Sociology," *American Sociologist*, 8 (November, 1973): 187–191.

4. For an early study of this kind, asserting its importance for many types of studies, see J. J. Moreno, *Who Shall Survive?* (Beacon, N.Y.: Beacon House, 1953). See also Theodore M. Newcomb's classic study *Personality and Social Change* (New York: Dryden, 1943), as well as Charles Kadushin's *The American Intellectual Elite* (Boston: Little, Brown, 1974).

5. In this analysis I do not distinguish awards from prizes, in part because their meaning overlaps considerably in English. In some contexts, a difference in usage may be observed. Typically the term prize is used when a definite ranking is announced, e.g., first prize, second prize, and so on. Sometimes the term award is used when there is one winner, but it is more often used when several people are given some type of distinction or honor, all of them receiving the same title or recognition, whether in money or scrollwork.

about which person is "really" faster, or who will win, but it is the reality context that determines "the" result. (Emphasis on *the* is required, since of course at another time the result might be different.) A device does the measuring, and the judges have almost no freedom in determining the winner, but their decision is crucial in ratifying the measurement.

Apparently far removed from that case, but in fact structurally similar, is an art show, in which judges have far more freedom to decide who has created the "best" painting in *that show* in various genres, such as still life, landscape, collage, and so on. Again, many people hold strong or weak judgments about whose work is best, both before *and* after the decisions. Nevertheless, the event is viewed as a confrontation of those claims or opinions with the "reality" as the judges decide it. Moreover, for various reasons to be explored subsequently, that judgment becomes in turn an independent and sometimes powerful factor in later judgments about who is best.

Some basis for this independent effect is to be found in the formal patterning of the decision process. That is, unlike ordinary, casual evaluations, these are organized to increase the likelihood the judges will be both competent and fair. Whether the "prize" is an honorary degree, a Pulitzer Prize for newspaper reporting, a Congressional Medal or other military medal, or the award for being Rookie of the Year, all require a formal definition of who may be a judge and who may be a claimant or contestant (whether or not the person to be judged has even asked for the honor), and a set of rules or criteria on the basis of which the judgment is to be made. Almost always, a formal vote is taken. In the case of the Oscars, the awards for various activities in film-making, the voting procedures are elaborate, since the number of "judges" is large: the voters are employees in the movie industry.

Some time after the vote, the winner or winners are announced, most often at a public, formal ceremony in which the winners, the organization, and the activity it encourages are praised. The meaning of this ceremonial performance will be analyzed later. For now, I should emphasize only that though our traits and performances are evaluated in our daily lives, we are not given awards for a high ranking, while the prize process is set apart in several important ways from that unbroken stream of daily judgment.

Two further differences, perhaps socially the most important ones, are that the formality of the contest 1) transforms all contestants (whether or not they asked to compete) into strangers, and 2) places all of them on an equal rank as competitors. In any field, many of the potential winners are known to one another, and they are surrounded by social networks who know some or all of the work to be judged. The contest asserts that all of their personalistic ties are irrelevant, and so are their prior judgments. The judges should pay no attention to those opinions, or even to their own. In addition, although it may be obvious (as in a tennis match, an art show, or a competition for a medal in science) that some people are superior to others, that *general superiority*, as well as the likelihood that only a few people are likely winners, is by social rule deemed irrelevant: All are equal until their work is judged at this particular time.

Finally, it is the achievement or performance that is being judged, not the contestants' loyalty, aspiration or ambition, hard work or intelligence, or kindness. It is rare that anyone is given a medal for having a fine character, just as one is not given a prize for an ascriptive trait, such as having the most aristocratic lineage.

PROMOTIONS AND PRIZES

Although it is safe to say that most people who are given promotions rank higher in prestige than those who are not, that a specific set of "judges" (managerial superiors) make those decisions, and that these are formally announced, promotions are also defined socially as different from prizes or awards. Let us consider these differences.

First, to accept a promotion is to agree to carry out a specific set of performances for as long as one holds the job. In this the promotion differs from most awards, even though at least some prizes require the winner to deliver a lecture or make a speech at some later time. Second, almost all who are promoted have not yet proved they can do the job at all, since most have never held that position before. No such contingency is encountered in the acceptance of a prize. Instead, one is certified as having *already* performed well at the task, and one is not even required to perform again at that level.

In this respect, too, the prize or award differs from another type of formal judgment, the election. In the United States, there are somewhat more than half a million local, state, or national offices that are won through formal elections. Here, then, there is a single time of judgment, a set of rules, and a set of judges, but winning is not defined as a prize or award. The outcome is partly a prestige evaluation: Who is ranked as the best? However, there is no certification that the individual has done an excellent job, merely that some people want that person to *begin* doing a particular job. The judgment is an expression of hope or trust about the future, rather than an evaluation of an achievement already made.

A third difference between formal awards and various kinds of promotions is that the range of performances required of one who has been promoted or who has been victorious in an election is wide, and the higher the job level the wider that range. By contrast, most awards, and almost all well-known ones, are given for a high achievement in a very narrow type of activity, whether it be lyric poetry or the hundred-meter sprint.

Fourth, a prize is not given for an ascriptive quality, but nearly always for a past performance. By contrast, although all societies utilize both ascriptive and achievement criteria in social placement, it is well understood that many specific promotions or positions have been given for ascriptive traits. For example, kings, emperors, and aristocrats were given those and other court-released posts through ascription. Even in modern society it is not difficult to observe jobs being given partly or mainly for such qualities as age, sex, race, ethnic membership, religion, or—being the owner's son.

This fourth difference, it should be emphasized, is not a sharp one, because sex and race especially have been used to eliminate many potential competitors from a contest beforehand, thus avoiding the charge of bias in the judging itself.[6] Nevertheless, the very narrowness of the performance being judged, and the definition of the judgment as applying only to the performance (not the performer), reduces the *immediate* effect of ascriptive criteria in formal awards; and in any event such prizes are not given for such qualities.

Thus, if people aspire to formal awards and prizes in *addition* to being generally esteemed, or specifically promoted, it is because the prestige they get from them is socially distinct and embedded in a different structure. The possible fruitfulness of further exploring this category of processes in the allocation of prestige, with reference to both the social control impact of awards and the kinds of social groups that offer them, is evident.

THE IMPORTANCE OF PRIZES

Although we must later confront the question of why some groups or organizations give prizes and awards, let us consider briefly why both participants and winners consider formal awards of great significance and so are willing to be evaluated.

Perhaps one important psychological basis may be found in a theory propounded by Festinger, who argues that people "need" to evaluate themselves by reference to others, that is, to rank themselves in relation to others by reference not merely to height, weight, location, and so on, but also to intellectual and psychological traits or attitudes as well.[7] It is as though a person is not entirely sure of his or her identity or self without making such comparisons. We need not pause to examine whether this is true psychological "need," for it is at least obvious that people constantly engage in such comparison behavior. Moreover, from time to time they appear to seek various types of social situations in which they can measure themselves against others. Awards, like examinations, constitute one of the few points where a person has a relatively full assurance, if not of real

6. For example, in the 1970's many female athletes, from Little League to college levels, were not allowed to compete with males. Although the topmost performers are almost certain to be males, many females below that level are superior to many males, so that the refusal violates a fundamental norm of athletics (the best should win). This norm is gradually triumphing over the sexist embarrassment.

7. Leon Festinger, "A Theory of Social Comparison Processes," *Human Relations*, 7 (May, 1954): 117–140.

achievement—of top performance—then at least of how he or she is judged by others.

In societies where that search for knowledge about one's worth in relation to others is much less intense, such awards would be far less common. This is likely to be the situation in most primitive societies of the past. In such social systems, most people learned more easily how their skills and qualities were judged, and they felt less doubt because the judges they faced (the members of the society) were more likely to agree on that evaluation. In most of these societies, people were less likely to experience failure in a competitive situation, for formal competitions were not common.

However, test situations did occur in some social systems. For example, the Plains Indian tribes did not actually give awards, but at least they defined the trophies of war raids as proofs of high merit. Similarly, in many warlike societies, loot or trophies were given to people as rewards for conspicuous bravery or skill in battle, though most of these were not true formal contests.

Phrased in Calvinist rhetoric, winning a formal award or prize is an "evidence of grace." It suggests that one's talents are worthy of respect. To the extent that the winner believes the judges are wise critics, he or she can believe for a while in his or her excellence. At worst, as an index of merit, to win is better than to lose.

Next, we note the peculiar relation of the formal award to the "career," or sequence of later events in life. Always afterward, one has earned the honor: Whatever happens later, the award is a proof that at one point one reached a certain level. It is more reliable than rumor or self-claim about how well one performed. It is thus like other physical evidences of high points in one's past, such as newspaper clippings, heirlooms, love letters, or the ownership of a few acres left from a family plantation.

For reasons that are already clear, such prize contests are newsworthy, attracting the attention of a far wider audience than just the participants. If they are only grammar school foot races, their news value is relatively low on a national scale, but even then they excite much discussion among the relevant families and permit the exhibition of pride. Contests arouse interest because they are viewed as dramatic. People typically want to know who is currently "champion" and who is closest in performance to the best.

Because of this news value and because presumably honest judges have decided or certified who has performed better or best, the outcome can have considerable effect on later steps in people's choices and careers, as they move from one school to another, one city to another, or one job or social network to another. Awards of lesser importance, at lower levels of achievement—high school prizes for excellence in German, field sports, or public speaking—of course lose most of their impact within a few years, but for a while they too may affect the individual's success in eliciting others' cooperation, encouragement, and support. They are viewed as indexes of other forms of excellence, and the advantages they yield in the short term may open opportunities which over a much longer term lead to still greater achievement.

In adulthood, of course, prizes are less frequent but are likely to be worth still more, in either money or prestige. Literary prizes may insure both publicity and financial rewards. Medals in science may increase the individual's chances of getting research grants, promotions, and further prizes. Ribbons or awards won in field trials for hunting dogs may help one to join an elite country club. All these may help in the same way as personal recommendations and general prestige rankings, but their presumed objectivity gives them a special independence in swaying decisions, especially of people in other networks who have little direct knowledge of the person in question.

Whether participants actively seek to be contestants, passively allow their work to be considered, or have little control over whether they are evaluated, most will not win. Consequently, one might suppose that many would not wish to participate, since the chance of failure is so high. However, the costs of not participating may also be high; and the added investment or cost of participating may not be great, since one is engaged in the activity anyway.

The cost of not participating may be high because thereby one asserts that one's work or skill is not up to the level of other possible participants. The cost of taking part in this particular award process may be relatively low, since one may not have to prepare any special work or activity for it. For example, one shows paintings already done; and even if one makes one or more paintings especially for this show they form part of one's life work afterward. A foot race is done especially for a particular contest, but the racer does not have to make many special investments for it, since he or she is training for more than one such race. The possibility of failure discourages fewer people than one might suppose, if one is considering only the likelihood of defeat.

However, the possibility of gaining an award or prize does exist, and most people experience direct pleasure at winning, whether the contest is a word game at a party or a national prize in literature or science. Awards at any phase of one's career may yield advantages later on. The contests themselves are experienced as dramatic by those who are eligible, as well as by others who are linked with them socially. The outcome affects the flow of information about winners and losers, and changes the prestige ranking of individuals and organizations. Thus, many social factors make prizes and awards important for all who participate in the evaluation process.

TYPES OF PRIZE-GIVERS

Structurally, most prize-givers fall into three main types. The first can be called institutional. Those who are eligible for formal awards are employees of an organization. Such organizations include corporations, schools, armies, and the employees but not the parishioners of churches.

The second can be called voluntary groups. The people who become competitors are part of the group who actually create or make up the organization. They have banded together in order to pursue and promote activities of their own choosing. Such organizations include dry cleaners' associations, church clubs, academic societies.

The third can be labeled award organizations. Their main goal is to set up such competitions, which include Miss America contests, stock shows, the Nobel and Vetlesen prizes, and athletic contests.[8]

Concretely, of course, these categories overlap to some degree. For example, some voluntary organizations such as academic or professional societies, or clubs associated with a church, may set up special committees to carry out the prize-giving. Organizations whose main activity is to regulate a competition may in addition begin to create subsidiary activities and programs, related to their general field of interest. A church may give a medal to a layman, for his or her contribution to church activities, or a government may give a medal to a civilian for special bravery in saving other people's lives. Nevertheless, in the main these structural types predominate.

Note that in the first of these types, the institutional, the participants spend much of their time working at tasks set by the organization, which in turn controls a large part of the flow of the other day-to-day rewards the individual gets. A corporation, school or army is engaged in a set of tasks specified by its charter; the individual is paid for his or her contribution to that on-going activity. The organization itself is central in the lives of these participants, who may or may not become competitors if it sets up some type of contest.

Prizes themselves are not very central to either the institutional or the voluntary type of prize-givers, for both are primarily engaged in other kinds of tasks. The voluntary type is distinguished from the institutional because it does not loom very large in the lives of most of its members. Most of their time is engaged in their day-to-day work as job-holders, or in family or neighborhood interaction, and their members may indeed belong to many other kinds of voluntary organizations.

By contrast to both of those, in the award organization the prizes and the prize process are central to its existence and thus to the members of that organization, but the organization itself does not play a large role in the lives of possible competitors. Some award organizations give a prize or some recognition to people who did not ask to compete and who have

---

8. A fourth type should be noted here, although it plays a lesser role in the interlinkages among social networks or the submarkets of prestige: the nonrecurring prize or reward typically given by the first or second types of organizations noted above. Sometimes a special prize or medal is given to an individual who has carried out some special or unique assignment, e.g., navigating a submarine under the polar icecap, developing a special type of wheat or rice, or serving a local community as a physician for fifty years.

little knowledge of the rules for the competition. For example, a goodly number of people are made members of the National Academy of Science, or the American Academy of Arts and Sciences, with only a vague knowledge of how they were chosen, or what membership might require of them, if anything. Perhaps for a large number of prizes, the organization that gives the prize does not loom very large in the lives of those whose work is being evaluated, though the prize itself may be viewed as important.

SOCIAL APPROPRIATENESS OF PRIZES AND AWARDS

Common to the three types above is that some achievement is given a special recognition, although the general activity itself is one that people go right on doing just the same. They are engaged in raising tomatoes, being beautiful, or doing research, and they are given some amount of daily esteem for their competence, achievements, or qualities. The question then arises: Why do people or organizations feel that it is appropriate, useful, or important to give such awards, to single out individuals in some special way? We might suppose that this is no more than a custom of our era, needing no explanation. That is, the number of contests and awards has increased greatly over the past generation, and has been steadily rising for well over a century, and we can take such contests for granted. They are part of our daily experience. Award contests now form a social model to be followed by any group or organization that wishes to emulate others.

However, we ought not take such competitions for granted. First, this custom has not been universal. Indeed, in most social settings in world history such award processes have not been usual (although they probably have been in all large-scale societies). Second, they require socioeconomic investments and costs—and even run the risk of failure—which must be set against the possible gains to the group. (For example, a subgroup or organization may have to be created.) There must be rules for entrance and adjudication, judges, set times for entry and judgment, an agreement on what the prizes will be, and arrangements for announcing the decision.

Much more important in cross-cultural as well as historical perspective is the question of why some kinds of activities are judged to be appropriate for some form of competition and award-giving. Here, as in several other analyses in this book, we face a problem in folk sociology. That is, we observe the groping attempts of human beings to develop some kinds of social structures or motivational systems that will elicit from others a behavior that is desired by the group or community. Awards and prizes are a very small part, but a dramatic part, of the total amount of earning or receiving esteem in a society, and we are asking why some types of activities are socially viewed as more or less useful for this kind of special recognition.

Let us first approach the problem of locating some social settings in which formal awards are viewed as socially inappropriate. Our three types of award-givers implicitly suggest a first regularity, for all of them refer to *organizations*. It is rare by contrast that an individual sets up such a contest or a prize, either for himself or for others. That is, an individual will only be laughed at if he organizes a competition in which he is the sole competitor and receives for himself a gold medal, announcing to the world that he is the World's Greatest Lover or Hero.[9] A person would also be received with suspicion, laughter, or rejection if he or she walked up to a group of strangers on a street corner and there attempted to pin a medal on some individual, proclaiming him or her as Our Neighborhood's Finest Citizen, or indeed any other honorific appellation. Such a prize-giver has little or no prestige to give, the recipient does not in fact believe that he or she was chosen in a genuine competition, and anyone who seriously accepts the medal would be laughed at by friends.

Similarly, families do not engage in such formal competitions and do not offer formal prizes to their members. Those few who do typically view this as one of their lovable idiosyncrasies, and as a type of game. I suppose that the members of most families would be reluctant to organize such contests because their ranking in various kinds of competitions is already well known, so that no judgments are necessary. In addition, they share in each other's prestige to a substantial extent, even without a prize. In any event, the number competing would typically be too small to legitimate a set of judges, a set of rules, or an award.

Correspondingly, friendship groups do not organize such competitions. Again, members usually know already where they stand relative to one another, or they do not wish to bring that standing into prominence. To introduce such a formal competitive pattern into their informal relations would undermine to some degree their friendship. As with a family, their numbers are too few to permit the organization of a committee of judges, a set of rules, and a group of awards. Once more, we can envision the possibility that a friendship group might establish a formal, voluntary organization that would attempt to give prizes for fun, and some neighborhood gangs do precisely that. Nevertheless, it would be generally understood that outsiders would not honor those prizes at all, but would view them as a joke.

A segment or aggregate of a population does not confer such awards. The population can be divided into those who have longer fingernails or shorter, rosy cheeks or pale, blond hair or dark, but such aggregates do not share much social life and do not often recognize that they together form a group. They are unlikely to meet for the purpose of deciding upon an honor to be given to someone who represents their activities, goals, values, or problems. Here we deliberately select trivial physical traits, but in fact the larger ethnic or racial aggregates in the population do not offer

9. And, since some people will enjoy the joke, some Times Square novelty shops sell just such scrolls, documents, or fake medals for that purpose.

prizes, either. Only when representatives of such groups set up formal, voluntary organizations are prizes given for activities related to some of the special interests of those segments of the society.

Audiences and clienteles are not usually groups, do not typically form organizations, and do not ordinarily give prizes. Perhaps the closest approximation to an audience giving a prize is the testimonial dinner, probably most often given to a politician or physician. In press releases, these are described to the public as prestige awards made by a clientele after serious deliberation. It is safe to say, however, that such dinners for political figures are almost never organized by a mass of grateful voters, but by political cronies. They do not typically confer much prestige, even when a formal scroll or plaque is presented to the official. Newspaper editors recognize this situation by viewing such affairs as "nonevents," and they give modest coverage to the speeches made on such occasions. The testimonial dinner to a physician is more likely to be an expression of genuine gratefulness, but even in this situation his or her clientele must organize a specific formal group for the purpose; and they cannot confer as much honor as a medical group could, for they do not possess it.

The question of whether a group is socially viewed as having prestige to give is especially relevant for another type of organization which does not often give prizes: a maximum security prison or a concentration camp. Administrators of such prisons are typically convinced that their inmates would view such a competition as a fraud, a sly attempt at manipulation. They believe the prisoners would view the prizes as embodying little prestige and having little value in the outside world. Viewing their relationship with prisoners as largely antagonistic, they are also convinced that prisoners would reject the prizes because accepting them would validate the prison authorities as a main source of prestige.

Their judgments are only partly correct. What little evidence we do possess on the very modest attempts to give prestige rewards of various kinds suggests that although prisoners do begin with such attitudes, they can be convinced that the prizes are worth something. In fact they are likely to alter their behavior somewhat in order to win them.[10]

Of course, prisoners may view each other as having prestige to confer, even when they view their keepers as having little authority. Under some circumstances both captured soldiers in an enemy camp and inmates of concentration camps have organized their own competitions, to keep up morale, to offer entertainment, to assert their own social structure. Such contests implicitly affirm the group's own capacity to give esteem to those who achieve well by its standards.

Groups do not feel it is appropriate to give awards for the "small virtues," such as being neighborly, wise, or honest. This is partly a problem of making judgments: Most ascriptive traits and most of the

10. Robert L. Hamblin *et al.*, *The Humanization Process* (New York: Wiley-Interscience, 1971).

small virtues are not graded by fine distinctions. More important, it is likely that even in our award-giving epoch, a competition in activities that by social definition should not be motivated by public payoffs would violate the meaning of those virtues.

Awards are not given for purely ascriptive traits, such as race, sex, or caste. At least two sets of factors make such an award unlikely. First, most ascriptive traits are, like the small virtues, not graded finely, and thus they cannot be used easily to determine who is "best." Indeed, they are typically used to create social *categories*, whose members are defined roughly as being at the same level with respect to that particular trait. The ranks of aristocracy are somewhat more finely graded, but again no more than a limited number of social categories is created (dukes, earls, and so on).[11]

The second set of factors that make awards for ascriptive traits unlikely are the felt principles of folk sociology that would define such a contest as absurd. I suggest that the social absurdity is based on these understandings: The award cannot be based on a contest, since all the "data" are compiled already. It cannot be a contest, since the participants would not be competing with one another; after all, they do not have to do anything. Since they do not have to do anything, the award cannot motivate anyone else—other possible competitors—to try harder, to do better. Even more violative of what an award-yielding contest must be is that possible competitors could not do better even if they wanted to. That is, the data and actions that are relevant are all in the past, and cannot (or should not) be altered. Next, there is no achievement to celebrate, since no living person has created his or her lineage.[12] Finally, the community would not feel it has gained anything from this nonachievement.

It is clear, then, that any group, or even an individual, could arbitrarily announce a competition and give a prize, to anyone, for almost anything; but most people would reject a wide range of such possibilities as socially inappropriate or absurd. What is viewed as an activity for which an award or prize might be given will vary historically and in different societies.

WHAT DO AWARDS ACCOMPLISH?

We have spoken of the importance of prizes and awards for both winners and participants. Let us continue our analysis of the social inappropriateness of award-giving by considering what goals, aims, or consequences of the group itself are served. Thereby we can see more easily why

11. Of course, for each special court function there may be a specific order of precedence, though it is not determined by the "most aristocratic lineage," and there is no such award or competition. Kinship with the royal family may determine precedence, but the reader should remember that many royal families would not rank very high on the nobility of their lineage.

12. Equally absurd would be an award for the "World's Richest Man" or "Most Politically Powerful Man," but such a contest would violate, I think, different principles of folk sociology—most notably, the community would feel such achievements are already rewards in themselves.

prizes and awards are more common, or historically appeared earlier, in some types of activities than in others.

The most obvious group or subsystem goal that is served by such prize competitions is that they sift and evaluate the participants, and thus furnish information about how each individual ranks in his or her achievement. They offer a basis for judgments about possible future achievements and are used in decisions about recruitment or the encouragement of people's talents. This may be especially important where members of the subgroup do not have accurate knowledge about the abilities or achievements of all other members.

Such prizes give prestige primarily to activities that do not pay off very well materially. This general statement will be examined in more detail in subsequent pages. In addition, awards and prizes are most common, or arise earlier historically, in activities that seem not to be central concerns of the society, such as play, athletics, and games; or they are given within some special subactivities of a central activity that are themselves not of prime importance. To some degree, then, prizes substitute for other types of benefits: This is a second group goal served by prize competitions.

A third goal of such competitions is to give prestige to achievements that seem so outstanding that not honoring them is to deny some supposed values of the society. This can especially apply to scientific prizes or medals, which can be seen less as motivating others than as celebrating achievement itself.

It is not easy to state rules for distinguishing among these goals or functions. Indeed, one might claim that the third overlaps to some degree with the second category, because the third category may also be viewed as attempting to redress a discrepancy between what has been accomplished and the material rewards that are likely to be forthcoming.

Let us now attempt to state these relationships in a more concrete way by examining the main areas in which prizes have been more common, or have arisen earlier, before the contemporary proliferation of prizes and awards in almost all kinds of activities.

The areas in which competition awards are viewed as socially most appropriate are the school, athletics (especially school athletics), and the arts. They are much less common in business and government—that is, the central activities of modern society—except for the military. They are common in one other area that is not merely peripheral to the central concerns of the society, but is a folk survival from older times: dog and horse shows, rodeos, and county fairs, for example. In its heyday, this last type offered dozens of competitions, from Largest Squash to Best Grape Jelly. After we consider these main areas, we shall go on to examine other specific types of award-giving, in an effort to illuminate this phenomenon still more.

Prizes of various kinds are common in grammar school, increase in number through high school, and drop off substantially in college and graduate school, though the awards themselves increase in prestige value at that level. Prizes are still less common experiences for professors, but these prizes yield still higher esteem.[13]

In school activities, the goals that such prizes and awards serve are not at all obscure. They have been part of school life for hundreds of years. Teachers offer them in an effort to improve scholarship, heighten an interest in school athletics, and recognize attainment and thus sift the best pupils from the others. Above all, they assert the independent importance of an activity that is widely understood to be no more than preliminary to life in the real world, outside the school. One important consequence of such contests in schools is to develop in pupils a general motivation to compete throughout adulthood.

It is not easy to teach pupils that scholarship is of high significance, for that is a judgment contrary to common sense. From grammar school through the university, students have always suspected that school work is mostly irrelevant to their later adult tasks. They have understood that to go through school was and is useful, but school achievement does not help much in becoming a good electrician or even a good corporation executive. Consequently, when permitted to do so, they have paid less attention to scholarship than to social activities, which are more fun and are even likely to be of much practical use later on.

Teachers have thus complained for generations about student resistance to their efforts. Backed by parents and the state, they could (and still can) for the most part enforce discipline and order in the classroom, but to make children study is a more difficult task. Teachers cannot offer real friendships, wages, or political power as rewards.[14] Their main resource for social control is prestige. Even their promises of future rewards in wealth or worldly success are not to be taken seriously, since those possible payoffs must be discounted by the necessarily long period before they occur. The chances of actually getting them are not very great even when all goes well.

To the extent that teachers can make the school into a real social system, however, with its own set of prestige rewards, they can overcome their large handicap by making heroes of those who perform outstandingly in that world. By creating, in addition, a wide *range* of different compe-

13. "Less common" than at earlier career phases, but the academic world almost certainly gives more awards, prizes, and honors than almost any other, with the possible exception of sports. Many thousands are given each year. For data on who knows about them, within a subarea of physical science, see Jonathan R. Cole and Stephen Cole, *Social Stratification in Science* (Chicago: University of Chicago Press, 1973), pp. 179ff.

14. On the other hand, it is possible that this is at least one reason for their frequent failure. See in this connection the work of Robert L. Hamblin *et al.*, *The Humanization Process*. This group has carried out a series of remarkable experiments, aimed at transforming the skills and motivation of children at various levels in different kinds of schools, through both prestige-giving and tokens that can be exchanged for both privileges and material goods. It seems likely that some part of the success occurs because the rewards are tied closely to the individual pupil's level of beginning competence and motivation; but the exchangeable tokens are of much importance, too.

titions, from making posters to attending school regularly, they can enlist a large percentage of their pupils, who can become interested in at least a few such contests.[15] Since these socialization processes occur in childhood, they are likely to have a maximum effect upon both psychological motivation and commitment to the values of the school.

Prizes for all types of school activities constitute one category of competition awards; a second, and related, category is that of athletics. Prizes, ribbons, and medals are deemed so appropriate in athletic contests that it is difficult for most Westerners to imagine a competition in the high hurdles, the pole vault, the giant slalom, or any other athletic skill without such tokens of victory. Until after World War II most such contests were amateur school events, which far outnumbered professional ones. It seems likely that the modern development of professional sports has been accompanied by a proliferation of awards and prizes because the social model is based upon amateur and school athletics. Since World War II, prizes have increased in professional sports, while many sports that were once mainly amateur and little noted (for example, women's bowling and tennis) have become commercial successes. Winners are paid more in both money and symbols. This fact is a strong reminder of what prizes do that money does not. The public is more attentive to who is "the best," or who wins in a particular tournament, than to who has earned the largest salary. Players assert that winning an important contest (for example, tennis at Wimbledon) is worth more than earning even more money somewhere else. Sports promoters use their ingenuity in creating new rules and contests for prize-giving, not primarily to motivate players but to excite the interest of the audience.

Schools have generally been more successful in exciting the interest of students in athletics, as participants or spectators, than in scholarship. Sports are more fun than irregular verbs. As drama, too, they are far superior for many reasons, not the least of which is that there is a definite conclusion, and one can both witness the performance and judge the winner oneself. Almost certainly, athletic contests and games were developed in human history long before schools, in part because they are a primitive form of theater.[16] Consequently, they were and are used as a social device for creating student allegiance to the school, and for making the school into a real social system whose values are respected. Like so many other such social devices, they may come to command more allegiance than the system they were created to support.

Let us pursue a step further the question of why such medals, prizes, or

15. For an earlier study of such contests, see Shu-Kuei Carol Chen, *Honors and Awards in American High Schools* (New York: Hillside, 1933), who asserts that about half of high school students try to win awards in nonathletic extracurricular activities, and from one-fifth to one-fourth of students seek prizes in citizenship, scholarship, athletics, and attendance (p. 111).

16. Very likely, the foot race is the most nearly universal award-yielding contest. It is found in almost all cultures, although the "award" may be no more than a token, a feather, a wreath, or a jokingly awarded symbol of victory.

awards are given in athletics. Both participants and spectators feel something is amiss if no such victory symbol is given. If scoring is possible, people want to keep score, for otherwise they do not feel they are really playing that particular game.[17] It seems clear that the prize or cup is a tangible proof of victory.

I am willing to hazard the guess that the social meaning of the prize originated in military raids and war generally. Aside from the material value of war trophies and loot in the distant past, they proved that the warrior was competent and brave. He did not carry back the enemy's shield or sword, scalp or gold drinking cup with the enemy's gracious permission; he must have been victorious. So, similarly, in athletic contests—which have often been viewed as a type of battle conducted under formal and less murderous rules—the ribbon or trophy remains as proof of one's achievement. This may be especially important in formal athletic contests, because they recur: there will be new champions. Fame and prestige are ephemeral. Thus both the group and the individual want such tokens.

It needs to be emphasized, in this period of rapid professionalization of athletics as an expanding branch of the entertainment industry, that until World War II most athletes were amateurs. Few could make an occupation of athletics. Some amateurs, mainly in college football, received token financial benefits secretly, but most athletes dropped competition soon after leaving school. Prestige was most of whatever reward they received from other people. For most of Western history, athletes have obtained modest amounts of prestige for their high achievements and their contributions to the group pleasure of spectators, but their material rewards have been minimal. Correspondingly, in the Anglo world until recently, a fairly strict social line—marked by the difference in prestige between those who competed solely for honor and those who were *paid*—separated the "gentlemen" from the "players" in cricket.

Thus, the material rewards of professional sports (fed by television's demand for drama) have grown, and the social importance of prizes and awards has very likely kept pace with that growth. Sports promotors deliberately create new contests and rules for declaring new kinds of "winners" in each sport, and the audience continues to feel that it is socially appropriate to give plaques and awards to winners in athletics, as in school activities.

A third area of competition awards—again, one that is not defined as one of the central concerns of the society—is the creative arts. There, success is highly contingent; even if it comes, it may not bring large material rewards. Some highly esteemed lyric poets and composers, paint-

17. However: in a private communication, Harry Edwards informs me that in some unofficial basketball games in China, young people were reported not to be keeping score, in a deliberate effort to make the game a fraternal and communal one. This may be a passing phase in China, with its new emphasis on international sports competition.

ers and sculptors, have earned large incomes, especially those who have lived to be old; but all are told early in their careers, and often correctly, that they should not believe money comes with esthetic esteem.

Thus, in contrast to academic teachers who believe that hard work at scholarship might pay off eventually in financial success, teachers of the high arts cannot do that. Those individuals who show talent at an early age are likely to be encouraged to take part in competitions, and winners are encouraged by the prizes they receive. These contests are more common in art than in writing. Such art competitions occur not only in art schools; they are also encountered in ordinary schools, colleges, and local communities. Of course they are also encountered in later professional life, though less often.

Creative as well as performing artists are paid esteem partly for their supposed selfless devotion to the activity itself, for it is widely believed that they could not devote themselves to the arts for the money alone. They are partly paid, too, for their contributions to the maintenance of high culture in their society. This was once mainly a concern of the aristocracy, who thereby proved their claim to being finer than lesser people. Both monarchs and aristocrats gained some esteem for their support of budding or ranking artists, whether musicians, painters, or sculptors (another link between different segments of the society). As the middle classes have also come to give wider support to the creative arts, practitioners are no longer seen as artisans, skilled workers, or servants of aristocrats and kings. Consequently, their class prestige has increased considerably over the past several centuries.[18]

More people now earn some money from the creative arts than in the past, but it is not certain that a higher percentage of aspirants can make a living from them than, say, a hundred years ago. This is especially true for painting, poetry, and sculpture, since far more people enter these activities than in the past, convinced by the art objects they see that they could do better.

Nevertheless, except for the teachers of creative arts, it is difficult to make a living from these vocations. Here, too, competitions help outsiders to learn who are the ranking or rising creative people. Prizes and awards thus yield prestige that is likely to be translated into sales, commissions, or jobs. Aside from the indirect effect, the winners are paid directly in esteem, for activities that the group honors but is not willing to pay for with substantial material rewards.

Note that as prize-giving itself has become a widely emulated model, and comes to be experienced as a dramatic element in modern life, prizes and awards are increasingly to be encountered in show business, not alone in the creative arts. Thus, there is an Oscar competition each year in the

---

18. The lowliness of that rank should not however be overdramatized; many creative artists were welcome in aristocratic or royal courts, as real artisans (bricklayers, carpenters) were not.

film industry. There are Emmy awards in television; awards are given for the Broadway musicals judged to be best, as well as to serious dramas; and similar awards or prizes are given for various categories of radio shows as well as for rock music.

What is notable about all of these is that the proclaimed and official justification for the awards is some type of esthetic criterion. One can imagine giving a prize to the Broadway show that has simply earned the most money during the year, but in fact that type of award is viewed as inappropriate. In effect, the social definition is that it is inappropriate to give special honor for simple financial achievement (which, unlike virtue, is its own reward). So, similarly, an award could conceivably be offered for the popular book that has earned the most money during a given year; but the various literary awards for books, whether in lyric poetry or the novel, are supposedly given for artistic merit, as decided upon by literary judges.

Although prizes and awards frequently occur in school activities, athletics, and the arts, contests are not common, as noted earlier, in business or government, except for military activities. Let us consider for a moment why it is viewed as appropriate to give various kinds of medals for achievement in military life, where they are typically not won as part of a formal contest as in athletics or the school.

The case is especially instructive because it must be conceded that war (unlike scholarship, athletics, and the creative arts) has been a central concern of all major and minor nations everywhere, for as long as we have records. People who excel in it are given more honor in wartime than in the peaceful episodes that have now and then marked even the history of warlike countries.[19] Nevertheless, the highest medals are given for a type of achievement that is not central to the main functioning of a war machine.

Moreover, the military instance is the more instructive, since the military gives many other awards than honor, and distributes many other resources in the form of promotions, raises, and interesting or comfortable job assignments. Presumably, that distribution is based upon competence or achievement in these occupational tasks. In addition, precisely because of the high emphasis in military training upon both personal honor and group esteem, awards and medals are distributed for a wide range of achievements, from sharpshooting to excelling in close order drill on the parade ground.

Nevertheless, these rewards do not yield the same kind of prestige that medals for heroism do; and winners of the highest award in the United States (the Congressional Medal of Honor) are, in some official ceremonies

---

19. Even in China, in whose official Confucian philosophy (supported by learned mandarins) learning but not military endeavor was supposed to receive the highest esteem, successful generals were honored just the same.

and social affairs, given precedence over high-ranking officers. As noted earlier, trophies and loot of various kinds commonly served in the past as symbols of victory. The capture of an enemy's battle plan was viewed as a triumph, to be exhibited later in museums or royal halls. On the other hand, formal medals were not common in military history until the creation of the mass army in Napoleon's time. His contemporary Wellington continued to give medals only to officers, but Napoleon gave them to enlisted men as well. The wars of mass movement that began in the Napoleonic era made it much more difficult for all the participants to know who had been conspicuously brave, quite unlike the small-scale raids or battles of previous centuries. The likelihood that substantial loot would fall to each individual warrior was also reduced, since battles were increasingly fought in the field, where few people could count on obtaining any loot at all; while the numbers of soldiers were so large that even a city might yield too little as an adequate reward for each brave person in the successful army. Thus medals became a symbolic substitute for loot.

On the other hand, field battles between mass armies have also made personal bravery far less important militarily than in the battles that occurred prior to the nineteenth century. It is likely that in the major wars of mass movement since Napoleon's time almost no important battles and no wars have been determined by individual or group heroism. Nevertheless, within the hierarchy of military values, heroic behavior elicits great admiration.[20]

Dr. Johnson once commented that courage is considered the greatest virtue because without it a person has no ability to preserve any other virtues. Very likely he spoke for most people in asserting that: "Courage is so necessary to maintaining virtue that it is always respected, even when associated with vice."[21] Prizes, awards, and ribbons may increase people's dedication to an activity, in the hopes of winning greater prestige, but it is difficult (for modern urban people) to imagine how individuals might be motivated much by the possibility of obtaining a medal for gallantry. At best, the chance of obtaining one will be small, but the chance of getting killed in the kinds of situations where one could win it will be high.

Military leaders have always maintained that courage in battle is of great importance, and some have indeed argued that battles are largely determined by which side runs away first. Militarily, of course, the brave will have a small edge over the cowardly; but in all modern wars, with only a few exceptions, both sides have shown great bravery and willingness to die. Perhaps the truth in the assertions of the military is that

20. On this point see Morris Janowitz, *The Professional Soldier* (Chicago: University of Chicago Press, 1966), chap. 11.

21. For a further discussion of courage and honor, see intro. to Arnold Wilson and J. H. F. McEwen, *Gallantry* (London: Oxford University Press, 1939).

bravery must be held up as an ideal, so that soldiers may be able to function adequately even when frightened by the prospect of death. Nevertheless, conspicuous bravery for which medals are obtained does not typically change the tide of battle or war.

Military leaders feel it is necessary to give medals in order to honor bravery, which is important in itself. Nevertheless, it does not seem likely that medals for gallantry motivate soldiers or sailors much in dangerous situations. It is very likely necessary to give medals, but the "need" is really felt by the *people who give them*. That is, it is felt that some public honor must be given as a symbol of the collective gratefulness of the armed forces or the nation, when no other possible reward seems fitting. The dead cannot, after all, enjoy material rewards, which in any event seem a paltry recognition for the risks taken, and are deemed socially an insignificant or even incongruous motivation for the willingness to die for a group goal.[22]

STOCK SHOWS AND COUNTY FAIRS

A final type of activity that is not socially central to the main work of the society and that has offered many prizes is made up of competitions related originally to agriculture: fat stock shows, horse and dog shows, county fairs, and rodeos.[23] They deserve a brief comment here for their relevance to the processes of prize-giving that help link parts of the society together.

Horse and dog shows have broken completely away from their rural background, rodeos have become part of show business, and agricultural fairs are continued mainly because they attract tourists. Such competitions actually continued to increase until well into the twentieth century in this country although the rural world had long been declining. However, they are not a recent social invention. They have graced agriculture for literally thousands of years, celebrating the gifts hard won from the earth. Since they arose and flourished when agriculture was important, they might be seen as denying our general hypothesis that such contests and prizes are more common in activities that do not seem very central to the main investments of the society.

But a closer look reveals a confirmation of that hypothesis. First, prizes were more likely to be given for achievements of small commercial significance. For example, one did not win prizes for the highest produc-

---

22. For further discussion of whether medals can motivate people to show gallantry, especially in civilian life, see John Smythe, *The Story of the George Cross* (London: Arthur Barker, 1968), pp. 48–49.

23. The serious reader should be reminded, however, that through most of its history the U.S. has earned much of its foreign exchange by exporting agricultural, not manufacturing, products; and that this most technologically advanced society has been a high producer of raw materials. Nevertheless, farmers make up less than five percent of the population, and the agricultural part of the Gross National Product has been both modest and declining for decades.

tion, the most efficient farm, or the greatest profit.[24] Instead, they were offered for much more peripheral achievements, such as Largest Pumpkin, Best Tomatoes, or Best Apple Pie. Jersey cows won because of their appearance, their conformity to an ideal type, not only their cream production. Almost all of these can be more easily judged at a fair than can real productivity or efficiency, thus solving the problem of measurement.

Most of these contests could be won by the poor as well as the rich, by children as well as skilled adults. For example, youngsters could carefully tend a pet Poland China hog or a bed of strawberries for such fairs, just as an ordinary cowboy might hope to win in a calf-roping contest. Women were not excluded, either, since many of their home products could win prizes. Moreover, in such competitions ribbons or prizes might be given for fourth, fifth, or even sixth place. Consequently, a wide range of the population could hope to win at something (as in school competition). Thus, most people had some stake in these festivals.

The esthetic, social, and entertainment elments ruled in this folk pattern. It is an especially striking instance, visible as far back into agricultural history as we can penetrate, of the human capacity to make games out of work. Rather than adding honor to material rewards, as would be the result of simply giving prizes to the most successful farmers, these contests gave esteem to the more playful aspects of their lives: sports, pretty quilts, queenly cows, commercially unprofitable but lavishly sized fruits and vegetables. They honored, then, the achievements that gave some grace and respect to their work life but that were only peripherally important to the grim realities of financial success at farming.

AWARDS AND PRIZES IN BUSINESS LIFE: A SPECIAL CASE

Prizes and contests like those described above have not been common in the main activities of getting wealth. They have not been viewed as appropriate, doubtless because socially the financial rewards themselves seem sufficient. On the other hand, we have also noted that, as this social model becomes more widely accepted, almost any organization or group can simply decide to set up a contest. As a consequence, such prizes may increasingly be seen as socially appropriate where once they were not. Prizes, plaques, and awards can be observed in several very special aspects of the business and manufacturing world. The first of these is in trade associations of various kinds, that is, organizations of businessmen at higher or lower levels of wealth and influence, which cultivate fraternal and communal ties among people who are by occupation dedicated to economic self-interest and competition with each other. Here again, the

---

24. Since agricultural agents shaped these fairs for decades, as they changed agriculture generally, youngsters could win prizes for models of good contour plowing, safe water supply systems, or flood control projects.

scrolls, certificates, and other awards they offer give esteem not to those who simply earn more money each year, but to those who "serve the industry"—contribute to the collectivity as a whole or serve as models of how an ideal businessman or manufacturer should behave.

A second, and more interesting, area of corporate life in which such awards have become common is sales competitions. This case is instructive, for such contests are organized by the corporation leadership itself, in its own interest: to increase its profits. In addition, the prizes can be viewed as almost a pure economic reward, for often the winners get vacations, consumer goods, or even cash prizes along with certificates or plaques as mementos of their achievements. Nevertheless, these are formal competitions and do convey esteem for an accomplishment; they are viewed by peers as proofs of excellence.

Granted that they do in fact elicit some extra effort, especially among those who believe that by a marginally greater effort they can obtain a still greater cash award (and those who do not compete may fear they will be fired), we face the question of why, since such salesmen often make substantial salaries anyway, the prestige reward is thought to be useful or necessary.

I suggest that corporate officials who organize such contests are guided by an intuitive folk sociology that can be articulated thus: commission sales personnel do not have the authority of line officials, or the esteem of technical or research staff, even when their annual salaries are equivalent to either. They feel that their prestige rewards are discrepant with their substantial contributions to the organization. Indeed, in literature as well as in jokes, the salesman as a social type is deprecated. Consequently, they are more easily motivated by an increase in prestige than are other personnel; and giving scrolls is surely less costly than money.

The acclaim that is given them when they win prizes for success in selling automobiles, insurance policies, or refrigerators not only yields direct satisfaction to the winners, but it makes all the members of the business feel that this work has been given some social recognition. As in other rewards, of course, these announcements form a link between sales personnel and other parts of the corporation, and they can be exhibited to outsiders. They proclaim that this activity, even with its somewhat lower prestige, should nevertheless be esteemed.

In addition to trade association awards and sales contests, a third type of competition that is sometimes created in business life is a campaign to elicit money-saving or money-making ideas from the rank and file (and sometimes, less often, from those engaged in research). Again, it should be remarked that this is a relatively recent innovation, since a hundred years ago high-level officials did not believe they should listen at all to the suggestions of lower-ranking personnel. Such campaigns are a message to higher-level people that they should give more respect to those at lower levels for their possibly useful ideas. It is also a way of announcing to such rank and file employees that they, too, are important, are contributing to the larger collectivity—not merely when they are typing or operating a comptometer, but also when they are thinking about the larger needs of the organization.

A fourth area in which contests are to be encountered in business or corporate life is in civic or community campaigns of various types. Here, most often, the "winners" are departments or subsegments of larger departments in the corporation, but sometimes they are individuals. They are rewarded for devoting time and attention to what is after all not essential to the money-making goals of the business, but is thought to enhance the prestige of the organization itself within the surrounding community. Once more, those contests constitute a message that civic accomplishments are also to be honored, although they are peripheral to profit-making.

Finally, of course, there are formal awards or prizes, usually not the result of competitions, for years of devoted service and responsibility. These are especially given for dedication to middle- or lower-level tasks on the part of people who are usually not socially recognized as central to operation of the business.

THE DECISION TO GIVE A PRIZE

Although the leaders of an organization can simply decide arbitrarily that they will henceforth give awards for some type of achievement or collective contribution, people who set up such a contest must face a sociological decision of whether the achievements and the participants in a given area of activity are worthy of much esteem. They must make at least a guess as to whether such an award will elicit any credence from people who learn about it. A contest may require that people actually enter (athletics, dog shows, school essay contests), as against the type of competition where a committee surveys the field in order to discover for themselves who are best (the Bollingen Prize, Critics Awards, the Pulitzer Prizes). The committee or organization runs the risks that no worthy person would bother to compete and that no one has done anything in the given area that seems worthy of high honor. When there are few competitors of any great worth, the winner will garner little prestige, and the award-giving organization may be considered a failure.

As fields of activity expand or develop, it is likely that some people will begin to decide that the contributions therein justify important prizes. It is only recently, for example, that the Nobel Prize competition was widened to include economics. And it was only about two decades ago that discoveries in underwater geology became significant enough to be considered worthy of a large award, the Vetlesen Prize. The still life has been recognized as a class of paintings in art competitions for generations, but collage was not until well after World War II.

Since prize committees are dedicated to the field in which they wish to give honor, they often seek a donor who will give cash in addition to a scroll or plaque. Such a philanthropist in turn receives esteem for the gift, and he will receive greater esteem if the prize comes to be coveted, so that persons of high prestige will wish to win it.

In the early history of award-giving in any field, the amount of prize money is typically small, commensurate with the lower amount of esteem its achievements are meant to honor. If considerable money is granted as part of the award, its prestige is greater. However, esteem does not come from the money itself. Rather, social norms require that if a large sum of money is to be granted, the procedures, auspices, and judges must be so chosen and organized that high-prestige candidates will compete or will be considered. Thereby, a competition or judgment acquires more prestige over time. Finally, the list of prestigious men and women who have won the prize in the past proves socially that the prize carries great esteem and, in turn, justifies the size of the money award.

In general, leaders in the field wish to establish prizes and awards, and seek philanthropic donors before the rank and file might agree that the time is appropriate. Announcing such a competition is an assertion that the contributions of the field are now worthy of public acclaim. Thereby the esteem of its leaders is enhanced. People outside the field typically do not concern themselves with that question at all; although once winners begin to be announced, outsiders may also take note of their achievements. It is clear how the processes of prize-giving make up some of the linkages among different parts of the social structure.

HONORIFIC OFFICES

Although honorific offices are not the same as prizes and awards, because the officer is usually required to carry out some activities during the course of his tenure, these offices are not usually onerous, and the incumbent does not often receive any salary for them. It is widely understood that the office is essentially an award of prestige, or a recognition of high esteem on the part of one's colleagues. For the most part, these offices are to be found in various academic associations or fields of learning.

Several regularities can be noted here. One is that, although winning the office is usually the result of formal election, social tradition has frowned on open campaigns for such an office. In some learned societies friends and supporters are not supposed to mount even a covert campaign. This pattern has changed somewhat in recent times, but primarily in the direction of campaigns that emphasize differences in political philosophy. Especially in social science associations, a left-wing versus conservative split has occurred.

Nevertheless, it is still not considered proper to mount a campaign that is aimed at persuading others that a given candidate has made greater intellectual contributions to the field than others have. Presumably, judgment is rendered by peers; the office is supposed to be earned by prior intellectual achievement and not artificially inflated by publicity, speeches, television advertisements, and the like. Often, short biographies of the candidate are distributed by the staff of the organization, but only to identify the person, not to persuade the reader that the individual's scientific contributions have been major.

Those who are given honorific offices in such societies have usually contributed more than others have to their field.[25] This is likely to be so whether we simply count the quantity of the articles and books written by the officer or the number of times his or her work is cited by those in the field.

Additional variables are also at work. How much they affect prizes and awards generally we do not know. It is likely, for example, that the persons who win such offices have produced some articles or books on "theory" in the field. In all scientific fields, there is a social division between the "methodologists" and the "theorists": High officers are less likely to be known primarily as methodologists. Theorists typically gain more prestige, and are more likely to be viewed as having made a contribution to the field as a collectivity.

As might be supposed from other sociological data, those who hold honorific offices in learned societies are more likely to be in major departments, and to have taken their Ph.D.'s from major departments. Critics and dissidents in the field are less likely to become officers, unless their contributions are thought to be especially eminent. Since the office itself represents the learned society to some extent, it is felt that those who are severe critics have made a lesser contribution to the prestige of the group.

A variable of less importance is whether the individual is widely respected for what we have called the small virtues, and whether he is widely liked as a person. Both have some weight. However, a cautious formulation of the relationship seems to be that a person who enjoys a wide friendship network and is widely respected for his or her character is more likely to win against one who is of equal eminence, but is less likely to win against someone thought to have made a higher intellectual contribution to the field. A similar formulation applies to guild services. People who have contributed substantially to committee work, served on small commissions, and aided generally in the functioning of the organization are more likely to win such honorific offices, but only over a person of equal or lesser eminence.

---

25. For the field of psychology, as an example, see Lauren G. Wispé, "Of Eminence in Psychology," *Journal of the History of the Behavioral Sciences*, 1 (January, 1965): 88–98.

THE PROBLEM OF THE JUDGES

Wherever there is a contest, there will be judges. Where there are judges, both their competence and their character may be questioned. If winning is important, contestants may consider whether they might improve their chances through the help of the judges—or whether their opponents might do so. Since everyone knows these possibilities exist, many people have some motivation to keep watch over the rules and the judges. Over time, in any activity where contests or competitions are common, new rules are constantly being proposed, to ensure fairness. Where it is possible, and especially in the modern historical epoch, the goal of contest committees is to reduce the possibility of affecting the judgment of the judges. That is most easily done, of course, where mechanical devices can replace the eye, as in racing of all kinds. The judges then serve to guarantee the honesty and accuracy of the measuring devices. The more important the contest, and thus the more significant the decision, the more likely it is that the rank of the judges will be high. Their presence does not so much guarantee the competence of the decision as it does the care with which the decision will be made and therefore the lesser likelihood that anyone will later challenge it successfully.

Doubtless, the problem of the judges has existed from the time the first contest prize was ever given, perhaps thousands of years ago. I suppose that even then the community and the contestants argued that a man of good judgment and honesty should preside. On the other hand, we can ask the unanswerable question as to what percentage of contest decisions were dishonest, or how often one or more contestants managed to persuade a judge to hand down an erroneous decision in their favor.

This specific question is a part of the larger inquiry into the subversion of prestige processes, to which a later chapter is devoted. I bring it up here because of its special relevance for contests and competitions of all kinds. I am willing to guess that the percentage of outright dishonesty has been very small. On the other hand, I also suppose that a fairly high percentage of contests have been somewhat affected by the honest biases of judges: In favor of the hometown team, their own race, sex, or class, their own prejudices about style and form, and so on.

If a contestant or aspirant wants to subvert a judge, the transaction must be private, both then and later. If the judge violates his or her role obligation as a fair evaluator, others will heap scorn on the judge and on the contestant as well. If the contestant has "won," others will not only disesteem him or her but will jeer in laughter. The prize itself becomes an empty object, devoid of honor, or indeed an evidence of shame. The other judges also lose respect and will be angry. Thus, within a wide network of people, only one contestant and one judge (or perhaps more) will stand to gain anything; and both they and the whole network stand to lose if they are exposed.

It should be emphasized that the "losing" contestants are not indignant primarily because they did not win the prize. That is a risk which they accepted upon entering the competition. What has been denigrated is their performance: It was not taken seriously. The social definition of what they thought they were doing—competing—has been violated. They were not in the competition at all. The intensity of their commitment, the integrity of their aspiration, have been voided of meaning. Nothing they were doing was of any relevance, for the decision was fixed in advance. They would not have bothered to take part, had they known. It is as though, contrary to the social charter, there was no contest at all: There was only one competitor.

Even in athletics, cheating, with or without the connivance of judges, is always a temptation. It occurred even in the early Olympics, two millennia ago. Cheating is more perilous in athletics than in other contests, however, because many spectators will be keenly watching, and the performance is observable. On the other hand, until the invention of the motion picture film, both athletics and the performing arts differed from many other kinds of competitions in that the achievement occurs in the contest itself, and only the audience can record what happens. In all games and in many athletic contests numerous ambiguous events occur on which umpires, referees, judges, or linesmen will make rulings, and most of these are not recorded for later rejudgment. In many other competitions (science, art, literature) the work is entered and it continues to exist afterward, to be judged independently of the contest itself.

On the other hand, once we move from athletics, though the work itself may continue to exist, it is more difficult to ascertain whether a judge has been either incompetent or dishonest because personal and group standards are understood to vary greatly. A judge in a piano competition may feel (without confessing it even inwardly) that a contestant who plays "perfectly" is "cold, and does not grasp the inner meaning of the music." A dog show judge may harbor a bias in favor of working dogs and against miniatures. Always, the judgments can be defended somewhat because there are many competitors whose achievements are fairly close to one another. As long as the "winner" is within that range, a dishonest judgment (if any) is not easily detected. On the other hand, since the judging committees are usually known, the members understand that they will have to answer their critics, informally or formally, for the decisions finally made.

Although there are strong norms that require probity from contest committees, no social group relies on the strength of those norms alone. Rather, the processes of judgment are created by human beings who have a high stake in the fairness and competence of the outcome and a motivation to watch carefully for violations. The rules for the contest are so organized as to make the risk of discovery high for anyone who might otherwise see an opportunity to "win" by persuading the judges to be dishonest.

TO ACCEPT OR REJECT AN HONOR

Some prizes, awards, honorific offices, and honorary degrees are offered even though the winner has not proposed himself for candidacy. Most of these are given for achievements in the arts, literature, and the sciences.

Usually people know that their work is being considered, but not always. Sometimes they can ask friends to suggest their names. In any case, they have to decide whether to accept or reject the prize or honor if they do win. It is difficult to turn down such awards. Almost no phraseology seems believable, persuasive, or socially acceptable to either the award committee or outsiders. Some nominees do succeed in avoiding these honors by privately requesting the judges to pass them over, but those who publicly reject such prizes are not usually viewed as having been highminded or noble. Their rejection is likely to be viewed as petulance and their arguments as specious.

To turn down the prize is to reject the group offering it, and they will feel disesteemed or angry. This is a usual reaction of people who learn that the amount of esteem they give others is viewed as insufficient. The candidate cannot say "it is not enough," for that is viewed as simple arrogance. Besides, the organization (just like a person) cannot confer more honor than it is able to give. An honorary degree from an obscure university, like a prize for lyric poetry from an obscure committee, is worth only so much, and there is no way to increase that honor.

If, by contrast, the winner tries to say, "I am humble, I do not deserve it," others will view the response as false modesty. The reaction to asserting that someone else deserves it more is similar. In both cases, rejection denies the authority or capacity of the community or group to make a decision about the person's contribution. The winner asserts his or her own right to judge, alone. Socially, we are not often permitted to arrogate to ourselves the decision that we do not deserve something, even though some of our friends might delightedly concur.

Winning an award or honorific office is likely to increase a person's prestige. It can often be translated into additional income, since the person is more likely to be able to command higher lecture or consultant fees, salary and raises, and job offers. On the other hand, it is not true that all such awards add to the individual's prestige. If an Eisenhower or a Linus Pauling accepts an honorary doctorate from a small college, or a medal from a little-known committee, it is likely that his presence at their ceremonies adds prestige to them, rather than the reverse.

Thus the process of choosing those who will be honored, and of deciding whom one will accept the honor from, can become a delicate set of balances. The lesser-known committee or group may not wish to select a candidate whose prestige is too great, for he or she may not accept the offer. The individual in turn must decide whether the time and energy required for participation, and even the sharing of prestige with that particular group, is too great a cost for the award. Nevertheless, in general, probably few people reject such awards, offices, or honorary degrees.

The balance is the more delicate because, when an individual accepts such an honor, he or she accepts simultaneously the right of that organization or committee to confer it upon him or her. That is, to accept is to concede that they have some prestige to grant, that they enjoy legitimacy as an honor-conferring group. The recipient accepts, in effect, a membership in a particular community, whose other members now share to some degree in his or her esteem.

Correspondingly, that very relationship makes still more difficult a rejection of the office, honorary degree, or award. For one who rejects it is thus refusing that membership, and their tiny portion of the esteem being granted—their essential linkage with his own contribution.

Chapter 8
Prestige Processes over Time: Changes in the Difficulty of Performance

In earlier chapters, we made reference to many social changes that have occurred over the longer term—the continued increase in the number of organizations that give awards and prizes and the lesser deference given to the nobility, for example. This and the succeeding chapter analyze the processes by which prestige allocations, and the social behavior they partly control, change over longer periods of time.

The matter merits separate attention because we know that over time new social structures (bureaucracy, the corporation) emerge and new kinds of behavior or social attributes (chariot-driving, piety) gain or lose in esteem. That is, we can not take for granted that the day-to-day prestige processes we have been exploring will necessarily be adequate to explain such new events or long-term processes. On the other hand, we cannot suppose that the important processes over long periods of time are fundamentally different from those over shorter periods, even if the events seem more massive. When viewed over historical epochs, social changes cannot contain any elements that are not found in short-run processes; after all, nothing else is there to constitute them. Nor is there any separate set of factors that cause change and another group of variables that cause stability. Everything changes and in changing alters everything else. The answer to the general question "what causes social change?" is the same as the answer to the question "what causes stability?"—everything.

Nor are we seeking a grand theory of social change. Looking to other sciences as a model, we see it is wise to limit our aspirations. Findings in the sciences more advanced than sociology are overwhelmingly made up of relationships that can be called timeless equations, because presumably they would be expected to hold true in the year 2,000 B.C. or 2,000 A.D. Little research in physics has aimed at finding special laws of change, and chemistry hardly recognizes the problem at all.[1] If sociology has not

---

1. In both physics and chemistry special subfields do focus on the phenomena or conditions that once existed at, say, the beginning of the solar system. Nevertheless, those investigations proceed only

discovered any firm principles to explain the grand changes of history, it has, at least, some distinguished companions in failure.

The longer view does yield one special advantage: We may not be able even to perceive great changes if we focus only on the shorter run. There are three major types of massive change that an adequate social change theory must be able to analyze, and all three simply do not "emerge" until much time has elapsed.[2] The first of these is secular trends, such as birth or death rates, or the decline in respect for piety. Many of these would appear to be no more than trendless fluctuations unless viewed over decades or generations.

A second type of massive social change that is difficult to perceive over the shorter run is structural transformations, such as the rise of bureaucracy, the appearance of a world economy, or a major revolution. Contemporary participants often fail to recognize that such processes have started; for example, even a major revolution may seem to most observers to be no more than a modest revolt at first. A third type of change is determinate sequences. These are hypotheses about social evolution of this form: If the social structure or institutional pattern is at Phase I at Time T, then it must go through Phases II and III at times $T+1$ and $T+2$. In technological developments, they seem to be obvious (the wheel must come before the railroad); biological evolution yields further illustrations. Such hypotheses were common in nineteenth-century social science. New attempts at them have been made more recently; they state that a particular evolutionary sequence is made up of steps such that each phase is required for the next one.[3]

But we need not analyze these problems separately, since any specific cases can be at least observed as secular trends of some kind—for example, the rise of bureaucracy (a structural transformation) also appears as a trend over time, in the form of increasing numbers of bureaucracies and bureaucrats. If our modest aim is the analysis of secular trends, we are likely to focus on the most common and important of massive changes.

More important, we have been analyzing the allocation of prestige as the outcome of social exchanges whose terms are generally determined by the relative supply of various qualities and performances, relative to how

on the assumptions that any laws and equations that apply to such time periods would also hold under any comparable set of extreme conditions, then or now. After all, they really have no choice: All their experimental data come from the present. In theoretical physics, the idea of time creates some special paradoxes. For a discussion of some of them, see David Layzer, "The Arrow of Time," *Scientific American*, 233, no. 6 (December, 1975): 56–69.

2. For a more elaborate analysis of the types of social change analysis (focused on the family), see my article "The Theory and Measurement of Family Change," in Eleanor B. Sheldon and Wilbert E. Moore, *Indicators of Social Change* (New York: Russell Sage Foundation, 1968), pp. 295–348.

3. For examples, see G. P. Murdock, *Social Structure* (New York: Macmillan, 1949), pp. 190ff. and chap. 8; and H. E. Driver and W. Massey, "Comparative Studies of North American Indians," *Transactions of the American Philosophical Society*, 47 (July, 1957): 165; as well as H. M. Blalock, "Correlational Analysis and Causal Inference," *American Anthropology*, 62 (August, 1960): 624–631; Robert M. Marsh, *Comparative Sociology* (New York: Harcourt, Brace & World, 1967), chaps. 2, 3; and Neil J. Smelser, *Comparative Methods in the Social Sciences* (Englewood Cliffs, N.J.: Prentice-Hall, 1976).

much they are valued (demand). Thus, in our time analysis we can focus on various kinds of performances whose supply becomes larger or smaller over time, usually as the result of changes in their difficulty or their facilitating conditions.

In this chapter we consider, then, what happens to the allocation of prestige when the difficulty of achieving some performance (or the rarity of some quality) rises or falls over the longer term. In the succeeding chapter, by contrast, we shall focus on how the demand for some qualities or traits rises or falls when new evaluations, norms, or values are accepted by a group or society, thereby making some types of behavior less or more respected than formerly. What prestige processes are then observed?

CHANGES IN RESPECT

With all these cautions, let us present some changes in the amount of prestige given for various qualities and behaviors over the history of the United States, without regard to whether behavior or evaluations changed first. The aim is no more than to note that patterns of prestige allocation change slowly but do change in different degrees, and that both supply and demand factors will affect how much esteem people feel or show for different types of traits or performances. Then we shall go on to consider some explanations of such changes in social control through prestige allocations. The evaluations of truth-telling:

There has been no perceptible change in the esteem paid to those who are able or willing to tell the truth, though the percentage of truth-telling may have dropped somewhat because of urbanization: There is less chance that others will discover one has lied.

In any event, the crucial variable has typically not been one of supply, but of demand: People have good reason not to want to hear the truth about themselves, while generally wanting to know the truth about events and about others.

Nevertheless, a grudging respect is still paid to those who are willing to run the risk of earning a reputation for usually telling the truth.

Deference to age:

Respect for age has gone from a moderate level (it was never as high in Western as in Eastern societies) to a somewhat lower level. Since World War I, some increase in overt disrespect for those over sixty-five may have occurred. Nevertheless, people still pay, and feel, more respect for older than for younger people.

Piety:

Esteem paid to those who are pious has dropped substantially, except in small circles (such as convents, special sects).

The "farmer virtues":

The rural skills, such as riding a horse adequately, shooting accurately, maintaining the land in good tilth, plowing a straight furrow, have dropped from widespread high evaluation to general irrelevance. Within the small circle of farm workers and owners, some of these skills have become curiosities and hobbies (the ability to rope a steer) rather than a widely used basis for judging others. Other achievements (maintenance of the land, for example) remain a general basis for ranking within this subgroup.

Bravery:

The willingness to use violence to protect one's "honor," or the "honor of one's wife," has dropped greatly in esteem. When bravery is exhibited in saving another's life it is still admired, but the occasions for it are too few to rank most men by such a standard (in spite of the rise in egalitarianism, women are typically not weighed by this criterion at all). Respect is paid to bravery when it is shown by people who are paid for it, such as firemen, policemen, coast guardsmen, soldiers, and sailors. Among boys, bravery is still widely esteemed.

Since World War II there has been a drop in the esteem given to those who risk their lives to defend their own money or that of others, as in a robbery. Money is increasingly thought not to be "worth" risking one's life for. Many or most men still feel respect for a man who "had the guts" to attack a hoodlum who molested his wife, however they might deprecate that violence publicly.

Drinking liquor:

Prior to World War I, there was a sharper distinction between drinkers and teetotalers than now, while many drinkers paid to respectability the tribute of hypocrisy by hiding their vice. In many circles it was taken for granted that men would be relatively hard drinkers, and in others drinking was viewed with great disesteem. As drinking has become more widespread since the 1930's, the ideological teetotaler is viewed as old-fashioned and has lost some respect. The heavy drinker is increasingly viewed as ill. Moderate drinkers have gained respect since World War I, since most people do not now disesteem them.

Thrift and saving:

In the earlier days of the republic, this quaint virtue was the theme of many speeches and exhortations: being thrifty was a moral end in itself, not merely instrumental to material goals. It is now generally held to be old-fashioned to evaluate another person by this criterion, but it is possible that a secret poll would reveal a continuing respect, though slighter than a century ago, for those who are able to be thrifty.

Accuracy, skill, speed, and diligence in work:

These work virtues have always been highly evaluated in America and still are, though again a minority dissents. Western aristocracies have usually contained a substantial minority that did not rank these virtues high, except in their subordinates.

The family virtues:

Chastity in the bride, divorce, housekeeping skills, and the acceptance of traditional maternal and paternal obligations have all lost some of their importance as a basis for personal esteem; the standard for an adequate performance is lower and is less clearly defined.

What is notable about such examples is how frequently we must conclude that there is little evidence that their basic respect patterns have changed by much. In contrast to these examples of achievements or qualities are the striking alterations in styles, fashion, and taste, whether intellectual or esthetic, that mark the history of any modern country. People make fun of what was high style or "good taste" a few decades ago.

Fashions come and go, in cooking, clothing, painting, poetry, philosophy, political beliefs, popular music, and religion. In such areas, the processes by which prestige is generated do not change much, and how much prestige can be achieved in a particular activity may not, either; but specifically what is considered excellent does alter.

Some people once earned some local respect for excellent cooking, and a few still do, but what is judged to be a fine dish has altered at all class levels. In circles where being in fashion matters, one gains approval by choosing what is "high style"; but what that is will change radically over several decades. So obvious are such changes that film-makers and novelists can use them to announce that a story is set in a particular historical period.

The changes that seem most significant to social scientists are not such matters of taste and style, many of which they view as trivial, but large alterations in the social system. Among these are the extensive bureaucratization of social life, the increased influence of corporate bodies and agencies, a more intensive division of labor, changes in the occupational structure (for example, the decline of farming, the increase in service jobs), the development of a huge peacetime military establishment, or the interpenetration of business and government. Nevertheless, all such changes simply offer sites or opportunities (mainly occupational) where prestige can be earned or lost. By themselves they do not alter in any determinate fashion the prestige evaluations of the society.

But though the bases of prestige allocation may change relatively slowly, they do alter, and social scientists have attempted to offer various explanations of these changes. Let us consider one common explanation, which may be seen as a search for the changing payoffs or costs of following different courses of action over time.

SOCIOECONOMIC EXPLANATIONS
OF PRESTIGE CHANGES

Socioeconomic interpretations of history are common, for both large and small social changes. Many sociological analyses are economic in their reasoning, even when they do not use the technical formulations of economics and even when they are presented as criticisms of economics. Let us consider a number of such interpretations in order to understand both their uses and their limitations for the analysis of prestige processes.

One of the more obvious examples of socioeconomic reasoning is encountered in explanations of the rise and fall of clothing fashions. Those who first adopt a new fashion gain much social approval for it (and pay more money). However, as more people adopt it, the latecomers receive far less. That is, with a greater supply, people will pay less money but also get less prestige with their coin.

Some sociological formulations presented as criticisms of traditional economic theory, especially the notion of the "rational economic man," are also economic in their reasoning. One widely used example is the assertion that peasants or tribesmen whose aim in working for wages was to gain only a traditional sum (a head tax in Africa, a dowry in Europe) did not work for a longer period if wages were increased. That is, they would not maximize their economic return, but sought instead a fixed social goal. Max Weber's description of migratory farm workers who came to East Prussia before World War I is such a case.[4] If they were maximizing, they were maximizing a total social return, not a monetary one: once they had earned a traditional sum, they felt it was time to return to their homes. However critical such cases may be, they remain economic in their dynamics. Most can be seen as instances of diminishing marginal utility: Beyond a certain amount, the unit increments of wages are worth less. Wilbert E. Moore has also countered that sociological criticism by asserting that if colonial capitalists had ever tried the experiment of paying good wages (and offered worthwhile goods for sale), then the marginal increment over the alternative of tribal subsistence would have been greater. Then tribesmen would have been willing to perform diligently as factory workers.[5]

Another classical sociological criticism of economic theory, that it failed to take account of the differences between individual and group responses, has much relevance for changes in prestige over time. Its underlying reasoning is also economic, however, for it focuses on what happens to individual behavior when the whole demand schedule shifts to the right or left (that is, the demand is more or less permanently higher or lower). Durkheim's criticism is an example. He pointed out that according to utilitarian economics and philosophy (as well as common sense) people are happier or more contented if their material condition improves. But if the whole society becomes better off, as occurred in nineteenth-century France, Germany, and England, it is not true that people are generally more contented. Rather, the standards by which everyone judges his or her condition also rise, and their discontent is as high as ever.[6] Similarly, he asserted, the rate of suicide will rise in an economic depression, but it will also rise during a boom period (when, again, the norm rises).[7] Upward mobility is valued, but in a group where it is common individuals are not likely to be generally content. Here, the underlying economic translation is also evident: With a greater supply of some social good, its value drops.

Another sociological formulation argues that if over time (and under the threat of hell or hope of paradise) the members of a religious sect move toward virtuous behavior and away from evil, they do not give one another any greater amount of respect or praise, but continue to be as censorious as

    4. See Weber's "Capitalism and Rural Society in Germany," in Hans Gerth and C. Wright Mills, eds., *From Max Weber: Essays in Sociology* (New York: Oxford University Press, 1946).
    5. Personal communication.
    6. Emile Durkheim, *The Division of Labor*, trans. George Simpson (New York: Free Press, 1964 [1893]), p. 253.
    7. Durkheim, *Suicide*, trans. John A. Spaulding and George Simpson (New York: Free Press, 1951 [1897]).

before. In economic terms, there is a rise in production or supply, and thus a lower price is paid for the level of virtue or piety that would previously have been considered adequate or meritorious.

Clearly, then, some traditional sociological analyses of social changes use a basically economic form of reasoning; although they are likely to focus on nonmonetary gains and losses and do not utilize the technical formulations of economics, they use a basically economic form of reasoning that will be useful in the analyses of prestige changes that follow. Leaving aside such classical accounts, we shall next consider socioeconomic interpretations of other historical changes in order to understand better how prestige allocation changes over time.

SOCIOECONOMIC INTERPRETATIONS OF SPECIFIC PRESTIGE CHANGES

One example of a social change that seems to fit an economic dynamic is the greater success of biomedical science in Germany than in France, from about 1840 to the end of the century.[8] In the decentralized German system (each state having its own university) there were far more important universities to bid for the budding or recognized scientist than in France, and thus a greater demand. Talent moved successively into the new fields in which opportunities for making discoveries (and thus earning prestige) were higher. If one German university would not offer enough facilities, honor, independence, or other rewards, others would do so.

Another example took place in the latter half of the sixteenth century, when the turbulent British nobility began to keep the public peace and reduced its brawling and skirmishing. In simple terms, it came to be permanently more costly in esteem, friendship, and even money than in the past to seek private vengeance or mount assaults on one's fellow peers. Elizabeth I made known her personal displeasure over such actions, banished peers from her court, dispossessed them from honorific posts, and where possible levied fines against the offenders, while the peaceful were rewarded with smiles, respect, and offices. Vice was thus made less profitable in prestige, and virtue was rewarded. To be sure, more than two additional centuries were required before the urban proletariat were persuaded to keep the peace; but during that long period they did not get the same rewards or punishments as peers did, either.[9]

Similarly, when James I (through Buckingham) granted many honors and peerages on the basis of personal whim or money rather than public merit, the number of persons so elevated increased, but the amount of

8. For this instance, see Joseph Ben-David, "Scientific Productivity and Academic Organization in Nineteenth Century Medicine," *American Sociological Review*, 25 (December, 1960): 840, 842; and, more generally, *The Scientist's Role in Society* (Englewood Cliffs, N.J.: Prentice-Hall, 1971).

9. A good account of this difficult step toward civil peace, including a discussion of the duel (which by rule accepts all gentlemen as prestige equals in the right to kill each other, and this requires them to use equal weapons whatever their warlike resources) see Lawrence Stone, *The Crisis of the Aristocracy: 1558–1640* (New York: Oxford University Press, 1965).

prestige given to such new titles decreased. That is, with a greater supply the worth or honor simply declined (as did the purchase price of titles that were bought). By contrast, too, since Elizabeth was stingy in granting honors, she could demand—after all, the monarchy was a monopoly—a higher level of performance (gifts, military or political achievements, loyalty) for such an elevation than could James.

Both fashion within a short span and sumptuary restrictions over centuries (and continuing in the Elizabethan period) yield further applications of an "economic" or market formulation of prestige changes. Sumptuary laws in many societies of the past (both East and West) forbade various commodities to the lowly in rank, often with lofty disregard for whether they could afford them financially. Each rank should be content with the food, mode of transportation, clothing, and decorations appropriate to its station. However, the economically more successful families in each social stratum violated those rules, because they prohibited exactly the socially most important indices of respect or esteem; and these rules were increasingly violated as wealth increased over generations. However, as more people came to possess any given indices of rank that money could buy, those commodities also conferred less and less prestige. That is, with increasing supply, the prestige value of such luxuries permanently lessened.

Thus, both in some traditional sociological explanations of social change, and in some specific cases of prestige changes in history, we can perceive some broadly socioeconomic forces at work. Many of the important ones are not primarily monetary, but are human attempts to obtain esteem or respect.

CHANGES IN MEANS OR CONDITIONS AND EVALUATIONS

So we see that both in long-term alterations of behavior in response to prestige changes and in day-to-day actions, people are engaged in various types of social exchanges with other individuals or with groups, and thereby are responsive to alterations in the prestige market. Both supply and demand are affected by many variables, and to simplify our analysis we distinguish (as common sense often does) between changes that are caused by changed conditions or new means and those that are caused by new evaluations or norms. We consider the consequences for prestige allocation when one of these two changes first.

The consequences for prestige allocation can be considered within two general categories. 1. The social or physical conditions change so that it becomes either easier or harder to perform at the same level as before. Then, a larger "supply" of esteemed performances may be forthcoming; or supply becomes more difficult or costly, and thus declines. 2. The norms, values, or evaluations of a group change, either requiring higher or different performance for a given level of respect or permitting a lower level of performance or quality (for example, the rejection of "manners" among hippies in contemporary society). That is, in the first general case, it can be supposed that the conditions change first, altering the difficulty of performance or achievement and therefore how much the performance is judged to be worth. In the second general case, the norms or evaluations change first. Let us consider this distinction.

Of course we do *not* take for granted what the sequence of these types of changes will be, that is, whether typically the facilitating conditions, or instead the norms, typically change first. Moreover, in any concrete historical case it is often difficult to be certain which did change first; the sequence is too difficult to unravel. Within any great social change, both processes are of course taking place at any given slice of time, so that proving which came first may simply be impossible.

We perceive this difficulty when we consider that no matter which action change is observed, it is often possible to locate at least someone who offered a prior ideological justification for it (for example, the ideological precursors of modern science); and no matter which new ideological or evaluational proclamation is examined, it would be possible to show that some people had already begun to act in accord with its provisions even before it was proclaimed (Turner's later paintings as precursors of Impressionism). Certainly there was some "protestantism" in religious behavior before Luther nailed his theses to the Wittenberg church door in 1519. Since ideology and evaluations interact constantly with all the elements that cause behavior, and completed actions affect people's evaluations of that action, the exact sequence may often be debatable.

Nevertheless, we can select some instances that seem reasonably clear, in order to analyze the dynamics of prestige changes when the conditions that facilitate one or another kind of behavior change first—the focus of this chapter—or instead when norms alter first, the topic of the succeeding chapter.

FACILITATING CONDITIONS OR MEANS

Let us consider the first type of case, one that is widespread in contemporary society: the development of new techniques or social conditions that facilitate higher performances. One large set of instances includes an apparently conglomerate range of activities such as depth, height, and speed achievements, including athletic records.

To achieve at the levels of the height, depth, and speed records of even a decade ago no longer elicits much esteem. If someone were to mount an assault on the land speed record, for example, and achieved only four hundred miles per hour on the Salt Lake Flats, people would wonder why he or she even bothered to try. A dive, of a submarine or a free diver, to the record depths of two decades ago is now routine. With reference to a given level of performance in such areas, the amount of esteem has fallen substantially. It would appear, then, that we could apply a simple economic formulation and note that the supply has risen so much that the prestige paid for that level has dropped.

There are, of course, exceptions here and there. For example, although the sheer number of baseball players today should increase the statistical chance that any given record of the past would be broken, some batting records remain difficult to equal.[10] However, the prestige of modern professional athletics has changed in many ways over the past half century, especially since the 1950's, when it began to form a large part of the television entertainment industry. First, within a given sport, as in the past, income is likely to be mainly determined by the athlete's skill and thus prestige. Second, with the expansion of total demand for athletic entertainment on television, many sports have become profitable for both practitioners and entrepreneurs, so that a far larger number of men and women can earn large incomes as stars. Third, because of this financial achievement and the public renown that goes with it, the general prestige level of sports has risen as well. That is, supply has risen, but demand has risen more.

In addition, the much higher performances of modern athletes have generated a greater amount of prestige to share. The higher rewards now available attract more talent into these activities and make a large investment of work in them a reasonable risk. This greater talent and amount of training, coupled with modern techniques and equipment, have all created a much larger gap between the achievements of even the gifted but untrained amateur and the gifted person who has mastered some specialty.[11]

The amount of prestige available for those at the top of a sports profession is greater than half a century ago. Supply in the form of higher performances, number of performances, or performances in different sports has risen greatly. Demand has risen more, certainly in part because those higher levels earn more respect and are more entertaining.

SUPPLY OF MIDDLE-CLASS SKILLS

Let us consider next a somewhat different set of instances, still within the general category of prestige changes created by new facilitating conditions. For various reasons, obtaining any given level of formal education has become easier over the past century for most of the population of the United States, and more recently for all major segments of the population. It has also become easier to be clean whenever one is not actually engaged in a dirty task; to obtain clothing that is not ragged or markedly shabby; and to master schoolbook or middle-class speech.

All of these were once used, and still are to some extent, as class

10. Babe Ruth's total batting performance has not been matched, although Hank Aaron has equaled a few of his records. As of this writing, few have surpassed his earned run average as a pitcher.

11. For an analysis of changes in athletic performance, see Henry W. Ryder, H. J. Carr, and Paul Gerget, "Future Performance in Footracing," *Scientific American*, 234 (June, 1976): 109–119.

indicators. Poor people were once shamed for being ragged and felt shame that they could not appear before others dressed respectably. But, as Michael Harrington has remarked, it is one of the technological and market triumphs of our society that the poor no longer need offend us by dressing in shabby clothing.[12] Regional, class, and ethnic dialects remain, but only a small minority in our society is so isolated as to be free from at least school pressures to learn "correct" speech. Most children are forced to go to school for many years, and thus they acquire at least an amount of formal education (completion of high school) that a century ago would have been deemed worthy of some respect. The low time and cost necessary to be clean, and the germ fear generated after World War I and still affirmed in schools and advertising, facilitate cleanliness in our society to the degree that most Americans find it difficult to understand how or why anyone could remain dirty.

With supply so much easier and more abundant than in the past, how could the esteem paid for it remain as high? Indeed, people who now use standard speech, dress respectably, avoid being dirty except briefly when a task makes it necessary, and get through, say, high school do not gain much respect for any of these.

But that single statement does not describe fully the social changes that have occurred in prestige. A further important regularity is that the standards have not continued to rise; it is not necessary to be extraordinarily clean now in order to obtain esteem. Rather, the person who goes beyond the level of cleanliness now viewed as adequate is considered to be excessively persnickety, or obsessive. That person, then, loses some esteem. Similarly, the person who follows meticulously the speech patterns of the schoolroom is thought to be faintly pompous, although of course there are social circles (mainly academic) where that behavior would not be noticed.

In the area of clothing, subtle but important class differences continue to exist for both men and women, but they are not relevant for the once powerful distinction between being respectably dressed or not. That this distinction has not lost all its ancient emotional force was amply proved by the hippie dissidents of the 1960's. By deliberately dressing shabbily, in mismatched costumes, in clothing left over from a generation ago or cut into rags, they proclaimed their rejection of that very "respectability" which the poor once vainly sought. They aroused considerable anger and resentment by their demands that they be treated respectfully even though they were not "properly" dressed and were actually disdainful of proper dress. To be sure, mainstream society had its usual ironic revenge, for soon it began to ape (in more expensive versions) many of those costumes. Today, as in other periods, those whose dress seems much more respectable than average are not given esteem, but run the risk of being considered stiff, formal, and reserved.

12. Michael Harrington, *The Other America* (Baltimore: Penguin, 1965), pp. 9–24.

By contrast, censure of excess is not often directed at education, unlike clothing, speech, and cleanliness. Over time, the general level of expectation has risen in all these areas. As a consequence, one might predict that a college education does not command as much respect as it did a century ago. However, that prediction does not fully describe what has happened over the past century. Let us consider the prestige consequences of the rise in the average educational level in the United States up to high school graduation.

The most obvious fact is that, while the supply of educated people has increased, so has the demand. Corporations and government agencies demand more education from their potential employees, even though very likely there is little correlation between performance at any given level and education.[13] More parents want their children to be educated for longer periods of time; more people want their friends to have acquired many years of formal education; governments spend more money on education. Indeed, education is one of the largest industries in this country.

Consequently, although supply has risen, so has demand, thus the general prestige of a given level of education, such as high school or college graduation, has not dropped as much as might be predicted.[14]

Other regularities also appear that sociological theory does not predict. For example, those who a half-century ago took a B.A. are not now required to take an M.A. or Ph.D. in order to obtain an equivalent amount of esteem, unless they plan to enter academic or professional work. At the bachelor's level there is inelasticity in the demand curve. A bachelor's degree is "enough" for any nonprofessional work and for engineering. In the United States, the Ph.D. remains the highest degree, and is enough for academic jobs, while its esteem may well have dropped somewhat. No higher degree has been created. If the individual plans to enter lower-level clerical work, a high school education is enough, and he does not gain much if any added esteem from additional education. In many circles, fellow workers would consider him a bit odd for being at that level.[15]

Thus, the result of a century of increasing supply of education is not a simple drop in the esteem paid for a given higher level of education, commensurate with the higher supply. Demand has also risen, while inelasticities in the curve of demand, and therefore in the esteem paid for education, can be observed. They are not so prominent or definite as in the instances of cleanliness, proper clothing, or schoolroom speech, but they are visible.

With reference to these last three behaviors, a further regularity is

---

13. For evidence on this point, see the body of data assembled by Ivar Berg, *Education and Jobs: The Great Training Robbery* (New York: Praeger, 1970), pp. 38–60.

14. In more technical terms, the demand curve has "permanently" shifted to the right.

15. Thus, contrary to George C. Homans, such people are not viewed as having made "bigger investments" that justify better pay or esteem. They are more likely to be viewed as foolish. See Homans, *Social Behavior: Its Elementary Forms* (New York: Harcourt, Brace & World, 1961), p. 75.

observable. As noted, to go above the norm may arouse slight ridicule, and it certainly does not add prestige. But to fall below the norm elicits disesteem, because in American society most people feel that to attain that level requires almost no effort—and, as already noted, generates no esteem, either. But as a further consequence, the first two have almost dropped out as indices of class position, and the third, speech, has become less important. Since most people perform satisfactorily, these items become of much less utility for placing people on some position in the broad spectrum of class. That is, an achievement can become so widespread that *it is no longer much used as an index of rank*.

This phenomenon is not confined to Western civilization or to consumer goods that become more easily available with greater affluence. To the extent that classes or castes, or individuals within them, try to gain more respect, they may try to acquire the traits, behaviors, or goods of the higher social ranks that are perceived as indices of rank. In the Indian caste system, this pattern has sometimes been called Sanskritization, that is, a lower caste emulates a higher caste (vegetarian diet, avoidance of certain occupations, rejection of foods from certain castes) in order eventually to claim a higher rank.[16] To the extent that such lower ranks or groups succeed, however, those very traits lose their importance as indices. Higher-ranking strata or groups are clever enough to emphasize still other traits or performances as the appropriate signs of acceptable social rank.[17]

SUPPLY BECOMES MORE DIFFICULT

Turning from prestige changes created by new facilitating conditions, let us now consider those prestige behaviors or qualities that for various technical reasons become more difficult to achieve than previously. If classical theory is correct as applied to social change, then people should gain as much respect for a lower level of performance, when because of technical reasons it becomes more difficult (and thus supply at that level is lower) as they once did for a higher level. How is prestige allocation affected by an increase in technical difficulty over time?

Let us first select what seems to be a clear-cut but trivial case, and then confront the most important sociological fact about this class of phenomena. Repairing one's own automobile has become much more complex than it was fifty years ago, because the number of mechanical subsystems in it (automatic choke, power steering, air conditioner, and so on), their inaccessibility, and the specialized tools necessary have all increased. Men could once obtain a modest amount of esteem for an above-average skill and knowledge of this amateur task.

But though some men can and do repair their own automobiles, the

16. For criticism of this conceptualization as it applies to Untouchables, see Owen M. Lynch, *The Politics of Untouchability* (New York: Columbia University Press, 1969), pp. 4ff.

17. For a more complex economic analysis of the bandwagon, the snob, and the Veblen effect, see Harvey Leibenstein, *Beyond Economic Man* (Cambridge: Harvard University Press, 1976), chap. 4.

number is now so small that most men are not ranked at all. The amount of respect has not increased for those who now possess what was once an average skill. Rather, the important sociological regularity is that *when few can be differentiated at all, that evaluation simply becomes less salient* for prestige. In some specialized circles (for example, amateur rally and race drivers) that ranking will still be made, but in most circles the man who is skilled at it does not so much receive esteem for a skill others do not possess: They do not feel they are competing at all and, rather, view him as taking part in an esoteric hobby. Since they themselves do not really take part, they do not even know how to rank him within its levels of achievement.

It is only at the lowest levels of ignorance that a ranking can still be observed for ordinary men: The male who is totally ignorant about how his automobile works is less esteemed. By a symmetrical contrast, women are not generally ranked at all in this area, but the few who have some skill are likely to receive a good bit of esteem.

INCREASED DIFFICULTY OF SOCIAL ACHIEVEMENTS

We can locate a few other instances where achievement becomes harder because of technical difficulty, but we shall probably find them most easily in frontier history, where technology becomes more primitive (to be considered in a subsequent section). Here, only note the two most striking facts about this category: the rarity of clear-cut examples where technology has made a given technical performance level more difficult; and, by contrast, the abundance of achievements that have become more difficult for reasons of "social conditions," "scarcity of time," "administrative difficulty," or "lack of cooperation," that is, diffuse, structural, social reasons rather than simple technological ones.

Very likely, a substantial minority of Americans would answer the question, "which things have become harder to do in modern life, with its high technology?" by saying "almost everything, except the things machines can do when they function well." Among these might be included: rearing children in cities; dropping in on friends with a sure expectation of being welcome; obtaining adequate servicing of the machines we use in our homes; keeping efficient domestic help; putting on an election campaign; giving formal dinners; maintaining friendships or marriages; generating community loyalty, cooperation, and safety; eliciting friendliness, help, or even civility from strangers.

Indeed, a central principle of what is the most socially acceptable "alternative sociopolitical philosophy" of our generation, supported by an articulate minority of the better-educated, is the claim that industrial progress has not led to social progress.[18] This is a centrist or liberal

---

18. For variants of this general view, see the works of Paul Goodman, and of Jane Jacobs, *The Death and Life of American Cities* (New York: Random House, 1961); Tibor Scitovsky, *The Joyless Economy* (New York: Oxford University Press, 1976); and of course, in a more romantic view of where progress might go, Charles A. Reich, *The Greening of America* (New York: Bantam, 1971).

position, which asserts that in pursuing the achievements that an industrial economy can most easily make, we have made it difficult to obtain many social or collective goals. These include (in addition to the foregoing list): protection of the mass consumer from shoddy or dangerous goods, clean air and water, conservation of natural resources, reduction of noise and garbage, neighborliness, and local influence in decisions about one's community life. In crude terms, they assert that in making many technological goals easier, we have made community goals harder. More precisely, many social commentators assert that a wide variety of goals requiring the *conscientious or responsible cooperation of other people* seems to have become more difficult over the last several generations, except when individuals are paid to give them (as in a corporation).

These goals are not to be dismissed as "middle-class wishes," as goals that lower-class people do not seek but that those in the middle class do. Most people at any class level view them as worthwhile even when they do not agree with the liberal or centrist political philosophy noted above. Of course the poor have always had greater difficulty in achieving any of these goals than have the affluent, but these problems are pervasive. For example, until World War I, the utilization of servants extended far down into the class structure, so that the "servant problem" was not confined to the rich. The shared neighborhood surveillance that once made child-rearing both safer and easier than now was more likely to be more adequate in middle-class areas than in lower-class ones, but it did once exist in many of the latter areas as well.[19] Most of the "social achievements" we have been noting have become more difficult for all classes. The affluent remain generally more protected than other classes, of course, but it is likely that the increase in difficulty has recently been greater among the well-to-do.

To analyze *why* all these activities have become more difficult would require a detailed description of the dynamics of contemporary society, and space does not permit it even if it could be achieved. Nevertheless, we should consider some "causes" for a moment, if only to be clearer about what this class of "tasks" contains and thus how these changes affect prestige allocations.

One powerful if crude variable is the increasing value of time and the lessening value of money.[20] Modern technology and the shortened work week have not apparently created much additional leisure for most people.[21] Since an increasing percentage of the adult population works for

19. For an architectural analysis of this problem, especially in high-rise apartment areas, see Oscar Newman, *Defensible Space* (New York: Collier, 1973). See also Gerald B. Suttles, *The Social Order of the Slum* (Chicago: University of Chicago Press, 1968).

20. In *The Harried Leisure Class* (New York: Columbia University Press, 1970), S. B. Linder has outlined the implications of viewing time as a commodity in daily life. J. K. Galbraith's *The Affluent Society* (Boston: Houghton Mifflin, 1958) points out many implications of the lessened value of money. See also the fundamental paper in this area: Gary Becker, "A Theory of the Allocation of Time," *Economic Journal*, 75 (September, 1965): 493–517.

21. Sebastian de Grazia, in *Of Time, Work and Leisure* (New York: Twentieth Century Fund, 1962), has attempted at some length to lay out the problem of ascertaining this crucial datum.

money, and the amount earned is greater, people increasingly calculate the worth of their nonwork activities. A substantial minority decide that the most rational use of their "free" time is part-time work in addition to their regular jobs. People feel pressed for time, and plan their use of it, so that "dropping by" without warning (an intrusion into others' time plans) becomes less permissible, or disesteemed. Because money is less valuable and time has become more valuable, more people try to use their leisure more intensely, to have more "peak experiences," through travel vacations, sports activities with heavy investments in equipment, expensive resorts, and sports lessons or guides. They may have to work more to get more money, because a given amount of money now brings less return in pleasure than in previous generations.

Men "tinker" with their automobiles less, not only because modern cars are more difficult to repair than early models, but also because they come to feel their more valuable time should be expended on something else. Even women who do not hold jobs feel that the time required to organize elaborate parties and formal dinners, to cook numerous or difficult dishes, to supervise a staff of servants, to maintain or supervise the laundry necessary for use of linen tablecloths and napkins or even clothing, to seek out and work with a seamstress in order to have one's dresses made, and so forth, is much too precious to be wasted in this fashion. In upper-class circles, it is now common to have one's more elaborate dinners catered. It is not that people cannot afford the *money* for servants (although comments deploring the cost of servants have been frequent for generations). Rather, servants require time and attention, which, especially among the rich, is less abundant than money.

Political campaigns, too, increased in cost until 1976, but they exhibit one other major problem that is observable in social achievements or activities that have become more difficult over time: They require more organization, and the enlistment and integration of far greater numbers of people in a common activity, than they once did. Almost any kind of reform campaign or informal community program, the creation of a neighborhood security force, or the maintenance of a volunteer fire department will require greater energy to be started or kept in operation than, say, fifty or one hundred years ago. This is partly because people have "other things to do," that is, time commitments. It is also partly because their normative commitment even to groups of which they are members seems lower than was reported in the period prior to World War I. An increasing percentage of people feel that they can avoid "doing for others" without being disesteemed—thus they will not unless they are paid money for it.

Of course, technology has decreased the cost of travel and communica-

---

Whether or not the amount of free time has increased over the past half-century, the difficulty of proving that it may at least show that the increase cannot be great.

tion, enabling more people to interact with more others at a distance than in any previous historical epoch. The paradox or irony of this social change has not escaped the observation of social commentators: We can communicate with more people than in the past, but we care less about them and have less interest in cooperating with them.

The reader will recognize the broad outlines of the category of activities that have become technically or socially more difficult because almost everyone will have complained, angrily or with detachment, about specific experiences of this kind, and newspapers bring numerous others to our attention each day.

Even though the causes for an expansion of this category are not clear, the question that is the theme of this chapter must be posed: How much esteem do modern people elicit for doing well in these areas? Since performance has become more difficult, the classical socioeconomic theory would assert that what was once a modest or average level of achievement would now arouse far more respect than before. Or, in economic terms, since the supply is lower (and surely the demand is no less) the price should be higher. What in fact do we observe now?

The category itself would have to be more precisely defined before a satisfactory answer could be stated. But with reference to some of these goals, it seems likely that most people suspect that success therein does not come from talent or hard work and that such "achievers" do not merit more admiration or praise than in the past. The housewife who manages to keep a servant or two for a decade or more is more likely to be viewed as lucky than as a wise manager. A couple who builds, repairs, or rebuilds a house without financial surprises or trouble with contractors is likely to be envied for their good fortune, rather than admired for their wisdom. Urban parents with "model children" are respected if it is thought they accomplished this by their parental excellence, but this is a rare case. That is, in many of the social areas where achievement seems to have become more difficult, people are often simply not ranked because success may not be viewed as proof of merit.

By contrast, community leadership, that is, success in the kinds of achievement that have become more difficult (goals that require the conscientious and responsible cooperation of other people who are not paid to give it), does elicit much esteem. Viewed as a collective contribution, it is not thought to be simply the result of good fortune. However, its apparently greater difficulty in modern society does not clearly cause such achievements to earn a great deal more respect than, say, a century ago.

There is no way to test this last speculation, but let us consider it for a moment. Among the large changes that characterize a modern industrial society is an increase in the number of social problems that people believe should or could be solved and, correspondingly, the creation of agencies or organizations to solve them. As a consequence, there are more formal and informal groups than in the past, whose aim it is to take care of some difficulty that once would have been left to the customary social adjustments of the community—ensuring contributions to the church, the discipline of children, raising a barn, maintaining neighborhood safety, organizing festivals and fairs. Very likely, most people feel that the difficulty of personal or community tasks requiring others' cooperation and responsibility has actually increased faster than the resources of informal and formal groups and organizations created to carry out such tasks.

However, because these tasks are more difficult than they once were, the belief is widespread that community leaders and their groups are failing to solve such problems (as most people fail to solve their personal problems). Thus, their collective contribution merits some esteem, but not a great deal, and certainly not as much as in the past when such groups accomplished more. Second, some of these tasks have become so huge (neighborhood safety, caring for the elderly, keeping the community clean) that they are now viewed primarily as the responsibility of government agencies. As a consequence, church groups, private philanthropy, and neighborhood improvement associations are seen as focusing only on the small problems overlooked by large corporate agencies. Again, people who contribute are thought to merit some prestige for their small achievement, but not a large amount.

By contrast with the present situation, informal and formal church or community leaders and their groups were once viewed as a major force in solving community problems or carrying out neighborhood tasks, and therefore they merited considerable respect. In the contemporary world, social contributions of this kind, as leader, organizer, or lesser participant, continue to elicit esteem from others, but the increased difficulty does not appear to yield much more respect than in the past. By comparison with what corporate actors (government agencies and corporations) can do, the accomplishments of individuals in these areas seem small even when they are as dedicated as informal leaders of the past were. I believe that the difficulty has risen, but so has the standard for achievement.

THE FRONTIER

Let us turn from this wide range of social achievements that seem to have become somewhat more difficult over the past half-century or so, to a much narrower historical process, in which both technological and social goals became more difficult for a few generations: the American frontier. People who ventured onto this ever-moving frontier, from the beginning of the eighteenth century until about 1900, had to leave much of "modern" technology and its social structure behind. At any given place, new settlers had to leave without much of the skill, machinery, and social experience of the older regions. Frontiersmen had to improvise or do without these aids.

Thus, while the main body of Western civilization was progressing technologically at a rapid rate, conditions on the American frontier (and frontiers in other countries, too) can be considered in many ways as having reversed that time process. That is, people arrived with attitudes, norms, values, and even skills that were adjusted to a more advanced society than where they now intended to live. Essays, letters, diaries, travelers' accounts, newspaper stories, and fiction describe these conditions, usually emphasizing the adventure, danger, and deprivation the settlers faced. Even people who were born on the frontier had somewhat similar internal experiences, because they were aware that by the standards of "normal" society "back home" their lives were much more "primitive" and difficult.[22]

Many of the standards these people brought with them were difficult or impossible to meet. Did the supply of "good" performances simply lower their standards, so that they paid more esteem for any given level of performance than would have been paid in the older settlements? Keeping in mind that "frontier" is a technological and social phase, not a specific geographical location or a specific time—for example, Indiana and eastern Texas were not frontier in the 1890's, but western Texas and Montana were—let us consider some frontier changes in the evaluation of various social behaviors.[23]

The most profound alteration, from which many others derived, was that prestige itself became much less important as a control system, while the resources of money and force or force threat increased in influence. The failure to live up to traditional standards of fairness or justice, elegance or beauty, piety or education aroused less group disesteem, and disesteem was less likely to generate other social losses. People felt less bound into a community whose prestige standards determined opportunities, friendships, posts, economic gain, or political support.[24] They felt more isolated, more dependent on their individual resources. Men felt freer to use

22. As Walter P. Webb notes in *The Great Plains* (New York: Ginn, 1931), even the basic geographic conditions on the plains made old skills useless and required new solutions. For example, the lack of trees made fencing and building difficult; lack of water made agriculture into a riskier venture, and in some parts of the High Plains led to a new area of litigation, irrigation law; poor river transportation raised the price of some commodities and increased dependence on the horse; without enough population for adequate government, individuals had to depend more on themselves for personal safety; and so on. However, at every point on the frontier, not alone the plains country, people faced their new problems without as much help from a settled community or from a reservoir of developed skills and tools as they would have enjoyed in the older regions to the east. See also James Willard Hurst, *Law and the Condition of Freedom in the Nineteenth Century United States* (Madison: University of Wisconsin Press, 1956).

23. Perhaps it should be emphasized that this analysis does not depend on the correctness of Frederick Jackson Turner, *The Frontier in American History* (New York: Holt, Rinehart, and Winston, 1962 [1920]), whose hypothesis that the American frontier, and its closing at the turn of the twentieth century, was decisive for the sociopolitical history of the United States. We are only considering prestige processes where the frontier existed at any given time, when the social and technological apparatus of the then modern world of the older settlements were left behind.

24. Edward Shils, in more abstract language, also makes this point in *Center and Periphery: Essays in Macrosociology* (Chicago: University of Chicago Press, 1975), pp. 3–16.

force or its threat on others without the permission or support of local governments, and with less fear that any community would organize in wrath to punish them.

When there is little community integration, people deal with one another much more *as individuals*, and they need not pay as much attention to others outside the immediate exchange or interaction. They can drive harder bargains without much fear of interference, if they can muster enough threat of force. They perceive fewer advantages from social prestige; but (unless the region becomes entirely lawless) gaining money is an advantage that does not diminish in importance even if many others disapprove, as long as individual objections do not become transformed into community disapproval.

This general situation can be seen most sharply in the absence of a genuine upper class on the frontier. Few members of the upper class came to the frontier, except as an adventure, a lark, or a flight from disgrace. In any given region or territory, some few families became rich, but even fewer were viewed as members of an elite. There were few equals to constitute a class. They lived too far from one another to interact frequently, so as to create a community that could set firm standards for manners, dress, comportment, or even morals. Moreover, all elites rest upon the concession by other classes that they are indeed the highest level of the society, and mere wealth did not generate that consensus on the frontier, as it did not elsewhere. Some of the newly rich on the frontier sometimes did exhibit pretensions to superiority, but their efforts were frequently mocked in literature, essays, and gossip. Again with reference to the theory we are discussing, such pretensions did not arouse more esteem because it was recognized that to be elegant on the frontier was harder than elsewhere. Rather, people did not agree as a community that such efforts were worthy of much respect.

Correspondingly, most people who moved to the frontier lost much of their claim to prestige because of family rank. Few of the others one might encounter would have known his family or its position, and in any event migrants can not easily transport family prestige. As in many other areas of action, the lower supply of family prestige does not increase its value when so few have much of it. Instead, it becomes of less importance.

On the other hand, it seems that even more esteem is given to those who are highly mobile in rank—i.e., who move from little to much, from poverty to ownership of a great ranch, from powerlessness to personal rule over even a small domain. Indeed, it was typical (and that rhetoric is still common among American entrepreneurs) for the successful frontiersman to exaggerate the lowly state from which he rose in order to emphasize his personal achievement and thus his claim to greater respect. One alteration in norms or standards is especially visible on the frontier, as it has been in the United States generally, compared with Europe: "old" family or money did gain some esteem, but "old" was a very short time span on the frontier. It was likely to be measured by decades, not by generations.

But let us turn from these broad points to a few specific changes. Certainly, a house on the frontier that would have been viewed as modest in the older settlements was viewed as more than adequate. Almost no one built dwellings comparable to southern or Hudson River Valley mansions, and no one could furnish them so elegantly. The necessary equipment and materials were not available locally, were extremely costly to transport, and in any event were socially unnecessary: One did not have to achieve that much to have the finest house in a frontier territory. And, at the other end of the scale, while no one thought a sod house or a log cabin was an excellent abode, they were so common that living in one was not disgraceful.

The lack of money and the difficulty of sheer survival when many daily necessities had to be scratched afresh from a harsh environment forced a decline in cleanliness, modishness of clothing, the excellence of cookery, formality of manners, and standards of fine artisanship. All of these required time, energy, money, and a surrounding social structure (all in short supply), and even a modest achievement in any of them aroused esteem commensurate with their difficulty on the frontier—though that level of excellence was less than in the older settlements farther east.

By contrast, elegant carriages were useless where roads were hardly good enough for wagons; they were thought to be silly rather than worthy of emulation. But though thoroughbred horses were also too delicate for frontier conditions, they were always admired: this was a horse culture. Manners especially require reciprocity: what one does for another, the other owes in turn. Eastern manners (especially table manners) were mocked, and a much more modest level was aimed at by "respectable" people. After all, the individual cannot impose his or her own high standard on others; for if they do not reciprocate, he or she then appears ridiculous or insensitive.

Living by the traditional standards of morals and religion requires considerable time, energy, and money, even when there is a community that punishes failure by some denigration. Men and women sometimes began living together without benefit of clergy, simply because no clergyman was available for months at a time. In the priorities of the frontier, a church was not preeminent; and church attendance once it was built was unlikely to be dutiful or widespread. People were more likely to settle arguments by gunfire than they were on the eastern seaboard, and winners did not lose as much in esteem as they would have in the more settled regions. (On the extreme frontier, they gained.)

In the last area of social behavior, we must consider another historical alternative. We have noted that people on the frontier responded to difficulties there by lowering the standards for adequate performance in some areas (for example, cleanliness); in others (upper-class manners) the standards themselves were dropped or became irrelevant. With reference to many traditional moral patterns, however, it is less clear that the norms and beliefs actually changed, in the sense that people no longer felt committed to them. Instead, people accepted or tolerated a range of behavior in others and themselves that they may not have felt was ideal. They saw that actually living up to the traditional norms was more difficult here; they also saw that others did not punish transgressors as severely; but they may not—on this crucial point, we simply do not know the facts—have therefore simply dropped their allegiance to those moral, ethical, or religious norms. That is, the decline (if any) in standards was probably of short duration.

By contrast with that theoretical ambiguity—"theoretical" because the problem can be encountered in many other types of situations, such as lower-class urban life, shipwrecks and other survival situations, and concentration and other hardship camps—it seems clear that in the areas of educational or scientific achievement the standards of adequate performance were simply lowered, as a function of supply and demand. People continued to respect education and (to a lesser extent) scientific work, but people with modest performances in either were esteemed far more than they would have been (or in fact were) in the older settlements.

That theoretical ambiguity noted above also contrasts with the apparent situation in the fine arts. Although a high percentage of towns of any size on the frontier eventually built an "opera house," and both Jenny Lind and Oscar Wilde drew substantial crowds wherever they appeared in the West, it cannot be inferred that people on the frontier thirsted for concerts, poetry, and "high culture." Aside from the fact that there was not enough economic surplus to support lavishly even the cultural enterprises of the east coast, it would be hard to deny that most people on the frontier viewed such activities as effete, ridiculous, and irrelevant. This was especially true of men on the frontier, who were likely to stereotype the poet as an effeminate, mooning fellow (they could exempt Wilde in part from that stereotype because he mocked almost everything sacred and could "drink like a man"). Essays, travelers' reports, and diaries suggest that at least a substantial minority of women, who were the "culture preservers" in the United States, did long for such refinements. By and large, however, it cannot be said that the standards for gaining respect in the fine arts were simply lowered (as they were for education); rather, few people on the frontier paid them any respect at all, or they made fun of them as pretentious at best.[25] That is, with lowered supply, the demand dropped too.

It should be kept in mind, too, that here we are speaking of high culture, which typically requires a genuine upper class for its support; and

25. Very likely, this has been the typical attitude among the urban lower classes in Western societies for at least the past two centuries.

that class in turn gains some of its rank from its supposed allegiance to such activities. Because people were generally hungry for any entertainment, performers who ventured to the frontier could usually attract an audience; but the taste of that audience hardly coincided with that of Boston Brahmins. Practitioners of the high arts were not attracted to the frontier because the rewards were few and the life was difficult. Thus the supply was lower than in the east, but so was the demand. Certainly few people on the frontier could have claimed much esteem by proclaiming themselves to be devotees of opera, symphonic music, ballet, or the poetry of Robert Browning.

Evaluations of more practical skills rose, however, not only because they were in short supply (at least, in comparison with the increased demand) but because life itself was precarious on the frontier. Men and women were admired for their ability to endure hardship, their audacity and imagination when facing disaster, their ingenuity in solving technical problems (from curing a sick cow or pulling a tooth to repairing a wagon) without adequate training, tools, or the help of a specialist. People were also respected for bravery. And, as in the older settlements, competence in the skills of farming or stock-raising was esteemed.

People were therefore more willing to associate with those who ranked high on such survival skills than with others, and more willing to select them as leaders of a posse, a new local government, or a long drive to a new territory. Such skills, it should be emphasized, were also respected in the eastern rural areas, as indeed they were (to a lesser extent) in urban capitals. On the other hand, most people in the more settled regions could not have been easily ranked along such dimensions, since the opportunity to observe them faced with such problems almost never occurred. That is, the difficulties of frontier living raised both the social evaluation of skills and character traits that facilitated survival and the chances of ranking people by those criteria.

Chapter 9
Prestige Processes over Time: New Standards for Giving Esteem

In Chapter 8 a range of time changes were considered in which increased or decreased difficulty in performing well seems to cause alterations in the amount of esteem given to individuals or groups. Let us now consider the dynamics of the reverse process, when higher or lower evaluations are first announced as a way of causing social change. That is, we shall now analyze what happens when changes in evaluations, norms and values, or philosophies appear to be the "independent," causal, or at least initiating variable, thus altering the esteem given to different kinds of behavior or traits. When a prophet announces a new doctrine, a fashion leader proclaims a new trend in dress design, an artist's manifesto castigates the Academy and promulgates a new esthetics, it is as though a new schedule of prices is being proposed. Henceforth, such announcements assert, we should praise these behaviors, and dispraise those, as against our customs of the past. If people then alter their evaluations, and change the esteem they give, perhaps others will alter their behavior to gain that prestige in accord with the new preachments.

In the last chapter, we were essentially focusing on unplanned changes in prestige processes, such as the adjustments to frontier or extreme survival conditions or the gradual expansion of industry. In such cases, the historical change in prestige allocation was an unintended consequence of many people's actions. It was, like most human activities, accompanied by at least some arguments about evaluations, but it did not begin as a set of stated aims about how prestige should be allocated, based on an announcement of new evaluations or a new religion.

Perhaps all history can be viewed as the blind working out of actions begun for entirely other purposes: History is made up of what people did not intend at all. Whatever the ultimate wisdom of that view, however, both leaders and their subjects follow a different one, for leaders seem to believe they can change things; when their careers are ended they believe they did so; and people at lesser ranks believe they are forced to change because of the actions and proclamations of leaders. We shall follow these assumptions, too, and ask whether prestige processes differ when the social change is inaugurated by changes in evaluations, or in standards for earning prestige.

The type of change focused on in this chapter is not symmetrical with that of the preceding chapter. Properly, it should be: How do prestige allocations change when people's evaluations alter before there is any change in behavior? But I believe that this logical parallel does not concretely appear as a common historical phenomenon. Almost never do the evaluations of a society or group change so rapidly that one can say that at some specific time they have in fact changed but as yet no behavioral adjustments have occurred. There are a few reported instances of mass religious conversions, but very likely no instances when almost everyone in the society is known to have changed political, esthetic, or moral evaluations before making any changes in behavior. Rather, we observe that prophets, rulers, or would-be rulers announce a new system of evaluations and by their persuasiveness convert some people but not most; and then gradually others follow if the new message is successful. For this reason, we must focus mostly on historic cases in which such rulers or aspiring leaders proclaim or announce a set of evaluations first.

In the last chapter, by contrast, we noted various changes in behavior that became relatively common before much argument about new norms and values. Such changes can sometimes have very different effects than changes in what is esteemed. Obviously, an *individual* can change his or her norms or evaluations with little or no change in behavior. One can, after all, make such changes inside one's head with little cost, but changes in behavior may be more costly. One may come to believe in sexual freedom but live in a restrictive community; to berate oneself for smoking and drinking but be unable to give up either; to esteem modern art but be surrounded with people who despise it. However, if *everyone* is moving in the same direction, many of those behavioral changes will no longer be costly. If everyone comes to believe that aristocrats should not be given much respect, the cost of refusing deference drops immediately. If almost everyone comes to believe in the importance of building the new revolutionary society, then all participants give each other esteem for their contributions, so that the individual believer can easily express his or her new attitudes by engaging in that behavior. Thus there may be differences in the consequences of action or normative commitment for the individual.

With reference to the group itself, since evaluations state what its members prefer, esteem, or wish, changes in one direction are likely to be translated into action—that action is not, to be sure, ever a complete conformity, but it is unlikely that one can locate a society that has changed its values and norms without changing its behavior, too. Individuals and subgroups may be internally dissident or nonbelieving, but when a society actually changes its attitudes and preferences, its members are also likely to be altering their behavior in order to live more closely by those new standards.

Historians are tireless in reminding us, correctly, that no significant change ever happens all at once (unless caused by a natural catastrophe); and that no political leader or prophet ever transformed the social patterns of a group merely by informing its members how much respect they should pay from that date onward. Even without plan or program, changes in means and conditions will change both behavior and evaluations, as noted in the previous chapter. However, when leaders attempt new plans, they are likely to change human behavior very little. Most programs for social change are failures over the long run.

Nevertheless, all changes that are planned are accompanied by attempts to change people's evaluations of what should earn esteem. All revolutionary proclamations announce that henceforth a different set of achievements or group contributions will be honored. A declaration of war and the speeches supporting it do the same thing. When conquerors begin the administration of a new territory, or a king establishes a new policy, they will invariably attempt to impose a new set of rewards or punishments in the realm of prestige and not alone in property or the courts. Evidently, it is natural for political or religious leaders to try to create social changes by altering the amount of esteem given for various activities.

Many social engineers assert that it is easier to change behavior by altering means or conditions than by changing people's attitudes, norms, or values. The latter are the product of childhood and adult socialization, and are not easily altered. It is easier to reduce cheating on examinations by separating students from one another than to change their moderate disesteem for those who cheat. If new jobs at good pay are opened for women, many husbands will object less to their wives' working, even if they do not alter by much their feeling that women who do so deserve less esteem than those who do not work.

On the other hand, most leaders have not usually confined themselves to that solution. First, it requires more managerial skill than religious or political leaders typically possess, while the use of commands or persuasion requires little. Second, most people who try to inaugurate any social change begin with few resources. They are leaders of a tiny religious group, members of a small revolutionary cell, young people and old whose aspirations are far greater than their means. Indeed, it is usual for even high political, business, or religious leaders to complain that they lack the means with which to press others to obey their wishes. Third, those who attempt any new program usually want others to feel committed, to believe, to have faith in the new system of practice or belief, and not merely conform in overt behavior.

If they succeed, then the costs of command are less, for those who accept the new evaluations are more likely to conform simply because they feel that this particular course of action is more desirable and they want the esteem that comes from following it. Leaders will feel more comfortable with believing followers, and the trust and respect between them will be greater. For all these reasons, then, it is typical that any attempt to inaugurate a social change is preceded and accompanied by attempts to persuade members of the group or society that different kinds of achievements or individuals should be esteemed from those esteemed earlier.

What happens to prestige allocation when a new set of standards is promulgated, such as a manifesto of rising artists, a call for revolution, or the preaching of a heresy? Believers form a covenant stating that they will pay respect to those who conform and believe and will denigrate those who do not. As noted before, the new standards may be harsher or more difficult to meet, or they may instead be more permissive.

NEW NORMATIVE EVALUATIONS OF MEANS

Let us first consider a relatively simple type of prestige change. Sometimes a social change occurs not because a major shift in religious doctrine is preached or a revolutionary junta proclaims the overthrow of the system, but because people learn how to achieve better a goal that is widely accepted. Then the new *means* to that end become the basis for changes in esteem. This type of change does not usually lead to significant alterations in social structures, though it may be as weighty as a new way of destroying an enemy. It may also be as trivial as the approved style of playing tennis. As the new means are accepted, people create, announce, or affirm new norms that give greater esteem to people who use the new procedures.

A good example is the change in Western ideals or norms of bodily attractiveness since World War I, in favor of slimness and against plumpness. Correspondingly, the social standard for a lavish meal has changed. An opulent Edwardian meal would now be viewed as little short of vulgar and piggish. The older phrase "a fine figure of a man" once referred to a body that would now be viewed as dangerously overweight—but also as not very attractive.

A major element in this evaluational change was the growing recognition that being plump is not evidence of good health. Here, the evaluational change has given greater admiration to a slimmer figure, and people have changed their behavior accordingly. (Of course, as in the past, many who are poor may remain slim through no choice of their own.) More recently, smoking has increasingly come to be viewed as unattractive and even antisocial, that is, dispraised, because more people now believe that it harms both smokers and those in the same physical area.

In both instances, there may have been little change in the admiration for those who are healthy or attractive, or in the desirability of either state. What has changed is the knowledge about how to achieve health, and thus the evaluations of people who appear to take effective steps toward it.

As a similar example, people have always preferred a beautiful countryside, clean air and water, and garbage-free streams, but only recently have ideological attacks been mounted against careless trash disposal, sewage and industrial pollution, the use of slowly decomposing pesticides, and so on. Those attacks have increased with the recognition that such practices are destructive and that the absorptive capacity of the planet is limited. In turn, the attacks have justified disesteem for people and organizations that engage in such practices and praise for those that help to stop such behavior.

Both these steps (attitude changes and attacks) have occurred before any substantial changes in pollution behavior. In fact, at present one can assert a substantial correlation between the amount of pollution a corporation engages in and the amount of advertising it buys to claim prestige for its ecologically sound achievements. As will be noted in the chapter on subversion, it costs less to claim virtue than to change one's behavior in that direction.

Doubtless the reader will think of many other cases, that is, those in which new knowledge about how to reach a goal already approved alters people's evaluations of the means. Then they give esteem or disesteem to people or organizations who use the better means. Esteem or dispraise is given to different patterns of action than in the past, and different behavior is elicited. Of course, as in all behavior, even when our evaluations change, and others wish to change their behavior to earn our esteem, giving up the old and following the new may be too costly. Thus, many neither slim down nor stop smoking.

EVALUATIONAL CHANGES AS "LOGICAL" INFERENCES

Let us consider another type of case in which evaluations alter before behavior. In the previous type, a change occurs in the knowledge about the means for attaining some broad goal or value, and people begin to give more esteem to those who use those more effective means. In this case, people—prophets, leaders, groups—begin to make "logical" inferences from some broad principle or value to new areas of conduct, norms, or social rules. Perhaps the most conspicuous case in the history of the Anglo countries is the Magna Carta. The barons who wrested that agreement from a reluctant King John would surely have been indignant at the suggestion that its provisions, which became the foundation of modern civic and parliamentary rights, ought to be extended to merchants, artisans, peasants, blacks, or women.

Such inferences are never logical to their opponents, who deny that the syllogism is complete. For example: All men are equal and should be guaranteed these rights; black men are men, too; therefore . . . . Or: "Men" includes women, for the term means "mankind." However, most broad principles and values are stated inclusively, and most can be extended to people, situations, regions, or organizations that had not been originally anticipated to be included (but that were not specifically excluded). That extension may not be successful; indeed, perhaps it is usually defeated. However, many cases do exist: the rights of workers in some corporate decisions, race relations, women's rights, rules of evidence, and so on.

Typically, when the new ideological assertion is made, which extends a broad value to a new area of action (denial of the divine right of kingship, of the husband's rule, of the legitimacy of decisions of a corporation president), only few will accept quickly the new norms that are proclaimed, while many will perceive that such an inference *could* be drawn (and object to it just the same). Then some who accept the newly promulgated norms, or who at least perceive some justice in them, may carry them out in action.

In the recent women's liberation movement—the latest resurgence in a long history—the inference was made from the notion of "equality" (under various definitions) that women were being blocked, deprived of their rights, discriminated against, and given less prestige than they had earned by universalistic standards. Many women, and still more men, roused themselves to deny the charge, but no great perception is needed to observe that even those who are staunchly conservative feel the pressure of these inferences. Similarly, many who accept the *logic* of the inference cannot feel in harmony with the newly proposed norms: that is, they still feel more comfortable if women are excluded, they admire men who can dominate their wives, or they give praise to women who do not wish to take a job.

Moreover, many women and men who accept the logic of the inference may carry out actions in its support without much emotional commitment to the norms. That is, they accept (as most people do) the broad principles before they have come to accept specific norms implementing them; and they may act before they have become fully committed to those norms. They may praise women who rebel against the stereotype, or applaud men who become "liberated" from traditional male roles, before they themselves are comfortable in executing the changed normative requirements. Nevertheless, they do announce new rules for giving approval and elicit some changes in behavior by offering praise for them.

ESTABLISHING A PRESTIGE COMMUNITY

Those who aim at changing others' prestige evaluations with reference to any particular activity may well have some group-like social patterns; after all, they do share some values and may cooperate in common programs. From time to time, however, important social changes have been set in motion by subgroups that genuinely create a small "prestige community." That is, members withdraw to a greater or lesser extent their allegiance to some values of the larger society, and pay respect to one another for conformity to a different set of norms or evaluations. Christ with his disciples formed such a group, and so have many heretical sects in perhaps all official religions. The Black Muslims did so more recently. Many revolutionary movements began with small groups, too, who constructed a community of like-minded comrades whose standards for granting esteem were counter to those accepted by others. Though they might be viewed as "outsiders," they defined themselves as insiders, the only society worth caring about. Of course, some groups go still further, and establish communes that are set apart physically from the rest of the society.

Such prestige communities mostly begin with few resources, although here and there some groups have been created by members of the elite (in modern times, for example, Opus Dei). Commanding little prestige themselves, they face the double problem of rewarding their members, as well as obtaining respect from outsiders who basically disagree with their evaluations. Both goals are important, but they are likely to be partly incompatible.

With reference to the problem of paying prestige to members, such groups are in effect setting up a separate social economy, agreeing among themselves about what each contribution or achievement will be worth in esteem and what is a tolerable performance for continued membership. Usually those standards are harsh: members make great demands of themselves, and expel those who are lax in their commitment.

They begin with little or no prestige capital. They have as yet no accumulated achievements that justify such payments. On the other hand, to the extent that members both accept the new standards and live by them, they do earn esteem from one another. Each makes contributions to the collectivity and thus justifies the respect he or she gets from the others.

At a deeper level, that set of steps throws some light on prestige processes generally. It suggests that a group may decide to pay its members some esteem for whatever they collectively decide to honor, thus maintaining its prestige economy as long as they live by those standards. Those who form a prestige community act as do those who found a nation and issue money as legal tender. The procedure is *not* the same as that of poker players who play for only chips and set arbitrary values for each type of chip. In that case, after the game is over no one can trade in a chip for a given amount of money.

By contrast, a newly established monetary system may be backed by bonds or gold, but it is at least backed by the future taxes and the productivity of the citizens, just as the payments of esteem by a group are backed by its members' production of valued acts. If ultimately the money of the new nation is accepted as payment for goods and services, it no longer has a merely arbitrary paper value, set only by the government's fiat. Nor is acceptance of the money only an act of faith: People accept it because they can observe that in fact others will change their behavior when given some of it, that is, they will hand over goods or services. So, too, a prestige community does not set esteem payments by whim alone. The test is whether members will in fact conform to the new standards in order to gain the esteem of other members, even though those standards are counter to those of the larger society.

However, the further challenge is whether the group, community, or even new nation can use the prestige it believes members have earned to exchange with still other, outsider groups. A new nation formed by revolution may especially encounter this problem in its relations with other nations. The new nation can sometimes impose a very different value on its money within its boundaries (for example, the Russian ruble)—as can a small group with its prestige—than others will accept. Here, too, the question is the ultimate backing for the money, or for the prestige; that is, goods and services of various kinds.

Obviously, if the achievements honored within the group (bombing a railroad, shooting a duke, doctrinal purity) are not esteemed by outsiders, the group's "accomplishments" may be viewed with abhorrence. Such groups and their members may not be able to get help or respect from others; no one wants *their* respect, and many will not interact with them at all, or only in financial transactions. They may be persecuted instead, at least until they have converted some of the larger community to their beliefs.

It is partly to avoid this disesteem in social transactions that some subgroups try to remain secret. Some, like the Hutterites or the Bruderhof, establish communities apart from the larger society, exchanging with it only those goods and services on whose value they can come to some agreement. The Black Muslims (like the early Christians) established themselves among people who were at least somewhat sympathetic to their cause even though the outside, white authorities tried to persecute them. The Black Muslims stated a set of rules that aroused some respect in the black community (sobriety, hard work, no drugs, praise of blackness, giving no deference to whites), and later their achievements were even given some respect by many whites. Thus, as against their lack of prestige capital at first, when they announced the standards by which they would give respect to members, they were able at a later stage to draw on considerable prestige capital. They were also able to exchange some of it for political influence and use it in gaining credit from banks for the formation of new enterprises.

The Black Muslims tried to keep their relations with whites to a minimum, in part because a beginning prestige community is at some disadvantage in interactions across the social boundaries with outsiders that are more influential. They were somewhat separatist even among blacks. Separation or secrecy, like nationalist restrictions on who may enter or leave a nation, makes it easier to control both internal prestige payments and exchanges with other groups. Separatism makes it easier to observe what members do, and thus to warn them early if they are straying from the path of conformity. Being separate, either socially or physically, makes the socialization of children easier. Both socialization and social control are more effective if members are not tempted by alternative evaluations or payoffs from outsider groups or communities.

To the extent that a prestige community is successful in gaining more members as well as social resources of all kinds, it comes to be disesteemed less—consider in this respect the many sects that have become relatively "respectable" over the past generation. The classical analyses of the changes a sect goes through as it gradually becomes a successful church also point out that the strict rules of the original subgroup are gradually weakened.[1] Expulsion of an erring member becomes rarer. Such standards are too difficult for a large population to meet, with its lower intensity of devotion or commitment. On the other hand, in a later and more successful phase the larger membership still gives high prestige to those specialists in dedication (the true revolutionaries, the pious elders) who continue to live by the more rigorous standard.

WAR AND REVOLUTION

Besides changes in behavior effected by the formation of a prestige community, more massive alterations are sometimes set in motion by a proclamation of new norms and values in wartime or revolution. Especially in the past (until World War I in many countries), a monarch and his advisors could simply announce a state of war, with little prior effort at mass persuasion. Revolutionary cadres typically do so. When only a small number of people has decided on the ideology of the revolution, then a ruler or would-be ruler "announces" a set of social demands. Everyone is to alter his or her evaluations and actions: An enemy is named who is henceforth to be denigrated along with his subjects or supporters; mobilization is ordered and patriotism invoked; new prestige schedules are created, by which military heroes are to be rewarded. Propaganda machines are set in motion in order to persuade unbelievers to the new evaluations, while believers are to be confirmed in their approved ways of thinking.

Even successful wars do not quite fit the class of events emphasized in this chapter, namely, long-term changes begun by proclaiming new values. True enough, a goodly number have led to massive long-term changes. For example, World Wars I and II are both to be seen as major watersheds in world history. Defeats in war have often led to rebellions or revolutions. However, it is rare that the changes announced as the goals of a war, or the new prestige evaluations, *become* the longer-term changes in the social structure. It is rather the complex social events of the war itself, and its attendant physical and social destruction, that cause the large

1. For an analysis of these stages see J. Milton Yinger, *Religion in the Struggle for Power* (Durham, N.C.: Duke University Press, 1946).

changes. Perhaps one minor exception is the wartime goal of combating Hitler's racism, which may have increased somewhat the disesteem given to racists since then.

Revolutions, by contrast, both announce and implement longer-term changes in prestige evaluations. The ideology of the revolution is supposed to become the ideology of the society after the fighting is over. The aim is not like that of war, to return to traditional ways, but to discard them. The task is greater, since the would-be leaders begin with much prestige and influence only among a handful of followers. They do not have the resources that the government has when it begins an ordinary war, while their goals are farther-reaching.

In view of the widely known difficulty of changing either actions or attitudes through propaganda, it is striking that both change quickly when war breaks out. Although traditional monarchies did not engage in much initial propaganda to prepare their subjects for the war to follow, while modern governments do, at a minimum leaders have always charged that the enemy has committed iniquities and merits disesteem. Justice is claimed for their side. They announce that henceforth different achievements will be honored than in peacetime, such as courage and competence in battle, leadership in marshaling resources, and sacrifice for the nation. Whether campaigns of persuasion could be mounted, or if mounted would be successful, if entirely different goals were presented instead of those of war (neighborliness, brotherhood, equality) is not known. It is, in any event, rare indeed that any populace has simply refused to be moved by those appeals and has instead asserted its unwillingness to fight. Nationalist sentiments can, it appears, be easily aroused, and they will support a wide range of short-term alterations in what is paid respect. The consequences also may lead to massive long-term changes.

Just as it is a puzzle why people so quickly alter their actions and evaluations to support a nationalist war, so there is a puzzle as to why successful revolutions seem to expand so abruptly.[2] Analysts of revolution can show that any revolution is "caused" by complex processes set in motion by a long history.[3] However, conflict and grievance are so widespread in most countries that, had a revolution occurred in an entirely different set of nations, it would be possible to show that there, too, it was "inevitable." Nevertheless, a high percentage of the actors in a successful revolution are surprised at how swiftly it unfolds.

Both these puzzles suggest the important fact that under some circum-

---

2. The paradox of the slow, by no means inevitable movement toward revolution and its swiftness at some point is one of the themes treated by John Urry, *Reference Groups and the Theory of Revolution* (London: Routledge & Kegan Paul, 1973).

3. A keen attempt to separate the inessential from the essential processes is that of Theda Skocpol, "A Structural Theory of Social Revolution," prepared for the American Sociological Association meetings, New York, August, 1973; some of this appears in *Comparative Studies in Society and History*, 18, no. 2 (April, 1976): 175–210, as "France, Russia, China—Structural Analysis of Social Revolutions." See also Jeffrey Paige, *Agrarian Revolution* (New York: Free Press, 1975).

stances a wide range of evaluations can change relatively quickly, when new ones are announced, and before any large-scale material rewards or threats have been used to change people's actions. Revolutions, moreover, cause or lead to longer-term changes that would be difficult to predict if the analyst did not study the ideological proclamations. That norms, values, or evaluations can change in these ways does not prove they are not deep, or are no more than fleeting impulses; after all, people sacrifice in order to live by them. Perhaps it proves only that we have not as yet understood their inner psychic structure.

In any event, in both large-scale wars and revolutions those who lead also command (or eventually obtain) huge resources other than mere proclamations of new standards for earning esteem. As in normal social life, disesteem or esteem is likely to be accompanied by additional punishments and rewards. For example, those who enthusiastically and effectively support the war are likely to be given more respect and higher profits or promotions as well. Those who help the revolution may gain higher posts and save their own lives as well. The allocation of offices, political influence, material gains, and prestige is likely to be highly correlated, and perhaps especially so when the political apparatus is pursuing a narrower set of goals than in peacetime. This range of rewards reinforces the norms and values that become salient during war and revolution.

The temporary character of esteem won in wartime has been remarked on many times. Heroes often experience with some bitterness the anonymity that peacetime brings. Unless military honor is quickly exchanged for job opportunities, people forget the exploits that were honored. Some heroes turn to politics, where their diffuse aura of esteem may yield votes. In the most successful exchanges, the specific or general skills of military service (with computers, shipping, administration) are used for civilian jobs. In general, however, when peacetime standards for prestige rule once again, the value of wartime exploits drops considerably.

I speculate (without adequate data) that successful revolutions differ from successful wars in this shift of evaluations (and that they differ still more from unsuccessful wars). After a war, leaders typically engage in a set of symbolic actions to mark the change to peace: the end of the war is proclaimed, the dead are mourned officially, speeches announce the new goals of binding the wounds of war and beginning reconstruction, medals and honors are issued, the men and women in uniform are helped to start their civilian lives once more, and plans for future progress are drawn up. That is, a different set of standards is proclaimed, a new set of goals.

Although some of these actions also mark the end of the revolutionary conflict, a central difference is evident. Far from announcing the victory as support for the traditional way of life, leaders point to it as proof of their legitimacy and the rightness of the revolutionary values. It is not the military aspects of heroism that loom large at this time, however, but its contribution to the revolution as a process. Now that the problems of conflict are out of the way, the real revolution, that is, putting into effect the revolutionary goals, can finally begin. Thus the heroes of the past are still to be honored, for they helped build the road to the future, and the same values are to be affirmed as during the military conflict. Revolutionary heroes are likely to continue to be honored (subject to the ironies of fate) unless a counterrevolution succeeds in denying those values.

By definition, the leaders of a revolution at its outbreak do not, as they praise and blame in their proclamations, express the evaluations of the citizenry. If their pronouncements were already in harmony with the people's ideology, there would be little need for armed conflict. That harmony remains to be achieved. Typically, even the leaders are not clear about what they are going to do. What a revolution aims at, as so many practitioners have asserted, is gradually discovered by actually making it. However, some themes are closer than others to the inner wishes of ordinary people. One is of course the promise of material rewards, especially land. Equally appealing is the theme of freedom from oppression, the demand for respect, or justice.

This latter theme takes many forms in Jacobin revolutions, including the abolition of elaborate uniforms or court costumes, confiscation of nobles' estates for public use, the norm that leaders should live simply, and the erasure of hereditary privileges. Here we note again the point that some long-term changes are more difficult than others, and some can be more swiftly implemented than others.

Very likely, deference toward aristocrats or elites is more quickly and easily wiped out than many other social patterns, and this begins to occur about as soon as announcements are made that such deferential behavior may henceforth be dropped. Almost certainly the change is easy because the previous pattern was costly to people's self-esteem. Once the threats of force or economic reprisal are reduced or eliminated, people do not continue to doff their caps to their former social superiors. These changes express complaints made in recurrent peasant or proletarian uprisings over the centuries. The courtier's polish and manner, the official seals of the king's ministers, the military duke's insignia of command are never enough to maintain their high esteem rankings in the new market of respect where all their former legal and economic supports have vanished.

It should be noted in passing that the prestige of the nobility disappears. It cannot simply be handed over to the new rulers, whose base of esteem is quite different. The land of the nobility does not disappear, although their rights to it do. As one consequence, who owns or uses the land after a revolution may remain a point of contention for some years afterwards.

Such changes in esteem after a revolution are not temporary. World history is too short to give us much understanding of the conditions under which a hereditary nobility might be reimposed after it has once been removed. However, the history of the past three hundred years suggests that that step might be very difficult. It seems easier to stave off the efforts of bondsmen or slaves to gain their freedom than to force them into their old status again. The ideological pronouncements or evaluational proclamations that originally inaugurated such changes are not easily refuted later. Machiavelli too noted the difficulty of maintaining a tyranny in a city-state that had once enjoyed its liberty.

By contrast, the high ideal of sacrifice for the communal good, the eagerness to work hard and long for the revolution, the willingness to give up comfortable, traditional ways, typically begins to falter before the promises of the revolution have been fulfilled. The human capacity for dedication to the collectivity does not continue for long. It was Mao Tse-tung's awareness of this social regularity that led him to engage in "purification" campaigns from time to time, calling the Chinese citizenry back to the values that launched the revolution. Thus, those beginning goals and values that emphasized sacrifice and hard work are likely to be honored still, but the person of modest esteem is not expected to live up to them in reality over the longer term.

CHANGES OVER THE VERY LONG TERM

Evaluational and behavioral changes over the very long term, that is, several generations to centuries, differ from most of the foregoing cases in that they can much less easily be linked with a single persuasive source that occurs at a particular time, such as a religious prophet, or a nationalist or revolutionary leader. They include such changes as the gradual deprecation of slavery and racism, and lowered overt deference given to the upper classes, the increased political respect paid to workers and union organizers, the greater esteem given to women who do "men's jobs," and the spread of civil rights.

In all these instances, nevertheless, without question the ideological or evaluational pronouncements did precede any substantial change in behavior. These and similar cases are different from most of the examples considered earlier in this chapter in that 1. it would be more difficult to locate the *first* such pronouncement or statement, because all of these are minority positions little noted or remembered for the most part, and they have appeared here and there over the centuries; 2. such earlier statements in the distant past did not convince many people, and there was little cumulative change in people's norms or attitudes about these matters until fairly recently in Western history; and 3. more important, although almost certainly the more recent changes have also been preceded by ideological and evaluational preachments, the persuasiveness of such statements was helped by alterations in other factors (political influence, economic developments) and not alone the evaluational.

For example, the increased persuasiveness or attractiveness of bourgeois virtues in England, the United States, and France through the eighteenth and nineteenth centuries was enhanced by the success of bourgeois revolutions (by force and force threat) in those countries, as also by the growing economic pressure of the middle classes. In England and the United States, the working class gradually won more respect, not only because of eloquent defenses of the worker in speeches, pamphlets, and essays. Nor was it alone because workers gradually acquired bourgeois virtues (education, work discipline, cleanliness). In addition, that changing opinion was supported by the growing political influence of workers (the spread of suffrage, the threat of revolution in England in the 1820's, the outbreak of revolution in many countries in 1848, the growth of labor organizations) and their greater importance as purchasers.

Consequently, even if we wish to analyze the independent and prior influence of evaluative changes on prestige allocations over several generations or centuries, in such cases we must once again concede that other changes also made the new evaluations more credible or persuasive. As Machiavelli remarked, the unarmed religious leader or prophet does not win. The historically "inevitable" triumph of a new set of evaluations takes place amidst the clash of arms and the laborious creation of new institutions that determine different prices for commodities, as for people and their services.

It is not possible at this time to force any genuine order on this set of complex cases, forming as it does most of the slow, great changes of world history. However, a few types of cases can be noted. First, some evaluative positions are relative oddities, proclaimed only occasionally over the centuries, and gaining new adherents or a supporting movement only under special circumstances, such as new powerful social supports (war, revolution, plague) or a charismatic prophet. Thus, until the advent of the English feminists of the early nineteenth century, few defenders of women appeared—Plato being a notably rare figure.[4]

A second type that might be closer to Sorokin's "trendless fluctuations" than to a real change are those minority positions that are steadily proclaimed through the centuries but that garner only a handful of followers. These are not likely to be social movements, although some become that. Perhaps an example can be noted. From the earliest period of the Roman republic, a bucolic theme has been found in Western social philosophy. It consists of such value assertions as these: rural life is morally superior to urban life; the tiller of the soil is simpler but nobler in spirit than city people; nature is benign and clean, while urban life is cruel and decadent. Further, freedom and dignity are to be found in even rural poverty, but not in urban riches (recall the tale of the city mouse and the country mouse); rural men are strong and virile, but urban men are weak and effete. The bucolic theme was partly a literary pose and never became

4. In his insistence that, although women were generally inferior, some were superior to some men and should therefore be given the same opportunity to develop their full potential.

dominant; its importance very likely shows a slow downward trend. Nevertheless, many decisions and actions were made in conformity with it (for example, sacrificing some profits in order to enjoy the prestige of owning landed property).

These rural-urban subthemes, and variations on them, have affected political philosophy and thus political action over many centuries. They have been more persuasive in Anglo countries than in Latin countries, without affecting by much the steady migration of populations toward cities whenever opportunity has opened. They have supported the continuing political influence of the farm lobby in the United States. They appear in thousands of political speeches here each year, in which the virtues of countryfolk and villagers are extolled—although the percentage of farmers has dropped to less than five percent of the work force. These themes gave a special piquancy to the pastoral games the aristocrats played at Versailles, and a special titillation to cross-class sexual liaisons in modern fiction (the lower classes are seen as closer to rural people and thus as having more authentic emotions).

But though these prior evaluations have had some effect on Western action and feeling, they have at best moved only a modest minority to any firm belief or norm commitment and still fewer to behavioral conformity. Most people who preached these rural sermons did so from an urban pulpit or coffeehouse. Doubtless that can be done most eloquently from a London townhouse while anticipating the pleasures of a weekend on a country estate.

These bucolic evaluations had little cumulative effect, but they were supported by more followers than any defenses of women's rights were until very recently in Western history. The latter is like the former in that both are minority evaluations over many centuries. The women's movement has become strong only in the past decade in the United States; but massive alterations in several social institutions were needed for its modern support here and in other countries. The bucolic set of evaluations, by contrast, was persuasive for a minority, and it never became a social movement.

The interaction of these complex variables becomes even more dramatic in a third type of case, the rare instances when kings become prophets (or prophets become rulers): Henry VIII, Peter the Great, Ivan the Terrible, and perhaps Oliver Cromwell, for example. All of them tried to change their subjects' evaluations of both beliefs and behaviors. They could issue tracts and essays, proclamations, and edicts—and thus the changes they began did start with the announcement of new evaluations. However, they could also command others to preach the new doctrines, too. Intensifying the persuasiveness of their message was not only their own prestige and that of their supporters, but their ability to use the threat of force, their personal friendships, and a wide range of economic rewards and punishments. Henry VIII's protestantism may have been idiosyncratic in origin and shallow in depth, but his success in wringing at least overt conformity was substantial.

The specific example of Henry VIII alerts us once more to the necessity of organizing other resources to support a proclamation of new prestige evaluations, but it also points to a fourth type of case, recurrent through history: the *unintended* ideological or evaluational effects of changes in evaluations. Success in gaining firm adherents—people who wish to live by the new rules for propriety or piety and who esteem others who will also follow those new standards—makes more persuasive a set of still newer doctrines that are likely to be radical. Before, they may well have been unthinkable. After the new doctrines have gained a better foothold, they seem only interesting or daring. As many students of revolution have commented, it is after the new regime has taken over that the more extreme leaders are likely to rise and gain a following.

The modern reader who learns of puritanism views it as strict, grim, and repressive. But the evaluational or ideological themes that have grown from ascetic protestantism generally must include such radically permissive beliefs (translated into action by giving or withholding esteem for conformity with them) as divorce, the rejection of monarchy, freedom of speech, civil liberties of the citizen against the encroachments of the state, attacks on slavery, and even the right to decide individualistically which sexual norms one is to follow: Leaders of the Mother Church, one might say, correctly foretold the evil effects that the Reformation would bring, although the protestants of the early seventeenth century would have been equally outraged by these indirect consequences of their doctrines.

Again, it is hardly necessary to note that so dramatic a set of long-term consequences could not have flowed alone from merely contemplating the early Puritan value assertions. As with the original "success" of ascetic protestantism, the new, more radical views were supported by economic transformations and doctrines, revolutions and wars, the emergence of persuasive rhetoricians, and the threats of discontented groups. Nevertheless, those political and economic changes were themselves guided by the growing influence of such new doctrines, expressed in novels, coffeehouse conversations, satires, theological debates, parliamentary confrontations. At each step in these slow developments, people continued to make further decisions as to whether the new modes of gaining esteem were more worthwhile.

Our understanding of such changes over generations or centuries is limited by the near impossibility of separating out the crucial factors, or perhaps by the deeper fact that over such longer time periods there *are* no grand, overriding factors. Almost anything we can point to, for example, "economic factors," "politics," "nationalism," are simply grab-bags containing many related variables and therefore ending as tautologies.

The difficulty is compounded by two contrasting observations. One, the more obvious, is that although kings, prophets, or revolutionaries may announce new standards for paying out rewards of all kinds, and may even elicit changes in behavior, people's resistance is often strong, and it is rare that large changes occur quickly. The ideals of the French Revolution were not put into practice while it was triumphant, and of course not afterward either.

On the other hand, the contrary observation can also be made: Sometimes people are told that an apparently well-supported custom is no longer to be honored, and forthwith it is dropped. The special vulnerability of high deference to aristocrats when a large-scale rebellion occurs has been noted. Some types of social patterns, when attacked, reveal either that people's emotional commitment to them was weak, or that the socioeconomic forces upholding them were fragile. As a consequence, historians can sometimes point to seemingly large swings of public attitudes and behavior over a relatively short run, that is, a few decades, even when the basic economic structure has not changed. Let us now consider one of these—again, with no presumption that we can "explain" it, but rather to note again the complexity of locating regularities in social change processes.

LARGE SWINGS IN ESTEEM EVALUATIONS

An obvious implicit hypothesis, applied to both revolutions and evangelistic attempts at reducing the prevalence of sin, is that some directions of change are simply easier than others, because virtue and hard work are difficult. Therefore, steady or quick changes in the direction of self-indulgence and fun are more likely. But though the hypothesis appeals to crude common sense, history is replete with contrary instances. Indeed, the continued existence of societies at all refutes the hypothesis; for if the trend were so easy in one direction, virtue or high contributions to the nation or community would long ago have disappeared. To the contrary, at any given time strong processes support the imposition of higher, stricter standards, while other strong factors oppose that trend. When these are in balance, forces that are not in themselves overwhelming may cause large swings in at least apparent behavior and attitudes of a country. The efforts of seventeenth-century ascetic protestants, in America and in England, to improve each other's piety and virtue (as well as that of nonprotestants) suggest such an instance.

These changes throw some light on a general question that may arise in any inquiry into change over the longer term: What is the sequence of adjustments between new norms for admirable behavior and its supply? What happens when a religious sect demands an even higher level of piety and virtue from its followers (and perhaps others), as did the New England Puritans? Presumably, members do try to fit their behavior to the group's announced standards, in order to gain esteem and avoid dispraise. Then, of course, the supply of "good" behavior has risen. What is the next step in that sequence? Sociologists have generally offered the hypothesis that the amount of esteem given the good will not rise, and the amount of dispraise heaped on the wicked will not fall. All that happens is that in the new stage the members now punish each other for acts that were viewed as acceptable before, or at worst unimportant. Some few people— "saints"—can meet the more rigorous demands, but since the standards or norms have risen, their performance is now no higher above the new level than the best previous behavior had been above the formerly acceptable standard. Thus, even the good people gain no greater respect than before the new standards were accepted. My interpretation of the swings in prestige allocation noted in this section is that they are, likely, the impact of social and individual costs on both supply and demand, when those who demand or esteem extremely virtuous behavior and those who must supply it are the same people—and then even modest forces can tip the balance in another direction. That is, both evaluations and behavior are likely to alter when those costs are high, although the change is supported by only moderately-sized factors.

However, let us first consider in more detail the hypothesis noted above, that when people press one another successfully toward more virtue, or more sacrifice for the group, they simply raise their norms for acceptable behavior, and no one earns any more esteem than before. This reasoning seems to apply, at least in part, to other, shorter changes in prestige evaluations, such as the attitudes toward criminality in a community during cycles of reform and corruption, or toward vice during a cycle of religious revival and relapse. However, the hypothesis also fails in some respects. One is that, as emphasized earlier, the supply of any kind of high performance or virtue is a pervasive difficulty in social behavior. It is not true that people can live by the most rigorous standards indefinitely. People will not adjust to any and all, ideological demands even if paid much esteem, although for the short run they may try.

Over the somewhat longer run, however, as those costs become too great, members of the group or community will not give either the same amount of respect to one another as before the more rigorous standards were imposed or a greater amount. Instead, they are more likely to change the norms or standards to a lower level, and accept a less demanding performance as adequate or praiseworthy.

Over a somewhat shorter run, the hypothesis is only partly correct with reference to the New England Puritans (during most of the seventeenth century, when the struggle against sin, doubt, and heresy was most intense). Although modern readers have learned with delight that some Puritans behaved improperly,[5] nevertheless it seems likely that those

---

5. For one analysis, see Kai Erikson, *Wayward Puritans* (New York: Wiley, 1966). The author offers another version of the classical "constancy hypothesis": If a new type of evil arises (e.g., the threat of Quaker heresy), then members of the society will relax their vigilance about the usual moral derelictions and turn their attention to that new form (pp. 107–136, 176–179), so that as a result the amount of "deviation" that is socially perceived remains the same.

sober immigrants did in fact ask more of themselves morally, and that their consciousness of sin did press them to live more austerely (as well as more censoriously) than most groups have done. As a consequence, that part of the hypothesis is correct: Those Puritans whose moral and religious performances would have been judged as adequate in even Cromwellian England would incur censure under the more severe New England standards.

Nevertheless, the hypothesis fails in a crucial way, for within that small society the higher level of performance *was* viewed as difficult to attain, and it brought greater rewards: Those who succeeded received much esteem (as well as inner assurance of future bliss). And if the less successful were censured for behavior that would have gone unnoticed elsewhere, or at an earlier period, they also enjoyed some self-respect as well as respect (however grudging) from others for being part of that grand aspiration—whether or not they were surely among those in God's grace. All who participated fully in that moral enterprise gained esteem from one another because they were conscious that they were outperforming people elsewhere, were in fact more virtuous than others. It was not a zero-sum game, with only so much esteem to be parceled out among the more and the less successful. That moral and religious venture created more esteem for the group to enjoy than had existed before it started. Over the long run, of course, the secular world corrupted their successors. Or, the Puritans prospered, and lost the pure focus of their theological attention. Divines continued to rule, but moral standards as well as behavior fell away from those earlier, austere times.

While the New England Puritans were wrestling with their harsh environment and their even harsher consciences, their spiritual cousins were ruling England with the help of Cromwell's inner light, and of course they were subject to more ample temptations. There, the swings in evaluations and behavior were much wider, because the pressures toward virtue were in greater tension with the temptations. As spokesman for the new order of piety and virtue, and as ruler, Cromwell was able to give out rewards and punishments for conformity in belief as well as in deed, and for nearly two decades in the middle of the seventeenth century foreign visitors could observe with astonishment the efforts of the Englishmen to live by the new standards.

With the restoration of Charles II in 1660, however, a sharp change in the publicly affirmed values and norms occurred, and thus in the behaviors to be observed. One cannot claim that Charles strove to create the new standards, the social style, of his reign—as Cromwell certainly did—since striving did not suit his temperament. Nevertheless, his accession was marked by substantial alterations in what writers and speakers praised, what they believed should be esteemed. The theater became risqué when not bawdy. Religious toleration rather than persecution became acceptable (aside from the witchcraft craze, which never reached the intensity of the continent at that period). Looser standards of sexual morality prevailed, and gaiety and fun among political figures became permissible. The evaluations and norms of Charles' reign moved in a direction opposite to those of Cromwellian protestantism, and so did people's behavior.

Leaving aside the cosmic injustice that Charles not only appeared to enjoy himself, but was well-liked both then and now, let us speculate about the trend of admiration and respect during those seemingly quick swings (that is, in the larger historical frame we are now considering) of evaluations and behavior in seventeenth-century England. If we accept the hypothesis that people remain just as censorious when standards of virtue are raised (as in Cromwell's rule), so should they pay the same respect to one another when those standards are lowered. A drop in the supply of virtuous behavior should have caused no decline in the amount of esteem given, since what was viewed as adequate would have dropped with it. That is, the citizens under Charles' reign who performed at a standard judged as barely acceptable under Cromwell, or as being almost lax, might now be given a fair amount of respect, since their virtue would be still higher than that of the average citizen of the 1660's. Perhaps, too, there would have been a few pious diehards who continued to live by the older, austere Cromwellian rules, and perhaps they might have been viewed as saints or moral heroes.

To push those lines of reasoning to such an extent once more reveals their weaknesses and ambiguities. For in fact the leaders (and certainly the lower classes) in the Restoration period did not pay high respect to those who continued to live by the more demanding religious and moral standards of the previous two decades. At best, they paid them no honor, and often ridiculed them as old-fashioned. With the new standards, the evaluation of that austere behavior had dropped (except among the unbending true believers)—and, as it happened, this swing of public opinion and behavior was not a temporary aberration. No succeeding regime, not even Victoria's, ever again imposed so strict a standard on the English population as had Cromwell's.

Perhaps, as suggested earlier, the central process is to be viewed as the effect of cost on both supply and demand, when those who supply virtue and those who esteem it are the same people. After all, our costs in normal times are modest, for then it is others who aim at sainthood or physical heroism. Few of us are competitors for that high rank. During periods of revolutionary zeal and religious conversion or intensity, everyone is being asked to aspire that high. As a consequence, few wars have continued for long when the entire populace is engaged in them without people reducing their praise for military heroism (and thus eliciting less of it). At such phases, even modest factors may tip the balance toward a rejection of the war. For in that situation, as in the moral heroism of a religious sect, a large part of the population must carry the burden that heroism demands—spoliation of property, disfigurement, and death.

But the swing to virtue cannot be viewed as the deviation, and the Restoration as simply a return to the ordinary, for that heady period did not become the normal pattern, either. After a revolution, people do not return to all the traditional standards for giving esteem. History is not a pendulum, and such swings or changes in how people evaluate others' behavior do not even typically restore matters to what they once were.

IDEOLOGY AS AN EXPRESSION OF CHANGING CLASS INTERESTS

Up to this point we have been considering what processes are set in motion when new evaluations are announced, that is, new schedules for giving out esteem or disesteem for different kinds of performances. This formulation takes for granted that such ideologies or value assertions do have some effect. By contrast, the folk wisdom incorporated in one or another version of the Marxist hypothesis asserts that all such ideologies are no more than expressions of class interests and have no real consequences.

Phrased in a more cautious way, a class is said to develop a set of beliefs that fits its aims, needs, or profits—its economic relations in the productive system. People's beliefs are, it is asserted, in harmony with whatever advantages they get from the socioeconomic system, and the official ideology of the nation simply justifies the exploitative advantages of the ruling class. Classes change their beliefs when it is advantageous to do so, when it enables them to claim rewards or to avoid punishments. The Marxist hypothesis would seem to be supported by our observations of individuals, at least, for we can see that many people do alter their ideas of what is worthwhile, what deserves esteem, as they rise or fall in social rank. As academics move upward from assistant to full professor, they are likely to believe more firmly that deference *should* be paid to full professors. In commonsensical analyses, we note that upwardly mobile persons were selected in part because their opinions already pleased a set of superiors; or because they were influenced by those superiors to alter their beliefs.

More broadly, our observations of special interest groups in a society also lends support to the Marxist view. Occupations, ethnic groups, or classes attempt to persuade others of their claims to respect as well as other types of rewards. It is typical that such ideological pronouncements are made before others in the society have changed (if they ever do) their behavior or attitudes in that direction. Often (for example, in the case of American blacks) these debates are passionately continued over generations with little evidence of much change in behavior, though rhetoric or style may alter.

In general, some version of a Marxist explanation for this class-protective behavior is accepted, but not tested: that special interest groups or classes develop an ideology that supports their privileges, and they simply try to mobilize the support of other groups in order to get more privileges. In the Marxist hypothesis, which doctrines a class proclaims (and whether a class succeeds or fails) is not affected by the wisdom or correctness of its ideas, but only by its position in the economic structure. As Marx states in a much-cited passage:

> The mode of production of material life conditions the general process of social, political and intellectual life. It is not the consciousness of men that determines their existence, but their social existence that determines their consciousness.
>
> [It is necessary] to distinguish between the material transformation of the economic conditions of production, which can be determined with the precision of natural science, and the legal, political, religious, artistic or philosophic—in short, ideological forms in which men become conscious of this conflict and fight it out.[6]

That is, valid explanations must come from understanding the economic relations. The ideological forms simply tag along, adjusting to the economic forces.

Michael Harrington has argued strongly that this and other passages from Marx do not convey his real message, and that Marx in fact gives much weight to the impact of the ideological. However, whether or not these and other passages convey Marx's message, a widely held hypothesis asserts that classes or groups change their ideologies only when their economic relations alter.[7] In a parallel way, it is asserted that a dominant class can impose its ideology on the nation as a whole. Since Marx himself was a good observer, he also noted that under some circumstances a class might *not* be very conscious of its own interests, that is, might exhibit a "false consciousness" by believing in an ideology counter to its own interests. Thus, servants who own nothing might nevertheless accept the ideology of their masters. Peasants unable to engage in much communication because of their physical separation might not come to a common understanding of their economic position. The poor have often supported a war that was not to their interests. So, similarly, in a period of social change, some people in one class or another may cling to values that no longer serve their new class interests.

A general test of these hypotheses requires that the ideologies of various ethnic groups, special interests, or classes be systematically analyzed and then linked with their positions in the socioeconomic structure. To my knowledge, that has not yet been done. At a very general level, these guesses assert a banality, that people in various positions or ranks perceive things differently. More concretely: They will create or believe in a set of ideas that justify whatever privileges they enjoy; explain why they do not

6. Karl Marx, *A Contribution to the Critique of Political Economy*, trans. S. W. Ryazanska, ed. Maurice Dobb (New York: International, 1970), pp. 20–21.

7. For judicious commentaries on the Marxist hypotheses and on the autonomy of, especially, knowledge in its relations with economic position, see Robert K. Merton, *The Sociology of Science*, ed. Norman W. Storer (Chicago: University of Chicago Press, 1973), chaps. 1, 6.

obtain other rewards, or must suffer various deprivations; and excuse their failures. At high ranks, such ideologies defend the privileges of rulers (for example, the divine right of kings); at lower ranks, perhaps excuses for failure are more common. Since people at higher ranks enjoy more influence and wealth, more of their assertions will appear in books and speeches. Thus, whatever ordinary people believed in the past, the historical record (made up of comments by the more privileged) will at least suggest that the most widespread ideology was that of the higher ranks.

It is true, as the Marxist hypothesis claims, that people with privileges also claim their right to them. But further, they also believe in that right. As Weber comments (with respect here to the legitimating function of religion):

> The fortunate is seldom satisfied with the fact of being fortunate. Beyond this, he needs to know that he has a *right* to his good fortune. He wants to be convinced that he "deserves" it, and above all, that he deserves it in comparison with others. [8]

If ideological arguments have any effect on others, it is clearly to the interest of landlords or manufacturers to justify their advantages. It is similarly useful for an immigrant to express agreement with the host society. However, the different versions of this hypothesis do not explain why people can be expected to believe their own arguments. For example, the corporation president serves his or her own interest by pressing for favorable legislation, but believing in those claims is not necessary, and needs to be explained. This problem will be treated later.

Like many other bits of folk wisdom, the Marxist hypothesis is difficult to put to the test, since it is not stated so that contrary data can refute it. If one points out that the leaders of the American Revolution were mostly privileged but nevertheless preached a rebellious doctrine, it is asserted in answer that they were not as high in rank as the English aristocracy or governors. If a substantial minority of working-class voters side with a conservative party, they are said to be victims of false consciousness. If it is shown that even at the higher socioeconomic levels there is much political disagreement, it can be claimed that people nevertheless "support the system"—as do those of the lower classes. That is, the general hypothesis can be easily adapted to apparent exceptions because it does not specify how much ideological agreement we should expect at various class levels, or how much harmony we can expect between class interests and ideology.

When stated in an extreme version, the hypothesis is palpably false, because it is self-contradictory. If in fact ideology has no effect, and is no more than a rationalization of privilege, its existence at all is a mystery. First, others would not believe it, for their own ideology, too, would be a

---

8. From "Die Wirtschaftsethik der Weltreligionen," trans. as "The Social Psychology of the World Religions," in H. H. Gerth and C. Wright Mills, eds., *From Max Weber* (New York: Oxford University Press, 1946), p. 271.

justification of *their* privileges; thus they could not be persuaded of an alien ideology that is in disharmony with their own class position. Second, there would be no motivation to engage in ideological propaganda if economic relations fully determine what everyone gets or fails to get. That is, if ideology is really epiphenomenal, and has no effect, then no class or special interest group would bother to create it. If possible, that group would try only to change their economic position. If their economic position were privileged they would not feel any need for the support of an ideology, and in fact it would yield no support.

In most versions, of course, the hypothesis runs counter to the descriptive facts, too, since in every special interest or class there is always a subsegment that does not agree with the other members on some important point. More relevant to the issues in this section, very likely all social movements are begun and supported by people who initially cannot use their new ideologies or evaluations as a simple defense of their existing class position, or as a way of getting immediate prestige payoffs from peers or superiors. After all, they are trying to alter that position, and they experience counterattacks from others.

Since the hypothesis is a bit of folk psychology, we must explore it at a deeper psychological level. Against its partial truth, people have many painful experiences that deny its widespread applicability. If we could find a rationalization for admiring ourselves just as we are, we could look upon ourselves as fine human beings. If we could only alter our values and norms to fit all our weaknesses, vices, and idiosyncracies, happiness would be within the grasp of all.

Few of us succeed, for our positions do *not* determine fully our attitudes, our perceptions of reality, or our values. We cannot, even if we wish to do so, alter them to conform with our "self-interests." People's attitudes and opinions, beliefs, values, or ideologies, over historical time or within an individual's life cycle, *are* correlated with their self-interests, but each clearly has some independent power to affect the other.

Although this hypothesis seems to be taken as psychologically self-evident (for example: people rationalize, or give good reasons for, doing what they want to do; people think well of themselves; arms manufacturers believe war is a splendid thing), in fact it is not stated precisely enough to be a formal part of personality theory; and a goodly part of psychodynamic theory is concerned with the contrary phenomenon, that is, guilt or self-denigration. In any event, whether we focus on individuals or classes, on life cycles or long-term trends, it is wise to be alert to the possibility that both factual claims and defenses of privilege may well be self-serving. On the other hand, groups do seek, and sometimes get, ideological support from others, and they sometimes believe in evaluations that do not serve their present class interests.

A more Darwinian view of what happens—that is, that under certain conditions certain ideas displace others—does not permit us to determine just which evaluations a group or class will choose, create, or believe in over time, either; but it seems closer to reality than the assertion that ideologies have no effect on class position but are in harmony with it. From that view, individuals, classes, or other special interest groups (religious sects, ethnic groups, occupations) make tentative or explicit justifications of what they want or the advantages they possess. Typically, they can do so without violating any sense of justice, because they are much more aware than others of their special difficulties, the problems they must solve, and what they accomplish, that is, *how much they contribute in relation to what they get*. This is so for groups that attempt to rise (occupations, ethnic groups), as well as for classes that attempt to gain civic or economic advantages over time. They make demands for more respect (as factory laborers have for more than a century), as they try to get higher wages or perhaps more obedience from others. More important, they try to persuade others that their contributions, qualities, and achievements are worth more. Peasants and workers do this, just as do people at higher ranks. Conquerors demand and get overt deference, but they also try to elicit real respect. Fathers and mothers try to convince their children and their friends that they are good parents and thus merit love and obedience. Every rising social group—primitive Christians, anesthesiologists, seventeenth-century merchants, nineteenth-century British manufacturers—similarly puts forth new arguments to plead its claims.

Such historic claims, like those of individuals, can vary greatly. At an extreme, a group, stratum, or occupation might assert that everyone else will burn in everlasting hell, unless all change their religious beliefs, rituals, and moral behavior and contribute their wealth to the new prophets. A stratum might argue that everyone else should be their slaves and that they themselves should be given every privilege and luxury without contributing anything in turn to the society. The normal aggrandizing direction of such claims is clear: It does not seem theoretically profitable even to consider the hypothetical opposite case, that is, a class that asks that its members be permitted to become slaves, to be denigrated, and at all skill levels to serve others without recompense.[9]

The creation of ideology to justify privilege or to assert dignity in the face of low respect from others is a pervasive process, and everyone engages in it from time to time. Free men who were made into serfs, farmers who were driven from land by enclosures over the centuries, or natives who were forced to become colonial subjects doubtless attempt to develop arguments or beliefs that permit them at least some self-esteem. That is, they privately denigrate those in higher positions, deny that those in higher ranks have justified all their privileges, and explain to one another

---

9. The direction of normal thinking and experience can be stated in another way: We are likely to believe someone who makes an aggrandizing claim, i.e., we believe he or she means it. By contrast, if some were to make the self-denigrating type of offer, we would not usually believe it: We would suspect that some trick or conniving probably underlies the proposed self-sacrifice.

why they cannot fight back successfully. Some will also emphasize (as do people in lower-ranking occupations in modern nations) how necessary their contributions or skills are for the community or for those in higher ranks. So far, some version of the Marxist assertion seems correct.

But such aggrandizing claims are constantly being confronted, refuted, denied, or met with counterclaims and thus are cut down to dimensions that are more acceptable to others. This "Darwinian" process is not simply determined by economic forces. Most such assertions are not successful until they have been tailored or shaped to fit somewhat better the beliefs of their surrounding hearers, the social environment in which ideas will flourish or fail. Other people with *their* own demands for prestige, their preexisting values and norms, and their own resources, will yield to such proposed claims only as much as they must.

Perhaps Brahmins, of all social groups, made the most extreme of successful demands when they put themselves at the top of the Indian caste system, but even they had to develop a set of beliefs that asserted their indispensability for all others' spiritual welfare both in this world and the next. That is, they claimed to make a large contribution to the community, but also had to persuade others of the correctness of that idea. Monarchs and aristocrats have evidently never believed that their force, fraud, and wealth are enough justification for their exactions and commands; they have also felt it necessary to try to convince their subjects of their real contribution to the nation or principality. However hollow the argument, that it is made at all underlines the awareness among even the powerful that they must shape their demands for privileges not just to reflect their own economic interests, as the Marxist hypothesis maintains, but to recognize the evaluations and beliefs of other people.

But if all such evaluations were only tailored to others' norms, there would be no changes at all. Some of these new claims, ideologies, and opinions at first transgress others' evaluations and yet come to be accepted eventually (for example, respect for unions, the right of blacks to vote and to be educated, the destruction of monarchy and aristocracy). Why do they survive and flourish? Again, we note that the cliché of self-interest can "explain," or at least make comprehensible, the generation of new claims to more prestige, or new schedules of prestige evaluations, but it does not help us much in understanding why others accept them. New religious sects or movements offer their converts the promise of greater self-esteem, more respect from sect members, and rewards after death, but this does not explain why some of these beliefs win in the competition with others. It was to the self-interest of the established painters of the 1880's, and the acknowledged experts and the public as well, to stick to their own tastes, and not honor the widely denigrated Impressionist artists of the nineteenth century. Nevertheless, it is these artists whose work is now considered classic.

At present, these historic shifts seem puzzling, perhaps not quite as difficult to understand as why some people come to like black olives, beer, or rugby and others do not, but surely more complex. Perhaps the areas of social science in which explanations of these matters have been sought most assiduously are those of market research, public opinion, and race relations. Huge sums of money and work hours have been invested in the apparently simple question of what are the conditions under which people change their attitudes, opinions, preferences, or values. By comparison with the large-scale, long-term changes we are considering here, such alterations are indeed simple. That body of research has in fact yielded some understanding of how attitudes or opinions can be changed by propaganda campaigns in an age of advertising.

Nevertheless, historians have not been able to use those findings as explanations for great sociopolitical changes such as the spread of communist beliefs among the Chinese masses, the growth of nationalist sentiments in post-Renaissance Europe, or the steady decline of monarchies and aristocracies. It is not clear that it is even possible to develop a body of general explanatory principles for such great changes, and certainly Marxist theory has failed to do that. Such principles cannot be derived from the crude insight that classes or groups develop ideologies that will partly express or harmonize with their position in the economic structure.

PROCLAIMING NEW EVALUATIONS

At any given time, and in any society or group, the evaluations that state how much esteem any given behavior should merit must be expressed as a *distribution*: that is, some people affirm them and others do not, in varying degrees. There are always some pressures in favor of, as well as against, any particular social change. Some physical problems loom larger to one segment of the population than to another, and people respond differently to them, for example, to floods, drought, or lack of arable land. Some people are more concerned than others with the obvious discrepancies between professed values and social reality and want to persuade others to close that gap: for example, ideal equality versus real oppression; achievement as an ideal basis of promotion versus real nepotism; honor by birth versus incompetence. Some people propose new norms because prior changes have created new problems: for example, enclosures of land without provision for the dispossessed, or factories without protection of the exploited. All proposals for changing who shall merit esteem offer new solutions but encounter resistance from some or most members of the society.

Whether the new evaluations are promulgated before behavior has changed much or afterward, all of them announce that henceforth some people and some actions should get more approval than before. Such pronouncements, like new types of plants or animals, suffer a high mortality rate, while a few survive to become dominant in later cohorts. Doubtless new proposals are more likely to be killed by indifference than by opposition; but let us note some of the typical dilemmas that advocates of changes in prestige allocations face, as well as some of the regularities in success and failure.

The most fundamental dilemma, and thus perhaps a widespread regularity, is that preachments are most likely to elicit approval and to gain at least superficial support if they simply affirm traditional values. But then the problem that has caused some people to want new norms or values is left untouched. In organizations, this is the dilemma of those who propose to change an agency by "burrowing from within," that is, working within its limits but suggesting changes or persuading others gradually. Such people usually arouse most admiration if they work to support its charter and traditional activities, or contribute to its maintenance, but then their movement toward change is slow. Since few are wise enough to know whether it is possible to go fast, or whether they will be successful with a moderate strategy, it cannot be asserted that either system is the more effective.

A second dilemma is related to the first, and emphasizes the fact that not all types of behavior can be successfully praised as a working ideal, that is, a standard that ordinary members can achieve with reasonable efforts. Specifically, those who set forth very high standards for excellence, or new evaluations that are difficult to meet, may well elicit some admiration, but few believers. It is especially when leaders attempt to persuade their followers to forsake their comfortable, slovenly ways and to return to austere standards that this dilemma becomes sharp. They elicit nods of approval, and even perhaps temporary emotions of certitude, but little inner change of evaluations or norms. Founders of sects often face this difficulty. Having set their standards high, in part to emphasize their radical departure from the parent church, they are likely to find only a few who are willing to live according to the new, difficult ways.

A third dilemma has been noted before, the extent to which people's ideologies simply defend their class or group rank. The dilemma is this: People would prefer to hear a message (new or old) that legitimates any advantages the social structure confers on them and that protests against any disabilities they suffer; but a message that is very self-serving may not elicit much belief from them, and still less from the larger society, which ultimately determines whether the proposed changes in evaluations will flourish. This dilemma sometimes appears in a slightly different form: A new set of evaluations that will appeal to the already dissident and arouse their intense approval will also be the least likely to arouse much approval from the rest of the society, and thus may not further the cause of rebellion.

A fourth dilemma involves our earlier discussion about the relative merits of changing behavior through manipulating the opportunity structure, or through new evaluations. As noted then, most administrators or leaders utilize both patterns when the goal is important, and they make many cost calculations as to which mode to emphasize at any given time. The dilemma is this: It is relatively easy to change behavior by manipulating opportunities, and it rather difficult to change opinions already formed; but the costs of such manipulation are sometimes so high that attempting to change attitudes will be wiser. For example, taking guns from all citizens will reduce the homicide rate whether or not existing evaluations are already set against the personal use of violence. But if they are not, then putting such a plan into operation without changes in evaluations would be politically difficult, if not dangerous. One can reduce the illegitimacy rate more easily by stopping all contact between unmarried, nubile persons of the two sexes; but this could not be carried out by even a radical dictator in the modern world, and a wise adviser would suggest it be preceded by a large-scale campaign to induce new evaluations of chastity. In short, administrators or rulers, and not alone prophets or revolutionary aspirants, typically do not have the physical or economic resources to alter the opportunity structure as they would have it, and they must often try the less costly method of altering people's preferences and feelings of approval instead.

They are also forced to do so, under most conditions of political rule. It is a widespread regularity that most people who encounter any change, or any proposal of change, demand (if it is not hazardous to do so) explanations or justifications for it. People who make changes must learn to expect such challenges, and in the modern world they often prepare for them by asking their staffs to prepare press releases or other documents that explain why the new patterns are being followed. Unlike white rats, even under monarchies people express their discontent with new rules or demands unless these are justified by normative or evaluational arguments.

Although, as we have noted before, most proposals for new ways of allocating esteem are ignored, many do gain some hearing, or even a small following. Many artists of even modest renown have proclaimed new esthetic norms and persuaded at least a few people to agree with them. In a large country such as the United States, it is possible to attract a few people to almost any new doctrine. Perhaps this was not true of countries in the past, where possibly social change was slow; but this may mean no more than that fewer people felt free to expound new doctrines. The relation between that freedom and the response is shown by the fact that people who suggest new principles have enough social experience to seek out listeners who seem to be more receptive to the new evaluations.

When even a few are persuaded to the new ideas, they are likely to show their allegiance by acting in accord with those precepts. That is, they conform with the new "rules," hand out praise or dispraise to others for their behavior, try to organize subgroups to increase support for the newly proposed norms. Next, whatever group or groups may be the target of the new principles will soon be divided somewhat by the different responses of its members: Many will be indifferent, but some will be antagonistic or supportive. Even if there are few formal debates, changes in the standards for giving esteem or disesteem will change the amount of respect each member now gets. If formerly some received general approval for conforming to the old rules, they will now receive it only from members who have not changed their attitudes. On the other hand, those who have changed their sentiments will give them less, or will give them dispraise instead.

The proponents of the new begin as a minority, and often are not the leaders, so that they command far less prestige with which to reward those who would be virtuous by the new standards. In addition, they command fewer resources of other kinds with which to reward any who favor their cause. However, they are usually higher in rank than average members. Thus they can sometimes form groups, group-like aggregates or co-alitions, or networks with which to generate some prestige for allocation. Commanding some prestige of their own as members, they use it as risk capital in paying out esteem or disesteem and in organizing the new subgroup's allocation of praise until the new criteria for respect have become more fully accepted.

Even though most such attempts fail, it could be argued that over time all such conflicts do affect, in at least some small way, the system of values and norms the group supports. Still, we must be wary of even that speculation. Our memories, like history books, mostly retain examples of initial successes, or of failed campaigns that ultimately succeeded, such as trial by jury, manhood suffrage, Impressionist painting, the abolition of slavery, women's suffrage. But that success is why they are remembered. Very likely, most attempts to persuade others of new values and norms not only fail, but also leave little trace in the later behavior or norms of the group.

A common appeal made by proponents of the new is that the new is in conformity with some traditional or widely accepted principle or evaluation. Thoroughgoing revolutionaries in China are able to locate supporting themes or ideas in literary or philosophic classics. Whether art moves toward representation or abstraction, or whether or not it turns toward "creations" that are no more than a paragraph of literary description, critics and artists can point to older principles that support what they now praise in the new: originality, freedom, inner strength, bold composition, and so on. Every proposal for new civic rights—for ethnic groups and colonials, blacks, women, and even pets—can draw upon centuries of rhetoric in favor of those rights, without regard to the omission of those same subgroups in the traditional arguments.

Thereby, people who still like the older evaluations or norms can feel less anxious about considering the new ways. That form of argument gives some legitimacy to the new. Thus, the American revolutionary leaders claimed that they simply wanted the liberties and rights that any freeborn Englishman already enjoyed, and were willing to rebel in order to guarantee them.

Although a few quick changes have been noted here, the overwhelming regularity in social change is that great changes not only do not usually occur within a short time; but perhaps most occur with the gradual succession of generations, rather than with the altering of people's deep convictions. Even in science, it has frequently been asserted that important new theories (for example, the quantum theory) often conquer only as the older generation dies out. What seems radical to one generation looks mild enough to the next. As the older generation is displaced, members may have to begin conforming to the new principles accepted by younger people (as older southerners must to the new racial etiquette)—although older people have not at all accepted those principles as proper.

We have often, in this and the preceding chapters, analyzed the impact of great leaders or social forces; but it is likely that for many long-term changes a different orientation is more fruitful. Specifically, we should heed the dictum that great events do not necessarily have great causes. Even when great changes have been preceded by a proclamation of new evaluations, and supported by many vigorous actions, the ultimate historical result seems often to have been shaped by myriad factors whose particular impact is difficult to untangle. Surely one of the great "events" of the past five centuries is the spread of civic rights, but it would be a rash analyst who would claim that any great cause lay at its roots, unless that great cause is simply a blanket term such as "industrialization."

Chapter 10
The Dynamics of Subversion

THE PERVASIVENESS OF SUBVERSION

Prestige is desirable and useful, but earning much of it by performance is tedious and difficult, while altering one's various acquired or ascribed traits, such as seniority, need, ethnic membership, or family background, is sometimes impossible. Consequently, almost everyone tries at times to persuade others that he or she has earned a bit more than a full disclosure of the facts would warrant. The temptation is continual, and a wide array of techniques can be used toward this goal. They range from the outright bragging lies that strangers may tell one another to the subtler hints a job candidate may use to encourage a personnel officer to infer a rich, successful work history. They include the use of cliques of cronies, claques, and friendly art juries. In some circles, "inverted snobbery" is the approved style, and the proper shabby jacket may suggest that one has so secure a rank that one need not put on airs at all. In all circles, people engage in name-dropping or place-dropping, not merely to let others know their location in social space, but also to let others know that they have close associations with the "better" people and places.

Such public relations techniques, though normal and observable in all societies, subvert the processes by which groups seek to reward the deserving, since thereby some people are being rewarded for their skill in affecting others' responses or decisions, rather than for their merit whether achieved or ascribed. If bribery, not service to the kingdom, is the basis for becoming a Knight of the Garter, then people may decide it is more effective to bribe than to make some contribution to the country. When such alternatives are widely available, many groups and individuals may use them to obtain more than others get for the same performance. Although much research in advertising and public relations has shown that propaganda persuades little when people can independently observe a contrary reality, doubtless some efforts, from the use of blackmail to self-advertising, do succeed in persuading others that a person or group should be viewed in rosier colors than his or their real qualities or achievements might otherwise achieve.

People may try to undermine in their own favor the processes of social control through prestige allocation even when they believe they are getting exactly the amount of deference they deserve, for they may simply want more. In addition, most of us are tempted at times to present ourselves as deserving more than we would otherwise get, and we succumb because of a pervasive tension between our self-evaluation and evaluation by others. Individuals, groups, organizations, and members of social classes accept others' evaluations in part, but they typically rank themselves somewhat higher than these general evaluations. Consequently, they are moved to use what skills they possess to evoke from others a more satisfying response.

In addition, people may not give as much esteem as a person or group should have received, even by widely accepted rules of the society. Sometimes others have manipulated events so as to bring unmerited dispraise on a person or group, or to take deserved praise from him or them. Consequently, those unjustly treated may be tempted to use various tools that in their opinion achieve justice, though in so doing they manipulate the prestige opinions of others. The fact that some others may deny that an injustice was done does not alter an individual's wish to improve matters; it only adds urgency to the situation, and perhaps a greater wish to engage in subversion of some kind.

In any event, we can easily observe that people do not automatically grant as much prestige as recipients think they should receive, and often the latter are not satisfied with that amount even when it seems "correct." If an individual or a group enjoys a certain amount of esteem, several alternative allocations of energy are then available to increase that amount. As one alternative, the actor can improve his performance. But that may be difficult or impossible. One may not wish to work harder. One may not know how to improve. One may not have enough talent to improve much. Or, one may not have the opportunity to demonstrate one's excellence—in the case, for example, of an unknown singer in a small southern town, or a black plumber in a city where white unions control all plumbing jobs. Thus, individuals and groups face a second alternative: attempting by various techniques either to change directly the prestige response or to alter the symbols of prestige.

Human beings are ingenious at both inventing social rules and evading them. If they cannot change one type of reality, they will attempt to change the symbols of reality; if these are difficult to change, they will try to alter the opinions or actions of those who distribute those symbols. It is not surprising that some people are tempted to manufacture deeds, such as claiming to have reached the North Pole without actually getting there, thereby stealing others' scientific discoveries. In addition, hints and gestures are often designed to move others' opinions only slightly, to make others *notice* what one has done or what one is. Thus one may simply warn family members to wipe their feet before entering, to call attention to a day spent in arduous housecleaning. Even if prestige is based largely on

ascribed or acquired qualities, and one is not well-born, one may nevertheless engage in acts designed to persuade others that one's family background should be given more honor. People have in the past bribed those
who control the issuing of coats of armor, knighthoods, and even titles of
nobility.

But though the temptation to subvert is pervasive in social life, so are
others' efforts to keep those attempts in some check. Others also have a
large stake in prestige allocations. After all, it is their prestige that is
being granted; and if some obtain unearned prestige, they have in effect
robbed the till of some of the common coin. What one person gets does
affect how much others get. Therefore, everyone has an interest in unmasking such attempts to get more prestige than the unwritten rule
prescribes.

Moreover, in some kinds of activities, both insiders and outsiders have a
large stake in the matter. For example, if one selects the most prestigious
neurosurgeon, but his rank is based on clever public relations work and
not merit in neurosurgery, the consequences for one's life may be disastrous. If Nobel Prize decisions are determined by opinion manipulations
or bribery, then the laureates would simply be those who are more effective in that métier and not in the arts or sciences in which they are
thought to have earned honor. Thus, there are strong counter pressures
against pervasive manipulations, and in some areas the success of such
manipulations would seem to be crucial.

On the other hand, as Erving Goffman has so dramatically shown in *The
Presentation of Self in Everyday Life* and writers of etiquette books have
argued for centuries, precisely because all of us spend some of our energy
in persuading others we deserve more esteem than we seem to be getting,
we also have some stake in refraining from an overly strict examination of
others' pretensions, lest our own be pitilessly exposed. Few of us are so
virtuous or so obviously superior in our achievements and qualities as to
need no charity when we succumb to the temptation of touching up our
self-portrait to our own advantage.

Thus, the processes of granting and rejecting claims to esteem exhibit a
basic tension between *charity* and *justice*. Ideally, perhaps, one would wish
charity for one's own pretensions but justice for others'. *General* charity or
even naive credulity toward everyone's claims would create a system in
which one's real acts or ascribed traits would be irrelevant, and prestige
would be granted merely on the basis of one's assertions about one's merit.
Then we would all be the victims of one another. Anyone would be
permitted to be accepted as a great pilot, hero, scientist, or surgeon. On
the other hand, general justice would require a strict examination of
everyone's claims, a time-consuming and tedious process that would
threaten most of us now and then. Impersonal justice is not ever a goal of
any social system for more than brief moments in history, not merely
because it is inhumane and humorless, but also because it is tiring. So

much energy would have to be expended on the checking process that the work of the society could not be accomplished.

Different subsystems of any society—occupations, institutions, clubs, kinship and friendship networks, sports competitions—are likely to follow very different rules about how much a person is permitted to affect others' opinions about his or her qualities and performances. In turn, for different types of activities within each subsystem, different sets of rules about permissible self-touting will be found. Similarly, in some societies, such as those of the Kwakiutl, Homeric Greece, and perhaps most monarchical courts in full bloom, self-dramatization can be widespread; while in others, such as those of the seventeenth-century Quakers, the New England Puritans, the Zuñi, or the polar Eskimos, people who exaggerate their achievements or qualities are likely to be chided and exposed. We thus expect to find a range of differences, whether we examine these subversion processes cross-culturally, over time, or in different segments of a single society at a given time.

Analysis of prestige subversion requires an understanding of the ways in which people gain more or less prestige for their qualities and performances than specified by the formal and informal rules of the group or subgroup. We shall attempt here to locate the kinds of situations in which individuals and groups engage in acts that may enhance their prestige beyond what they would get for certain qualities and performances without that added, active intervention. In this examination, we locate four types of subversion: 1. getting unmerited approval; 2. avoiding merited disapproval; 3. preventing others from obtaining merited approval; 4. causing others to receive unmerited disapproval. Our focus will be on the first of these, getting unmerited approval, in the belief that far more energy is directed toward that end than toward the others, though it is perhaps the least disapproved of all four types. Nevertheless, all of us have at times tried to avoid merited disapproval by lying, evasion, or covering up in some fashion, and perhaps most of us are at some times the victims of others who prevent us from obtaining merited approval. And, however deprecated this action may be, some do plot successfully so as to cause others to suffer the burden of unmerited disapproval.

In this chapter, then, we introduce the general phenomenon of subversion, and focus on the dynamics or processes to be observed within it. We consider both its possible rewards and its costs. That is, we analyze the factors that increase the likelihood that anyone will make an attempt at subversion, or instead avoid it. In that process, we also note the actions of others, who have some stake in exposing those attempts at subversion.

In this exploration, somewhat more attention will be given to *informal interaction* in this chapter, and somewhat less to different *contexts* in which subversion is more or less widespread. The latter structural factors will receive emphasis in the next chapter.

In making this separation, we shall not lose sight of the basic sociological dictum that any dynamics always occurs within, and is affected by, structures; and structures have no effects at all except through processes. In any given interaction, as in any attempt at subversion, basic social dynamics are at work; and how they operate is affected by various features of the social structure. For example, it is much more difficult to subvert prestige processes successfully within an informal social setting, where everyone is under constant observation. Correspondingly, the consequences of "being exposed" are not very harsh in a social system or a subsystem that permits considerable public bragging or deceit, as in commercial advertising for rock singers and bands, public relations campaigns of corporations, or the political propaganda of nations.

Therefore, although in this chapter we focus more on *dynamics*, some comparative references to structural differences will be made; and although in the next chapter we shall focus more on *structural* factors, we shall continue to point out the dynamics of subversion. Throughout, the larger aim remains the same: to determine the extent to which people or organizations are more or less controlled by the prestige allocations others make. It is, after all, the importance of prestige processes that makes people and organizations attempt at times to subvert them.

THE PROBLEM OF DEFINITION

Throughout this and the next chapter, we describe how people, groups, and organizations try to gain unmerited prestige. In order to describe the patterns of prestige subversion, we must wrestle with the difficult problem of defining "unmerited" esteem. Technically, it would be efficient to define as unmerited any esteem that is more or less than the amount the group sets as appropriate for that level of excellence in the performance of some task. Then, we could consider all the ways by which love and affection, bribery, ethnic membership, force, seniority—that is, a wide range of variables extraneous to the task itself—might lower or raise the amount of esteem given by the group for any kind of performance, from foot racing or typing to sculpture or scientific discovery.

Unfortunately, these added or subtracted increments are not all viewed by the group as unmerited. Ascribed traits are thought of as legitimately raising or lowering people's prestige. The performance itself is never viewed as irrelevant in any society, but even in a modern industrial society there are only a few special situations in which performance alone is even "supposed" to determine the prestige given. It is instead typical in human interaction that prestige decisions based on nonperformance variables are not seen as "deviant," but as permissible or prescribed group rules.

Consequently, although we can observe that some people become indignant within a work group or a school if a superordinate hands out praise or dispraise on some other basis than performance, some (and especially those who receive the praise) will defend that recognition whether it is based on need, seniority, loyalty, race, or kinship. That is, even though it would be convenient to define as subversion any behavior by which groups prevent achievement alone from being used as the sole basis of respect, such a definition denies the social rules that in fact determine the "legitimate" allocation of prestige.

A more useful definition would accept whatever standards the group uses for allocating prestige, that is, whether prestige is given for achieved, ascribed, or acquired characteristics of performances, but would view as subversive any separate, additional activities that are aimed at moving others to grant further esteem or prestige. For example, a singer performs in an opera but also hires a claque in order to induce the audience to feel a greater pleasure and prestige response than they would otherwise. A politician works hard in a successful campaign, but also sees to it that his or her supporters organize a testimonial dinner in his or her honor.

That is, we distinguish: how much the individual has done or what his or her qualities are; and the separate acts or activities that are aimed at obtaining more prestige rewards (or less punishment) for those qualities or performances. Both these variables can range from zero to a great deal. An individual may do much or nothing, or be possessed of many highly valued ascribed qualities or none, but might also do much or nothing to increase the respect that would ordinarily be given for those performances or traits. Our definition is not, then, evaluative. Whether some will view that additional act as improper depends on their norms and values, but the definition itself does not make that evaluation. On the other hand, obviously our term, subversion, *is* value-laden. However, the possible alternative terms in English (undermining, destruction, warping, deviation, and so on) seem to suffer from the same defect—while in fact the acts we consider *are* aimed at subverting the prestige processes.

THE QUESTION OF INTENT

To speak of a separate act "aimed" at enhancing one's prestige may appear to be inappropriate, for much of this kind of behavior is done without great thought or without conscious intent, and much of it is not viewed as a violation of prestige rules. "Complaints," for example, frequently occur in informal conversations between people in the same social position, such as fellow workers, friends, neighbors: Professors complain that they work long hours and cannot do research because they must spend so much time in administration or student counseling; parents tell each other what a burden children are; typists agree with one another that their bosses make unreasonable demands.

But these comments are less complaints than requests for shared sympathy, affirming that both hearer and speaker believe in certain values or subscribe to certain norms (what obligations bosses owe to typists, or vice versa) and reminding others that one is trying—that is, that even if one's work is not spectacular one does deserve esteem. People make such announcements as a matter of course, without having made a specific decision that others have *not* granted esteem, and without any conscious intent at manipulating others' opinions. If someone were to suggest that those comments are self-advertising, the speaker would be annoyed. The comments do claim slightly greater respect than the speaker believes others would concede, but it would be difficult to prove intent or aim.

Nevertheless, if those claims go beyond well-understood limits, if the "complaints" become sharper, others do begin to interpret them as attempts at manipulation. The underlying message *is* a reminder of what respect the speaker believes he or she deserves, beyond what would be forthcoming without that message. Thus, it seems to be no great distortion to speak of "aiming" at such a goal, even when that goal is not consciously planned.

Indeed, much of social action "happens naturally," without a conscious plan, but we can easily perceive that people are trying to do something just the same: for example, moving toward a more animated group at a cocktail party, showing deference to a person with authority, thanking a clerk for help in filling out a form. In each such case, we can see what the aim is (or at least some of the aims), and the behavior is clearly goal-oriented. Thus even in informal, unself-conscious talk about who deserves how much esteem, it is still reasonable to use the rhetoric of aim or goal as long as we do not assume a rational, explicit plan.

COMMON PROCESSES OF SUBVERSION:
REWARDS AND COSTS

In order to understand better the place of prestige subversion in social interaction, let us take brief note of the wide range of behaviors that might be included.

Cheating

Plagiarism

Stealing another's idea

Taking credit for another's contribution or work

Bribing

Purchasing titles or honors

Use of force and force threat in obtaining positions or honors

Putting blame on another person

Currying favor with influentials

Using blackmail to gain membership in a club, to obtain an honor, to get a position

Lobbying

Public relations operations

Hypocrisy

Name-dropping

Place-dropping

Proclaiming one's talent

"Passing" of all kinds, including passing as a member of a dominant group or covering one's stigma

Testimonial dinners

Claques

Cliques

Use of favoritism

Excuses and explanations

The list on the left is deliberately separated from that on the right to remind the reader that some subversive behaviors are morally more censured than others. However, all such behaviors shade into one another in concrete fact. Those on the right often take forms that are viewed as more or less acceptable, within different social circles. Thus, we sometimes engage in name-dropping and place-dropping partly as a way of locating ourselves in social space, so that others can identify us better. The self-proclaimed talent may indeed be a great talent, even though the person may not yet have produced a great work.

It is also to be noted that everything in the list essentially falls within our definition of separate acts, aimed at manipulating the process of allocating prestige. In plagiarizing, the actual achievement (other than the work of copying) may be set at zero; and the "extra" act of making the associated claim is extreme, though of course in actual fact the range may be from a claim that one thought of the idea independently to a denial that one ever heard of the real source of the idea. In bribing a court official to grant a court honor, post, or the right to bear arms, the act is separate from whatever ascribed rank one's family can rightfully claim. In cheating on an examination, whether in school or on state tests for professional licensure, the achievement may be low relative to the claims made. Preventing another from attaining an honor that is rightfully his is again a separate act, though in this instance it aims at a negative goal. The activities of people with stigmata are often attempts to prevent others from knowing precisely how serious their defects are; that is, they engage in "passing", just as members of an ethnic group may prevent others (for example, by telephone) from knowing their social status. [1]

As noted before, not all these separate acts are far removed from ordinary behavior that is aimed at presenting one's self in a better light or hiding one's faults from others. Some of these variations are widespread enough that, when challenged, people may give a cynical response, alleging that "everyone does it." If the behavior is aimed at helping someone else, as when one helps a friend, one cites a social rule that permits people to give extra credit to others or help them get extra credit on the grounds of obligation or personal ties.

What is tempting about these techniques is that they offer the possibility of a high gain from a small beginning or investment. One has not had a good idea, but one can steal it from someone else; one's family is obscure, but one can purchase a court title. One does not know the answer to an examination, but one may be able to attain the bar by copying someone else's answers, or the answers one has secreted in a purse or cuff.

What is forbidding about them is that the possible loss may be great. One may be excluded from ever attaining the bar or the status of physician; one may be publicly humiliated for one's family pretensions or

1. See Erving Goffman, *Stigma* (Englewood Cliffs, N.J.: Prentice-Hall, 1963).

rejected by a social club upon being found out; or one may be challenged by the originator of an idea.

As in other types of temptation, the first question a person may ask is *how much is the goal worth?* Some people hunger for honor and glory, while others have only a modest wish for it. Some people have a keen wish to garner prestige for their families, while others are content with only a small amount of it. We may resist the temptation to put the blame on others, or to inflate our presentation of self only a trifle, simply because the potential gain is small in our evaluations. It is easier to be virtuous if our wants are few. Indeed, in many situations we may prefer to ingratiate ourselves by self-deprecation; that is, we do not seek added esteem, but rather hope that the other person will simply like us more. On the other hand, the potential gain may be great: a talented singer may believe that if only he or she is given a chance, which some amount of manipulated praise might generate, the success would follow. The gain may instead lie in *not* being accorded one's usual social standing, as when a person wishes to escape unnoticed in a resort because his companion is not his wife. Or, in the midst of a revolution—when former high rank becomes disesteemed—a nobleman may assiduously engage in "extra acts" to convince others that his ascribed rank is that of an ordinary workman or a member of the lower middle class, and that he should not be the object of any conspicuous attention at all. Thus, the potential gain in esteem from a given opportunity for subversion may range from a large minus value to a large plus.

The second question is, *how normatively committed people are to the means or rules themselves?* They may, for example, simply be unable to enjoy the honor or prestige if it is falsely based. If a person knows, for example, that he or she was awarded a medal for literary achievement because friends conspired to give it without thought of literary merit, that person might feel that the honor is worthless. Some academic honors, bestowed by learned associations, are given when a scientist or scholar is well on in years, and he or she may feel cheated if it is given out of compassion rather than for achievement. Athletes are not only morally indignant if they feel that a referee has been bribed or is unfair against them, but they typically do not even wish to win if that can be done only through such a subversion of the proper and accepted rules.

On the other hand, people may sincerely avow that normative commitment and yet predict inaccurately what they would do when confronted by such a possible gain. It is rare that the individual has truly no hope of a promotion, honor, or high reward, and is therefore sure the rules have been violated in his favor. People adjust a bit more comfortably (as noted at various points in this book) to getting somewhat more than they deserve than to getting somewhat less. Most people can develop fairly good rationalizations for being given an honor. They do not often question seriously the process by which it was decided.

As an added factor that makes people's commitment to the appropriate means somewhat less powerful, some manipulations of the rules may be viewed as proper in order to redress injustice. That is, one believes honestly that one deserves a post, a job, or an award and therefore feels it is justifiable to manipulate the prestige processes simply to get what one in fact should have. Or, even while conceding that one is violating the accepted rules for achievement or recognition of merit, one may argue defensively that the need for it is great, so that one can still enjoy an award that is falsely based. One can view this as a "special case," while upholding the traditional, legitimate means of gaining esteem.

Besides the worth of the goal and the degree of normative commitment to the rules, a third question in the temptation to subvert the prestige processes is *how well the technique would work if used*. One might be willing to try to persuade a friend to help in a decision about promotion, and thus gain more esteem, if one were sure that step would work. Often, however, one does not even have such a friend. Many short stories and novels have focused on daydreams in which individuals adopt upper-class or middle-class accents, or dress impeccably in order to be accepted as equals in an upper-class country club or resort; but most people know that they simply do not command such techniques, or they are sure that they would be found out by some other failure or fault. Many students do not cheat on examinations because they feel they are bound to fail. Many people who are conspicuously wicked might be willing to use the technique of hypocrisy, that is, to affirm loudly and publicly their allegiance to values they privately violate, if they believed that technique would be sufficient.

Much more important, however, is the fourth question, *what are the costs of being found out?* Here several complex subvariables must be considered, not the least of which is the chance of being caught.

As to the costs, although everyone lies at times, most people are much more willing to gloss over the truth, to be evasive, to be silent, or to sin by omission than to tell a direct and open falsehood, simply because the censure is much greater if one is caught in an out-and-out lie. One can comment knowingly about a distant or romantic place, without actually asserting that one has been there. The costs of restating someone else's idea without full credit are much less than simply copying his specific words without a citation or quotation marks.

However, the costs can be great. One can be put in jail for passing oneself off as an officer of the United States Army, or for treating patients for profit without being a physician. One can lose one's job and suffer the obloquy of a nation, as Nixon did, by claiming a high moral posture though engaging in criminal activities.

How great the costs are will vary from one historical epoch to another in different societies, and among different kinds of activity within the same society. An explorer who claimed to have climbed to the peak of Mount Everest, or to have gone to the North Pole, without having done so would be treated as an outcast in the social circle of explorers.[2] However, a politician who is discovered to have paid for his own testimonial dinner could, in most cases, laugh it off with wry amusement.

As to the chance of being caught, if people believe that the likelihood of being found out is small, they are more tempted to subvert. In turn, the likelihood of being caught is a function of other variables, especially whether an effective system of checks and disclosures is operating. All people have a modest stake in preventing others from obtaining more prestige than they have earned, but the amount of that stake varies greatly from person to person. In some specific circumstances, for example—state examinations and most college examinations—people are specifically hired to keep others from cheating. On the other hand, monitors in college examinations may have little stake in the system itself. At an expensive resort, almost no one has much stake in checking the social pretensions of anyone who can pay his or her bills. By contrast, baseball scouts have a high stake in their reputations as people who cannot be easily fooled by a self-proclaimed baseball talent. They are likely to check out fairly carefully the pretensions or claims of a would-be aspirant to the major leagues (or his press agent's claims), not merely because they are paid to do the job, but because they have a professional reputation that rests precisely upon that capacity.

Although the role of monitors will be discussed again at a later point, it should be noted here that often monitors are appointed precisely because individuals feel the *cost of unmasking someone* may be great. A person is humiliated if he or she is proved to have garnered unearned prestige; but one also feels humiliated if one challenges someone's right to esteem and that challenge is shown to be unfounded. It is an assumption of the ongoing social system that people question each other's right to esteem only under rare circumstances.

Getting caught is a lesser likelihood when the individual is *part of a larger aggregate* or mass than when he or she attempts subversion alone or in a small group. In such mass situations, the temptation to overstate one's claims may be greater. This is true for examinations, where students in large examination rooms are much more likely to cheat than are those in smaller groups.[3] It is less risky to claim that one was reasonably brave in a large battle than in a situation where only four or five members of one's squad were engaged. In the crowded hubbub of a cocktail party, it is easier to seem sprightly and intelligent, thus earning a bit more esteem than one might otherwise get, and even to suggest some distinction in one's achievements, than to achieve the same goal when talking with only

2. As Dr. Cook was for his claim that he had reached the North Pole before Peary. For a defense of Cook, see Hugh Earnes, *Winner Lose All* (Boston: Little, Brown, 1973).

3. William Bowers, *Student Dishonesty and Its Control in College* (New York: Bureau of Applied Social Research, Columbia University, 1964), p. 29.

one person. Of course, one is also less tempted to do so in the latter situation.

The greater the discrepancy between one's claims and the reality, the more likely one will be found out, and the greater the humiliation. This is indeed one of the elements of social control that reduce the extent and success of all of these subversive processes. In general, to make great claims successfully would be most advantageous, but it is also least likely that other people will accept them. Instead, people are more likely to check them out or to perceive quickly their incongruity, whereupon the consequence is that one is thought to be either a scoundrel or a fool.

We have thus seen that the worth of a goal, the depth of a commitment to the accepted rules, the possibility of success in subverting prestige processes, and the costs and chances of being caught all affect the extent to which a person may be tempted to try subversion. Another determinant of whether to succumb to engaging in subversion is the calculation of whether *one might win anyway*, if one followed the usual legitimate techniques for gaining recognition from others.[4] For though some of these techniques, such as bragging or the use of friendship cliques, may take less energy than creation or work, they nevertheless take some energy. They represent some investment, and they are attended with some potential costs or punishments. Thus, consciously or not, the individual may calculate whether he or she might not pursue a strategy of avoiding the cost of humiliation or failure, and instead focus on the job or task itself. In such a calculation, a student who perceives that the examination is completely beyond his or her capacity may feel less tempted (other things being equal) to gain a few points by copying, since it will help very little. At the other end of the scale, the individual who knows the answers has no great need to risk the punishment for cheating, since he or she expects to do well anyway.

The temptation is greatest for those at one or more marginal points along the curve, that is, where a relatively small amount of cheating might be just the crucial factor in moving over the line from failure to passing, or from a fairly good grade to a much better one. The person whose creativity is high will feel relatively little temptation to steal another person's idea. By contrast, a professor under great pressure to publish but with little hope of having an idea worth publishing may feel that a lowered conscientiousness about citations might be just enough to help him produce a publishable article.

It should be noted, however, that *where* one is on such a curve is not merely a matter of what the objective observer might perceive. Some people believe, for example, that they are close to getting into medical

---

4. Statistically, but not experientially, this is equivalent to the first factor: how much the gain from a successful subversion might be. For example, if the chances of winning by subversion are high and those of winning legitimately are equally high, then the relative gain (comparing those two courses) is little or zero. Nevertheless, we experience these as different decisions; thus they are separated here.

school and that a bit of cribbing, judicious use of family friends, or even a bribe to a chemistry professor might put them over the line—when in fact they are not even close to that point, and that help will not be enough. Similarly, one might feel fairly highminded in refusing to brag to an interviewer for an important job in the strong belief that he or she will get the job on merit; but that prediction might nevertheless be incorrect.

In any event, it seems likely that individuals who believe that they are likely to win if they follow the traditional modes of behavior for obtaining prestige are more likely to avoid any of the subversion techniques than those who believe that they are more likely to fail. In simple terms, the former are likely to perceive the cost of being unmasked as high and the cost of following the socially approved pathways to merit as low.

SUBVERSION AS AN ORDINARY EXPERIENCE

Although the rhetoric of "temptation" is used here in order to present decisions in a stark way, we cannot use that vocabulary to describe much of daily experience. For example, in the course of any given day few of us are presented any tempting possibilities of cheating, plagiarism, bribery, or the use of force threat to gain some position. With reference to gentler subversive patterns, such as exaggerations, fibs and evasions, and hypocrisy, perhaps most of us engage in them somewhat during most days, but even then we are likely not to be conscious of any *intent* to do so, and certainly few people work out any program or plan for building an entire career out of such activities.

Hypocrisy (to be analyzed later) is indeed an extra act *intended* to increase our standing with respect to general virtue. However, in real life *others* are more likely to press individuals toward false affirmations of various values, and against any public denial of those values, than those individuals are to plot such hypocritical claims. The costs of being exposed as a hypocrite may be relatively high, but the day-to-day costs of telling everyone of our dissident beliefs may also be high; consequently, we are not typically conscious of much evasion of the truth when we nod sagely now and then when someone affirms those pieties.

Just as most people are not consciously hypocritical, most are not likely deliberately to plead with friends in higher positions to violate their standards and vote for one's promotion merely for the sake of friendship. One might, however, talk with them about the great need for promotion, and how the possibility of not getting it causes anxiety and unhappiness.

Like individuals, most large corporations do not see themselves as attempting conscious subversion. They engage in both lobbying and public relations activities, and it is evident that their allegiance to the truth is halting or tenuous at best; but the representatives of those corporations would typically argue that they are not engaged in subverting the prestige processes, but in "educating the public." On the other hand, they are aware that the costs of exposure are low for most collectivities, whether the American Medical Association or the General Motors Corporation; that the financial costs are relatively low as well (since they are deductible as business expenses); that few people have any stake in monitoring their effusions; and that at least some of these assertions may aid in achieving their goals.

At a still more distant remove from serious violation or plan are all of those normal civilities that Goffman has described in such detail, by which people express various small pretensions to virtue and achievement and their hearers make no attempt to expose them but instead express their own, with some security that all will protect one another.[5] It is safe to say that these activities do not undermine the processes of prestige allocation. After all, no one is fooled. Each person is permitted some modicum of self-esteem and is encouraged to yield the same pleasure to others. No one typically supposes that others in the outside world will view those compliments as objective judgments, or that they will award jobs, promotions, or titles on that basis.

There are not many situations, from one day to the next, in which we feel that others are attempting to dupe us by their bragging, or to persuade us of their great achievements; as a consequence, we usually feel no great impulse to check out others' stories. We usually see no great loss even if we do perceive that another person is name-dropping or place-dropping as a way of presenting himself or herself in a better light. We may simply decide the other is not worthy of our friendship, or we may prefer to avoid him or her. But since in any event we are not faced with any decision about that person's fate, we have no great motivation to examine the claim in detail. Where the stakes become higher, as in jobs, membership in an exclusive club, or the handling of money, we are much more likely not to take such claims or hints at face value.

Small-scale acts of subversion may be very common in ordinary life, but they are likely to stimulate little effort at correction, and they are not usually seen as part of a conscious plan. At most, they are likely to arouse a little indignation, amusement, or rejection, which in turn has some control effect on such attempts.

VARIATIONS IN SOCIAL CONTEXT

The analysis up to this point suggests that different patterns of subversion will be encouraged more or less in different social structures or contexts. It is useful to note some of those differences at this point, to illustrate further one element in the processes we have been discussing: the effect of widespread subversion on the costs of being found out.

A person will be more tempted to cheat on examinations, or to cheat generally, when the maximum loss is small, and this is likely to be so when such subversive patterns are common social behavior, or when the social norms are somewhat tolerant of such deviations. For example, the simple purchase of a title in present-day Great Britain would be a public

5. Erving Goffman, "On Face Work," *Interaction Ritual* (Chicago: Aldine, 1967), pp. 4–45.

scandal if it became known. But it was considered almost a normal transaction in James I's time.[6] Indeed, so much was this the situation that after a while both the monetary price and the amount of prestige a title yielded began to drop as the number of titles increased.

In the heyday of Tammany rule in New York City during the last decades of the nineteenth century, people who gave or accepted bribes for putting someone in office (and thus giving him some prestige) risked little. Although convictions did occur from time to time, bribery was common, there was no real civil service, and the competence of Tammany Hall appointments was of relatively little concern to insiders or outsiders.

The "arts of the courtier" were widely cultivated at the courts of Louis XIV and Louis XV. Consequently, it cannot have caused any deep twinges of conscience among those courtiers, or any great fear of being punished for self-praise, name-dropping, place-dropping, or self-advertisement, when any of them expressed grandiloquent compliments to one another, described the glory and greatness of their own family line, or announced what great feats they would perform on the battlefields of the future. It is equally safe to say that few people were deceived by such behavior. It is reasonable to suppose that such courtiers became relatively adept at discounting all such attempts at manipulating the system, that is, they were skeptical of others' self-praise and could perceive quickly when others obtained posts of honor or battle awards on the basis of favoritism or bribes. Of course, as in all systems, those outside the court may have supposed that the honors were at least in part merited.

With reference to costs in the dynamics of subversion, then, I suggest the hypothesis that there is a correlation between the prevalence of attempts at prestige subversion, and both low cost of being exposed and skepticism or lack of belief with which outside observers view those who succeed in getting honors and desirable positions.

AVOIDING MERITED DISAPPROVAL

We have mainly been focusing on attempts to gain more prestige than an act merits, and have noted that although such activities are widespread, we do not know whether a large percentage of people succeed in such attempts, that is, whether they gain substantially more than others through them. By contrast, we can point to specific facts that prove much success at avoiding merited dispraise. More cautiously, the data suggest that very little of the total amount of deviant behavior in American society leads to a person's being labeled as deviant. If, as is likely, such persons are dispraised somewhat, their efforts succeed at least in reducing the full amount of disesteem the social rules seem to prescribe. Here we shall emphasize criminal behavior, to simplify analysis.[7]

6. For a lighthearted historical treatment of how honors have been obtained in England, see James McMillan, *The Honours Game* (London: Leslie Frewin, 1969).

7. Much of this section is an adaptation of material in chap. 5 of my *Principles of Sociology* (New York: McGraw-Hill, 1977).

Each year, employees take two to three billion dollars' worth of property from the companies they work for. What they steal ranges from the tools they use, or the goods they make or sell, to summer homes built on company time by subordinates for a manager.[8] Few such employees are ever formally charged in court for these offenses. In a study by Sutherland, all the corporations investigated, and thus their corporate officers, had committed offenses defined as crimes, but almost none of these persons was labeled a criminal even when his corporation was fined.[9] Most criminal acts are not even reported, and the overwhelming majority do not lead to prosecution.[10] Studies of respectable citizens have been done in which they are asked whether they have committed various offenses. Most people admit that they have committed various crimes in the past without ever having been arrested.[11] Shoplifting, fraud, and embezzlement—amounting to well over two billion dollars' worth each year—do not often result in imprisonment, and typically the culprit faces no public loss of esteem, especially when he or she tries to pay back the money or pay for the stolen goods.

All this applies even more, of course, to activities that are only moderately disapproved. Many forms of gambling are against the law, but millions of people gamble just the same, and gambling syndicates may well handle as much as two to three billion dollars annually. Customers of prostitutes are not punished or labeled as deviant. A majority of students cheat on examinations at times, but it is rare that any are publicly dispraised for it.[12]

The list is long and could be extended but the conclusion is evident: A considerable number of people manage not to be dispraised as much as the rules call for when they violate either the law or social regulations. At first glance, this is almost self-explanatory. The major social processes of respect and disrespect are not aimed at full punishments, which might soon encompass everyone, but at social control; they are aimed at pressing people back toward conformity. Relatively few people incur the full penalty for any violation; and since most people do violate rules at times, this restraint is wise; it keeps people within the group.

But beyond that simple notion—that groups generally do not punish everyone to the fullest extent of the law because very soon there might be no one unpunished—we must consider the equally important factors and processes by which some escape more than others. With reference to many

8. Confining the figure only to retail stores, the National Retail Merchants Association estimates that 2.7 billion dollars of store goods "disappear" each year: *Newsweek* (November 24, 1975), pp. 103, 107.

9. Edwin H. Sutherland, *White Collar Crime* (New York: Dryden, 1949).

10. On this point see Austin T. Turk, "Prospects for Theories of Criminal Behavior," in Mark Lefton *et al.*, eds., *Approaches to Deviance* (New York: Appleton-Century-Crofts, 1968), pp. 367–368.

11. One of the earlier studies was done by James S. Wallerstein and Clement J. Wyle, "Our Law-abiding Lawbreakers," *Probation*, 25 (March–April, 1947): 107–108.

12. Bowers, *Student Dishonesty*, p. 193.

of the factors that reduce the amount of dispraise, we can speak of individuals taking extra steps to accomplish that end, but other factors will be noted as well.

Visibility decreases the likelihood that an individual will escape being dispraised for a violation or deviation. Being exposed in the newspapers increases censure for the same act; higher officials can more easily hide their errors or deviations from subordinates than can the latter from their supervisors. People in small towns feel that their acts are more visible than do people in large cities.

That is, visibility is a matter of degree, affected by social position as well as geography. The alcoholism of secret drinkers is less visible and thus more likely to escape disesteem than is the alcoholism of public drinkers. People who engage in activities that are called sex offenses take many measures to hide what they are doing, to avoid criticism as well as for esthetic reasons. On the other hand, some types of violations do not permit low visibility: for example, to manage an enterprise in gambling, prostitution, or drugs requires at least some publicity, else customers will not know where to go—yet the customers want to avoid publicity so as to avoid disesteem. It is a condition for successful swindling that the nature of the activity not be known until much later. In the perfect swindle, the victim does not learn that he or she was a victim and thus does not denounce the criminal. At the other extreme, it is difficult to hide a murder or a suicide, and most cases of either cause some lowered prestige for all who are involved.

Besides visibility, the *intensity with which the group disapproves* the type of offense will of course affect how much dispraise a culprit will be given. He or she can not easily manipulate this norm.[13] In any society, these norms are complex. For example, physical assault is more strongly disapproved than are crimes against property; physical assault against an elderly woman more than against a strong, young man; physical assault by a young man more than by an elderly one. People disapprove more when the amount of loss (money, personal injury, physical damage) is greater.[14]

The *frequency* with which a person commits any disapproved act will also affect whether he or she escapes much censure or loss of respect. The higher the frequency, the more likely that more people will know about the offense; and the less likely it is that they can excuse it as a temporary fall from grace, or that the offender can effectively use various techniques for avoiding dispraise.

Since all these esteem processes are transactional, *how high the stakes are*

---

13. An ingenious technique for measuring the norm has been developed by Peter H. Rossi *et al.*, "The Seriousness of Crimes: Normative and Individual Differences," *American Sociological Review*, 39 (April, 1974): 224–237.

14. One small-scale inquiry into labeling theory reported that the most important factor determining whether a shoplifter suffers the disesteem of prosecution is simply how valuable the merchandise is. See Lawrence E. Cohen and Rodney Stark, "Discriminatory Labeling and the Five-Finger Discount," *Journal of Research in Crime and Delinquency*, 11 (January, 1974): 25–39.

for anyone involved—like the visibility of a culprit and the degree of disapproval of an act—will affect both the ability and the desire of the offender to escape much censure. An offender's high rank, for example, may yield some protection and also increase his wish to avoid dispraise. An enemy, a competitor, or a supervisor will each have a different stake in whether a given individual gets away without adequate censure. The police have a high stake in seeing to it that the killer of a police officer not be allowed to escape. People have a greater stake in assuring disesteem to erring or deviant people in their own neighborhoods than to criminals or deviants in a distant town. On the other hand, up to some point the members of a group will have a greater stake in protecting a fellow member from exposure than in letting an erring outsider escape dispraise.

By contrast, if an individual has been fooled by a swindler or a confidence man, he or she may have a low stake in assuring a full measure of punishment for the offender: The culprit is then exposed as a crook, but at the same time the victim is exposed as a fool. Moreover, the case can be even more denigrating for the victim. A considerable number of confidence games and swindles are successful only because the victims are tempted to engage in swindling, too (for example, purchasing a "money-making machine"). To press the case for censure of the swindler is to announce that one was aiming at a swindle of one's own.

Even more important than the high stakes involved, the *relative resources* of the individuals or groups in prestige processes may have considerable effect on who gets how much public praise or dispraise. People who are well-to-do can hide their offenses more easily than others. They can also defend themselves more effectively if someone finds them out. In a murder case, the stakes are high (often, on all sides); but the advantages of wealth can be seen in the statistical fact that only a minute fraction of prisoners waiting on Death Row have been well-to-do.

The greater the resources in money, prestige, or political influence, the more people can sway officials, reporters, and others to turn their attention away from the deviation, or persuade them to treat it as a minor offense, calling for only a small loss in esteem. Corporate crime is defended by an elaborate legal organization. Juvenile delinquents of upper middle-class families often avoid much loss in respect, and are less likely to be convicted and sentenced to reform schools, than are other children. Such families can make restitution, offer gifts or bribes, or persuade officials that their resources will enable them to reassert control over their children.

To the extent that "outsiders" learn of such events, people who commit various offenses do lose some prestige; but even for the same offense the losses vary greatly, depending on the interaction of the factors considered here. There is, in short, a variety of steps that people with resources can take that will reduce the visibility of their offenses, divert other people's attention from them, reduce the severity of the accusation, or permit a claim of innocence in open court. If accusers have many resources or feel they have a high stake in publicly branding an offender, of course the chances of getting off with less loss of respect will be smaller.

In addition to resources, the use of *good excuses* as a way of avoiding merited disapproval is widespread. This set of steps overlaps somewhat with the previous factor, because those with more political or economic influence can more easily contrive believable excuses, or obtain help toward that goal. Various steps can be taken to reduce the amount of dispraise or punishment thought to be appropriate for a deviation, among these are good excuses ranging from real alibis (proving one was somewhere else when the violation occurred) and the denials backed by weak proof, all the way to explanations (it looked like theft, but I was borrowing it for a while.) The category also includes offering additional information that reduces the amount of merited censure (I did not stop when I knocked the old lady down, but I was running home where my child had been injured). Perhaps one should also include here the plea that one was under great temptation (I stole, but I was starving); or incapacity (I grabbed the woman, but I was drunk and did not know what I was doing). In some instances, the person being charged may even adopt the tactic of making a confession and asking for forgiveness, or asking to be allowed to make restitution in some way.

All of these techniques work at times, depending on the artistry of the individual and the willingness of others to suspend disbelief. Very likely, most such attempts do at least reduce the severity of disapproval and weaken the desire of accusers or others to punish the culprit to the fullest possible extent. In all of these techniques the accused person claims that he or she had good motives, still affirms the group norms, and wishes to be viewed as a respected member. The accused concedes the right of the group to give censure or praise.

A transactional and processual view of the factors that alter the chances of avoiding merited disapproval suggests that success may often attend these efforts. Indeed, groups that hope to survive or flourish cannot afford to be very censorious, demanding the full measure of disapproval for each transgression. Human beings err so frequently that the members of most groups would all be soon in jail. But though day-to-day social processes seem to press the deviant back toward conformity, rather than expose him or her to the amount of dispraise called for by the rules, many structural and personal factors affect just how much esteem the offender will lose.

CONTROLS IN INFORMAL INTERACTION

To challenge another person's right to esteem within an informal group is risky. Evidence that unmasking another would be experienced as awkward can be obtained by imagining situations in which we do wish to subject a person to such inquiries (for example, at a party we see someone pocket one of the host's silver spoons). We could also make informal experiments in real life. That is, we can observe another's reactions when we deliberately subject him to a serious inquiry into his "right to be there." The reader will recognize at once, if he or she considers such an experiment, that it is likely to arouse much emotion.

Typically, when one person subjects another to a close examination of credentials, he hides the attempt. He or she will mask the inquiry by feigning a genuine interest in such matters as where the other person went to school. Where was he or she born? What kinds of jobs has he had? And so forth. Joshing, irony, and joking can be used as ways of eliciting more data, or perhaps of obliquely informing another person that his pretensions have not been fully accepted and are under examination.

Most people become angry or resentful when they perceive that another person is actually trying to check out their claims. The questioner is viewed as pretentious: How does he arrogate to himself the right to make such an inquiry? The individual who undergoes such an inquiry may also be angry because he or she perceives no great gain in it; that is, the person is forced to run the risk with no perceived profit, by contrast with a formal test. The individual sees no profit from the inquiry because he or she feels his position is already settled—by contrast with the formal test, in which taking the test is an admission that one has not yet proved one's achievement.

Also, we are typically not psychologically prepared or set for such an examination, for it intrudes itself as a violation of civility and friendly discourse. An unwritten assumption in social encounters, felt as a right, is that all parties are already accepted as true members, while this particular form of questioning states in effect that the person under inquiry is not yet accepted.

So fraught with resentment and annoyance is such an inquiry that once a person is in a social encounter or group, few will risk challenging him even when some may wish to do so. If one is introduced by a physician as a fellow physician, one may proceed in white jacket and mask to join the other in observing an operation without further questioning of one's credentials or right to be there. At a literary cocktail gathering, almost no one will ask another person whether he or she has had an adequate college education. It is precisely because people do not feel able or willing to pursue very far any informal inquiry into others' pretensions that formal tests are widely used in modern societies where we do not know much about the persons we meet, and where the stakes may be high. We consider this relationship in a later section.

ENCOUNTERS WITH STRANGERS

The temptation to inflate one's claims is greater when the costs of exposure are less, and the likelihood of exposure is less when people have a lower stake in the untoward consequences that may flow from accepting those claims at face value. The consequences are likely to be especially low in encounters with strangers. Simmel once noted that people may confess to strangers what they might not be willing to tell their intimate friends or spouses.[15] Almost everyone has had such an experience, for example, traveling on a train or airplane with someone whose social position is far removed from one's own (in geography, social network, or rank), so that one can be very frank and open, expecting that there will never be another encounter with that person and so there will be no costs in revealing one's peccadilloes.

It seems likely that the frequent behavior pattern is for both strangers to present themselves in a somewhat better light than they would to their own intimates and spouses, again because for both the cost of doing so is low, and they would prefer to be the recipients of undeserved admiration rather than merited scorn. That is, neither risks much by somewhat larger claims than usual because neither has any great stake in challenging the other's claims to virtue, competence, or widespread esteem. Strangers are not likely to invest their money or risk their reputations even if they do accept such claims. They have little motivation to stop a pleasant exchange of compliments by subjecting each other's stories to a close interrogation or a reality test.

This ideal-typical situation of "the stranger" occurs not only in mass society or at a cocktail party, but also in frontier or boom towns of the past or present, where a large percentage of the population are strangers with unknown (and often untestable) backgrounds. Often a genuine social norm has been reported for American western frontier towns, that one should not inquire very closely into others' pretensions but rather should let each person's acts speak for themselves. Each person, in a sense, creates his or her own history as he or she chooses, and only infrequently will others feel they have any stake in exposing self-praise.

Of course, in such a situation almost everyone develops competence in "reading" the symbols, gestures, modes of speech, and so forth, in short, the cues by which people ascertain to what extent the claims are justified. Thus, though people who meet as strangers in frontier or boomtown settlements are freer than people in settled traditional villages to make large claims, others are equally free not to believe those claims and especially not to risk any investment of political influence, money, jobs, or even friendship without further inquiry.

Consequently, even the situation of strangers in interaction may encourage only a modest amount of self-inflation in most people. It is easier to make large claims to strangers or to people outside one's own social

15. Georg Simmel, "The Stranger," in *The Sociology of Georg Simmel*, ed. and trans. Kurt Wolff (Glencoe, Ill.: Free Press, 1950), pp. 402–408. See also the extended comments on visibility or observability, the extent to which others can easily see how an individual or group lives up to the accepted norms, in Robert K. Merton, *Social Theory and Social Structure* (New York: Free Press, 1968), pp. 395ff.

circle. But typically these people have very little stake in whether our stories are true, or indeed in our fate; thus, large claims may not be helpful, either. Strangers have no special interest in cooperating with us even if they do believe our stories. It is people who are closer to us, involved in day-to-day interaction, whose respect and esteem we most need, but these people are also in a better position to scrutinize our claims and to discount them if they do not bear examination. This relationship is discussed further in the following chapter.

Many interactions between people of different classes also have the character of encounters between strangers, in which either side may claim more than is justified, but in which once again neither has a sufficient stake in the other to bother to find out the facts. After all, that manipulation is of no great utility unless some useful results flow from it, and this will happen only if both will continue to give each other enough evidence to check out their stories over time.

THE SUCCESS OF HYPOCRISY

Since we read each other through our inadvertent signals and cues, our involuntary expressions of motives, and since some of our prestige ranking is based on our perception of others' motives and emotions (their evident respect for teacher or parent; joy in greeting a kinsman or friend after an absence; patriotism; dedication to science), *external* indices of inward emotions are widely used by everyone. For much of social life, there are norms about how we should feel, and not alone how we should act, but people are typically willing to accept behavioral conformity as proof of our appropriate feelings.[16] At a minimum, outward conformity suggests *inner* agreement with the norm; and that external affirmation is at least more worthy of respect than a public negation would be. Consequently, all of us are at times guilty of hypocrisy, that is, presenting ourselves as virtuous or diligent not only in behavior, but also in *attitude*, when inwardly we do not believe in the norm. That is, we try to avoid merited disesteem.

The individual who behaves hypocritically, that is, presents false claims to inner virtue, may be forced into some public virtue just the same. For example, if one behaves prudishly or chastely, whatever one's inner feelings, fewer others will try to assault that pretended virtue. If one presents oneself as virtuous and avoids situations in which one could be interpreted as being available—for example, being alone with a member of the opposite sex—and rejects most overtures, one simply has less opportunity for dalliance. As an ironic consequence, those who are trying to hide their less approved wishes behind a mask of public rectitude will have somewhat less opportunity to violate the norms.

Similarly, the employee who shows his assiduousness by bustling

16. For a more extended discussion of the relationship between behavioral and feeling conformity, see William J. Goode, "Norm Commitment and Conformity to Role-Status Obligations," *American Journal of Sociology*, 66 (November, 1960): 246–258.

about, especially when his boss is around, may in fact be forced to do some productive work, if only to fill in the time when he is under observation. He may feel no devotion to hard work. His gestures and movements are designed to seem not a communication to anyone, but ordinary acts of work. They are created in order to lead any observer to infer that he is concerned with carrying out his task.[17] Unfortunately, the most effective set of cues is precisely hard work, a mischievous trick that the social structure often plays on its unbelievers.

But though many or most of us do try to gain a better moral reputation than we deserve, and are thus guilty of hypocrisy—which Oscar Wilde defined as the tribute vice pays to virtue—we need to know whether many try to claim *much* more than they deserve, and whether they succeed if they try.[18]

At one extreme, it is a condition of their trade that embezzlers must succeed in presenting themselves as law-abiding until they are found out. So must all white collar criminals. The illegal stock manipulator will fail unless others believe that his operations cover no chicanery, that since he is publicly esteemed he is really worthy of trust. The confidence man fails, too, if his intended victim penetrates his disguise as an honest person, though in this instance he may be known to police and to other practitioners of his occupation. Most of the time, the professional thief must also pose as an upholder of the property institutions in ordinary matters if he is not to be arrested, though of course he cannot easily do so while he is engaged in his work.

All these more extreme cases prove that one must create a "career" in moral achievement, in esteem, if one wishes to engage in seriously disesteemed activities; one must develop a sustained pattern of subverting ordinary prestige processes.

Unfortunately, in these dramatic cases we have no way of knowing how many succeed. A low percentage of property theft cases are ever solved; but few who devote their lives to such theft are able entirely to subvert the disesteeming processes, even though they exhibit honest behavior through most hours of the day. They do not for long prevent law-abiding citizens, and especially the police, from learning that they do not deserve their respectable self-presentation. Not many confidence men or embezzlers continue indefinitely to avoid exposure, though many escape physically by leaving the scene. The victims do learn they were cheated.

In all of these categories of crime, not many criminals remain undetected throughout their lifetime, and fewer still are unknown as criminals.

---

17. See Erving Goffman's comments on excuses in *Relations in Public* (New York: Basic Books, 1971), pp. 100–105.

18. For the pervasiveness of hypocrisy in the American country town, see Thorstein Veblen, *Absentee Ownership and Business Enterprise in Recent Times* (New York: Huebsch, 1923), pp. 142–165. For the widespread masking of real feelings in European villages, see F. G. Bailey, *Gifts and Poison* (New York: Schocken, 1971).

Note in this connection how many people are brought to trial, and are noted in the newspapers as followers of the criminal professions with many arrests but no convictions behind them. They have escaped imprisonment but they have not fully succeeded in subverting the dispraising processes: "Everyone knows" that they are not respectable. It is only strangers who do not know. Since, however, they remained free for so long they did succeed in avoiding the full measure of disesteem the law demands.

By contrast, it is likely that most corporate crime—violations of laws against pollution, collusion on price or production, the manipulation of pension funds, and so forth—remains unknown, and thus most white collar criminals very likely keep their respectability unsullied. Here, hypocrisy is rather successful. The social rules are subverted that prescribe dispraise and stigma for having committed crimes.[19] However, in view of the fact that those who violate such laws do not typically see themselves as criminals, or the laws as even morally binding, it should perhaps be asserted instead that in most of these instances the violators are known to one another (as among confidence men) but see no great discrepancy between their acts and their claim to virtue. Without public opinion data from both the victim society and such criminals, we cannot assert just what public opinion is or how successful is the virtuous self-presentation of corporate criminals. Because of this possible disagreement, we cannot easily use this large class of cases as a clear-cut instance of successful hypocrisy. Nevertheless, in a technical sense, this is a large category of cases where efforts at self-preservation do manage to avoid disesteem for the violation of such laws.

Daily newspapers present exposures of hypocrisy upon the twin assumptions that the reader will be interested and that this is news, that is, uncommon enough to justify reporting. Bigamy, police protection of criminals, income tax evasion, acceptance of bribes, parental abuse of children—a considerable part, perhaps most, of these violations are committed by people who have claimed the moral respect of their fellow citizens up to that point, and who have proclaimed their allegiance in church and lodge, in community speeches and daily talk, to the values and norms they violate.

In general, the greater the discrepancy between the offense and the prior moral pretense—for example, when a minister seduces women in his congregation, or a physician cheats his poor patients—the greater the newsworthiness. Both the discrepancy and its newsworthiness correlate, in turn, with the moral indignation outsiders feel upon learning of the violation, though they do not correlate well with the legal punishment the violators eventually suffer.

Nevertheless, not only do such reports fail to tell us how many people are successful in concealing moral violations behind good reputations;

19. The classic work in this area is Edwin H. Sutherland, *White Collar Crime*.

perhaps they are not even good instances of that special type. Instead, they are merely examples of temporary escape from public censure. Most such sudden public labelings occur not only after but *because* outsiders and insiders have come to know about the violations, to report them to others, and accordingly to dispraise the violators: That is, the concealment was not ultimately successful. The public event both validates and intensifies a private process of prior disesteeming. Long before the police intervene, child-abusing parents have usually aroused abhorrence among their neighbors, whatever their protestations of parental virtue. The "secret sins" of the clergyman arouse gossip before he is denounced. It is even hard for the housewife to be a secret alcoholic, since deliverymen, friends, meter readers, and prying children soon penetrate her efforts to conceal. Her reputation as a sober citizen is lost before any public labeling occurs.[20] The fibber earns that pejorative reputation even when the rules of civility protect him or her from overt denunciation.

The basic reason why most such attempts at falsely presenting oneself as virtuous fail is that people have a strong motivation to evaluate whether others merit the respect paid them for their supposed inner affirmations of virtue. They evaluate by reading others' bodily gestures, intonations, unspoken or half-spoken attitudes, appearance at inappropriate places at suspicious times with the wrong companions, time schedules, telephone callers and correspondents, budgets.

People are quicker to suspect the worst than to suppose the best, because of their motivation not to pay more respect than others deserve. Consequently, many innocents suffer, but correspondingly it is unlikely that many of the guilty fully escape suspicion. Of course, the higher the social position of the individual, the more likely it is that people will gossip about him or her, and the more likely some of that gossip is disesteeming. People in high social positions, as noted earlier, are more protected from direct observation, so that facts are not so easily ascertainable and are more protected from direct challenge. Nevertheless, others about them spend more time and attention in analyzing what they *can* observe about those in higher positions, and they have a stronger motivation to look for disesteeming facts that will reduce the claims of upper-rank persons to prestige.[21]

We are all taught to disesteem hypocrisy itself, that is, to condemn anyone who poses as excellent or virtuous when he or she is not. The social

20. See Everett C. Hughes' comments on the apartment superintendent for an example of how an outsider can read what is going on behind apartment walls: *The Sociological Eye* (Chicago: Aldine-Atherton, 1971), pp. 343–344.

21. It is useful to reread Erving Goffman, *Strategic Interaction* (Philadelphia: University of Pennsylvania Press, 1969), in this connection, who analyzes the problems of informants, spies, and counterspies in carrying on a dialogue of penetration, self-presentation, double-dealing, and so on. His instances are simply more formalized and more carefully plotted "patterns of hypocrisy." These are people who affirm a publicly approved set of values when they are in public, but who inwardly do not believe in those values and do not conform with them in action.

aim is to reward a genuine inner commitment. However, these "hypocrisy processes" must themselves be viewed as one part of all prestige dynamics. Hypocrisy really *is* a tribute that vice pays to virtue. When we are hypocritical (as all of us are from time to time), we are at least conceding the group's ability to punish us if we openly deny its norms, and perhaps often we are also affirming our approval of virtue, at least philosophically. For the surveillance that everyone undergoes may be based on a very high standard. The gossip we spread about each other asserts that others are not living up to that highest standard, and sometimes it contains an accusation that they do not even affirm the appropriate values: They are hypocrites. When we try to present a better front than our actions would command, we at least claim to affirm the standards of performance that we cannot in fact achieve. We do gain more prestige, or at least lose less of it, by affirming these values and norms publicly than we would by rebelliously asserting our right or obligation to violate them in action. Rarely, we engage in a shared conspiracy of hypocrisy and fool others entirely. Often we understand that others may well see through our pretensions, and may even guess at our lack of faith, but that they see no need to challenge that self-preservation if the discrepancy between reality and our public affirmation is not great.

Some part of the data about hypocrisy will not become known. We shall never know how many religious hypocrites have gone to their graves undetected. In an epoch or society where disbelief would be met by incredulity or punishment, few dare to assert their lack of faith in the gods and rituals, as in any other dominant sacred values or doctrines. Doubtless there were atheists among the cathedral builders of Mont St. Michel and Chartres, but we shall never know who they were. In the modern and more skeptical world unbelievers abound, and so do social researchers who ask them to confess. Researchers do not ask them how often they have posed as believers when they are not, in fact. Anthropologists have reported that even in primitive societies not everyone is to be counted among the faithful in heart.[22]

But though social pressures demand both attitudinal and behavioral conformity—and thus generate hypocrisy—only the outward behavior is fully observable if the individual so wills it; and he can often control to some extent even the inferences that others draw from his unwitting gestures and comments.[23]

During past historical epochs, doubtless the clever observer might have been able, as might a survey researcher, to uncover some of the underlying dissident religious beliefs. We can suppose that some medieval peasants might have noted that their neighbors did not attend mass as often as

22. See Paul Radin, *The Primitive Man as Philosopher* (New York: Appleton, 1927), and his reference to Dorsey's acute earlier observation among the Sioux on pp. 359–360.

23. See in this connection William J. Goode, "Norm Commitment and Conformity to Role-Status Obligations."

seemed right, but they would only rarely have entertained the thought that the neighbor was simply an unbeliever. In our own time, when it seems easier for people of similarly weak or dissident faiths to flock together, it must not be forgotten that most others of a similar feather are caught in more traditional social networks, where they feel they cannot safely express their agnostic or rebellious attitudes.

A favorite theme in the modern novel, as in much Western literature, has been the Promethean hero of small or large stature, who challenges the gods, or who grows up to challenge the philosophy of his respectable family or community—usually, it should be remembered, by escaping to the big city. However, it seems likely that most people in real life have harbored such challenges in their breast but have decided it would be practical to keep quiet about them in order to reap the advantages of being judged a loyal member of the faith. Litterateurs and historians may admire rebels, but ordinary people are more likely to pay their respects and offer jobs to men and women whose outward behavior and expressions of faith support the belief systems of their communities. To hide one's inner rebellion is a subversion of the prestige processes whose cost may be relatively low because there are no easy techniques for exposing false pretensions. On the other hand, the irony remains that to the extent that people hide both their lack of inner faith and their outer deviations, others are affirmed in *their* conformity, and the traditional social patterns are maintained.

Chapter 11
Structural Bases of Subversion

In the preceding chapter, we focused on the dynamics of subversive processes in prestige but made many references to differences in social settings or contexts. In this chapter, we focus on social structures but do not lose sight of dynamics. In general, I believe that structural factors account for far more subversion than do any manipulated errors in individual perception. A reminder to the reader: By "subversion" is meant any special, additional efforts people make in order to get more prestige than their achievements would otherwise elicit, or less disesteem; or to prevent others from getting the respect they would otherwise get, or to cause others to receive disesteem they would otherwise not receive.

In order to emphasize how differences in social structure can make some kinds of subversive behavior more or less likely, we need only repeat that it is not alone the immediate interpersonal transactions that determine how much prestige people will get. Society-wide expectations and beliefs set the stage for those interpersonal dynamics. How much merit an individual, organization, or group will claim, or get, is not determined even mainly by what happens within a specific exchange or interaction, but more by the larger social structure. It is partly individuals' knowledge of those broader social patterns that shapes much of their interpersonal dynamics.

WHERE ARE SUBVERSION ATTEMPTS MORE COMMON?

Just as it can be asked whether different types of societies experience more or fewer subversion attempts, it can also be asked whether within a given society subversion is more common in some social sectors than in others. In some areas of activity the temptation to subversion may be less because the attitudes or norms against manipulation or excessive claims are severe, monitoring is widespread, and the costs of being found out are high compared with the possible rewards. In other areas the reverse holds. As a simple illustration, most professors would be shocked to learn that another had hired a press agent to inflate his or her public reputation, or had used bribery to obtain a coveted award, although some help from a friend in getting a job would not be viewed askance. Similarly, fellow employees would be troubled to learn that the new chief accountant of the corporation had praised his own excellence beyond the apparent evidence, and had been hired without an elaborate investigation; but if a salesman had been hired mainly on the basis of his or her self-presentation, or promises for the future, or unexamined claims of past achievements, some people would be amused and few offended. Still more manipulation occurs in love and politics, where people may make almost any claims to high excellence. Although these may be denied immediately or investigated eventually, far more license is observable in these activities than in most others. It is understood that a would-be lover might be tempted to paint his or her qualities in a rosy light, and that an aspiring or incumbent politician is incapable of admitting any accusatory truth about his or her achievements. Let us examine these differences further.

Amateur athletes are likely to confine their claims to no more than a modest expansion of the truth, less because the norms against self-glorification are severe than because the risk of exposure is great. An athlete can prove—more likely fail to prove—that he or she is superior at running the hundred-meter dash, or capable of beating all competitors in the giant slalom or fanning more batters than all other pitchers. There are effective mechanisms, actual contests, for deflation. The monitor is reality itself. Friendship, bribery, self-advertisement, or even a press agent will not help much once the individual faces his or her opponents.

Norms against self-aggrandizement are stronger in team sports, probably to prevent individuals from angering their teammates by excessive claims to prestige that is rightfully theirs. The costs of violation may be high because fellow members are quick to punish the offender with disesteem. A becoming modesty may be useful in other ways. A quarterback who claims too much glory for himself, for example, may be informed how dependent on his blocking linemen he is when in the next game they step aside to let him receive the opponents' charge alone.

Although flamboyant personalities may be almost as common in university life as in show business, professors are thought to reveal bad taste if they make large claims for their discoveries or achievements, or even allow others to do so. Correspondingly, Nobel Prize winners have been known to comment at the end of their careers that they did not accomplish very much. To be sure, scholars may take greater care in footnoting their own work than that of others, and may be diligent in sending offprints of their writings to important colleagues, but the style and norm are clear: Expanding one's claims is not well received.

Of course, as in athletics, monitoring is widespread in the academy, and one's work is visible. Again as in athletics, violating the norm is viewed as self-glorification at the expense of others' rights to prestige. In this instance, and especially in modern research, "the others" are often in fact one's team, for most investigations are not the work of an individual. In fact, every person's research is partly based on some earlier work, and there are giants of the past compared to whom almost anyone knows that he or she is a dwarf.[1] To make excessive claims is likely to arouse indignation or scornful smiles.

The case of the professions is different from that of academic life, for it is much easier to manipulate clients' opinions, and the payoffs for that kind of success are substantial. Clients are not trained to detect most deceptions—perhaps every medical charlatan has had numerous grateful patients. Exposure is therefore rare.[2] Here, then, the norms are severe. The traditional professions subscribe to codes of ethics forbidding several kinds of "extra steps" (kickbacks, denigrating others' work) that can be taken by someone who wants to gain more esteem than his work justified. The norms are imposed by a collective, a formal organization, and implemented both by informal gossip and professional associations. These in turn are supported or helped by many links with other organizations (government agencies, hospitals, medical schools). The norms are essentially enforced as part of an implicit bargain between the society—that is, a set of potential victims—and the professions: The latter agrees to engage in self-policing, and the society grants it a monopoly over its special work. Those who defend the professions explain the norm and its enforcement as ways of preventing the potential client from choosing a professional on the basis of advertising, cut-rate fees, kickbacks, or bribes instead of merit. But a careful reading of the rules against self-advertisement in the professions will show that they serve far more to protect professionals from one another than to protect the client from such claims.[3]

By contrast with the traditional professions in which the possibility of victimization of clients is great, in the highly technical subprofessions of engineering both the norm and the controls by fellow professionals are weaker. As in athletics, reality is the monitor. Few would be tempted to make excessive claims, since it is almost certain that the client is a corporation with a fairly good capacity for investigating their validity.

Although excessive claims are discouraged in amateur sports, the academy, and the traditional professions, in the creative and performing arts, both popular and elite, almost all these subversive activities are viewed as "normal" if not approved. They are generally interpreted as the outgrowth of confidence or an expansive ego, rather than as a Machiavel-

---

1. On this phrase, the bitter controversies about who first discovered what, and the dependence of successive cohorts of researchers on the work of the past, see Robert K. Merton, *On the Shoulders of Giants* (New York: Harcourt, Brace, Jovanovich, 1965).

2. For an extended analysis of why the professions exhibit their particular structures, see William J. Goode, "The Theoretical Limits of Professionalization," in *Explorations in Social Theory* (New York: Oxford University Press, 1973), chap. 14.

3. As noted earlier, professional associations do not help the client by furnishing accurate, adequate information about the merit of each professional. For a stronger set of accusations, see Marcia Millman, *The Unkindest Cut* (New York: Morrow, 1977).

lian attempt at manipulation. Especially in the creative arts self-proclaimed talent has been visible for perhaps hundreds of years. It often takes the form of a young person announcing that he or she is indeed a genius and that people should applaud now and be prepared to applaud his or her work even more when and if it ever appears. In the performing arts, too, almost any form of self-advertisement is viewed as acceptable. Manipulation through friendship, seduction, claques (in opera), or bribery may be viewed as permissible, if sometimes excessive, ways to focus the attention of the public on the individual's real excellence.

It is also widely assumed that a manager or agent, someone to whom to delegate these useful if not entirely admirable activities, is necessary for a successful career. This is because it is thought that even the first-rate person may fail if these efforts are not carried out—and especially because competitors, the other rising stars, are helped by such methods. Fans of the arts are therefore not surprised, and usually not offended, if they learn that a painter, sculptor, opera singer, or rock leader has engaged in a wide range of machinations in order to enhance his or her reputation with critics or a larger public.

These observations help explain why, as various sports become professional and thus part of the entertainment business, the norm against self-advertisement relaxes somewhat. Here, too, the star may hire an agent whose task it is to carry out all of the advertising and self-compliments that are generally disapproved of in amateur athletics and somewhat less in professional sports. (Individual sports, such as boxing, permit a wider latitude of behavior.) Whether or not such efforts do increase the esteem or reputation of a star performer, he is at least partially convinced of their effectiveness, since he or she continues to pay for them.

Several examples have been noted in order to remind the reader of the differences among various kinds of activities, with reference to the consequences of successful subversion. In referring to *costs*, we must distinguish the cost to the individual if he or she fails to live up to the advance billing; the cost to team or subgroup of performers when one individual tries to obtain esteem they view as theirs; and the cost to the client or the society when someone manages to elicit more respect than is merited. These costs must be calculated by reference to the chances of concealing one's efforts. Where that is possible, as in the professions, social mechanisms of monitoring, by colleagues or teammates or by formal agencies, are likely to be created. That is, precisely where the temptation is great because the payoff is large, and the cost to colleagues and the society is high, both norms and monitoring efforts will be set against such attempts at subversion—and, of course, those efforts at control will never be fully successful.

By contrast, in the arts the cost to society of successful subversion is small: Few customers could argue convincingly that they were harmed by a poor performance. The risk of performer humiliation is substantial, of course; however, the case is not like that of athletics, where overly large claims are soon reduced by a public test. The test in the arts is not so much whether the performer is well trained, but whether the public will respond with enthusiasm, and there are no objective measures that can predict that response. Thus, many performing and creative artists can stubbornly claim, even after initial failures, that they are nevertheless "great," and some indeed have gone on to ultimate success afterwards.

We have been focusing on rather dramatic cases, occupations and activities much in the public eye. But the structure of opportunity (costs to various segments of the society, the chance of being punished) increases the likelihood of subversion attempts in other activities as well. One of these is the large category of jobs for which the standards of performance are not high, that is, in which a wide tolerance for mediocre achievement is found. Then both the prospective employer and the candidate know that errors in judgment will not cost much, and the candidate will not be humiliated by a merely modest performance after a self-laudatory introduction. Perhaps the occupation of cook in the United States is a good example, but so is that of waitress, and so are most unskilled and semi-skilled jobs. Often employers demand some experience, or claims to experience, but the potential recruit feels it is safe to gloss over his or her deficiencies by an adroit presentation of self, praise from kin or friends, or the manufacture of references.[4]

Subversion attempts are also rather common in a second type of case: where performance is simply hard to measure, either in advance or later on (in the major professions, it is only the client who cannot measure performance accurately). Then the risk of exposure is low. We have already noted the difficulty of measurement in especially the creative arts, simply because of the widespread disagreement as to what is excellent. Corporate management is not so extreme a case, but a similar problem exists there. Although economic criteria are fully accepted as a measure of excellence in corporate life, and every effort is made to ascertain an individual's performance both before and after hiring, in fact that kind of evaluation is very difficult to make at higher levels of management. Employers use a wide range of recruitment tests, such as recommendations, personnel tests, and education as screening devices, and in response all clever aspirants know many tricks for creating an impression of past, present, and future success. Although in corporate life it is generally agreed that certain men have been spectacularly successful as managers, the immense amount of research on this topic has not disclosed adequate criteria for evaluation. Thus, the chance that one's claims to excellence will be exposed as fraudulent is not really high, and the temptation to engage in some subversion is seen as no worse than an expression of a healthy self-confidence.

As a next type of case, the temptation to engage in subversion is

4. It is not that we are pleased with a mediocre meal or inattentive waiting on table, but that in this country few people object very strenuously to either.

especially high wherever occupational gatekeepers are found, but (as one would predict) certain safeguards are typically created to keep the gatekeepers honest. We have already noted that gatekeepers in the performing arts may control the few doors through which an individual can obtain the opportunity to become both rich and respected. Gatekeepers play a lesser role in amateur sports, where an individual can usually prove himself or herself without a sponsor, as well as in business, where there are many alternative ways to enter the job market.

Besides instances in which standards of performance are low or measurement is difficult, subversion is especially tempting in an activity where there are few gatekeepers and these few have great influence. This is the situation in many professions.

Fewer people actually try subversion than are tempted in an occupation with a few important gatekeepers, because as the gatekeepers' influence becomes greater more responsibility is put on them. For example, a baseball scout who could be bribed would be worthless to the major league team that hired him. It is usual that as gatekeepers become of greater importance in any activity (such as those who direct the Social Register), they develop a set of norms that emphasize their integrity and their skill at correct evaluation.

The final category of activities in which subversion is common, and perhaps even accepted, is the small but important case where standards are high and the performance can be measured, but only rarely and not in advance. This includes perhaps high political offices and high military posts, especially prior to World War II. Let us consider this latter type, for it illuminates both the ordinariness of subversion attempts and the extent to which not all of them are disesteemed. Although we describe these processes in the historical mode, clearly they apply to some extent to modern military life in many countries.

In most Western countries, such men spent their adulthood trying to work themselves into positions of command. Though seniority counted greatly, and their achievements at various types of peacetime tasks (including much technical learning) also counted, it was always understood that many other ascriptive and personalistic criteria (class background, family connections) might play a large role in promotions before the test of a war occurred.

Until perhaps the middle of the nineteenth century it was still possible to purchase a military command in many countries, and bribery was not unknown. Because physical courage was a conspicuous necessity for most staff officers until World War II, as it still is for junior officers, those in command (however they got there)[5] were usually men of high confidence, willing to put themselves and their claims forward with some energy.

---

5. Often, of course, through family connections. Note the many times Churchill's mother pressed people to give him military opportunities; see Ralph Guy Martin, *Jennie: The Life of Lady Randolph Churchill*, vol. II (Englewood Cliffs, N.J.: Prentice-Hall, 1969–1971).

Unfortunately there is no clear relation between a man's ability to put forward large claims effectively and his actual competence in war. Success in these manipulations were no index of any ability to win battles.

To reduce the effect of these conditions under which people are more likely to use subversive techniques in prestige in order to gain their ends, societies develop formal ways of preventing excessive claims. To these we now turn.

FORMAL VERSUS INFORMAL SYSTEMS FOR VALIDATING PRESTIGE

Formal monitoring is used much less in a tribal society,[6] a rural village, or a small group than, for example, in urban or larger groups. In the former, testing others' claims goes on automatically and without much consciousness because most people are under observation much of the time, by almost everyone else. Similarly, people who are close in social position, or who enjoy similar rank and general prestige, are less likely to engage in much inflation with one another than with others of different position. That is, in such cases formal monitoring is less common because informal monitoring is effective.

As in most settings, people of the same rank in frequent interaction do, of course, pay one another the civility of not challenging small claims to virtue (professors' oblique assertions that they are attentive to their students' needs, plumbers' claims that they "always give a good day's work"). However, they are less likely to make larger claims to more esteem than they deserve. Each has opportunities for checking out the other's claims and is likely to be a competent judge. Each is able, since all are likely to be socially linked, to expose any fraud and to impose costs on any who attempt subversion.

By contrast, in a larger society where most individuals are strangers and where correspondingly all must respond to others' external symbols—in short, to their self-presentations—people are more likely to be victimized by fraudulent claims and are less likely to discover that they have been. Moreover, as a society becomes technically advanced, the costs of incompetents getting jobs and honors through manipulation rise in many sectors, while their opportunities multiply. The costs rise because technical failures in one area are likely to create problems in others. The opportunities multiply because people cannot spend enough energy and skill to check every claim made by strangers.

Consequently, where self-enhancement or subversion might be easy and rewards high, formal licensure or organizational monitoring of various kinds is likely to be inaugurated. It might be thought that this step is unnecessary in activities that are self-validating. After all, whether one

---

6. Interesting exceptions have existed, as noted earlier. War-like tribes seem to permit more boasting. Among the Kwakiutl, subversion became a major social activity. Some tribal kings had spokesmen to sound their praises, and so on.

can fight a bull adequately, drive a trailer rig, work on high steel, or extract an appendix is a question that can be answered quickly if the claimant attempts the task. But in many self-validating activities people are not permitted to set themselves up as experts, especially where others may suffer as a result. They are not allowed to attempt the job at all until they have been checked out by some formal organization. Thus a bureaucratic solution spares individuals the burden of unmasking others, and society the costs of failure.

Note that in military heroism, where one can get away with much puffery, since often there are few or no witnesses, one is not permitted to write up one's own exploits without external validation. Others must do so who were witnesses. Even in Vietnam, where there was widespread subversion in such claims, this form continued to be followed; and in fact, that eventually led to its exposure. That is to say, sometimes the senior officer commanded subordinates to produce the appropriate descriptions that extolled his bravery under fire—but eventually some began to report that subversion. So it was proved that subversion is possible under such procedures, but also that the method may eventually expose the subversion. As in sports, to subvert the rules it is necessary to put pressure on the "referees," but the dishonest referee may also leave evidence of the violation.

Such mechanisms are part of the insurance system that prevents great losses to credulous people. There are many validation systems: social registers for a number of American cities (now consolidated into one), civil service classifications, membership and credit cards, licenses of all kinds. All these procedures permit us to avoid asking whether the individual can perform in a certain way. We do not need to test the person at all; we need only ask whether he or she has passed through the monitoring process in the appropriate fashion, that is, has the proper credentials. Thus we accept symbols of competence as sufficient; and even when we are being especially careful, we are still likely to do no more than check whether someone does indeed hold such formal memberships, certificates of achievement, and so on.

Such formal testing is more common in a highly technological society, not only because there are more competencies that need testing (because there are more specialized jobs and posts), but also because we do not have much direct experience of the performance levels of people we encounter each day. We have some information about people under our surveillance (for example, a physician), but even then we do not know how well they can perform some technical task such as surgery. Thus, when the allocation of prestige becomes relatively important, but we no longer trust our ability to judge, we hand over the task of testing to formal authorities. In turn, because it is easier to check a person's credentials than his or her competence, a person who may be able to do a job even better than others, but lacks the credentials, is likely to be excluded.

One may, then, view the myriad formal examinations in modern society as a form of quality control, a set of mechanisms for reducing the prevalence of prestige subversion at crucial points where subversion might be likely. Let us consider this further.

QUALITY CONTROL

In such a formal gatekeeping process, typically those who are in charge of it are of high rank, if only for that moment (although often more generally as well), so that candidates are faced by others who have been validated as possessing more competence. The experience is often deflationary. It forces individuals to bring their pretensions into line with the social rules and their own achievements. Consequently, such passages from being unlicensed to being licensed, from being a candidate to passing the examination, become a focus of personal and social concern. People may become so attentive to it that they concentrate more on getting through the test than on being genuinely competent, that is, they try to subvert the examination itself. After they have passed the test they are socially defined as competent, and few will question them on that point thereafter. Thus the payoff from the validated competence, whether it is a license for driving a truck or a certification in neurosurgery, may be relatively high. (The higher the selectivity, the greater the payoff.) Indeed, if it is not high, no such testing system is likely to be developed.

These formal occasions are structurally different from ordinary day-to-day informal surveillance or penetration of others' pretensions. For before the formal test, inquiry, or examination, the individual claims only to be a *candidate*. He or she does not yet claim the prestige of the status itself (as one does in peer social interaction). Indeed, if the person did so, in many situations he or she would then be barred from the test. Someone who claims to be a lawyer or physician would be excluded from the examination if this were publicly known. Failure in the examination is always a stigma, but far less so than if a person is exposed as fraudulently attempting to claim the level of achievement before the examination.

Such situations are typically threatening, even when the test itself is trivial. In all of them the candidate is not merely asserting that he or she is worthy to be a candidate; rather, the individual claims to have already the competence of a member, a full-fledged possessor of a license or validation. However, that claim may be hollow and soon revealed as false. One is asserting that one should get the prestige and all the rights of true membership because one has earned them. The test is not to be a new, higher accomplishment. It simply examines whether in fact one has already achieved that level. If one passes, one has proved the possession of that competency and the right to that rank or status. If one fails, one loses esteem in one's own eyes and in the eyes of other people.

The individual deliberately makes himself vulnerable because of the potential rewards. Indeed, there is no other choice if one wants such a position. The vulnerability consists in running the risk that the examiners will deny one's claims. Because such experiences are threatening, painful, or exhausting, groups do not often impose them, except in school. Most people would find intolerable an adult life in which they frequently had to prove themselves by formal examinations. These examinations are more threatening than the judgments people face when they seek promotions, partly because they seem to be more effective in testing skills; being turned down for a job, on the other hand, is not socially defined as being unable to *do* the job.

On the other hand, formal examinations need not be frequent, because there are not really many points at which the costs of inflation or subversion have to be kept in check by much, or at which the society can create an adequate test at modest expense. In addition, the standards for examinations are generally higher than the day-to-day demands of the work itself (driving licenses of all kinds are an exception), so that their frequency can be low. In the course of a year's work, for example, the plumber almost never encounters all the complex problems that he had to be able to master in order to pass his journeyman's examination.

As noted earlier, formal examinations also reduce the social awkwardness of frequently trying to find out whether another person indeed has the competence he or she claims. If a friend possesses a driving license obtained after a reasonable examination, we do not seriously query whether he or she can in fact drive an automobile. We are content if our physician displays his various certificates of examination or residency; we do not often probe his or her claims to professional excellence. Indeed, most people do not even read the certificates, but accept the mere symbols of the physician status, for example, the appropriate office, nurse, and examining room with its various instruments, as adequate.

STRUCTURES AND LINKAGES

Because this chapter focuses on structural elements in prestige subversion, we have unavoidably noted many interlinkages among parts of any social structure. Although this topic was explored earlier in the chapters on prizes and interlinkages, it is also appropriate here to note some specific interlinkages in subversion: that is, how position in social structures can afford opportunities to subvert.

Since everyone carries out many role obligations and is thus visible in many different sectors of the larger society, it is sometimes possible to manipulate others' responses by adroit behavior in one sector, which is designed to obtain prestige in another.

Prestige from outsider activities

One type of extra prestige generation through such linkages can be observed when professors or businessmen serve in governmental roles during leaves of absence from their usual jobs. If the individual performs only modestly well, he or she may gain added esteem from this combination of performances. Let us consider the example of professors. Since their colleagues in government have little access to the professors' achievements in academic activities, they are likely to assume that those achievements are respected. Academic colleagues, in turn, are likely to take for granted that those professors' performances in government are at least adequate. Both sets of observers are thus likely to assume that those professors are doing well in the activities that are not under their observation. As a result, professors on leave who work in government jobs gain additional credit, for they are viewed as contributing to both sectors.

A high-level manager or employer can also use control over subordinates to earn prestige from outsiders, who have no post from which to observe his or her competence. The manager may, for example, require subordinates to pay overt deference and respect, whether or not they agree internally that he or she has earned it. Outsiders, seeing this apparent admiration or deference, may then suppose that the individual has earned it from his subordinates, and that outsiders too should pay more respect. In military organizations, such a superior is called by various kinds of pejorative titles behind his back, "chicken" being only one of them.

Exchanging other kinds of "power" for prestige

It is also possible, as we have repeatedly noted, to make various kinds of exchanges of other resources for prestige, especially in the manipulation of prestige symbols. Prestige cannot be bought directly with money, just as the inner prestige response cannot be commanded by power; but both wealth and political influence can be used to take some extra steps that will enhance an individual's reputation. These take various forms: trading one resource or another for the symbols of prestige, such as a coat of arms; using resources to engage in activities that directly generate esteem; and hiring people whose task is to gain publicity and respect for real or illusory deeds that yield prestige.

As many novels and short stories have shown, a person can exchange a resource for the symbols of prestige. The person with money can buy upper-class clothes, an elegant house, an address in the proper neighborhood, or the kind of art that is acceptable in elite circles. People can use business connections to gain entrée into private clubs. As Veblen argued more than half a century ago, all this attests to the individual's economic prowess, but also to his or her taste and acceptability in the right circles. People can choose vacation spots, restaurants, or nightclubs where they maximize the chances of associating with others of somewhat higher prestige, who may then assume from those external indices that they really do enjoy prestige or have earned it.

The wise person with money can also employ this resource in activities directly yielding esteem. He or she can become a philanthropist, support struggling artists, or give grants to string quartets or to museums or universities. Within more limited circles, he or she can give money to a local church, a community fund drive, or a hospital. By becoming involved conspicuously in such circles, a person earns esteem directly, for all these gifts to the collectivity yield prestige. Further, such activities divert any possible questions about the individual's social background. They also permit the organization of attractive social gatherings or parties to which he or she can invite high-ranking guests whose presence partly validates the claim to greater social standing than the individual actually possesses.

Of course, at higher levels of prestige, political power, and wealth, ranking individuals find it useful to hire public relations experts who can carry out, or suggest, many of the separate steps that enhance their reputations. Such experts may urge their clients to engage in activities that directly yield prestige (such as philanthropy), but they also try to publicize any real or supposed achievements that might generate further esteem.

Similarly, the possession of office or political power of any kind yields some prestige and can be used to generate even more if properly used. An individual can give political or legal support to people with higher social standing, as when he or she helps build a public road that will largely be used by members of a country club; in turn, these people may be grateful enough to give that person entrée into a more select social circle. An individual with political influence can sometimes appoint friends to posts that yield prestige for them—and these can be as trivial as the chairmanship of a village library committee or as exalted as the vice royalty of India. That is to say, trades can be made among prestige, political influence, and money, though usually not directly.

Being an outsider

Another structural arrangement that permits manipulation of the rewards people obtain is the common differentiation of "insiders" and "outsiders." Groups typically pay more prestige to members than to nonmembers for the same qualities and performances, thus determining to a large extent how much the outside society pays to those same individuals. This occurs especially when the group serves as a validating organization for achievements or merit (for example, boards or committees that award prizes). In addition, members who are in a central location within the group, or who are leaders of the group, are paid more for the same accomplishment than are the less important members. Not only are such people spontaneously paid more respect; groups often engage in various manipulations as well, to prevent lesser members or outsiders from being given full recognition for their qualities and performances.[7]

---

7. Some confirmation of this can be obtained from research on the flow of communication in groups, especially how the structure of a group affects how much is known about and communicated to the individual. See, e.g., G. A. Heise and G. A. Miller, "Problem-Solving in Small Groups Using Various Communication Nets," in A. P. Hare, E. F. Borgatta, and R. F. Bales, eds., *Small Groups*

These patterns are most observable in professional groups, which often fail to give credit to nonmembers or to members who enjoy little prestige. Often, too, they remain ignorant (purposely or accidentally) of relevant work done by outsiders. In part, this result grows from the selection and validation processes already described. That is to say, members have already been selected for their worthiness, and need not be further examined as to their general right to some respect; the group needs only to examine whether some additional performance is worth some added esteem.

If a neighborhood faith healer in the United States were to report that he or she had made a medical discovery, for example, the statement would at best be treated as a kind of human interest story in the newspapers, while physicians would give it no credence. Such a person has not gone through the selection and validation that physicians have, and the performance itself would not be examined by the usual array of medical researchers. Likewise, physicians have either ignored or attacked the therapies (osteopathy, acupuncture) of outsiders, often condemning such people as quacks and charlatans without investigating seriously whether their medical knowledge is correct.[8] Similarly, churches ignore the saintly behavior of nonbelievers and have often taken vigorous steps to persecute or destroy them.

Several processes support the pattern of giving less prestige to outsiders, or barring them from prestige, for worthy qualities or performances. First, of course, networks or groups are likely to view their own worth in general as substantial and their command of their particular field of endeavor as high. To do otherwise is to deny their reasons for existing as a group. Next, not being in close relations with outsiders, and indeed being unwilling even to take their efforts seriously, they do not observe what outsiders do, or they view it as irrelevant or hardly worth attention.

Next, in giving prestige to their own members, or to their leaders, groups are rewarding those who affirm the wider range of group values, as against those people who simply perform well at a given task. The bone setter, the osteopath, or the chiropractor may at times have helped some of his patients, but typically he did not accept the full range of professional discipline, or undergo the full curriculum of education required of a physician. Thus, the group judges that his achievement is worth less than that of a physician.

(New York: Knopf, 1955), pp. 353–367; and Alex Bavelas, "Communication Patterns in Task-Oriented Groups," in R. J. Ofshe, ed., *Interpersonal Behavior in Small Groups* (Englewood Cliffs, N.J.: Prentice-Hall, 1973), pp. 594–604. On the problems of whose knowledge is more accurate, at different positions in the social structure, see Robert K. Merton, "The Perspectives of Insiders and Outsiders," chap. 5 of *The Sociology of Science* (Chicago: University of Chicago Press, 1973).

8. Perhaps the most notorious case in the nineteenth century was the persecution of Semmelweiss for his discovery that physicians themselves were spreading puerperal fever to their patients. With reference to some of the general processes, see my article "Encroachment, Charlatanism and the Emerging Professions: Psychology, Sociology and Medicine," *American Sociological Review*, 25 (December, 1960): 902–914.

Perhaps of even greater importance is the fact that if the outsider were given as much prestige as the insider, the group could not share much in the prestige. Society would see that the outsider had accomplished the feat without the group, so that the group has little incentive to grant him esteem. The outsider has in effect stated that he or she owes them nothing and that what is earned is his or her own. The outsider has not in fact made a contribution to the specialty group, whatever the contribution to the larger society. Of course, one consequence is that the outsider, and often the person of lesser importance in the group, feels much less committed to the group and its aim than do its established members. That is, the failure to reward creates a lesser allegiance to the smaller social system.

Using collusion

The differences between insiders and outsiders draw our attention to a further structural factor in the subversion of prestige processes: collusion. It is difficult to carry out any kind of manipulation without the cooperation of others. Usually, then, some people are in close social contact with the person who attempts subversion and know what is going on. The usual aim of the manipulator is not so much to persuade these close associates that greater esteem is deserved, but to persuade others: a club, a corporation, the higher levels of an organization, the larger society.

Thus, a fundamental tactical question is whether an individual can use the people close to him or her to carry out such a subterfuge (attacking others, avoiding disapproval) without others farther out in the social circle or network learning from those closer to the source that some type of fraud or subversion is going on. In politics, for example, the members of a trusted inner group who tell the newspapers a poll was taken showing their candidate to be more popular than any other, when in fact no such poll was taken, could reveal the fraud. That danger was neatly illustrated by the Watergate episode, in which several highly-placed inside participants eventually disclosed some damaging facts.

Examples of collusion abound. Normally, several people are required to engage in a bribery exchange for a political office. In propaganda and public relations campaigns, at least those on the inside typically know what is going on. People who are heroin or cocaine users, and most respectable secret alcoholics, must give possibly hurtful facts to at least their suppliers, who may or may not keep the secret. Spies that pose as legitimate members of a country must report to others who know they are not.

We have already discussed the problem of exposing others, but it is to be noted here that some insiders may wish to keep the secret because they themselves are profiting from it—fellow spies, those who sell liquor to the alcoholic, fellow politicians, and so on. Victims, by contrast, have no special stake in maintaining secrecy, except the shame of confessing their foolishness or their guilt. Still others may keep the secret in the ordinary course of events, but confess if they are caught, in order to escape punishment.

In examining the structural arrangements of manipulations, it is necessary to ask who can observe what is going on, and then in whose interest it is to keep the secrets. Complete outsiders, of course, have some social stake in exposing many of these operations, since otherwise they are paying esteem to the wrong people, but they are not moved to expose secrets unless someone closer to the event challenges what has been going on. Moreover, as already mentioned, anyone takes a risk who attempts to expose another. Thus it is that in many organizations the chicanery of prestige manipulation may continue for many years unpunished and unexposed, even though some people have considerable knowledge of these machinations and others at least hear about them at a distance.

LABELING

Our discussion of the structural bases of subversion has mostly focused on widespread machinations aimed at getting undeserved prestige or avoiding deserved disrespect. But our comments on the differences between outsiders and insiders and on the collusion of close associates in prestige manipulations leads to another type of subversion: robbing others of deserved esteem, and defaming them. This is often accomplished by unfairly labeling them—as criminals, juvenile delinquents, or deviants of some type. We must consider how this process works.

Although "labeling theory" takes many forms, all of them assert that we cannot assume as correct the observation and cognitive processes by which people decide that others are "deviant," deserve dispraise, or should be categorized as criminal or improper. Some theorists even appear to argue that those who, for example, are labeled as juvenile delinquent have committed no more crimes than those who have not; or that people who are labeled as mentally ill have come to be that way because of the process of labeling itself.[9]

Whether or not that extreme view is actually held by anyone,[10] labeling theories point out that the gradual or quick process of labeling may come to push the "deviant" into a deviant role, for others react to him or her as a deviant and thereby elicit counterresponses that reinforce that social view. Sooner or later, the deviant comes to accept that role, that is, labels himself or herself as a deviant and organizes subsequent behavior in conformity with that self-view. This is called "secondary deviation."[11]

9. For a thoughtful discussion of the empirical and definitional problems of this issue, with special reference to mental illness, see the comments by Thomas J. Scheff, Robert L. Chauncey, and Walter R. Gove, *American Sociological Review*, 40 (April, 1975): 242–257. Of course, people know that they are being judged and labeled, and this may affect their behavior as subjects, rendering suspect the results of many experiments. See R. Rosenthal, *Experimenter Effects in Behavioral Research* (New York: Appleton-Century-Crofts, 1966).

10. So far, I have found no one who makes this extreme claim.

11. See the discussion by Walter R. Gove, Patrick W. Conover, and Edwin Lemert in *The Uses of Controversy in Sociology*, Lewis A. Coser and Otto N. Larsen, eds. (New York: Free Press, 1976), pt. 6, "To Post the Limit of Labeling and Redirect the Study of Deviance," pp. 219–249.

Thus, the process of labeling a person "crazy" leads others to view him or her as indeed mentally ill, to treat that person accordingly, and to elicit such behavior, outside or inside the asylum. Similarly, in a rural Sicilian or Greek village, to label a girl "loose" leads people to treat her so. This cuts off all alternative paths that virtue usually offers, excludes her from respectable society, and may eventually push her to leave the village for the city, if she is not killed by a member of her "dishonored" family. Policemen in the United States subject a boy to more careful scrutiny than they give others if he has been labeled a juvenile delinquent, suspect him more quickly, disbelieve his explanations or alibis, and more often report to the judge or social worker their opinion that he should be sent to the reformatory, where in fact he is more likely to be confirmed in criminal ways.

Goffman himself, though often categorized as a labeling theorist, has warned us in *Relations in Public* that we must not suppose that labeling is a free-floating variable or process, accidentally or whimsically alighting on one individual or another.[12] It may be useful, therefore, to state the issues somewhat more systematically in the context of our present focus on subversion. Specifically, we now ask how much effect the labeling process has on either deviants or the "respectable"; if the theory applies to the one, it should be applicable to the other. Or, phrased differently, if people can be made deviants by false labeling, can they also be made virtuous by false labeling?[13]

A second question is, what is the percentage (in statistical language) of Type 1 and Type 2 errors? That is, what percentage of deviants (with respect to any rule of ethics, morals, law, achievement, or merit generally) can manipulate others so as to escape that label—and for how long? And how many innocents, that is, persons deserving respect, can unjustly be labeled—and again for how long?[14] If we could answer these questions satisfactorily, then we could more easily ascertain the consequences of such labeling processes. For example, if some deviant persons can persuade most others that they have earned respect, does this confirm them in their subversive ways; or does the labeling instead "convert" them to the path of righteousness, just as labeling theorists claim that those who are labeled deviants come to be deviant? Having attained some success (even if unde-served), do deviant persons no longer feel the temptation to cheat a little?

A version of labeling theory that is general enough to answer these questions has not been formulated as yet, and of course has not been tested. Even within the narrower sectors of behavior that labeling theorists have explored, that is, deviance, these questions have not been answered.

12. Erving Goffman, "The Insanity of Place," in *Relations in Public* (New York: Basic Books, 1971), pp. 335–390.

13. It should not be forgotten that labeling theory is anticipated by Charles Horton Cooley's "Looking Glass Self," and more generally in W. I. Thomas' dictum that if something is defined as real it is real in its consequences.

14. For a good discussion of this and related points, see Howard Becker, *Outsiders* (New York: Free Press, 1963), pp. 9ff.

Almost certainly the answers will vary with the extent to which there is surveillance, a body of rules and techniques for ascertaining or measuring merit, and a sharing of knowledge; and these in fact vary in different arenas of social life, as well as over time.

Even if our general view of subversion is correct—essentially, that others do learn much of what the reality is—labeling may still have much impact, for the following reasons.

First, though one might argue that "murder will out," most mislabeling (malicious, manipulative, or accidental) refers to acts in which others have a much lesser stake than in murder, so that fewer people will expend any great effort to unmask others, or to protect the innocent. Second, even if we are correct in asserting that most innocents who are erroneously dispraised do move successfully toward reclaiming the respect they have lost, and some people do unmask those who have been clever enough to create a good reputation while not deserving it, at any given time both the victims and those who are helped by the mislabeling *are* in an undeserved position. They are either gaining some rewards or incurring some punishments that have been created by manipulatory acts, though unjustly. Consequently, the reality of the social structure at all times is that *the allocation of some part of all disesteem and praise is based on labeling error*.

Moreover, since it is not in the interest of everyone to expose others, and few wish to spend much effort redressing injustice (it takes energy, and risks the anger of others), some people will continue to be labeled wrongly for a long time. Consequently, over both the short and the long term, all those processes are in operation by which people act on their misperceptions, press the mislabeled into those roles, and shape their life chances and alternatives so as to confirm the label. Whether or not the result is pervasive and general injustice, widespread injustice only in certain subsectors of the society, unfairness to categories or groups, or specific inequities to individuals, there is enough mislabeling in most social systems to persuade at least some people to give little credence to the system.

Although labeling is of much social importance, labeling theory is not a theory, or even a hypothesis. It merely states that labeling does occur; that is, sometimes being labeled presses an individual toward the kind of behavior described by that label. Like so many other common observations, folk sayings embody it, as well as its contrary: A rose by any other name would smell as sweet; but give a dog a bad name . . . .[15] That is, the "theory" merely asserts that one can sometimes observe such a process in the area of deviant behavior.

15. For those who recognize the second adage but do not know the rest of it, the final clause in one version is: "and *hang* him!" The adage is given in the *Oxford Dictionary of English Proverbs*, 3d ed. (London: Oxford University Press, 1970), which cites James Kelly, *A Complete Collection of Scottish Proverbs Explained and Made Intelligible to the English Reader* (1721), and Sir Walter Scott, *Guy Mannering* (1815), chap. 23: "It is pithily said, 'Give a dog an ill name and hang him'; and . . . if you give a man, or a race of men, an ill name, they are very likely to do something that deserves hanging."

THE DYNAMICS OF "SUCCESSFUL" LABELING

By contrast with a narrow focus on the fact that some people are labeled as deviants, our discussion has been concerned with many kinds of labeling, and specifically with the conditions or factors that increase the likelihood of attempts at labeling; increase their success or failure; and alter the social control effects of various kinds of labeling. A more adequate labeling theory would in short state the conditions or factors that increase or decrease the success of labeling and specify when counter-labeling or rebuttals are successful. It would also predict whether negative labeling is more successful than complimentary labeling; and whether a group's or individual's efforts to self-label in complimentary ways are likely to be more successful than efforts to pin a negative or positive label on another individual, group, or organization.

Although the phenomenon of labeling has usually been reported in observations about deviance processes, it should also be visible in activities that are generally esteemed. In science, Merton and Zuckerman have noted, for example, what they call the Matthew Effect, that is, the process by which those who have been given some advantages and honors come to be given still more.[16] In analyses of socialization in the professions, it has been pointed out that small distinctions in favor of an individual give that person the opportunity of gaining a better education, richer apprenticeship experiences, more influential sponsors, more interesting job opportunities, and so on, so that by the time actual professional practice begins, the person's ability is in fact higher than that of someone whose initial talent may once have been equal.

But though the labeling process is visible at either end of the prestige spectrum, we also know from observation that most people who are given some approving label at an early period in their careers do *not* gradually accumulate still more advantages at each successive stage. The positive support they receive does not guarantee continued success. Indeed, most people are gradually sifted out, leaving only a few who reach the higher levels of achievement and honor.

It must be concluded, then, that the Matthew Effect is not stated correctly. It would be more accurate to say that those to whom more is given are more likely than those to whom less is given to receive still more; but most who are given more at each stage do not move on to get even more. Few have enjoyed an easy ascent to greatness. Most fail, even among those who once enjoyed many advantages.

Neither does negative labeling at one phase lead to an accumulation of disrespect. Most boys and girls whose neighborhood reputations are negative at one time period do not continue to be disesteemed and to behave deviantly so as to earn that reputation still more. Instead, they perceive

---

16. Robert K. Merton, "The Matthew Effect in Science," in *The Sociology of Science*, chap. 20.

the costs of that path and the advantages of conformity. By the time they are mature adults, most have become respected citizens.

In both types of cases, it is not that labeling has no effect. Rather, labeling is not a powerful enough variable to outweigh other influences, especially that of actual changes in behavior and performances. In fact, precisely because most people believe that labeling has some importance, many people, families, groups, and organizations engage in deliberate efforts both to change their behavior and to engage in counter-labeling efforts, such as advertising, anti-defamation suits and programs, moving away from those who label negatively, changes in social networks, and so on.

COUNTERACTING LABELING

From this perspective, we can at least point to some of the factors that alter the effectiveness of any kind of labeling—whether self-labeling by organizations or individuals, or the labeling of other organizations or individuals.

The first is the possible gain to the social actor who attempts to label. How much is it worth to anyone to pin a complimentary or negative label on another, or, as discussed in this and the previous chapters, on oneself? The individual who enjoys a complimentary but undeserved label has little reason to alter that situation; here, the gain is obvious. The ghetto adolescent who begins to perceive that others are labeling him in uncomplimentary ways may feel the gain from combatting that opinion is worth little. By contrast, the graduate or medical student whom others label as irresponsible or careless may decide that his career will be hurt if he or she does not fight that label. It is worth something if others label one's enemies negatively, but we may see little advantage in trying ourselves to pin any label at all, negative or positive, on most people, except to the extent that we believe we are correctly judging their actions.

A second factor is the cost of labeling another person. Any process of labeling requires some investment of time and attention. The juvenile delinquent has few resources with which to create a counter-label that is more appealing, while a corporation may be willing to spend millions to combat the label of "polluter" (it might even, in rare cases, actually improve its behavior.) The person or organization with prestige can more effectively deploy considerable influence in order to label another, either negatively or positively, or to create an improved self-label.

A third factor affecting the success of labeling and again related to cost is the structural position of the actors involved. Each person or organization occupies a different position within the social structure, and some have greater access to the target audience. Some are already at the center of attention, so that others will listen. A greater use of resources will surmount the disadvantage of poor access, of course. However, structural position, that is, opportunities for presenting the message, is independently important, as many communications studies show. Thus, a stationery store owner in a poor neighborhood may be more successful in labeling others than more affluent people in the same area.

A fourth factor is the discrepancy between claim and reality. The more obvious the discrepancy, the more difficult it is to create a new label or a counter-label. In asserting that there is a reality (although some might dispute that assertion), we are not stating that a youngster is (or is not) a juvenile delinquent, a housewife a kleptomaniac, a businessman a crook, and so forth, but merely that observers have noted some real behaviors and have usually made inferences from them that we call "labeling." (In social psychology, this is called the "attribution process.") Refutation can deny "the facts" if there are bad witnesses or none; can offer a more kindly explanation if the facts seem clear; or can assert new and improved behavior if that is the only alternative. But "the facts" are socially defined, and if the discrepancy between what the target audience sees as the facts and what the labeler aims at is very great, the chances of success in creating or altering a label will be correspondingly lower. Again, that likelihood of outcome will be weighed against the probable costs and the resources that can be deployed.

A fifth factor affecting labeling success is the receptiveness of the audience to that kind of message. A grimly prudish society is quicker to seize on very small cues as a basis for labeling a person as lascivious or lewd. In the rural South of half a century ago, a young man of good family earned some disesteem (and envy) for "sowing his wild oats," but that label itself would excuse his behavior for a few years, and even a short beginning at reform would usually rehabilitate his reputation. The label itself suggests a self-limiting process, and people were not willing to believe that "improper but normal" behavior deserved a permanent loss of esteem. Upper-middle-class social networks are not very receptive to the label "juvenile delinquent," thus any attempt to give that label to one of their boys requires some effort. A group is likely, on the other hand, to be willing on scant evidence to believe the worst of its enemies.

At various points in these complex processes, the efforts of labelers and counter-labelers clash, and one or the other may decide the effort is not worth the goal. The gossip who seeks to denigrate a neighbor may perceive it is costly, and invest no more in the labeling attempt. A young man may leave his home town because he does not have enough resources with which to build a better reputation. Few wish to rebut their own reputations as honorable to brilliant, but even fewer would succeed: others have a stake in defending that reputation, and the efforts at rebuttal would probably do no more than add the label "modest" to the list. In any event, at various stages the organization, group, or individual may decide the costs of counter-labeling or of label-refutation are too high.

Even in so briefly considering the main factors that influence such labeling attempts and successes, we can see that: pejorative labeling of others is more likely to be successful than complimentary labeling; complimentary labeling of others is more likely to be successful than complimentary self-labeling; and those who enjoy a complimentary label at one stage of their careers can use that edge to gain further advantages (because they have more resources) more easily than those who suffer from negative labeling can remove that onus.

STEREOTYPING AND DISCRIMINATION

Though everyone engages at times in individual efforts at subversion, it seems likely that most of the successful efforts at gaining more than merit justifies, or at preventing others from receiving what they have earned, fall into one large type: some form of discrimination against a whole social category, such as a class, race, or ethnic group. That is, if we could obtain a quantitative measure of the total amount of successful subversion in any large society, the behaviors by which especially cunning persons aggrandize themselves at the expense of specific others would be but a small amount compared to the subversion that is accomplished by the structure of the class, sex role, ethnic, racial, and religious patterns. Such patterns are defended by standard arguments against the fitness of the excluded or disesteemed candidates: They are not intelligent enough; they are too aggressive to be good team members; they are lazy; and so on.[17] Relatively little space will be devoted to this topic here, even though I am asserting that quantitatively most subversion gets done through race, sex, ethnic, and religious discrimination. This analysis is restricted simply because I do not believe that much can be added to the large body of published analyses of esteem and discrimination in these areas of behavior.

Most such barriers to opportunity and thus to obtaining prestige are ascriptive (such as sex, race), but not all. For example, in societies with high educational levels, many jobs require a minimum of formal schooling, although candidates with less could acquire the needed skills, and organizations hardly pay any attention to the quality of schooling once the person is hired.[18] Age and sex bars are common in all societies, but political ones are too. Whether they apply to ascriptive or acquired traits, however—whether to age, sex, race, experience, ethnic identity, or even achievement—all restrictions have in common a pattern of stereotyping others, that is, viewing others as a category and supposing that all people in that category exhibit certain disesteemed traits. They are all prestige rankings, by which almost everyone in that stratum or segment is viewed by other groups as less worthy. Specifically, they are not worthy to be *candidates*, to be given adequate opportunities; and they should not get as much prestige as others for the same achievements.

17. The standard textbook for much of this behavior is George E. Simpson and J. Milton Yinger, *Racial and Cultural Minorities*, 4th ed. (New York: Harper and Row, 1972).

18. For persuasive documentation on this point, see Ivar Berg, *Education and Jobs: The Great Training Robbery* (New York: Praeger, 1970), pp. 85–101.

It might be argued that, since other social strata do in fact give such people a lower worth, that worth is simply their "market value." Consequently, there may be injustice but not subversion. Throughout American history, almost any contribution made by a black was given a lower evaluation than an equivalent or even lesser achievement made by a white person. We may deplore that fact, as we might the low wages of unskilled labor, but in both cases it can be claimed that such injustice has been the "social price" of such people. We need not assume that manipulation was involved.

However, much of this discrimination does fit our definition, because it is possible to ascertain historically and to observe now that people do engage in *separate* acts designed to reduce the prestige or respect given to members of such categories. Here, too, the allocation of prestige has by no means been a free market. Both individuals and groups have mounted private or public campaigns of propaganda, legislation, vilification, formal restrictions, quota systems, false documents, violence and threats, blackmail, and bribery to prevent such disadvantaged groups from obtaining as much prestige for their qualities or performances as they otherwise might. The literature on racial, ethnic, and sex discrimination in this and other countries documents this pattern overwhelmingly.[19]

Moreover, this flood of both action and propaganda over the centuries is, in turn, a major factor that supports the evaluations and behaviors themselves. People grow up firm in the belief that the other sex, or other castes, races, religions, or classes, exhibit various disesteemed traits, because people have been subjected to precisely that flow of information and emotional argument. Because all this has been so extensively documented and analyzed in social and psychological research for decades, it is not worthwhile to devote much space to "proving" that these patterns are pervasive.

If higher-ranking social categories believe, on the basis of objective observation and without any flood of propaganda, that others *cannot* live up to the challenge of a given opportunity, we might speak of error but not subversion. However, the denigratory messages are widespread; thus discrimination is typically a self-fulfilling prophecy.[20] If people with deprecated social traits are barred from the chance to try (because they are not worthy anyway), only a few of them will embarrass anyone by achieving greatly. Perhaps because dominant social groups suspect their judgments might be false (or because they do not wish to confer even the esteem of admitting the lower-ranking categories to equal candidacy), it is rare that equal encouragement is given to individuals in the less esteemed groups, or equal prestige for the same achievement.

---

19. For some of the more genteel types of discrimination, see E. Digby Baltzell, *The Protestant Establishment* (New York: Random House, 1964).

20. See Robert K. Merton, "The Self-Fulfilling Prophecy," in *Social Theory and Social Structure* (New York: Free Press, 1957), chap. 9.

But this widespread pattern of subversion, based on the large structural elements in most societies, is under general attack. One might argue that it is one more instance in which social research has had a substantial impact on politics. Subversion loses some of its persuasive or deceiving influence when both victims and oppressors can read detailed reports on how it is done. The justifications for racism, sexism, and other discriminatory patterns have been undermined by social and psychological research, and again the victims can and do acquire this knowledge. It is the experience of the Western world for well over a century, and of the entire world since World War II, that increasingly such disesteemed categories of people come to reject those stereotyped judgments publicly, and to resist or denounce all such private or public campaigns of disparagement: in short, to "demand their rights." They accuse the dominant social strata of subversion; they claim they have been weighed by false scales. In addition, and in part because of such protests, more people in those categories can now point to specific high achievements, so that the bars and disevaluations are more harshly revealed as tricks and frauds, that is, as subversion in our specific sense.[21]

SUBVERSION AND SUPPORT OF THE EXISTING SOCIAL SYSTEM

Since no society rests on the belief that the wicked should or will flourish, and the good will or should perish forever, all these efforts toward the subversion of prestige processes are of theoretical importance for understanding how much credence the members of a society will give to its social structure or leaders.[22] Both theological and political doctrines reveal the importance of this relationship between subversion and the credibility of a social order, for all of them attempt to explain why the wicked are not always punished in this world but sometimes prosper. It is necessary to devote some thought to this apparent injustice, since the most obvious answer might suggest that the rulers' love of justice is at best restrained. Simple, unguided observation cannot easily conclude that all the good prosper and all the iniquitous are scourged, as long as such contrary cases lie ready at hand. Priests and rulers, then, sense the necessity for guiding their followers along the correct thoughtways.

We do not know how successful that guidance is. However, it seems likely that most people in Western societies would concede, if pressed

21. One consequence of this movement is that "passing" becomes less significant as a phenomenon in racism. Just as some people have purchased the symbols of higher-class position, not possessing the reality, so some Caucasoid-appearing "blacks" have entered white society as whites—and of course many disadvantaged people may "pass" temporarily by telephone or on trips or vacations. Erving Goffman, in *Stigma* (Englewood Cliffs, N.J.: Prentice-Hall, 1963), notes many such techniques. Passing has no effect on racist social structures; attacking their subversive effects does.

22. E. Digby Baltzell, *The Protestant Establishment*, argues in his conclusion, pp. 380ff., that the failure of the Protestant upper class to "bring in" the true elite, i.e., to recruit the best, has eroded their own authority and prestige.

hard, that most people do get about what they "deserve." More cautiously, only a tiny percentage are in favor of radical changes in their society.

Official ideologists invariably try to explain why those who rule actually deserve the deference we find it wise to give them publicly. Theological doctrines promise that evil people *will* be punished, at least in the *next* world. Such philosophies need not explain all anomalies, all deviations from justice, since it is assumed that accidents and luck play a role in any system. They must, however, proclaim that over the long run, most of the best will not be defeated by the machinations of the worst. They must assert that the system offers few general opportunities for subverting the rules of merit, whether achieved, acquired, or ascribed. In this fundamental sense, all official ideologies must both explain and justify the existing social system, since within it the leaders have presumably deserved their rich rewards. Correspondingly, social theorists of widely different political persuasions have generally claimed that unless people do believe in the rightness of the system, and in the difficulty of general subversion of the rules, they will not continue to support that system.

Many civilizations have asserted that human beings are rightly born to their social rank, high or low, and nothing should be done to alter the apparent injustices that result. At a less general level, in many monarchies the "grace and favor of the king" was once thought to be a proper basis for allocating prestige, at least to nobles and courtiers. However, even in such systems where the king's favor was little questioned, if it was widely believed that he was easily fooled into rewarding the unworthy or punishing the worthy people did object to such subversion, by any means that lay in their power. For in that case he is not giving honor on the basis of the values affirmed by the nobles or people surrounding and supporting him, but on his erroneous, manipulated view of what others are achieving.

Two further regularities can be noted in the relationship between subversion and the credibility of the social order. One is that there is a correlation between class position and belief in the system; put another way, toward the lower classes, a higher percentage of people believe the system is rigged.[23] This first regularity, discussed at various points in this book, needs no extensive comment. Most people accept their rank, and most do not claim they should be given lavish rewards for their present qualities or achievements. On the other hand, more people toward the lower ranks than toward the upper ranks do harbor the suspicion that, had the social structure been differently arranged, they might have achieved more and thus obtained more.[24]

---

23. William H. Form and Joan Rytina, "Ideological Beliefs on the Distribution of Power in the United States," *American Sociological Review*, 34 (February, 1969): 19–31. Class patterns are also discussed in our chapter on interlinkages.

24. On both points, see Richard Sennet and Jonathan Cobb, *The Hidden Injuries of Class* (New York: Vintage, 1973), chaps. 4, 5; and Studs Terkel, *Working* (New York: Avon, 1975).

The second regularity is that, toward the upper social strata, more people have actually witnessed subversive behavior at those privileged levels than have outsiders. The structural position of insiders, leaders, or those with influence affords opportunities to observe both more honesty and more chicanery than others can observe. These people can see that many of their fellow members live by the approved norms of ethics, even if it is partly because they do not have to sacrifice much to do so. The esteemed professor of medicine does not have to steal patients, pay kickbacks, advertise, or denigrate other physicians in order to earn a good living and obtain deference. People who are esteemed and well paid can afford to be highminded about small matters. Such insiders and leaders do not usually believe they manipulate the system unfairly, for it has given them more opportunities for achievement than others get, and more legitimate ways of publicizing their achievements. They are more likely to affirm the system: Manifestly, if it gives them, the deserving, more rewards, it must be a just system.

Of course, insiders and leaders are also in a position to observe some of their fellows whose allegiance to principles of merit is somewhat weak, who take some steps to get more esteem than justice might bring—the physician or lawyer whose charm or country club membership rather than professional excellence gives him or her great success; the scientist whose control over the laboratory and the research grant, rather than scientific creativity, yields many co-authored publications. However, those on the inside are more likely to see such things as deplorable anomalies, not as the main reality. After all, they are not deceived by that subversive behavior.

It is possible, however, that this general regularity affects another important social pattern, the recruitment of revolutionary leaders from social strata close to but not at the top.[25] For such people are not only more likely to command the resources with which to mount a revolt, but are also better situated to observe the chicanery of the people who enjoy the highest ranks in the political system, and thus to feel morally indignant about it. Their lack of credence in the top leaders lowers their support of those leaders.

But though we can point to some of these consequences of subversion, we cannot as yet specify when a social segment, such as the college dissidents of the 1960's, blacks, women, or the natives of a colony, will come to fight openly against an official ideology or the social rules that have barred their way to esteem. Perhaps if we had secret polling data from past generations, we might have evidence of a slow growth in the belief that these systems were fraudulent, and we could then speculate about when public protests would become widespread.[26]

25. See in this connection my analysis of revolution, "Social Mobility, Family, and Revolutionary Potential" in *Explorations in Social Theory* (New York: Oxford University Press, 1973), pp. 287–315.

26. An extensive analysis of these conditions is found in Ted Gurr, *Why Men Rebel* (Princeton, N.J.: Princeton University Press, 1970).

It should also be noted, finally, that though few political leaders have been famed for their sensitivity to public opinion, their awareness that people are watching and do become indignant at wrongful manipulations of the esteem processes has caused many rulers to make some effort at either improving their behavior or mounting programs aimed at persuading others of their goodness. At a minimum, they may erect statues and triumphal arches, present circuses and games, pay for a mass of printed or spoken propaganda, or even offer displays of armed might to show that they protect the nation. They may make official visits to hospitals or to well-selected, scrubbed, poor but deserving citizens; or even attempt for a while to give honor to those who achieve greatly, as part of a campaign to influence their subjects to believe that those who rule did not obtain their privileges by subversion of the society's approved prestige processes. That is, their knowledge of one possible consequence of subversion for the social system leads them to make some effort at forestalling that threat. Even when favoritism and ascribed rank are defended philosophically, they are not thought to justify the manipulation of others' opinions about esteem. If the rewards given are thought to be the result of opinion manipulation and not worth, leaders who hand out rewards have believed that they would increasingly lose political support.

Loss of credence may not lead to open revolt, for that may be too dangerous. Command of arms, prosperity, or success in war against an invader may keep a set of leaders in power even when they are not widely respected. Many foolish monarchs have survived for years: for example, James I continued to reign while losing esteem. However, eventually, widespread subversion may result in the complete undermining of a regime: James's successor Charles I continued to lose esteem and eventually lost his head as well. It can plausibly be argued that the final overthrow of the French aristocracy, though delayed by the military might of Louis XV and Louis XVI, was caused by the increasing popular conviction that they enjoyed great privileges which had been fraudulently built into the legal system: Their honors were not commensurate with either their political services or their military contributions.[27] They had received honor by manipulation, not by merit either ascribed or achieved, and other social strata withdrew their normative support.

Besides the dissidence resulting from a large-scale undermining of the social order, we have also noted a few subsidiary consequences of widespread subversion. For example, it seems likely that more talent and energy are then invested in manipulation than in individual performances or contributions to the group. At such times, too, people come to suspect the worst of even fairly honorable men and women. Quick upward and downward mobility at the higher levels is common, but often on the basis

---

27. See the analysis of this point by both Alexis de Tocqueville, *The Old Regime and the French Revolution*, trans. Stuart Gilbert (New York: Doubleday, 1955), pp. 86ff., and Franklin L. Ford, *Robe and Sword* (Cambridge, Mass.: Harvard University Press, 1953), pp. 27–29, 114–115, 249–252.

of gossip, machinations, flattery, and self-serving plots rather than hard work or talent in public service.

We have also suggested that within a given historical epoch those sectors of human activity where acclaim is thought to rest mainly on manipulation will enjoy less respect. Military and artistic achievement exhibit the two sides of this assertion, for trickery and manipulation have been widely used in both to gain the coveted opportunity to prove one's talent, but in both the test of reality will ultimately face the aspirant. At that point, the honor given to the aspirant will be determined far more by achievement. The winner in sports is given some esteem, but less in a sport where it is thought that the system is rigged (for example, modern professional wrestling).

Without question, the honor that is given in contemporary Western society, where tens of millions of dollars are spent each year to make or unmake reputations in most kinds of endeavors (and nations too attempt to gain esteem by manipulation, as when they defend their imperialism as the road to justice), is partly determined by the subversion of prestige processes. It is my belief, to be tested by better data, that in such an era most people are not grossly deceived for long. However, over any time scale new deceptions are tried, too. As a consequence, at any given time much injustice in the allocation of prestige does occur, most of it in the form of stereotyping and discrimination against the major social categories of sex, race, caste, ethnic group, class, and religion.

Chapter 12
Disapproval and Dispraise

Century after century, wise, worldly advisers have asserted that praise and flattery are effective in wooing women, persuading men, winning enemies over to one's side, and obtaining the favor of kings. It is not yet clear whether praise is in fact that efficacious because it is in short supply compared with disapproval or dispraise (and therefore the more valued); or whether those in power reward those who give this advice because they would prefer not to hear criticism, wishing rather to keep their monopoly over this form of social control.

Although we cannot answer that question here, we can examine the control effect of dispraise, or withdrawing respect from others. That control effect is the focus of this chapter; but we should at least note in passing that dispraise is used in other ways as well. One of these ways can be categorized as a set of "distancing" mechanisms, in which the aim is to keep the other person away, to precipitate a quarrel or fight, or even to make an enemy of the other. Thus, a parent will sometimes begin to criticize a child when he or she knows that the child is annoyed by the parent's behavior. A boss may begin to scold an employee to forestall some complaint.

These are diversionary tactics, and may take a more extreme form, as when one spouse stops an inquiry into his or her behavior by beginning an angry diatribe about the other's behavior. By escalating the discussion into a bitter quarrel, one avoids a serious rational inquiry (or even nagging about some defect in one's character) that may be much more threatening.

These distancing or diversionary tactics are not the same as the dispraise that is used as the preliminary to an intended conflict, such as a street fight or duel, or as a signal that henceforth the dispraiser will view the other as an enemy. Psychologically, some such preparatory interactions are instead ways by which one individual generates enough anger and ego strength to be able to challenge the other. Socially, they are announcements of conflict to others who may be involved in the same network. They are also expressions of moral justification for the attack. But it should again be noted that although most people possess this repertory of tactics, they do not typically choose these role behaviors in a calculating manner.

Dispraise is often used, of course, to assert one's own superiority, but this assertion may have other audiences than the person criticized. For example, a rising intellectual may use the occasion of a book review to announce his or her superiority, not alone to the author of that book, but to others of the group. Criticism is a widely accepted vehicle for displaying one's skills, standards, and acumen and has more than once been consciously used as a technique for job-seeking.[1] Similarly, strong criticism of one's own group may be used not only as a signal that one is willing to leave it, but as a way of persuading people at higher levels of other groups that one deserves to be accepted as a new member. In this case, the target audience is not one's own group; instead, the person who dispraises his or her own group is announcing his or her superiority to that group. But though such uses of dispraise or disesteem are not trivial, and are often dramatic, the various forms of disapproval are used in a much wider set of situations for the purpose of shaping human behavior and attitudes. It has occasionally been suggested in this study that the control effect of approval might be less or more than that of disapproval, and of praise more or less than dispraise, under some circumstances; but up to this point a specific inquiry has not been made into disapproval. We have taken note of the fact that in the daily round everyone constantly judges others, disapproves or approves more or less, and tells others about those responses or not. To the extent that we have preferences, attitudes, norms, and values, we engage in such activities continually, and in turn we are guided in our course of action to some extent by our knowledge of others' positive or negative responses.

Why does disesteem warrant separate analysis? Of course, we can view praise as gain, profit, or reward, and dispraise as simply its opposite or negative: loss, cost, or punishment. However, both experimental evidence and personal experience suggest that the two are different, and not merely opposites. We evaluate them differently in weighing our future conduct. Even in the supposedly simpler and more rational world of economic transactions, profits and losses may be experienced differently even when of the same magnitude. That is, a financial loss does not give a message that is simply the opposite or negative of the message that a financial gain announces. A loss is not only "bad news"; it is also "news," for in reasonably good times it is of some interest to outsiders and of special concern to insiders. Successive losses will bankrupt a business, or cause a manager to be fired. At a minimum, losses announce that something is wrong. Corporation management is usually given a relatively free hand when the company enjoys a profit, but banks and directors scrutinize policies carefully when the year ends with a loss.

---

1. For example, Willard Waller's elaborate editorial criticisms (before publication) of Robert MacIver's *Society* in 1936 was aimed at bringing himself to MacIver's attention. See William J. Goode, Frank F. Furstenberg, Jr., and Larry R. Mitchell, eds., *Willard Waller: On the Family, Education, and War* (Chicago: University of Chicago Press, 1970), pp. 66–67. However, this course of action is not generally to be recommended when the person criticized will decide one's job future.

The experience of physical hurt or punishment, too, is a message about the cost of a given behavior, but again it seems to be qualitatively different from that of pleasure or reward, not merely its negative. However, the problem of ascertaining the impact of punishment is not simple, and indeed psychologists have designed thousands of experiments in their effort to ascertain how animals and human beings respond to punishment.[2] There is considerable, if puzzling, evidence that the curves describing behavior shaped by punishment are not merely the reverse of curves describing behavior shaped by rewards. Therefore, since dispraise is experienced as a kind of punishment, perhaps its control effects cannot be inferred by simply reversing the curves or results from giving praise. That is, both experimental evidence and personal experience suggest that the control effects of dispraise might be different from those of praise and thus deserve separate attention.

In this chapter it is neither appropriate nor possible to solve what is essentially a psychological problem in learning theory. The task is rather to analyze the social structure of disapproval and dispraise. Nevertheless, in order to explore the conditions under which disesteem or dispraise occur, and what control effects either is likely to create, we must at least consider the general effect of punishment.

PUNISHMENT AS BEHAVIOR CONTROL

Ideally, we should begin with a clear definition of reward and punishment, but psychologists have disagreed among themselves too much to warrant much boldness in an outsider. The problem is simply that though we can label as "punishment" any noxious stimuli such as an electric shock, extreme heat or cold, sudden loud noises, and so forth, we do not know just what an animal's experience is when it encounters what we are sure is either punishment or reward. Moreover, "punishment" in English suggests, especially in a human context, the notion of retribution or reprisal for "bad" behavior. Indeed, though psychologists take care not to use that meaning in their interpretations of animal experiments—after all, the animal did not know what was the "right" way to act—noxious stimuli are used as a kind of reprisal, such as when the animal has taken a wrong turn in a maze. Nevertheless, we cannot suppose that experimental animals "believe" they are being punished for not following the rules set by their experimenters.[3]

Accepting that ambiguity, and assuming that the term in the context of animal psychology does not imply any reprisal, we can first note that some versions of modern learning theory suggest that punishment not only has less positive effect than reward; it may even be of little negative

---

2. See the excellent summary by Richard L. Solomon, "Punishment," *American Psychologist*, 19 (April, 1964): 239–253. See also *Deterrents and Reinforcement*, by Douglas H. Lawrence and Leon Festinger (Stanford: Stanford University Press, 1962), for some related complexities.

3. But see Robert Rosenthal, *Experimenter Effects in Behavioral Research* (New York: Appleton-Century-Crofts, 1966), pp. 158–179.

importance. An animal can most easily be taught a behavior pattern by inducing it in some way to carry out part of the desired behavior, then rewarding that behavior at each successive step in its acquisition of the entire pattern. It is not necessary, and it may even be less effective, many argue, to punish the animal at any step for a failure; it is preferable simply to withhold a reward when it makes an error.

To extinguish the learned behavior, the experimenter typically ceases to reward the animal for it. Punishment does not speed the gradual process of extinction, although it does cause a temporary reduction of the learned behavior. In general, during the period of acquisition, punishment for "wrong" behavior neither accelerates the process of learning nor makes it harder to extinguish the learned behavior subsequently. Indeed, experiments have reported that punishing "correct" behavior may reinforce correct behavior under some laboratory conditions.

Such findings, especially the finding that the effect of punishment is not clear and obvious, are puzzling to laymen. Punishment is not as well understood as reward, partly because it has been less investigated (and less investigated partly because it yields less tidy results). However, if these findings are correct, they present social analysts with an enigma. Human beings are fairly clever in intuiting how to control one another, but in no society have the members ever tried to shape each other's behavior by reward alone.[4] Societies do differ in how they punish, but all have used a wide array of punishments: fines, shaming, public confession, ostracism, flogging, torture, flaying, beheading, and so on. Not only do people spontaneously punish one another in various ways, but if questioned they argue that sound theory and observation support the efficacy of such practices. They are especially firm in their belief in the necessity of punishing children, as proverbs from a wide array of cultures will attest. Certainly, few parents would argue that scolding and disapproval, one form of punishment, are unnecessary.

Obviously, people utilize their own experience in predicting the response of other people. It is likely, therefore, that they cannot be entirely wrong. That is, since they know punishment affects *them*, they reason that therefore it must affect others.

However, common sense is often wrong about its supposed verities and thus possibly about social control as well. Only rarely does a layman try to test a hypothesis that runs counter to received folk sociology. For example, at the end of the eighteenth century in England, scores of crimes were punishable by death, and that severity was defended publicly and privately; but the best evidence indicates that so grave a threat did not curb crime at all (any more than did the elimination of that threat). The physical punishment of children has many serious consequences, often

4. See, in this connection, B. F. Skinner's *Walden II* (New York: MacMillan, 1948), and *Beyond Freedom and Dignity* (New York: Knopf, 1971).

among them its failure to change either their attitudes or their behavior in the desired direction; yet when challenged, most people will defend it vigorously. We cannot at all assume, then, that existing customs eventually will be vindicated when we have greater scientific knowledge about human behavior.

Despite our limited understanding of punishment as a form of social control, some simple but powerful facts about the effect of punishment on learning can be stated.

First, punishment teaches quickly. The survival value of this trait is obvious. The animal that does not quickly learn which things hurt will quickly die, and thus will not pass its genes on to the next generation.

Second, not only is punishment-learning fast; it also requires little reinforcement, and it is difficult to unlearn. Many human beings spend years of their lives in psychotherapists' offices trying to unlearn fears or disgusts they acquired through punishment in childhood.

Third, punishment-learning is both crude and constricting. People (and other animals) learn more ineradicably and easily that some things will bite, sting, burn, or kill than that these things might under some circumstances be useful or pleasant. A good part of learning in later childhood and early adulthood consists in finding out that earlier rules (for example, about honesty, paying taxes, traffic) are not to be obeyed mechanically, but qualified and differentiated in many ways (for example, white lies).

Of course, some part of socializing (as we argued earlier) does not aim at precision or differentiation; indeed, it aims at the opposite. Parents once tried to develop in their children a general taboo against sexual exploration, so that any approach toward it would arouse feelings of fear or anxiety. Military training has typically relied on both prestige punishment (humiliation, degradation) and physical punishment, in the explicit belief that in the heat of battle the soldier must be guided by his superiors' commands and not by primitive fears that the threat of death might arouse.[5]

A major reason for this is that much of social structure is made up of "forbiddens," actions that people should not engage in. Everyone knows them well enough to be able to count on others' conformity, with little innovation or flexibility: friends will not steal when they visit one's home; visitors' children will not harm the baby in its crib; people will not set fire to each other's houses, even if they have hurt one another's feelings, and so on. Indeed, the training usually results in our not even being aware that we are avoiding these behaviors.

A fourth effect of punishment on learning is that it can create some-

5. Consider in this connection the two very different modes of training Air Force officer candidates as analyzed by Gary L. Wamsley, "Contrasting Institutions of Air Force Socialization: Happenstance or Bellwether?" *American Journal of Sociology*, 78 (September, 1972): 399–417; but the data are not clear as to how widely the results differ.

times paralyzing emotions and cognitive confusion if it is not clear to the person or animal which response is being punished. That is, if the "correct" response or choice is sometimes punished and sometimes rewarded or not punished—or if the subject lacks the capacity to discriminate between two situations that appear the same but have different consequences—the person (or animal) may become emotionally upset, unable to function well, or muddled.[6] Many such experiments have been carried out with animals, but we can observe this pattern in human beings as well. It is likely that the failure of the social environment to discriminate among the responses of the lower-class black child, that is, its punishing indiscriminately too many of his or her responses, hampers learning substantially. Child-abusing parents sometimes achieve the same result by punishing infants for their failure to make discriminations or adjustments beyond their capacities, such as being toilet trained at six months, picking up their clothes neatly at age two, and so on.[7]

Beyond these four rudimentary observations, understanding the effects of punishment on human learning poses more complex problems than understanding its effects on animal behaviors, for human beings have several aims in punishing that are not quite like those of animals. In childhood socialization, and to a great extent in adult socialization as well, those who socialize others have three analytically separable intentions: 1. to teach the person to *discriminate*, for example, among colors, dangers, kin statuses, words, foods, and so forth; 2. to teach the child or adult to *prefer* certain behaviors, results, music, beliefs, and so on; that is, to acquire attitudes, norms, and values, so that he or she will autonomously and spontaneously act and feel in ways approved by the group or socializer; and, 3. whether or not the person internalizes these norms, to teach him or her to *act* in conformity with them just the same; that is, to use 1. and 2. in deciding to obey the social rules.

Animals, mindlessly punished or rewarded by the natural environment, learn to discriminate among edible and inedible substances, colors, predators, territories, habitats, seasonal changes, and so on. Social animals also punish one another, and so teach some necessary discriminations and required conformities. Predator parents will harry their cubs into the den when threatened, a silver-backed male gorilla will cuff a youngster who in play disturbs him, a calf that insists on grazing in poor forage will be punished by being left behind, and so on. Note that many such social learning experiences are also instances of control as well.

But though human beings also use physical punishment for the two aims of teaching discrimination and enforcing control, the aim of inculcating norms, attitudes, or values may require other techniques. For that

---

6. See Martin E. P. Seligman, Steven F. Maier, and James H. Geer, "Alleviation of Learned Helplessness in the Dog," *Journal of Abnormal Psychology*, 73 (June, 1968): 256–262.

7. Here I am omitting any analysis of the effect of punishment on the punisher. Among other results, it can be psychologically satisfying or cathartic.

reason, caution is necessary (as experiments have reminded us for generations) in extrapolating from animal experiments in learning, and from many human experiments as well. It is not only that the experimental task seems at times artificial and silly (for example, posing a problem that can only be solved by trial and error, or memorizing nonsense syllables); but that it does not utilize a ubiquitous type of social punishment used only in human relations, that is, shaming, dispraise, or disapproval, that shapes attitudes and values as well as behavior.

It seems unlikely that even the most thoughtful and sympathetic white rat really cares whether the experimenter is happy with its performance or is ashamed if it makes an error.[8] Giving it an electric shock is not likely to cause it any pangs of conscience, or stimulate it to organize a revolution against that injustice. In and of itself, such a shock (as when electric wires are accidentally crossed) is not likely to elicit twinges of guilt from a human being, either. On the other hand, a profound difference in social structure differentiates the two types of animals: outside of laboratory experiments, one human being almost never punishes another, or even his or her pets, without also scolding or dispraising.

Besides adding the act of scolding to a physical punishment or a legal fine, people can use dispraise alone as a punishment, because from their infancy human beings are emotionally dependent on one another. Any disapproval is a "cost" to be borne, a punishment. Almost certainly, however, its impact on socialization is greater than any other kind of cost or punishment, especially if disesteem is expressed (as usually it is) as a withdrawal of affection, love, or warmth.

Approval and disapproval both contain messages, not only in the narrow sense that they are sometimes one side of a conversation, but in the broader sense of being signs, that is, others can "read" them as they can understand the meaning of a cat's purr. Thus, people learn to perceive unspoken disapproval, and to discriminate what is socially acceptable from what is not. An involuntarily raised eyebrow, a turning away of the body, the avoidance of a subject, a less than enthusiastic "hello"—all may tell another that his or her act is disapproved. Even a reassuring, warm "it doesn't matter" can convey the same message—that the performance was not good enough.

In addition to giving cognitive information about the state of another's opinions, both the anticipation and the perception of disapproval can control another's behavior before the action. Most people want approval or respect because it is pleasing in itself and because it is useful. Most wish to avoid disapproval because it is painful and it is costly. It reawakens or triggers all the childhood experiences (when dependency was so great) of

---

8. Again, however, see the work by R. Rosenthal, *Experimenter Effects in Behavioral Research*, pp. 158–179. Even without intending to do so, experimenters sometimes do convey messages about what they want, and subjects (animals or human beings) respond positively.

others' anger, rejection, deprivation, humiliation, or physical punishment. In general terms, it is a loss of prestige, and few people are so secure in their possession of others' respect that they do not mind that loss. Consequently, they do not merely note calmly that others express disapproval; they also react to this disesteem with both emotion and some alteration of behavior. Thus, dispraise not only affects discrimination and conformity; it also affects greatly the emotional responses we call shame, guilt, "conscience," attitudes, values, and norms.

TESTING THE INTERNALIZATION OF NORMS

Although dispraise seems to affect attitudes, values, and norms, testing that effect is difficult. Two of the major constituents of social learning or socialization, discrimination and behavior control, are better understood than the third, the internalization of norms: how the child (and to a lesser extent the adult) comes to believe in or accept as his or her own the norms or beliefs of those who socialize. We understand this much less than the other two for several reasons.

One is that although experimentation with animals can yield much information about the first two sets of processes, almost all analysts believe that animals do not internalize norms, do not come to "accept values," and do not experience pangs of conscience. Therefore such experiments do not focus on this part of socialization. Second, although experimentation with the first two processes of learning can also be carried out with human subjects, the process of internalizing norms is thought to be slow and not easily carried out in laboratory experiments. And by the time the human being is old enough to be experimented on, he or she has already internalized many norms. Third, meddling experimentally with the values and norms of young human beings is viewed as improper, by both their parents and by researchers, and therefore is not often tried.

A fourth reason why we understand the internalization of norms much less than the other two constituents of social learning is that, unfortunately, observation is not a good substitute for experimentation in the process of internalizing values because the time periods necessary for observation are so long that many other, often unknown, variables intervene to contaminate the results. Equally important, observation alone will not easily yield data about the dependent variable, that is, whether or not the person young or old has actually internalized the values or attitudes. An individual may be observed to conform even though he or she has not accepted the values of the socializers; and everyone at times fails to conform with values and norms he or she does accept.[9]

Because of these complexities, we cannot neatly test many of our

---

9. Interviewing can partially provide the data on internalization, but complex research designs are also needed on all the points noted in this section. For summaries of these studies see Frank Furstenberg, "Transmission of Attitudes in the Family" (Ph.D. diss., Columbia University, 1967).

hypotheses about the effects of dispraise either in the internalization of norms or in social control.

FORMS OF DISPRAISE

Keeping in mind the difficulty of testing precisely the socializing effects of dispraise, let us see what regularities we can observe in them, beginning with a consideration of the forms by which people express disapproval.

Like approval, disapproval is ubiquitous. The initial responses of low, high, or average respect for others' qualities and performances are inner feelings or articulated decisions. Eventually, however, both the judges and the judged come to have at least some guesses or knowledge about each other's rankings, for such evaluations are translated eventually into observable actions, even when the deprecated person does not learn why. He may be left out of conversations, receive fewer social invitations, lose customers, be passed over instead of promoted, and so on. Thereby people not only learn in general how well they are respected or disapproved, approved or disesteemed; they even come to learn with some accuracy who harbors which judgments (though with less accuracy about pejorative evaluations). Because of these reciprocal processes, by which both those who rank and those who are ranked come to learn about each other's evaluations, disapproval usually appears as the social phenomenon of *dispraise*, whether public or private. Much of our discussion focuses on overt disapproval, or dispraise, which we distinguish from inner or covert responses.

The acts or feelings, the qualities or performances, that cause overt disapproval also cause a break in the social routine, whether work, play, or informal social interaction. The normal expectation that things will continue to go well is violated.[10] To do very well is an occasion for congratulations, and to do reasonably well usually causes no comment; but to do poorly requires adjustment from others. They must shoulder a small or large burden they had not anticipated. They must step in to correct the error, to reorient the disrupted social situation, or to repair the social or physical damage.

The dispraise itself also causes a break in the smooth flow of interaction, for it diverts the attention of both parties (whether groups or individuals) from the goals and sequences that each had in mind. Indeed, it is partly for this reason (and not alone because the person disapproved may react

10. Several of Erving Goffman's analyses (e.g., *Asylums* [New York: Anchor, 1961], *Behavior in Public Places* [New York: Free Press, 1963], *Stigma* [Englewood Cliffs, N.J.: Prentice-Hall, 1963], *The Presentation of Self in Everyday Life* [New York: Doubleday, 1959]) have focused on the social maintenance and recovery activities by which a failure in the presentation of self is remedied. Much of what he reports can be fruitfully perceived as efforts to generate or recapture esteem, and to manage the interaction when disrupted by such actions as dispraise. Here I am extending one of Goffman's insights to the ranking of performance in any area of life.

with anger) that people often refrain from criticism even when their inner response is disapproval. Expressing dispraise requires, at a minimum, several additional phases of action (counter-argument, analysis, reconciliation, and so forth) before both can return to the previous flow of interaction.[11]

Both dispraise and the inner response of disapproval are observable in many forms, though these types are not clearly demarcated one from the other. Some obvious differences in forms of disapproving responses can be briefly noted:

Whether or not the gestures or actions of disapproval seem intended or planned;

whether the disapproval is observable only as gestures or facial signs, or is also expressed in words;

whether it is expressed (by gesture or words) to others, or only to the one who has fallen below the norm;

whether or not disapproval is expressed to those who have either the influence or authority to penalize the individual disapproved of;

whether it is expressed to others while the person is present, or while he or she is absent;

whether it is stated as a formal charge or charges, or only made in passing, obliquely, or in a semijoshing fashion;

whether it is accompanied by assurances of continued affection or respect, or accompanied by threats of future sanctions, or even by physical punishment.[12]

All of these and still other possible distinctions alter the social definition of the event and the psychological experience of disapproval as well. But the forms of dispraise often overlap (for example, *both* gesture and words), and we do not possess sufficient data to specify the conditions that will produce one form of response rather than another, or the consequences of each. However, we can at this point note that such differences exist and are worthy of study, and that together they make up the wide range of disapproval and dispraise from which everyone obtains cues as to how others evaluate his or her performance and qualities.

Such forms also constitute a range or repertory of choices open to anyone who feels the impulse to criticize another. For if we rank another's performance or qualities below an acceptable level, that is, if our response is a disapproving one, we face the problem of whether to do anything about it: whether as a group member or leader to propose ejecting or firing the person; whether to hide our feelings or let them show, or express overtly what we feel.

Usually, whatever we do, we respond with little thought about whether

---

11. Erving Goffman, "Fun in Games," in *Encounters* (Indianapolis: Bobbs-Merrill, 1961), pp. 17–81, and "Alienation from Interaction," in *Interaction Ritual* (New York: Anchor, 1967), pp. 113–136.

12. Note that each of these dichotomies applies to every dispraise interaction.

our response will be effective in changing the other's behavior. (Of course, we may decide to comment or not for other social reasons than control. For example, we may refrain from dispraise if we are in a crisis and wish to focus on the task, rather than on a criticism; or if we are afraid to let a superior know how we feel.)[13] Our spontaneous or unthinking response is likely nonetheless to be perceived by the other as a rebuke or punishment, and is part of the ongoing flow of rewards and punishments the person experiences each day, by which that person decides how to chart his or her behavior.

Similarly, even if our criticizing response was initially unplanned, usually we are immediately aware that we *have* criticized. From repeated experiences, we are also aware of the possible consequences of expressing our disapproval: that the other person may feel hurt, leave the group, retaliate, and so on. In short, all those in such interactions are conscious of the costs and rewards as they may follow from a given level of performance, the responses to it, and the counter-responses to those responses. Indeed, that knowledge is precisely what is required to be a genuine member of a group; and one can spot a stranger by his failures in those perceptions.[14]

Thus, everyone must choose more than once each day: whether to express one's disapproval; and how to respond to disapproval when it is directed against oneself. With reference to the former, the decision is that of weighing (consciously or not) the costs or advantages of expressing disapproval in some fashion. With reference to the latter, the question is whether to respond with a counter-attack, passive acceptance, or improvement in one's behavior.

Of course, costs are incurred if one praises, too, but they are not the same ones. Let us review both types of risks, that is, offering esteem or disesteem. Since the costs of paying respect are analyzed elsewhere in this study, we can note most of them briefly:

When one individual expresses to another his or her approval of that person, the one who approves will sometimes feel a cost or loss in self-esteem;

when one individual tells others about his or her respect for someone who is a competitor, he or she may be concerned that the others will decide that he or she should be ranked below the competitor;

to praise a superior may arouse in one's peers, and in that superior, the suspicion that one is trying to curry favor;

to praise a subordinate may cause him or her to expect a promotion or other reward, and his or her peers to be hurt or miffed;

13. We sometimes deliberately dispraise another as punishment for previous misdemeanors, because he "deserves it" and because it gives us pleasure, with little concern about whether his behavior will improve.

14. As Goffman has analyzed at length, the spy must master this knowledge, while counter-intelligence must devise subtle tests of whether a suspect possesses it. See Erving Goffman, *Strategic Interaction* (Philadelphia: University of Pennsylvania Press, 1969) and "On Face Work," in *Interaction Ritual*, pp. 5–45.

to praise anyone or anything risks making others doubt one's good taste or judgment.

Since we shall later discuss people's responses to disapproval more systematically, here we need only note the obvious, that others react to disapproval with hurt feelings, defensiveness, and counter-attack; that their friends may respond similarly; and that the work or social group may be disrupted as a consequence. Even when members of a work group rate others as falling below the average, only under special conditions will they approve firing the less competent.[15] *Few social norms oppose the expression of approval.* Far more oppose dispraise, that is, the expression of disapproval, especially in face-to-face encounters. We feel spontaneously and easily the psychological impulse to disapprove, but the social costs are likely to be great enough to curb the expression of that impulse.[16]

ELEMENTARY PROPOSITIONS ABOUT DISPRAISE

Given this general opposition to expressing disapproval, we now inquire about the factors that affect the likelihood that disapproval will be widely felt, that it will be openly expressed, that third parties will agree with that disapproval, and that it will be accompanied by other forms of punishment. We can begin by succinctly stating some simple propositions about disapproval.

First, the greater the *amount* the individual falls below the norm set by those in interaction with him or her, the greater the *frequency* of any performance below the norm, and the greater the supposed bad *effects* of the inadequate performance,

the higher the percentage of the group who will feel disapproval;

the greater the likelihood that someone will dispraise, that is, express disapproval overtly;

the greater the likelihood that others will approve the overt criticism;

the greater the chance that other sanctions or controls will be applied against the offender (firing or ejection, economic or physical punishment, and so on);

the greater the likelihood that the criticism will contain moral overtones or be expressed in moralistic rhetoric; and that the critic will display anger.

Second, the curve of disapproval, dispraise, anger, moralistic rhetoric, and likelihood of other controls will rise more sharply than the degree of deviance or failure to conform, perhaps because members suppose that the erring person does not even accept the rule.

However, third, the higher the social or occupational position of the offender, the less likely he or she will be overtly criticized.

---

15. William J. Goode, "The Protection of the Inept," *American Sociological Review*, 32 (February, 1967): 5–19.

16. Here a type of case noted earlier is omitted, in which a man and woman both use overt dispraise in a joshing fashion to convey their genuine attraction to one another, as when one says to the other, "I would never be interested in even having a cup of coffee with you," and the other responds, "Who says I'd ever ask?" but each understands the other's real meaning: approval and liking.

Fourth, the higher the rank of the person criticizing, the greater the likelihood that others as well as the person criticized will agree with the criticism. Let us now examine several regularities in the interaction of rank and dispraise.

Many social rules curb overt criticism of the offender because it is socially disruptive and because people do not like to receive criticism. However, the social rules also permit and even require some persons to criticize openly: those who have the larger hand in making the rules, who have the larger responsibility for the group effort. That is, the rules permit little public criticism of superiors, but permit and obligate superiors to dispraise subordinates as a group or individually, privately or publicly, indirectly or explicitly. Such superordinates may or may not enjoy high social rank, but they usually rank higher than those they criticize. These superiors include parents; teachers of all kinds; critics and consultants; straw bosses, foremen, and managers; policemen and guards; political or moral leaders; conquerors and colonial rulers. An examination of their social interaction with the people they seek to control reveals several important regularities.

The difference between the esteem or prestige due to a social *position*, office, rank, or status and the deference or respect due to an individual's *performance* in that position is of course well known and has been noted earlier.[17] Here, its relevance is that the person of higher rank is more likely to express *both* forms of disesteem downward,[18] that is, a lesser respect for those of lower rank generally and disesteem for anyone of lower rank whose performance is not up to par. Obviously, higher-ranking persons can do this with less chance of counter-attack than people of somewhat lower rank. Thus they are less restrained in expressing disapproval, though this privilege has been diminishing for generations.

Whether expressing disesteem for the performance of a person who is in a lower rank is only a social pattern or is also a norm is a complex question. People of higher rank are certainly more indignant when chided by those of lower rank than are those of lower rank when chided by higher-ranking people. However, the normative question is whether the values of third parties in higher or lower ranks are in accord with the responses of the participants.

It can be supposed that in both formal and informal settings third

---

17. However, I remind the reader that I do not reserve the term "prestige" for the former and "esteem" for the latter, as is common in lists of sociological definitions. I see no warrant for that in either the English language or the nature of the response.

18. It is possible, as Joel Telles argues, that this statement applies primarily to public criticism. It may be that at least as much disapproval upward is expressed by subordinates, but not where it can leak back to the superordinates being dispraised. Subordinates may feel more disapproval, because they are more likely to be affected adversely by what their superiors do.

It can also be argued that in absolute terms the downward criticism of subordinates as a class is greater than the criticism of particular individuals. But that qualification does not contradict the above, since it is criticism of their performances that is being discussed, e.g., how badly the switchboard operators are performing, how undisciplined the laboratory assistants are these days. It is not deprecation of their positions.

parties of higher rank would generally side with the person of higher rank to whom anyone of lower rank had expressed his or her disapproval, unless that disapproval was clearly justified. Third parties of lower rank would be much more divided in their commitment, but in most situations (unless the "fault" clearly lay on the side of the higher rank), at least a majority would still feel the lower-rank should not express his or her disapproval to the higher-rank individual, independently of how safe it would be to do so.

Put otherwise, and in a more complex fashion:

The higher the rank of one person relative to the other, the lower the relative justice must be on the side of the person of higher rank for third parties to concede generally the right of those at the higher level to scold openly.

The greater the justice that is perceived to be on his or her side, the lower can be the rank of a person who criticizes, relative to another, while still enjoying the support of third parties.

Both these relationships are intensified if the third parties are of higher rank. That is, third parties are more likely in general to side with the person of higher rank, and so the person of lower rank must be viewed as having more justice on his or her side in order to obtain the support of higher-ranking third parties when he or she dispraises openly a higher-ranking person.

Each of these three variables, then—the balance of perceived justice on one side or another; the relative rank of the two persons or groups; and the relative rank of third parties—will affect how much moral support one or the other side enjoys in such a conflict and therefore the likelihood that scolding or dispraise will be directed downward or upward. As is obvious, by and large the thrust of these variables is toward a higher likelihood that people in somewhat higher-class rank or power positions will openly scold or dispraise those in lower positions, rather than vice versa.

DISPRAISE FROM SUPERORDINATES

The extent to which the upper-rank person is permitted to show his deprecation of a lower-rank person, that is, to exhibit a lower respect for that *rank*, is a function of many more complex variables, and it differs greatly from one society to another. The trend in the past two hundred years in the Western world has been toward a diminution in general social approval of this kind of condescension, deprecation, or even dispraise.[19] Blacks no longer step off the sidewalk in the south to permit whites to pass. The modern taxi driver is not likely to express the same deference as a public coachman of the nineteenth century would have paid to an English gentleman. What would have been considered appropriate behav-

---

19. See Edward A. Shils, "Deference," in E. O. Laumann, P. M. Siegel, and R. W. Hodge, eds., *The Logic of Social Hierarchies* (Chicago: Markham, 1970), pp. 434–435, for a relevant comment on the less overt respect of lower ranks for the higher in modern times. I have of course commented on this before.

ior by a gentleman of the nineteenth century toward an honest workman would now be viewed by most people as rude and in any event unwise. The workman might simply walk off the job, complain to his union, or tell his friends not to come and repair the plumbing or electrical wiring. Complementary to this trend is a diminution of overt flattery or respect in salutations, endings of letters, and recommendations.

These changes in behavior express the alteration over time in the evaluations of each other by classes, subcastes, groups, or strata. Presumably they are caused by the increase or diminution of one or more groups' military or political power, economic resources, supply and demand for their social or economic output, education, and so on. The impact of such variables is slow, indirect, powerful, and obvious. For example, people within a given social stratum will be given more respect over time if they acquire the vote and thus come to affect the destinies of those who make the laws. If their total income as a class rises over time, so that sellers who treat them rudely will lose much business, they will also be treated with more respect. If they are protected by union rules about how they are to be treated on the job, employers will become more gracious toward them. If their education and style of life become more like that of the higher social ranks, so that deprecation seems less legitimate, they will demand and get more respect from others, and so on.

Perhaps these changes can be described as a decline in distinctive class boundaries, or an increase in the pervasiveness of status inconsistency in the society.[20] But it is not now possible to disentangle the impact on each causal variable separately. Rise in prestige ranking will augment both political power and economic rewards, and so on. Only a rash optimist would assert that mankind's cruelty to man has diminished over the past several centuries,[21] but the rights, respect, political influence, and range of economic options of the common man have all increased in most Western countries, and in most other countries at least over the past generation.

People's respect (or lack of it) for another social stratum shapes everyone's life chances substantially, and the competition among classes or occupational groups for esteem is a slow, pervasive, and powerful set of forces that may eventually alter the social structure of a country. Generally, however, this set of factors is not as salient in our experience of daily life as in our immediate perception of how other specific individuals are actually responding now. That larger set of interclass forces looms as less striking, since both ego and alter mainly take for granted their mutual

---

20. For a discussion of these arguments, see Robert Nisbet, "The Decline and Fall of Social Class," in Laumann, Siegel, and Hodge, *The Logic of Social Hierarchies*, pp. 570–574; as well as Donald J. Treiman, "Status Discrepancy and Prejudice," *American Journal of Sociology*, 71 (May, 1966): 651–664.

21. Fyodor Dostoevsky makes this comment in "Notes from the Underground," in *Three Short Novels*, trans. Constance Garnett, rev. and ed. Avrahm Yarmolinsky (New York: Anchor, 1960), pp. 198–201.

rank differences, and thus how much approval or respect each should give to the other. For the most part, we do not often consider in our daily lives the gradual or slow trends toward a greater or lesser respect being paid to our general social position, occupation, or class.[22] We are most aware of those larger forces when a person of higher or lower rank behaves toward us with much less or much more respect than we had anticipated.

In any event, the deprecation by one class of another, most often the deprecation of a lower class by a higher class, does not usually aim at improving the style of life or the behavior of the other.[23] That type of deprecation merely expresses a class judgment, or it articulates the basis on which the class judgment is made: For example, members of the upper class may disparage the lower classes as rough and uncouth, dirty, improvident, alcoholic, immoral, and so on, while many members of the lower classes return part of the compliment by affirming among themselves that people in the upper strata are drunkards and morally loose. Particular persons in one class or in a supervisory position may deprecate a particular *person* at another rank in order to make him improve, but general deprecation of a lower rank does not often aim much at that type of control. Rather, the aim is to reaffirm the right of the persons in the higher ranks to their various privileges. Such disapprobation or lack of respect (for example, prejudice toward ethnic groups) also confirms the values and style of life of the higher social rank.

Of course, since individuals bear the brunt of this disapprobation, some perceive a message in it and try to change in order to move upward. Reciprocally, in our generation some people in higher social ranks also try to ingratiate themselves with people in lower ranks by imitating some aspects of their clothing, style of life, and so forth. For the most part, however, class deprecation or rank deprecation is simply a group affirmation; it is a way of saying, "We are not like those other people; we are better."

We have been noting that far more open criticism is directed downward than upward in any hierarchy and have been asserting that this pattern has two powerful sets of supports: the influence or resources of those who have higher positions, and who can thus dispraise others with less danger of counterattack; and the normative support that third parties give to that

22. However, note that some analysts have examined this feeling of a subclass that it has lost prestige, in order to explain right-wing political leanings; see S. M. Lipset, *Revolution and Counterrevolution* (New York: Basic Books, 1968). These are, however, themes of daily conversation, e.g., the lesser respect of wives for their husbands, or of children for parents, since "the good old days" when what I have called the classical family of Western nostalgia is thought to have existed.

23. See, however, the acute analysis by Reinhard Bendix of the attempts by English entrepreneurs in the nineteenth century to persuade the working classes that they should ape their betters in order to rise in social position. They tried to supplant the doctrine promulgated by the gentry to the effect that the working class could never be like the gentry, being of an entirely different order of people; the entrepreneurs urged instead that they *could* rise as a class or as individuals through education, hard work, thrift, rational calculation, cleanliness, godliness, etc. (*Work and Authority in Industry* [New York: Harper and Row, 1963], pp. 99–116).

general pattern. In an organization or an informal social structure, a further set of factors is to be found in the general structural position of those in higher rank, that is, the extent to which people in a higher position are able to criticize others simply because they have a greater opportunity to see their errors.[24]

Both the physical and social structure of most groups and organizations make the acts and thus the errors of subordinates more visible than those of superordinates. Superordinates more often work behind doors. They can enter the work space or performance space of subordinates, but the latter must ask permission to enter the work space of superordinates. Superiors have the right to read the memoranda subordinates write and receive, but they keep to themselves the memoranda they send upward or receive from their superiors or subordinates. Teachers read the examinations of students, foremen look at the output of their workers, and overseers watch the performance of their slave or native laborers, but the latter do not usually have much opportunity of checking the efficiency or intelligence of the former. Again we must not forget certain special statuses that do enjoy such reciprocal advantages: the private secretary or executive secretary; the valet, and the houseslave. Superiors try to organize matters so that they can choose when to be "on stage," but their subordinates cannot.

This basic result of the structure of supervision gives the superordinate a real advantage in dispraising his or her subordinates. This ability to see errors proves the superordinate deserves the higher position. After all, he or she has not committed such errors; the subordinate has done so. Of course, the superior has not typically tried to carry out the same task, either, but in any event he or she did not fail at it. Usually, in addition, the superior does have more knowledge, which also helps him or her to remain superior. Having already won more than once, he or she has an additional prestige advantage that permits him or her to criticize or dispraise without much fear of a counter-attack. The structure of the lower-level task or performance also requires a smaller range of talents or achievements. The subordinate may be superior in some things, but that does not help; rather, he or she is to be judged only by those activities that

---

24. Although this assertion about structural differences is correct in general, those at a lower position do have some opportunity to observe some aspects of performance at higher levels; and those in high positions cannot, obviously, see everyone at lower levels. For example, workers on the assembly line can learn from the newspapers whether the company, under the president's direction, is earning profits, and they hear at least by gossip something of his performance on the job. Correspondingly, the president can wander at will through his plant, observing what he can, but the event is startling and not likely to yield much good observation. Nevertheless, in general, immediate superiors can more easily observe subordinates than vice versa, as detailed below. See, in this connection, Robert K. Merton, *Social Theory and Social Structure* (New York: Free Press, 1968), pp. 395–407.

Subordinates may try to hide by using several available social roles, as analyzed by R. S. Warner, D. T. Wellman, and L. J. Weitzman, "The Hero, the Sambo and the Operator," *Urban Life and Culture*, 2 (April, 1973): 53–84, precisely because it is they who are more easily observed and thus more likely to be punished.

are relevant to a particular task. As a consequence of these structural factors, the subordinate comes to feel inferior in various ways, but especially to feel vulnerable.

If we now examine several different types of social control relations in which this superordinate-subordinate pattern is observable, we shall uncover several additional regularities. All of them are continuing interactions and therefore exhibit a complex interweaving of many variables. We shall try to focus, however, mainly on why people who have the responsibility of controlling others use more or less disapproval or dispraise as a technique.

USE OF DISPRAISE IN TRAINING

We might suppose that denigration would be used when trainees are to be pushed toward the outer limits of human capability, as in the sciences, competitive sports, or the performing arts. The goad of possible humiliation would, it might be thought, spur those whose attention, energies, or achievements drop below the standard set. In advanced training in the sciences, however, this form of social control is much less common than in the arts and sports. Let us consider the differences that create this contrast in control patterns.

The content of a dispraising message is in part a cognitive mapping, and since in all three of these activities people believe that it is possible to measure performance objectively, correction could take the much less punitive form of simply telling the trainee that performance has fallen below the norm. However, dispraise has an additional message beyond that of stating a discrepancy between performance and standard. An equally important aim is to influence motivation. It accuses the person of failing to try hard enough to live up to the ideal set. It is experienced as a loss of esteem and, usually, of affection as well. It is an assertion that, at a minimum, one was not a true member of the group when one did poorly. At a maximum it is a threat that in the future one may be rejected or ejected. It therefore creates anxiety which can be reduced only by trying harder.

This experience is common in the performing arts—classical ballet dancing, instrumental and vocal music, and to a lesser extent acting, in which formal training is less common than in these other areas—and also in sports. The student is usually exposed to high drama and humiliation; criticism is frequent and severe. It is often accompanied by sarcasm and irony, though less often by true anger in spite of the tone. The performer in the arts and competitive sports usually internalizes this recurrent disapprobation and scolds himself or herself for the least falling away from an ideal performance.

However, the dispraise is usually interspersed with affection, and both coach and pupil know that ordinary standards are not being applied. For ordinary people could not even come close to meeting those standards.

By contrast, the trainee is, or could be, a higher order of being who should not be satisfied with less than a great performance. There is, then, a kind of perverse honor in being so criticized: the less competent are not so maltreated; instead, they are ignored.[25]

This use of often severe dispraise in sports and the performing arts, where standards are high and trainees carefully selected, calls into question a common hypothesis about the use of dispraise, as of force and force threat: namely, that such punishments are mainly used by institutions or organizations that must accept all who are sent to them. By contrast, the hypothesis asserts, highly selective organizations with much prestige to dispense need not use those techniques in their efforts at social control. Examples of the former would be the draft army, a prison, or children in a family. An example of the latter would be an elite private school: its pupils are presumably already highly motivated when they arrive.

But that formulation does not apply at all to the most selective military academies in the past, either here or abroad, or even to the elite English "public" schools. It does not hold for the traditional training program of the United States Marines (almost all volunteer, throughout its history). And, as we have indicated, it is not correct for the performing arts and competitive sports. All of these are both selective and punitive.

We need not assume that the traditions followed in one type of training are necessarily wise, though it can hardly be doubted that they rest upon some residues of experience, knowledge, and folk social theory. Certainly coaches believe their methods are efficient, but even relatively inefficient methods may work just the same, so that people do not test alternative ones. In any event, we can look at those social patterns in order to guess at the kind of psychological or motivational structure the human beings in charge are trying to create in their trainees or pupils.

On the other hand, in the equally selective training of young scientists, dispraise is far less common than in sports and the performing arts. Professors do not typically humiliate their students for an unimaginative experimental design, or scold them unmercifully when they fail to put in the appropriate twelve hours a day in the laboratory. What differences between these two kinds of training cause such differences in social control?

Perhaps the most striking differences between these two extremes is that dispraise is more common in training in which the body must be subdued. In competitive sports and the performing arts, control over the body (voice, fingers, hands, legs, toes) is a core problem, second only to the cognitive mastery of the form itself. We cannot now explore the

---

25. This point can be generalized. As Cynthia F. Epstein has noted, in professional training and work many women are given less praise for their excellent work, and less dispraise for poor work, than are men: It is a mark of not being taken seriously; see "Women Lawyers and Their Profession: Inconsistency of Social Controls and Their Consequences for Professional Performance," in Athena Theodore, ed., *The Professional Woman* (Cambridge, Mass.: Schenckman, 1971), pp. 669–684.

further implications of this striking fact; but it should be noted that in both military training and in the case of the novitiate in the ecclesiastical orders, where dispraise is also widespread, the body must also be subdued. In the military, motivation must exceed the rebellion of body, for the military person must act bravely, function effectively, and carry out orders in the face of exhaustion or death. Training for religious orders demands submission to ecclesiastical authority, denial of hunger, cold, and discomfort, and acceptance of a generally harsh spiritual and physical discipline. No such control of the body is demanded in training in science, though of course professors do try to convince their students that most of their waking hours should be spent in the laboratory or study.

Competitive sports and the performing arts differ fundamentally from the sciences in a further aspect of body control. It is only by driving one's body to its limits in the first two areas that one can even find out how talented one really is. The coach or teacher's aim is to goad the candidate to make that trial. Whether, as some experiments with pigeons would suggest, human beings can be as easily enticed with rewards as animals can to push their bodies to the limit, cannot be asserted with conviction. However, teachers in these areas have not believed so in the past. By contrast, professors in the sciences do not commonly believe that their students can ascertain the limits of their talents only by driving themselves to exhaustion for years on end.

Another difference between trainees in the performing arts and competitive sports and those in the sciences is that the former are more dependent on the coach than the latter and must tolerate dispraise, whether or not that is the most effective technique. It is widely believed in the performing arts that almost no one can realize the highest levels of his or her talent without the help of a coach. In singing, for example, it is taken for granted that the singer cannot even properly "hear" his or her own voice, and thus cannot learn to shape it correctly over time without a teacher. The success of Leopold Auer in training great violinists is legendary, as are the stories of talented young musicians plotting to obtain an audience with a great teacher in order to get the best training. Generally in competitive sports, too, it is believed that the talented individual is not likely to become a peak performer without training from a fine coach (running was once an exception, since some boys could and did become outstanding before any coach helped them). By contrast, even though great scientists have usually worked with science professors who have themselves contributed substantially to a given field, it is not generally believed that the talented young man or woman will fail if a fine teacher is not available.

The dependency is contrasted further in the extent to which the young scientists can publish the results of his or her research without the sponsorship of a professor, while few sports competitors or concert artists could simply present themselves to the public without some imprimatur from a teacher-coach. As in 1905, when the unknown Swiss Patent Office employee Einstein published his astounding three papers, so can an unknown physicist still get a good paper published.[26] By contrast, although it is possible, it is considered laughable for an unsponsored and untutored concert singer to hire a hall and make his or her New York debut.

Between sports and performing arts on the one hand and the sciences on the other, not only is there a difference in the dependence of the trainee on the coach, and thus in his or her being forced to tolerate dispraise; but also there is a difference in the dependence of the trainer on the performer's success. Specifically, how much loss does the coach incur if his or her charges do badly in public? The answer uncovers other interesting differences between activities in which more or less dispraise is used in training. To consider an extreme case, the athletic coach may well be fired if his charges do not do well. A poor concert debut may raise questions, aired in newspaper reviews the following day, about the competence of the music coach. Such teacher-coaches depend for their reputations on the success of their pupils. By contrast, the teacher-scientist gains most of his or her esteem from his or her own research.[27]

Perhaps a more crucial difference between athletic or artistic training and training in science seems at first trivial: The performing artist and the athlete must perform at a high level at a specific time and place, usually chosen by others. If he or she is not in top form on that day, the results may be lamentable. Even if the athlete wins because opponents do poorly too, the record will show the low achievement. Even if the performing artist is warmly applauded (almost all are), critics and peers will know when the performance has been poor. Performing well on other days is not enough. The only way to guarantee a consistently high achievement is to build a technical or artistic "floor," a level below which one is not likely to fall even on off days.

By contrast, the scientist who does badly on a given day is almost never giving a public performance. Poor work can be corrected in time, or discarded. Errors can be caught before outsiders see them. The published article in science is somewhat like the refined and polished recording in music. Many people have used their technical skills to erase poor phrasing, bad logic, incorrect calculations, or erroneous citations in that article. When the scientist is asked to present a paper or a colloquium at a specific occasion, of course, he or she may run the same risks as the concert artist or athlete. He or she may forget the line of logic, use muddled

26. See in this connection the work of Stephen Cole, "Professional Standing and the Reception of Scientific Discoveries," *American Journal of Sociology*, 76 (September, 1970): 286–306. Typically, papers in this and most other fields are judged after the authors' names have been removed.

27. Some of this research, of course, is done with advanced students. For an analysis of the problem of allocating esteem in these situations, see Harriet Zuckerman, "Nobel Laureates in Science: Patterns of Productivity, Collaboration, and Authorship," *American Sociological Review*, 32 (June, 1967): 391–403, and "Patterns of Name Ordering among Authors of Scientific Papers: A Study of Social Symbolism and Its Ambiguity," *American Journal of Sociology*, 74 (November, 1968): 276–291.

theoretical reasoning, exhibit errors in calculation, and be humiliated by critics in the audience.[28]

However, science training is not aimed at producing an excellent set of colloquium skills, but at producing a fine published paper. Training in the arts and sports attempts far more to motivate the performer to be at top form on any given day, which simply means so high a level of technical or artistic skill that even the "poor" performance will be relatively excellent. On a bad day, Rudolf Serkin is still likely to be perceived as a great pianist. On an especially muddled day in his laboratory, Linus Pauling's work is not likely to be seen by anyone at all.

The difference in the use of dispraise seems, then, to be founded on the danger that errors may not be detected and corrected before they have resulted in a catastrophe. The withdrawal of prestige, or disapproval, is a means of social control that creates anxiety about making errors, and it is more widespread in activities where the individual's errors cannot easily be stopped "in time," once he or she enters professional life. Two other contexts have already been noted in which this is true: military training and ecclesiastical training for religious orders.

To these examples we might speculate that law can be added. In law schools, the courts, and the Anglo parliaments and congresses, the aim is early prevention of error, not innovation or creation.[29] The law contains a broad range of behaviors and subsystems, all of which (with the possible exception of legislation) rest on the goal of avoiding the error of deviating from a body of statutory and customary law. Legislation is by definition innovative, but the social pattern of such assemblies in the English tradition (and most others as well) is a confrontation between and among political opponents, and thus it both permits and demands dispraise when errors occur.

In the court, both judges and lawyers lay great stress on avoiding error, dispraising any who commit blunders. In addition, however, the court is conducted under the theory that if two opposing sides are motivated by the threat of punishment (incarcerations and fines in criminal cases, financial losses in civil ones, loss of prestige for prosecutors and criminal or civil lawyers), then all the relevant facts will be uncovered, or *the errors exposed*, so that a correct decision will be made. It is essentially an adversary proceeding, permitting and requiring attack and thus dispraise of the opposition. As a cynical saying in the legal profession has it, "When you have no case at all, attack the other lawyer." Thus, in addition to the norm that legal tradition is to be followed and deviations from it punished by loss of prestige (and other resources), court behavior supports dispraise of opponents by each other.

28. So may the business executive who presents a report within the corporation. Both may then be criticized for "not doing their homework."

29. Both belief and practice may be partly based on folk myth: i.e., most issues are not settled by oral confrontation. Still, enough are to make a poor court presentation an unwise risk.

It is not surprising, then, that American law schools also use the technique of public disapproval, far more than any other academic training does.[30] The ill-prepared law student may well be tongue-lashed for his or her ineptitude, lack of scholarship, muddled logic, and general unfitness for the law. The aim is partly to prepare the student for future attack in law briefs and the courtroom; and in any event the emphasis, as in the performing arts, is on avoiding errors, that is, mastery of the tradition. The tradition must be so mastered that even at lower levels of performance the work will be well done, because the opposing lawyer will aim at exposing all errors.

BUREAUCRATIC CONTROL

We have been focusing to some extent on the training phase of several types of work because it is there that most of adult occupational socialization occurs, where the trainee learns and acquires the values and norms of professional behavior. Where the work emphasis is on avoiding deviation or error—physical, moral, spiritual—denigration is more likely to be used as a technique of teaching and social control.

However, most of occupational life does not fall into the two neat categories of error avoidance (for example, concert performances) and rewarding innovation (for example, artistic or scientific creation). Most of it in a modern society is bureaucratic.[31] Outside the research and development sections, innovation in most bureaucracies is little sought and generally resisted. The new employee receives considerable overt disapproval if he or she begins work by offering a plan for reorganizing the system. The recruit is taught the routines, rules, and traditions and is warned that deviations will be punished.

At the lowest levels of the bureaucracy, this means that both fellow employees and superordinates will scold the new employee for his errors. In the novice period, at most ranks, failure to observe the rules arouses

30. See Wagner P. Thielens, "The Socialization of Law Students" (Ph.D. diss., Columbia University, 1965), and contrast James D. Watson, *The Double Helix* (New York: Atheneum, 1968). See also *One-L*, by Scott Turow (New York: Putnam, 1977), a personal account of legal instruction at Harvard.

31. Most work even in the professions occurs within some kind of bureaucracy, and this holds for scientists as well, as I have noted in "The Theoretical Limits of Professionalization," in *Explorations in Social Theory* (New York: Oxford University Press, 1973), pp. 341–382. However, not all work in bureaucracies is "bureaucratic," and the system of control varies greatly from one type of organization to another. For example, physicians work within the bureaucracy of a hospital, but to a substantial extent they control it; see Mary Goss, "Influence and Authority in the Outpatient Clinic," *American Sociological Review*, 26 (February, 1961): 39–50, and Eliot Freidson, *Profession of Medicine* (New York: Dodd, Mead, 1970), esp. pp. 115–119. The most salient controls over the scientists' innovations and creation are collegial, not hierarchical; see E. Litwak and H. Meyer, "Administrative Styles and Community Linkages of Public Schools," in A. J. Reiss, Jr., ed., *Schools in a Changing Society* (New York: Free Press, 1965), pp. 53–73, and E. Litwak, "Models of Bureaucracy Which Permit Conflict," *American Journal of Sociology*, 67 (September, 1961): 177–184, and so on. Indeed, when error avoidance is most important, organizations or subsegments of it are most bureaucratic and also dispense less praise as a mode of control.

deprecation; later, the persistently deviant employee will be threatened with more severe punishment as well and may indeed be fired. Before or simultaneously with discharge, he or she will also be dispraised for ineffectiveness, because of the errors made.

But though such errant behavior arouses scolding—since most deviations ignore or deny a system that does, after all, work—in all bureaucracies it is nevertheless the successful innovator, that is, the deviant, who receives the highest praise: Patton and MacArthur in the military; St. Francis and Pope John XXIII among the religious; Knudson and Sloan in automobile manufacturing; Justice Taney and Oliver Wendell Holmes in the law.

Although I have been suggesting that the prevalence of dispraise or overt disapproval as a technique of training or social control is linked with the main type of goal a collectivity aims at, it must be reemphasized that I do not assume any harmony between the needs of an organization and its wise use of praise or dispraise. That a family system, organization, or society uses a certain mixture of praise and dispraise, reward and punishment, force and prestige does not at all prove that this is the most efficient way of controlling the people in it. Certainly many bureaucracies have performed poorly because they did not evoke or encourage worthwhile innovations. The United States railroads can be cited as a conspicuous example in recent corporate history, but alternative cases will doubtless come to the reader's mind—for example, most of the European monarchies just prior to World War I; the industrial system of Great Britain over the past two decades; and so on.[32]

It is not a paradox that in most bureaucracies one can almost guarantee a modest success by making no "errors," that is, by not deviating from the rules and thus avoiding disapproval, but that nevertheless the successful innovators gain the highest esteem. Some of the relationships that produce the greater esteem given to the successful innovators can be stated briefly:

1. Some bureaucrats rise high by creating effective innovations, but almost none rises from the bottom that way. Those few high ascenders who begin at the bottom usually rise the first few ranks by doing very well what the rules demand, that is, by avoiding errors.[33]

2. Making errors is never a profitable road to pursue, but with each upward step the bureaucrat is also given more subordinates to help him or her avoid errors, so that he or she can concentrate on solutions rather than routine responses.

32. And, of course, many inefficient units do not go under because they face little competition—e.g., for many decades, the U.S. railroads, and the southern slave plantations because the demand for cotton continued to rise.

33. Joel L. Telles notes that innovation at the bottom will not be listened to and may be seen as a threat. See also Peter Blau, in *Exchange and Social Power* (New York: Wiley, 1964), p. 43. In addition, people at the bottom are unlikely to think of improvements, because innovations usually require either knowledge of the system (most often acquired by working up through the system) or technical competence (also achieved while working up through the system). Those, of course, who enter the system with such competence and can thus easily think of new ways of doing things, generally do so far above the lower-status levels.

3. With each upward step, the bureaucratic employee is also given greater latitude for innovation, because:

The higher-level employee commands more of the resources that have to be invested in order to implement changes;

persons at higher levels command a larger "credit line," a longer period of suspended disbelief from others, before superiors decide that his or her new program will not work;

higher-level bureaucrats will have more immediate subordinates who feel that it is in their own interest to applaud their superior's good ideas;

the problems are more difficult at higher levels, that is, old routines do not work well, and their solution usually requires that some innovation be made;

the curve of prestige allotment rises with rank, so that a creative change will yield more esteem at higher than at lower levels of a bureaucracy.

If these relationships are correct, they conform reasonably well with our previous analysis, which proposes that dispraise is more likely to be used where the task emphasis is on the avoidance of error, while rewards are emphasized more for tasks or jobs that permit or encourage creativity and innovation.

DISPRAISE IN PRIMARY RELATIONSHIPS

Although subordinates often end the work day with anger in their hearts at their bosses (and reciprocally), fellow employees are much less prone to murder one another than are friends and kin. This is a fair index of the intense disapproval that is sometimes created in intimate relationships, for surely most homicides may be viewed minimally as an expression of strong disesteem, publicly expressed.[34]

As they are the main source of our pleasure, so do primary or intimate relations create much of our disappointment. Although such quasi-quantitative statements are not easily proved, it seems likely that most people experience more disapproval (and, of course, approval as well) in their kin and friend interactions than elsewhere. They do so because the discrepancy between what is wanted and even thought to be "right," and what the other actually does, is greater than in most areas of social relations. The discrepancy is greater, not because people are less conscientious there, but because the relationship is diffuse (that is, it includes so many aspects of life, therefore almost everything the other person does will be judged and thus the chance of some failure is maximized); and because we care so much, that is, a less than adequate performance hurts more, no one else can or does quite substitute, and we are emotionally dependent on the other.[35] The factors that make others in our kin and friend networks important to us and capable of giving us great pleasure are

34. For an analysis of the interaction that leads to homicide, see my "Violence Between Intimates," in *Explorations in Social Theory* (New York: Oxford University Press, 1973), pp. 145–197.
35. The "performance," it should be remembered, typically includes responses we literally cannot produce at will: i.e., the "correct" or "appropriate" feelings such as love, respect, etc.

also those that make them the source of possible dismay and hurt. Indeed, it has plausibly been argued that the fragility of the modern American marriage arises from our burdening it too much emotionally. We expect more from our spouses than they could possibly achieve.[36]

The amount of dispraise that is experienced in intimate relations is also great because the feeling of disapproval is so quickly expressed in overt dispraise (the line of communication is short). This is so for several reasons. First, the other individual is likely to be *there*, so that often we do not enjoy a time lag in which we can consider whether we ought to express overtly our disapproval. Second, unlike the work situation, and unlike many semipublic networks of acquaintances, in intimate relations it is much more difficult to complain to a third person, in the hope that he or she will pass on the message to the one we really wish would read it. In a bureaucracy a fellow employee can tell another individual about the faults of a third, with the notion that eventually this information will reach him or her, with or without the source attribution.[37] The closer and more intimate the personal relationship, however, the less it is likely that a third party can be used in this fashion. Many complaints of spouses about one another are defined as too intimate to be relayed to each other through a third person.

Another factor that increases dispraise in intimate relations is the lack of a formal hierarchy of authority. In bureaucratic settings this often reduces the face-to-face dispraise by subordinates of their superiors. Hierarchy sometimes reduces the amount of dispraise in the family. Children, of course, are intimidated somewhat by their parents' authority, at least until their teens. We are told that in the past (and it has remained true to some extent in our generation) the formal rank of elders was more explicit, as in Victorian England or in India or China; as a consequence younger people and women would have suppressed much of their felt disapproval of elders and men.

More important in the overt expression of disapproval in intimate relations is that even when we might wish to hide our disapproval in the interest of a higher harmony, we are much less able to do so than in other relations because the other person involved learns to "read" even our subtle gestures better than outsiders do. So much is this the case that sometimes we deliberately use a movement, gesture, or act that will communicate to the other person that we are trying to *hide* our disapproval, knowing full well that he or she will penetrate that attempt, and thus receive the message just the same; in turn, we claim the righteousness of having tried to avoid hurting the other person.

Moreover, in the interpersonal dynamics among intimates, showing that one is hurt, or that one feels righteous, is often seen as a counter-

36. I have discussed this in *Women in Divorce* (Glencoe, Ill.: Free Press, 1965), pp. 7–8.

37. See, for example, William A. Rushing, "Social Influence and the Social-Psychological Function of Deference: A Study of Psychiatric Nursing," *Social Forces*, 41 (December, 1962): 142–148.

attack, as an overt expression of anger. It is especially in intimate relations that the line between covert and overt disapproval is thin, and even the difference between disapproval and dislike is difficult to perceive. One person not only learns to translate the other's actions and gestures as expressions of hidden disapproval, he also learns to penetrate the overt expression of disesteem about one action and perceive that still another act is the real source of the annoyance; that is, what really generated the disesteem or disapproval is not being expressed in the oral argument.

But it is also especially in intimate relations that we are typically not simply trying to give our friends and kin a cognitive message, that is, that we would prefer they stop what they are doing or improve their behavior. Indeed, we want them to change their motivation, to recoil spontaneously from what they are now doing. We want in effect an inner and *willing* change. This aim is never far from the social control technique of denigration generally, but it is much less salient or even important in bureaucratic relations, where instead it is enough that our fellow workers act in correct ways, whether or not they feel the appropriate emotions, or even feel that the approved ways are excellent. (Of course, the motivational elements do rise in salience toward the upper levels of a bureaucracy.)

As a consequence, when we "correct" our kin and friends we do not easily and cooly inform them what it is they have done, and what it is we would like them to do or stop doing; we express considerable emotion in our protests. We withdraw some affection from them.[38] However, as emphasized all along, much of the deprecation that is expressed to others does not have a conscious, rational social control aim, even though it may have that effect. The individual protests because he or she feels righteous and punitive; the other person has been bad, and often bad to the one who is scolding. One protests or dispraises because one's self-esteem has been wounded. The other has not done his or her duty. He or she has not given what is owed. And the other could have done so if he or she had really wanted to do so.

This is especially observable in the relations of American parents with their children. Although many surveys report that most parents do not use physical force on their children, few observers would accept that description. Only few will be able to remember that their parents never pulled, jerked, pushed, or hit them.[39] The parental use of force is almost always accompanied by scolding and deprecation, and even when punishment does not escalate into the use of force, much of what parents say to their

---

38. A further complexity should be noted here. Although in intimate relations with kin or friends we do learn to "penetrate" or read their gestures or cues, we are often not sure whether we are perceiving disapproval or disaffection, disesteem or withdrawal of warmth. One may, to check one's guess, tell one's wife, for example, that she doesn't really disapprove what one has done or believe one has done a poor job, and that instead she is really angry or full of rancor about something else. Often this probe fails; and sometimes it is not a probe but an attempted diversion.

39. See in this connection my article "Force and Violence in the Family," *Journal of Marriage and Family Living*, 33 (November, 1971): 624–636.

children expresses their disapproval of what their children have done recently or in the past. The scolding expresses the justification for the use of force now or for any other kinds of threats in the future. Almost no reader will have observed parents who have uncompromisingly attempted to rear children only by giving them various kinds of rewards, without the punishment of face-to-face disapproval for their errors, failures, and general lack of consideration for others.

USING PRAISE
RATHER THAN DISPRAISE

It is especially in the interaction among intimates that social controls aim at preventing deviations from what is viewed as right or proper—what we have called "errors" in our analysis of occupational training—rather than supporting innovation or new social patterns. Consequently a bias may exist that favors the use of dispraise. This is so in the first instance because the received or traditional social patterns (moral, ethical, esthetic) are viewed as appropriate: very few "innovations" in these areas are considered acceptable. Thus, disapproval of nonconformity is more likely than praise for innovation.

There are several further reasons why praise is not widely used as a reinforcer in these situations. First, it may be difficult for people to think of an efficient operant schedule, or to exercise the care that applying it requires. Second, few of us are patient enough, as we are not with the pet dogs we try to train, to wait for our friends, lovers, or spouses to behave as we want, so that we can reward them with praise and thus elicit more of that behavior in the future.[40]

Next, social disapproval of one kind or another is used, and punishment generally, because it is difficult to think of an alternative reward schedule—for example, giving far more rewards for "being good"—that would tempt the misbehaving individual into goodness, without at the same time undermining the disapproving individual's self-esteem and sense of what is right by requiring him or her to forego demanding what is due and punishing what is "bad."

Socialization is directed toward making others love virtue and hate vice, and that effort in part succeeds over time. However, the pleasures of laziness, slovenliness (if others will clean up after us), gluttony, selfishness, sexual adventure, irresponsibility, and so on, constantly beckon us. These avenues of action or inaction are attractive, and thus they are quite different from the avenues of a maze that the psychologist, using electrical shock, tries to keep the white rat from entering. Fundamentally, one avenue in the maze is about as attractive as any other to the white rat, but this is not so for the activities that social punishment aims at preventing.

The wife nags, scolds, or deprecates her husband for slovenliness on

---

40. Both these comments were suggested by Joel Telles.

Sundays not only because she feels punitive, but because she has no alternative tool, and she recognizes at some level of consciousness that the slovenliness is pleasurable for the husband. She cannot use force or economic threat, and she cannot easily persuade him that to be neat is more pleasurable than lolling about unshaven in his tee shirt. If that were so, he would have chosen to be neat. She can only show by her dispraise that she has withdrawn esteem and some of her affection from him. Her effort is to show him that the cost of his pleasure comes high. The effort may not succeed; but few of us are so ingenious as to think of a reward schedule effective enough to tempt others from pursuing a course that they experience as satisfying, even if we are willing to spend all our energies and resources in controlling others by that means.

Even if the wife can perceive that her scolding technique does not change her husband's behavior, she is likely to feel that to work out a better reward schedule is to demean herself. After all, she is already giving him as much esteem as he deserves, or more; and he is paying insufficient respect to her by behaving as he does. She is likely to believe, correctly, that not to reward him for his slovenliness will not extinguish that behavior, although not rewarding a white rat may extinguish a pattern of entering into a particular avenue of a maze. In short, it is "unjust" to ask her to manipulate his behavior by giving him additional rewards for some alternative behavior, instead of punishing him by disapproval of his undesired behavior.

For most people the conscious choice, when indeed there is a conscious decision at all, as to which social control technique to use, is not just whether overt disapprobation will in fact have its desired effect and whether the cost of the dispraise will be too high, but also and perhaps primarily how much it costs the individual in self-esteem or sense of rightness to *forego* an act of punitiveness that he or she feels is appropriate.

Thus, we can say that cost-reward calculations are made, even if unconsciously, but they have a particular form that can easily be overlooked. That is, we can loosely say that we dispraise others when the costs are not too high. We also calculate, however, how much it costs an individual in self-esteem, frustration and so on if he or she does not punish the other person. Thus a cost-reward ratio must contain at least two kinds of costs: how much it costs an individual to punish, since the one being punished may counterattack; and how much it costs oneself not to punish. Both must be set against the possible conformity (behavioral and emotional) that might be forthcoming from the other person, who is after all independently calculating his or her own cost-reward ratio.

An additional element, again largely not conscious, is the *lower credibility* of an individual who foregoes disapproval. If one merely says calmly that it would be better if the other individual did so and so, or stopped doing so and so, the effect might conceivably be the same, but most people believe that it lacks impact and persuasiveness. The added element of expressing dispraise, disapprobation, or deprecation informs the other person that one means it seriously; just as violence, anger or the use of physical force do. Overt dispraise not only tells the other individual that one is angry now about the violation, but that very possibly there will be an escalation in the future if the bad behavior continues.

COMMUNITARIAN GROUPS

Expressions of disapproval are common among members of social groups: to define the limits of appropriate behavior; to affirm or proclaim their values and norms; to inform erring members indirectly or directly that a proper member does not engage in such deviations; or to distinguish one group from another. Even in groups or social systems where open dispraise is uncommon, such as the Zuñi of the southwestern United States, backbiting, gossip, and a flow of disapproval punish those who do not conform.

It is not possible now to state the main variables distinguishing social groups that permit much overt dispraise from others that do not, but one apparent difference is worth noting.

A first approximation appears to be the extent to which a specific social organization constitutes a real community, that is, one whose members feel they share a destiny, accept common values and norms, and are linked by many cross-ties of kinship, property ownership, and political influence. Then (as in kin or friend networks), each person may feel both the obligation and right to correct openly an erring fellow member.

On the other hand, differences of rank in villages or primitive societies inhibit the free expression of disapproval. Adults may scold children other than their own, but not other adults if they are higher in influence or rank.[41] Moreover, other norms may also restrict overt dispraise, for example, the New England village norm in the past and present that frowns on intruding upon "other people's business."

But overt dispraise is especially widespread in one type of community or social group, that is, successful communes and political or religious sects that set themselves ideologically against the dominant beliefs of the larger society or social system.[42] These have especially used the social control technique of public confession and dispraise within the closed group. Among them may be noted the Pilgrims, the Communist party, the Oneida Community, the Bruderhof, and the Moravians. Such communities emphasize, as the traditional sociological literature on sects has noted, a set of beliefs that each member must obey and must accept

41. See Benjamin Zablocki, *The Joyful Community* (Baltimore: Penguin, 1971), pp. 228–229, for a discussion of who can dispraise whom in the Bruderhof, where official norm affirms the duty of public criticism.

42. See Charles Nordhoff, *The Communistic Societies of the United States* (New York: Schocken, 1965); Gillian Lindt Gollin, *Moravians in Two Worlds* (New York: Columbia University Press, 1967); Kai T. Erikson, *Wayward Puritans* (New York: Wiley, 1966).

implicitly: a strict observance of rules, a willingness to reject or expel stubbornly deviant members, opposition to influences of the outside majority, a sharp separation of members from nonmembers, and a subordination of the individual to the needs of the group. Each member is responsible to and for every other member, and has the duty of reporting errant behavior to others. Meetings are held in which charges and confessions are made and punishments meted out. Although most people cannot tolerate this lack of privacy, high dedication, stern discipline, ideological purity, and yielding of self to the sect, many such groups have not only succeeded in maintaining themselves over generations but have also achieved considerable influence over much larger groups or social systems.[43]

Clearly, such communities lay great stress on disapproval because they aim at preventing errors or deviations, or even a slight falling away from virtue. They do not set up a system of rewards for innovation, since the rules are presumably laid down by higher spiritual authorities and by an accepted theology. All of them do, however, typically offer a high set of rewards for conformity. Most notable is the contentment that comes from knowing one's conduct is accepted by one's fellow members, and that this behavior is superior to that of outsiders. Since most have perhaps been religious in their orientation, a further powerful reward is also promised: the approval by the deity, now and after death.

RESPONSES TO DISPRAISE

We have continually noted how disapproval in its various forms, that is, the loss or threatened loss of prestige, increases the likelihood that those who encounter it or learn of it will conform more than they would otherwise. We have also pointed out all along the many complexities in determining the actual social control effects of disapproval, particularly on the internalization of norms. We often conform behaviorally when faced with criticism without at all altering our feelings or norms. Or, we may conform overtly because we know we would be emotionally upset by strong disapproval; but there are many situations in which that anticipated intensity of our emotional response does not lead to conformity at all, but instead to rebellion, withdrawal, or sabotage. In this section we shall sketch briefly the main responses to dispraise, without attempting to determine its effects on the individual's commitment to values or norms.

Earlier, we noted some of the social variables that increase the emotional impact of criticism, without attempting to formulate a rank ordering. Public scolding is generally experienced as more humiliating or emotionally hurtful than is criticism given to a person privately. At its

---

43. Zablocki, *The Joyful Community*, pp. 143–144 notes that one factor that makes this vulnerability tolerable is the deep conviction that members are superior to outsiders. For a discussion of the problem of bearing the criticism, see Takie Sugiuma Lebra, "Reciprocity-Based Moral Sanctions and Messianic Salvation," *American Anthropologist*, 71 (June, 1972): 391–407.

most extreme form, a public attack is most hurtful when the criticized person must listen to it, but the message is also directed to others present. On the other hand, precisely because this is so, few people ever muster sufficient indignation to carry it out, except perhaps within the family.

Rebukes that are expressed by gestures, intonation, or oblique verbal references, that is, face to face but not explicit, are generally experienced as less hurtful than disapproval one hears about indirectly (and which was therefore expressed to others). However, the reader will doubtless know of a common class of exceptions: Husbands and wives, parents and children, and siblings in conflict may use such obliquities as well-recognized "triggers" or "code gestures" referring to previous battles, so that a special laugh, intonation, or closing of a door may precipitate a rush of intense anger or hurt.

It also seems likely that the failure to praise in a situation that specifically calls for it, as when one has just given a public performance, creates less emotional impact than direct dispraise. Next, in a worker's adjustments to a new job, or a trainee's learning of a new skill, criticism or disapproval in the early phases is experienced as less hurtful than later— but the teacher-supervisor is also likely at the early stage to offer mostly simple correction ("no, it is done this way") but little dispraise. In general, at an early stage people expect some criticism because no one takes it for granted that he or she will do the job well at the very start.

Early or late, however, dispraise that accuses the other person of poor motivation, attitude, or dedication is more likely to arouse hurt or anger than is dispraise focused only on errors in technique. On the other hand, as noted earlier, few people are able to correct others without expressing disapproval, and readers will not be able to remember many situations in which they made errors under supervision without being dispraised.[44] People are especially hurt if accused of not trying hard when they feel they have been. They are also angry if their errors are held up for disapproval when they already know they have made them. However, that irritation may be less than when they believe they *are* doing well and then are criticized for a poor performance.

In any event, in the face of dispraise few people are simply able to shrug their shoulders and say, "that's the way it is," with little emotional feeling about the matter.[45] Without attempting a deep analysis of this set of emotions, it can be supposed that in most such situations the person dispraised usually recognizes (at least internally) the rough correctness of the facts adduced, but denies they are quite as described. In addition, he

44. The main variables that seem to increase the likelihood that a teacher or supervisor will, instead of scolding, simply inform the other what is wrong and how to correct it are these: 1. when the task is very difficult, so that the teacher does not expect the student or subordinate to become proficient quickly; 2. when the stakes are low or the loss is not great if there is failure (chopping firewood vs. piloting an airplane); 3. when the student is paying for the instruction (speedreading, psychiatric treatment).

45. It is easier to dismiss the criticism with less emotion if one believes the other is upset for some other reason, is being pressed by his or her boss to correct others more, etc.

or she is protesting the justice of the accusation. At a minimum, the person knows that someone else believes he or she has failed in some way.[46]

RULES OF DISPRAISE

People know what the "rules of dispraise" are, as they show by their anger when anyone violates them. Others are expected to know which kinds of disapproval are appropriate or inappropriate to express under what conditions. Thus, an employee may be indignant because his or her error that was criticized was not really important enough to justify public criticism from the boss. The rules of greeting, renewing an old acquaint-anceship, or simply returning home at the end of the day call for an unbroken sequence of interactions from the people involved. If either person (or, for that matter, another person) intrudes a criticism in the midst of this sequence, the other will feel hurt or angry.[47] One should wait for an appropriate occasion.

That is, people also dispraise others for violating the rules of dispraise out of ignorance or willfulness. Workers typically feel that if the boss criticizes them often, he is "picking on" them. The worker picked on knows there are many other workers; to be the butt of repeated dispraise therefore means the boss is being unfair, has singled out him or her as a scapegoat. In short, the violation is willful. This response to recurrent dispraise can be observed more widely: If one learns that someone has expressed disapproval in several contexts about one's behavior, one is likely to define the critic as an "enemy," rather than as a person who wants to see one's behavior improved.

The social rules, and the psychological mechanisms that parallel them and are perhaps created by them, also define as impermissible a logical alternative: punishment without dispraise. If the parent, bureaucratic superior, teacher, judge, or military officer were to hit, deprive, fine, sentence, fire, or otherwise punish another person without any comment, that person would be bewildered and, very likely, indignant. The dispraise contains a moral justification of the punishment while being a punishment itself. It is also, as noted earlier, a role obligation under appropriate circumstances.

EFFECTIVENESS OF DISAPPROVAL

But though high emotional impact and high control effect can be distinguished, the former may after all create a fear or anxiety about further denigration or disesteem and thus press toward the latter. People

---

46. André Modigliani, "Embarrassment and Embarrassability," *Sociometry*, 31 (September, 1968): 313–326, suggests that how embarrassed one feels is determined more by what one believes others believe about oneself than by what others *really* believe, or what one believes about oneself; thus, one is likely to feel emotionally upset even if one feels one is "right."

47. This is true as well in many other sequences, e.g., the beginnings of a sexual interaction between husband and wife or lovers. In this connection, see also Erving Goffman, "Fun in Games," in *Encounters* (Indianapolis: Bobbs-Merrill, 1961), pp. 17–81.

do prefer to receive praise rather than dispraise, if the cost of conformity is not great. On the other hand, as much research and observation have shown, a strong emotional impact may well alter behavior without moving it in the desired direction. Nevertheless, and in spite of the various complexities to be noted, the relationships sketched below can be stated briefly; for essentially they assert that when individuals or groups perceive that the prestige cost of failing to conform is more than the cost of conforming, they are likely to move toward conformity even if their attitudes do not change.

Several personality variables have been linked with the effectiveness of disapproval in altering behavior. In a common type of experiment, carried out hundreds of times over the past generation, social psychologists present people with ambiguous stimuli, or problems of maintaining their opinions or judgments without any external standards, and then subject them to social pressures aimed at altering their responses.[48] People who rank high on the personality variables of independence, autonomy, high need for achievement, self-confidence, self-esteem, and so on are less likely to conform when faced by differing opinions or dispraise than are individuals who rank low on such traits.[49]

Correspondingly, first-born individuals are more likely to yield than are later-borns.[50] This relationship is thought to be based on the link between the need for affiliation (stronger in first-borns) and yielding to criticism. In a parallel way, a substantial number of studies have shown that women are less able to tolerate social disapproval, and conform more than men when faced by it. Again, this is interpreted to mean that their personality patterns are less autonomous, and they have a greater need for affiliation than do men.[51] An individual ranking high on the authoritarianism scale is more likely to conform when faced by dispraise.[52]

On the other hand, individuals who have had some success in being right, in having their own judgments confirmed, or in exploring new ways of doing things and getting rewards from that, are less likely to

48. See, for example, the early classical experiments of S. E. Asch and Muzafer Sherif in S. E. Asch, "Studies in the Principles of Judgments and Attitudes," *Journal of Social Psychology*, 12 (November, 1940): 433–465, and "Studies of Independence and Conformity, I: A Minority of One against a Unanimous Majority," *Psychological Monographs*, 70, no. 9 (whole No. 416, 1956); and M. Sherif, "A Study of Some Social Factors in Perception," *Archives of Psychology* (New York, 1935), no. 187; and M. Sherif and O. J. Harvey, "A Study in Ego Functioning," *Sociometry*, 15 (August-November, 1952): 272–305. For a good conspectus of much of the literature in this area, see Richard Ofshe, ed., *Interpersonal Behavior in Small Groups* (Englewood Cliffs, N.J.: Prentice-Hall, 1973).

49. D. C. McClelland, J. W. Atkinson, R. A. Clark, E. L. Lowell, *The Achievement Motive* (New York: Appleton-Century-Crofts, 1953).

50. W. C. Carrigan and J. W. Julian, "Sex and Birth Order Differences in Conformity as a Function of Need Affiliation Arousal," *Journal of Personality and Social Psychology*, 3 (April, 1966): 479–483.

51. See in this connection the studies cited by Walter Nord in "Social Exchange Theory: An Integrative Approach to Social Conformity," *Psychological Bulletin*, 71 (March, 1969): 184, 199.

52. See the studies cited by Dorwin Cartwright, "Influence, Leadership, Control," in James G. March, *Handbook of Organizations* (Chicago: Rand McNally, 1965), p. 35.

conform under criticism. Similarly, if individuals have strong judgments about what is right or wrong, or about the best mode of carrying out a task, or about what they think they perceive, the personal cost of yielding is higher than for those without strong convictions, and the former are less likely than the latter to conform. If, however, the situation or stimulus is ambiguous, others' opinions or attitudes will weigh more heavily even on such opinionated individuals.[53] A major social result of dispraise is to dispel any such ambiguity, by announcing what the standards are.

Some persons are not so much insulated against dispraise by self-esteem as by an internal "bargain" or cost-accounting, by which they decide simply to pay the cost of some disapproval in exchange for not working very hard. After all, doing any task well requires some care and expenditure of energy. If the task is difficult, failure may be recurrent. But though recurrent criticism is likely to hurt, many individuals decide either to run that risk or, having no choice, to accept the cost because they cannot maintain a high level of dedication for long. Both bosses and parents sometimes create in others this kind of internal bargain with fate by setting standards so high that their employees or children must fail repeatedly and thus be criticized. Consequences for both sets of social relationships are often disastrous.[54]

A further psychological implication of this weighing of costs is that when the gap is great between a person's performance now and what the group desires, the positive influence of disapproval will grow less and less as the individual moves toward the approved level.[55] That is, the difficulty of conformity increases, and thereby the cost of being criticized drops relative to the cost of conformity, whether it is the difficulty of technical performance or living up to moral norm.

Such situations lay bare one of the ways in which conforming to avoid punishment may not be wholly rational. The common observation that intense scolding does not improve others' behavior (however satisfying it may be to the scolder) sometimes reveals good sense on the part of the nonconformist. Specifically, in the above situation where living up to group standards may be difficult, if one is dispraised much but the

53. Note that the situation or stimulus is not ambiguous when the individual's allegiance to a group with different values is strong; e.g., a member of a street gang or of a lesbian organization or a religious sect can simply reject as irrelevant the dispraise of nonmembers.

Utilizing alternative values that may justify one's action is a widespread group and individual neutralization technique. It is not confined to juvenile delinquents. See Gresham Sykes and David Matza, "Techniques of Neutralization: A Theory of Delinquency," *American Sociological Review*, 20 (December, 1957): 664–670.

54. In this connection, see the article by Day and Hamblin on two modes of supervision, in which the authors note that many of the workers whose foreman was punitive accepted the foreman's mode of dispraise without much emotion, simply because they had known of it in advance and viewed it as an expectable part of their daily routine. Robert C. Day and Robert Hamblin, "Some Effects of Close and Punitive Styles of Supervision," *American Journal of Sociology*, 69, no. 5 (March, 1964): 499–510.

55. The influence of disapproval also lessens as a person moves further *away* from approved behavior.

punishment is not escalated (there is no increase in firing, criticism, physical punishment, and so on) one is in a "no win" game, and it does not pay to invest much in trying to do so. One can concentrate on hiding, sabotage, or devious hostility, but improving one's performance may not reduce the dispraise enough to be worth the effort. Here of course the causal variable is not psychological, but sociostructural.

One of the more widely tested social relationships, drawn from both observation and experimentation, is that an individual will yield more when everyone in the group is set against his opinion, behavior, judgment, or attitude. This general relationship contains, however, several interesting complexities. One, noted early in the Asch experiments, is that if the lone innocent dissenter gains a supporter, as for example in judging the length of lines, others who before were yielding to the unanimous group will now see the lines "correctly," that is, they will begin to dissent, too. Some evidence suggests that the supporter need not even judge correctly in order to crack the majority; a nonveridical dissenting partner will have a similar impact, if the ambiguous stimulus is physical.[56] However, if the problem is one of social opinions, then the new supporter will not have the same impact if his or her dissent does not correspond closely to the "truth."

This relationship between the disapproval of a consensus group and the response of a lone dissenter may be viewed in a slightly different way by asking how many alternative modes of behavior are available to the person who faces criticism. In the relatively isolated primitive society, compared to urban civilizations, fewer behavior patterns were acceptable as alternatives to traditional modes. To this degree, the individual faced a kind of unanimity, so that even without much overt dispraise he or she was likely to conform. Phrased in sociostructural terms, an individual in a relatively isolated primitive society could count on fewer supporters and had no alternative group to join. In modern society, this can be translated into the observation that people will yield more to criticism if they do not have an alternative employment, another or better social circle to join, or a different friendship group that will offer as much praise or affection.[57] Similarly, if one's group is more desirable than any others, so that alternatives are costly, one is more likely to yield in the face of its dispraise.

Correspondingly, a number of experiments have corroborated common sense by showing that when an individual fears rejection, or has only a shaky hold on membership in a group, he or she is more likely to conform

---

56. Vernon L. Allen and John M. Levine, "Social Support, Dissent and Conformity," *Sociometry*, 31 (June, 1968): 138–149; see also Gary I. Schulman, "Asch Conformity Studies: Conformity to the Experimenter and/or to the Group," *Sociometry*, 30 (March, 1967): 26–40, who suggests that high-status persons conform less to a group, not because they resist the group more, but because they conform more (if unconsciously) to the experimenter.

57. See, for example, L. Festinger, S. Schachter, and K. Back, *Social Pressures in Informal Groups: A Study of a Housing Community* (New York: Harper, 1950), pp. 101–113, 151–177.

when faced by possible disapproval.[58] On the other hand, if the individual does not like his or her group, its dispraise is less likely to cause him or her to comply with its wishes. And intense dispraise typically generates hatred, willingness to leave the group, sabotage, or active dislike, thus insulating one against the group's control impact.

Clearly, disapproving an individual is especially likely to be effective in groups that are cohesive or integrated. However, the general pattern contains a further complexity worth mentioning. True enough, a member of a cohesive group who wishes to remain in it is more likely to yield to criticism than a member of a less cohesive group.[59] But though the cohesive work group will usually outproduce noncohesive ones, as many studies in industrial sociology have shown, it does so only when the members of the group are agreed among themselves on the value of high production. Thus, the cohesive group may dispraise the fellow worker who turns out low production if their norm is high production; or they may subvert the superior's orders and instead join him in regulating output at a lower level.[60]

Furthermore, the dispraise of a group engaged in any task is likely to have more influence on a member if social life outside that task is also shared. If activities are not compartmentalized, but are common, the individual is likely to feel that he or she will lose far more by resisting group criticism.[61]

People are also more likely to comply when faced with dispraise if their faults and errors are costly to others in the group (and of course others will press them harder); but they are much less likely to comply if they can define their faults and errors as merely individual idiosyncrasies, causing no harm to anyone.[62]

RESOURCES AND THE EFFECT OF DISPRAISE

I have left until last the social variables that most determine whether people conform in response to dispraise: whether the person or group that dispraises commands high resources in prestige, wealth, force or force threat, or even attractiveness. All of these variables merely determine

---

58. J. M. Jackson and H. D. Saltzstein, "The Effect of Person-Group Relationships on Conformity Processes," *Journal of Abnormal and Social Psychology*, 57 (July, 1958): 17–24, and J. E. Dittes and H. H. Kelley, "Effects of Different Conditions of Acceptance upon Conformity to Group Norms," *Journal of Abnormal and Social Psychology*, 53 (July, 1956): 100–107.

59. Dorwin Cartwright, "The Nature of Group Cohesiveness," in D. Cartwright and A. Zander, eds., *Group Dynamics* (New York: Harper and Row, 1968), pp. 91–109.

60. See an early analysis of this in W. J. Goode and Irving Fowler, "Incentive Factors in a Low Morale Plant," *Explorations in Social Theory*, pp. 319–329; repr. from *American Sociological Review*, 14 (1949): 618–624. Also see W. J. Goode and Nicholas Babchuk, "Work Incentives in a Self-Determined Group," *Explorations in Social Theory*, pp. 330–340; repr. from *American Sociological Review*, 16 (1951): 679–687.

61. For example, see Festinger, Schachter, and Back, *Social Pressures in Informal Groups*, pp. 101–113.

62. One version of this process is to be found among delinquent boys: see David Matza, *Delinquency and Drift* (New York: Wiley, 1964), esp. pp. 81–85.

whether the content of the dispraise contains an added message or threat, the possibility that the erring person or group will lose in affection, money, and so on. People who rank high in such resources can, in short, command a range of punishments, and their dispraise has greater impact.[63]

The supervisor's criticism hurts because of his or her expertise and general rank, but also because he or she may eventually fire the employee who does not conform to his or her requests. Since the expert enjoys prestige, not following his or her advice is thought to be foolish: people are more likely to fail if they do not follow his or her suggestions. Fellow workers are therefore likely to drop their social support of the member who rejects criticism of the expert. Peers will scold the person who resists the criticism of his or her boss; they will tell the person to "do what the boss says." Here, of course, the impact of such threats varies with the likelihood that they will in fact be carried out. As in all social situations, whether the failure to conform will be observed by others, that is, how visible it is, determines that likelihood in part, as does the extent to which people report to superordinates the deviations they observe.

On the other hand, dispraise is like other kinds of punishments in that severe use of it does not guarantee conformity. Over the past several hundred years in the West, the higher classes have increasingly moved toward less overt disrespect toward the lower classes. Employers have moved toward less dispraise, possibly because industrial psychologists and sociologists have told them to do so, but also because its frequent use creates a hostile labor force in the modern world. If the president of a large company expresses disapproval of a typist for her behavior, the typist may be frightened by the implicit threat, but his or her peers may also dispraise the president (though not directly) for inappropriate behavior. The middle-level manager who frequently harangues subordinates will lose the respect of both superiors and subordinates, except under special circumstances. Further, many people perform poorly under a disapproving eye, often focusing on the person who threatens rather than on the task itself.

Perhaps most important as a change over time is the growing awareness, in policy and theory, that heavy use of dispraise makes it necessary to invest more heavily in other resources (affection, money, and in some situations force), so that while the cost of being criticized is high for the subordinate, so may the cost of criticizing for the superordinate. Thus, when a person of higher rank in an organization expresses public, severe disapproval of an individual at a lower rank, the latter is likely to tolerate that punishment. However, if the superordinate expands that practice

---

63. Note that in *Shantung Compound*, Langdon Gilkey reports how the shaming or dispraise that thieves, malingerers, and loafers encountered did not move them at all: Not only was the compound not a cohesive unit, but the dispraise did not contain or embody further threats. The inhabitants would not create an effective force system, or even a system of economic losses or fines (New York: Harper and Row, 1966), pp. 118–119, 160 and passim).

into a general policy and scolds widely and severely, the organizational costs of the resulting hostility of subordinates will be high. Then, people still higher in the organization may decide that the superordinate's momentary pleasure in punishing others comes at too high a price.

Whether we refer to overt behavior or to attitudinal change, the evidence seems to be that, used as a widespread control device, mild dispraise is somewhat more effective than severe dispraise.

Phasing of dispraise also determines how effective it is. The person who has been criticized does typically feel some hurt or anger, but this is reduced when his or her standing is restored by a phase of approval. Correspondingly, if an individual receives some disapproval after some experiences of approval, he or she is likely to become somewhat more anxious about future performances, and to try harder. [64]

The process of conformity in response to dispraise or disapproval is even more complex than sketched here, but space does not permit so speculative a set of comments. Essentially, however, attention should be called to the fact that most conformity to dispraise is not to overt disesteem, that is, to the reality of it, but to the threat of it, that is, to the person's knowledge or anticipations about the possibility or likelihood of experiencing disesteem. For this reason, it is not sufficient to take note of the fact that people in higher rank, or with ample social resources, can protect themselves against dispraise, that is, they do not have to conform, and could resist dispraise. Of course the rich and powerful, like the beautiful, can afford to be rude and thick-skinned. Dispraise from the lower orders can be discounted or shrugged off.

Nevertheless, most people would prefer to avoid dispraise, even covert dispraise, even if it comes from subordinates. Proud barons have generally preferred to feel the approval, rather than the hidden disesteem, of their peasants or villeins. Indeed, it is not a paradox that rulers with great force at their command, both traditional despots and modern dictators, have tried to engineer overt applause and happy faces in their subjects: Though possessed of enough resources to resist disapproval, they have typically wanted to avoid it or, where possible, to generate approval or enthusiasm. Dictators especially seem to crave joyous enthusiasm, not mere obedience, from their subjects.

At higher social ranks the relation between dispraise and compliance becomes still more subtle and complex. In general, at higher ranks of bureaucracies or the professions as of informal social life, people are less likely to engage in overt dispraise of one another. On the other hand, because the standards of performance may be very high, some inner dispraise may be common. People are, I think, more likely to react to the possibility of disapproval, that is, to conform without any disesteem being actually expressed, at such levels. This is so even among peers, where

64. With reference to liking-attracting and phasing, see Kenneth J. Gergen, *The Psychology of Behavior Exchanges* (Reading, Mass.: Addison-Wesley, 1969).

resources are high for both attack and defense if that were the outcome. At such higher levels, whether the potential dispraise comes from a slightly higher- or a lower-ranking person, the impact may be great because of one's general prestige standing and expertise. For example, on a military command staff even a lowly colonel may be an expert and thus command not only prestige but the cognitive key to a military puzzle. In a corporate staff meeting, a higher-ranking person may "win" against another's disapproval but lose ultimately because he or she was simply wrong.

Indeed, much of committee work is likely to be viewed as temporizing, muddled, or indecisive, precisely because even the members who command higher prestige or general influence do take others' opinions into account; that is, they try to avoid the disapproval of lower-ranking members even though it may be covert. In addition, of course, at higher levels of both occupational and informal social life, the people in interaction are more likely to form a real group, and thus members are less willing to incur the disesteem of the others. Here, that is, though each individual can protect himself or herself substantially from attack, the disapproval of others at the same high level is viewed as costly just the same. We can also see once more the possibility, stated as a hypothesis in an earlier chapter, that at higher prestige levels the threat of prestige loss is greater than at lower levels.[65]

65. And, as the Watergate experience reminds us if Machiavelli and others had not, even powerful leaders can be brought low by subordinates, so that the prestige responses of the latter are too important to be ignored.

Chapter 13
The Problem of Justice

In this chapter, the charter of our inquiry will be broadened to analyze the problem of justice. In so doing we are not broadening the charter by much, for throughout this book we have taken note of people's moral indignation at unfair allocations of prestige, their attempts to get more than others think they deserve, and their resistance to unfair terms of exchange.

We shall broaden the inquiry somewhat more by considering allocations of other resources, such as wealth or political influence, not alone prestige. Or, more cautiously, while continuing to emphasize the justice or injustice of prestige distributions, we shall also take note of other distributions.

In thus confronting the problem of justice, we follow other social scientists who in recent years have increasingly paid attention to the problem, returning to a task that social science and philosophy had assumed throughout their history. That return to an ancient theme can be viewed as no more than a belated recognition of a deeper truth that our forerunners saw clearly: Almost any theory of society is likely to be a theory about justice as well, even if the analyst protests against that interpretation. Any substantial theory of society must explain social order and conflict. It does so through its explanations of social control, while these must focus implicitly or explicitly on whether members of a society believe its social arrangements are reasonably just. Such a focus is necessary, for that belief will affect somewhat the willingness to maintain the society, or to destroy it.

The earliest social analysts dealt with justice in part because they were moralists and did not typically make a sharp distinction between moral judgments and empirical observations. However, even as observers they could see the immense importance of people's ideas about justice as a basis for their actions. From the earliest traces of legend, poetry, religion, and law one can note that people have been preoccupied with the problem of justice. Homeric warriors were indignant that their exploits were not justly applauded and rewarded. Job complained of the afflictions visited upon him by the Lord because he could not see their fairness. Tyrants have chiseled in stone their claims to have meted out justice in their reigns, and have recorded the mountain of skulls they made by lopping off the heads of rebels who denied those claims too spiritedly.[1]

The religions of all major civilizations have proclaimed the ultimate justice of the cosmos, and thus have had to explain the embarrassing fact that evil befalls good people just the same. Often, they assert that a final judgment will redress all evil. Most Christian theologies maintain that evil people will eventually be punished, even if they appear to win now. Many Hindu theologies hold that each person's conduct of life determines whether a next reincarnation will be at a higher or lower level—and whether the soul will finally be able to escape the wheel of life altogether. Acting appropriately in the face of injustice will yield its later reward.

Nor has that concern diminished over time. From the personal to the international level, groups and individuals invest much energy in redressing what they view as injustices. People are passionate about the standards of justice, and no less passionate because others disagree. Fights among children are expressed in both violence and arguments about fairness. Adults divorce or kill their spouses because of resentment at felt injustices. Groups mount revolutions in defense of their ideas about justice. All of us focus much of our emotional attention on justice and injustice—whether the specific issue is God's creation of an imperfect world, or the obligation of one's son to clear the table after dinner.

So pervasive a human concern will, then, enter social theories in one form or another, even if the analyst wishes to avoid the problem of justice. But several recent changes in social science have increased the explicit attention paid to justice as a problem. Among these are the political attacks on mainstream sociology, the greater interest of social scientists in social conflict, and the reemergence of social exchange theory.[2] Let us consider each briefly.

The Durkheimian or Parsonian theoretical orientation that dominated mainstream sociology from World War I until the early 1960's focused explicitly on *social order*—why does social life not fall apart, but instead exhibit so much regularity?—but it contained an implicit solution to the problem of justice.[3] That orientation explained social order (as did many organicist theories of past centuries) mainly as the result of some degree of

---

1. And some chose instead to assert that they had redressed by their bounty the injustices of life, as did Mereri (2160–2130 B.C.) in Dynasty IX of Egypt, who had this message for us inscribed on his tomb: "I gave bread to the hungry and gave clothes to the naked. I rescued the weak from the strong."

2. I use the term mainstream sociologists rather than functionalists in accord with my analysis in "Functionalism—The Empty Castle," in *Explorations in Social Theory* (New York: Oxford University Press, 1973), chap. 3. What has been attacked as "functionalist doctrine" is a set of beliefs that no group of serious sociologists ever accepted; and in any event the notion that most members of a society view its social structure as legitimate and right is held by social analysts of many different orientations and should not be confused with functionalism. On the political issues, see also my "Place of Values in Social Analysis," *ibid.*, chap. 2.

3. See William J. Goode, "Norm Commitment and Conformity to Role-Status Obligations," *American Journal of Sociology*, 66, no. 3 (November, 1960): 246–258, and "A Theory of Role Strain," *American Sociological Review*, 25, no. 4 (August, 1960): 483–496.

consensus. That is, members of the society are socialized to believe that its social patterns, its religious and family values, its institutional arrangements are just, or generally good. Social institutions were not created by specific acts, but they do continue because they are willed; people approve them and support them.

If justice means that most members of the society approve of its social patterns, or accept them as legitimate, then mainstream sociologists were asserting (as a fact) that most people saw their society as just. This view doubtless contains some truth, and is generally correct for most primitive societies, with conspicuous exceptions here and there among societies ruled by the great tyrant kings of Africa.[4] It is very likely not correct, however, for almost all Latin American despotisms since the Iberian conquest of the New World, most reigns in Russia, the late phases of several Chinese dynasties, many reigns in the late Roman and Ottoman empires, the reign of Louis XVI, and so on. Western sociologists were writing primarily with data on liberal Western democracies and primitive societies in mind. Even in modern liberal democracies many specific subcategories of the population believe that at best they are victims of injustice in particular ways, and some of them protest about it. However, from a broader perspective of time and space, and even without a precise measure, it seems reasonable to assert that perhaps in most large societies much of the citizenry did not believe their rulers or their social system were just. Later in this chapter we shall again consider how widespread is the belief that injustice is common.

The strong attack in the 1960's on the political bias of mainstream sociologists was effective despite the fact that the leaders in mainstream sociology were already more liberal or left politically than most other sociologists, and as a group sociologists were more so than other academics or the population of the United States as a whole.[5] In addition, the specific research findings of sociology furnished the main empirical basis for the 1960's attacks on injustices in the American social system. In any event, these often bitter polemics argued that sociology had not been dealing adequately with the relations between social order and justice, or with how the existing social institutions create justice or injustice. As a consequence, in the succeeding decade more sociologists have paid theoretical attention to this problem.

Sociology has also begun to give more prominence to conflict in social life, as well as to the importance of force and force threat in maintaining order, a focus that the political left had always emphasized. Thus, factual

---

4. For a concrete analysis of that political pattern, see E. V. Walter, *Terror and Resistance: A Study of Political Violence* (New York: Oxford University Press, 1969), with case studies of some primitive African communities.

5. See Everett C. Ladd and S. M. Lipset, *Professors, Unions, and American Higher Education* (Berkeley, Calif.: Carnegie Commission on Higher Education, 1973). Also see Seymour M. Lipset, *The Divided Academy: Professors and Politics* (New York: Norton, 1976).

data on the extent of dissensus in the society, or the lack of agreement with many forms of social arrangements, as well as theoretical arguments that force and force threat are prime massive social forces, both pose the problem of justice as again worthy of serious inquiry.

A further factor that has pressed in the same direction is the development of exchange theory. Because in any voluntary exchange a primary issue is who gets the better of it, as exchange theory has developed the problem of equity has become prominent in its formulations. The oldest of frameworks for social analyses, as Homans remarked, exchange theory has always been inextricably bound up with justice. Durkheim pointed out long ago that the theory is embodied in even the most ancient of criminal codes, which viewed equal retribution as the proper payoff for crime (an eye for an eye, a tooth for a tooth). In its sophisticated development, which began when Adam Smith published *The Wealth of Nations* two centuries ago, exchange theory continued to encounter the problem of justice. In his work, Smith addressed what the untutored mind sees as a recurring problem in exchange: the possibility of not getting a fair bargain in daily economic (or other) transactions. If everyone seeks his or her private advantage in exchanges, the ordinary person might reason, then one person may take advantage of the other; and since no one is concerned about the public good, people may make satisfying bargains with one another that in turn hurt others. In short, rationally seeking one's advantage seems to permit or generate a good bit of injustice.

Smith's answer—and economists have generally followed his reasoning since then—was that people need not accept a poor bargain, for if it is really poor others will offer a better one. A corresponding statement frequent in elementary economics is that both sides gain in exchanges since each wants what the other has more than what he or she has. In answer to the larger question of justice if in fact there is no better bargain available, Smith said that individuals must offer what others want and must be efficient in competition with others. The greatest production for the benefit of the most will occur if people are permitted to seek their best advantage in an open market, for then they will try to produce what most want. Public needs will not suffer, if people want them to be filled, for enterprising individuals will produce for those needs and will be paid to do so. Governmental controls can be held to a minimum, to prevent theft or fraud. In most things, market controls will press everyone to fit action to others' demands as expressed in what they are willing to pay for.

Generation after generation of skeptical students has questioned this line of reasoning, since it seems to run against much observation and common sense. In part, the field of welfare economics was developed to confront some of these problems that mainstream economics had not analyzed adequately. In addition, political strife has often centered on whether those basic economic assertions are correct. It is at least clear that if action is not guided by collective goals, then justice cannot be taken for granted. If exchange is guided by the textbook rules of the market, each person need have little concern about whether the other is paying too much or receiving too little, or whether the benefit of the entire collectivity is being neglected.

Much of the analysis in the foregoing chapters shows that not all the injustices one might expect in social exchanges occur, because even though market patterns operate in social behavior, the rational self-seeking of the market does not fully control most social transactions. Individuals in work teams do not labor at maximum capacity because members reduce productivity to a tolerable average in order to maintain good relations with one another. Workers organize in order to create a labor monopoly that will oppose domination by employers, support one another's demands for respect, and keep individual competition within some bounds. Persons in social interaction do not always take advantage of others' weaker positions because they also want to be esteemed by friends, neighbors, or a wider public.[6] Third parties intervene to redress injustices now and again when a dominant individual seems blatantly unfair.

Even where the doctrines of unrestricted, individual exchanges and competition are most widely preached, that is, in the upper ranks of business, one finds the strongest pressures in favor of group (or monopolistic) adjustment, favors given for friendship, economic exchanges based on esteem, and economic sacrifices made for corporate goals.

However, this does not mean that justice is thereby achieved against the pressures of market economics. It is rather that market economic exchanges do in fact generate unacceptable social results, that society will not even achieve order if it is based only on such exchanges, and that much of social behavior (as we have argued throughout) rests on other bases. For all these reasons, then, the analysis of the problem of justice is a natural step to take in the unfolding of this exposition about prestige as a set of social control processes. Nevertheless, our aim is modest in the face of this great task, for at best only a few of its subquestions can be resolved here.

DISAGREEMENTS ABOUT JUSTICE

The problem of justice is simple, and it is insoluble. It is, as Plato stated it, the problem of who should get what. No answer, not even his—that individuals should receive according to their tasks or their contributions to society—has ever commanded general assent. People do not agree on the criteria by which justice should be measured. Nor do they agree on how those standards are to be applied to this or that specific situation. One person or group may view as just what another considers obviously unjust. Individuals and groups may agree on one standard for themselves but a different one for others; for example, that they should be

6. This general point is widely made by sociologists. Peter Blau uses it as an important element in his analysis of justice; see *Exchange and Power in Social Life* (New York: Wiley, 1964), pp. 157–158.

rewarded for seniority but that others should demonstrate merit in order to win a promotion. And every person and every group believes in diverse, even contrary, standards (merit *and* family influence; quantity *and* quality; seniority *and* productivity) at different times and in different situations. Indeed, in many judgments about justice, people assert one principle (merit, honesty) because it is socially acceptable, when they are really moved by very different principles (ethnic membership, liking). Although they often do not know they have been doing this, they frequently suspect others of doing so.

In view of these difficulties, it seems unlikely that anyone can arrive at a solution acceptable to most people. Modern analysts have offered new solutions and revived some of those Aristotle suggested without convincing more than a small number of readers. Most philosophers and social scientists have actually contributed to these difficulties by supposing that their own values about ideal justice are the values most other people would really accept, if they understood things better.[7]

These difficulties have not persuaded people to accept general disagreement as normal, and to give up trying to work out a satisfactory definition of justice. Is it possible that scientific knowledge can be of use even in a question whose answer seems mainly to be determined by ideology, ethics, or religion, that is, by value judgments that are inherently unprovable?

"CORRECT" STANDARDS FOR JUSTICE

During the past decade the charge has often been directed against mainstream sociology (as against the other social sciences) that it has hidden behind a false doctrine in the midst of political conflict—that, unwilling to take dangerous political positions, it has proclaimed the doctrine of value neutrality (that sociology should be value-free) and asserted that science cannot prove the truth of any political belief, or any norm or value whatsoever. In fact, sociologists have never made the former claim, that sociology could be value-free. After all, science is social activity, and is constantly shaped by values. Nor did Max Weber make that claim. However, most sociologists have asserted and continue to assert that sociological research cannot demonstrate the truth of a value judgment. Cautiously put, most social scientists agree that a value assertion does not add any empirical truth-value to any factual description, and that facts cannot prove any value judgment.[8]

7. See John Rawls, *A Theory of Justice* (Cambridge: Harvard University Press, 1971). For further comment on these difficulties, see James S. Coleman, "Inequality, Sociology, and Moral Philosophy," *American Journal of Sociology*, 80 (November, 1974): 745–747. Whether Rawls' principles are ideal standards or whether rational people would choose them is also discussed by Raymond Boudon in his review, "Rawls: *A Theory of Justice*," *Contemporary Sociology*, 5 (March, 1976): 102–109.

8. For further discussion of this seeming paradox, that radical critics have attacked mainstream sociologists for opinions they have not held, while mainstream sociologists have supposed erroneously that their radical critics have believed science can "prove" politically left-wing values, see William J. Goode, "The Place of Values in Social Analysis," in *Explorations in Social Theory*, chap. 2.

So it is with justice. Any "solution" to the problem of justice will be a value assertion. It may be more or less persuasive, but no scientific methodology exists to prove its correctness.

However, as with any value assertion, social science can help in coming to some solutions concerning justice. First, it can gather data on what people prefer, admire, or value. If we believe it is *just* that people have what they want, these facts will guide us in helping others. Similarly, if we can find out which kinds of social arrangements people actually believe are *unjust*, we can work with them to reduce that injustice. Social science can also find out some additional facts that are relevant for handing out justice, if we can once agree on a standard. Thus, if we believe it is just to give equal training to people of equal abilities (our standard), it can obtain measurements of ability, which then forbid us to allocate training on some other basis, such as class, caste, race, or religion.

Furthermore, it can examine various kinds of existing social arrangements and describe their real consequences. Then people can decide, on the basis of their own standards for justice, whether they approve those results. Some of these principles or descriptions are obvious and some less so. Even a casual observer can now see that in the modern world the social structure of South Africa is likely to generate increasing strife, because a majority of its citizenry view it as basically unjust. Somewhat less obvious is the hypothesis that the greater the number of ranks in an organization, the lower the morale of the lower-ranking people; or that there is a correlation between rank and the degree to which people believe the system is just, so that those toward the lower ranks are less likely than others to grant that the system is fair.[9] Besides analyzing the consequences of existing social arrangements and then evaluating them by our own standards of justice, of course, we can analyze hypothetical social structures with the same goal in mind, as Coleman and Boudon do when they analyze Rawls' proposed system of reward allocation.[10]

Finally, but more speculatively, we can ask whether certain kinds of social actions or structures are even possible, that is, whether such a society can exist or continue to exist and whether an existing system can be changed in a desirable direction without great force—and with what consequences. Most social analysts would, for example, assert that it is not possible in a modern society to allocate rewards on a completely egalitarian basis, that is, an egalitarian industrial society is not possible. With reference to the second form of question, it now appears to be politically possible (as it was not two decades ago) to put into effect some kind of guaranteed annual wage in the United States as one step toward a more

9. Amitai Etzioni and Eva Etzioni, eds., *Social Change* (New York: Basic Books, 1964), pp. 75–76. On the other hand, Joseph Lopreato reports that in one northern Italian city where left-wing attacks on managers are common, alienation is common at all ranks; see *Peasants No More: Social Class and Social Change in an Underdeveloped Society* (San Francisco: Chandler, 1967).

10. Coleman, "Inequality, Sociology and Moral Philosophy," pp. 746ff.; and Boudon, "Rawls: A Theory of Justice," pp. 104–107.

equal income distribution, and social scientists have been attempting by actual experiment to find out what the consequences of such a plan might be.[11]

None of these empirical and theoretical aids to clarification, of course, resolves the ancient question of what justice "really" is, for that question is beyond the capacity of any scientific analysis. On the other hand, to the extent that deciding what is a just course of action can be based on hard facts or good theory, they can be useful.

JUSTICE AS RHETORIC

Many analysts continue to claim that the question of justice is a false one because the concept is derivative, epiphenomenal, a mere rhetorical device. The idea of justice, it is held, has no independent existence. This assertion is not only made by Marxist thinkers, who argue that a dominant class simply creates an ideology to justify its privileges, by principles that only seemingly apply to everyone. In one form or another, this hypothesis is also entertained at times by almost all social critics, since one can frequently observe people claiming justice while they are exploiting others.

One can argue that the idea of justice is epiphenomenal in another, related sense: It does not help us to predict others' behavior. That is, it can be asserted that people's behavior is shaped by the reality and expectations of rewards and punishments, and the idea of justice may be seen as no more than a rhetorical device by which they express disapproval or approval of what they get; or by which they hope to enlist the support of others. They are angry if they lose out, as they are pleased if they win, but applying the label of justice to either event adds little to our knowledge of how they will act.

Some of our observations support these claims; but some do not. When people get less than they feel they deserve, they seem more indignant than when they get more; but numerous experiments show that they may in fact be troubled as well about getting too much. In many situations, they take steps to restore equity even if that requires them to give up some gains. People fight for claims that others view as excessive, but daily observation as well as history presents many cases of their fighting for the justice of *others'* claims. They even give their lives to free others from unjust exploitation, slavery, or serfdom. People defend their own interests with the rhetoric of justice, but they also turn it at times against themselves in guilt at their own violations of fairness. Indeed, if people were motivated only by profit and not also by more complex factors such as standards of fairness, human behavior would be relatively easy to predict.

Perhaps equally important as evidence for the idea of justice having real effects is that conquerors or leaders are never content with mere exploita-

11. See Peter H. Rossi and K. C. Lyall, *Reforming Public Welfare: A Critique of the Negative Income Tax Experiment* (New York: Russell Sage Foundation, 1976).

tion or the imposition of injustice based on the force threat at their command. Evidently they believe that the idea of justice has an impact on social control, for they try to persuade their subjects or fellow citizens that they deserve their high rewards. Presumably they do so because success in this persuasion increases their self-esteem and prestige and over the long run lowers the costs of rulership. Or: A citizenry that believes the ruler is just is also less prone to revolt.

None of the above observations is, however, a full answer to the question of how hollow or epiphenomenal justice is. From our difficulty in resolving the issue, we might infer that the question itself has not been formulated correctly. Nor can we merely ask what specific percentage of the time people will sacrifice a certain amount in the interest of justice. As so often in social analysis, we must begin to inquire under what conditions some principle of justice is followed, rather than the principle of pure self-interest. That inquiry must also begin to ask under what conditions individuals or groups think the idea of justice is even relevant as a basis for a decision or action. That is, what is the social definition of a "justice situation"?

Such formulations bypass the question of whether the talk of justice is only rhetorical and do not attempt to answer the question of what justice should really be. Instead they ask what kinds of exchanges people consider just in the real world. Several such inquiries into what people view as just have been attempted, and we shall comment on them in succeeding sections.[12]

JUSTICE AND UNEQUAL CONTRIBUTIONS

In asking about the social conditions in which people make different kinds of decisions about justice, we are emphasizing that justice decisions are "public," in that always some other people are concerned, other than the minimum two persons who engage in any social transactions. Social exchange theory has (in the version developed in this study) suggested at least some partial answers to the question of how interpersonal fairness can ever be achieved, or the common good served, if social transactions are based only on rational self-seeking—that is, third parties do intervene; people seek love and respect from others and not only material gain; people lose their political influence and their ability to threaten others when they are respected less; and so on. Consequently, it is important to know what people consider just or unjust, even while we understand that such facts are difficult to obtain or interpret.

Certainly such an inquiry does not presuppose that there is one main principle that all or even most members of a society will accept. Indeed, we already know, from observation as well as research data, that several contradictory principles coexist. Nor does this question even assume there

12. A recent inquiry is that of Guillermina Jasso and Peter H. Rossi, "Distributive Justice and Earned Income," *American Sociological Review*, 42 (August, 1977): 639–651.

is general agreement on a few important principles of justice, although sociological theory asserts that this is so because it seems unlikely that a social system can function adequately if there is widespread disagreement on values. We do know that in large-scale societies with fully developed class systems, for any one such principle there will be a distribution of opinion. That is, opinion will range from strong agreement to strong disagreement. We also take for granted that people's behavior will correspond only in part with their sincere beliefs about what a just action would be. After all, doing good to others costs something, and the cost may be greater than the gain in esteem from self or others. Here as in other areas of behavior, belief and action are correlated, but we cannot expect that correlation to be very high except under special circumstances.

The principle widely proclaimed as the most general rule that people either believe in or follow is called by Homans the Principle of Distributive Justice. Homans reminds us that it was also enunciated by Aristotle (it was stated earlier by his mentor Plato, somewhat more loosely) and called "equity" by many social psychologists, who have carried out hundreds of experiments in order to find out the various ways it is expressed.[13] This principle states essentially that persons who are equal in important ways should receive equally. Or, more specifically, those whose costs, investments, or contributions are the same should be rewarded equally— and if the contributions are not the same, then rewards should be proportionately *unequal*.[14] Slightly different versions of this relationship have been presented, but all essentially contain a ratio between some qualities or performances of one individual, and his or her rewards, compared with those of another person or class of persons.[15]

Homans believes that some version of this rule "is either explicitly stated or stands as an implicit major premise in the arguments and behavior of many men in many, and probably all, human societies."[16] It "represents what many men in fact find fair." That many social psychologists

---

13. See George C. Homans, *Social Behavior: Its Elementary Forms*, 2d ed. (New York: Harcourt, Brace, Jovanovich, 1974), chap. 11; and Leonard Berkowitz and Elaine Walster, eds., *Advances in Experimental Social Psychology: Equity Theory: Toward a General Theory of Social Interaction*, vol. 9 (New York: Academic, 1976). John W. Thibaut and Harold H. Kelley use the notion of "comparison level" to interpret very similar observations in *The Social Psychology of Groups* (New York: Wiley, 1959), esp. chap. 6. Aristotle's statements are to be found in his *Nichomachean Ethics*, bk. V, chap. 4, and *Politics*, bk. V. Also see Peter H. Rossi *et al.*, "Measuring Household Social Standing," *Social Science Research*, 3, no. 3 (September, 1974): 169–190, and Peter H. Rossi and William A. Sampson, "Race and Family Social Standing," *American Sociological Review*, 40, no. 2 (April, 1975): 201–214.

14. Homans, *Social Behavior*, pp. 247–248, 250.

15. J. Stacy Adams, "Inequity in Social Exchange," in Leonard Berkowitz, ed., *Advances in Experimental Social Psychology*, vol. II (New York: Academic, 1965), pp. 267–299; Elaine Walster, E. Berscheid, and G. W. Walster, "The Exploited: Justice or Justification," in J. Macaulay and L. Berkowitz, eds., *Altruism and Helping Behavior* (New York: Academic, 1970), pp. 179–204; and Peter Blau, *Exchange and Power in Social Life*, pp. 151–160 and passim. In a more recent formula, Walster, Berscheid, and Walster have emended the Adams ratio by specifying whether the inputs are negative or positive, and by including the costs the individual incurs, in "New Directions in Equity Research," in Berkowitz and Walster, eds., *Equity Theory*, pp. 2–4.

16. Homans, *Social Behavior*, p. 240.

call this "equity" in their research suggests some agreement with Homans, and of course with Aristotle and Plato. Moreover, it is likely that the reader, like most heirs of the Western cultural tradition, will feel that somehow the rule does sound fair. Even if we make exceptions to the principle, we are likely to agree that it is a kind of ideal, to be followed under some circumstances. Because the rule seems as applicable to the problem of justice in allocating prestige as in allocating any other benefit, it seems worthwhile to examine it more closely.

As an empirical description of what people actually find just, this rule is extraordinarily weak, in spite of its distinguished history. Its loose quality is also evidenced by its focus on equality, when it is mostly used to justify *unequal* rewards.

Some part of its persuasiveness, like so much of folk knowledge, arises from the fact that it teeters on the edge of tautology. In its most precise form, it is a comically perverse rule of logic: People who are the same in all ways should be the same in all ways; if they get different rewards or punishments, then they would not be the same. As soon as the case moves from that perfect equality, however, people fall to bickering among themselves as to whether the ways any individuals are the same are really the ones that should be counted. Throughout human history, societies have seized on differences both large and small as the crucial ones that determine large differences in rewards or punishments. Sons may be alike as sons, but in many social systems it has seemed obviously just that eldest sons should be given the family property and title; in polygynous marriage systems, first wives were thought to deserve particular honor and influence.

More precisely put: We can list dozens of ways in which two individuals are the "same," but other groups and individuals may view all of these as irrelevant; instead, they seize on one of the ways in which they differ, as being crucial and overdetermining. Brilliant women have achieved far more than most men without being honored commensurately; and so for many other categories of human beings: blacks, slaves, colonials, subordinate employees, outsiders, the poor, and so on. If we qualify the principle of distributive justice to account for this range of behavior, asserting that people should be rewarded equally for qualities or performances that the group views as appropriate for rewards or punishments, we disclose the tautology: People should be rewarded equally if they are thought to be equal in the qualities or performances that should be rewarded equally when they are equal.

Precisely because it is both persuasive (as a tautology is likely to be) and difficult to apply, however, it can be used effectively in making demands. Over the past several hundred years in Western societies, it has been used especially by the disadvantaged in claiming more equality: Children of high talent, though poor, should be given more opportunities; since aristocrats are not different in any other way than in ownership of property, they should not have more political rights than other people; since all persons are inherently equal in civic rights, European empires should not rule over any colonies. However, in times past it seemed equally self-evident to aristocrats that in crucial ways they were superior to others and should be given more honor and material rewards, though in Christian theology their souls had no special superiority. The rule has been used to support conflicting claims and usually, despite its focus on equality, to justify unequal rewards.

The universality of the rule cannot be saved by arguing that, although people generally accept the principle of equity, they do not always agree on how investments, costs, or contributions should be evaluated. If there were very little agreement in judgments about justice, people would not be able to invoke the rule with any effect; they could not use it in settling disputes; and they could not concur on who deserves more. In fact, people do agree a great deal within the specific context of the group itself, where the rule has a concrete meaning defined by the group's evaluations or norms. Therefore, if we try to reformulate the rule with precision, it is likely to be stated thus: If a group views a particular set of traits or performances as the one by which rewards are to be allocated, while others are to be mostly irrelevant, then people who are about equal in that set should be given about equal rewards.

Similarly, most of the modern attempts to formulate that rule assert that if the costs, investments, or performances are unequal, then the rewards should be, too. This is a rule of proportionality that will be considered further in a subsequent section. In order to work out a more accurate formulation of what the rule means, it is first necessary to map variations in standards or norms in order to uncover the general patterns that shape them. At some point, such an analysis will lead to the difficult question, Why do different kinds of groups, communities, or societies believe in those *particular norms* or evaluations which they consider most relevant for their decisions about justice?

COSTS AND INVESTMENTS

Many analysts of justice have introduced costs or investments into their formulations. We must therefore consider them as part of the rule of distributive justice as we ask what people really consider just or unjust in the allocation of prestige or other rewards.[17]

In an earlier chapter, we noted the central facts about costs and investments in both market and prestige exchanges, and they can be sum-

---

17. No one has, as far as I know, analyzed in detail the differences among the actual formulas presented by Homans, Adams, Blau, Berscheid and Walster, and others. Some of the differences are substantial, and none is supported by empirical data about how people actually make their decisions about justice—i.e., to what extent they take account of costs or investments, whether they subtract costs from profits, whether they actually calculate "rates" of profit, and so on, all key elements in the formulations of each of these theorists.

marized briefly here. In the textbook version of the market, as well as in the real commodity market, the seller's cost does not, for the most part, determine what the buyer is willing to pay. Buyers will not and need not pay more for the commodities produced by a factory with high costs, since factories with low costs can offer lower prices, still make a profit, and drive the inefficient factory out of business. Buyers do not feel that any of this is unjust. So it is with a wide variety of qualities and performances that bring esteem or disesteem: The individual's cost does not affect the amount of esteem he or she is given. A corporation executive may hate his or her job, and thus the costs of a good performance are high for that individual, but peers and superiors will not therefore lower the standards for performance.

It is obvious that these relationships hold for investments, too, since economically these simply become costs. How much an individual or firm has invested, over how many years, in the development of a commodity for either the economic market or the prestige market is largely irrelevant to the people who evaluate that commodity. The crucial question is whether it is desirable, and what the supply is relative to demand. Years of practice on the violin may still fail to create a tone that anyone wants to hear. We do not esteem the poor teacher more, if he or she has spent a lifetime in trying to learn how to be better. It is true that when we learn how much an individual has tried, suffered, or improved in order to achieve something, we may admire that person more. However, we pay more esteem not for the quality of the performance, but for his or her personal character.

People are not willing to give more prestige for a performance to someone whose competence is less but whose costs are higher or investments greater than those of another. More important, people do not believe they should do so. Justice does not require that we give more respect (or money) to those who do poorly because they have made a large investment in that activity.

It seems clear that, on the whole, achievement has much greater weight than costs and investments in determining who should be paid more prestige, or given any other reward. Homans asserts that others will view it as justice if a higher education or other "investments" are rewarded more, but he neglects to add the special conditions under which that claim holds true. Of course, the prestige and wages of jobs that require a higher investment are generally higher. However, if we observe persons who are overaged, overtalented, or overeducated for a given job, we see that such people are not paid more respect for their work by their fellows or supervisors. These others do not feel they should be paid more.

On the other hand, we apply a somewhat different standard in our own case, or that of people whom we cherish. Then we do care about costs and investments, and somewhat less about actual performance or output. If my background is upper-class, I may well feel that it is just to be given special privileges on the job. If I was once a ghetto child, and suffered many deprivations in order to get a professional education but am evaluated as only mediocre in my work, I am likely to feel it is unjust that I get so little respect. Others suffered less, invested less, but got more. Very likely the merit of the performance is never irrelevant; but these other factors are given more weight in the calculus of justice when we have an intimate relationship with the individual or group being judged.

Although performance appears to be the principal basis for judging those not close to us—this standard being modified by considerations of investments and costs in intimate relationships—these regularities do not fully encompass the observable facts. After all, no one would appeal to outsiders or nonfriends for justice based on his or her investments or costs if it were certain that others would not accept such a standard. In fact, such claims to justice are common, not the least in business, where businessmen extol the salutary effects of competition but nevertheless complain when one of its effects is losing money. Under some circumstances their appeals are persuasive.

Individuals or corporations that invest heavily but lose are often thought of as victims of fate, or simply as foolish. Indeed, as the experiments on equity research have shown, one way of "restoring" justice is to blame the victim and thus deny that injustice has occurred. However, one reason why people may successfully claim justice on the basis of costs is that when many people or corporations in the same general position have invested much and lost, they may organize to protest the system under which they have lost. Their collective complaints may urge politicians to change the rules of investment or payoffs by erecting protective tariffs, forbidding the importation of competitive labor, changing the rules about who may enter a craft union, or limiting entry into a profession. Much business, financial, and occupational legislation over the past generation has arisen from just such complaints. Similarly, one can see in the women's movement, the Italian protest organizations during the late 1960's and those of blacks in the early 1960's and the organized political campaign of Jews beginning in the late 1930's a set of attempts to claim that investments in education and training required a new allocation of esteem. These people were not getting as much respect as their investments or accomplishments justified.

Some of these appeals can be persuasive because people's calculations of justice distinguish among several kinds of investments or costs. People who invest a lifetime of training and effort in the performing arts (painting, music, writing) but achieve little success are not viewed as victims of injustice. Further, when people or corporations invest in the development of new inventions, products, movies, or selling campaigns, but then lose, they are not viewed as having a right to claim injustice. Similarly, missionaries who have worked a lifetime to convert natives, and imperial governments that have invested in armed control over their colonies, have not been given much sympathy when they failed. Some of these are viewed as high-risk ventures to begin with, and failure is an anticipated possibility. Others are viewed as activities that ought to fail, and still others are viewed as the outcome of socioeconomic change, as when traditional occupations (blacksmithing, glassblowing) lose their economic base. Further, if one invests in illegal or improper enterprise or activity that is designed to pay off in money or prestige, but fails, that is not seen as an injustice.

Of course, the *sheer political influence* of a class of individuals or corporations is the prime determinant of whether a solution will be found for a poor return on investments or costs. However, the more persuasive the message or solution itself, the less the amount of political strength needed to change the situation for such groups or people. Clearly, many such claims do not persuade many others that injustice has been done.

People make such appeals, or find them persuasive, when they feel that the group has taken part in an unwritten compact with the society: A given level of reward will continue if the group carries out the necessary and socially approved tasks with some competence. When what they get is reduced to an unsatisfactory level by their costs or investments (relative to those with whom they usually compare themselves), they feel the terms of that contract have been unfairly altered. People in unskilled jobs, for example, make these complaints, mainly with reference to costs, rather than investments. Because their political influence is small, we suppose that this implicit contract is a main factor in the passage of social welfare legislation: Far too many people have had nothing to live on after a lifetime of diligent work. Police organizations point to the high costs of their jobs, and craft union members and professionals to their investments in apprenticeship and education, in making a case for legislation or administrative rulings that will raise wages or respect, or limit competition. The argument is extensible: Shipping and oil companies lobby for legislation that limits their liability for oil spillages on the grounds that they are doing a public service and the costs will be too high if they must bear the full economic responsibility for the resultant damages.

These elaborate corrections of the principle of distributive justice do not deny the importance of costs and investments in weighing the justice of prestige or monetary rewards. They do show, however, that neither can be simply inserted into a formula for distributive justice if the analysis is to be realistic. It is only under specific conditions that either cost or investment becomes crucial, and here I have tried to begin that specification.

THE COSTS OF SELF-SACRIFICE

It seems clear that Homans and others are wrong in supposing that most people believe distant others should be paid more when their cost or investment is higher but their output the same as or lower than that of similar individuals. With reference to most evaluated activities, people believe rewards should be commensurate with accomplishments or output, rather than costs and investments. As noted above, we do not apply so severe a standard when we are weighing persons who are close to us, and we give more weight to costs under certain specific conditions.

At least apparently different from these special circumstances is the conspicuous case of heroism, and self-sacrifice generally, where costs are of great importance in evaluating the justice of prestige awards. Here the esteem paid is highly correlated with the real or likely costs, if it is not supposed that people engage in it in order to get that payoff.

Some respect is paid for heroism of almost any kind, even for going over Niagara Falls in a barrel; but the greatest amount is given when an individual risks or loses his or her life for the group or another person. Eulogies and poetry have echoed this view through the ages. The highest military medals for bravery in the United States and Great Britain, the Congressional Medal of Honor and the Victoria Cross, have often been given posthumously because the kind of deed that earns them is likely to end in death. They are always given for helping or saving others.

However, it is not the saving of others' lives that makes an act heroic. After all, physicians do that every day, and so do drivers when they swerve to avoid a collision. Rather, the greater the potential loss (the risk of death) and the more successful the exploit, the greater the honor. An officer or a member of the upper classes has typically been given more esteem for risking his or her life for the group than have enlisted personnel or members of the lower classes—since the lives of the former are viewed as worth more, they risk more. If a person rushes into a fire to save others' lives but is killed along with them, the self-sacrifice is accorded less honor (the effort was ineffective). If an individual has a high personal stake in saving another (her own baby, his new bride) the esteem is less. In this case the potential loss from attempting the rescue will be weighed against the alternative costs (in self-esteem and the respect of others) of not even trying. Thus, the net potential loss is not as great as it would be if the rescuer were not also pursuing his or her own needs.

It can be argued that here (as in the economic market) it is mainly through restricting supply that costs affect the honor paid (since it costs a great deal to make a Steinway grand piano or a Ferrari, supply will be limited to the few people who can pay a high price). We honor more those who risk their lives for others because the contribution may be crucial, and thus demand high; and because the supply of willing self-sacrificers is low. The argument is not entirely convincing, however, since the honor is paid mainly by those who derive little benefit from the heroism and whose demand for that particular act would seem to be somewhat modest. At least, it seems likely that the spontaneous feelings of respect are more direct than such a calculation implies.

Heroism is perceived, I believe, as an extraordinary free gift of the self, made with little thought of reward and with the knowledge that survival is chancy. To revert to the imagery of supply and demand, though supply may be somewhat low, the more important fact is that group demand is high—not simply the demand to save a life or win a skirmish, but the demand to preserve the group itself. Specifically, individuals feel their own needs and wishes to be so imperative that groups and societies expend much energy in persuading them that group needs should instead be given priority. This is not a preference that individuals would easily accept without pressure. Such a priority is however necessary if the group (and its advantages) are to survive. As a consequence, people in all societies are taught to pay respect to those who give much of themselves to group needs, whether that gift is a lifetime of community service or an act of self-sacrificing heroism.

Devotion to group goals, as against self-interest, may be common enough and its consequences large enough to be of practical importance in many groups or organizations. It has certainly played a large role in the success of revolutions. Heroism in either military actions or civilian life, however, has too small a practical effect to explain the great respect it arouses. One therefore looks for its symbolic meaning: It represents an extreme conformity with the ideal of putting group interests ahead of one's own, and asserts dramatically that the ideal is not mere rhetoric but lies within human capacities. Here, then, it appears that costs do figure significantly in calculating the justice of the prestige rewards the self-sacrificer gets.

THE RULE OF PROPORTIONALITY

The general formula of distributive justice is imprecise with reference to costs and investments, since people apply a kind of sliding scale to the worth of costs and investments: If they are our own, or those of persons we care about, they should be counted more than those of outsiders. Other variables, too, alter the extent to which prestige and other allocations are based on investments or costs: the type of investment or cost; whether a group is organized to demand a larger allocation of rewards for its costs and investments than that given to other groups; the political influence of a group; the extent to which outsiders can be persuaded to feel a group has an implicit contract with society; and so on. The various formulations of distributive justice also assert that when persons compare their rewards, they calculate whether their own ratio of profits to costs, investments, or contributions is equal to that of other persons, usually individuals in similar social positions. This is the rule of proportionality referred to earlier.

The rule asserts that (whether one weighs costs or investments) if the productivity or contribution is doubled, the person's rewards should double as well, compared with those of other persons. In concrete terms, if we double our output, but get only one-third more in monetary or prestige rewards, then we shall be indignant and claim an injustice.

This is surely incorrect. The various formulas that state this relationship do not fit the wide range of judgments that people actually make.

First, it is difficult to give a precise meaning to, say, being "twice as excellent" a violin player as another. This is not a trifling problem in applying the rule of proportionality to prestige allocations, though it is surmounted easily in real judgments about who is worth more, since these are not likely to be spuriously quantified. People actually make extremely refined evaluations of an ordinal kind, weighing what several people may justly claim by a range of disparate variables: age, experience, loyalty, responsibility, quality and quantity of work—all applied simultaneously, and resulting in a decision to award a job, prize, or raise to one rather than the others.

A more important deficiency in the proportionality rule (analyzed at some length in Chapter 4) is that what is viewed as a justly larger or smaller reward in money or prestige actually varies in a curvilinear way with output or contribution. To turn out "twice as many" research reports or anything else of high quality may yield only little more reward, or a great deal more, depending on *where* along the curve of productivity the doubling occurs. If two workers are, for example, both below an acceptable level of competence, both may be fired even though one of them is twice as productive as the other. As pointed out before, where achievement can be measured, even if only intuitively, and its upper limit is not set by an organizational norm (for example, the speed of the assembly line, the pressures of peers), rewards are highly skewed and peaked, but so is productivity likely to be. In science, for example, most of all scientific contributions are made by a small minority of researchers.[18] Or, differently phrased, the prestige that most scientists enjoy because they share the esteem paid to their field of activity is mostly produced or generated by the work of a few outstanding people within it.

At such higher levels it seems likely that the payments or rewards seem to rise at a steeper rate than the achievements. In sports, of course, at higher levels there is no possibility at all of achieving "twice as much" as close competitors—in land speed records, batting averages, hurling the javelin—but the added payoff from being just ahead of them is likely to be large.

Thus, at both the higher and lower levels of contribution the rule of proportionality does not appear to be correct. Actual judgments about justice give a different weight to a greater or a lesser productivity or contribution depending on where a given person falls on the curve. There

---

18. Perhaps the earliest attempt at a precise statement of this relationship is Lotka's Law (1926): The fraction of the persons in a field who publish a given number of articles equals $\frac{1}{n^2}$. Thus, for the fraction of people who publish four articles, we obtain $\frac{1}{16}$ and for one article $\frac{1}{1}$. For a substantial number, say 10 articles, the fraction is $\frac{1}{100}$ and of course the curve rises sharply. See also James Shockley, "On the Statistics of Individual Variations in Production in Research Laboratories," *Proceedings of the Institute of Radio Engineering*, 45 (March, 1957): 279–290, and Derek J. De Solla Price, *Little Science, Big Science* (New York: Columbia University Press, 1963), as well as Robert K. Merton, "The Matthew Effect in Science," *Science*, 159 (January 5, 1968): 61: "It took thirty other men to contribute what Kelvin did."

may be points where others will agree it is just that persons doing twice as much or as well should be paid or honored twice as much, but without research data on this relationship we do not know where those points are. They are not likely to be found at the higher and lower ends of the curve.

The issue of proportionality also raises the question of whose ratio of profit to investment, whose total rewards, we are weighing, that is, the question of *comparison*. Social psychologists who use the formula of proportionality[19] have done most of their experiments with students, whose rank is about middle class. Comparisons refer, then, to one another and to the contributions or payoffs within the experiment itself, and do not often extend to high or low positions in the larger society. The question of whom one compares oneself with is more problematic for sociologists than for social psychologists.[20] In deciding whether their rewards or punishments are just, people do not compare themselves with everyone. Usually they choose others like themselves in important ways, most often people in the same group. More generally, for many kinds of comparisons, and not alone justice, people use the standards of a reference group, of which they may or may not be a member.[21]

Research has not disclosed a precise rule by which individuals use this or that set of other persons as a reference group. It has amply confirmed the observation, however, that how contented we are, or how unfairly treated we feel, depends on whose standards we use for comparison as well as on our objective situation. One may feel one is the child of fortune because of a modest business success, if one's reference group is the poverty-stricken set of friends one grew up with in the rural south. When the clerk or typist complains of injustice in gaining esteem, he or she does not ordinarily adduce the case of the scientist in the corporation laboratory, but is more likely to note that other clerks or typists are better off in another office, or on another floor; or that some other lower-level white collar workers are better treated. When members of the English working class in one study were asked whether they knew others who were better off, most said they did not.[22] Of course they read of such people, or saw

19. For example, Walster, Berscheid, and Walster, in "New Directions in Equity Research," pp. 3–4.

20. For example, Joseph Berger, Morris Zelditch, Bo Anderson, and Bernard P. Cohen, in "Structural Aspects of Distributive Justice: A Status Value Formulation," in Berger, Zelditch, and Anderson, eds., *Sociological Theories in Progress* (Boston: Houghton Mifflin, 1972), pp. 119–146, present a formal set of relationships to explain how this choice is made. See also their later work: Joseph Berger *et al.*, *Status Characteristics and Social Interaction* (New York: Elsevier, 1977).

21. Homans uses the terms comparison group or comparison person (*Social Behavior*, p. 252). The term reference group has been widely used since the Merton-Rossi article of 1948, now extended as "Continuities in the Theory of Reference Groups and Social Structure," in Robert K. Merton, *Social Theory and Social Structure* (New York: Free Press, 1957), p. 281–368; Herbert Hyman, who coined the term in 1942, has also developed his thinking further in "Reflections on Reference Groups," *Public Opinion Quarterly*, 24 (Fall, 1960): 383–396. See also Herbert Hyman and Eleanor Singer, eds., *Readings in Reference Group Theory and Research* (New York: Free Press, 1968).

22. W. G. Runciman, *Relative Deprivation and Justice: A Study of Attitudes of Social Inequality in Twentieth Century England* (Berkeley: University of California Press, 1966). For Runciman's commentary on Homan's theory of distributive justice, see "Justice, Congruence and Professor Homans," *European Journal of Sociology*, 8, no. 1 (May, 1967): 115–128.

them on the street, every day, but they did not choose them for comparison.

However, such data have been stretched to suggest that, in general, people who live in miserable conditions, or who are exploited, do not feel as discontented or unjustly treated as one might suppose. Since their comparison level or group, or their reference group, is made up of others like themselves—the poor, the natives in an imperial colony, migratory agricultural laborers, blacks, slaves—and the members of each group get about the same amount as other members in that group, no one should feel relatively deprived, or unjustly treated.

By phrasing the last statement in so strong a fashion, I have not biased the question but merely raised to prominence the hidden assumption in much of the literature on comparisons and proportionality in justice processes: Since people mainly compare their lot with that of others like themselves, most people will be relatively contented. They may of course be discontented because, within that restricted set of comparisons, some specific others may be getting small, unearned rewards that loom large, but not because they compare their lot with others in very different circumstances. Is that general description correct?

First, the fact that people usually compare themselves with others in a similar situation can be explained simply: It seems silly to do otherwise. If one of average accomplishment is measuring how well one is doing, even a modest success seems minuscule if one is contrasting oneself with the rich and highly esteemed; and one's listeners would view the comparison as pretentious.

However, the reality is somewhat more complex. Second, the fundamental assertion that people evaluate their rewards with reference to others like themselves is challenged by the observation that, in many conversations, people do compare themselves with others who are not their reference group. Manual laborers, for example, at times compare their situation with that of the rich, their employers, or even professionals and express their sense of injustice about the factors that give them less respect than those others.[23] It is not only "when society is badly shaken up," as Homans puts it, that such broad comparisons are made[24]— although they are made more frequently then.

Next, in the comparisons a person makes to decide what is just, whether the reference group consists of peers or superiors, calculations of the ratio of profits to costs or investments are variable. If an individual believes his or her achievements or contributions are superior, it is less likely that he or she will calculate closely whether investments or costs are high and thus "profits" lower. Nor does an individual give much weight

---

23. For example, see Richard Sennet and Jonathan Cobb, *The Hidden Injuries of Class* (New York: Random House, 1973).

24. Homans, *Social Behavior*, p. 253.

to others' investments or costs if those others are not people he or she cares much about. If an individual's own achievements or contributions are not superior, he or she is more likely to give much weight to personal investments, needs, costs, or loyalty, and thus may well consider whether his or her own "profits" are equal to those of others. Moreover, when people do make such comparisons of profits, they are much more likely to make them with reference to other individuals, rather than to specific occupations. That is, I believe that if people are asked whether they could name many occupations whose payoffs in prestige or money are unjustly high compared with the investments and costs needed to engage in them, compared with how much those occupations contribute or are "worth," many would find the difficult questions unnatural and puzzling. It is not a common comparison, and many people would answer, "few or none."

Indeed, I believe that although a large percentage of respondents in both Western and socialist countries would agree that extremely high wealth, or respect or deference, such as might be enjoyed by a rock celebrity or a very rich person, is not deserved, that judgment would be made without conscious or explicit regard to investments. Or, more cautiously, most people simply do not believe that anyone who gets enormous returns can possibly have earned it. Certainly, calculations about investments are not common. A few respondents might also mention specific occupations they do not believe contribute much to the society (stockbrokers, politicians), and which deserve little—but again I do not believe that judgment is based on any supposed investments, costs, or rate of profit.

When people do make comparisons of "profits" with reference to occupations or groups, the comparisons are frequently with occupations close to their own in the occupational structure. Policemen assert that their own investments and costs justify their getting more respect and higher wages than firemen, while firemen assert the principle of equal pay. Members of the various craft unions (electricians, plumbers, carpenters, sheet metal workers) argue among themselves as to whose training is more demanding, whose work is more difficult, and which craft deserves more respect, in justifying or rejecting differentials in wages or esteem.

EQUALITY AS A RULE OF JUSTICE

In the preceding section it was pointed out that the generally accepted formulas of proportionality—twice as much contribution or achievement for twice as much payoff, or, equal profits for equal costs, investments, and contributions—are very likely not correct for either prestige or money, especially at the upper and lower levels of achievement or contribution. We considered this matter in the context of reference groups, since without that datum we cannot know which "proportion" or whose "profit" is being considered in a decision about justice. We expressed some skepticism about how often people implicitly or explicitly calculate others' profits, but noted some of the structural circumstances under which this type of calculation is likely to be made.

Throughout the past several sections we have been suggesting various emendations in the general formulations of distributive justice, so as to make it more harmonious with the judgments that people actually make about justice in daily life. In this section we consider another principle of justice that is sometimes followed, in opposition to the notion of unequal rewards for unequal contributions: the principle of equality. Throughout its history the Western cultural complex has reserved a special place for the norm of equality.[25] It has been a widespread "ideal ideal": what people feel they ought to value highly, or how people could or would act under ideal or utopian conditions. It has played a special role in major revolutions in Europe and the New World from the seventeenth century onward but had risen to high prominence in various peasant revolts as early as the fourteenth century. Perhaps its origins lie in the emphasis given to political equality in Athenian Greece, but we shall not try to explore how it came to be so attractive in Western culture—which in practice has certainly given greater weight to other principles of distribution. After all, no nation in this long historical succession has ever taken more than minute steps toward achieving that ideal.

We have already noted that although the rule of distributive justice, or equity, is often phrased as "equal rewards to equals," in fact it really states that people who accomplish more, or invest more, or have higher costs, should be given greater rewards. That is, although phrased as a rule of equality, it is a rule of inequality, specifying that the standards for unequal treatment are based on unequal performance. Some of its persuasiveness doubtless comes from that emphasis in rhetoric.

The seductiveness of equality as a rule is evident in the sentimentalized view, now over two centuries old, of primitive societies: namely, that they practiced a kind of early communism in which everything was equally shared. The ideal of equality shaped (but did not determine) the organization of communes in the nineteenth- and twentieth-century United States. It has dominated the rhetoric, and partly shaped the practice, of communism in its various forms. Modern social security and welfare politics in all nations are similarly molded in this ideal, even though few people would claim a strong allegiance to it as an exclusive principle.

Deutsch has asserted that equality is the dominant principle in "solidarity-oriented groups," or in "cooperative relations in which the

---

25. For a brief summary of its most common norms, see Nicholas Rescher, *Distributive Justice* (New York: Bobbs-Merrill, 1966), esp. chap. 4. Using a different framework from mine, Morton Deutsch suggests that when the goals of the group are different (economic productivity, enjoyable social relations, or personal development and welfare), the standard for justice will be different ("equity," equality, or need, respectively); see "Equity, Equality, and Need: What Determines which Value will be Used as the Basis of Distributive Justice?" *Journal of Social Issues*, 31, no. 3 (Summer, 1975): 137–149. Although my orientation is different, and I have developed a number of different hypotheses here, I have found his ideas most helpful.

fostering or maintenance of enjoyable social relations is a primary emphasis"[26]—what we might call conviviality. Although most readers will feel intuitively that this hypothesis is correct, it is difficult to think of nontrivial causes that confirm it.

The trivial cases lie at hand. We try to give equal respect as well as equally good food and drink to our dinner guests. Friends try to "be fair," which usually means that they try to give equal respect and affection to one another. A group of deer hunters or campers will try to divide most burdens and pleasures equally, showing as nearly equal esteem to one another as they can.

However, it is equally clear that sororities and fraternities, lodges, country clubs, or boys' gangs—to name some of the obvious examples of continuing social groups whose goal is solidarity or enjoyable social relations—do not follow the norm of equality in many important ways. Communes do not. Social networks do not, although smaller friendship groups may. Some individuals are given more respect as well as influence than others, and often material rewards as well. I am not asserting merely that the norm is not followed in practice; that might be said of many norms. Rather, members would deny that that *is* the real norm, except within the actual situations of conviviality. For example, at a sorority party or dinner (a short-term occasion) some effort is made to make all the comforts and fun available to everyone equally, and to give more attention or esteem to anyone who seems to be neglected. In convivial situations the rules for deference are usually relaxed somewhat, permitting a larger number of individuals to interact with some superiors as equals. However, we should not forget that in time past, when rank differences were clearer and more strongly institutionalized, it was common that even at dinners or festivals those in high offices or statuses were given special privileges, such as curtseys and bows, expensive dishes not served others, or areas set apart from the rest. (When dinners are very large in the modern world, some of this deference is still observable.) That is, when the somewhat lower-ranked persons were once grateful enough for smaller relaxations of deference rules, the powerful conceded only that much.

In any event, aside from such delimited occasions, solidarity or fraternal groups do not follow the norm of equality in other activities, such as recruiting new members, deciding on policy, or raising money.

It is tempting to conclude, then, that the hypothesis cannot apply to concrete groups or relationships, but simply to the various *phases* or social *occasions* in almost any group or organizational life, when the goal is simply to engage in enjoyable social relations. At such times, members are more likely to use the rhetoric of equality, and to aim at giving equal treatment to everyone.

However, we can instead try to refine the hypothesis, by beginning

26. Deutsch, "Equity, Equality, and Need," pp. 146–147, 148.

from the facts about equal sharing as we observe it in daily life. Though apparently very different, the situations in which equal sharing is considered just seem to have in common the important characteristic that *the people involved see each other as members of the group or community* and are socially defined as equals with reference to that particular situation. Most of those people do not, however, have close solidarity or conviviality as goals.

In both experiments and real life, there are some situations in which there is a payoff, or chores to be allocated, but it is simply difficult to think of an obvious rule by which to divide them. For example, if the experimenter presents a collective problem-solving task such that no individual seems to contribute more than others to the solution, but a special windfall profit occurs, it is likely (in the United States at least) that participants will decide everyone should share equally. Similar social behavior occurs in real life: A children's friendship group cuts into equal portions a cake baked by one of the mothers; members of a subunit of a corporation equally divide a prize won for reducing costs and feel they share equally in the honor, or young people in a summer camp hand out tasks by lot and then rotate them on an equal-time basis.[27] As can be seen, not all of these are occasions for conviviality. Some are work situations. In this set of cases the common element is that no simple rule of unequal division seems justified while everyone is defined as equally a member of the group.

A second type of equal sharing is found in many collective goods: highways, parks, fire departments, national defense. They are difficult to have at all if they are to be divided. Further, they are so expensive that one person, or even a few, cannot pay for them independently in order to monopolize them. Yet the cost per person is modest enough, and is not objected to very much if those who pay know there will not be many free riders.[28] Nearly all such collective goods can be seen as a gradual historical development, by which a benefit once enjoyed by a few rich families (parks, collections of wild animals, guards against marauders or thieves) comes to be defined as properly available to the entire community. More succinctly, the definition of who is an equal member gradually widens, and the costs are more broadly distributed.

Political and civic rights form a third type of equal sharing. Like the previous two, they seem self-evident (as America's Declaration of Independence asserted two centuries ago), but of course most of the world's population does not yet enjoy them equally. In this case, such rights have

27. However, if tasks are defined as requiring a higher order of skill and thus a rarer one (higher demand, lower supply), people's belief in the justice of equality is likely to weaken somewhat, in favor of the doctrine that such higher contributions deserve some extra payoff in respect and—usually—a reduction in doing chores.

28. On these points see Martin Bronfenbrenner, "Equality and Equity," *Annals*, no. 409 (September, 1973): 19. Also see Mancur Olson, *The Logic of Collective Action* (Cambridge: Harvard University Press, 1965).

typically been divisible, and not shared equally (for example, the vote). Again, however, equal sharing of these rights is the result of extending membership in the political and civic community to include almost every adult in the population. It should be emphasized that esteem, or philosophically and formally defined equal respect—from whatever political conflicts it was gained—is the central factor in this development over the centuries, that is, the belief that everyone is equally entitled to certain formal civic rights, backed by law.

A relationship that prescribes or suggests equal sharing is, in perhaps all societies, ideally a friendship between peers. Obviously, on the other hand, in most of the cases we have noted, not all group members are really equal, most are not friends, and convivial social relations are not the main goal. Even in the few cases of small groups made up of close friends, some individuals are in fact more respected, wealthy, or influential than others. In such cases, of course, the differences may be small. But in most of the cases under discussion the differences may be large, although as members of the group, individuals' benefits may be defined as *appropriately, justly,* the same.

Why people of lesser wealth, prestige, or influence might be willing to receive treatment equal to that of individuals with greater advantages in certain circumstances—those involving conviviality, the sharing of a special benefit to which no one obviously contributed more than others, the allocation of public goods or civic rights—is obvious enough. It is usually more desirable to get more benefits rather than less. Why, however, are people with greater advantages willing to concede such benefits?

The first step toward an answer is that such concessions are relatively limited; we do not find societies in which those with great resources, skills, or influence share equally with others in all ways. Great hunters did share in the past, but they did not share equally in a genuinely communal hunt. The nobility in every country has gradually withdrawn its claims to "more than equal" public deference and monopoly over high posts and political influence, but only under threat, and as slowly as possible.

A second part of the answer is that such concessions are given because the alternatives seem worse. In the case of political and civic rights, as argued earlier, a major cause has been force and its threat. Of course, with each step in gaining such rights, a class or group has a greater ability to press for still more equality. As more people gain the vote and the legal capacity to use the courts, they are given more deference and are better able to make more specific demands in other areas (jobs, housing, education, the right to unionize). It was noted earlier, too, that as the collective economic market within any lower class becomes larger—as it did in the more advanced European countries from at least the eighteenth century onward—it becomes less wise to treat members with disdain.

More broadly, I speculate that in many or most types of equal sharing, those who could have used their advantages to take more than an equal share do not exploit that advantage, so that they will be liked more, or disliked less. As the community widens to include classes or persons once excluded from real membership, those who already had greater resources will feel a need to be liked by them, too. Differently phrased, the liking and respect will become of importance—and may become important politically and economically as well. That is, to the extent that more people are viewed, within a given context, situation, or relationship, as peers, at least some steps will be taken toward equal sharing with them because their support, esteem, and liking then becomes important.

To the extent that rules for unequal sharing are relaxed, those at both the top and bottom gain some advantages: Those at the top will feel they are liked more (and they are correct); and those at the bottom will enjoy being treated in a more egalitarian manner by people who have been less respectful or generous with them in the past. On the other hand, it should not be forgotten that equal sharing, or egalitarian social interaction, is likely not to extend to more consequential matters: For example, the vote may be shared equally, but political influence is not; some economic benefits may be extended to everyone, but most are not; a minimum civility or public respect is given to most people, but high esteem is not.

We have thus expanded somewhat the range of relationships or situations in which equal sharing is more likely to occur, and have suggested that the central dynamic is a (nonconscious) exchange of some economic, political, or prestige benefit for liking, and as a way of avoiding still greater political or esteem losses. The main types of situations and relationships seem to be the following:

1. Genuine peership, as between friends;

2. political relations where the threat of force or the possibility of being outvoted exists;

3. convivial situations or phases in any group: office parties, festivals, dinners;

4. where it is difficult to divide, but all contribute to the cost of the good: the village green or water well, police departments, national defense;

5. where a benefit or burden can be divided (a cake, an accidental windfall or profit in a game, chores in an ideologically egalitarian commune) but no obvious or traditional rule exists that specifies that any particular person should receive more than others. Usually, it is not clear that anyone has contributed more than anyone else to the special benefit or outcome. With reference to chores, they are defined as within the capacity of all, and can be divided equally;

6. early stages in survival situations.

It is typically reported that survivors consider it to be just that sharing be equal. Under those circumstances, it is also clear (as Hobbes pointed out in his analysis of individual vulnerability) that anyone who tries to take extreme advantage could very likely be overpowered. Whether this is the central dynamic, or instead it is the common catastrophe that creates a kind of elemental feeling of peership, does not seem clear. As stress becomes much greater, and the threat of death increases, at least one or more of the survivors is likely to feel that the doctrine of equal sharing has lost much of its persuasive quality. If survivors die off one by one under the stress of cold, hunger, or thirst, it is common that equal sharing dies out too.

So far, our analysis has referred to the equal distribution of benefits. However, the justice of sharing punishments equally does not appear to command the same agreement. On the other hand, it is a general rule of justice—again, in the sense that people in many or most cultures will agree it is just—that those who are guilty of the same offense should be punished equally. This rule is widely accepted, even though one can point to obvious qualifications and exceptions; for example, aristocrats have never accepted the rule; ecclesiastics in the medieval period did not; and (as with benefits) people who have a more intimate stake in the outcome (the culprit, friends of the victim) also believe the rule should be modified somewhat to fit their wishes.

Unlike benefits, punishments are imposed. This is true of individuals as well as for the pattern of punishing an entire group by disrespect, fines, or imprisonment when one or more members have committed an offense. Rarely if ever do we observe a group or social unit that asks for a collective punishment instead of an individual one imposed on a particular culprit. Nor does the person with power or authority give the group the choice of actually dividing the punishment, so that each individual member would receive a part of the total that otherwise would all have been given to the individual culprit.[29]

In a number of authoritarian structures (the armed services, the classroom), those in command will sometimes punish collectively (by public scorn, or the imposition of taxes) rather than waste time in searching out the individual offender. One aim, aside from saving time, is to press the group to police their own members. It is reported that this is fairly successful in Soviet schools,[30] although it has had but modest success in U.S. classrooms.

In Western cultures, I suppose, those who undergo a collective punishment when the offense was committed by one or a few individuals generally believe they are victims of injustice. Whether they would respond differently if they were collectively sharing no more punishment than the culprit would have received if found guilty as an individual is open to experimentation. I would speculate that highly cohesive groups

29. When an authority figure arbitrarily singles out one victim to be punished, a group may express its solidarity by sharing some of that punishment if it can be done, e.g., helping to clean up a parade ground or classroom. (Suggested by Mark Johnson.)

30. See Urie Bronfenbrenner, with John C. Condry, Jr., *The Two Worlds of Childhood: U.S. and U.S.S.R.* (New York: Russell Sage Foundation, 1970).

would accept that choice, whether the punishment is disesteem or physical pain, until the person in command began to escalate the punishment
beyond the amount that would usually be meted out to an individual.

Though uncommon at present, patterns similar to the latter can be
found in the past. In pre-Roman law in Europe, especially in Germanic
societies, kin were generally held liable for crimes committed by individuals, and that rule has been followed in family vendettas in other regions.
Since the Germanic law (which included, of course, Anglo-Saxon law in
England) required payment (as did many other early systems) for violent
crimes, kin members did in fact divide and thus share the punishment,
though not equally. Often the punishment was public disesteem, such as
banishment and exile. The closest modern parallel probably occurs when a
family bribes a prosecutor or judge to free a kinsman.

Sharing equally, like egalitarianism generally, arouses a false nostalgia.
Modern intellectuals especially respond positively to it, and in some form
or another it arouses sentimental responses from most people, primarily
because it evokes images of an uncomplicated friendship, bonded in a total
sharing. The success of many novels and short stories depends on the
author's ability to evoke such emotions. The theme of equality has great
political appeal, however people violate it in daily practice. Here, some of
the structural factors have been sketched that increase the likelihood that
some form of equal sharing will be seen as justice, or will be followed.
They are not all trivial. Some are major steps in political development over
several centuries. All seem to rest on the social definition of who is a "real
member," and thus on the factors that press toward the widening or
narrowing of the boundaries of membership.

NEED AS A STANDARD FOR JUSTICE

If we analyze how people actually make judgments about justice, we
must also consider the principle of need. It sometimes overlaps in application with the rule of equality, because need is more likely to be invoked
within the more intimate relations of peers, and because it is often set
against the principle of inequality (distributive justice, or equity) based on
differences in performance. It is often linked, too, with such criteria for
justice as seniority, loyalty, or humble service to the group, because these
may, like need, be viewed as alternatives to the inequality that is based on
productivity or achievement. However, all three of these are a kind of
contribution or output, and are not to be confused with need, which is
invoked as a separate standard of some justice in some relations and
situations.

The principle of need is surely the most primitive rule of justice, at
least in the psychological sense, for babies know no other. What is just is
that they should get what they want, right now, and what they want they
need. All of us recognize in ourselves that same imperious urge from time
to time, an inner scream that what we feel we need, we ought to have. In

socializing their children, parents must therefore try to convince them that their wants are not the same as their needs, and that though real needs are more commanding than wants, the rules of justice may at times disapprove of meeting even real needs. Children, and therefore the adults they become, frequently fail to accept this unwelcome lesson in self-denial or the austere pleasures of ideal justice.

From an early age, others try to teach us to distinguish between our needs and our wants, and so as adults we are quick to point out to others that they have confused the two. The issue arises especially in the family, the institution that is shaped most by the principle of need: In general, allocation should ideally, in most cultures, be decided by who needs a given service or good. Although in fact families do not base most of their allocations on the principle of need, perhaps all societies would view some version of the early French socialist principle as ideally appropriate for family behavior: From each according to ability; to each according to need. At least, ideals emphasize the help the competent adults should give to the less able young and aged. The principle of need arises as an issue in the family, of course, because the key problem of justice there becomes, "Who shall define my needs?" Or: "Why can I not define my strong desires as my *needs*, and so gain social support for them?"

Many people in the modern generation share the notion that each person has the right to define what his or her own needs are, and that people should fulfill their own needs where possible.[31] This principle of justice has the advantage that it is not easily refuted: No one can deny that the claimant really feels that need. However, it suffers from the defect that claiming a need often fails to persuade others it should be filled. In the real world a rule of justice cannot survive such a defect.

Although need is recognized as one principle of justice in all adequately functioning societies,[32] it is not individuals who are permitted to define their own needs, but members of the society. Or, more cautiously, anyone including a baby may define his or her own needs, but others may not validate them. That is, they will not agree that justice requires they be fulfilled, and they will not help to meet those needs.

This crucial point is especially evident when a family, group, or community defines some allocations as needs which the individual or another group does not even want. Probably most children would claim that they need love, respect, various privileges, play, rest, food, and warmth, and they also want them. However, their parents, teachers, and the commu-

31. For a sometimes amusing account of this variegated social movement, whose earlier representatives certainly included Satan (in Milton's version of the Fall), Eve, Prometheus, and Faust, as well as the somewhat less mythical Romantics of the early nineteenth century, see Tom Wolfe, "The Me Decade and the Third Great Awakening," *New York*, 9, no. 34 (August 23, 1976): 26–40.

32. This is not a definition. When societies begin to break down, individuals drop the social standard of justice in favor of a standard that defines their own wants or needs as dominant. This also happens when survival groups begin to die out under stress. For an apparently concrete instance of such a society, see C. Turnbull, *The Mountain People* (New York: Simon and Schuster, 1972).

nity will also insist that they "need" such unwelcome experiences as mathematics, formal education, balanced diets, exercise, work training, and many kinds of medical attention. Consequently, those who proclaim the right to define as needs whatever their inner impulses find attractive are less likely to gain much social support for their goals.

One might indeed view a society as an elaborate system for preventing the individual from defining what his or her own needs are, and especially from confusing needs with imperious urges. The moral authorities of the society—parents, kin, teachers, physicians and psychotherapists, governmental officials, and clergy—are all part of a system that determines not merely whether an individual's wishes are to be viewed as permissible, but which ones are legitimate enough to justify community support.

Because need is socially defined, it varies historically and cross-culturally. American children "needed" their teeth straightened long before British children did. Orwell pointed out (in *The Road to Wigan Pier*) in the depression of the 1930's that British welfare was expensive because the higher classes could not force the poor to be as thrifty as it was possible to be. Since the lower classes *would* be wasteful, and would not live on rice and beans, they "needed" a higher allowance than that necessary for basic subsistence. A lower allowance would in fact have led to starvation.

So, similarly, one may argue that it has not been truly necessary to bail out large corporations that have been mismanaged, since other companies would have been able to produce all they had been producing, and those workers might be more wisely put to doing something other than redundant manufacturing. Nevertheless, both those workers and many business and political leaders have defined that need as great enough to justify financial aid. They have thought the negative consequences of a rejection for the economy (and themselves) would be intolerable. In sum, the meaning of need or necessity is not absolute, but variable, and is socially defined by the group evaluations of various alternative allocations.

It is indicative of our widespread bias in favor of inequalities based on performance or achievement that we do not often analyze need as a criterion for granting some benefit to one person or group rather than another. In the economic market, the suggestion that the price should be higher or lower because of the seller's or buyer's need would be met with incredulity or laughter. In the prestige market, the notion of granting a science prize or a medal for bravery on that basis would be viewed as incongruous. As for the allocation of love and friendship, to be sure, a moment's thought will tell us that those who love ardently have often asked for tokens of affection on the grounds of need. Men especially have made that plea, and almost certainly their suit has often been successful. In fact, many women have thereby been moved to fall in love—thus casting some doubt on the notion (Willard Waller's Principle of Lesser Interest) that the person who loves more commands less. But even in love and friendship it is generally felt that greater or lesser need is not an appropriate criterion for choosing among various suitors.

Nevertheless, in three important social institutions—the family, school, and government—the allocation of many benefits, including prestige, is often justified by relative need, and we can think of numerous other situations in which many people view it as proper to allocate more benefits to others because their need is greater. Here are a few of the commonly observable patterns of allocation based on need:

> Social welfare: Need determines the allocation of aid to dependent children, old age and disability payments, disaster grants, relief to victims of catastrophe in this and other countries.
>
> Promotions: When other differences between candidates seem small, the greater need of one may determine the outcome. Job recommendations often cite the candidate's need. Thus, one consequence of a socially defined need comes to be higher prestige, from getting the job.
>
> Fellowships: Very likely most are granted partially on the basis of relative need—though not the candidate's need for prestige. Nevertheless, the award yields prestige.
>
> The economic market: At higher levels, where many of the principles of the textbook marketplace break down, both corporations and whole sectors of the economy (automobiles, garments, shoes, shipping) demand remedial legislation or subventions based on the principle of need.
>
> The family: Decisions about who needs something the most will determine many allocations (education, toys, musical instruments, psychotherapy).
>
> Schools: A common argument in favor of new teaching programs, the distribution of praise, admission to extracurricular activities, or special teaching help is that the students need it.
>
> Individual and group psychotherapy: need may be invoked to justify giving more approval or esteem to one person than to another.

These do not exhaust the situations or contexts in which need is felt to be an appropriate standard for justice. They may serve, however, to stimulate the reader to think of other concrete cases, and to suggest that need as a rule of justice is not just an anomaly or a residue from an older historical era. It grows from and is supported by the normal social forces of our time, and it will continue to be of importance in the future as well.

Several of these situations refer to the allocation of prestige on the basis of need. But I have pointed out other types of cases as well so that the general dynamics of allocation by need can be better understood. These observations suggest a number of relationships that shape the pattern of judgments about need in distributing both prestige and other benefits.

The most fundamental relationship is that the individual or a group in need is socially defined as a "member." In many times and places some who are defined as outsiders have been allowed to suffer without help (natives, peasants, nonmembers of a parish). Similarly, the closer or more intimate the potential helper is to the one in need, the more likely it is that aid on these grounds will be given. If the person is "one of ours," he or she ought not be allowed to fall below a certain level of income, influence, or esteem.

Moreover, need appears to refer to group imperatives: Unless this need is fulfilled (food, training, a disaster loan, respect), the group or individual cannot discharge some important social role. Without it, normal functioning is unlikely.

However, one consequence of this social definition is that if the individual or group cannot function adequately even with help, assistance may not be forthcoming. Differently phrased, the response to need seems to be curvilinear: At extremely high levels of need it may seem useless to help. This rule applies to decisions about a wide range of problems: medical therapy, survival of individuals or groups in a disaster, education, training, fellowships. At very high or low need levels of prestige benefits, then, some of those in authority are likely to decide that resources should be allocated on other grounds.

When it occurs, giving on the basis of need, whether of prestige or money, is not typically an exchange. The recipient is not expected to pay back any equivalent; he or she "deserves" the help. The giver usually does not gain much if any power over the recipient. More commonly, the recipient only owes the obligation of using the help as expected, for example, doing his or her best, studying hard, becoming productive, or perhaps someday helping a similarly placed person (for example, a student). Because, however, people are likely to respond to any help or aid with gratefulness or an impulse to reciprocate, and because the inability to reciprocate often causes some distress, it is likely that most people who are given help when needy will not feel they have received only what they deserve, and many will feel some shame.

On the other hand, when some of the poor come to perceive their situation not only as a personal difficulty but also as a class problem, they are able to assert that fulfilling their need is *justice*, that it is no more than their right. This change is part of a slow secular trend toward giving the disadvantaged more respect as well as material benefits, and toward understanding that much of human misery is caused by structural factors, not personal failures.

Although we have cited a number of instances where something is granted on the basis of need, there are very few situations in which need is the primary principle. In most allocations, need is viewed as a just standard only after some other criteria have been met. One might formulate this principle as follows: If two persons are otherwise similar in qualities and performances, then the person in greater need should be given more. For this reason, it is likely that most people with regular jobs still feel that only the *virtuous* poor should be given some form of welfare—as was the rule in all countries until recently in world history. Conservative opinion in the United States continues to be slightly offended that mothers who bear illegitimate children should be given any but the most minimal welfare: They are enjoying themselves, but getting paid for it. They may need esteem, but they do not deserve it. In the extreme situation where someone is about to lose his or her life, no further criterion has to be met, but that is not common. More usually, an individual's greater need for a job is considered if he or she otherwise compares adequately with other candidates.

Correspondingly, when the person's greater need seems to be caused by his or her greater fault, and especially by character faults such as laziness, drunkenness, or irresponsibility, that person's claim to a job or respect is felt to be less justified. Whether this is because the suffering itself is viewed as justice, because people feel less sympathy with self-inflicted troubles (such a person is not "one of ours"), or because people who cause their own trouble are seen as *willing* their own problems, thus one should not help them out of these problems—we do not know.

Because everyone knows that under some circumstances need is an effective plea, and there are in fact hundreds of local and national programs in which eligibility is based on need, it is possible to engage in subversion, that is, to claim need where none exists. In many situations it is socially inappropriate to arouse sympathy by asserting need; but my observation is that even when the hearer is slightly offended, the plea has a positive effect just the same, whether the aim is more respect or a better job. For most government programs, of course, that plea is a necessity, and thousands of people each year succeed in presenting themselves as needy when they are not, at worst, *that* needy; and very likely many of the needy will not swallow their pride in order to accomplish that goal. Indeed, the principle operates so as to face many people with a dilemma: If one does too well because of the aid one gets, one does not deserve to continue getting it, because one's need has now become less; but if one does poorly, others will feel one is unworthy.

The above formulations make it clear that the principle of need embodies several implicit hierarchies of evaluation. One is the gradation of emotional or social closeness of those to be helped to the persons or groups making judgments about relative needs (again, the needs of people closer to us are more important). Another is the extent to which those to be helped will be able to function adequately if aid is forthcoming. Still another is the gradation from simple biological threat (fire, drowning) through economic necessities to perhaps respect and then love.

In contemporary debate about whose needs should be met, the focus is most often on economic needs. At least some discussion in recent decades, however, has also come to center on the need of some groups or population segments (enlisted soldiers, Chicanos, Indians, women, blacks) for greater respect in order that they may fulfill their potential, develop as persons, and take their proper place in society. For many decades, it has been agreed among psychologists as well as popular writers that troubled children may need more love in order to function adequately as adults.

Whether debates concerning whose needs should be met focus on economic or other essentials, most such discussions center on people at the lower socioeconomic levels because their needs are greater in all realms: money, prestige, love and friendship. However, at higher levels too one can observe that some people or groups may be in need of some resource in order to function as well as their peers or members want. Of course that need may be money, as when friends or kin help a fellow member of the upper class to get a job. Within organizations, however, the more likely need at higher levels may be prestige or esteem.

At such levels, an organizational decision may be made to arrange for more prestige to be given to an individual. For example, where the doctorate is viewed as an academic necessity, and a person who is named professor does not have the degree, easier ways toward it may be opened (for example, acceptance of a published book as a doctoral dissertation). Both time schedules and minor rules may be similarly relaxed for the younger person who needs a doctorate in order to keep or get a job. In the past, when high social rank was thought to be necessary for ambassadors (the association is still close, of course), some were given decorations and medals, or even elevated in title, before going abroad to serve.

The most common type of need for esteem at higher levels is easily overlooked: the need for deference or overt esteem in the allocation of various organizational resources. At such levels, as we have often noted, the individual enjoys considerable prestige. Whatever subordinates may feel internally, their overt esteem or deference is shown, not so much in bowing or scraping, as in meeting the superior's need for facilities, services, time, and privacy.

Much of the deference in any job is not personal and is not determined by how much real respect each coworker has for the other. It is rather based on the need of the worker for various resources, if he or she is to function adequately in the task. In a smoothly operating team, those who need this pervasive deference normally get it.[33] Nurses pay to doctors the deference of getting out of their way physically, permitting interruptions of their own activities, handing them instruments, cleaning up the patient for them, and providing many other services and aids that help maximize the efficiency of each hour of the physician's time and energy (and also make him feel central and important). This "deference of effectiveness" is the most common overt way of expressing esteem in an organization. Such overt respect is taken for granted—it is indeed based on the widely accepted principle of inequality justified by achievement—and is not much resented. However, bosses who demand more overt

---

33. For an extensive analysis of this and other aspects of deference, see Joel Telles, "Deference Processes as Studied in Intensive Care Units" (Ph.D. diss., Columbia University, 1976).

esteem paid to them than seems necessary for the job (a much bigger or more lavish office, an overly elaborate system of protection from callers, demands for personal services) are likely to be disesteemed behind their backs.

With a few exceptions here and there (for example, the group surrounding Nixon), modern organizations and groups do not, as certainly kings and emperors did in the past (for example, Louis XIV, Nero, Caligula), require more ceremonies of deference in order to function. On the other hand, from time to time they may decide that persons in authority do need more overt esteem or deference in the task itself, that is, more deference of effectiveness. That is, they try to give more scope and authority to their decisions, and to furnish them with more privacy, priority in time allocations, or more facilities and services so that the job will be done better.

Such discussions and decisions have been carried out, for example, with reference to the place of the foreman in industry, during the 1940's and 1950's, when studies suggested that his structural position was one of considerable stress. That is, he was superior to a workman in rank, but not really equal to managerial staff. He was thus in need of more authority and deference in order to do his job better. Examples have often occurred, too, in communes that were originally intended to be egalitarian, but in which leaders arose over time; or that turned toward a more spiritual orientation with a charismatic leader.[34] Decisions may, of course, move in the opposite direction, as when private schools are founded with the explicit philosophy that, for the students' more adequate personal development, teachers should yield some authority and deference to them. That is, the daily schedules, modes of decision-making, allocation of services and facilities, and style of social interaction, should be adjusted to the needs of pupils rather than teachers, since children "need" such an atmosphere in order to thrive. As in all such problems, the decisions are not always correct.

RESPONSES TO INJUSTICE

We have analyzed one by one the main standards of justice actually followed by people in their social relations—unequal allocations of prestige or other benefits, based on unequal contributions or personal qualities, on equality, and on need—and have shown from observation and common experience that each of these principles is more or less likely to be adduced or followed under certain social conditions. However, we shall also look at the most important findings of social experiments about justice, for they may help us to understand further how people actually define, apply, or respond to different principles of justice.

---

34. A fuller analysis of the internal structure of communes will be found in Benjamin Zablocki, *Alienation and Charisma* (New York: Free Press, forthcoming).

Hundreds of experiments have been carried out, largely by social psychologists, to ascertain how people respond when they encounter what they perceive as injustice. Space does not permit an adequate summary of this work here, and in any event an excellent one is available.[35] We shall however note its more significant findings, as they help to understand the ways in which people actually define justice. Generally, this research has used a restrictive and stringent standard for justice: How willing are people to *restore* equity or justice when injustice or harm-doing has occurred? Such a step is much less common (because it is more costly) than a decision that some injustice has taken place.

The cost of restoring justice is not only (as in so many of these experiments) that we may have to give up some of our gains. More generally, we could never get through the day if we were to put off our other goals while we correct each and every evil we encounter or observe—here, a harsh mother striking her child; there, a biased advertisement or news story; down the street, a family living in misery. Such a policy would require more energy, time, and influence than we possess. Nor could we bear the costs in hostility and reputation for eccentricity that we should incur. Because of this range of difficulties and costs, it is not correct to assert that we are approving all the evils we do not fight. Restoring justice or fighting injustice could be a full-time activity.

The formal definition of justice, called "equity" in these experiments, is much the same as that of Homans, Blau, Adams, or Aristotle, although specific details of such formulas differ.[36] In much of equity research, the experimenter creates a situation in which one or more persons are harmed in some way, or are rewarded too much or too little, in relation to their contributions or achievements; thereby, an unjust situation is created. Then the focus is on the conditions or variables that affect the participants' willingness to restore equity. These findings are drawn from artificial groups in artificial settings, but they throw much light on how people act in real life.

Groups and communities punish members who act unfairly and reward those who are fair. The rewards and punishments most commonly take the form of esteem or disesteem. As long as groups make it more profitable to be virtuous, people have some stake in behaving equitably; further, everyone has been socialized to believe in fairness. Consequently, people become indignant if treated unjustly and feel troubled, distressed, or guilty if they do harm to others or treat them unfairly.

As one result, under some circumstances people will try to restore

35. Elaine Walster, Ellen Berscheid, and G. William Walster, in "New Directions in Equity Research," pp. 1–42; and J. Stacy Adams and Sara Freedman, "Equity Theory Revisited: Comments and Annotated Bibliography," in Berkowitz and Walster, eds., *Equity Theory*, pp. 43–90. The various issues of equity discussed in this chapter are treated differently in the experimentation on helping others. For that work, see J. Macaulay and L. Berkowitz, eds., *Altruism and Helping Behavior*.

36. As I noted earlier, the differences are not all trivial; but since I believe that most of the formulas do not fit reality closely enough, there is little need to criticize them here.

equity. They do this by *actually* righting the balance between contribution and payoff, or by *psychologically* altering their perceptions of the balance. Righting the balance might include these activities: If an employee now works too little for the prestige or pay received, he or she might begin to work harder; if too much, he or she might loaf more on the job, steal or destroy company property, or increase the employer's costs in some way.

Everyone is familiar with psychological ways of righting the balance, many of which are disesteeming processes. Juvenile delinquents use some of them to justify vandalism or violence,[37] and some can be observed in social relations between races. The employer who underpays his workers may actually perceive them as stupid or incompetent. The delinquent can see members of middle-class society as crooks, too, or as having provoked an attack. A husband who exploits his wife may feel or believe that she gets far more from taking care of him than he receives in enjoyment. That is, the harmdoer or exploiter can convince himself or herself that the balance is not so inequitable as an outside observer might report; that it is actually fair.

Of particular relevance to prestige processes is the psychological technique of derogation, or blaming the victim, which may be used by both observers and harmdoers. The more responsible one is for the harmdoing, and the greater the harm done, the more likely one is to derogate the victim. The relevance of this for the exploitation of one class by another is obvious. If the victim is viewed as bad or incompetent in some way, then he or she "deserved" some of the misfortune, and little injustice was done.

Another psychological technique for "righting the balance" is to minimize the suffering of the victim (an example of this is the assertion that the poor "like to live that way," or that field hands in agriculture "are used to that kind of work"). In addition, the harmdoer can often claim that he or she is not responsible: The harm was caused by fate, or by order of a superior.

One can, then, alter the reality of the imbalance, which often requires compensation or restitution; or one can alter one's perception or judgment about the reality by distortion or justification. The two are not commonly used together—perhaps because that seems illogical: for example, if the victim was not "really" harmed, then he or she ought not to be compensated; there is no inequity to be corrected.

We can easily observe that people are less likely to restore equity if that is very costly, but a related finding is less obvious: If some restoration is possible but is not viewed as adequate by those faced with the problem, they are less likely to take the step. It is as though people calculate that inadequate compensation is a loss to themselves, the givers, but does not

---

37. Gresham M. Sykes and David Matza, "Techniques of Neutralization: A Theory of Delinquency," *American Sociological Review*, 22 (December, 1957): 664–670.

wipe out the inequity. On the other hand, those who might be helped by that step would, I suppose, ordinarily prefer to get something rather than nothing. One practical implication of this finding, if it is correct, is that the victim should calculate precisely whether his or her claims might be seen as so large that others see no way of making adequate recompense, for in that case they may do nothing at all.

Distortion or rationalization is less likely to be attempted, the less it fits the apparent facts; thus it is less likely to occur when the victim and the harmdoer are in much social contact, or the harmdoer expects to have much social contact with the victim in the future.

Besides the actual or psychological righting of the balance, other methods for restoring equity can be observed. When a victim of inequity retaliates, the action typically wipes out any distress the harmdoer felt, if indeed he or she felt any. In that situation, the harmdoer does not usually derogate the former victim. If the harmdoer apologizes—a behavior that may contain several elements simultaneously, such as a plea for forgiveness, an explanation or justification ("I could not help it"), or a claim that one has already suffered ("I have felt so guilty")—he or she feels the balance is righted. If the state or an outside agency (the supervisor, the school) intervenes either to retaliate or to restore what was lost, the harmdoer is also likely to feel that the matter has been corrected, and will no longer feel distressed.

In addition to situations in which a person or persons are harmed, or awarded too much or too little in relation to their contributions or achievements, another type of "inequity" occurs when people help others even though they did not cause the harm or loss. That is, by helping others they have created an imbalance; something is owed to them. People help strangers, for example, and at times even risk their lives for others. What, then, ought the receivers do to pay them back? Private and public agencies engage in aiding those in need. In such situations, both helper and helped face the problem of restoring equity. Here again it is possible for the receiver to derogate the "victim," that is, the person who has helped and thus created an imbalance between contribution and payoff. By disesteeming the person who helped, one can wipe out the debt in part. As more than one cynic has commented, "Why does he dislike me? I never did him a favor."

The ability to pay back reduces the distress that some people feel when they have been given much help when in need. In addition, folk rules about which kinds of presents or aid to accept from strangers or people in the "wrong" kind of relationship to oneself aim to prevent the receipt of aid or gifts one cannot recompense. For example, it was once common for young women to be warned not to accept lavish or intimate presents from men who were not their fiancés; two friends attempt to give each other presents that are roughly equal. People feel more friendly toward others who give aid or presents that they can pay back. People are embarrassed if others express great admiration for them but they cannot sincerely respond in kind. Even when the imbalance is in our favor, and good rather than harm has been done to us, if the imbalance is substantial and not easily restored, we who are the gainers may well feel some distress about this inequity.

These and other findings do cast some light on the complex dynamics of decisions and actions concerning justice and injustice. Even though people are more likely to complain at injustice to themselves than to restore equity when they have caused inequity or harm, under some circumstances they do take such steps.

On the other hand, it is difficult to reproduce or create a stratification system within a laboratory experiment, although of course class variables do affect the results. The participants generally begin with goodwill toward one another and a Western collegiate egalitarian bias in their definitions of equity. One might guess that if the person who gained by the manipulations of the experimenter were a seventeenth-century Spanish or French marquis, he might feel the imbalance was entirely proper; such a marquis was, after all, "worth" that much more. More important, cross-class, cross-caste, or cross-group attitudes in real life permit imbalances between contributions and rewards, which seem fair to those who gain from them, and decidedly unjust to those who lose from them.[38]

Within the dynamics of class systems, most of the losses or harm are not viewed by the upper ranks as anything they do to those lower down; and very likely a high percentage of those at lower ranks feel that way too. People do not generally feel that anyone or any group specifically created the class system, though of course most can see that those toward the upper ranks do take steps to preserve or increase their advantages.

When viewed as a class phenomenon, a psychological technique for restoring equity such as blaming the victim becomes more complex than in an experiment on equity. In the experiments, the loss or harm comes first, and the harmdoer then creates the derogation. In real life, people learn early in life which kinds of persons or traits should be valued or disvalued; they learn to disesteem other castes, classes, races, or ethnic groups long before they have had much opportunity to exploit those whom they derogate. In class relations derogation can also be a rationally chosen program, a propaganda technique, by which one presents oneself or one's group as honorable and another as worthy of denigration—in order to justify a planned victimization. One can do this without at all believing the accusations made.

More important than the disesteem and propaganda in actual class relations is the likelihood that most people do not know that a common

---

38. For a complex program of experimentation, designed to ascertain how a range of status variables affects others' judgments, see Joseph Berger *et al.*, *Status Characteristics and Social Interaction* (New York: Elsevier, 1977).

pattern in their thinking about others who receive lesser rewards at lower ranks is a process of blaming the victim. Most people would be indignant at the charge that they are distorting reality in order to "right the balance." I do not believe this knowledge is part of folk wisdom at lower levels, either. Some experimental evidence suggests that victims may come to disesteem or blame *themselves* under certain conditions (for example, when both retaliation and restitution are impossible); they may impute special virtues or abilities to those at higher ranks; or they may even claim they have gained something (wisdom, spiritual growth) through their losses. These processes, too, have been observed in the daily interaction among castes, classes, or ethnic groups, although I believe that self-derogation by the victim (such as Uncle Tomism) has been less common than supposed.

Like so much of exchange theory, from which equity theory is an offshoot, interaction in these experiments occurs between and among individuals. Not only are classes and ethnic groups lacking, as we have noted, but so are corporate actors, such as governmental or business bureaucracies. In corporate structures, some procedures exist for restoring equity because employees who feel the system is unjust are likely to become less diligent or efficient in their work, while inequity is likely to reward the less competent. In the community or nation, likewise, disaffected citizens may become rebellious. On the other hand, as we have repeatedly noted, when the injustice itself is caused by the structural arrangements—such as the disparagement of achievement by the lowly or disesteemed ranks, the bars to opportunity—then the system contains few formal procedures by which victims can count on any restoration. Mostly, they must carry out their own program of propaganda, lawsuits, retaliation, denigration, sabotage, or revolt.

TRADITION AS A STANDARD OF JUSTICE

Ours is a society in which people are urged to strive upward. At any given time the person we interact with may be in passage from one level to another. In any social encounter we may not know much about the other person. For these reasons, people are now more likely than in most past societies to question openly whether a given person actually deserves what he or she has received. Certainly people in Western society are less likely than in past societies to argue that they should be given a certain amount of respect or money because it is traditional to do so; that is, that they were in the same position in the past, and always got that much.

By contrast, in perhaps most societies of the past, whether great civilizations or small tribes, the question of why a chief, baron, or other person should receive more or less deference or material rewards would far more often have been answered by the statement, "it is our tradition." That is, "we have always done that," time has given authority to that practice. This answer would also apply to their laws and customs generally.

Can it be asserted, then, that tradition is another rule of justice? Although I believe not, let us consider this question. Both jurists and sociologists have often viewed tradition as one major basis of law. If the lord of the manor has "always" handed out annual payments or gifts to his tenants at Christmas, not to do so is an injustice, unless the tenants have first failed in some of their obligations. When it was a longstanding custom for the Polynesian chief to distribute food to his subjects at certain feasts, not to do so aroused indignation—as did the disesteem of placing any object above the chief's head. For almost all such expressions of respect, salutations, gifts and exchanges, or rewards that have been recorded in the past, most participants would not have supposed that any other justification than tradition was needed.

The explanation that tradition is the only justification necessary is not entirely hollow. It can easily be observed how quickly some social pattern becomes regularized, legitimated, or at least expected. There is at least some truth in Homans' hypothesis that what ought to be is determined "in the long run and with some lag" by what people find is the case; or that "whatever is, is always on the way to becoming right, though it may not long remain so."[39] It is a widely offered hypothesis of social change that social patterns are often legitimated simply because they arise and continue for some time, such as fork and knife rules in the United States (once important for social acceptability), or driving on the right or left side of the road. Certainly for many such patterns it is not easy to see any obvious explanation: Almost any orderly pattern seems reasonable enough, and no normative principle appears to be evident, except, "we've always done it that way." Other rules, I guess, could once have been justified by a reason, but we no longer know what it was. Later, various other social patterns grew about them, so that change became costly. Such growths about small beginnings occur in patterns of social settlement, too; for example, a winding road grew from a horsepath, and shops, houses, or farms were oriented toward it.

Some traditions of gift-giving, such as at Hanukkah and Christmas, are supported by ancient tradition, but it is obvious that these exchanges are also supported by the associated pleasure-giving festivities. It is doubtful, however, that most traditional rules of distribution rest on bases no more substantial than their having been followed many times before. It also seems doubtful that people typically come to view as just whatever may be the distribution of rewards and punishments they personally experience, or perceive in the lives of others.

People in all societies do come to accept what they cannot alter; it is a large leap of optimistic faith, on the other hand, to suppose that they will view as just whatever they cannot alter, however painful. If that were so, most of us would be much happier. If landlords control the legal system

---

39. Homans, *Social Behavior*, pp. 249–250, 263.

and exact heavy rents from their peasant tenants, these people may adjust, in the simple sense that they carry out their rental obligations if they can, but they are not thereby gradually persuaded that those terms are just. To say a monarchy is supported by tradition means no more than that it has been strong enough to hold onto its rule through successive reigns, and that no class or group sees any way of taking over the government.

Over the several centuries of slavery in the New World, there was never a time when slaves were able, by their own efforts, to gain their freedom (with the notable exception of Haiti), and millions "adapted" to that life: that is, they did not revolt. However, while under slavery they never came to believe that slavery was just, and they rejoiced when they were freed. Of course, in all societies some people have come to believe in the rightness of their lowly position. In Western societies, perhaps a high percentage of people would even agree that on balance what they receive from their jobs is about what they are "worth," or that their prestige rankings are about what they merit. But there is little or no evidence that a majority of those who must accept terms they consider unjust will eventually come to see them as just—in short, come to believe that continuation, or tradition, is enough to make them just.

The persuasiveness of tradition has several bases other than justice. First, the distribution of rewards and punishments it prescribes has survived objection and protest in the past, and people who grow up in that tradition perceive its strength. It was once tradition for a Russian peasant to show deference to his lord by doffing his cap, as once a Southern black was expected to bare his head when talking with a white. In all such cases, the subordinate knew that failure to show that traditional respect had always been met with indignation and force. It would be foolish to test it again.

Similarly, peers have often used tradition as a way of educating or persuading the reluctant or rebellious, for most people have at least some stake in peace even at the expense of justice. For example, fellow students or pupils, fellow workers, members of the same army squad—all may point to tradition as socially visible proof that whoever is in charge is likely to maintain a given practice. The tradition rests, then, on a continuing advantage in power and a continuing set of payoffs to the more powerful. When, as in friendship relations, the distribution is more equal, so that both parties gain about the same, continuance of the tradition rests primarily on those gains.

In addition, any traditional distribution comes to be buttressed and linked with still other exchanges or social patterns, so that others in the total network or community have a stake in maintaining those allocations. Each such link may give only modest support to it, but the sum may be great. The overt respect or deference that nineteenth-century factory workers paid to the foreman also buttressed the authority of higher-level managers and subforemen, as well as the social rank of the foreman's wife in the neighborhood. Whether others in the network believe the amount given is somewhat too high or too low, they derive some benefit from the system as it exists. All the gradations of the nobility have some stake in the system as a whole, even if individuals believe that Marquis X should justly be no more than a baron; but thousands of other people, from servants and tenants to sellers of all kinds of goods, also have an interest in the continuation of those traditional distributions of high social rank.

More crudely put, tradition becomes so because people with greater resources of power continue over time to maintain the same pattern of allocation, and at a minimum others accept that distribution as a reality not easily altered. Felt injustices are not easily transformed into felt justice by simple continuation. In spite of numerous philosophical comments to that effect, it is not likely that many prisoners come to love their chains. It is far more likely that force and force threat, or power, has maintained many traditional allocations.

On the other hand, certainly much of tradition persisted because its allocations were not viewed as very unjust, and instead reflected at least a general agreement that the exchange was reasonable—the modest respect paid to craftsmen in medieval towns, the esteem traditionally given to whaling captains over many generations, the division of the catch on Newfoundland fishing boats, the deference paid to chiefs in many tribes. That is, tradition was not the cause but the result of many generations of judgments about what the contribution or achievement of various kinds of persons, occupations, posts, or groups was worth. They were not seriously challenged, and thus became traditions, because they were thought to be more or less fair.

Tradition, then, does have some social weight, because it sometimes expresses a social evaluation that has stood the test of many negotiations over time. It is often expressed in the rhetoric of justice, but whether it rests on felt justice is an empirical question to be tested by the data.

HOW WIDESPREAD IS THE BELIEF IN JUSTICE?

The recognition that force and force threat, rather than felt justice, have maintained many traditional allocations of social benefits points out that, inevitably, any serious analysis of justice must explore its connection with power.[40] Formulations of distributive justice argue reasonably that people or groups are given more rewards if they contribute or achieve in ways that are valued, and that evaluation will be higher if supply is low relative to

40. Here I shall continue to mean "force and force threat" by the term "power." It seems loose to use that term to mean the ability to get one's way by any means whatever, including purchase, affection, or prestige. The meaning I use is narrower, but more precise; and linguistically there is no point in using the term unless one at *least* means force and force threat, including legal systems, property institutions, and the ability to call on force as even a distant threat (e.g., alimony payments, ejecting a student from class or a guest from one's home). For a fuller theoretical discussion, see William J. Goode, "The Place of Force in Human Society," *American Sociological Review*, 37 (October, 1972): 507–519.

demand. Unfortunately, such formulations appear to be tainted by the same blind cheerfulness that once claimed that an invisible hand wisely guides economic processes, or that asserts that both sides gain in all economic exchanges. These formulations seem unsatisfying because they seem to assert that whatever prices or rewards exist in reality, people have affirmed them or approve of them—and thus, there can be no justice.

Such formulations seem to overlook the central assumption implicit in distributive justice: that there is a free market, that supply and demand themselves are not determined by individual or corporate power in any major way. That is, theories asserting that the rewards, prices, or prestige rankings encountered in a society are simply what most people have agreed upon assume that the power of no subgroup or set of leaders is enough to affect those payoffs, directly or indirectly. If the assumption of a free market were to hold, then we would have to concede that women are respected and paid as well as men for equal contributions, and that the failure of women to equal men's achievements is not caused at all by men's control over training, opportunities, and awards. We would similarly have to agree that physicians earn large rewards in prestige and money because their clientele freely pay them, and very little because of their organizational and legal control over every aspect of medical practice, from admission into medical school to the availability of hospital facilities. Simple observation at least suggests that at various points in the acquisition of prestige, as of money, the structure of power determines to some degree the rewards people get.

Since people do feel some grievance or resentment when they do not get what in justice they think they should get, social analysts have suggested various links between power and people's beliefs about whether they are being treated justly. Here are a few:

When people threaten to take power from the hands of the privileged, the latter are more likely to hand out justice than when no such threat is made.

When people believe they do not get as much as they deserve, the use of power prevents them from doing much about it. Thus, social stability does not prove that the citizens are content.

When people in power hand out justice, people of lesser rank are more likely to pay them loyalty and obedience in turn, thus reaffirming their power.

It is necessary to have power in order to dispense injustice, because injustice will mean an unfair division in favor of the person with more power, and such a division would (without the power advantage) arouse resistance.

Presumably, if everyone got what he or she believed justice dictates, fewer people would try to use force or its threat (through the law or directly) in order to get more; and fewer people would seek political offices or other ways to get power.

Doubtless, the reader has encountered many statements about how the maintenance of power is dependent on citizens' belief in the justice of a system, or how injustice must be sustained by power. Their content can be expressed by this statement: The amount of power used by power-holders is measured by the gap between a fair or just share of social benefits such as respect or money and what most people actually get. Presumably, where most people feel they are victims of exploitation or injustice, the privileged must use more power to prevent protest or revolt. Correspondingly, where most people feel their shares are just, they will be less moved to use force or its threat.

If that line of traditional reasoning is correct, major powerholders face a dilemma. If they mete out justice, and exploit their subjects or fellow citizens' less, they gain allegiance but lose some exploitative advantage. If they exploit more, they lose in loyalty and face the risk of revolt. Many analysts have asserted that a third option exists, that is, persuasion, fraud, deception, or socialization (i.e., changing others' beliefs or attitudes). Powerholders may establish or maintain an otherworldly religion (for example, medieval Christianity, Hinduism) that promises later rewards for accepting life's difficulties without complaint. All societies explicitly "train" or socialize their children to believe that the system is just, and that people get what they deserve. It is obvious that in all ongoing societies, all three patterns exist, and reliance on one more than another of them will vary from time to time and from society to society. Greater efforts will be made in some societies than in others to socialize children (or to persuade adults) to believe their lot is just.

Compared with large civilizations, in most primitive societies with the exception of some (perhaps all) large African kingdoms, it seems likely that there was a much smaller gap between what most persons received in prestige and material goods and what they believed they should get, and between both of those two and what most others believed they should get. This occurred partly because rulers, elders, or ruling strata commanded a much lesser advantage in power and other resources over others, and partly because in such intimate social interaction the respect or affection of others was very important. Under those circumstances, it was less likely that groups or families would be able or willing to exploit others for long. Indeed, it is more characteristic, as theorists of the primitive economy have pointed out for several generations, that "big men" in all but tribal kingdoms commandeered greater resources or won them through hunting and then redistributed most of them in large festivals, thus buttressing their high rank.[41]

By contrast, in great civilizations, for certainly more than two thousand years, powerholders have exploited people with lesser power, erected legal structures to keep them in their place, supported ideologies that asserted

---

41. This point is elaborately dealt with in William J. Goode, *Religion among the Primitives* (New York: Free Press, 1951), chap. 5, "Religion and Economic Action." See also Marcel Mauss, *The Gift* (Glencoe, Ill.: Free Press, 1954), Karl Polanyi *et al.*, *Trade and Market in the Early Empires* (Glencoe, Ill.: Free Press, 1957), and Peter Ekeh, *Social Exchange Theory* (Cambridge, Mass.: Harvard University Press, 1974).

the system was just, and seemed to concede the smallest possible share of wealth and respect to their lowly subjects. That statement appears obvious enough as we contemplate the poverty and disesteem of the lower classes all over the globe, for most of world history—but we have no way of demonstrating our central factual assertion here: that in most great civilizations of the past, at most times, much of the population actually felt that the system was unjust, and that what they received in prestige or wealth was unfairly small, relative to what they contributed or achieved. I believe they did, but we shall always lack the data necessary to prove they did.

Granted that the poor and powerless received little of prestige and wealth, did they—by their own standard of what was just—concede that the powerful and rich deserved the greater amount they actually received? In the European middle ages, peasants, villeins, and serfs could perceive that lords and kings were "superior." For example, they commanded a more elegant language (sometimes, two of them); appreciated poetry and music; possessed several skills (hawking, jousting, swordsmanship) and areas of knowledge (law, history, ceremonies); and sometimes protected their subjects from brigands, invaders, or overreaching minor lords or fellow citizens. Did all that justify, in the hearts of the silent lowly, the greater privileges the lords enjoyed? Did they come to believe in the rightness of those privileges because (as Homans claims) people come to accept the reality as just?[42] Or can we accept as an adequate negative answer that revolts were recorded in many reigns, and thereby people proved they did not affirm the justice of their lot?

We do not know whether the revolutionary attacks on the class system that were made in the various peasant rebellions of the fourteenth and fifteenth centuries in England and Europe, for example, were simply the result of historically unique injustices, or whether they were inner judgments that were widespread over many centuries but came to expression only when the lower orders felt more powerful (or more resentful).[43] We do know, surveying the slow changes in successive reigns, in many civilizations, that when there were "just kings" and stability, neither the social structure nor the lives of ordinary citizens changed much. Good King X, whether Wenceslaus or Alfred, did no more than show personal kindness or respect, or protect his lesser subjects from force, fraud, or humiliation at the hands of grasping lords and merchants. He did not alter the fundamental division of privilege and prestige by which the lowly got little and the highly placed got much. He could not, in the unlikely event he so desired, change the distribution of power and prestige by which that system was maintained. Only the slow, massive enfranchisement of the whole population over many centuries and the increased esteem it com-

---

42. Homans, *Social Behavior*, pp. 249–250.

43. For a good analysis of the Wat Tyler revolt in 1381, see Rodney Hilton, *Bond Men Made Free* (London: Temple Smith, 1973), esp. chap. 3.

manded could accomplish that in a few Western countries. Other countries had to wait for the few genuine revolutions over the past several decades, while the large remainder have at least been affected by both those salutary examples.

Not only do we lack these data about the past. In addition, we still lack a reasonable measure of the extent to which the present distribution of power even in the more enlightened democracies, such as the Scandinavian countries, prevents the attainment of justice, by the standards of ordinary citizens. Nor do we have such a datum for the other Western democracies. I suppose that most of these citizens would agree at present that the system as a whole is generally fair, compared to real alternatives, that a smaller percentage would agree their particular share is just, and that a fairly high percentage would deny that the very rich merit their extreme wealth. By contrast, I would guess that a fairly high percentage would concede that those who enjoy high *prestige* do deserve it. We know that is true for the prestige of occupations, since half a century of research supports that conclusion. On the other hand, the percentage of those who agree that their share of the benefits such as wealth, influence, and respect is just is correlated with class, so that a lower percentage of those toward the lower class agree, and several large segments of a population (many women, a majority of American blacks and Indians) still feel the system deprives them of their just rewards.

Over world history, most people have not enthusiastically pursued justice for themselves for very long; that pursuit is fraught with danger. Powerholders have repeatedly demonstrated their willingness to kill, in their preference for order over justice. Because those who have felt most strongly they were not obtaining justice have also been the weakest in the society, they have not, except in unusual conditions, been willing to risk their lives for it. Those, by contrast, who believe most strongly in the existing social arrangements are also the most likely to be gaining advantages from that system, and therefore they feel the least motivation to alter it; happily for them, they have the greatest power to resist any reduction in their privileges. Preferring order (with its continuing advantages) to justice, they are more likely than others to achieve their preference. As for the less powerful: Whether or not most people in most societies prefer order (as seems likely, since order is necessary for any kind of social life at all), they get it just the same, since it is imposed on them.

I believe that this harsh description applies much less to Western democracies than it applies to most class structures throughout most of world history, but it is not possible to obtain adequate data to describe how far from it the modern world has moved.

Chapter 14
The Problem of More Equality

Throughout this inquiry I have sharply criticized many inequalities in this and other nations. At the same time I have insisted on the inevitability of heroes,[1] of a skewed and peaked distribution of prestige and other social rewards in modern societies. I have not, however, systematically addressed a question that has been a focus of liberal as well as revolutionary thought for centuries: Can more equality be achieved? If so, how would we set about achieving it? These are important theoretical and pragmatic issues, which come increasingly to the fore in this most unstable of eras. There is no country in the world in which these issues are not passionately debated at present, and every recent revolution has promised equality, or at least more of it.[2]

In the modern world, over the past several centuries and increasingly in the past generation, people's concern with the esteem (and not alone the income) they get has supported a trend toward less overt deference and toward universal respect. Since the prestige any class or group earns is very dependent on opportunity, and opportunity is in turn partly determined by legal structures, this great trend often takes the political form of demands for "equal rights"—in voting, jobs, free speech, residential location, protection from discrimination. Since subnational groups in many countries are given less respect than the dominant society, their modern solution for inequality is sometimes a call for independence—the Scots in Great Britain, the Quebecois in Canada, the Basques in Spain.

The Harijans or outcastes in India and the Eta in Japan, although they are not subnations or ethnic groups, also seek more respect as well as the economic and civic rights that are part of that goal. All over the world, oppressed or disesteemed categories or groups as well as classes and castes have been demanding to be treated with more overt deference and real respect. *More equality*—in political power, economic goods, and esteem—has become a theme in the rhetoric of revolt, political pressure,

1. For a psychoanalytic treatise on this inevitability see Ernest Becker, *The Denial of Death* (New York: Free Press, 1973).

2. For a sober discussion of modest proposals toward this end, see Herbert J. Gans, *More Equality* (New York: Vintage, 1974). Every empirically based analysis of class systems describes the details of this widespread inequality, and most attempt to explain its inevitability.

and social change. It is a theme which has great appeal to the down-trodden all over the world, and it is these downtrodden who have formed a majority of humankind throughout most of world history.

Increasingly, people who have been disadvantaged by their ascribed statuses—women, blacks, colonials, subnationals, members of many religions—are demanding to be considered as full members of society. And dominant groups are moving toward granting at least some of their demands. As noted in the last chapter, full membership is often defined as properly equal in a wide range of civic rights and public goods, from voting to the use of highways or the right to a pension in old age. That is, regardless of the additional privileges some individuals get, true members should be "equal" in enjoying many goods, rights, and services that would not have been theirs even fifty years ago.

In the area of prestige, however, it can be argued that no such trend ought to be supported. We should be allowed to heap large honors on the heads of our heroes. We give our admiration freely to people who perform well or who exhibit esteemed qualities (nobility, beauty): We *want* to applaud. Why reduce our freedom to express our natural feelings?

Perhaps most people in this and other societies (including socialist ones) would also argue that lowering inequalities would undermine the social control system we have analyzed in this volume. That is, people would not try as hard. We would not then have as many heroes to celebrate, or as great ones, because people would not strain to reach the heights if they were not rewarded as much as now. More equality, it might be alleged, would remove part of the sheer color and drama from the world; we would all then be at the same dull level. Perhaps most people in modern nations (including again those in socialist countries) would also assert that un-equal rewards for unequal performance *is* justice; that is, it would be wrong to give equal rewards to the shirker and the diligent, to those who accept little and those who accept much responsibility or leadership.

Such arguments pose false alternatives between continuing the exact inequalities we now observe and moving toward complete equality. We do not have to choose either of them. Regarding the first, in fact there are great differences in the amount of inequality found in various societies, and over various historical epochs. The specific inequalities we now see cannot be viewed as a natural harmony worthy of preservation forever. They were created by human action, and they enjoy no privileged stand-ing. Regarding the second alternative, it is theoretically inconceivable that every person and every action would or could be ranked the same. As long as people evaluate some performances and qualities as more excellent or worthy than others, large inequalities will remain.

Since people will always evaluate and judge, no one's freedom to admire heroes is likely to be taken away. However, as pointed out many times here, especially in the chapter on structural subversion, many individuals, groups, and social categories are given far less respect (or more) than they would deserve if there were more equal opportunities for education, training, jobs, and other achievements. That is, even under our present social arrangements (in every major country) people's prestige responses are shaped by external social pressures, customs, legal systems, and patterns of discrimination. How much esteem people give is partly determined by the social barriers of any society, rather than entirely by a free, autonomous reaction. To reduce those barriers would yield more real freedom, both to achieve and to respond positively to that achievement.

As to whether potential heroes—be they kings or entertainers—would strive as hard if the discrepancies in reward were not exactly as great as they are now, two answers can be given. The first is that if the difference were as large as that between a Japanese prince and an outcaste Eta in the Tokugawa period, or as small as between a very creative Swedish nuclear physicist and a less creative one, that difference would still cause people to strive hard, for it is worth something. And if the rewards at lower levels were higher, many more people at these levels would strive harder. Second, if people at lower levels were esteemed more, the esteem they give to others would be worth more, so that the total amount given to the upper levels (if not the discrepancy between their share of respect and that of others) would be as large as, perhaps even larger than, at present.

As to the problem of just rewards, it was pointed out in the last chapter that the principle of unequal rewards for unequal contributions, and the present amount of inequality, are both rejected by most persons under some circumstances and in particular relations. Just as we can assert that more individuals should enjoy more nearly equal political rights, or income, so can we aim at a reduction in the indignities or disesteem some people suffer, or at a movement toward a somewhat greater equality of respect for all. Neither principle is to be followed blindly in all circumstances. In any event, individuals and groups increasingly see the justice of greater equality rather than less.

One might instead give the argument for more equality of esteem a political form: Such equality will increase the relative esteem given to persons at lower social strata, and that in turn will give them more influence or social control over those at higher ranks. When people at lower levels are disesteemed, others are less willing to listen to them, or agree to their wishes; as a consequence, their legitimate interests are more likely to be disregarded, as at present.

EVALUATING CONCRETE PROPOSALS

Although some of the social changes that I believe could increase the equality of prestige will be listed here, space does not permit an evaluation of each, though arguments for and against all of them can be made. I rather hope to stimulate further suggestions and thus to persuade others to give more thought to ways of increasing equality. In this section, a few theoretical principles will be offered that might guide our thinking about such proposals. Some of these principles set broad limits to what can be done, and others assert that some steps can be made toward increasing equality.

As to the most general question, that is, whether any such change is possible at all, ordinary daily observation in different countries reveals large differences in the amount of equality people enjoy. For example, if we observe the difference in the treatment of people in the lower social strata in Denmark as contrasted with the treatment of such people in India, or blacks in the United States as contrasted with the lower classes in Germany, it seems clear that societies vary considerably in the amount of inequality that is taken for granted. Over longer historical eras, still greater differences in inequality seem evident. Since the discrepancies between top and bottom do vary, and are created by human action, it seems cautious enough to argue that they can be altered by human beings.

Additional support can be based on related phenomena in economics, for proposals aimed at reducing inequality can be viewed as ways of changing or fixing prices. Economists are fond of reminding us that price-fixing does not reduce demand or increase supply, and thus black markets arise to supply unsatisfied demand at a "real" higher price. Although such statements correctly describe the forces at work, they do not describe the real outcomes. Price control was generally successful in World War II. Zoning regulations do determine what land use is permitted and thus also fix prices to some degree. Import regulations effectively fix prices, too, by reducing foreign competition. Rules that determine who may be trained to become a craftsman or a professional (thus limiting the supply) are price-fixing systems that work. For generations, corporations have controlled prices informally or formally. From time immemorial, societies have fixed prices in the prestige market by preventing women, lower castes and classes, and lesser-ranked ethnic, racial, and religious groups from enjoying their full share of opportunities or their full share of prestige for their achievements. To be sure, some prices or rewards are harder than others to control—for example, overt deference is easier to control than the inner esteem of others—but the reality of control is surely a reasonable proof that it can be done.

How it is to be done is a more difficult matter. It is intellectually easy to "solve" the problem of more equality by postulating a major revolution, in which egalitarian socialist ideals will be imposed on everyone by mass propaganda and force or force threat. Apocalyptic solutions are tempting because they are simple: Henceforth, we shall do everything right. Marc Bloch comments somewhere that grand policy changes are likely to be based on astrology or alchemy. The first asserts that the inexorable movement of the stars, or fate, will inevitably lead us to the new and better world. The second tells us that suddenly we shall be able to transform lead into gold. The comparable modern solution is to postulate a revolution in which the leaders are omnipotent and everyone soon follows willingly. By definition, if they have enough power they can transform the society.

Aside from the fact that most revolutionary leaders find it difficult to transform their societies, we do not have the right to pursue so ethically perilous a solution. It appears more justifiable when the old regime was despotic, corrupt, massively exploitative, and oppressive of human dignity, as in such countries as China or Cuba. It is reasonable to argue that most of those populations would have agreed with those accusations, and did prefer the alternative that history finally offered, at least at the time the military part of the revolution became successful.

On the other hand, it would violate what we know of people's beliefs and opinions in many democratic countries (such as the Scandinavian and Anglo nations) to make the claim that they would prefer the same alternative. Almost certainly they would approve of more equality, but they would also reject the authoritarian controls of modern communist countries.

Thus, the intellectual problem of working out possible steps toward more equality is somewhat difficult: One cannot, without denying citizens a real voice in their own fate, simply wipe out the existing sociopolitical arrangements. Any practical steps must at least be in harmony with some of the major values or beliefs of the people whose lives are to be shaped by them. The impatient will feel chafed by such restrictions. The radical will sneer at their timidity. Still, there is wisdom in Alexander Herzen's comment that we have not the right to grind the face of this generation as we step upward to make a better world for the next. Good results are at best chancy, and the destruction of what people do enjoy in their present lives may be certain. Thus, any proposals should at least pay respect to the opinions and values of the people who will experience the consequences of those proposals.

Major revolutions have accomplished a great deal; I am simply pointing out that we cannot offer an authoritarian solution for countries that enjoy greater freedom and less exploitation than the people who have experienced modern revolutions. In several countries, those great cataclysms have introduced a strong ideological support for egalitarianism, altered who gets which rewards, eliminated the stratum of the nobility or imperialist rulers, and raised the esteem given to agricultural and factory workers.

On the other hand, even that solution generates its own problems. Revolutionary societies become less revolutionary after a while. New classes arise, which exhibit large disparities of privilege, deference, power, and wealth that sadly remind us of other countries. When, as in Russia, the main national goals remain the same, that is, high material production, military success, and domination or conquest of neighboring countries, there may not even be much discrepancy between the distribution of prestige and other rewards (except for money) there and in capitalist countries. In any event, as noted earlier, even revolutionary leaders encounter great difficulty in persuading their followers to believe firmly in all the new prestige evaluations; aspiring citizens do not suddenly begin to use all their personal influence to gain a lowly factory job and to reject managerial positions.[3]

Whatever combination of forces may be effective in achieving more equality in prestige, changes toward equality need not be mere allocations of a fixed sum, a kind of zero-sum game in which whatever one group gets, another must lose. Prestige is rather like wealth or economic production: It is only in the very short run that the total is simply redistributed; over the longer run, what people produce or achieve may well yield far more to be distributed within the society, to the lowly as well as the privileged.

These observations bring to mind a major principle on which effective social programs must be based: Large effects do not typically proceed from large causes. It is rare in social history that we can point to a massive trend (industrialization, modern capitalism, the Russian Revolution, the Protestant Reformation) and confidently assert that it was caused by a single large event or factor. As in the socialization of children so in the shaping of nations; change is mostly caused by innumerable small and large forces that continually or recurringly press in one general direction rather than another. Thus, if I do not suggest the unleashing of large forces it is not alone that we do command them; it is also that I believe a more effective program is made up of many small parts, often undramatic, that support one another.

TOWARD MORE EQUALITY

Writing a half-century ago, Tawney commented on the effects of inequality in this fashion:

> One of the regrettable, if diverting, effects of extreme inequality is its tendency to weaken the capacity for impartial judgment. It pads the lives of its beneficiaries with a soft down of consideration, while relieving them of the vulgar necessity of justifying their pretensions, and secures that, if they fall, they fall on cushions . . . . It causes them, in short, to apply different standards to different sections of the community, as if it were uncertain whether all of them are human in the same sense as themselves.[4]

Arguing in favor of more collective (or public) goods, as well as more economic equality, he pointed out that thereby workers would enjoy more human dignity and social consideration.[5] Any set of practical steps toward

---

3. For data on these points, see Alex Inkeles and Peter H. Rossi, "National Comparisons of Occupational Prestige," *American Journal of Sociology*, 61 (January, 1956): 329–339; and Robert W. Hodge, Donald J. Treiman, and Peter H. Rossi, "A Comparative Study of Occupational Prestige," in Reinhard Bendix and S. M. Lipset, eds., *Class, Status, and Power* (New York: Free Press, 1966), pp. 309–321. See also Murray Yanowitch and Wesley A. Fisher, eds., *Social Stratification and Mobility in the U.S.S.R.* (White Plains, N.Y.: International Arts and Sciences Press, 1973).

4. R. H. Tawney, *Equality*, 4th ed. (London: George Allen and Unwin, 1952), pp. 24–25.

5. *Ibid.*, pp. 28ff.

more equality in prestige must be linked with equality in other realms of social behavior, since various social resources, such as political influence or wealth, can be used to increase prestige, just as esteem can be used to get other kinds of resources.

These interconnections are exhibited by the historical trend toward lesser deference paid to rulers or the upper classes, the decline of nobility and monarchy, and the greater respect that disesteemed groups or classes have come to demand over time. Indeed, we can draw a lesson from the latter historical movement toward somewhat greater equality. It was rooted in a wide array of changes, in which two large sets or processes can be discerned.

First, the lower classes, ethnic groups, races, groups, and peasants really have "improved" and thus merited more respect, as measured by many values or norms of the dominant groups. They have become cleaner and better educated. Their language has moved closer to standard school speech. Their economic productivity is higher. Fewer of them do dirty work (sweeping chimneys, shoveling manure) because there is less of it, and a smaller percentage of them engage in menial jobs because these use a smaller segment of the labor force. That is, the obvious discrepancies in skills and appearance between the better-off and the less well-off classes are simply narrower.

Second, and perhaps of greater weight, successive revolutions, political threats, and laws have given more political influence to classes or groups that once had little; and both labor and political organizations have made of the lower and lower middle classes a considerable economic force. As a consequence, people in the privileged classes as well as their representatives must cater somewhat to the needs or wishes of those at lower-class levels. When blacks become a larger economic market or a large voting bloc and sharply retaliate when they encounter disesteem; when immigrant Eastern European Jews show their vote does count[6]; when outcastes in India form political organizations—in short, as various submerged or oppressed groups get more economic and political resources—they can demand and get better social treatment. Their trades and exchanges become part of the larger social control processes by which one group or another changes its behavior in order to obtain the help (or avoid the difficulties) that another group can produce. As a consequence, both direct and indirect influences can increase the amount of esteem that various groups or classes will obtain. Let us consider, then, a range of these influences.

OPEN OPPORTUNITIES

Equal or open opportunity as a policy has been subjected to much attack, in part because some view it as a quota system, depriving some

---

6. For details of this process, see Irving Howe, with Kenneth Libo, *World of Our Fathers* (New York: Simon and Schuster, 1976), esp. chaps. 11, 12.

people of their rights in order to help others who have been disadvantaged. It has been especially attacked by those who have done well under the existing structure of narrower opportunity, and it has been especially supported by those who feel their chances of advancement have been restricted unfairly—in the United States by blacks, Indians, Chicanos, women, and the poor. The various proposals or actions under the label of equal opportunity have not typically aimed at increasing equality of rewards for various kinds of achievements, but the equality of opportunity to earn them.

Education has come to be used more and more as a criterion for hiring, even when the skills for a job can be learned by people of modest education.[7] Consequently, many people have been restricted from getting a job they could do well simply because they do not possess the formal educational credentials it demands. Partly for this reason, numerous programs have been suggested or carried out that essentially increase the number of people with at least the necessary formal certificates or credentials. These include "open-door" colleges or schools, with or without remedial education to develop quickly some of the educational skills students may lack. Some systems offer school credits for "adult equivalencies," that is, credits for knowledge, experience, or skill that an adult may have acquired outside the school itself but that are equivalent to the scholastic experience. Compensatory education usually aims at helping adults to obtain classwork they once missed but now need.

To the extent that education is respected and helps to obtain jobs that are esteemed, such programs increase the number of people who gain in prestige, and thereby some equality of esteem is achieved.

So, similarly, the many programs of affirmative action have tried to open the doors of opportunity to less-esteemed categories of people who were formerly viewed, without being tested, as unworthy of the jobs.[8] Again, hiring on the basis of affirmative action opens up occupations to traditionally less-esteemed people, who thereby gain some prestige; for many of them could do these jobs well enough if given the chance.[9] Allied to these attempts are programs for training or retraining for specific jobs, to give some advantage to those formerly deprived of such opportunities.

All such efforts are in harmony with at least some major values of this and other Western societies. However, their effects on equality—even if they are carried out adequately—are somewhat complex. First, the allocation of prestige to *individuals* would not be less peaked or skewed for the

---

7. For a cogent summary of data that show the irrelevance of education to much of achievement, see Ivar Berg, *Education and Jobs: The Great Training Robbery* (New York: Praeger, 1970).

8. See, e.g., the U.S. Supreme Court's decision in Griggs vs. Duke Power Company (a high school diploma is not an adequate test of job skills, and requiring it discriminates against black applicants).

9. See, for example, American Tel. & Tel. Co. vs. U.S. Court of Appeals, 408 F.2d 228 (5th Cir. 1969)—the telephone company must allow women to apply for traditional male jobs; and Lenore J. Weitzman, "Affirmative Action for Academic Women," in Alice S. Rossi and Ann Calderwood, *Academic Women on the Move* (New York: Russell Sage Foundation, 1972).

resulting achievements. There would be more skilled competitors, since more people with more talent would be trained. On the other hand, a lesser percentage of them would be from the higher social strata or groups that are now given more initial advantages. Competition would be keener, achievements higher, and the amount of prestige to be distributed greater. Thus, the curve of prestige distribution would probably not be flatter for the highest achievements or contributions: The individuals at those levels would still get a large portion of the prestige being paid.[10]

As against that consequence, two flattening or broadening effects (that is, more equality) would be discernible. First, the present restrictions now imposed by reason of class, sex, age, or ethnic factors would be reduced. The discrepancies of reward now linked to class would be less likely, since the chances that an individual born within a given class would remain there would be smaller. The myths of class—the notion that members of a class have a right to privilege without regard to their achievements— would be weaker, and thus the class discrepancies in esteem would be less. Second, some movement toward more equality would occur if a larger part of the society were viewed as eligible to compete, as contrasted with the present social system.

MORE PRESTIGE FOR DIFFERENT ACHIEVEMENTS

Although various open opportunities may help achieve greater equality of esteem, I do not believe it is possible to broaden the granting of esteem so much that almost everyone can be ranked as noble or heroic for at least a few minutes in his or her lifetime, in some kind of activity—be it only the exquisite grace with which someone wrings out a mop or the patience with which someone meets family crises. Perhaps the world would be the better for it, but the change is unlikely. Probably even a modern dictator would not dare to announce that henceforth we shall not give adulation to football or rock stars, but instead to excellent waiters or bus drivers. Whom, what, and how we honor is determined by evaluations that are not easily altered.

However, which evaluations are dominant or salient at a given time will be affected by war, revolution, and other national crises, by group membership, class position, and many other factors. Consequently, it is possible for a group, organization, or nation to give more prominence to some evaluations than before, and thus to give more rewards to some activities or some aspects of achievements that formerly were viewed as secondary. Social support can be elicited for some of these changes, since they are in conformity with existing values. Medals, awards, and even salary increases can be used to emphasize the greater esteem that the group judges should be paid for a particular behavior.

10. Plato's "equal-opportunity system," described in *The Republic*, would not have had a flat distribution curve for prestige, either, since the greatest honor would still have been given to the topmost class. However, other rewards were to be given to the lower strata.

In universities and colleges, for example, it is possible to give more esteem or other rewards for teaching, in which the curve of prestige distribution is somewhat broader or flatter, and somewhat less to research. Since many people do in fact want better teaching, and it may be possible to measure its quality, this change is in conformity with existing values. Some individuals would, of course, rank high in both teaching and research; but recognizing the contributions made by teaching would in general move toward a smaller discrepancy in prestige between those who do well in research and those who do well in teaching.

In a parallel way, it is possible to give more esteem to hospital staff who try to make life comfortable for patients, rather than simply convenient for higher-level medical personnel. Again, many people (including even some medical personnel) do value this aspect of achievement highly, but at present it is given little recognition. Similarly, in law, community service is given a modest amount of prestige (less than corporation work), but it is possible for communities, groups, and even law firms to pay more respect to such work publicly. It seems likely that closer scrutiny would disclose many such possibilities; that is, greater esteem could be given for desirable performances, or qualities of performance, that are not given much at present. The result would be an improvement in the quality of life and a greater equality in the distribution of respect.

A redistribution of disesteem, similarly, could reduce inequality somewhat, if it were directed at persons who now gain much esteem for doing well some tasks that perhaps should not be done at all. One of the innovations of political dissidents in the 1960's, in several industrial countries, was public protest or criticism directed at organizations or persons whose achievements seemed morally dubious when weighed against the collective good—for example, the manufacture of napalm and other war goods used against the Vietnamese, research aimed at solving the problems of authoritarian regimes, and the destruction of natural resources. Work in all industrial societies yields esteem because the occupations of such societies are esteemed, but one can raise the question of whether what a particular person is doing hurts the community.[11] Many people do not view the claim that "I am only doing my job" as an adequate answer. Various consumer protection agencies raise that issue indirectly when they reveal the adulteration of food, cheating in repair services, or the consequences of pollution.

Here, too, there is some support for steps toward giving disesteem when an activity may actually harm the quality of life of members of a community. Generally, the disesteem is directed at those whose class rank is high; and any improvement in their behavior is likely to help people of

11. For example, attorney Richard Wasserstrom of U.C.L.A. argues that lawyers who follow "legal ethics" and ignore the larger value implications of their work are legally correct but morally wrong; "Value Conflicts and the Professional Role," *Learning and the Law*, 3, no. 3 (Fall, 1966): 45–61.

lower rank. A further shift in the direction of handing out disesteem on this basis would, then, contribute somewhat to equality.

THE OMBUDSMAN

Ombudsmen could greatly assist in directing disesteem at high-ranking offenders and thus could help achieve greater equality of prestige. Invented in Sweden, whose dedication to more equality is considerably greater than that of the United States, the office of ombudsman has been tried haltingly here and there in this country. The ombudsman has the duty of uncovering (and trying to rectify) injustices in an organization, governmental agency, or community even when victims are afraid to protest publicly.[12] Like a newspaper reporter, a consumer advocate in city government, or a quality control unit in a factory, the ombudsman has a stake in—is paid money and prestige for—locating failures, deviations from the norms, or serious evils, when other people have a stake in keeping them hidden. The ombudsman's actions are therefore likely to arouse criticism, especially from those who lose esteem when their errors or injustices are revealed. It is not surprising that the office of the independent ombudsman has not been viewed by most leaders as a step toward enlightenment.

Once established, however, such activities and offices obtain social support because people who have suffered from the system or from particular individuals see that they can get some protection. These people are also likely to have few resources with which to protest effectively or redress their wrongs, and those in high positions are more likely to be forced to answer for their actions. The activities of the ombudsman increase equality of prestige by criticizing those in high ranks, where the social control effect of disesteem is likely to be greater than that of esteem; and by requiring more respectful treatment for people in lower ranks. In addition, the organization, community, or social system profits, since leaders are forced to be more effective, or to act more in conformity with group values.

COLLECTIVE PUBLIC GOODS AND SERVICES

As noted in the last chapter, when societies move toward viewing a larger percentage of the population as true members, more goods and services become available to all, on a relatively equal basis. This change is partly caused by widening the number of people accepted as worthy; but in turn their use of such benefits raises the standing of those people. In modern societies, these include schools, entertainment in parks, police protection, recreational areas, libraries, museums, roads, agricultural advice, public health measures, research on a wide range of problems, and in some countries complete medical and dental care.

---

12. See Walter Gellhorn, *Ombudsmen and Others: Citizens' Protectors in Nine Countries* (Cambridge: Harvard University Press, 1966).

Which services and goods are chosen to be made available is partly determined by the sheer affluence of the country or political unit and by the official ideology (who is worthy of being a real member) embodied in the laws. Socialist nations are committed to an official ideology of equality of goods and respect and the inclusion of everyone as members. They are thus more likely than capitalist countries to assert that a wider range of goods and services should be available to all.[13]

Collective goods and services differ from welfare or transfer payments primarily in that they are presumed to be given more or less equally to everyone and are not reserved for the poor; one is not required to prove one is without a job in order to enter Yosemite National Park or the New York Public Library. They are organized on the assumption, however, that not all will use most of them, except rarely. For example, if everyone eligible were to get on the roads, enter the parks, and use the libraries within any short time period, those goods and services would be swamped. Indeed, many such things, in the United States at least, *are* being overwhelmed, and without that much use.

Any step toward an increase in collective goods arouses opposition, precisely because many persons do not recognize all others as true members of their community. In addition, many see that they themselves will never use the opportunities offered, and so they feel they are paying for others' pleasures or services. Part of the opposition arises from the wish to pay for one's own goods and types of care (medical therapy, transportation), and thus to avoid any responsibility for paying for anyone else's expenses.

The classical problem of who is the free rider—who is disesteemed for not contributing enough, and what should be defined as a collective responsibility—is never solved, although the line between the appropriately public and private continues to shift. At any given time, people in any country are likely to view as self-evident that everyone should pay for his or her own in one area and not in another, while the citizens of another accept a very different division.

Within smaller, specialized communities, far more items can be dispensed on an egalitarian basis (all members are defined as equally worthy), especially if the community is what Erving Goffman calls a "total community" that encompasses most aspects of daily life. Some retirement and recreation communities have gardening, landscaping, and general maintenance staffs to take care of the myriad tasks of keeping up the occupants' homes. In some, communal meals are made available. In total communities such as monasteries and convents, military training schools,

---

13. The assertion of equality typically falls short of reality, partly because poor socialist countries may have some difficulty in commanding enough goods and services to distribute. In one area especially, the equality of the right to purchase, Russia falls far short of the U.S., since sociopolitical rank determines whether one has the privilege of buying goods of higher quality, or better prices, or without waiting. For fair observations on this widely reported pattern, see Hedrick Smith, *The Russians* (New York: Ballantine, 1976), chaps. 1–3.

prisons and jails, and mental institutions, almost all services are handed out on a roughly equal basis (though need is also recognized as binding in some things).

Services to help the ill or elderly make short trips, day care and nurseries for children, free mass transportation for local journeys, free street telephones for local calls, medical and dental care, and many other benefits have been suggested or put into effect in such smaller communities. All of these have the result, as did those that have existed for generations, of creating a floor or base level of equality below which no one need fall. Everyone who is a member of the group or nation can enjoy at least that much without having to demonstrate poverty. By raising this floor or base, a larger number of people are guaranteed that minimum, and thereby the amount of equality is increased. Since those who take advantage of such services and goods do so by right of membership or citizenship in the community, and not because they have failed in some way, this use is not socially stigmatized.

Pascal remarked that the law in its majestic impartiality punishes the rich and the poor equally when they steal a loaf of bread or sleep under a bridge. Many ordinary people have felt that irony in some forms of "equality." If properly dressed and possessed of enough cash, both rich and poor may be treated respectfully in the finest restaurants and resorts in the United States, and one need not even be well dressed to buy a luxury car or home.[14] Nevertheless, many equal-opportunity goods and services— public health measures, immunization, parks, medical care, help to the elderly—do not quite merit that irony. That the powerful, esteemed, and rich get more or better in all countries is clear enough. However, many of these goods and services are, and many more can be, handed out with a closer approximation to equality than ever in the past. By reducing at least some part of the discrepancy between those who have much and those who have little, such steps do reduce inequality a bit.

TRANSFER PAYMENTS

Industrial nations have instituted a wide range of pension, welfare, and subsidy systems, some of which can be called collective goods or rights because one has a right to them even if one is not living in poverty (for example, job pensions, veterans' benefits, and social security).[15] Thus they offer a small claim to equality. Others are "transfers," in that they presumably take from the well-to-do and give to the needy. Welfare, medical services for the poor, aid to dependent children, food stamps,

14. Even so, the irony should not be exaggerated: Historically, this was not an equal right. Even with the necessary cash, people of the lower orders (not to mention Jews, blacks, Chicanos, Orientals, women, and so on) were not permitted to enter certain restaurants, hotels, and resorts, or to buy homes in certain areas. Still earlier in history, the lower orders were not permitted to buy or consume certain commodities, as stipulated in numerous sumptuary laws.

15. See Charles Reich, "The New Property," *Yale Law Review*, 73, no. 5 (April, 1964): 733–787.

guaranteed annual income, foster home care, and other programs all aim at helping people who either temporarily or chronically cannot buy the goods and services they require in order to achieve a minimum quality of life, a modest degree of dignity. All such programs also yield some esteem, because through them fewer people are forced to suffer the humiliation of obvious poverty and deprivation.

The latter programs have been attacked because their cost has risen greatly in recent decades. The cost rises because governments feel they should take care of many groups or categories of people who once would have been taken care of by their kin, or not taken care of at all. Every study of those people shows that most are really in need; but critics continue to harbor the suspicion that they are being duped, that the needy are lazy or worthless families or individuals, simply parasites who should be disesteemed. Critics argue that welfare systems increase the power of the state, undermine economic freedom, and reward the idle and improvident, while burdening the hard-working and thrifty.[16]

In the face of such attacks, expansion of these programs continues in all countries. The main variables that affect how large a percentage of the Gross National Product is spent by a government on such items (including social security systems) are: how large a fraction of the population is made up of the elderly; how old the welfare system is; and the amount of GNP per capita.[17] The fraction spent on all these payments does not depend on whether the ideology of the country or the ruling party is collectivistic or individualistic. In general, the United States, Russia, and Japan expend small fractions of GNP on social welfare; Austria, Sweden, and the Netherlands spend about twice as much.[18]

Under modern conditions, welfare and military expenditures have a negative effect on one another (if one rises, the other falls); but in large wars of the recent past (especially losing ones), with full mobilization, nations that were in effect asking for collective dedication and thus accepting everyone as a real member have moved toward more equality. That is, they have granted more respect and material benefits in exchange for political support. One manifestation of this is help for the needy. In industrial nations, most people both approve of these forms of help and affirm an ideology that asserts everyone should work hard and be capable of taking care of himself or herself.[19]

Calculations of the equalizing effects of social welfare programs are difficult.[20] However, Wilensky's analysis suggests that although their

16. For an excellent, succinct cross-national study of these payments, see Harold L. Wilensky, *The Welfare State and Equality* (Berkeley: University of California Press, 1975); for the arguments mentioned here, see esp. chap. 2.

17. *Ibid.*, p. 22.   18. *Ibid.*, table 4, p. 122.   19. *Ibid.*, pp. 32, 71ff.

20. For various schemes that aim at a guaranteed annual income, see Herbert J. Gans, *More Equality*, and Peter Rossi and Katharine C. Lyall, *Reforming Public Welfare: A Critique of the Negative Income Tax Experiment* (New York: Russell Sage Foundation, 1976).

effects do not all run in the same direction (for example, public higher education is a net transfer payment *to* the well-to-do), on balance the result of all the taxes and transfer payments together is highly progressive; that is, they do add up to an egalitarian transfer, from the well-off to the poor.[21] They do not have large effects on the total income distribution, and there may be little or no long-term trend toward still more equality in wealth or income. Nevertheless, their egalitarian effect is measurable. More people command some minimum of respect because they need not suffer the shame of doing without things most other people can have.

Here again, such programs serve to create a floor or base below which the society prefers not to let a family or individual fall. Not all are strictly income payment, but all do add somewhat to the ability of individuals to live adequately and to avoid the abject poverty that members of the society experience as humiliating.

PROGRESSIVE INCOME AND INHERITANCE TAXES

The expansion of collective goods and services, and of transfer payments, requires the creation of taxation systems that are progressive, that is, that require the well-to-do to pay more than others pay. These changes also achieve more equality of prestige. The nominal taxes on high incomes and estates are high in the United States, and they vary from one industrial nation to another. But real taxes in this country are considerably less than nominal taxes because of tax loopholes that the privileged have written into the laws. In addition, the rich receive various forms of subsidies, indirectly to the corporations they own or directly (to farm operators and landowners).[22] Much dispute centers on how much redistribution of income could occur if all loopholes were eliminated; but it is clear enough that income taxes are at present only modestly progressive, and thoughtful lawyers can cut inheritance taxes down to very small amounts if given time. As a consequence, the amount of inequality of wealth and income does not change much from one decade to the next.

The effect of these inequalities on esteem and civility is seen in that extremes of income and wealth command overt deference, even abject servility in historical periods of economic scarcity. If people are to command respect from one another, what each can do must matter to the others; if they can do almost anything they want without some control by the others, they will not be motivated to change their own behavior, to compromise, to negotiate. People will try to perform well because they

21. Wilensky, *The Welfare State and Equality*, chap. 5.

22. For discussions of tax advantages at different class levels, see Gabriel Kolko, *Wealth and Power in America* (New York: Praeger, 1962); Robert J. Lampman, *Ends and Means of Reducing Income Poverty* (Chicago: Markham, 1971); Joseph A. Pechman, "The Rich, the Poor and the Taxes They Pay," *Public Interest*, no. 17 (Fall, 1969): 21–44; Rose Sanford, "The Truth about Income Inequality in the U.S.," *Fortune*, December, 1972; R. Barlow, "The Incidence of Selected Taxes by Income Classes," in J. N. Morgan, ed., *Five Thousand Families: Patterns of Economic Plagues*, vol. II (Ann Arbor: University of Michigan Institute for Social Research, 1974), pp. 213–245; I. Sharkansky, *The Politics of Taxing and Spending* (Indianapolis: Bobbs-Merrill, 1969).

need the help or admiration others can give them. However, if one stratum has great wealth, prestige, or influence, its members need not compromise or negotiate: others must conform without their needing to do so in return.

When people's interests are widely divergent, as they are under the condition of high inequality, it is difficult for them to compromise, to negotiate.[23] The gap between them is too great. With greater equality the higher ranks and the lower can more easily come to acceptable terms. People would be much more likely to agree about how much civility or esteem each should pay the other if their wealth and political influence were more equal. Moreover, dignity and self-respect, difficult to achieve at the poverty level, would be increased by heavier assessments at the upper levels of wealth and income, which would both reduce the economic advantages at the top and raise those at the bottom strata.

ORGANIZATIONS THAT DEMAND INCREASED RESPECT

Like a more equitable distribution of wealth through graduated taxation systems, organization for collective influence can increase the amount of respect accorded low-ranking individuals. One important problem in any democracy is the "permanently outvoted minority," that is, the less-privileged segment of the society, whose votes are too few to be worth special attention. In this society (and most other large ones) this minority has included most ethnic or racial groups, the old and the young, women, and the very poor. Their increase of political influence through organization has commanded greater esteem from others. The behavior even of southern sheriffs toward blacks improved substantially when their votes began to determine elections. When Italian organizations began to protest slurs against Italians, that disesteeming behavior diminished. In a world populated by large corporations and agencies, individuals can often make a greater impact by joining with their more or less respected fellows, so that their aggregate influence is substantial.

Organizations such as unions demand and get both money and overt respect. The behavior of foremen has changed remarkably over the decades, most notably where strong unions have developed. The effects of organization are several. Union members get more money and security, and thus have more economic influence as well as respect from others (not to be fired on a foreman's whim—or to work at a steady job—yields more respect). Both corporation officials and ordinary supervisors not only treat subordinates with greater civility, but they are likely to feel more respect for them, too. In the larger sphere of politics, groups or segments that are represented by organizations are treated with more concern.

Organizations of various kinds can, then, increase equality by representing or supporting the claims of the disesteemed to greater dignity. That some of the greater civility paid is rationally calculated and overt

23. Gans, *More Equality*, p. 23.

rather than representative of an inner change of heart, goes without say-ing. However, it is no small step to obtain a modest amount of overt deference. In addition, people whose various claims are supported by effective organizations are in fact given more real respect, not merely external gestures.

DECENTRALIZATION OF POWER

When individuals organize they can demand more respect from large corporations and agencies; the decentralization of the power of large cor-porations and agencies is another means of achieving greater equality of esteem. Because great political influence can make great profits possible; and because great wealth can be used to gain political influence; and because high prestige both leads to and is generated by achievements in the other realms, many proponents of more equality have argued for smaller nodes of power, smaller concentrations of political influence.[24] Major threats in modern times are the ever-increasing power of the state and the multinational corporation, of awesome size and capacity. Al-though these threats to the quality of life seem evident, it is not easy to perceive any adequate countervailing forces that might arise in the near future. Most technical, political, and economic problems seem to become larger and more complex, requiring a still larger concentration of political and social control for their solution and adequate execution. The various efforts at community control seem to be on too small a scale to have much effect on this massive secular trend. Such attempts, which aim at reducing the inequality of influence, wealth, and even respect between large sociopolitical units and local people, do result in some greater equality of prestige. But that effect is likely to remain small.[25]

Somewhat more successful is the impact of giving a larger voice to workers in corporations. That is, some decentralization of political and economic influence within the corporation decreases the inequality in prestige between the various occupational levels of the organization. Most such plans, in this country and in Europe, have been modest in scope,

24. For a further analysis of the democratization of power, see Frank Levy and Edwin M. Truman, "Towards a Rationale of Decentralization: Another View," *American Political Science Review*, 65 (March, 1971): 172–179.

25. Although the countervailing forces are not large, it should at least be noted that considerable evidence exists in support of the notion that large size does not always yield economies of scale. Many problems are more efficiently solved at the local level: e.g., crime control, supervision of small children, care of the aged or mentally ill, small crises, and even some economic tasks.

For cogent reviews of data, and not only arguments, see the following essays and their bibliog-raphies in vol. I of Alex Inkeles *et al.*, eds., *Annual Review of Sociology* (Palo Alto: Annual Reviews, 1975): W. R. Scott, "Organizational Structure"; D. Mechanic, "The Comparative Study of Health Care Delivery Systems"; D. H. Smith, "Voluntary Action and Voluntary Groups"; T. N. Clark, "Community Power"; G. T. Marx and J. L. Wood, "Strands of Theory and Research in Collective Behavior"; and R. R. Alford and R. Friedland, "Political Participation and Public Policy." Also see Paul and Percival Goodman, *Communitas: Means of Livelihood and Ways of Life* (New York: Vintage, 1960); Jane Jacobs, *The Death and Life of Great American Cities* (New York: Modern Library, 1969); and Tibor Scitovsky, *The Joyless Economy* (New York: Oxford University Press, 1976).

ranging from workers' committees for planning some details of production to inclusions of workers' representatives on the boards of directors. Such units can be given still more influence by law, and by changes in corporate policy.

However, here as elsewhere, I do not suppose it is necessary to make large increases in voting rights in order to persuade leaders to give more respect to corporate employees' opinions. The nearly invariable result of giving more respect and influence to subordinates is that higher officials learn their opinions are worth more than they had supposed, and thus that those subordinates are worthy of more esteem.

It is one of the commonplace myths, always seductive and mostly proved incorrect, that organizations or nations are more efficient if a single leader or oligarchy is given great influence. Most leaders have resisted decentralization of influence, even though giving more respect and weight to the opinions of people at lower levels increases not only their loyalty but often the effectiveness of the group effort as well. Consequently, although I believe that the main social forces of our era move toward greater centralization, any political steps against it are likely to increase equality of prestige and improve the quality of the productive process, and are worthy of some social support.

As noted at the beginning of this chapter, a wide array of possible moves can be made in the direction of greater equality of prestige and other social rewards without accepting the intellectually easy but unrealistic solution of postulating a total revolution in which egalitarian norms are imposed by force threat and massive propaganda. I continue to suppose that many such steps toward equality would in fact be supported, or could be shown to deserve support, by at least some norms and values already affirmed by the citizens of many modern countries.[26]

Such aims do not seek a dead-level mediocrity, into which all are equally forced. On the contrary, I believe that a substantial amount of historical and contemporary inequality—in prestige, wealth, and political influence—did not and does not grow from a free market, in which everyone has a fair chance to develop his or her own talents. Thus, most of these steps toward equality would have the greatest undermining effect on social arrangements that were created by human beings in order to enjoy privileges that at best have been only partly earned.

AN END TO HEROES?

Many humanistic essays have deplored the passing of heroes, the decline of dash and glitter, the dull mechanization of warfare, the bureaucratization of daily life. Coupled with that thesis, a romantic conservatism has often suggested that since artists have been supported by kings and

26. For example, I believe the data amassed by Richard F. Hamilton, *Class and Politics in the U.S.* (New York: Wiley, 1972), persuasively support the general thesis that legislators vote far more conservatively on these steps toward equality than the population would.

nobles, heroes of all kinds are more likely to flourish in the full-blown gaudiness of a highly inegalitarian class system. Peasants and the poor may suffer, but great achievements abound.

Against that general view, it has been argued here that heroes abound in modern life, in all senses. Not only are the achievements of men and women in the arts and sciences, invention, sports, in courage, and in many other realms abundant; they are also given more admiration, by more people, than in the past. Moreover, I insist that there are thousands of unsung heroes as well, people who have achieved greatly in activities that are given only modest or local attention—automobile mechanics, mothers, frisbee hurlers, calligraphers, harmonica players, first-grade teachers. People's behavior is constantly being shaped by the wish to gain the respect of others, and in a large-scale society there are some people who will admire others for almost any kind of fine performance, in at least a local setting.

I believe, too, that a higher percentage of the populations in Western democracies have been granted more respect and more opportunity for individual development, and have responded with a wider range of high qualities and achievements, than in any prior historical epoch—if there is a single exception it is Periclean Athens, which itself aimed at that kind of broad development for at least all its free male citizens. It is also to be noted that the citizens of these countries have paid less deference to the upper strata, and have not even tolerated a nobility, but they have admired greatness when they could observe it.

Perhaps of equal importance is our thesis that the decline of deference to a noble stratum, or of servility to people of higher position, need not mean a lesser admiration for greatness when it appears. Esteem or prestige, like wealth or political influence, need not be and mostly is not a zero-sum game in which the other gains what one loses. If more people are encouraged to achieve greatly or well, if indeed we move toward greater equality in all the ways suggested above, we shall in fact honor more people for more kinds of contributions to human beings everywhere. As the esteem of people who are respected more is worth more, those who are seen as heroes will be given no less honor than before; there will be more prestige to allocate. Moreover, we shall continue to celebrate our heroes, in open admiration for their achievements, which after all we do share as fellow members in the same society.

Index